D0938713

ORGANIZATIONAL
DIAGNOSIS

ORGANIZATIONAL DIAGNOSIS

Harry Levinson

with Janice Molinari
and Andrew G. Spohn

Harvard University Press
Cambridge, Massachusetts
1972

*Whatever a man's achievements, they are unquestionably a product
of affectionate people who nurtured his aspirations. Those who hold one
in high esteem, who encourage him in moments of confusion and despair,
who support his self-confidence by sharing his dreams, and who urge him
into the future by their expressed faith in his capacities, are surely the
agents of his unfolding. Many have done that for me; some have indeed
been exceptional allies. I dedicate this book to them:*

Deane E. Ackers
Nelson A. Crawford
W. G. Clugston
Robert K. Greenleaf
Alfred J. Marrow
Claude R. Miller
Albert Pick, Jr.
Murray E. Sholkin
Earl D. Scott
Thomas W. Childs

CONTENTS

ILLUSTRATIONS

PREFACE

After an initial survey of mental health in industry from January 1, 1954 to June 30, 1955, I organized, and for 14 years headed, the Division of Industrial Mental Health at The Menninger Foundation. Dr. William C. Menninger sponsored the initial investigation out of unearmarked contributions to the foundation and obtained funding for the first three years of the work of the division from the Rockefeller Brothers Fund. This work took the form of a 2-year case study in the Kansas Power and Light Company which led to the first steps in conceptualizing the relationship of work and the work organization to mental health (*Men, Management and Mental Health*. Cambridge, Harvard University Press, 1962). The Kansas Power and Light study and the several briefer studies which followed it led to initial methodological formulations resulting from the work of an interdisciplinary team (*Interdisciplinary Research on Work and Mental Health*. Topeka: The Menninger Foundation, 1961), some of which are incorporated in this volume.

Initially my concern was with the symptoms and problems of the individual at work. An early focus, for example, was on accidents, absenteeism, and alcoholism as reflections of the psychological problems of individuals. It became increasingly evident to me that the way an organization was managed had considerable import for the mental health of the people who worked in it. Logically, then, an important mode of preventing emotional distress was to understand organizational malfunctioning, and the symptoms that resulted, and to evolve ways of ameliorating both simultaneously.

But there are no generally accepted systematic ways of examining organizations to assess their well-being and to decide what, if anything, needs to be done to help them. Our own initial efforts to formulate an examination procedure were crude. We found other methods to be too limited or too mechanistic. As my early colleagues went their own professional ways, I continued to work on evolving a diagnostic procedure.

It became evident that the very factors and forces which made our and other diagnostic efforts inadequate dictated what an adequate diagnostic process should be. An organization is a living system. It has components which, taken together, comprise its whole. These components interact with each other and the whole with other wholes and its own environment. It grows and develops, has a history, experiences crises, and adapts. An organization, then, is like any other living system. Therefore modes of systematically studying and evaluating other systems might be extrapolated to the study of organizations.

The most highly systematized examinational procedure for a living system is that used for the physical and psychiatric examination of the individual person. For years physicians have been examining people for the purpose of assessing their health and diagnosing their ills. The psychiatric examination is a direct extension of the physical examination, with a heavier emphasis on the adaptation of the person to his environment.

Perhaps the most detailed psychiatric examination outline, and most highly elaborated diagnostic system, both of which lean heavily on open-system theory from biology, is that of Karl Menninger (*A Manual for Psychiatric Case Study,* New York, Grune and Stratton, 1952; revised and enlarged 2nd ed., 1962; *The Vital Balance,* New York, Viking Press, 1963). There it was, right in my own backyard. What easier way than to extrapolate from the centuries-long efforts to study the individual person summarized in the form of Dr. Menninger's books? Because I was clinically trained and immersed in a clinical setting, the extrapolation seemed to me even more appropriate, for my whole effort to learn more about mental health in industry was from a clinical, specifically psychoanalytic, point of view.

I began with a crudely extrapolated outline which I used for teaching Fellows in The Menninger School of Psychiatry. My intention was to have them extend the basic examination method in which they were trained to the study of organizations. I used revised forms of the outline in my teaching at the Sloan School of Management at Massachusetts Institute of Technology in 1961–1962; at the University of Kansas School of Business in 1967; and at the Harvard Graduate School of Business Administration, 1968–1971. In addition, clergymen who were in the Pastoral Care and Counseling Program of The Menninger Foundation helped me formulate revisions as they undertook to study church institutions.

In the course of this work it became clear to me that the *organization*, not business, hospital, school, church or some other institution, was the subject. Experience demonstrated that the kind of organization was irrelevant to the method for studying it, just as the psychiatric method may be applied with equal facility to a young child, an old man, a menopausal woman, a delinquent adolescent, a depressed executive or a candidate for submarine training. In practice, the outline was used with equal success in monasteries, public schools, hospitals, and businesses. However, examples from one kind of organization do not always make sense to those who are more knowledgeable about another. Yet, to offer multiple examples for each topic would make the book too long. Therefore the reader will frequently have to interpret examples in light of his own area of interest. All examples not identified by source are taken from case studies conducted by me or my students.

Part I is a guide to using the outline and entering an organization. Part II describes the data to be gathered and how to classify, interpret and summarize them. Chapter 4 is the outline itself. It is this with which the reader will most frequently work after he has become experienced. Each topic in these parts is explained, followed by examples. Many of the examples drawn from the literature and contemporary publications were selected by Mrs. Janice Molinari. She not only did yeoman work with the examples, particularly in the spring of 1968, but she also used an effective editorial pencil on those six chapters.

Part III (Chapter 10) is an example of a complete case study, prepared by Andrew G. Spohn. Part IV discusses what to do with the data once gathered and written up, and it includes a sample report, also by Mr. Spohn. The appendixes include examples of questionnaires, both objective and subjective, and other material which may help the reader use the outline more effectively.

In the references, where possible, I refer to the literature on each topic for the reader who may want to pursue a given topic in depth. However, the references are likely to become quickly outdated so the reader is urged not to depend on them alone. While these references are authoritative, and in my judgment helpful, they do not constitute an exhaustive survey of the literature.

In order to be comprehensive, this book is necessarily detailed. As an instrument for teaching, its detail will help the reader understand more clearly the multiple dimensions of an organization. I assume the reader who attains some skill in organizational diagnosis will abstract from and condense the outline to meet his own needs. However, the purpose of writing a diagnostic study is to specify the data one is using so that he may check the sources of his diagnostic inferences and hypotheses. If he eliminates his data, he risks vitiating the purpose for which he uses this outline.

Although the concept of the outline arises from psychoanalytic theory and clinical practice, combined with organizational theory, it should serve a wide range of people who have varied orientations and skills. Most of the fundamental data should be the same for all.

My intention in preparing this book is to help formalize and professionalize the organizational consultation role. I write it for graduate students who will become consultants and for all those who want to sharpen their diagnostic skills as part of their aspiration to become more effective managers and executives. Society's greatest need is for people who can help its organizations do their work ever more effectively. I hope this volume will be a contribution toward meeting that need.

Harry Levinson

ACKNOWLEDGMENTS

I owe an important debt to the many colleagues and students who helped me in myriad ways to evolve this manual and to the many organizations that lent themselves for research and study. The former are too many to list individually and the latter must remain anonymous. I owe special appreciation to Jean Senecal, who did most of the typing and retyping of Parts II–IV and who was responsible for much of the transcription of interviews and studies which subsequently became a part of those chapters.

Among those whose assistance has been particularly helpful are Sallyann Sack; Yolande Lynch, Charlton R. and Helen F. Price; Father Leo Thomas, O.P.; F. Marshall Valier; Dr. D. Ian Thomas; Ralph M. Hower, and Paul R. Lawrence.

During the period when the background work for this book was done at The Menninger Foundation, the activities of the Division of Industrial Mental Health were supported in part by grants from the American Natural Gas Service Company; the International Harvester Foundation; the Detroit Edison Company; the Sears, Roebuck Foundation; the Northwest Paper Foundation; the Marathon Oil Company Foundation; the General Electric Foundation; the General Foods Corporation; the California Portland Cement Company; the Consolidated Natural Gas System Educational Foundation; the Standard Oil Foundation; the Michigan

Bell Telephone Company; the Kansas City Power and Light Company; and the Kansas Power and Light Company.

Beginning in July 1968, I continued in this work in the Harvard University Graduate School of Business Administration. Deans George P. Baker, George F. F. Lombard, and Lawrence E. Fouraker have been most encouraging and supportive. Financial support has been provided from general Harvard Business School research funds as well as from the Thomas Henry Carroll Endowment and a Ford Foundation grant.

To the many individuals, financial supporters, organizations, and to the administrators of The Menninger Foundation and Harvard who facilitated this work, I extend my appreciative thanks.

I am indebted to The Menninger Foundation for permission to use as part of Part I material drawn from *Interdisciplinary Research on Work and Mental Health: A Point of View and a Method.* (Topeka: The Menninger Foundation, 1961). The project members were Harold J. Mandl, Charlton R. Price, Howard V. Perlmutter, and Kenneth J. Munden. The formulation of that report includes much of their joint thinking. Dr. Mandl did the actual writing.

Throughout this book are a number of extracts from books and periodicals which illustrate topics under discussion. I wish to express my thanks to the publishers for their permission to use that material.

The following are reprinted by permission from *Time,* The Weekly Newsmagazine. Copyright 1967, 1968 by Time Inc.

"The Plum at First National City," June 16, 1967; "Ranching: A Kingdom for .8 of a Calf," October 20, 1967; "Seminaries: Uproar at Drew," February 2, 1968; "Colleges: A Search for Distinction," October 27, 1967; "Railroads: Toward the 21st Century, Ltd.," January 26, 1969; "Opening the Books," September 22, 1967; "Opinion: The Great Mogul," February 16, 1968; "Photography: Rollei Rolls Again," February 2, 1968; "Railroads," January 26, 1968; "Churches: Programming the Flock," March 29, 1968; "Store with its Heart in the Work," June 23, 1967; "Abandoning the Planets to Russia," January 5, 1968; "Building with Air," June 2, 1967; "One Out of Three," February 2, 1968; "A Brotherhood of Terror," March 29, 1968; "The Chain That Doesn't Bind," May 17, 1968; "Ecumenism," May 3, 1968; "Universities," January 6, 1967; "Airlines Competing with the Freeways," June 9, 1967.

"A Rueful Memoir: The Collier's Affair," Paul S. Smith, *Esquire,* September 1964. Copyright 1964 by Appleton-Century-Crofts. Reprinted by permission.

The following are reprinted by permission from *Fortune* magazine. Copyright 1960, 1965, 1966, 1967, 1968 by Time Inc.

"The Instant City," Walter McQuade, ed., June 1, 1967; "The Losing Battle of Waterloo," June 15, 1967; "Farm Technology Plows Ahead at John Deere," Gene Bylinski, December 1966; "There's Another Generation of Whiz Kids at Ford," Dan Cordtz, January 1967; "Union Carbide's Patient Schemers," Gilbert Burck, December 1965; "How They Minted the New Penney," John McDonald, July 1967; "Antidisestablishmentarianism of Wheeling Steel," Dan Cordtz, July 1967; "The Roche Team at G.M.," December 1967; "The Rise of the Ancient Mariner," September 1960; "Olivetti: Elegant and Tough," September 1960; "Spare time on Tuesdays," September 1960; "The Two Billion-Dollar Company that Lives by the Cent," Hubert Kay, December 1965; "The $4 Billion Business Garfield Weston Built," William Rukeyser, June 1, 1967; "Litton Down to Earth," William S. Rukeyser, April 1968; "The Fall of the House of Krupp," James Bell, August 1967; "How to Build a Superb School," Walter McQuade, ed., April 1968; "The Search for a Safer Cigarette," Gene Bylinsky, November 1967; "A Cadillac is a Cadillac is a Cadillac," Robert Sheehan, April 1968; "Dupont Under Pressure," Gilbert Burck, November 1967; "Hughes Aircraft: The-High-Flying-Might-Have-Been," Gene Bylinsky, April 1968; "What Went Wrong at Underwood," September 1960; "A Troubled Reflection," September 1965; "Hill & Knowlton's World of Image," T. A. Wise, September 1, 1967; "CBS: Bad Days at Black Rock," Roger Beardwood, May 1968; "The Second Battle of Britain," Walter Guzzardi, February 1968; "Big Board, Big Volume, Big Trouble," Carol Loomis, May 1968; "The Strange Death of Liberal Education," Irving Kristol, May 1968; "The Big Skid at Yale Express," Richard Whalen, November 1965; "The Maritime Industry's Expensive New Box," November 1967; "U.S. Business' Most Skeptical Customer," Philip Siekman, September 1960; "A Red Umbrella in a High Wind," Robert Sheehan, August 1965.

The following are reprinted with permission of *Holiday* magazine. Copyright 1967 by The Holiday Publishing Company.

"Antioch College," Arno Karlen, June 1967; "Bennington College," Richard Atheson, September 1967; "A Country Comes of Age," E. J. Kahn, Jr., December 1967.

The following are reprinted with permission from *Forbes* magazine. Copyright 1965, 1967, 1968 by Forbes Inc.

"The Dropouts," September 15, 1967; "Lockheed: Can it Make a Commercial Comeback?" October 1, 1967; "The Southern Hospitality Approach," September 1, 1967; "Never Underestimate the Fickleness of a Woman," October 15, 1967; "When it comes to Management is the Man in the Button-Down Shirt Smarter than the Man with the Mutton-Chop Whiskers?" September 15, 1967; "Business: Cheaper to Buy 'Em," February 15, 1967; "They Call it Geneen U.," May 1, 1968; "Xerox Corporation," October 15, 1965; "Dark Clouds at Sunbeam," June 15, 1968; "Situation, Lousy, Progress, Imperceptible," June 15, 1968; "Grace's Fall from Grace," June 15, 1968.

The following are reprinted with permission from *Harper's Magazine*. Copyright 1966, 1967, 1969 by Harper's Magazine Company.
"The Saturday Evening Post," Otto Friedrich, December 1969; "A New Direction for Negro Colleges," Howard Zinn, May 1966; "The Cooper Co. vs. The North Cascades," Paul Brooks, September 1967; "Notre Dame: Our First Great Catholic University," Peter Schrag, May 1967.

The following are reprinted with permission from *Business Week*. Copyright 1959, 1963, 1964, 1965, 1967, 1968 by McGraw-Hill, Inc.
"Yes, they sell more bananas," July 8, 1967; "TV that can bite," May 27, 1967; "Salvation Army beats a bigger, better drum," June 19, 1965; "The old bookworm keeps turning slowly," September 12, 1964; "Still a Target," July 8, 1967; "Reading, Wheeling and Able," March 16, 1968; "How Gillette has put on a new face," April 1, 1967; "The Edsel dies and Ford regroups survivors," November 28, 1959; "Marathon Oil pulls back," March 16, 1968; "Trying to cure Parke, Davis' ills," March 2, 1968; "Shipbuilding's leader heads into a storm," October 7, 1967; "The power behind the Post," May 27, 1967; "Hospitals try to cure a high-cost syndrome," July 15, 1967; "Caltech trains a new kind of scientist," March 16, 1968; "What makes the going great at Pan Am," February 17, 1968; "Kidde books passage on U.S. Lines," February 24, 1968; "Growing Complexity," June 19, 1965; "Kaiser finds a catalyst for growth," February 17, 1968; "Chrysler Corp. assembles a new identity," April 29, 1967; "New Garden tries more varied crop," November 11, 1967; "Russia: the next 50 years," April 29, 1967; "Can IBM keep up the pace?," February 2, 1963; "Aerospace shoots for diversity," December 9, 1967.

The following are reprinted with permission from *Newsweek* magazine. Copyright 1967, 1968 by Newsweek, Inc.

"From an Icy Quagmire Half the World's Oil," October 2, 1967; "Transportation: Way to run a train," May 6, 1968.

The following are reprinted with permission from *Science* magazine. Copyright 1967, 1968 by American Association for the Advancement of Science.

"Reed College Hunting for Money, a President and a Mission," Bryce Nelson, September 15, 1967; "Pitt Pick Chancellor Agrees that Modesty is the Best Policy," Bryce Nelson, February 3, 1967; "Naples Station: Crisis Italian Style at Marine Biology Center," J. Walsh, May 26, 1967; "California: Reagan, Draft Put Gloom on University's 100th Year," D. S. Greenberg, March 29, 1968; "Harvard: Beginning to Worry About Maintaining Faculty," Bryce Nelson, May 19, 1967; "Fund Raising: Yale Launches Marathon Campaign," R. J. Samuelson, June 19, 1968; "Dartmouth: Medical School Shows Good Recovery from 1966," D. S. Greenberg, June 19, 1968; "Huntsville: Alabama Cotton Town Takes Off into the Space Age," L. J. Carter, March 10, 1967; "DuPont and Delaware: Academic Life Behind the Nylon Curtain," P. M. Boffey, May 10, 1968; "Financial Plight at McGill: Quebec Favors its French Universities," May 31, 1968; "Harvard Faculty: How can you keep 'em after they've seen California?," May 31, 1968; "Student Unrest: Administrators Seek Ways to Restore Peace," June 14, 1968.

The following are reprinted with permission from *Think* magazine. Copyright 1967, 1968 by International Business Machines Corporation. "Renaissance in Appalachia," Paul Deutschman, September–October 1967; "The Ideal City — Can we Build It?" George A. W. Boehm, January–February 1968.

Organizational Authority, Robert L. Peabody, New York, Atherton Press, 1964. Reprinted with permission. Copyright 1964 by Atherton Press.

The following are reprinted with permission of Harper & Row, New York. Copyright 1962, 1964, 1967 by Harper & Row, Publishers. *Management by Participation,* Alfred Marrow, 1967; *The Executive: Autocrat, Bureaucrat, Democrat,* Eugene E. Jennings, 1962.

The following are reprinted with permission from *Life* magazine. Copyright 1967, 1968 by Time Inc. "The Gun Law — A Step Toward Sanity," May 10, 1968; "In U.S.

Universities the Humanistic Heartbeat has Failed," James H. Billington, May 24, 1968.

The following are reprinted with permission from *Dun's Review*. Copyright 1966, 1967 by Dun & Bradstreet.

"International Business — Italian Tourism," Jean Ross-Skinner, May 1967; "Borden, Land of Milk & Honey," Robert Levy, May 1967; "The Plant Moves House (Special Report on Industrial Facilities), March 1966.

The following are reprinted with permission of Beacon Press, Boston. *Voices in the Classroom,* Peter Schrag, 1965. Copyright 1965 by Peter Schrag; *Kohler on Strike,* Walter Uphoff, 1966. Copyright 1966 by Beacon Press.

"The Los Angeles Police," Paul Jacobs, *Atlantic Monthly,* December 1966. Reprinted with permission. Copyright 1966 by Atlantic Monthly Co.

My Forty Years with Ford, Charles Sorensen, W. W. Norton, 1956. Reprinted by permission of W. W. Norton, Publishers, New York. Copyright 1956 by Charles Sorensen.

The Invisible Scar, Caroline Bird, David McKay Company, 1966. Reprinted by permission of David McKay Company, Inc., Publishers. Copyright 1966 by Caroline Bird.

1

OVERVIEW

Man's interdependence with his fellow man has led him to form ever larger agglomerates of people. Individuals are necessarily members of families. Extended family units evolved into kinship communities, then tribes. As specific complementary family and occupational roles became defined, and as power had to be distributed differentially among people according to their responsibilities or their capacity for taking it, groups of people became more formally organized. Their organizations specified rights and responsibilities, codes of behavior, value systems and rituals, and leadership.

Larger social units — communities, states, nations — required organizations, rather than individuals, to carry out their adaptive tasks, particularly as technical developments led to specialization of functions and the physical facilities for carrying them out. A ship requires a crew, a school needs a faculty, steel manufacturing must be done in a plant. This functional specialization in turn increased work group interdependence. Sales is necessarily dependent on manufacturing, manufacturing on engineering, engineering on research, research on sales. Thus organizations are composed of interdependent groups having different immediate goals, different ways of working, different formal training, even different personality types within them. These differences make for different styles of functioning within units. An accounting department does work that is different in style, method and goal than sales. Accountants as a group are

different people than salesmen. Each group has its own process — its own
way of carrying through its work from beginning to end — based on whatever technology it uses. This process may be regarded as a *system,* a series
of interrelated steps, functions, activities, yielding a palpable result. Both
the process and the result may be explained, measured, controlled, and
interrelated with other systems.

An organization as a whole therefore is a system of interrelated subsystems. In its turn, it is also a component of larger systems — an industry,
a community, an economy. It affects and is affected by other systems. We
speak of an organization therefore as being an *open system,* utilizing a concept drawn from biology. This concept calls attention to the need for
studying living organisms in their contexts and to the limitations and difficulty of understanding information about living organisms when that information is taken out of context.

A conception of an organism, whether an amoeba, a person, or an organization, as an open system requires that one think of such a system as
having a major threefold task: maintaining equilibrium (1) among its internal subsystems, (2) between itself as a system and other systems, and (3)
between itself and the larger systems of which it is a part, in order to
survive. Failure to maintain an adequately adaptive equilibrium results
in collapse or destruction. But any system is more than the sum of its subsystems. A person is not merely interconnected gastrointestinal, cardio-
vascular, motor and nervous systems. He has uniqueness, personality, and
the capacity to act on his environment in a host of spontaneous ways. He
is, of course, a product of his history as well as his capacities. So it is with
organizations. They achieve uniqueness in their ways of performing their
functions despite the similarities of their organizational structures,
marketplaces, personnel, techniques. There is less visible structure in the
composition of all of these components into a unique whole.

Living organisms have energy. They can act forcibly on their environments. They are not merely acted upon. They adapt — that is, they master
the environment for their own survival — by modifying or controlling
their own behavior as well as the external influences on them.

Like all other living organisms, organizations have their problems in
adaptation. Sometimes their internal subsystems do not function well together; sometimes their environments change so significantly that former
modes of adaptation no longer work effectively. Subsystems can become
so specialized as to be almost foreign to other subsystems. A data processing
department in a public utility is a total stranger to most of the operating

units. An organization plan which is highly defined to let each person know his job, his reporting responsibility and his goals, is fine for a stable organization. It is not much help for a construction firm that must form new teams of people for every major job or for an organization that shifts from stable work processes to operations based on individual projects.

Subsystems tend to develop their own autonomy and to have internal norms or shared beliefs, goals, and values. They become behavioral settings for the people who work in them, shaping their thoughts, aspirations, and feelings about themselves, their work, and the organization.

Organizations, too, suffer insult and injury from their environments or conflict because of contradictory goals and purposes. At times it becomes necessary to assess both the nature and degree of dysfunction.

But there are no widely accepted comprehensive diagnostic procedures for assessing and evaluating organizations comparable, for example, to the examination process in medicine. True, there are many diagnostic processes for part-functions. The social psychologist may examine an organization's morale. The financial analyst may judge its financial health from statistics on profitability, return on investment, new products, market penetration, and similar data. The marketing consultant has his own ways of judging marketing strategies. Each specialist also has his own remedies for resolving or ameliorating the problems he perceives. Often efforts to resolve problems in one area create new ones for the organization as a whole or for other areas. This is especially true if examination of the environmental context of the organization is limited to that part of the environment in which the specialty operates, for example, the customer market, the blue collar component of the work force.

Traditional efforts to look at whole organizations tend to concentrate on its bureaucratic structure: What are the organizational units required to do its task, and how do they relate to each other? Or on its role structure: What roles are required to do the organizational task, and what are their requirements? Or on status arrangements and communications systems. These highly intellectualized analyses, however useful for other scientific purposes, do not easily lend themselves to perceiving the organization as an active, unique, living entity.

A comprehensive method of studying and assessing organizations for the purpose of ascertaining their points and nodes of dysfunction should cover a number of major areas. It should include an evaluation of the relationship of the organization as an open system with the other systems with which it interacts. It should be an ordered, systematic gathering of data as a basis for intervention or organizational change efforts. To understand an organization as a living entity, it will be important to see organizational purpose as being akin to the issue of identity for the individual. An organizational purpose implies a concept of the organization, a self-image, if you will. This concept, in turn, is or should be related to what the organization does and how it does so. The organization should be structured to carry out these goals and purposes, this concept. It should also be directed to the future for any conception of purpose implicitly anticipates the future. The leadership of an organization is a central factor in its adaptation, and the style of management says much about how its organization will adapt. These, too, need careful scrutiny.

Such a method, then, should require a student of organizations to fully describe an organization's concept, objectives, plans, its view of itself as well as its relationships with others, and its leadership. It must enable the consultant to understand systems of communications, coordination, guidance, control, and support. It must help him to delineate relevant environments and behavior settings. It must be a guide to unfolding the rationale of the organization, explaining its activities, and critically evaluating the organization's adaptive adequacy, followed by a reasoned series of recommendations.

An organization diagnostic method should be usable with equal facility by persons in a wide range of disciplines and by those with varying points of view within a given discipline. Ideally, such a method should make it possible to specify the data on the basis of which anyone intends to act to change the organization or upon which he will make choices of alternative action possibilities. Since any diagnosis is a hypothesis, it becomes important to be able to return continuously to the information on which the hypothesis is based if the diagnosis proves incorrect or inadequate, or if the mode of intervention fails to produce the anticipated results.

A diagnostic method should also be a basis for training people for organizational consultation, for fostering and formalizing a professional consultation role. It should provide students of organizational consultation with a basic professional tool for gathering information, putting it in some reasonably sequential order, and making inferences and interpretations. It should also serve as a device for training executives to better understand organizations and to continuously assess their managerial efforts. It should be capable of modification and refinement, based on experience, and of including within its purview more specialized diagnostic devices, just as a physician will make use of X-ray, blood tests, and more highly specialized measures as necessary.

Such a diagnostic procedure is outlined in this book. This manual is a data-gathering guide. It serves to sharpen perceptions and to organize them into a systematic whole. The reader would therefore do well first to read it quickly to get an overview of it. Then he should review the outline itself, Chapter 4, followed by more careful examination of the examples in the subsequent chapters.

Then, as he proceeds with his study, he will have in mind the kinds of information he must obtain. He will then be able to complete various parts of the outline as he works, rather than waiting until the end of the data-gathering process to put his material together. As he does so, he will be formulating and testing hypotheses in his own mind about how the organization operates. He will be able to follow up new leads, develop fresh ideas, and confirm or reject impressions.

While the outline is intended to be encompassing, many topics are re-dundant, as they depend on the same source material. Rather than rigidly following all categories in detail, the reader will need to use his judgment and be appropriately selective. The outline is a checklist. How much de-tail one will pursue depends on the problem he is working with and his own time constraints. However, he should be careful to note that while many items touch on the same material, each approaches the material from a slightly different point of view. These subtleties of difference should not be taken lightly, for the capacity to understand and make use of subtlety distinguishes the sophisticated consultant from the herd. Any fool can tell that a river flows. Only he who understands its cross-currents, its eddies, the variations in its speed, the hidden rocks, its action in drought and flood, is the master of its functioning. So it is with organiza-tions. The person who uses this manual to sharpen his awareness of sub-tlety and the bases of his inferences will find it helpful. If he uses it in rote fashion, it will be just a chore or at best an exercise.

One other advantage of the manual is that the references enable the con-sultant to refer to the literature on given fields. This permits him to be-come knowledgeable about the latest in practice or technique and to com-pare that with what he sees in the organization. He has a reference point in the yardsticks of the literature. But most important, he has the oppor-tunity to establish for himself and his clients, when they ask, the source of the information he is feeding back and the basis on which he is making certain recommendations or raising topics for consideration. Nothing is more comforting to a consultant than to be able to specify how he arrived at his conclusions. This enables both him and his client to weigh appropriately the emphasis to be given to a particular point, the need for more information, the holes in the study, and the weaknesses of the data. In a word, the outline helps to keep him honest with himself and his client.

Ideally, with enough experience, he will build the outline into his mode of working as a personal device, a way of looking at organizations almost automatically. This will also help him to organize his reading and weigh new concepts and ideas, to have a psychological hook on which to hang them and a basis for critical judgment.

One of the disadvantages of much social science theory is that it is comprised of first order inferences and limited, unrelated concepts. The inadequacies of such limited conceptual thinking become apparent when one has to work with it to solve problems. This kind of outline and diagnostic manual requires that one evolve his own overall theory, his own way of tying together what he knows, and that he rise to the level of being an organizational generalist. In short, it should compel him to raise his sights, broaden his purview, and see himself in a more comprehensive role. Such a conception and the study method to go with it become two legs of a professional role, the third being conceptually-based modes of intervention, or treatments of choice.

This book, then, outlines a mode of gathering data. It speaks to the question: "What do you gather, and how do you order it?" It is not in itself a source of answers: "What do you do about it?" It provides structure in a professional field that depends primarily on ad hoc actions and structure that is related to personality theory, for the outline itself is based on psychoanalytic conceptions interwoven with organizational theory. This method provides a cross-sectional view of the organization at a given point in time against the context of its history and environment.

However, it should be clear that the effectiveness with which the information is used depends on the skill and competence of the user. A technician can take an X-ray picture; a skilled radiologist is required to interpret it. This caveat is critical for there are too many practitioners in all fields who equate knowledge about a given technique with professional proficiency. To make such an equation is to blind oneself to what one does not know and therefore to be irresponsible in practice. There is not, as yet, a defined practice of consultation, outside of the clinical professions. This inadequate delineation of professional role, and the absence of an ethic to support it, leaves the individual consultant heavily dependent on his own ethics and judgment. Without a tradition and a well-defined mode of practice, he is his own guide. That is indeed a heavy responsibility.

2

INTRODUCING
THE STUDY

There are two reasons why one person comes to another for help: either he has some kind of pain (suffering, discomfort, problem) or he is causing someone else to have such pain, who is in turn compelling him to do something about that problem. There is one other kind of relationship between a professional person and others, that in which the professional comes to the other person for information, as in research. The same is true of relationships with organizations. Organizational leaders come to professionals for help or professionals seek them out for learning.

While the purposes of the relationship are different in these two cases, the procedure for gathering case study information may be much the same. From time to time, as necessary, distinctions will be made between these two purposes. Otherwise it will be assumed that the reader will keep them in mind.

The Initial Contact

If a person seeks out a consultant on behalf of an organization, the process of entry into the organization is a relatively simple one: he is invited in. He should obtain a clear picture of the nature of the problem for which he is consulted; how it is viewed both in its causes and manifestations by the person who seeks his help; who are the other influential persons involved whose cooperation must be obtained; and why he was chosen. He should establish both for the client and himself what expectations are being held of him, how realistic they are, and to what extent they are possible of fulfillment. This is especially important because the client may have implicit expectations of which he is not himself clearly aware and upon which the consulting relationship will ultimately flounder.

Having clarified the expectations, the consultant should then convey to the client the methods by which he works, the steps he is likely to take, the probable time span, and the cost. In some cases he will want to propose a formal contract with a definite beginning and end. In others, particularly in psychological consultation, it will be preferable to propose a limited contract to be followed by option or negotiation about renewal. Some consultants prefer to have a trial relationship with an organization, either based on time (three months, six months, one year) or the successful conclusion of the diagnostic process with its recommendations for action.

The initial contact is the most important one of the whole relationship. In a thousand subtle ways both the consultant and the client communicate with each other. If the client cannot like and trust the consultant in this initial period, their relationship will be a rocky one, if it continues at all. A consulting relationship, like a therapeutic or teaching relationship, should be an alliance of both parties to discover and resolve problems. This means that the relationship must be continuously examined by the consultant and that he must be particularly alert to the effect of his own behavior on the client and the client system.

It is wise for the client and consultant to review their relationship periodically and to renegotiate their goals and expectations. Unless this is done, both will struggle with outdated agreements or unresolved disappointments that will intrude upon their work together. If both parties do not feel equally free to change or dissolve the relationship, the client will feel himself increasingly dependent on the consultant and become angry for being in that position.

In addition, the consultant should arrange a regular meeting with the client executive to bring him up to date in a general way on what is being learned and what issues are arising. If the consultation is a long one this meeting should be scheduled weekly. Appropriate spacing should be arranged for shorter consultations. The reasons are first to ease the client's uneasiness about strangers in his firm and second to start his thinking in the directions which are likely to appear in the subsequent final report. Ideally there should be no surprises in the report as far as the client executive is concerned. He should have come step by step with the consultant.

Without betraying confidences or making too early commitments, the consultant must sustain his relationship in such a way that he maintains trust, keeps his client informed, and helps prepare his client for the steps he is likely to have to take on the basis of the report.

If the consultant does not do this, a long gap ensues between the initial contact and the report. Not only does this gap stimulate self-critical fantasies on the part of the client, but also when the report comes it is likely to be overwhelming even though the findings themselves are relatively modest. Unless this process is followed regularly and carefully, it is almost a foregone conclusion that nothing will come of the report, and the consultant will end his relationship with the organization with that presentation.

It should already be apparent that the distinction between diagnosis and intervention is an arbitrary one. The consultant is affecting the organization from the very moment he enters it. Therefore the diagnostic process really refers to the early stages of the relationship between consultant and organization, a series of interactions and transactions which hopefully will lead to constructive organizational change. From the beginning of his fact finding, the consultant, by the questions he asks and the fact that he asks them, may bring into sharper focus the problems experienced by organization members. He may cause them to think more critically about their leadership and to question its effectiveness. His report, rather than being a private document for his own technical use, becomes an instrument of confrontation for the client organization which compels them to decide what they want to do and what further use they want to make of the consultant.

In the initial diagnostic period discussed in this book, both consultant and organization gain a clearer picture of the condition of the organization, begin to think about possible modes of change, and decide whether they wish to commit themselves to a longer term effort to understand and change major aspects of the organization. As Anna Freud once remarked, the diagnosis is never complete until the therapy is finished.

Early Negotiation

The kind of preparation preceding a consultation study can profoundly affect its process and outcome. Any study is necessarily an intrusion into the daily and weekly work flow. In addition there are often fantasies that the arrival of a consultant means that the consultant, particularly if he is a psychological scientist, will diagnose individuals and prescribe treatment for them. The entire tone of the study period is affected by these fantasies and how they are or are not resolved. Here are some of the steps the consultant must take to deal with people's feelings and expectations in order to function effectively in the field.

At the outset, the consultant is in touch with a representative of the organization, preferably the top administrator. The major task of the consultant is to establish a realistic picture of the study and an open, positive relationship with this person. The organizational representative must have the opportunity to raise questions at length about the study. If the first contact is with the president of a company in which a branch is to be studied, further comparable contact will be necessary with the branch manager. In this instance the period of preparation will take more time. It becomes the responsibility of the consultant to recognize and deal with the meaning of the study to these people. The study is often seen as a means for headquarters to "spy," and realistic clarification must be made.

The consultant should indicate not only what he wants to do but also why he wants to do it in this organization, what risks the host organization runs, and how much time, cost, and effort will be required of the organization. Allow free give-and-take conversation to lead to a common recognition of the complexity and nebulousness of relevant issues and the realization that completely detailed definition of the steps in the study is not possible in the beginning. Discussions of such issues conveys acceptance of this ambiguity and confidence in the effectiveness of the consultant's collaboration with the organization.

Three points must be made during this initial contact: (1) information about the organization will be held in confidence; (2) confidentiality will be maintained so far as specifics about any individual organization member or group are concerned; (3) the general results of the study will be reported to all members of the organization who are part of the study, although the exact way of presenting these results is yet to be determined. It is irresponsible not to provide feedback to people who have allowed themselves to be questioned, observed, or interviewed, because inevitably a consultant creates expectations on the part of those from whom he seeks information, no matter how much he may believe that no one really cares what he learns. The feedback should be carried to the lowest level employees interviewed or questioned, and the consultant should have the concurrence of his client that this will be done. If the study is for research purposes, he should also work out the conditions of publication.

After the preliminary negotiations it becomes important to familiarize the organizational representative and his key associates with the consultant's associates, if any. A face to face meeting between such persons and the consulting team overcomes the often unrealistic fantasies which the organizational representatives have about "the team."

When the concept of the study has been accepted, the organizational representative and the consultant should plan how and when the study will be introduced into the organization. Here it is very important to set some limits. The consultant will do well to: (1) specify that all persons in the organization who are to be involved in the study must have knowledge of the study and its aims before the formal field work begins; (2) require that time be allotted for answering questions about the study and assure all members of the organization about confidentiality. In those cases where there is a union, clearance should be obtained from the union leadership. For research, joint sponsorship by union and management, if possible, is desirable.

If interviews are to be tape recorded, it is important to indicate that fact to prospective interviewees at the outset and also to indicate how confidentiality will be maintained with respect to the tapes and transcription.

Obtaining Consent

Management may, in given instances, find it difficult to assemble all members of the organization who are to be involved to be told about the study directly. In this case a written statement should be formulated and there should be assurances that supervisors will feed back any reaction to the study. However, preparation for the study is most effective when the consultant has been able to talk to every person in the organization who is to be involved. This is the ideal situation for which one should constantly strive.

It is useful to make a short presentation of the purpose of the study to groups of employees, after management and supervisory meetings at successively lower echelons. Production groups should be seen separately from sales groups in order to facilitate the questions that follow. The presentation should include: (1) a statement that the study is being done to learn about organizational processes and problems, not to diagnose people, and that interviews, conversations, and observations are confidential. (2) It should indicate that management has given approval to the study as evidenced by their presence in the room and the confirmatory statement made by them in the presence of both the consultant and the members of the organization. (3) There should be an explanation of the field operation: (a) introduce all team members and describe their professions briefly; (b) describe how the team will operate. For example, "Some people will be interviewed, some will be seen on the job, some will be seen in a group." (4) Emphasis should be placed on the important statement that some people will not be seen, that there are time limits, and choices are made on the basis of the consultant's judgment about how he best might learn about how this organization functions and how people within it work together. (5) Information should be given about exactly when the team will arrive and how long it will stay. After this presentation, allow for questions which will usually take up ten or fifteen minutes.

In my own practice, if I am undertaking a research study as distinguished from consultation, I prefer to explain a research request to the head of the organization I want to study, obtain his permission to do the study, and to get his approval to approach the next lower echelon. I then present my request to the next lower echelon, ask their concurrence and their permission to address the next echelon. At each echelon I make clear the purposes I have in mind, how I will proceed, and how confidentiality will be protected, and I introduce the members of the research team. I also make it clear that I want to be in that organization for *my* purposes, that I am not at that time a consultant, and that my findings will not affect anyone's job. If a group at any echelon turns the research proposal down, then it is killed unless the study can be done without that group and its subordinates.

Just this happened in a police department where the proposal was voted down by the sergeants. Though I regretted losing the research opportunity, nevertheless the turndown reflected the distrust of the lower level men for their chief. Had I attempted to proceed without their permission, cooperation would have been minimal even though the policemen knew that one of the conditions of the research was that no one who did not want to be interviewed need have been.

If the person through whom I am entering an organization is responsible to a board or higher level management, I want to be certain that those levels understand what is being done in the organization and have authorized it. This protects both me and my contact, particularly if subsequent publication of the research is intended.

I also carry the quest for permission to the lowest level of the organization in which the study is to be done. This means that I must obtain clearance from union officials and from the work group as a whole. Work group meetings, particularly, must have time for question and discussion, especially to make clear the limits of the study. I indicate clearly to employees that this study does not involve their family or home life. (If I were to study those aspects of living, I would not do so through the place of employment.) In a study in the Kansas Power and Light Company, this orientation and permission process was carried to forty different points in the company over a wide geographical area before the actual interviewing was begun.

For consultation, especially if the problem is a limited one, this procedure need not be followed in such detail. However, I like to make it a practice to inform lower level supervision where practical and possible what I am doing in the organization to forestall rumors. In addition, wherever possible, if the consultation involves work with groups of executives, I prefer to have their wives together in group meetings to explain what is being done and why. The anxiety of the executives about being studied or interviewed is quickly transmitted home and magnified there. Far better to allay unnecessary concern. Even if one is not in a position to offer more than generalities about what he is doing, such a statement, plus the opportunity to meet the consultant, relieves much concern.

In consultation a person may have no choice about whether he is to be interviewed. If that is the case it should be made clear. But the degree to which the informant is willing to cooperate is something he can control. It is important for the consultant to understand that his informants can dry up in subtle ways if they do not trust him. People can easily answer questionnaires falsely or make them useless.

One of the major advantages of carrying the introductory and permission seeking processes down through the organization is that it gives the consultant an opportunity to evaluate the kind of reception he is likely to get at different points in the organization. It is particularly important for him to understand resistances or negative feelings toward the consultation or study and to understand why they occur. He can then bring the negative feelings to the surface, discuss the reasons for them, and, ideally, dispel them. No matter how warm the welcome, there are always negative feelings in a research or consulting relationship. No one likes to be scrutinized or studied. Many people are likely to feel threatened. Such feelings cannot be wished away or ignored.

Some of the resistances or negative feelings can be sensed once the pre-

sentation is made to a group. Clayton P. Alderfer, reporting on his presentation of a proposal, speaks of four kinds of resistances by labeling the men who made them as "producer," "pilot," "checker," and "leveler." *
The producer wondered how the researcher could begin to understand what happens without learning what working on the line was like. In other words, how could he really know without working there? This was a suspicious, aggressive reaction from a man who thought he would be exploited and exposed.

The pilot was worried about the same issues but instead of acting aggressively, he told of his concern about having been tape recorded without his knowledge on a social occasion. Then he said he was worried about provoking antagonism among employees. His words reflected a different kind of defensive reaction. Instead of attacking, he used an earlier event to betray his anxiety, his fear of being exposed. This was a method of fleeing.

The checker reported that he had done research once, too. He recalled that the company he studied had not done anything right and did not even make good use of his findings. In effect he was saying that many things would be found wanting in the present organization but nothing would be done about them. He was not expressing fear or anxiety but questioning the usefulness of the effort.

The leveler reported that the hourly workers did not trust the managers, and he then asked for data about his own department so he could work on the problems there.

Neither the checker nor the leveler was threatened. However, the first three used fantasies to reflect their concerns. They had stories about what might happen or what had happened. Alderfer reports that in the cases of the producer and the pilot there were fewer participants from the units they headed. Furthermore, as might be expected, there were conflicts between the producer and his people as a product of his distrust.

The consultant, then, can infer from the questions he is asked, and the metaphors used in asking, what kinds of difficulties he is likely to have when, where, and with whom. He will also have from the beginning some clues to the kinds of organization problems he is likely to discover.

Some consultants prefer, in the name of scientific objectivity, to ignore such matters. Pure objectivity or detachment is impossible in the behavioral sciences. There is a significant literature on the impact of the re-

* Clayton Alderfer, "Organizational Diagnosis from Initial Client Reactions to a Researcher," *Human Organization,* 27:3 (Fall 1968), 260–265.

searcher or consultant on the results he gets. Better to recognize this problem and take it into account than ignore it or pretend it does not exist. A measure of objectivity can be obtained by having interviews coded by judges or similar efforts. However, I think it wiser for the consultant to continuously evaluate the effects of his own behavior and to respond to people as human beings.

The Initial Tour

Sometime during the entering process, and in a large organization many times during his contacts with various work groups, the consultant (and his team) will be taken on a tour of the physical facilities. In this way the responsible people can show their organization, asking and answering questions of the team members in the process of getting to know them better as the consultants demonstrate interest and understanding and provide a sample of how they will behave in the organization. If he is not invited to tour (and that is a datum, too), the consultant should ask to be shown about. This is done not only to become familiar with the various work areas and to obtain a general idea of work processes and work flow but also to form some initial psychological impressions of the organization. These will include his impressions of the building and work sites, attitudes of his guides and others he meets, the way he is received, what things he is shown, what is omitted, and similar issues.

The consultant's initial impressions are critical ones. He must attune himself to his own subtle feelings as he goes along because these reflect the impact of various environmental stimuli upon him. Others are likely to be affected in the same way; but because the stimuli may be fleeting or sensed preconsciously, their impact may not be understood. It is helpful to ask the following questions:

What did I see on tour?
What are my first feelings about the organization, the setting?
What were people's attitudes toward me?
What occurred on the tour that made me feel good, bad, indifferent?

It is important that he note even his hazy impressions immediately as they occur or he will lose considerable data. Since the consultant is his own most important instrument, he should begin on tour to use his antennae for sensing subtleties.

For example, in one factory a workman deliberately flicked a small bit of grease at the consultant who was being conducted on an initial tour. Since the tour was being conducted by a member of management, one might be inclined to feel that there were hostile feelings between workers and management. In another situation, the consultant was struck by what seemed to be amazingly cramped, inadequate office space for the company president. During the course of the tour he noted that the management seemed to be treating the employees as if they were children. He sensed a strong feeling of collective inadequacy which could be explained by any one of a number of possibilities: market reverses, marginal economic success, a lack of awareness of their own potential, nepotism resulting in inadequate key personnel.

On tour, the consultant should keep a careful eye out for slogans, bulletin boards, display cases, and other forms of communication, all of which are indicative of what the organization is emphasizing and how it does so. He should also note how the buildings and grounds are kept, where different groups eat, coffee break locations and facilities, points of informal gathering, modes for receiving visitors, parking, transportation, kinds of magazines in reception rooms and offices, and similar cues about the organization. These cues offer the consultant the opportunity to formulate hypotheses about some of the issues and problems he is likely to encounter in the organization. He can then follow them up in his formal study.

The consultant will find it helpful to keep a diary of his experiences in the company, to record events and observations which will not be likely to be reported in interviews or questionnaires. If he keeps such a record of the process of his relationship to the organization, he will be able to trace the consulting relationship from beginning to end. The diary should include his notes of the tour.

The guided tour is one way to be introduced to a number of settings. If the person in charge of these settings conducts the tour, he can introduce the consultant to his key subordinates at various levels and he will be likely to give his version of current problems in each area along the way. He is likely to know the reasons why general procedures are what they are. He can describe relationships with other settings in the organization. He is likely to communicate which setting functions are of greater or lesser importance to him and to the company, trouble spots, new ventures, and so on. While hearing about these matters, the consultant should already be asking himself how this person's view may fit with those of others in the setting.

The orientation of the person in charge to the people in the setting merits special attention since he is in such a strategic position to affect their experiences. Does he focus on people primarily, or does he give his attention to the functions and processes they carry out? Are people, when referred to, described primarily as problems or resources in the setting? If one observes a crisis such as a machine breakdown or someone approaching the supervisor with a special question, how does the supervisor react and what are its implications? One may find considerable consistency in the supervisor's reactions. Perhaps he takes a teaching position in all such interactions. Perhaps he expresses disgust by manner, facial expression, or what he says, feeling that people should not bother him with these things or that such occurrences reflect their excessive dependence on him. All such observations must be correlated since they aid the consultant in understanding the nature of experiences which people probably have as they interact with this person in authority.

Several types of phenomena are possible during the tour to which the observer should be alert:

1. How interested is the supervisor-guide in showing the consultant around? Is he actually bored with what he shows the consultant or is he involved in helping him understand these important phenomena?
2. What particular facets of the setting does he emphasize: the people; the product; the processes; the services performed; the history of the setting or organization?
3. How do people appear to the consultant? Are they tense or relaxed; hurried or casual? Do they seem confident in what they are doing or harassed and uncertain, "running to catch up"?
4. What is the quality of interactions with the consultant and the authority figure? Does he seem to see people as resources or problems? Does he have a differentiated view of them or are they merely a mass who populate the area? How are they approached by the guide as they are introduced (or are they)? How do they react to the supervisor and the consultant? Do they put on a good show of working hard? Do they ignore him? Do they look fearful? Do they seem to welcome the contact?
5. What crises occur during the tour? Does something go wrong? How is it handled? Do people bring problems to the supervisor? How does he respond? What kinds of situations arise which require people to divert attention from orienting the consultant to taking care of regular work?

During the guided tour the consultant pays attention to the use of space within the total territory inhabited by the organization. The territory includes office, factory and warehouse buildings, the space between and around them, and the floor area within them, or similar facilities in nonbusiness organizations.

It is also important on the guided tour to learn about the distribution of persons and equipment or other physical facilities over the various areas and the activities taking place in various sectors of each area. This will lead to the preliminary catalogue of settings and work roles which subsequently must be sampled.

3

THE STUDY
PROCEDURE

After having entered the organization, the consultant begins the formal study procedure. Usually this involves several steps: (1) a breakdown of the organization to be studied into its component parts; (2) the planning of a sample of interviewees to be representative of those parts and of the organization as a whole including careful attention to leadership; (3) a supplementary sample of people to be questioned by printed form; (4) observations of people at work; (5) an examination of already available records and relevant data; (6) and interviews with important persons outside the organization. The last may include former employees, others in the community who know the organization, competitors, suppliers, and other similarly informed people. The consultant may not know who the relevant others are until the study is under way. The five steps outlined above may not be taken in sequential order for much will depend on geographical proximity, seasonal pressures, and the results of periods of observation which the consultant undertakes.

Relating to the Organization

As already indicated, a study involves relating to an "organization." But what does that mean? One does not relate to an organization except as he relates to people in it and particularly to the leadership. These people may be representative of a group or class of employees. In many of his interactions in an organization, a consultant speaks with more than one person at a time. The organization has subdivisions which are psychologically distinct for the members of the organization. For instance, a consultant may be working with a member of the sales department. The sales department setting is the dominant reality for those who work in that area. The consultant is not at that moment relating to the organization as a whole. Thus, he must recognize the sectors of the organization which are most significant psychologically to each person and group seen. Such awareness minimizes disruption of the boundaries of the organization and permits respect for the feelings of people about such things as who should be talked to, who first, and why.

The consultant will be treated in many different ways. Sometimes he is seen as an evaluator who judges instantaneously the innermost competencies of people. He may be the "unwelcome guest." He may be sought as the hero, the ally that is needed to give "management" or "the workers" the right point of view, or as a punisher or as one who rewards. (These relationships often suggest the kinds of relationships people experience with one another in the organization.) His approach must be one of reassurance and support. Yet he may have to move into sensitive areas which are important for his understanding of the feelings and behavior of people.

An organization is composed of persons in authority and "siblings" who relate to these authorities. Each setting within the organization has some favored or disfavored position with respect to key figures. Personnel in each setting have a message to send to the president. This will include some messages of affection and some of hostility. Each member of a setting tries to obtain some reaction from a consultant which will indicate the consultant's views or stance and how the setting stands in his eyes, for example, "production is having it very hard," or "this is one of the best sales divisions." It is tempting for a consultant to begin a conversation by mentioning what he has observed in his earlier contacts. The content of his remarks and the tone conveyed can very easily influence what is then learned. For example, if a consultant says, "Production people are really having a difficult time," to a member of sales who feels that they are not, the consultant communicates that he has already taken a stand in the organization. He may, in fact, prevent the person in sales from talking about some of the difficulties he has in dealing with production. Furthermore, such evaluative statements have considerable potentially destructive impact on people. Personnel read a great deal into such statements and often project their fears in their interpretations of what they hear. Consultants must exert care to avoid encouraging such distortions however tempting it may be to show that they are "in the know." This temptation is extremely hard to resist, but failure to resist will be costly.

The consultant does not have the comfort of his own office in his field work. He may be given a space, but it is "borrowed." For long periods of time he finds himself moving from relationship to relationship and imbedded in the organizational process. He cannot withdraw for an extended period and examine what has taken place. The consultant is not only learning about the feelings, thoughts, and behaviors of other people but he is also altering his own behavior in response to others. In the uncertain situation of field studies, in which next steps are not always clear, some resolution of a consultant's anxiety may take place in a process of adaptation without recognition of just what he has done to adapt.

The consultant himself has needs for inclusion in the organizational life. In a certain sense, he wishes to "belong." He needs some affectional interchange; he wants to be liked, accepted, recognized. But he needs to have control over the situation insofar as he is seeking information from people, and he needs to have this information before he leaves the situation. Too often, the consultant, trying to "be a nice fellow," may not ask questions which he needs to know and leaves the field without the information he must have in order to evaluate what he has seen.

The consultant must remember that the members of the organization have some idea of what the consultant needs to know in order to understand their work situation. The members of the organization will respect the consultant more if he can maintain some distance and sustain his interest in more and valid information rather than giving all of his energy to winning them over. The consultant must recognize and control his own behavior and preoccupations. If he adopts the favored style of an organization without being aware of it, he may forget that this style is a quality of the organization.

One other consideration: Every organization must have a "back room." There are some secrets which are part of organizational life but not readily accessible. To understand what is happening in an organization often involves a problem of judging; for example, deciding whether one should gather the personal history of a key executive who had a major personality disturbance or whether to permit a confession about a shady company transaction at a given time. The goals of the study must be kept in mind. One certainly should not go into explorational ventures aimed at getting "intimate, sexy, or dramatic information" except as these bear on and contribute to consultation goals. And sometimes these must be avoided, even if they would contribute substantially, if the consultant will not have the time or opportunity to deal constructively with the anxiety which revealing such information provokes in people. For example, suppose he learns in the course of interviewing an employee that the employee's boss is embezzling funds. What is his responsibility to the company? To the employee? If he encourages the employee to talk, he must be prepared to help the employee deal with both the reality and his feelings about telling or not telling.

Factual Data

Every organization has at least some of its policies and procedures on paper. Some have historical data on file. All have financial reports or records. Most have annual reports. Many have job descriptions, personnel statistics, and consultants' reports. The consultant should become acquainted with what is on paper and develop for himself a perspective on how it all fits together. In some instances he will be the only person who has ever thought of these data as being interrelated. Usually he will be the first to think of their collective import for the organization. He must therefore be particularly alert to the language of these materials. Implicit in both the kind of written materials and the language used in them are attitudes toward the people who are to be governed by them and assumptions about what motivates people.

Every policy and every practice implicitly carries some assumptions about motivation for each intends people to behave in certain ways. Much of the time these hidden assumptions have dubious validity. An example is the safety program which includes publishing the names of those who had accidents on the assumption that people won't want their names published and therefore will avoid having accidents. Performance appraisal systems, management by objectives, zero defects, and similar programs implicitly assume that pressure and judgment by superior of subordinate are important devices for motivation and imply a carrot-and-stick philosophy. Incentive compensation systems put heavy weight on money as motivator. Paternalistic orientations count on people to be motivated out of loyalty and guilt. Managements rarely examine their assumptions. More often they become angry when their practices do not work well and attribute the failure to the negativism of their employees.

Outside Information

All organizations have relationships outside themselves — with competitors, suppliers, cooperating organizations, agents, professional associations, and so on. The consultant will find it useful to understand how the organization looks to these respective publics and should arrange interviews with their representatives, with the permission of his client. In these interviews he should indicate that he is trying to be of service to his client and would like to understand how the outsiders view the organization and its operations. These perspectives will enable him to understand how his client organization operates and what impact it has on others. Again, he may be the only one who has ever thought of this issue, not in narrow marketing terms, but in terms of the way the organization fits into its host environment.

There are a number of ways, in addition to interviewing, to get such information. Most newspapers have morgues, or files of clippings, filed by subject. Historical societies often have much information on file. Large organizations will frequently be the subject of articles in trade or professional magazines which may be located through libraries. Organizations, of course, vary in the amount of information available about them. The sheer availability of various kinds of information is a datum of diagnostic value.

In the process of developing his data, the consultant should keep his contact person informed about what he is doing. That person will be getting information from others anyway, some of which may be disturbing to him. Of course, the consultant should not discuss confidential matters with or "report" to his contact, but he should be able to indicate what part of the organization he is working in, in general the kind of reception he is getting, what problems he needs help with, and so on. The consultant should remember he is engaged in more than an information gathering process. He is building a climate of trust and confidence so that subsequently people can hear what he has to report and be willing to give it serious consideration as a basis for action. He cannot do that by isolating himself in his professional ivory tower. Trust is built out of repeated contacts in which people learn they need not be afraid, that the consultant is an ally, not an enemy.

Pattern of Organization

The consultant should remember that he is undertaking a holistic approach to the organization. He is to be interested in understanding the whole system rather than the interaction of one or two forces. He will be less interested in measurement and rigorous experimental control of variables than in how the whole system works. I raise this caution because as I discuss the next steps it will be easy for the reader to become preoccupied with parts of an organization.

Almost all organizations have some form of organization chart or plan which defines responsibilities. The consultant should get one from the person who is his major contact. However, he should not take the organization chart to represent the way the organization actually operates. Frequently the organization chart is not up to date. Sometimes it has not been distributed. It is not unusual for working relationships to grow up informally, particularly if a table of organization has not been published, which may be at variance from what the organizational leadership intends. Then, too, the informal organization, or the way the business of the organization actually gets done, may vary considerably from the way it is supposed to be done.

The consultant will find it informative to ask different people in the organization to draw an organization chart for him and to compare these with what he has been given. He will also find it helpful to know from each of his informants to whom they feel responsible for what, whether on the chart or not, and how they are evaluated by whom. This will help him round out the pattern of organization. If the organization chart is secret information or if no chart exists, problems of leadership may be of special significance. Members of the organization may struggle with questions of legitimate and illegitimate authority.

An early overall description of the organization must include enough detail about its internal structure and activities to guide the direction and depth of later stages of the study. The principal methods for accomplishing this early objective are the guided tour, to which I have already referred, and interviews with informants.

Settings

The concept of setting has particular application to organizations. One arrives at the observational units, called "settings," in the organization by discerning first overall organizational purposes and then how these purposes are subdivided into specific functions performed by definable groups within definable temporal and physical space.

If an organization is in the business of producing corrugated board, for example, it is apparent on a guided tour that this involves the production process; the supervision of that process; certain "front office" activities including customer contacts, sales, and bookkeeping; and maintenance functions so that the production machinery can be kept working. Each setting will be engaged in certain of these activities. The consultant must learn where and by whom essential functions of the organization are carried out.

The organizational purposes and subpurposes which a setting exists to perform influence the behavioral requirements which a setting imposes on people within it. The following central purposes or primary organizational tasks are similar to those identified by Bennis* to characterize different kinds of organizational functions:**

1. *Service:* complying with the request of another for materials, assistance, information, and so on, in a comparatively passive fashion.
2. *Problem solving:* responding to an environmental demand or opportunity involving creative selection from a variety of personal and organizational resources in order to satisfy the demand or capitalize on the opportunity. Problem solving activities may be distinguished from service activities by the greater requirement for active integration.
3. *Production:* performing automatic, repetitive, cyclic, or periodic activities with an identical outcome and involving a mandatory sequence of operations that attain the desired result.
4. *Indoctrination:* endeavoring to insure conformity with essential requirements from people who are joining or changing work roles.

---

* Warren G. Bennis, "Leadership Theory and Administrative Behavior," *Administrative Science Quarterly,* 4:12 (December 1959), 259–301.

** It should be recognized that although we can characterize a setting as far as its central purpose, this purpose itself may require subsetting or work roles with essential purposes of a different type. For example, a control setting may include data gathering and analysis functions (e.g., production data analysis by a production data analyst) and service functions (e.g., record keeping by file clerks), and problem solving functions (e.g., coordination, decision-making, or control).

5. *Control:* causing people or groups to undertake, cease, or alter task behaviors to meet organizational requirements.

This typology of setting purposes becomes clearer when it is related to specific purposes often seen in industrial organizations. *Service* activities are usually essential to support the purpose of some other setting. Hence a service setting usually is active in response to demands from a "parent" setting. Recruiting is one such type of activity often found in a personnel office. *Problem solving* settings often collect and correlate information about organizational activities to provide a basis for decision making. Many production planning or expediting departments serve such functions. Problem solving activities also characterize many innovative staff functions such as those in advertising or design departments. *Production* activities are characteristic of most factory settings in which "input," "conversion," and "throughput" or "output" phases can be discerned. Some raw material is changed or added to in a standardized way as it moves through the setting. The end product is a standardized unit or flow which can be produced only if the activities are performed in an unvarying sequence. *Indoctrination* settings are relatively rare in organizations; formalized industrial training programs are one specific example. *Control* activities include setting goals, evaluating process, and correcting deviations from established procedures. Most management settings are of this type, especially in their relationship to other settings in the organization.

Another feature of settings which can be assessed by questioning in the course of the guided tour is the *time* dimension to which Rice has given attention.* The reference here is to temporal boundaries within which the setting's central purpose is accomplished. These may be narrow and specific, such as a factory shift work, or long term and vague, such as planning activities in a management group.

Task Patterns

There are characteristic *task patterns* in each setting. This is essentially a group-level variable. It refers to the task-required pattern of relationships existing in any given setting. There are at least four such patterns.

1. *Complementary activities:* the group working toward a shared goal, the contribution of each group member distinguishable from, but intertwined with, others in the group.

* A. K. Rice, *Productivity and Social Organization: The Ahmedabad Experiment* (London: Tanistock, 1958).

2. *Parallel activities:* each group member performing essentially the same task.
3. *Sequential activities:* each group member performing some phase of the group task in a tandem relationship to coworkers.
4. *Individualized activities:* unique functions performed by each member of the group, neither complementary nor sequential.

Some problems will confront the consultant in discerning which of these patterns characterize a setting. *Informant interviews* are particularly useful here. Informants should include those whose job assignments require them to pay attention to the location of settings and the boundaries between them. Such informants may be (a) formal leaders of work groups; (b) cost accountants whose accounting systems often include a subdivision of activities according to setting and personnel; (c) industrial engineers whose jobs require them to introduce new people to settings or to understand the details of work activities within any given setting; (d) maintenance people whose repair and maintenance activities require them to make fine distinctions between various kinds of superficially similar tasks and machines.

Setting boundaries in general can be recognized by looking for agreement between several such informants. People inside and outside a given setting should agree on where a setting boundary exists. The following kinds of questions and observations will help to clarify the location of settings and the relationships between them:

What area do you work in?
What part of the operation are you responsible for?
Who works with you?
Where does the work go when your group has finished with it?
Where do you get your work (instructions, information, help) from?
Does anyone else use this space where you work for some other activity?

The consultant must distinguish *subsettings* within the organizational space. For example, a production setting may have two shifts with different personnel performing the same operations in the same space at different times. It then is useful to speak of this production setting and its subsettings, day shift and night shift. Even finer distinctions may be necessary at a later stage in the study if more intensive analysis of settings is undertaken. For example, within any given subsetting such as the day shift of a production area one may find various discrete activities (for example, the manufacture of different kinds of products) or various kinds of episodic events (a conference of supervisors) which involve only some of the people in the setting. Here we might speak of *situations within subsettings* which in turn form part of settings.

The preliminary mapping stage of the study is effected by drawing together the initial catalogue of settings, subsettings, task-required relationships between settings, a description of the activities in each, and the people formally in charge of each setting. At the same time the consultant also draws together his general impressions as they have emerged from the early overview of the organization. These range from current preoccupations of members of the organization to favorite expressions and the special vocabulary used in different settings and in the organization as a whole. Some settings seem favored; in others, people seem to be constantly under pressure or falling behind. Some names come up repeatedly and lead the consultant to consider these as key people, or someone who should be key by virtue of his formal position is not mentioned. These observations become orientation points. They are guides to what might be learned in the study and a consolidation of early experience which permits acceleration of the acquaintance of the consultant with as broad a group of people and situations in the organization as possible.

Plan of Study

From the initial mapping of the organization and early impressions, the general plan of the study is developed, to be modified on the basis of later observations. If more than one consultant is involved, this will require later coordination of results. A balance will have to be established between overlap of coverage for cross-checks and independent observations and activities for purposes of broad coverage. Enough flexibility should be built into the general plan so that the information to be forthcoming can be implemented in planning successive steps.

Some settings and subsettings will receive more intensive attention. These should include all settings with large populations or having central purposes which are particularly indispensable to the accomplishment of the organization's basic activities.

Although every setting is in some sense indispensable to the accomplishment of organizational purposes, there are clear priorities. In a production organization it would be essential to analyze intensively the various factory settings, the management function, and probably some of the office settings. If the organization is engaged in the sale of its products, the sales settings would also be selected for intensive analysis. And those particular production, sales, and office settings which had most members and were mentioned most frequently in the descriptions heard during the guided tour should get most intensive analysis. Cues such as these make it easier to decide which settings are indispensable to the accomplishment of organizational purposes.

The consultant will then have to arrange his interviewing and questionnaires so that he can be certain to have a representative sample of the organization. He should interview all of the top management group, however that is defined; the heads of each of the major functional groups he will cover; and randomly selected members of each of those functional groups. The remaining members of each of the groups may be sampled by questionnaire. Questionnaires should be administered in groups as soon as possible after entering the organization, before the formal interviewing, and they should be collected immediately on completion. This prevents contamination of the replies and provides data to be pursued in interviews and observation. Samples of an interview schedule and questionnaires are in the appendixes. However, the consultant may use whatever forms he chooses.

The number of people to be interviewed will depend on how much time the consultant has and the cost either to the research budget or the client. He should allow between an hour and a half and two hours with people at the senior executive level and at least an hour with those below that level. I, for one, find it easier to make notes during the interview and to dictate a comprehensive summary afterwards than to tape-record the interviews. Transcription from tape recordings takes at least four times as much time as the interview itself. There is considerable repetition in a series of interviews in the same organization, and often much of it is incidental to the purposes at hand.

The consultant will have to make appropriate adaptations in organizations which do not follow the usual organization chart pattern. George Fitzgerald offers these considerations from his study of a church institution:*

I. Every congregation seems to have a threefold division.
  a) *Staff:* This includes the pastor, secretaries, custodians, and frequently choir director. The unique thing about this is oftentimes, indeed it is

* George Fitzgerald, private communication.

even most desirable, the secretary is not a member of the congregation and, yet, of course, the secretaries have a great deal of influence in congregational life. In relation to the staff there would be those questions which have to do with job description (I [Fitzgerald] wonder if this isn't especially pertinent in relation to the pastor), job training, retirement plans, etc.

b) *Church Leader:* This is usually a slot made up of lay members who have been elected by the rest of the congregation. It would be revealing I [Fitzgerald] think to examine what training they have had for their position and also to try to understand what power they wield:

c) *Congregational members:* The pertinent questions in this category seem to be in terms of membership preparation and what relation this has to the whole process of reciprocation.

II. There seemed to be three questions about the church as an institution.

a) The relation of this congregation to its denomination.

b) It seems to me [Fitzgerald] there is increasing concern for interdenominational relations. This would be on the local, state, and national level. Of course the international level could also be included in terms of the World Council of Churches, etc.

c) The ideology of the congregation as to whether it is oriented to worship, education, local tradition, etc.

A school will involve students and teachers as well as administrators. A hospital may have a visiting staff who work in the institution but who are not employed by it nor part of its administrative activity.

Approach to the Setting and Its Incumbents

For administrative reasons and effective functioning, the consultant should move into a setting in steps suggested by the persons with formal authority: successive introductions from top executives through intermediate management and supervisory personnel to the line personnel. Unless this is done, people at each level are uncertain about the legitimacy of their spending time with the investigator.

The consultant may find it easy or difficult to enter a setting for general contacts or detailed observations and interviews. He may find that the detailed observation he wishes to make is strenuously resisted either by all the persons in the setting or those in the setting with formal authority who must be seen in any case in order that the request to enter the setting be honored. Whether a setting is difficult or easy to enter is an important datum in itself, since this often tells the consultant something about the way in which people in the setting see themselves or are seen by other parts of the organization. It will also tell something about the personality

and favored working style of the key figure in the setting. The consultant
may find, for example, if he is doing research, that researchers are barred
from a certain setting because it is a "secret" area in the organization.
There may be objective reasons for this: activities there may involve confidential relationships to customers or classified military information. Or
people in the setting may be preoccupied with a serious organizational
problem which cannot be revealed to the consultant until greater trust has
been established.

The analogy here to the psychotherapeutic relationship is obvious. In
psychotherapy, avoidance and denial as well as attack may occur when
topics or relationships are introduced which trigger an awareness of
conflict or problems. Similar psychological processes may be operating in
the organizational situation when the consultant is denied access to certain settings or activities for reasons which may not be apparent.

The practical question is: What is to be done when access to a setting
is difficult or denied? Usually this will occur in the initial contact with
the person or people in formal authority in that setting. It is helpful at
this point for the consultant to communicate that he accepts the fact that
there is no time to cater to him at the moment. But he should also communicate that he would like to understand this lack of time as it helps
him understand work in this setting, if not at the moment, then when it
is more convenient.

The general tone of this approach by the consultant is to invite those
in the setting to work with him on the understanding of this problem,
even if it is appropriate for him to leave the setting temporarily and
come back at a more convenient time. In any case the consultant should
attempt to establish a collaborative relationship rather than an exploitative one. Often resistance is mobilized because the consultant is seen as
allied with top management against lower levels. The consultant can
grant that he has been able to penetrate this far into the organization
only because management has allowed him to do so. However, he can
demonstrate that his orientation is, not to get answers which will be used
against people by management, but as an independent professional functioning with the agreement of management to learn and to understand
for constructive purposes.

In undertaking his interviews, the consultant should remember that
the interview has much more psychological meaning to the interviewee
than is likely to be apparent. Renato Tagiuri points out that man reaches
an optimum balance with his environment by working out his *technical*

role, his *power* position and his *sentiments* in relationship to others, particularly in his organization.* He must work them out again in relation to the consultant, and the consultant must do so with respect to him. So both parties have not only their relationship with each other but also their more enduring relationships to the organizations in which they work. The interviewee will want to state what he has to say in his own way and at the same time to avoid being shown up. He needs to maintain his position in the organization and his self-esteem after the consultant is gone. The consultant needs to satisfy his own organization (whether a university department, a consulting firm, or a group of colleagues), the client, and himself. But he cannot let the pressure to satisfy his needs result in his exploiting the interviewee. Thus, Tagiuri notes, the consultant must listen and observe, letting the client give and generate information that helps the consultant understand how the client experiences the organization and his work life.

The consultant should precede each interview or questionnaire administration by reintroducing himself to the interviewee, restating the purposes of the study or consultation, recalling its confidential nature, and, if that is the case in this study, indicating to the respondent that he need not be interviewed if he does not want to be. Even if a clear description has been given when permission was sought and granted for the study, most people will remain hazy about the intent and purposes. Some will have heard rumors which need to be corrected. The consultant should take nothing for granted about the respondent's understanding no matter how often he has indicated publicly the nature of his work in the organization. When the interview is completed, the consultant should permit the respondent to ask any questions he has to further clarify the consultant's function. Often individual interviewees will ask if their answers are like the replies of other respondents. This usually is a question to test the interviewer. He should repeat that inasmuch as the interviews are confidential, he cannot disclose what other individuals have said, but sometimes he can offer a general response which satisfies the questioner but does not reject him or his questions.

The interviewer should indicate to the interviewee that his interview will be examined along with others and a summary of the study reported to the group as a whole. He should indicate the same to groups to whom he is administering questionnaires.

* Renato Tagiuri, "Of Change and the Consultant," *The Arthur Young Journal* (Winter 1967), 1–3.

Observation and On-the-Job Contacts

One of the major problems with consultants and researchers is that they depend too much on interview and questionnaire data. Too few spend time observing the actual processes of work, work flow, communications, and work relationships. The on-the-job contact is a way of ascertaining how a person feels about his situation while he is in the setting.

I prefer to spend as much time as I can observing these events by being on site, asking people to explain to me what they do, how they do it, and the problems inherent in getting their work done. This may involve sitting in executive offices or keeping notes on the events of the day or walking from machine to machine or attending various kinds of meetings (including those for distributors, salesmen, outside visitors, boards of directors) or sitting in on training and orientation programs. On the plant floor I prefer to bring my lunch bucket to be able to take coffee breaks and lunch with the employees.

On both the plant floor and out in the field, such as riding the trucks of a public utility company, the consultant should wear clothes appropriate to the setting. On the floor, a gray work smock is sufficient; he need not wear overalls. Nor need he pretend to be "one of the boys." Employees will know that he is not one of them so pretense will only offend them. His interest in their work and the problems related to it will generate confidence and he will learn much informally. He will find it helpful for later analysis to sketch the layout of the work site and the points at which people congregate for coffee or lunch and to note who goes with whom and what the various topics of conversation are. Such sketches and accompanying notes will give him a picture of the organization as a combination of interdependent behavioral settings. He will readily observe the required role performances, the work to be done, and the nonrole performances. It will also give him an opportunity to observe how authority figures function and how people relate to them.

The consultant will often be asked about himself and his work, which will give him an opportunity for further explanation. And he need not be afraid of entering the conversation on noncompany topics like baseball. In smaller organizations I have found it helpful to visit the plant floor regularly. In some instances I have also found it helpful to explain to visiting guests, like distributors, what the study is all about if I am asked to do so by the management.

There are no simple rules for initiating contact and conversation on the job. "How long have you worked here?" can provide an easy start for someone since the answer is simple and it refers to the past which is generally less threatening than the present. Such a question leads naturally into such things as "What led you to work here in particular?" or "What had you expected this place to be like?" Such questions will often stimulate expression of attitudes about the setting. "What do you do?" or "How do you spend your time?" is often an incisive way to enter into the area of the person's functions and skills. Variations of this are necessary when one is right on the job with the person. Even though the functions seem clear, it is best to hear his description. If nothing is mentioned of other people, it is important to note this and to ask "How does your work fit in with the others around here?" or "I noticed that somebody comes by every once in a while. Why do they do that?" If the investigator notices a look of chagrin or pleasure, he should ask the person, "What happened then?" The most important principle is that of digging deeper, particularly in finding about sources of feelings which are observable. "What's wrong?" or "That seemed to come out well," are comments usually worth more than those which provoke straight information.

Observe different levels of comfort in dealing with the investigator. Perhaps, for example, only a small proportion of people in a setting may look the consultant in the eye when speaking. He then must ask himself why the others do not and learn more about this phenomenon. Are those people in this setting ashamed? Angry? Fearful? Of what?

Note how work is initiated and terminated. There may be a rush from the job at break time and heavy sighs of relief. As a supervisor passes, one may see a subordinate grit his teeth or turn to a coworker and say something which leads the other to laugh. The consultant must keep his attention sufficiently dispersed to understand interpersonal relations which occur "naturally."

A consultant should look for experiences which appear stressful to people. What kinds of occurrences disrupt or disorganize people and lead them to seek help? What situations stimulate worry? While one can and should ask about these, there are many opportunities to observe them in everyday life on the job. For example, when something dramatic occurs that is visible to all of the people in a setting, the consultant should scan the setting to assess reactions. If, for instance, an assembly line is shut down or breaks down frequently, that may not be as disruptive as it might seem. People might welcome the respite. Do people help get it started or do they evidence relief and wait for others to solve the problem? Do supervisors move in smoothly and calmly or do they become peremptory with the persons involved? In the office situation, what occurs when a new person comes into the setting on business? Who handles him? What do the others do while such a transaction occurs? What do persons in and out of a setting say about those who work in that setting? Is background information necessary to a fuller comprehension of usual or characteristic setting experiences? Which are the persons most talked about? Which are favored and disfavored? What kinds of personal characteristics and work characteristics tend to be the focus of conversation?

For example, the person whose name comes up repeatedly in a setting may be a young, aggressive, outspoken lad about whom people seem to agree regarding his characteristic behaviors. Some resent his outspoken qualities, particularly his supervisors, while others at and below his level have mixed feelings. They feel he adds some life to the place and respect him for speaking his mind but think that he is sometimes aggressive just to be aggressive. Such a pattern, along with other information and observation, can lead to understanding a general pattern in the setting in which conformity and smooth relationships are valued particularly highly. The action of this aggressive person can be the focus of attention as a means for supervisors to express their concern about aggression. Some gain vicarious pleasure out of this one person's independence while others view his behavior ambivalently because they themselves fear that outspokenness and the aggression associated with it is dangerous.

There are other questions that will aid in a general assessment of characteristic setting experiences:

1. Do people enjoy leaving the job to talk with the consultant so they can get away from it? How do they break off the interview when they are called by their supervisor?
2. Do people go into some detail in explaining their jobs or do they brush over what they do? Do they feel their work is a sufficiently important aspect of what goes on in the setting and organization that they feel the consultant should know it well?
3. What are difficult, frustrating, or trying aspects of the job? Which are most gratifying? Can and do people resolve many of these difficulties themselves? From whom do they get support or technical help? Do they feel comfortable calling on others?
4. What other people are brought in during conversation? Which are viewed positively and negatively and why?

5. In the total contact, does the person focus primarily on his job, the setting, or the organization as a whole? How much focus is there on the purposes served by his activities? Does he see himself as a specialist with considerable skill or as doing something which anyone can do?

There are many analogous questions to ask. But all must be directed to the consultant's objectives.

How can conditions of observation be sufficiently standardized to permit later comparisons? Work roles differ enormously in the activities they require and the time spans necessary to accomplish any given activity. Continuous observation over an indefinitely long time span would be the only way to be assured of getting "the whole story" of work role requirements confronting a given person, and that is obviously impossible. On the other hand, brief time spans for observation probably will yield an unrepresentative sample of activities in a given role, since behaviors conforming with some role requirements may occur too infrequently to fall within the observation period. A minimum of two hours of work activity should be observed to provide a reasonable opportunity for a satisfactory sample.

Recording Data

The observation record includes descriptions of *episodes*. This is the basic unit of the observation record. An episode is an event of work activity with a recognizable beginning and end. The definition of what would constitute an episode for a given work role should be decided upon in consultation with an informant and by a trial period of observation. Over a two-hour period there may be a dozen or several hundred such episodes, and they may be characterized as *task related* (for example, running a machine) or *nontask related* (for example, talking with a fellow worker about vacation plans).

For each episode, the following information is recorded:

a. the *time span* in minutes
b. *task or nontask* content
c. *source of the stimulus* that initiates the activity: within the setting; another organizational setting; an extraorganizational setting
d. *orientation of the subject* to the stimulus: compliant (responding to an instruction), collaborative (mutually sharing in a common task with some other person), or initiative (is himself the source of the stimulus)

e. *process* of activity *during the episode:* task related — producing a given item (or monitoring the production of an item by a machine), solving a problem, providing a service, or exercising managerial control over the activities of others; nontask related: relationships with persons other than coworkers or a personal "work" project

f. *outcome* of the episode: within the setting, in another organizational setting, an extraorganizational setting

g. *orientation of the subject to the outcome:* compliant, collaborative, or directive

h. *interpersonal relationship of the subject during the episode:* to a superior, a subordinate, a peer, or someone in another relationship to him (for example, friend outside the organization, relative, customer)

A half hour should be allowed at the end of each observation period to clarify with the subject any information in these categories which may not have been clear to the consultant when a given episode occurred.

Data Summary

For each person observed, the following information can be readily computed from the observation record:

a. *Average time* per episode

b. *Total number* of episodes during the observation period: total task related; total nontask related

c. Of task related episodes: relatively *most frequent source* of stimulus and subject orientation; relatively *most frequent activity* process; relatively *most frequent outcome* and subject orientation

d. *Total interactions* with: superiors, peers, subordinates, others

Setting Data Summary

From the summarized records and process notes taken by the observer, the following items of information for the total setting are prepared:

a. *total number* of episodes

b. *average episode time*

c. *number of stimuli* and *orientation* of setting occupants for each type of stimulus

d. *type of task process* for each setting occupant

e. *outcome* of setting activities and orientation of setting occupants to each outcome

f. *patterns of interpersonal relations* in the setting, both task and non-task.

Work Experience: Rationale

On-the-Job Interview

An on-the-job interview can make a unique contribution to the understanding of how a man's work influences his total psychological experience. The setting of the interview enables the consultant to see and sense what goes on in a man's life at work, and the consultant may talk over his observations with the subject.

As the consultant interviews a person at his job, the latter can demonstrate what he means in describing his situation. This is apparent enough in the factory-machine situation where a man shows the machine part or process he could not adequately describe in an office. This also holds true for the desk job. An executive may have an interaction during the interview with someone he had mentioned earlier. Discussion can then clarify what was meant in terms of this shared interaction.

The fact that the consultant interviews someone at his work site assures him of the consultant's interest in his work. The consultant demonstrates that he is interested enough in what he can learn not only to come to the organization but also to come "all the way" to the interviewee and that part of the company which the latter knows best. Whether he be a man on a machine, at the warehouse dock, or at the executive desk, the consultant is meeting him on his home ground.

The on-the-job context for the interview insures a heavier focus on work than is likely if the consultant sees someone in another place. Gouldner* illustrates this point in his description of research in the mining industry. He describes how interaction between field workers and miners *in the shafts* facilitated communication. Obviously, if the same employees interviewed on the job were seen in the consultant's office, the interviews would change drastically. The same principle holds true as the consultant moves any distance from someone's work situation, even to a special office within the company.

* Alvin W. Gouldner, *Patterns of Industrial Bureaucracy* (New York: Free Press, 1954).

The consultant must approach the setting and its personnel as an empathic learner. He must communicate to each person interest in the person's view of the setting. The person knows best how aspects of the setting, superiors, tasks, peers, are important *to him*. His assessment of others and their reactions to the setting have some validity. The person himself is the best informant about how he himself feels about his job and its many facets.

The consultant should communicate in feeling and words: "I want to learn about your work and what it means to you and people around you. You are really the only one who has access to your inner experience. I want to learn about what you feel, see, and think. I need and will appreciate your help. I do not want to interfere with you too much, but I cannot learn from you without visiting with you. I hope you will be willing to help me at this time. If not, I will understand." As rapport is established, the interviewee may give a rather general description of what he does and how he feels about doing it. The consultant always seeks further understanding of the person and his situation. The consultant frequently must ask the person to "show me what you mean" or "tell me more about that so that I can understand better." At times he may even ask the person to teach him some part of his job since this will make it easier to share experiences which the person is having or has had in the past.

Such endeavor can communicate to the subject not so much the consultant's prying but a reflection of his sincere interest in understanding what the person feels about what he does and the clarity with which he himself sees his work. Even after more inquiry, some avoidance or omission of his work life, consciously or unconsciously, is usually evident. The person may begin to fear what the observer might do with the information to be gained. He may feel that certain areas about which he is keenly concerned or preoccupied are "inappropriate." People often need help from a consultant to enable them to communicate freely.

The consultant may have to reassure the subject that an interview is not intended to be judgmental. When the emphasis on the person and *his* views seems too threatening, the consultant can turn to talk of less anxiety laden areas, perhaps other people. The consultant from the outset indicates that what he learns from an interviewee and others is confidential. If a consultant is asked what "others" say, he can reassure the interviewee that his own view is most important. What specific "others" say is, of course, confidential. This is not a reprimand, but a reminder and a way to tell the person that the consultant means what he says about confidentiality. As indicated earlier, however, if appropriate, he might make some general statement which satisfies the interviewee but does not distort the consultant's effort.

Negative feelings are often difficult to communicate. People experience deeper unconscious concerns which psychologically magnify to them the effects of their conscious hostile feelings toward the company, their supervisor, their colleagues, or their task. The consultant can aid them by demonstrating the acceptability of these consciously experienced negative feelings. "No one has a perfect job," "Everyone finds some parts of his job less satisfactory than others," or similar statements communicate that the consultant is not himself afraid of anger or hostility. Such communication asserts that the consultant is sincerely interested in all facets of the person's experience at work.

The on-the-job interview permits the consultant to observe a person reacting to his job situation — its demands, its uniqueness — a small sample of his total work life experience. The consultant sees what the subject's task demands of him in thought and motor skills; the number and quality of interpersonal transactions; sources of gratification and frustration. Such observations alone help the consultant to learn much about those experiences that have peculiar psychological and emotional impact on the person.

Interviewing on the job extends what the consultant can learn. What an individual says about what the consultant observes provides a check on what the consultant thinks the person's experiences mean to him. Or, when he has told about an experience, the consultant can stay alert to observe it in the person's work life. Sometimes, the individual is unaware of those facets of his work experience which the consultant's observations tell him are important to him. He may tighten up, flush, or betray some other sign of stress when his supervisor approaches. One might infer the stress whatever he may say about his relationship to his boss. But its significance differs if he *describes* this relationship as stressful or pleasant or lacking in conflict. Thus the consultant's presence in the situation helps him judge and differentiate what an individual wants to be true, believes to be true, and what is true about his psychological reactions to his work situation.

The on-the-job interview contrasts in form and goals with other study contacts with people at work such as those occurring during tours or incidental visits. In these contacts, the consultant is getting acquainted with people and giving them the opportunity to perceive his purposes accurately. Chance strongly determines what sample of their work the investigator observes. Sampling across the organization is rarely representative. The consultant is seeking general themes shared by numbers of individuals.

The consultant may learn from one person about his reaction to some union problems; from another, certain characteristics of his supervisor which he likes; from another, his reaction to a recent change in job functions or product. If the consultant happens to have many contacts with one person, he may come to know him well and know his reactions to these many conditions. But what is learned from him cannot be compared systematically to what is learned from each of the others because the depth and extent of contact is not equalized for all people seen.

Sampling errors in visits and tours around an organization are bound to occur. Sections vary in their visibility and accessibility. Some people are rarely seen because they work at "the other end" of a plant. The consultant spends more time in the "favorite" settings of the person who conducts a tour. These are some of the natural conditions of field work which makes it exceedingly difficult to acquire equivalent data from all parts of the organization.

The on-the-job interview procedures compensate for such sources of error by sampling job roles and settings and standardizing the duration and form of the interview and the representativeness of the job sample as much as possible.

Selection of Interviewees

The consultant should base his selection of individuals for on-the-job interviews on the number of major settings and job roles in the organization studied. The early mapping of the organization and general impressions provide this information.

Ideally, for purposes of understanding influential factors throughout an organization, the consultant should see two individuals in each of the major job roles existing in each setting. If one setting becomes the focus of special interest, increase of this sample is necessary to provide more comprehensive understanding. Similarly, if time restricts the number of people whom the consultant can see, sampling should be decreased in those settings or job roles which appear less likely to contribute knowledge being sought by the consultant. Such decisions must often be arbitrary.

The sampling for the on-the-job interview or other methods is a function of the consultant's goals. In an exploratory study which seeks to understand a total organization, weight must be given to broad coverage in as many settings and job roles as time permits. However, if a study seeks to understand the work problems of a given group of individuals (perhaps at a particular level in the hierarchy of an organization) or the impact of some particular organizational problems or events, the consultant must heavily sample those individuals most directly concerned. Such sampling decisions are never of the "either-or" type, since one setting or group is never isolated from others and all settings are not equally critical for understanding the experiences of people in an organization.

The consultant should be fully aware of his areas of heavy and light sampling so that he can appropriately qualify or assert his findings. For example, if no one has been seen in the local sales setting of a company, a consultant cannot know that general themes he discovers in contacts with other people in other settings are relevant to local salesmen. Similarly, if the consultant has seen twelve of the fifteen people in the shipping setting, he can feel confident of the generality of his findings for the setting as a whole.

Structure of Interview

The on-the-job interview should be conducted in a reasonably standard way. However, this does not mean that exactly the same things should be done and said with each individual. The standardization sought is that each interviewee is given maximum opportunity to reveal those aspects of his work experience which are psychologically significant to him. This requires that the consultant compensate for individual differences in anxiety and its expression, talkativeness, clarity of description, and investment in the study process. The consultant may have to guide one person away from being repetitive, while in another instance he may have to prod for more depth in a specific area which the person is skipping over.

Despite such differences as these, there are ways in which the form of the interview can be standardized to achieve equal opportunity of expression for each person. One way is to control *the duration of the interview*. An interview of 50–60 minutes provides a balance between the consultant's need to cover large numbers of people and the time it takes to enable a person to reveal his major involvements in and reactions to various facets of his work life. Clearly, if one person is seen for fifteen minutes and another for two hours, the latter is likely to discuss a wider range of topics.

Specific behavior in the interview (standing, sitting, shouting, whispering) will vary considerably depending upon the actual work situation, but some standardization is possible and necessary. The consultant should structure his interviews so that he can *converse with the interviewee at least one-half of the scheduled time* (whether this is distributed over the interview period or in blocks of time). He may spend some of his time doing the interviewees' job. Special attention must be given to loud noise or lack of privacy without so distorting the interview situation that the on-the-job conditions no longer prevail. The variety of situations defies simple rules. The consultant may talk with the interviewee during periodic breaks in work rhythm or away from the job site for five- or ten-minute intervals during the hour or discuss confidential topics when others are out of earshot.

Representativeness of the work sample during which the interview is held should be controlled whenever possible. The attempt consistently should be to find a representative hour of a person's work experience. Planning the occasion of the interview with either the interviewee himself or someone else familiar with interviewee's job role is helpful. Seeing a personnel interviewer during one of his interviews or a machine adjustor while he is setting up a machine is highly desirable. When this is not possible or it turns out during an interview that another time would have been more representative, the consultant seeks to understand the other situation as well as possible from the person's description.

Conducting the Interview

In conducting his interviews on-the-job, the consultant, as he has with others, must first meet the individual's need for a rational, reasonably unconflictive understanding of the study and the consultant. The consultant should introduce and identify himself at the outset of the interview. He must clarify or reclarify as necessary the purposes and structure of the interview. He must recognize what threat and discomfort may be experienced by the individual and allay or control these so that they do not become dominant or accentuated. The consultant must make the experience as constructive as possible for the interviewee within the limits of the relationship and its purposes in order that the interview be fruitful for both.

The purpose of the interview should be described as a means of "learning from you, because you know your job and reactions to it better than anyone else." This rationale for the interview and its goal, learning what his work means to the interviewee, must often be reasserted in one form or another during the interview. Some individuals will persist in trying to give "right" answers. The consultant must continually reemphasize that he wants this person's individual reactions to work and its components.

The consultant can encourage a frank, individual reaction by stating from time to time that all people respond differently. He should be careful not to convey judgment about the person's statements or answers to questions, since this would communicate that there are right and wrong or acceptable and unacceptable answers.

At times, in order to more fully understand something the person has said, it may be helpful to ask him to show the consultant what he means. Beyond this, it is sometimes appropriate, depending upon the consultant's predilection and the type of task, to ask the person to show the consultant himself how to do something. This not only can convey the interest in the person's unique situation but also can provide insights into areas of experience which cannot be described. And this further asserts the person's expertness in the job compared to that of the consultant.

Hence, the tone throughout the interview is one of the consultant and interviewee working together during their time together so that the consultant will know as well as possible what this person's work experiences are and what they mean to him. Asking in one form or another what the individual does in his job or how he spends his time provides an opening for conversation if the individual has been unable spontaneously to describe his reactions to his work situation. Asking him about something the consultant sees him do serves a similar purpose. As the person talks about his work and its requirements, the consultant questions him further about those areas which he does not understand so well and particularly those areas which seem of special affective significance. "What happened then?" asked after a person grimaces or smiles can yield important insights.

After fifteen minutes to a half an hour, the interviewer should deliberately assess for himself what he has and has not learned about the person, separating those areas which he feels he knows well, those in which he wants further information, and those in which he knows little, if anything. This assessment should guide the consultant in the remainder of the interview.

The general questions to be kept in mind to insure coverage of key areas during the interview are:

What are this person's sources of involvement and lack of involvement, satisfaction and dissatisfaction?

How does this person's work contribute to his knowledge and judgment
   about himself?
How does he perceive and respond to others at work?
What meaning does his activity and productivity have for him?
What are normative stresses for him and what coping techniques does he
   utilize in dealing with them?

At the end of the hour, as in every contact, time should be taken to
thank the person and to demonstrate the help he has given by illustrating
something learned from him. It is important to leave him with an experience of having contributed. This is not meant to be an insincere gim-
mick. There is no interview in which the consultant does not learn something. For example, saying to an individual at the end of an interview
that there are many more facets to his work than appeared evident before
the interview and exemplifying one of those, conveys to him that the consultant has learned something of how the interviewee sees his task. The
particular statement and example will vary for each person. The statements which are most successful are those in which the consultant incorporates his awareness of positive or negative feelings the person has revealed about his work. By this the consultant conveys that he has sought
to understand this person as an individual and that the person has been
successful in contributing to this goal.

Recording the Interview

The interview should be recorded as soon as possible from the notes
that were taken. The particular form and exhaustiveness of these notes
must vary depending upon the bent, skills, and memory of the consultant
and the particular situation, including the response of the interviewee to
note taking. But every effort should be made to record sufficient data during and after the interview to permit an adequate analysis.

The consultant should record, in order of their occurrences throughout
the interview, what the interviewee says, does, and feels; his reactions to
others including the consultant; and the consultant's reaction to him. The
record of the interview should highlight specific occurrences during the
interview period such as interactions with others, specific job activities,
the interviewee's emotional reactions, and his references to himself. Any
topics concerning nonwork, tasks, coworkers, or the person's setting
should be included as well as questions that the interviewer asked which
might have led to these, since spontaneous and requested statements often
differ in their significance.

The Impact of the Consultant

As already indicated, the consultant will have a significant impact on the information he gets and the feelings of those with whom he works. He must gauge that impact continuously. One way of doing so is suggested by Howard V. Perlmutter.*

a. What information did I spontaneously offer or give on request to which members of the organization?
b. How was this information used?
c. Thinking of two or three of the "richest" relationships I had with persons in the organization:
    1. What did this relationship mean to the person involved?
    2. Why? (How was I seen by him?)
d. From contacts with me, what did persons learn about previously unrecognized potentialities in interpersonal relationships?
e. How did people attempt to "modify" me and how did I cope with these efforts?
f. What kinds of emotional support (empathy, structuring, etc.) did I provide and to whom?
g. In carrying out my work, what did I convey about my view of the organization which represented new learning (especially integrative, synthesizing operations) for organization members?
h. What kinds of spontaneous overtures were made to me by organization members and (1) what induced these overtures, (2) what was their psychological meaning?
i. How did my intervention affect (1) authority relationships and (2) peer relationships in various parts of the organization?
j. What was the impact on organization members of my raising questions concerning:
    1. the meaning of the product
    2. the meaning of work
    3. supervision
    4. peer relationships
    5. fantasies at work
    6. relationship between work and home?
k. In what ways did people in the organization try to use me for purposes which I felt were inappropriate?
l. In what ways did people in the organization *fail* to use me for purposes which I would have considered appropriate?

* Howard V. Perlmutter, private communication.

The Person Who Seeks Help

Sometimes, if the consultant is a psychologist or psychiatrist, people may want to ask him about personal or family problems. When the clinician sees a nonpatient, the "contract" is a different one but just as binding an arrangement as the one made with a patient. In the case of consultation, the nonpatient is an employee who is approached by the clinician and is asked to volunteer information about himself for organizational purposes. Thus the contract involves an agreement between two parties to work toward a goal that does not assume that the clinician and the employee will become therapist and patient. If they do, it constitutes a breach of the contract.

Because of the nature of this contractual arrangement, the clinician as an organizational consultant with nonpatients explains clearly at the beginning of each interview in what role he is placing himself and what he expects of the other.

A breach of the contract may occur when either:

a. the interviewee expects and wants the consultant to treat him as a patient, that is, to assume the role of a diagnostician and therapist or
b. the consultant interprets the interviewee's references to psychological difficulties, for example, the statement that he has been a psychiatric patient, as a request that the consultant act as a therapist

In some cases the interviewee may refer to the consultant as a person skilled in treating patients and ask for help and advice spontaneously. It would be callous and inhuman to refuse to respond to this plea, but the consultant must be absolutely certain of the interviewee's motive and purpose in introducing such a request in the interview. This will insure against such unfortunate and destructive situations as an interviewee claiming that despite the consultant's claims about the purpose of the consultation, he is in fact trying to find out who the crazy people are in the plant.

To deal with the situation where a person asks for advice the consultant should:

a. ascertain clearly the nature of the employee's request by repeating his statement, to confirm how correct the consultant's impression has been
b. tell the employee that his request has been understood
c. call to the employee's attention, by a brief review of the opening state-

ments made at the beginning of the interview, that the purpose of the interview is not to have the consultant act as a psychological consultant

d. give appropriate advice about ways of getting professional help

e. tell the person that he must assume the responsibility for future contacts with the consultant if he wishes to discuss the matter further (it must be made very clear in the person's mind that the consultant is willing to be of help, but that this is the person's choice)

Termination

Whatever the length of his work in the field, the consultant is faced with the task of anticipating and dealing constructively with the termination of his relationship there. Unrealistic expectancies, inaccurate perception of his motivations, and concerns about the consequences of what they have revealed occur frequently and understandably in the people he has studied. Administrators and others will often ask for information about specific findings and impressions about sections of their organization. These requests will occur even though the consultant had said consistently during the study that he would take considerable time to analyze his data and that he would not, in any case, divulge confidences.

People will have asked him to carry their messages to others even though he had pointed out that what he learned would go no further in any identifiable way. People will demonstrate guilt for unloading information and reactions they had held back earlier, feeling that they had behaved unfairly by not being frank enough.

Such reactions are a small sample of the many ways in which people demonstrate the importance of the consultant's relationship to them, the power which they perceive in him and his study, and their fears and hopes about what he might accomplish. The difficulty people have in taking him at his word, their sometimes inaccurate and irrational perception of his power and motives cannot be attributed to a few peculiar individuals. For each person who blatantly evidences these reactions, there are many who reveal them subtly and others whose reactions have been too insensitive to recognize.

It is important not only to clarify the "contract" of the study through the field work but again at the last stages of the field relationship. Particularly at this time, it is important to help people recognize their concerns and inappropriate hopes along with showing them appreciation for their investment and faith in the consultant.

Is it needless for the consultant to demonstrate that he is not omnipotent and omniscient? Not at all. Such unrealistic perception of the consultant is characteristic. And it is important to confront people with the reality of his limitations, not out of simple scientific objectivity or modesty, but as a means to aid them to recognize their strength and independence. Those who doubt the potential of a consultant to trip off such dependence and transference in a period of, say, a week should reflect on field studies in which they have taken part and even speeches they have given. Are not the people who linger, question, and later phone often expressing a view of the scientist, clinician, or professor as all-powerful? Why else would people ask, "What should I do if . . . ?" when the consultant so often tells them that there is no simple formula for handling human behavior constructively?

The general procedure for the consultant to follow includes such things as mentioning his imminent departure to people and, ultimately, a walk through the settings, saying goodbye and thanks individually. He should give people a chance to ask further questions and express any last minute opinions and ideas they had not taken the opportunity to do earlier. They should be reassured in whatever ways are appropriate that they have been helpful. The consultant should refer to particular shared conversations with individuals, conveying that he had in fact come to know them to some degree. He must tell all that he will be coming back at a later date with a report on the study.

The last contacts are usually with the organizational representative who allowed entry and with whom the consultant planned the overall study. They should review where things stand, the general reactions of people to the study, and the consultant's own reactions. This review is usually carried on with considerable give and take in the conversation. The consultant usually picks up whatever loose ends, uncertainties, questions, and future plans need attention.

The feedback report is itself a critical part of the termination process even if delayed several months (see Part IV). Resolution of the fantasies about what the consultant might do with the information he has gained cannot occur with any completeness or finality until he has returned and reported. Only the report, a face-to-face experience, permits such resolution. After the feedback and discussion of it with people in an organization, termination can be seen as reasonably complete.

Part II

ORGANIZATIONAL
CASE STUDY
PROCESS

4

CASE STUDY
OUTLINE

This outline lists the individual topics to be covered in the case study. Chapters 5 through 9 explain the outline and elaborate it with examples. After the reader becomes familiar with this manual, he is likely to find himself working directly with the outline. He will then refer only occasionally to the discussions and examples in the text and to the references. The references at the end of the book are ordered sequentially according to their relationship to the outline topics. At the top of each page of references are listed the pages in the text to which those references refer. The reader may go directly to the reference for a given topic by using the page numbers as a guide, or go from references to text and vice versa the same way.

I. GENETIC DATA [Chapter 5, pp. 66–92]

A. Identifying Information [pp. 67–74]

1. Organization name
2. Location
3. Type of organization
4. Organizational affiliation

5. Size

    a. *Financial condition*
    b. *Stockholders*
    c. *Employees*

6. Situation of the initial contract

    a. *Consultation*
    b. *Research orientation*

7. Circumstances of the study
8. Special conditions affecting validity of the study
9. First overall impressions

B. Historical Data [pp. 74–92]

1. Chief complaint or events leading to the initiation of the study
2. Problems of the organization as stated by key figures

    a. *Long-range*
    b. *Short-range*

3. Background of the organization

    a. *Key developmental phases*

        (1) *As reported by organizational participants*
        (2) *As reported by outsiders*
        (3) *As reported by the consultant*

    b. *Major crises experienced by the organization*

        (1) *Natural catastrophies*
        (2) *Loss of key personnel*
        (3) *Labor problems*
        (4) *Financial emergencies*
        (5) *Technological changes*

    c. *Product-service history*

        (1) *Change and development of organizational goals*
        (2) *Sequence of development in product or service*
        (3) *Relative success or failure in various stages of service or product history*
        (4) *Geographical patterns*
        (5) *Special skills of the organization*
        (6) *Performance reputation and record*

    d. *Organizational folklore*

4. Circumstances surrounding study

II. DESCRIPTION AND ANALYSIS OF CURRENT ORGANIZATION AS A WHOLE [Chapter 6, pp. 93–169]

A. Structural Data [pp. 95–143]

1. Formal organization
   a. *Chart*
   b. *Systems concept*
   c. *Formal job description*
2. Plant and equipment
   a. *Location: territory covered*
   b. *Value*
   c. *Kinds of equipment: size, function*
   d. *Relative efficiency: age, obsolescence*
   e. *Special demands plant and equipment make on people*
   f. *Varieties of work environment*
3. Ecology of the organization
   a. *Spatial distribution of individuals*
   b. *Spatial distribution of activities*
   c. *Implications of the data on spatial distribution*
4. Financial structure
5. Personnel
   a. *How many people are employed*
   b. *Where do they come from and what is their ethnic composition*
   c. *What are the various educational levels*
   d. *What is the average tenure*
   e. *What is the range of skills*
   f. *What is the absentee rate*
   g. *What is the turnover rate*
   h. *What is the accident rate*
6. Structure for handling personnel
   a. *Recruitment*
   b. *Orientation*
   c. *Training*
   d. *Growth on the job*
   e. *Promotion*
   f. *Compensation*
   g. *Performance analysis*
   h. *Kind and intensity of supervision*

i. Rules and regulations for employees
j. Medical program
k. Safety program
l. Retirement program
m. Recreation program
n. Other fringe benefits
o. Labor contract

7. Policies and procedures

   a. Scope
   b. How they are communicated
   c. Who knows about them
   d. What discretion is left to lower supervisory levels

8. Time span and rhythm

   a. Seasonal cycles
   b. Diurnal cycles
   c. Planning spans
   d. Degree activities are regulated by time
   e. Attitudes about punctuality
   f. Urgency
   g. Concern about deliveries

B. Process Data [pp. 143–169]

1. Communication systems

   a. Incoming: reception and routing
      (1) Amount and types of materials
      (2) Modes of transmission
         (A) ORAL OR WRITTEN
         (B) FORMAL OR INFORMAL CHANNELS
      (3) Timing, rhythm, urgency
         (A) ACCORDING TO PLAN
         (B) ERRATICALLY OR SPONTANEOUSLY
      (4) Source and audience

   b. Processing: integration, decision
      (1) Amount and types of material
      (2) Modes of processing
         (A) ORAL OR WRITTEN
         (B) FORMAL OR INFORMAL CHANNELS
      (3) Timing, rhythm, urgency
         (A) ACCORDING TO PLAN
         (B) ERRATICALLY OR SPONTANEOUSLY
      (4) Source and audience

c. *Outgoing: routing and response*
  (*1*) *Amount and types of materials*
  (*2*) *Modes of distribution*
    (A) ORAL OR WRITTEN STATEMENTS
    (B) FORMAL OR INFORMAL CHANNELS
  (*3*) *Timing, rhythm, urgency*
    (A) ACCORDING TO PLAN
    (B) ERRATICALLY OR SPONTANEOUSLY
  (*4*) *Source and audience*

2. Current and previous studies in, and reports to, the organization
  a. *Consultant reports*
  b. *Special staff studies*
  c. *Marketing studies*
  d. *Engineering studies*
  e. *Accountants' audits and reports*

III. INTERPRETATIVE DATA [Chapter 7, pp. 170–247]

A. Current Organizational Functioning [pp. 172–247]

1. Organizational perceptions
  a. *Degree of alertness, accuracy, and vividness*
    (*1*) *To stimuli from within the organization*
      (A) FROM PERSONNEL
        i. Employees to management and vice versa
        ii. Supervisor to subordinate and vice versa
        iii. Departments to each other's needs
      (B) FROM PHYSICAL PLANT
    (*2*) *To stimuli from without*
      (A) PRIMARY EXTERNAL STIMULI
        i. Marketing conditions
        ii. Purchasing conditions
        iii. Labor conditions
      (B) SECONDARY EXTERNAL STIMULI
        i. Legislative (tariff and tax laws)
        ii. Transportation
        iii. Competitors
        iv. Research developments
        v. Economic, social, and political trends

  b. Direction and span of attention (selectivity)
     (1) Dominant foci of interest
        (A) LONG-TERM FRAMEWORK
        (B) SHORT-TERM FRAMEWORK
     (2) Significant neglected foci

  c. Assessment of the discrepancy between reality and perceived reality
     (1) Of reality within the organization
     (2) Of reality outside the organization

2. Organizational knowledge

  a. Acquisition of knowledge
     (1) Methods of obtaining new knowledge
        (A) RELATED TO PERSONNEL AND PLANT
        (B) RELATED TO PRODUCTS, SERVICES, OR COMPETITORS
        (C) RELATED TO FINANCIAL RESOURCES
        (D) RELATED TO FORCES AND TRENDS AFFECTING THE ORGANIZATION
        (E) BY WHOM (SOURCES WITHIN AND OUTSIDE THE ORGANIZATION
        (F) RESERVOIR OF INTELLECTUAL SOURCES
           i.   Talents and skills within the organization
           ii. Consultants
           iii. Affiliations with specialized institutions or universities
           iv. Library facilities and services
     (2) Degree of receptivity to new knowledge
        (A) BY WHOM
        (B) TO WHAT
     (3) Level and range of knowledge
        (A) CONCERNING THEMSELVES, THEIR PRODUCTS, THEIR SERVICES AND RELATED FACTORS
        (B) OUTSIDE THEIR IMMEDIATE AREA OF INTEREST

  b. Use of knowledge
     (1) How is it brought together
        (A) WHO THINKS ABOUT IT
        (B) LEVEL OF ABSTRACTION
     (2) How is knowledge organized and systematized
        (A) COMMITTEE SYSTEM
        (B) RECORDS AND STORAGE SYSTEM
        (C) OTHER MODES OF ORGANIZATION AND SYSTEMATIZATION
     (3) Amount and kind of use (retrieval)
     (4) Organizational conditions affecting the use of intellectual sources
        (A) ABILITY TO DEAL WITH ABSTRACT PROBLEMS

(B) FLEXIBILITY

(C) CHARACTERISTIC STYLE AND VARIATIONS

   c. *Dissemination of knowledge*

3. Organizational language

   a. *Themes and content of employee publications*

   b. *Organizational ideology*

   c. *Advertising themes*

   d. *Organizational symbols and slogans*

   e. *Language of policies as distinct from the policies themselves*

   f. *Language of customs, taboos, prohibitions, and constrictions: direct and implied*

4. Emotional atmosphere of the organization

   a. *Prevailing mood and range*

   b. *Overall stability or variability of mood*

     (1) *Intensity of reactions*

     (2) *Duration of reactions*

     (3) *Appropriateness to stimulating factors*

   c. *Intraorganizational variability*

     (1) *By hierarchical level*

     (2) *By department*

     (3) *Other (geographical location, profession)*

5. Organizational action

   a. *Energy level*

     (1) *Consistency or variability of application (rate of discharge of energy)*

     (2) *Points and periods of peak expenditure energy*

   b. *Qualities of action*

     (1) *Degree of directness*

     (2) *Degree of flexibility*

     (3) *Planning and timing*

     (4) *Degree of persistence*

     (5) *Effectiveness*

     (6) *Constructiveness or destructiveness*

B. Attitudes and Relationships [Chapter 8, pp. 248–309]

1. Contemporary attitudes toward, and relationships with, others

   a. *Range, diversification, depth, and constancy*

     (1) *Customers*

     (2) *Competition*

       (3) *Employees*
       (4) *Occupational associations and representatives*
       (5) *Stockholders*
       (6) *Legislative bodies*
       (7) *Executive and regulatory bodies (governmental)*
       (8) *Control bodies (internal)*
       (9) *Suppliers*
      (10) *Financial community*
      (11) *Host community*
      (12) *Dealer organizations*
      (13) *Plant builders*
      (14) *Consultants*
      (15) *Others*

  b. Major attachments

       (1) *Positive*
       (2) *Negative*

  c. Masculine-feminine orientation

       (1) *Of organization*
          (A) MASCULINE
          (B) FEMININE
          (C) DEGREE OF ACHIEVEMENT
          (D) HOW PERVASIVE
       (2) *In relation to the industry*

  d. Transference phenomena

       (1) *Related to the consultant*
       (2) *Related to the organization*
       (3) *Related to each other*

2. Relations to things and ideas

  a. Quality and intensity of relations to plant, equipment, raw material or supplies, product, and services

       (1) *Symbolization*
       (2) *Unconscious personification*

  b. Time: how is it regarded

       (1) *Past, present, future orientation*
       (2) *How is future planned for*
       (3) *Is time valued as an investable commodity*
       (4) *View of work cycles*

  c. Space: how is it conceptualized

       (1) *As a local concern*
       (2) *As a cosmopolitan concern*

  d. Meaning of work for the organization

       (1) *As a device for coping with the environment*

(A) IN ECONOMIC TERMS
(B) IN TERMS OF SKILL
(C) IN TERMS OF THINKING
(D) IN TERMS OF PSYCHOLOGICAL DEFENSE

(2) *As a device for fulfilling psychological contract*
(3) *As a device for channeling energy*

(A) CONSTRUCTIVELY
(B) DESTRUCTIVELY
(C) AS A PROCESS OF REGRESSION

    i. Within the work setting
    ii. In nonwork activities

e. *Authority, power, and responsibility*

(1) *How does the organization regard power*

(A) THE POWER OF OTHERS
(B) THEIR OWN POWER VIS-À-VIS THE WORLD OUTSIDE
(C) POWER INTERNALLY

    i. Generally
    ii. By ranks

(2) *How does the organization handle authority*
(3) *How does the organization handle responsibility*

(A) OUTSIDE THE ORGANIZATION
(B) INSIDE THE ORGANIZATION

f. *Positions on social, ethical, and political issues*

3. Attitudes about self

a. *Who do they think they are and how do they feel about it*
b. *Where do they think they are headed and how do they feel about it*
c. *What are their common aspirations*
d. *How do they look to themselves*

4. Intraorganizational relationships

a. *Key people in the organization*
b. *Significant groups within the organization*
c. *Implications of a and b*

IV. ANALYSES AND CONCLUSIONS [Chapter 9, pp. 310–365]

A. Organizational Integrative Patterns [pp. 314–352]

1. Appraisal of the effect of the environment on the organization

a. *Historical*
   (1) Beneficial
   (2) Harmful
b. *Contemporary*
   (1) Beneficial
   (2) Harmful
c. Anticipated
   (1) Beneficial
   (2) Harmful

2. Appraisal of the effect of the organization on the environment
   a. *Historical*
      (1) Beneficial
      (2) Harmful
   b. *Contemporary*
      (1) Beneficial
      (2) Harmful
   c. Anticipated
      (1) Beneficial
      (2) Harmful

3. Reactions
   a. *Of the environment*
      (1) To the injury
      (2) Toward source of the injury
   b. *Secondary reaction from the organization*

4. Appraisal of the organization
   a. *Special assets*
      (1) Material or tangible (financial, patents, physical plant, equipment, geographical distribution, transportation, communication, personnel)
      (2) Functional (including leadership and mental set, or attitude)
         (A) REALITY ORIENTATION
            i. To external environment
            ii. To internal environment
         (B) VALUES AND IDEALS
            i. Degree of institutionalization
            ii. Congruence with reality
         (C) TASK MASTERY
            i.   Psychological contract unfulfillment
            ii. Growth and survival
            iii. Task-directed behavior

b. *Impairments*

    (*1*) *Material or tangible (financial, patents, physical plant, equipment, geographical distribution, transportation, communication, personnel)*

    (*2*) *Functional (including leadership and mental set, or attitude)*

        (A) REALITY ORIENTATION

           i. To external environment
           ii. To internal environment

        (B) VALUES AND IDEALS

           i. Degree of institutionalization
           ii. Disparity from reality

        (C) TASK MASTERY

           i. Psychological contract unfulfillment
           ii. Growth and survival
           iii. Task-directed behavior

c. *Level of integration*

    (*1*) *Normal adaptive activities*
    (*2*) *First-order adaptive activities*
    (*3*) *Second-order adaptive activities*
    (*4*) *Third- and fourth-order adaptive activities*

d. *Overall effectiveness and facade*

B. Summary and Recommendations [pp. 352–365]

1. Present status
2. Explanatory formulation

    a. *Genetic*
    b. *Dynamic*

3. Prognostic conclusions
4. Recommendations

5

GENETIC
DATA

Portion of outline covered in chapter 5

I. GENETIC DATA

A. Identifying Information

1. Organization name
2. Location
3. Type of organization
4. Organizational affiliation
5. Size

   a. *Financial condition*
   b. *Stockholders*
   c. *Employees*

6. Situation of the initial contract

   a. *Consultation*
   b. *Research orientation*

7. Circumstances of the study
8. Special conditions affecting validity of the study
9. First overall impressions

B. Historical Data

1. Chief complaint or events leading to the initiation of the study
2. Problems of the organization as stated by key figures

   a. *Long-range*
   b. *Short-range*

3. Background of the organization
   a. *Key developmental phases*
      (1) *As reported by organizational participants*
      (2) *As reported by outsiders*
      (3) *As reported by the consultant*
   b. *Major crises experienced by the organization*
      (1) *Natural catastrophies*
      (2) *Loss of key personnel*
      (3) *Labor problems*
      (4) *Financial emergencies*
      (5) *Technological changes*
   c. *Product-service history*
      (1) *Change and development of organizational goals*
      (2) *Sequence of development in product or service*
      (3) *Relative success or failure in various stages of service or product history*
      (4) *Geographical patterns*
      (5) *Special skills of the organization*
      (6) *Performance reputation and record*
   d. *Organizational folklore*
4. Circumstances surrounding study

A. Identifying Information

The data listed in this section are used primarily for adminstrative and classification purposes. As in the lead of a newspaper report, this section contains the who, what, when, where, why, and how of the study. With the exception of numbers 7., Circumstances of the study, and 8., Special conditions affecting the validity of the study, the items discussed here should be written up immediately after the initial visit to the organization.

1. Organization name

2. Location

Name and location are simply stated. Although the name and characteristics of a given location may have a significant influence on the nature and functioning of an organization, the purpose at this point is merely to identify the organization and to anchor it geographically. The question of possible significance of both factors is treated in Chapter 9.

3. Type of organization

All types of organizations may be studied with this outline. Here exactly what this one is, is specified: a plant that manufactures electronic equipment, an elementary school, a law firm, a church, a life insurance firm, and so on.

4. Organizational affiliation

Is the whole organization being studied or one part of it? What is the relationship of this unit to the larger system of which it is a part, if this is the case?

5. Size

Here the organization is ranked relative to other organizations of the same type (No. 3), within the organizational whole (No. 4), and within the same geographic location, with respect to assets, employees, membership, stockholders, plant size, volume of business, and other comparative characteristics. Such data are frequently available from the organization's annual report. For business organizations data may be obtained from such sources as Dun and Bradstreet publications, investment firm analyses, Chambers of Commerce, and *Forbes*. Similar compendia provide statistics for churches, hospitals, law firms, educational institutions, and other specialized organizations.

a. Financial condition

Indicate relative strength in terms of financial resources and condition.

b. Stockholders

Indicate approximate number of stockholders in total, with an indication of locus of control — family ownership, majority held by a few individuals, less than (for example) 5 per cent held by any one person.

c. Employees

For certain types of organizations there may be no direct equivalents of stockholders and employees. For universities, churches, and other institutions, individuals in the study may be members, students, constituents. A major concern in this study is with the organization's relationships with those people for whom it has psychological meaning. The consultant should make appropriate substitutions which would differentiate kinds of power in the organization and varied perceptions of those who have different relationships to it.

The first five items can be stated in paragraph form:*

With assets of $15 billion First National City Bank of New York City ranks only behind the Bank of America ($18 billion) and Chase Manhattan ($15.8 billion) . . . First National City's domestic branches have spurted from 84, all in New York City, to 166 . . . spilling over into the suburbs . . . the overseas branches have more than doubled to 206 . . . it had 24,000 employees and 67,721 stockholders. (*Time,* June 16, 1967, pp. 86–87.)

St. Mary's High School of Ventura, Minnesota, is a four-year Catholic secondary school established and maintained by the archdiocese of Minneapolis. It is the third largest of nine Catholic high schools in the archdiocese and the fourth largest of seven high schools in Ventura. St. Mary's is the sole parochial secondary school in Ventura. Its student body numbers 970 and its faculty 47. St. Mary's has a current annual budget of $220,000 or $230 per pupil as contrasted with the $503 annual expenditure per student of the Ventura Public Schools.

6. Situation of the initial contract

Here the consultant must specify for himself the psychological contract of the study, both the unconscious expectations he thinks the leader(s) of the organization may have about him and the study as well as the mutual understanding which has been reached between the organization and himself. The "unconscious" part of the contract is often difficult to ascertain. In many instances the organization might not know what it really wants or might specify the wrong problem. The latter part of the contract may be verbal or written. In small organizations or when the study is limited to only a few individuals in an organization, it is usually verbal. When a large number of people must be informed about the reasons and purposes of the relationship between the consultant and the organization and the conditions of that relationship a formal statement which can be read to employee groups is preferable. Such a presentation should allow for questions and discussion to clarify the contract. It is usually not wise to wait long before converting a verbal agreement into a fairly specific written

* Examples for which sources are not cited are drawn from case studies conducted by me or my students or are drawn from personal experience. H. L.

statement. There appear to be two major categories of contract, based on the purpose for which the study was initiated.

a. Consultation

When an organization has had some kind of difficulty, it often seeks expert advice toward resolving its problem. Typically, it employs a consultant to analyze the problem, evaluate it, and make recommendations for action. The consultant may not necessarily be involved in the action to follow upon his recommendations.

When the president of a company told a consultant of the company's need for new, young leadership and his expectation that the consultant would bring such an event about, the consultant pointed out that he was not a miracle worker. He said he was there to help the leadership evolve modes of defining and meeting its needs, but that leadership development was intimately intertwined with the way in which a company was managed; he [the consultant] was not there to manage the company. He added further that his initial visits to the company were to be a mutual trial. The company was to be free to terminate the relationship whenever it wished without giving reasons. If either the executives or he felt that the relationship was not serving its purpose, it would be wise to break it off. Subsequently as the consultant visited other executives, he made the following statement: "At the request of the vice-president of personnel and the president, I am here to assess the organization's management development needs and to make recommendations for a management development program. To that end I am interviewing each of the members of the corporate management committee to obtain his perspective on management development needs and a perspective on the organization as a whole. These interviews are confidential. You and I will be the only persons who will know what was discussed during the interview. The results of all the interviews will be summarized and reported back to the president and subsequently to those who were interviewed. However, you need not be interviewed if you do not want to be. After the report is made, you as a group will decide what you want to do about the recommendations."

b. Research orientation

A study of an organization can follow upon the request of a researcher for research or teaching purposes. In this case, there may be no major problems of which the organization leadership is aware; even if there are, the organization may neither need help in alleviating them nor look upon the investigator as a source of that help. The consultant should state clearly that he has initiated the study.

This study is being undertaken to further our own education. It is being made for the purpose of trying to learn more about how psychological forces can contribute to getting the job done more effectively and to the maintenance of an emotionally healthy atmosphere within which people can work. The usual area of administration and management with which typical management consultants are concerned are not our particular focus. We were not called in as consultants nor do we pose as experts on hospital administration. Our intention is to learn from confidential interviews. After the interviewing is completed and we have prepared a statement of what we have learned, we will return to share those findings with you.

Although the leadership of the organization may not have looked upon the researcher as a source of help for the organization's problems, if the study discloses difficulties, the organization may then request help from him. At that point, another contract is negotiated. This second contract would be a consultation rather than a research-oriented relationship.

7. Circumstances of the study

Exactly how was the study conducted? The duration of the study, the number of investigators, the frequency and length of the visits should all be included. Often these details will be agreed upon at the initial meeting with the responsible organization executive; they may even be included in the contract. Sometimes, however, it will be impossible to establish a work schedule until a preliminary view has been obtained from discussion with one or more members of the executive group. It is not unusual for plans to be altered during the course of the study. Therefore, the recording of this section may have to be delayed or even rewritten before the report is finished.

A group of six graduate students from the University of Kansas studied Menorah Medical Center the week of April 3, 1967. This study included 96 oral interviews and 25 written questionnaires. The sample included the entire Executive Committee, 9 people who reported to that committee, 15 department heads, 8 head nurses, 14 registered nurses or licensed practical nurses, 7 nurse's aides, 2 surgical orderlies, 6 laboratory technicians, 19 nonsupervisory service employees and 9 clerical workers. Functionally, the sample included 48 members of the nursing staff, 19 members of the laboratory staff, 23 employees of the administrative staff, and 31 service employees. The medical staff was not interviewed or included in the study. The data and observations included in the study were gathered in a one-week period. Therefore, certain aspects, functions, or problems of the hospital — those which were not constant — could not be adequately studied.

8. Special conditions affecting the validity of the study

Organizations, like people, are not static. Conditions change constantly; some events may occur prior to or during the study which materially affect its validity. Among such events are strikes, the death of the chief executive, economic reverses, accidents, impending mergers or unusually rapid growth of the market. These should be detailed here.

What are the conditions under which the consultant entered the organization? Who brought him in? Why? What are the special problems in the organization? Are there any factors which might affect his judgment of the problems? Any biases? What controls have been placed on the consultant? These comments are illustrative:

There is no doubt that many of the employees took a great interest in the organization and in the outcome of the study; however, a smaller number of employees felt imposed upon, defensive, and resistive to any type of questioning or intrusion on my part. This was manifested on the questionnaire by flippant remarks or "I don't know." In some cases whole series of questions were left unanswered. Indirectly, I have heard that some people did not answer honestly or candidly. I have no way of knowing how frequently or how many of the people responded this way.

Among the special conditions affecting the validity of this study are these: First, this study of St. Anselm's Abbey was begun immediately following the last session of the Ecumenical Council in Rome. There are many anticipated, if not real, changes in the Catholic Church and in Catholic philosophy. These changes in attitude and philosophy have generated considerable discussion and anxiety among some Catholic people, especially priests and nuns. Second, realizing that there is considerable dissatisfaction among his faculty, particularly with the vagueness of the seminary's objectives, the president of the college recently appointed a committee to consider goals and objectives. Third, the college is anticipating a visit by a committee from the regional academic accrediting agency and there is some concern about how that committee will react to the low ratio of Ph.D.'s and inadequate library resources.

9. First overall impressions

The initial impression will differ from the previous data by being subjective rather than objective, but it should include impressions of the physical plant as well as psychological considerations. It cannot be arrived at by measurement. The consultant is his own instrument. He should ask himself: What does this place feel like? How effective and efficient does it seem to be? How would it feel to work here? He should ask questions about what he observes; he should think about the psychological, social, and economic costs and implications of what he observes. What are the effects of the architecture? the site? What kinds of perceptions or psychological stances do people have? What are the underlying assumptions about people? The consultant must attempt to recognize his first feelings about the organization, some of which will be fleeting. He must be alert to momentary negative feelings because he will tend to disregard them, particularly if the atmosphere is subsequently cordial. Such feelings should not be disregarded. Chances are that his immediate and subtle feelings are shared by others who may not be able to grasp or verbalize them readily. It is from these feelings, this impact, that he establishes the necessary working hypotheses about the problems of the organization. The consultant continually checks his working hypotheses as the study progresses. He will discard some, reserve others, and add new ones. Here also he should try to summarize his experiences from his initial tour. These illustrations are drawn from studies:

We noticed a number of potential hazards in the plant: pervasiveness of carbon black on all surfaces and in the atmosphere; the way in which chemical compound dusts were distributed in the atmosphere near the moulding machines; the isolation of individuals and work groups from each other, particularly on some of the highly mechanized operations where one operator controls a large complex of machinery; the absence of natural light in the center of the plant; the intensive machine vibration and noise in many areas. On at least four occasions the group barely escaped being bumped by forklift trucks, which scooted around the plant and even around blind corners and in tight areas with considerable speed.

The first overall impression was that St. Mary's school was a spotlessly clean, new physical plant which was darkened as the school day was over. The administration section has glassed-in windows with a small waiting room with two hard-backed chairs in front of a long, large counter. Two secretaries' desks were behind the counter; on the wall was an elaborate speaker system. This system goes to every room in the building and can be used to transmit or to listen to activities in the classrooms. The principal was friendly, cooperative and almost overly solicitous of us. He pointed out some of his frustrations and gave hints of feelings of inadequacy. He expressed a great deal of genuine interest in the study, looked forward to the feedback, and hinted at possible publication.

The second meeting was held with the staff. I felt the atmosphere of the group to be somewhat rigid and constrained. I decided to move slowly in a supportive manner to avoid undue anxiety or stress. I had a continuing question for myself: Would these people, particularly the nuns because of their compulsivity and concept of religious obedience, be able to participate freely in a study of this kind? During the first two visits, very few of the staff were formally introduced to us by the principal, but a number were active in the group interchange.

B. Historical Data

To have meaning for the purposes of facilitating change, the description of any organization must be viewed in its historical context. The consultant must know not only how the organization is functioning now and why but also how those forces evolved and what historical forces continue to influence its activity. However, one must strive for the truly salient points and not get lost in details. For example, nineteenth-century discrimination led to the development of Roman Catholic parochial schools; in many communities, they still maintain an outward defensive stance. Many businesses operate with labor policies intended to deal with problems of the 1930's.

This section is devoted to systematizing the objective data which delineate the organization's development. The data incorporated here should be verifiable. They provide the factual basis for all subsequent diagnostic hypotheses and for the conclusions which will follow. They form the foundation for answering the questions: How did this organization evolve? and Why does it ask for this particular kind of help now? Therefore, as does a mystery novel, this section must contain all the facts needed to substantiate the subsequent inferences. An interview form and a questionnaire for gathering some of the data are in Appendix A.

1. Chief complaint or events leading to the initiation of the study

As already indicated, a study may be undertaken either as part of a consultation at the request of an organization seeking help or for research and training purposes. When an organization seeks consultation, it does so because it has one or more major problems. The chief complaint is the problem as stated by the executive who asked for the consultation or who gave permission for the study to be undertaken for research or training. The chief complaint and the events which culminated in verbalizing that complaint to the consultant should be stated here. The chief complaint is a concrete, specific component of the situation of the initial contact.

[In 1952 Clarence Stouch, head of Crowell-Collier, approached Paul C. Smith and asked that he look over the ailing corporation and restore it to health.] Crowell-Collier was an old and respected outfit and had been successful for many years. Although *Collier's* and *The American Magazine* began to lose circulation and advertising in the post-World War II years, the gross volume of business ranged from 50 to 60 million dollars, and the encyclopedia and book division made plenty of money. The situation had deteriorated, however . . . at an alarming rate . . . [Stouch] disclosed that although the company would do a gross business approaching $60,000,000, it would lose in excess of $4,000,000 in the current year . . . The balance sheet listed current assets of more than $32,000,000, and total assets exceeding $42,000,000, [but the organization's] current liabilities nearly equaled its current assets (*Esquire,* September 1964, p. 132).

In addition to describing the direct contact in which the chief complaint was made, the consultant should infer the psychological meanings or implications, if any, of both the complaint and the conditions under which it was made. These inferences should be treated as hypotheses for further testing and should be entered later in the outline (IV, Bld, Chapter 8) under transference phenomena.

The executive vice-president complained that the three major executives were having increasing difficulty working together. He asked for consultation to help reduce the barriers because they were deterrents to decision-making. Several years prior to his request for consultation, the executive vice-president had applied to participate in a human relations seminar but later cancelled his reservation. He applied a second time and did participate. Subsequent to that participation, he requested an interview with the psychologist who conducted the seminar. The psychologist told him he would be in the executive's community for a two-week period. He indicated the times he would be free and invited the executive to call him on his arrival to designate the most convenient time for himself. The executive called a day before the two-week period was up, when it was obviously too late for an appointment. The corporation again made a reservation for an executive to attend a seminar, cancelled it, and finally, two years later, sent another. After the second participation, the company formally requested consultation.

In this instance the consultant should grasp the depth of the resistance of the executives to outside help and the implications of that resistance for the consulting relationship. He should have a mental note of this matter at this point, even though he will not formally write about it until later in the outline.

2. Problems of the organization as stated by key figures

Every organization has some kind of hierarchy in which people holding certain positions have formal authority. List what these people state are the primary problems facing their organization. These statements may differ from that of the chief complaint.

In many instances there are people who have de facto, rather than de jure, authority. These are the informal leaders. Their roles are usually discovered from the repeated references made to them in the course of interviews or when people are asked to whom they turn for help or information. View these people as key figures in the informal structure and record their opinions in Part IV, B4 (Chapter 8).

"Problems as stated by key figures" might be interpreted in several ways. It might be a simple statement of what the interviewees actually say; it might be what the same persons see after a skillful interview by a psychologically oriented consultant; or it might be what the interviewer perceives that the officials actually mean although they are not aware of the full import of their words. But in keeping with the intent of this section of the case study, the consultant lists only what the person *actually says* at this point.

There is also the chance that the statements offered may represent the actual way top management visualizes the problem; they also may represent how the management wishes to present it because they do not yet trust the consultant. The manner in which the problem is stated also reflects the degree of sophistication with which the problem is viewed. But these inferences and interpretations must be reserved for a later section of the study.

The statements should be divided, separating those which are viewed as long-range problems from the short-range issues. Problems which must be faced at some undefined future date are considered to be long-range. Developing the survival potential of the organization has a long time perspective. Problems which must be faced by a certain known date are generally considered to be short range. For many companies, immediate profitability is an urgent short-run problem. It is the consultant's responsibility to place each problem in its proper time perspective.

a. Long range

Humble bought about 30,000 acres in 1938 because there was oil and gas beneath the sweet, lowland grass . . . In the late 1950's the Houston Chamber of Commerce told Humble that the big ranch was blocking the city's rapid growth. The oil company turned to Lehman Bros., the New York investment house, for advice. Lehman suggested that Humble could develop part of its land lying along Galveston Bay for heavy industrial use, and reserve acreage inland for houses, shops, and offices. In this way, the workers in the plants on the bay would provide a market for the houses inland. It was, in effect, a long-range scheme for a new town.

Humble formed a 70–30 joint venture with . . . Del E. Webb to build the houses . . . Webb brought in California-style houses and California's semi-prefabricated building techniques . . . [But] the people expect[ed] Houston-style houses that look[ed] bigger and [were] hand built . . . (Therefore Humble's long-range problem was to encourage the growth of Houston toward its own development in which it had already invested $30 million.) (*Fortune,* June 1967, pp. 135–138.)

b. Short range

The economics of meatpacking worked against Rath most bitterly when the company changed its business strategy. Once mainly a fresh-meat operation, Rath has now concentrated its limited working capital on "the higher profit potential" of processed and packaged pork products (*e.g.,* Rath's Black Hawk bacon and canned hams), which it is marketing nationally. Last year [1965] Rath Packing dropped the last of its lamb, veal, and beef operations. Unfortunately for its 1966 results, the company cast its lot entirely with pork at a time when the hog cycle was more unfavorable for packers than it had been in years. (*Fortune,* June 1967, p. 232.)

For the immediate future the Temple faces several problems. It must expand its membership and financial base; improve its services to the community, particularly its religious school and social program; and develop more leadership in the present congregation. Although the rabbi has talked repeatedly about the last problem and it has been discussed in Board meetings, neither he nor the Board seems to know what they really mean by "develop leadership," and no concrete steps have ever been taken to do so.

3. Background of the organization

Some organizations have compiled or have had written organizational histories. Others have little or no historical information. Seemingly, the former instance should be the easier for the consultant since otherwise he must compile the history himself from talking to knowledgeable persons in the organizations. However, such is not the case. The consultant has no way of knowing the degree of distortion in an organization-compiled history. Nor is history as reported by organization informants as valid as that compiled from objective sources. He must therefore seek outside sources of information, if such are available, to complement both the data he obtains from informants and that from the record. Local newspaper files, historical society files, and similar repositories may be helpful; but they are invariably incomplete, biased, and give details rather than useful summaries. Business publications — *Fortune, Forbes, Business Week, Dun's Review,* and others — carry articles about companies which often give adequate background. There are similar publications in most other fields which discuss specific institutions.

a. Key developmental phases

A key developmental phase is an experience which significantly changes the direction, size, effectiveness, or strength of the organization. It is a period in organizational maturation which can be located in time. It can result from the development of a product or the adoption of a strategy or from natural occurrences or fortuitous circumstances, as an outgrowth of which the organization takes a new or different direction. (The consultant should distinguish between conscious choice of a strategy and one which arrives by itself.)

Such a phase may be positive or negative in the long run. A positive key developmental phase is one which reflects growth, greater sophistication, greater maturity, greater stability through diversification or financing, or greater access to personnel or financial resources. A negative developmental phase is a type of organizational aging or failure. One evidence of such a phase might be a decline in profitability because products become obsolete, declining membership, or lower quality of job applicants by virtue of uncontrollable external events. Positive or negative phases depend heavily on the organization's ability to perceive its environment objectively. Two magazine excerpts are examples.

John Deere and Co. spotted early the exodus of labor from the farms and the shift to more efficient, more highly mechanized farms . . . It aimed its research, design and development toward meeting the needs of the top 20 per cent of the farmers who get most of the farm cash income. While its competitors hesitated,

Deere boldly developed new machines and now has a leading place in the U.S. market. (*Fortune,* December 1966, p. 148.)

In 1853, Yellow Springs, a small spa in the prosperous corn- and hog-belt of southwestern Ohio, became a college town when Antioch, which had just been founded by Horace Mann, accepted its first freshman class. After Mann's death a few years later, Antioch continued with no special distinction until 1920 when engineer Arthur E. Morgan became its president. Morgan was one of the first men to apply to college the ideas of "progressive" education — concern with the student as a total human being, fitting the curriculum to him rather than him to the curriculum. He abolished fraternities, and intercollegiate sports gave way to intramural; Morgan wanted participants, not spectators. A democratic community was formed of students, faculty, and administration, with a joint Community Government (CG) that worked out new guidelines for classroom and living; rules were replaced by "Community Standards" and left largely to informal regulation under an honor system.

Most important, Morgan initiated the first complete program of alternate study and off-campus jobs at a liberal arts college . . . Antioch took on the personality of a career revolutionary — or, a hybrid of guinea pig and under-dog . . . It acquired a tone that combined Greenwich Village and a Quaker work camp. Despite underendowment, scorn from orthodox educators, attacks from local and national rightists, Antioch distinguished itself. (*Holiday,* June 1967, p. 48.)

(1) *As reported by organizational participants*

Organizational participants are people within the organization who have themselves experienced the key developmental phases or who have entered into the organization as a result of the change. They are therefore in a position to have some knowledge of the organizational situation both before and after the event. Firsthand reports by political and business figures are frequently best-selling books. Their value often lies in the difference between the perceptions of the participants and those of more objective writers.

The kinds of data that are summarized and entered here will often be much longer and more detailed than the example presented next.

The Pineland Presbyterian congregation is approximately 75 years old. Members of the congregation deny that the church has ever had major difficulties, although they report that one factional split took place in the 1920's. All other problems mentioned seemed to be centered around pastors who served in the church — thus in the eyes of the congregation were not really congregational problems at all. The factional split involved the pastor, the Rev. Mr. F. He wanted to use more authority and power than the then existing Session wanted him to have. The leader of the Session was a businessman who had happened to be a former minister at Pineland. The Rev. Mr. F. carried the struggle to the congregation and won his point, but the congregation split and many left the congregation. The Rev. Mr. F. and his faction remained. Mrs. R. is reported to have infused new life into the church in the early 1930's following this factional split. She did this by organizing a married couples' group. Undoubtedly the energy she still displays must have entered into her successful activities. Congregational members expressed dissatisfaction over the way that various pastors had served. The Rev. Mr. G. did not do much work in the church, partially because his wife did not like the ministry. Another minister refused to allow a more "Bible centered" curriculum to be introduced into the Sunday School. The Rev. Mr. B. had "expensive ideas" in hiring a secretary — and then suddenly left the church with large financial obligations to be met. The Rev. Mr. W. found disapproval because of his strong civil rights stand. There seems to be a widespread feeling of responsibility — even guilt — in the congregation over the fact that a recent interim pastor worked, too hard apparently, at visiting the sick and many other functions that the congregation expected of a pastor. His subsequent breakdown is something for which they seem to blame themselves.

(2) *As reported by outsiders*

Such people as local political officials (the mayor, city council members), newspaper officials, businessmen, social service professionals, and others in authoritative observational positions are referred to here as "outsiders." Persons in other companies in the same industry, trade association officials, suppliers, customers, fellow professionals, are also relevant outsiders if they have information or opinions about the organization. In this instance the consultant will be dealing with the issue of history as written by historians versus that reported by those who actually lived the events they describe. The two accounts may differ; thus, an observer may relate something which happened to an organization, saying, "I think this made a difference." Those within the organization may not feel that this occurrence was significant. The consultant will have to arrive at his own conclusions.

As with history from participants, data from outsiders can be so comprehensive and detailed that it becomes confusing rather than illuminating. The consultant will have to glean much information to discern trends and forces. He should observe the caution stated by a researcher who organized a company history from published sources:

Published sources often give incomplete records of important events in the company's history. There are often "blanks" which one would like to fill. An inference is a shaky and somewhat nebulous construct at best, and to draw one when facts are scarce and one's personal knowledge of a particular subject is small is to invite erroneous conclusions. Consequently there are blanks in the company history which the writer has not attempted to fill by inferring the "hows" and "whys" of the missing details. Only when there seems to be ample material on a subject to lead to a fairly sound conclusion is an inference made.

This next example shows how the researcher drew conclusions from an outside source: press clippings.

The Kansas press, particularly the Topeka press, appear to have consistent ways of covering various developments in the Kansas Power and Light Company [KPL]. Newspaper clippings as far back as the early 1900's contained many a glowing sentence about the prospective value and growth of the electric light and power industry. This is not to imply that there was accurate and detailed reporting on many of the areas in which we are interested (for often there was not), but rather that there were numerous articles on the social changes initiated by the introduction of electricity, on the glowing future of electricity, and on the symbiotic association between company and consumer. Newspaper articles are mostly neutral presentations of factual information; but when any value judgments are made, they are, in an overwhelming amount of the time, favorable to and in support of the company. In time of crisis to the company the newspapers have nothing but sympathy for the company, praise for the courage of company employees, and hozannas for the efficient dealing with threats. Early newspaper responses to the development of electric utilities centered around idealistic expectations and beliefs. The future worth of public utilities to the people was unlimited, and the newspaper greatly idealized the relation of a public electric utility to its owners and to the people. The owners and managers of such utilities were dedicated to serving the public, and the public must consequently be thankful for the progress made by a utility company and tolerant of its failures. KPL did not have to acquire prestige; it already had it by virtue of being a public electric utility.

(3) *As reported by the consultant*

The consultant may discern aspects of organizational history whose import had not been perceived by persons inside the organization or by outsiders, as in these illustrations:

The pastor feels that at the present time the congregation is in an intermediate stage; it is no longer a mission although many people still see it that way. One of the leaders described it as "being on a plateau." Another leader stated, "Everyone has to be active and a participating member in many areas to make it go. The demands seem far greater to us than in any other place." A charter member said, "The charter members were dedicated . . . evangelism was a prime goal when we started . . . 75 per cent of the people had no church background. They seemed more dedicated than the old transfers. As the transfers increased, evangelism died. The transfers were not as dedicated, they didn't realize what it really took. After the first building unit was finished, the spirit slacked off and it hurt us for awhile. The changing of pastors helped by bringing a momentary burst of enthusiasm." With the change in pastors and the departure of some of the naval base people, the leadership shifted naturally to the civilian community. There is more threat of naval personnel leaving, as both pastor and parishioners see it. What neither pastor nor parishioners nor members of other churches see is the disappearance of the sense of purpose with the end of the missionary phase of the church's development.

The company is recruiting promising young M.B.A.'s from nearby universities. While these young men come from the same cultural background as the present executives, their conceptions of management are vastly different. In a few years there will be a major clash, the outcome of which is likely to be sale of the company because it will be impossible for the president and his old colleagues to accept the defeat of giving in to the younger men's ideas or for the younger men to stay if the old ones win out.

b. Major crises experienced by the organization

Major crises may sometimes be the same as key developmental phases. A crisis can precipitate a developmental phase or it can be independent of any. The vital consideration here is what the crisis means to the organization.

(1) Natural catastrophies

The great Morro Castle, pride of the Atlantic Gulf & West Indies Steamship Lines, was on its way back from a Caribbean cruise in 1934 when it was destroyed by fire. To keep its government subsidy, it was necessary for Atlantic Gulf to build a replacement for the Morro Castle, but the company lacked the nerve to make the necessary investment during the depths of the Great Depression. Thus, it was that the fire which destroyed the proud ship also all but sank a once-great company. (Forbes, September 15, 1967, p. 161.)

In the mid-1950's, the United Fruit Company's Latin American banana plantations suffered a one-two punch as disease and winds decimated the tall Gros Michel banana plants that had been United Fruit's mainstay for fifty years.
    The heavy costs of recultivation, plus competition from lower cost growing areas, torpedoed profits. Margins skidded from a healthy 20 per cent range in the early 1950's to 0.6 per cent in 1960. Finally, in 1958 the company was slapped with a Justice Department consent decree requiring divestiture of banana lands and other facilities able to produce what then amounted to about 33 per cent of United's U.S. imports. (Business Week, July 8, 1967, p. 90.)

(2) Loss of key personnel

Keeping a balance of managerial types is one of the Ford chief's greatest concerns. But it's a trick that can only get harder as time goes on. For men who rose patiently through the ranks like Patterson [the Executive Vice President] are gradually fading out of the picture, and in today's company it is all but impossible for others to follow in their footsteps. Ford officials acknowledge the problem, but they argue that by the time the last of the old-timers has retired, the bright young men will have had many long, hard, sometimes disillusioning years behind them. *They* will then be the veterans whose hard-won judgment can temper the impetuosity of the next generation of brash newcomers. (*Fortune*, January 1967, p. 108.)

(3) Labor problems

Walter H. Uphoff (*Kohler on Strike*, Boston, Beacon Press, 1966, pp. 55–68) describes in detail how, during the Kohler strike, ferocious mobs of angry people, employees, and nonemployees, attacked the factory itself. The strike was disruptive for years, not only for the company but also for the town of Sheboygan.

In 1954, Consultant Anna Rosenberg told the management of the Studebaker Company and its UAW (United Auto Workers) local that unless management assumed its responsibility for managing and stopped permitting union stewards to bypass foremen, the company could not recover. The union accepted this statement. In a subsequent election the union membership replaced its officials with others who could work differently with management. Shortly thereafter, a new management took over the company. Its emphasis on production was viewed by the employees as a "speed up." The local thereupon reelected its former, more militant officials.

(4) Financial emergencies

The financial condition of the church is by far one of the most crucial concerns. In the 9 years of its history, the congregation has never succeeded in meeting its commitments without substantial assistance from outside sources. Both the building and the current expense budgets have been subsidized by large grants and loans from the Board of National Missions. While some support is normal and necessary in new church development, in this particular case the continuing support has greatly inhibited the congregation in accepting its full responsibilities.

(5) Technological changes

Television had played a large part in killing the *Post,* of course, not malevo-lently but simply by coming into existence, the new medium, more dramatic, more immediate, and cheaper. The heirs of Cyrus Curtis and George Horace Lorimer had been strong when television was weak, and there had been a time when they could have bought control of a whole network, but they had chosen instead to ignore the new competition. And so it took away Curtis's audience and Curtis's money, and then it came with lights and cameras to record the death of Curtis's old magazine, and nobody really seemed to mind the intrusion. Everyone wanted to take part in the show. (*Harper's,* December 1969, p. 120.)

The change from Latin to English in the Mass produced a negative reaction on the part of the older parishioners of the Church of the Assumption. To them it was not the same Mass, the same Church. When, to add insult to injury, the priest came down from the altar, pulled up a chair at the crossing in the tran-sept, and began to carry on a dialogue with the congregation instead of giving a sermon, they were certain group dynamics was going to replace the dogma of the Virgin Birth or that some equally devastating doctrinal catastrophe would occur.

c. Product-service history

The product-service history of the organization is a recounting of what key products or services the organization has offered at various times. A description of these will demonstrate how and why the key developmental phases occurred.

(1) Change and development of organizational goals

What changes have occurred in organizational goals at different times and how have they developed? The problems that precipitated and were precipitated by the shift in goals indicate sources of conflict in the organi-zation. Change sometimes means diversity for the survival of the organiza-tion. Whenever a change occurs, someone in the organization will suffer. A change in goals will always have some effect on status, self-image, and power of different people in the organization and of the organization vis-à-vis others as they see it. The pain will be less if the people involved are themselves changing the goals. For some organizations change has been a natural unfolding; for others, a slight veering; for still others, a drastic shift. The degree of strain becomes more acute when the shift has been dramatic. How much stress has the change precipitated? How has the new dimension hurt the employees geared to the status quo?

In 1920 . . . Prest-O-Lite and Linde practically created the synthetic organic chemical industry now known as the petrochemical industry; and the parent company organized a Carbide & Chemicals subsidiary to exploit the new products . . . Chemical research constantly got it into new fields and . . . [its] product line grew more diverse . . . By the late 1930's the corporation was an arch-example of . . . the conglomerate . . . The [then] Union Carbide and Carbon Corp. was . . . a mere holding company . . . between 1949 to 1951. It [Union Carbide] did absorb its subsidiaries and change[d] itself from a holding to an operating company . . . divisions [were encouraged] to break down their mono-lithic structures into vertically integrated product groups . . . each [with commitment to common goals]. (*Fortune*, December 1965, p. 148.)

The Ionian monks came to the West Coast at a time when the needs of the Church were quite primitive. Although its traditional work was pursuit of truth and communication of that truth within the dimensions of contemplation and community, the order found itself having to serve the parish needs of newly arrived immigrants while at the same time being required to support itself. Different goals were imposed on the order by local bishops and the hostile environment. Over the years it seemed unable to escape from these pastoral and teaching responsibilities, yet it recruited monks on the basis of its ideal goals. Now those monks are demanding that the order live up to its stated historic goals and their aspirations based on those goals.

(2) Sequences of development in product or service

To pinpoint who is hurting and specifically why, the consultant must know the steps of change. Who was there first, in the sense of what people with what skills and status? People who are older, have given longer service, and are more entrenched are usually more drastically affected by change. Sometimes valued skills are made obsolete. What were the technical problems? Who was involved and who acquired power when the problems were solved? What skills and talents were made obsolete? Which were pushed into the background? What contributions were no longer rewarded? How long has the resulting resentment been simmering? What has happened historically? These excerpts illustrate developmental sequences and resulting obsolescence of some part of an organization:

When Pope Paul VI reorganized the Vatican Curia, defined five-year terms for its membership, placed the financial affairs of the church in the hands of a finance ministry, this action upset the long-standing power of many members of

the Curia. Competence replaced seniority as the dominant value for officehold-
ers; loyal opposition rather than conforming agreement had already become
paramount in the Ecumenical Council. These changes only increased the intensity of the resentment of the more conservative cardinals in local sees over
the world, as reflected in their punitive prohibitions against younger priests
who wanted to implement approved changes.

CPC International, originally the Corn Products Company, began as a corn
crushing and refining business. Its emphasis was on production. When the company diversified into an international organization, which included food products, its internal emphasis had to shift from production to sales. Product innovation and marketing superseded production as the central activity. This meant
a shift in the focus of the research laboratory as well as in the kinds of executives who had to be recruited, all at the cost of the prestige of those who had
come to the organization earlier.

(3) Relative success or failure in various stages of service or product history

How does success or failure affect the organization? What impact did
success or failure have on the people within the organization and why?
In some instances success is crippling because, deluded by their victory,
people can no longer learn from their errors. Contented with success, they
fail to see the need for continued innovation. Or, having failed, they may
lose courage. Why do things succeed or fail in this organization? Efforts
may fail because they are poorly timed or inadequately studied or beyond
the resources of the organization. Some people cannot tolerate success
and must make "stupid" errors which lead to failure. Failure can be a
mode of circumscribing one's life or a mode of learning. Some people
cannot tolerate failure and must turn it to success. What happens in the
organization under study? One example illustrates a product failure; the
second, a program failure.

[In 1967,] General Electric Co. struggled with a safety call-back crisis akin to
some of Detroit's headaches over auto defects. The company announced that
up to 90,000 of its large screen color TV sets could emit low-level X-rays in a
small beam directed at the floor under the set . . . Service expenses to modify
the sets could cost G.E. more than $1 million; the news could damage the com-
pany's color sales and lead to lawsuits . . . [This crisis occurred when] color
sets . . . [were] already sagging, and some makers fear[ed] publicity over the
G.E. incident . . . and Congress . . . [had] already gotten Senate approval on
safety-in-the-home-legislation . . . G.E. discovered the radiation emissions . . .
in the course of its own testing program, and came to the PHS [Public Health

Service] for advice and help. There is no hint that anyone in government forced the recall on G.E. (*Business Week,* May 27, 1967, p. 61.)

The Immanuel Lutheran Church is experiencing failure while simultaneously achieving great success. It began as a small suburban group of 107 and grew in 5 years to 2,269 members. The church now has a beautiful edifice, five pastors and a busy program that is the envy of all of the other churches in the community. It was so intensely preoccupied with growth, budget, and activity that it began to lose members, and there is increasing complaint about its having become too big and less friendly. The pastoral staff responds to this complaint by trying to increase the number of program activities to "involve more people."

(4) Geographical patterns

The geographical distribution of the organization's activities has great influence on many aspects of its operation. It is more difficult to maintain a sense of unity in an organization that is widely distributed. Yet a large organization heavily concentrated in one area seems impersonal to its employees. International organizations attract more sophisticated employees because such people must have a broader knowledge of languages, cultural differences, and political and social forces than companies limited to a small area. The wider the geographical range of the organization, the more competitive it is likely to be; the greater its breadth of choices for new employees, the lesser the influence of local economics and politics. On the other hand, the more extended the organization, the greater the problems in administration, distribution, and flexibility. The delineation of the geographic pattern of the organization allows the consultant to compare aspiration against resources with the resulting strains and stresses. The geographical location of an organization says much about the degree to which it is likely to be influenced by the currents of social and economic change, its relative attractiveness for certain kinds of employees, the power it is likely to wield in its host community, and even its style of management. The more isolated the locale and the more dominant the organization is in its community, the more likely it is to be paternalistic. (A paternalistic philosophy of management means that the organization treats its employees like children and does for them what they might better do themselves.)

[In the Northern Alberta wilderness] the Sun Oil Company has spent nearly a quarter of a billion dollars and . . . has doubled the world's proven reserves of oil . . . [Getting the oil out of the earth is a superhuman feat. The rich oil land is located in Fort McMurray, an isolated town located between the Arctic Circle and the United States border. In addition to the remoteness of the site, there are even bigger problems.] Timber wolves prowl; the temperature drops to 60 degrees below zero, and, for summer . . . the muskeg swamps breed 82 different kinds of mosquitoes . . . In the summer, equipment sinks out of sight; such jobs as laying pipeline become physically impossible. On the other hand . . . 60° below zero temperatures [in the winter] turn metal brittle; bulldozer treads snap and diesel engines freeze up; welding becomes impossible. It is only when the temperature soars to a comparatively balmy 20° below zero that the work can be accomplished.

Under these conditions, it was difficult for the Sun Oil Company to find a construction crew. Clarence H. Thayer, the soft spoken, intense president of Great Canadian Oil Sands, Ltd., Sun Oil's Athabasca subsidiary, and the man who ramrodded the whole job, advertised for workers as far away as Korea — but when the men came, they seldom stayed long in the frozen muskeg or the dubious delights of Fort McMurray's boomtown saloons. Thayer offered free housing, excellent board and lots of overtime work at double pay, but still the work force turned over at the rate of two and one-half times a year. He brought in men from England and Scotland, promising to pay half their passage if they stayed four months and the whole bill if they stayed a year. Rural towns all over the West were flodded with slick brochures describing everything in Fort McMurray except the mud; one of them noted disingenuously that "ski facilities at Banff are among the world's best." But the brochures did not mention that Banff is some 425 miles from Fort McMurray. (*Newsweek*, October 2, 1967, p. 78.)

In 1949 the Mennonite Central Committee opened a voluntary service unit at the Valley State Hospital. Two years later, Valley State Hospital was the first employing agency in the Sidney, Montana, area prepared to accept conscientious objectors under the new selective service law, which provided that in lieu of military service these men must serve in some way in the interest of public welfare. By June of 1952 more than 150 such men — some married — were working at the hospital. They came from Mennonite communities across the country. By 1961 the Sidney Mennonite community expanded, and, slowly, a church was built to accommodate the families. However, the members of the new church lived in homes located in various sections of the metropolitan Sidney area. There is no Mennonite neighborhood. The Mennonites are so scattered that the church cannot so easily serve the socializing and mutual support functions characteristic of Mennonite churches.

(5) Special skills of the organization

What does this organization do better than anyone else? What is its unique capacity? How broad, narrow, limiting, capable of expansion are its talents? The special skill of an organization may lie in its leader, its laboratory, its depth of management, its capacity for mobilizing financial resources and making major financial commitment. It may lie in the public's identification with the image it holds forth, though its products are no different than anyone else's. Special skill is special power which can be used competitively or defensively.

What distinguished the . . . Whiz Kids [at Ford] was . . . their youth and their application of new tools and techniques to management problems . . . Ford's management today is set by the spiritual descendants of the Whiz Kids. (*Fortune,* January 1967, p. 106.)

Bennington is the most expensive college in the country. It costs $3,850 a year, for the simple reason that education of this intensity, on such a small numerical basis (a student-faculty ratio of seven to one), is a terribly expensive proposition. The faculty is full of creative people, the only kind that Bennington wants. The college does not recognize academic rank or hierarchy, does not regard a Ph.D. as a requirement for teaching, and allows that excellence in teaching might simply consist of teaching very well. Bennington's special skill is its teaching. (*Holiday,* September 1967, p. 91.)

The Tildon, Davis & Rossi law firm is a power in terms of law practices and also in other respects in the community. The firm maintains a good working relationship with the State Bar Association as well as with the bench, although it professes not to be political. There is almost a conscious effort in the firm to restrain itself from speaking of its power. There is an emphasis on gentility; however, this seems to be a thin veneer over the feeling of being the community's most powerful and influential law firm. The special skill of this law firm is its knowledge of and manipulation of the city government. For example, with zoning problems and other such municipal affairs the firm keeps close tabs on what is happening. When they feel an opportune moment has come, they will move in for their client in an effort to have an area zoned or rezoned, or some other such business handled at the municipal level. Often they allow other firms to do the leg work and the test case; then they will actively become involved in the proceedings. In this respect they are highly oriented and responsive to changes in reality.

(6) Performance reputation and record

Organizational reputation is what its publics — customers, employees, competitors, financiers — think and say of it. The organization's performance record is how it actually performs. Here the concern is, not with its performance on the stock market, but the way in which it serves its clients or customers. How much does the organization value its products? How carefully does it make them and how thoroughly does it back them up, as contrasted with what it says it does and what others think it does? The organization's reputation is a type of contract with the public, a promise to do or to deliver in certain ways. Its performance record is the degree to which that contract is kept. The effort with which the organization strives to fulfill its reputation is a reflection of organizational conscience, often epitomized by its slogan (discuss slogan in III A3d, Chapter 7) the gap between what an organization says it does and what it actually does has much to do with the organizational self-image. The greater the gap, the more resentment there is likely to be among employees and customers or clients.

Performance record can also be a point of vulnerability. As noted earlier, the more successful an organization is, the more likely it will continue to maintain the status quo and the less likely it is to change how it performs. Once a standard or demand has been created, an organization feels obligated to continue to fulfill it, even at some expense to itself. This may mean, for example, conflict between a historic premium quality line and the need for products for mass sale. Thus an organization's reputation can also suggest to the consultant where and under what conditions there are likely to be intraorganizational conflicts. Here are two statements reflecting reputation from published sources:

Although Reed [College] may sometimes be abrasive and has always been poor, this college does count on the American educational scene. An extraordinary high proportion of its students are awarded Woodrow Wilson, Fulbright, Rhodes and N.S.F. scholarships. One study indicated that, in the 1950's, Reed led other liberal arts colleges in the percentage of male graduates awarded Ph.D. and M.D. degrees. It is not surprising that Reed produces many top-flight scholarly performers. Since its founding, Reed has been concentrated almost solely on the academic side of undergraduate education . . . Basically, Reed is an "honors" college with little provision for the less intellectually motivated student . . . When compared to other liberal arts colleges in the western section of the United States, it is apparent that Reed has an unexcelled academic reputation. (*Science*, September 15, 1967, p. 1283.)

[Seattle's] Boeing Company . . . is telling the airlines, "Look, we've shown you we can build good planes. We happen to be a bit busy right now, but don't do anything until we can show you our plane." At least one big airline, Northwest, is listening. Says a Northwest executive: "We're an all-Boeing airline." This sentiment is understandable. With labor costs mounting, the airlines are reluctant to service different types of equipment, preferring the economics of standardization . . .

[In contrast, when Lockheed announced plans for their junior jumbo jet, the L-1101, the major airlines did not accept the Lockheed announcement with breathless anticipation because they had been out of the jet business for too long.]

What seems to concern the airlines most about Lockheed is not its ability to build a plane, but to support it once it has been delivered . . . [One major airline executive] said, "Before we bought Lockheed's plane jets, we would have to satisfy ourselves that they [Lockheed] could move up on problems rapidly and provide adequate spare-parts support at reasonable cost. An airplane is like a razor. It's not what you pay for it at first that counts, but what you pay for all the blades you have to put through it." (*Forbes,* October 1, 1967, p. 39.)

d. Organizational folklore

Folklore is part of the culture which is preserved in beliefs, myths, legends, songs, rituals, and practices. It is an integral part of tradition and, as such, becomes an important part of the contemporary scene. Folklore arises out of common experience, often from shared events in a given location, and is frequently an effort to explain that which is otherwise inexplicable, to differentiate those who belong and believe from those who do not. Folklore defines who is to be loved and who is to be hated. Organizational folklore serves to create models, embellishing their charisma with stories of eccentricity, insight, skill, and competence, or explaining their failures by attributing them to environment, economics, or malevolent forces. It also serves to create identification symbols, convictions and traditions which are sources of strength, and taboos. It is reinforcement for the organizational self-image.

About the only thing that has not changed in some respect in the Penney company [after reorganization] is a bit of private terminology. By long tradition harking back to founder James Cash Penney's early partnership days, Penney's employees are referred to as "associates." The word "employee" is out of order. J. C. Penney himself was, in fact, an associate — *i.e.,* he had partners in ownership, when he opened the Golden Rule drygoods store, his first, in Kemmerer, Wyoming, a tiny frontier mining town in 1902. When the company was incorporated in 1924, it had 570 partner associates, each a store manager who owned one-third of his store. Since incorporation, of course, the stores have been owned entirely by the company, but the old term lingers. (*Fortune,* July 1967, p. 111.)

Somewhere in the back of the collective American mind lies a quaint and engaging folk memory that surfaces once a year on Thanksgiving. The Pilgrims. Stout-hearted, pious, gray-clad churchmen marching to their meetinghouse with bell-mouthed musket and faith in God. Brave Miles Standish, Gentle Priscilla. "Speak for Yourself John" Alden. The Mayflower Compact, that cornerstone of American democracy. Freedom of worship in a new world.

Myth, much of it, the creation of patriotic 19th century romantics . . . The
Pilgrims do not deserve the sentimental image created for them by Longfellow
and his contemporaries. (*Time*, November 30, 1970, p. 69.)

4. Circumstances surrounding study

In the discussions in A7 and A8, the consultant described exactly how
he conducted the study and the special conditions which occurred during
or prior to the study which were likely to affect its validity. Here the concern is with the broader context in which the study is taking place,
with placing the organization in its contemporary environment. That
position will influence the circumstances, issues, problems, and forces of
its functioning. What major trends or forces are playing upon the organization now that may contribute to its feeling that it has problems? What
is happening in the industry or in this particular denomination? What
socioeconomic trends are affecting this organization now?

For many people . . . the Salvation Army stands for . . . trumpet-playing officers in blue uniform urging passersby to "Come to Christ . . ." Nowadays,
though, the Salvation Army is pressing in more and more on the business community, not only for a corporate donation, but for advice on growing business
problems . . . [Throughout the organization there is great push for new methods and techniques. The Army finds itself constantly reviewing its practices,
procedures and goals to make sure that it is making the most of its funds.] One
of the constant problems is keeping up to date in the new fields of service. This
often boils down to knowing what medical equipment to buy, or finding the
right kind of civilian professionals to staff its hospitals and counseling services
. . . it also means coming up with new services — such as the residential program for narcotics addicts — as the need arises. Part of the new stress is on
education for its officers and civilians. As the organization has expanded and
diversified, the operating budget has grown. To help meet the budget, the Army
has joined the Community Chest and United Fund drives for the "public" portion of its budget. The Army is feeling the rapid expansion and diversification
in its structure, too. The increasing size has spoiled the simplicity of the structure with a maze of staff functions, committees, regional commissions and advisory boards. A new staff organization — the national headquarters — has been
added to the chart, providing an appendix that coordinates policy and offers
consulting services, but has no chain-of-command authority. (*Business Week*,
June 19, 1965, pp. 118–123.)

6

DESCRIPTION AND ANALYSIS OF CURRENT ORGANIZATION AS A WHOLE

Portion of outline covered in chapter 6

II. DESCRIPTION AND ANALYSIS OF CURRENT ORGANIZATION AS A WHOLE

A. Structural Data

1. Formal organization
   a. *Chart*
   b. *Systems concept*
   c. *Formal job description*
2. Plant and equipment
   a. *Location: territory covered*
   b. *Value*
   c. *Kinds of equipment: size, function*
   d. *Relative efficiency: age, obsolescence*
   e. *Special demands plant and equipment make on people*
   f. *Varieties of work environment*
3. Ecology of the organization
   a. *Spatial distribution of individuals*
   b. *Spatial distribution of activities*
   c. *Implications of the data on spatial distribution*

4. Financial structure
5. Personnel

    a. How many people are employed
    b. Where do they come from and what is their ethnic composition
    c. What are the various educational levels
    d. What is the average tenure
    e. What is the range of skills
    f. What is the absentee rate
    g. What is the turnover rate
    h. What is the accident rate

6. Structure for handling personnel

    a. Recruitment
    b. Orientation
    c. Training
    d. Growth on the job
    e. Promotion
    f. Compensation
    g. Performance analysis
    h. Kind and intensity of supervision
    i. Rules and regulations for employees
    j. Medical program
    k. Safety program
    l. Retirement program
    m. Recreation program
    n. Other fringe benefits
    o. Labor contract

7. Policies and procedures

    a. Scope
    b. How they are communicated
    c. Who knows about them
    d. What discretion is left to lower supervisory levels

8. Time span and rhythm

    a. Seasonal cycles
    b. Diurnal cycles
    c. Planning spans
    d. Degree activities are regulated by time
    e. Attitudes about punctuality
    f. Urgency
    g. Concern about deliveries

B. Process Data

1. Communication systems

    a. *Incoming: reception and routing*
        (1) *Amount and types of materials*
        (2) *Modes of transmission*
            (A) ORAL OR WRITTEN
            (B) FORMAL OR INFORMAL CHANNELS
        (3) *Timing, rhythm, urgency*
            (A) ACCORDING TO PLAN
            (B) ERRATICALLY OR SPONTANEOUSLY
        (4) *Source and audience*
    b. *Processing: integration, decision*
        (1) *Amount and types of material*
        (2) *Modes of processing*
            (A) ORAL OR WRITTEN
            (B) FORMAL OR INFORMAL CHANNELS
        (3) *Timing, rhythm, urgency*
            (A) ACCORDING TO PLAN
            (B) ERRATICALLY OR SPONTANEOUSLY
        (4) *Source and audience*
    c. *Outgoing: routing and response*
        (1) *Amount and types of material*
        (2) *Modes of distribution*
            (A) ORAL OR WRITTEN STATEMENTS
            (B) FORMAL OR INFORMAL CHANNELS
        (3) *Timing, rhythm, urgency*
            (A) ACCORDING TO PLAN
            (B) ERRATICALLY OR SPONTANEOUSLY
        (4) *Source and audience*

2. Current and previous studies in, and reports to, the organization
    a. *Consultant reports*
    b. *Special staff studies*
    c. *Marketing studies*
    d. *Engineering studies*
    e. *Accountants' audits and reports*

A. Structural Data

Having identified the organization, outlined its history, and defined the purposes and conditions of the study, the consultant now describes the organization as he finds it. This section, too, is largely a factual notation about how the organization is put together and how it operates. Much of the data for this section may come from formal reports and records which the organization maintains; some of it will be formulated by the consultant from his observations and interviews.

1. Formal organization

Formal organization refers to the mode of organizing and allocating functions and responsibilities and to the distribution of power. It denotes who reports, or, at least, who is officially supposed to report, to whom for what purposes, and the interrelationships of units, divisions, and departments. The degree to which an organization is formalized or rationalized will vary from organization to organization and sometimes even within an organization. The task of the consultant is to learn and delineate the chain of command and the extent to which the interrelationships of the subsystems and parts are defined.

a. Chart

In most organizations the formal structure can be readily charted by members of top management who either have a chart or can easily draw one. It should be made clear that this is the *formal* chart — that is, the way the chain of command is officially supposed to be. In many organizations the informal chain of command is often very different. When an organization does not have a ready-made chart, the consultant should have the member of top management with whom he is dealing draw one as he sees the situation. Under such conditions, it is also helpful to have other top executives describe how they perceive the organizational structure; conflicts in perception will be evidence for subsequent inferences and conclusions. Flexible organizations recognize the need to change the organization chart frequently as people move from one position to another. The varying assets and talents of individuals make it necessary to adapt their occupational roles to take advantage of their strengths and counteract their weaknesses.

In addition to obtaining the formal chart, the consultant should include a written description of it at this point. The following excerpt from a case study is an illustration of such a statement.

The Ionian Order is comprised of 53 provinces headed by a Master General. He has a *curia* (administrative body) to assist him in governing the order. He has direct authority over all members, houses, and provinces of the order which he exercises through Provincials. He must approve the election of each Provincial by the members of his own province and appoints, on the recommendation of the Provincial and his council, the other officers of the province. In his *curia* he has a *Socius* for each major language group and frequently deals with the various provinces through them. His Procurator General handles all business with the Holy See.

The Provincial, elected by the Provincial Chapter for four years, has also a *Definitorium* to whom he must report. The *Definitorium* is a body made up of four priests, also elected by the chapter for four years to enact legislation which will govern both the Provincial and the province. The Provincial is the chief executive officer of the province and the respective Priors report to him.

There is a Provincial Council, composed of all previous provincials and certain specified others, who are advisory to the Provincial, except in financial matters where he must have approval by majority secret vote.

The Provincial appoints the members of his *curia*. These include the *Socius* (the deputy provincial), the *Syndicus* (financial officer), the Promoter of Vocations, and the Promoter of Missionary Activities.

The Prior is the head of a House or priory, which is formally designated as such because of the number of men assigned and the permanency of the House. A smaller, less permanent installation is headed by a Superior. The Prior is elected by the priests in his House, subject to the approval of the Provincial. The Superior is appointed.

The Prior has a subprior and a *Syndicus,* appointed with the approval of his House Council. There is also a Regent, whose duties are roughly equivalent to those of the President and Academic Dean of a secular college, responsible for theological education. For each of the subgroups within a House there is also an immediate superior: Master of Novices, Master of Students, and Master of Cooperator Brothers.

b. System concept

Traditional charts depict formal lines of authority and functional departments. As organizations grow in complexity, the formal charts are less useful for describing the actual interactions of people. Many different people are related to each other in varied ways which are not reflected on the organization chart, particularly in those organizations which alter the composition of task groups for new projects. Thus there is a need to understand how an organization operates as a system. This can be done by constructing another kind of chart which reflects interrelationships. Such a chart might have a list of job positions in their administrative order on its horizontal axis and a list of tasks and activities on its vertical axis. Then symbols can be placed in the squares to indicate the kind of relationship between a given task and the persons involved in that task.

c. Formal job description

Many organizations have elaborate descriptions for each job, while others have none. The dègree to which there are formal job descriptions reflects how carefully conceived the formal interrelationships are in any organization. It indicates also how people ostensibly are controlled, evaluated, appraised, and charged. The detail of such descriptions may suggest rigidity; the absence of detail does not necessarily indicate flexibility. Employees in organizations which lack formal job descriptions often are confused about what they are supposed to be doing. The absence of a formal job description makes it difficult to appraise performance in other than subjective terms because there are no concise criteria for effective performance. Some company presidents prefer it that way. Said one president when asked what the company's evaluation system was, "You are looking at it. I decide who will get a raise and who will not."

2. Plant and equipment

The consultant's interest in plant and equipment is primarily from two points of view: How do they affect the people who must work in and with them? What relationship do they have to the efficiency of accomplishing the intended tasks? The answers to both questions will have something to do with how people feel about themselves and their organizations. The description of plant and equipment may be stated in general summary terms; the consultant is not called upon to write an analysis as an engineer might.

a. Location: territory covered

The consultant need make only a simple statement about where the plant is located; its geographical relationship to its host community; its approximate absolute size in square feet, acres, and floors; its relative size with respect to the host community; its accessibility; its architecture; and similar data which will suggest its impact on people.

Roosevelt Elementary School is one of the 22 grade schools, 3 junior high schools, and 2 high schools in the Forest Heights Unified School District. This school district operates under the K-6-3-3 plan. Kindergarten and the first six grades meet in one building, the junior high students meet in a separate building, and the grades ten through twelve meet in the senior high school. With 17 classrooms and 515 students, Roosevelt Elementary School is somewhat larger than the average elementary school in the district. It serves an area with a radius of approximately one-half mile so that all children are within walking area. During the past decade, the Forest Heights School District has grown from 5,400 pupils to more than 14,000, and the number of schools has increased from 12 to 22.

In 1955 the Kaiser Aluminum & Chemical Corporation built a plant in Ravenwood, West Virginia, which then had only 1,100 people, mostly elderly. Today, the world's largest integrated aluminum plant employs 3,450 people; covers some 3,600 acres; consists of both a reduction plant and a rolling mill; and resembles a college freshmen's nightmare of a chemistry lab, with giant-sized beakers, retorts, bubbling cauldrons, and buzzing electrical devices. In the process, Kaiser also succeeded in changing Ravenwood, the surrounding Jackson County, and almost the entire valley. In 1955, Jackson had one of the lowest per capita incomes in West Virginia: $1,106. Now it has the third highest in the state: over $2,700. Where once there were only 200 people employed at salaried jobs, there are now almost 2,000 Jacksonites working in the aluminum plant alone. (The remainder of its employees come from the outlying counties.) Retail sales are over $17,000,000 annually as against the previous $8,200,000. Assessed value of county property has jumped from $27,000,000 to almost $75,000,-000. School enrollment (a prime developmental consideration in this area of dropouts, never-wents and "unemployables") has jumped from 3,600 to 5,700 for the county; more significantly, from 758 to 2,185 for the town of Ravenwood itself. Kaiser's presence in the county has, of course, brought new problems. The charming little river town is now not too dissimilar from any of the other bustling little industrial cities all over America. But the benefits far outweigh the problems. (*Think,* September–October 1967, pp. 4–5.)

b. Value

Value is difficult to measure because so much of the evaluation of an organization's assets hinges on appraisal and accounting methods and on current market conditions. Therefore, here the consultant will be concerned with an estimate of assets employed in the business at current value. Some organizations publish a statement of their assets in their annual reports, others do not. Fixed assets may be carried at either book value (their original cost) or current market value. It is important to know which and why. The way assets are listed indicates the impression the organization is trying to make. Sometimes an estimate can be made indirectly from local tax assessments. The value of an organization's assets says something about the permanence of the organization, its self-regard, the regard it has for its employees, and the way in which the community is likely to look upon it. Inferences about these matters will be made in those parts of the outline discussed in Chapters 7 and 8. The first excerpt reports on the assets of a manufacturing company as evaluated by that company. The second excerpt evaluates the physical plant of a school.

In its financial statement for the year ending December 31, 1967, Arrowhead Tool and Die Manufacturing Company valued its 15-acre site, plant, and equipment at $289,765.30, an increase of $31,956.45 over the previous year. It made no estimate of the value of its patents.

St. Mary's High School was completed in 1962 at a cost of $1,000,000. The building itself covers about half a block on 55 acres of land owned by the school.

c. Kinds of equipment: size, function

Here the consultant is interested in noting the differences in working demands and in opportunities within one company. These may require different kinds of people as well as different management procedures. The difference may have various effects on people who otherwise may be much alike. They may constitute unique working worlds. Size and function of equipment gives one a picture of the range of activities which the organization carries on. How much of what it fabricates does the organization manufacture itself? How much is done by outsiders? What implications does this have for the organization's vulnerability because of its dependence on others; of its control of others by making them dependent? What does the organization do with what it owns? In some cases equipment sits unused; in others, it is misused. Sometimes it is purchased to be "up-to-date," as electronic data processing equipment, but the organization is, as yet, unable to use it effectively. In many instances it is inadequate for the needs of the organization.

Another excerpt about Arrowhead Tool and Die will illustrate the kind of information that should be recorded here.

There are five major working areas in the Arrowhead Tool and Die Manufacturing Company: a front office suite for managerial, administrative and accounting functions; a machine shop; a welding shop; an assembly and paint shop and a warehouse. The dictating, typing, and storage equipment in the front office is relatively new. The executives' offices are furnished with modernistic walnut easy chairs and desks, the latter with overhanging tops. The clerical offices have gray metal furniture. The accounting equipment is rather primitive, limited to adding and billing machines. There are twenty welding stalls, physically separated from each other. The company has recently acquired five auto welders which function with more speed and ease than the older "hot rod" welders which they have replaced. They expect to acquire more such auto welders. The jigs used in all three shops are constructed in the plant itself. In the machine shop there are eight lathes, eleven drill presses, and seven assorted grinders. They are laid out around the walls of the machine shop and along a center half-wall so that there are four rows of such equipment in a herringbone pattern. There are floor fans beside each machine to cool the men in summer. In the assembly area, there is a large cutting torch machine; a few stamping machines, which stamp out small metal parts; and a large open area for putting the tools together. Hydraulic equipment for the tools must be ordered from other manufacturers because it cannot be made here. Delivery delays by the vendor hold up Arrowhead assembly work. The tools are assembled and then hung on trolley hooks which carry them in a U-shaped pattern through the paint shop where they are spray painted by hand sprayers, and then permitted to dry. The warehouse has forklift trucks, shelves, and addressing machines. There are only a few roller tracks on which to roll large boxes.

d. Relative efficiency: age, obsolescence

The relative efficiency of equipment has much to do with how people feel about using it, particularly, if they are under pressure to produce specified quantities. If machine tools cannot hold tolerances, if utility crews do not have protection from the weather in their truck cabs, if the air conditioning repetitively fails to cool the hot kitchen, the feelings of the workers will be worn on their sleeves. One way for the consultant to infer something about relative efficiency is for him to question the people who are using the equipment. The following excerpt from a magazine article is an example of the kind of information the consultant should be seeking.

Examples of inefficient operations and wasteful use of manpower kept turning up everywhere [at Wheeling Steel], Morris [the president of the company] recalls. During a routine visit to a galvanizing plant, he noticed seven coal shovelers stoking fires under the zinc . . . pots [into which] garbage cans [are dipped for coating] . . . It cost only $35,000 to change over to gas and it saved $70,000 a year . . . A new materials-handling manager discovered 56 firemen working as crewmen on the company's diesel railroad engines "when even the over-the-road carriers have gotten rid of them." Thirty-two have now been eliminated, but only after a struggle. Two full-time elevator operators were found running the elevator in a two-story warehouse building . . . Morris exclaims in amazement, "Wheeling Steel even employed lamplighters!" It actually has kerosene lamps on the railroad switches and the lamplighters trim the wicks and snuff them out. U. S. Steel got rid of its lamplighters 18 years ago.

[A major problem developed with its collapsing slab furnaces.] Steel slabs begin their passage through the hot-rolling mill by being heated up to 2000°F in one of three gas-fired furnaces. The slabs at Wheeling can weigh as much as nine tons, and the hearth supporting them must be made of special heat-resistant material — corundum brick on the upper layers, with less costly and less sturdy firebrick below. Designers of the furnace, reasonably enough, had left slight gaps between the upper bricks to allow for their expansion at furnace heats. Unfortunately, the corundum brick's coefficient of expansion is almost nil. After about six months, molten slag from the slabs worked its way down through the cracks and consumed the firebrick on the bottom, allowing large sections of the furnace floor to settle unevenly. Eventually, all three furnace floors had to be rebuilt, a two-week job for each one.

The six enormous rollers through which the hot steel passes as it is lengthened and reduced in thickness must be held accurately in place under fantastic stresses. But the specially designed hydraulic devices that had been intended to keep each roller axle positioned securely kept failing with such discouraging regularity that they were eventually abandoned. (*Fortune*, July 1967, pp. 107–108.)

Another illustration comes from a newspaper article:

During the fire at a fraternity house, two of the City of Lawrence's five pumpers became unserviceable. A 35-year-old pumper failed due to a cracked cylinder head and the engine of a 12-year-old pumper failed beyond repair. The city's fire department is now operating with only three pumpers, one of them 39 years old. Of the remaining two pumpers, one is used for response to fire alarms outside the city where the City of Lawrence has a contract. During the time of outside response, the entire city is dependent on only one reliable pumper. Three of the five pumpers have a pumping capacity of only 750 gallons of water a minute, compared to a minimum standard of 1,000 gallons a minute. The lone aerial truck is already 20 years old, considered just 5 years from the maximum useful life of fire-fighting equipment. Using the Kansas Fire Inspection Bureau's standards which call for all runs to be made within a two-mile radius of a fire station, there are major areas of the northwest and southwest of the city completely unprotected. There is no reserve equipment available to save a home which is burning at the same time there is a major fire in the central business district or at Kansas University. The Kansas Fire Inspection Bureau has said that since its last inspection in September 1961 the Fire Department has not been expanded to keep abreast of the city's growth. It said the "fire protection capability remains the same as in 1961." Commercial fire rates have been raised temporarily with a 15 per cent surcharge, with assurance that the hike will be permanent if the fire stations are not built, because of the city's current condition. In addition, some nationally respected companies have refused to write insurance in Lawrence because of the inadequate fire protction. (*Lawrence* [Kansas] *Journal-World*, October 18, 1967).

e. Special demands plant and equipment make on people

Here the consultant should consider what the plant or equipment make people do or hinder them from doing and what pressures they exert on people. The following examples illustrate the effects of the plant and equipment on those who work in and with them:

There must be a close working relationship between the mixer, the pallet lifter, the two forklift operators, and the man who packs the new pallets for the autoclave machine at Sunflower Brick Products Company. Because of limited space, the material coming out of the machines had to be moved through the various stages very quickly. But these men could not work effectively as a group because they were stationed at various points in the highly mechanized production process where they worked in relative isolation from one another.

Because of the physical lay-out of the hospital, the degree of task specialization, a departmental rather than hospital-wide orientation program, and a lack of emphasis on interdepartmental cooperation, the nurses at St. Agnes' Hospital have little knowledge of what is going on in other departments. Consequently, they often work at cross purposes.

The Department of Social Relations of a New England University was formerly housed in an antiquated, inadequate building. The faculty and assistants were forced to share offices and other facilities. As a result, there was much face-to-face informal communication among all members of the department regardless of tenure or rank. When an elaborate twelve-story building was erected for the department, offices and facilities abounded. However, a noticeable increase in formality and a decrease in the amount of sharing of ideas followed as full professors and others of long tenure were assigned to the second and third floors, and others were assigned elsewhere in the building depending upon their rank.

f. Varieties of work environment

A garment factory located in a dingy loft with poor lighting on New York's Seventh Avenue will be a different working environment from a colorfully decorated office suite in Rockefeller Center just a few blocks away. The kitchen help and the bell boys employed by the same hotel have vastly different work environments. The varieties of work environment, the uplands and lowlands, are the context for what might be referred to as the "sociological temperature" of the organization. Degrees of such sociological temperature are related to the organization's status system and also say something about the kind of people who can be attracted to different parts of an organization.

The consultant must note the range of environments from that of the chief executive to the janitor. The questions to be asked are: "What does this total work area look like? How centrally located are drinking fountains, toilets, elevators, dining rooms? What differences are there in furniture, pictures, carpeting, air conditioning, parking, and so on, in the various environments. Is an employee free to change his environment to the extent of hanging his own pictures? Who has to approve changes, and what does that mean for the environment?" There can be many more questions, depending on the perceptiveness of the consultant. With respect to executive offices, or other areas where an employee or work group has the freedom to construct its own environment, the question may have to do with how the office symbolizes the individual's self-image, aspirations, fantasies and needs. In many companies, official approval is required before an executive can hang a picture not taken from the company collection; other companies ban pictures entirely. Some companies seem bent on suppressing manifestations of individual taste. "When we moved uptown, we wanted everything absolutely uniform," explained a Mobil executive. "We wanted to get away from all that individuality down at 25 Broadway."

The following excerpt is an example of a description of work environments:

There are marked physical differences in the environment of the office and the plant of the Michael Manufacturing Company. As one enters the office from the flower-lined, flagstone walk, he is immediately impressed with the newness, cleanliness, and order of the surroundings. Although the noise of the factory is perceptible in the distance, the office is essentially quiet. It is furnished with a modern decor which harmonizes with the one wall of walnut paneling, muted gold-olive painted walls, and amber carpeting. Large potted plants are scattered effectively throughout the area, and an abstract painting decorates the walnut paneled wall. The secretaries and clerks are fashionably dressed; the men wear suits and ties. Upon entering the plant, the contrast is vivid. Considerable noise comes from the grinding machines, the pounding of metal on metal, the shrill sound of whistles and horns alerting the supervisors of messages and phone calls. Above the din workers call to each other. In addition, the welding shop is smoky, and fumes spread into the machine and assembly shops. During the summer, the open doors and windows provide greater ventilation for the shop area. Throughout the plant there is an odor from welding fumes and the various oils used in the machining process. Considering the tools and equipment produced in relation to the debris, the plant is clean. The main aisles are never cluttered; dirt, slag, and debris around each worker's area is usually limited to the immediate task at hand. The men in the plant area work in heavy duty bib-type overalls.

3. Ecology of the organization

Ecology is that aspect of biology which deals with the mutual relations of organisms and their environment. Sometimes it is referred to as bionomics. The concept has been adapted to sociology; it refers to that branch of sociology which is concerned with the spacing of people and institutions and the resulting interdependency. It will be used in the latter sense in this book.

a. Spatial distribution of individuals

The consultant should determine how and where people are located within the organization, and what relative distance or proximity they have to each other. Individuals may work closely together while sharing a common task, operate in a complementary manner, or work independently. They may do all three at different times. They may be scattered as in an electric power generating station where there are few people and much noise; they may be congested, as in a machine shop, with 25 men in a relatively small area. Even though the machinists may be physically close to each other, each may have to watch his machine carefully and therefore be psychologically distant from the person next to him.

These two excerpts are illustrative of the kind of information to be noted here.

At the Phoenix Card Company, the artists and designers are located within the same area on the same floor, but they are separated from each other by partitions. Each division is further subdivided into small groups, and each individual within a group occupies a separate cubicle. Each artist functions as an individual within his group yet can easily call upon a peer for advice or comment on a project.

Linemen in the Kansas Power and Light Company may work very closely, as when two are on a pole among hot wires, or they may be working on individual tasks hundreds of yards apart. Because they often must work closely together physically while under dangerous conditions, the men must be sufficiently close psychologically so that each can tell when another "has had his toast burned" by the way he greets his coworkers when he arrives at work. Unless one is particularly alert to the moods of the others, "he can hand you a hot wire."

b. Spatial distribution of activities

How are different components or activities of the organization related to each other spatially? What activity is where, and what are the routes to each? The consultant should consider those questions here. The spatial distribution of activities may be different from that of people because a given activity may be carried on in several different locations. For example:

The electric business of the Kansas Power and Light Company is concentrated more heavily at the eastern end of the state and the gas business, more heavily in the southwest. Headquarters for electric production and distribution are in Topeka; for gas, in Salina, 110 miles west of Topeka. The gas compressor stations, manned by a dozen men each, are even farther west, one almost 200 miles away. Thus the gas employees are farther away from each other than are the electric employees, farther away from company headquarters, and even farther away from their headquarters than are the electric employees. Where both activities are in the same community, the communication channel is through the general superintendent. Otherwise, the channel is through the vice president in charge of gas operations to his counterpart in electric operations.

The Tarantino State Hospital is divided both spatially and organizationally into separate divisions. There is no direct way to get from the out-patient services to the rest of the hospital without going outside the grounds and entering through a separate entrance. Central facilities like the lab are in the administration building, a half-mile from some of the outlying ward buildings. The administrative offices are distant from the wards and have become more distant as new sprawling ward buildings have replaced the older units which were attached to the administration building. Efforts have been made to decentralize as many activities as possible so that each section is almost a self-contained hospital, sharing central facilities.

c. Implications of the data on spatial distribution

In this part of the outline the consultant should be concerned only with an objective description of the organization. By combining his observations on spatial distribution, he can report on the implications of con ditions, circumstances, or requirements that are descriptively valid. These could include clique development, nodal points within the organization, who talks or is unable to talk with whom, what empires have resulted which are then to be guarded, or the points at which invisible lines are drawn purely on the basis of spatial arrangements.

Two excerpts from case studies exemplify some of these points:

Located in an old colonial style house, the Brice House Publishing Company uses the former living quarters for editors' office space. The editors have individual cubicles, in whatever nooks and crannies are possible. They tend to associate at coffee breaks and other informal social gatherings on the basis of their work location. The need for association with others after working intensively but alone on manuscripts reinforces the transformation of the social groups into cliques. One of the cliques is the "Sunshine Club." Certain girls whose work areas offer a choice view of the west invite their special friends to watch the sunset whenever the view is picturesque. Those who are not allied with this clique do not share the view or the social reciprocity which goes with it.

The men of All Saints Province perceive the large metropolitan area to be the place where the real Ionian life goes on. Those stationed elsewhere feel isolated from the order and think of themselves as separate entities. To intensify this feeling, those stationed further away from the metropolitan area are not given the logistical support that those closer receive: Although a man may ask for books or a typewriter, he is actually expected to scrounge for the funds to purchase these items. For those living away from the main house, transportation presents an enormous problem since the men are not allowed to own cars. It is often difficult to get a car when it is needed for professional work. One of the demands made by the work setting is that community living as prescribed by the constitution of the order is impossible for the majority of the men if they are stationed in houses with less than five Ionians since this is too few for community activities.

4. Financial structure

In Chapter 5, Section A, we detailed the organization's financial condition. That was a generalized statement of its assets and relative financial position. Here we want to know, in the case of business organizations, how the company is financed: how many shares of common stock, preferred stock, bonds, debentures, long-term mortgaging, and similar financial facts which will indicate the financial limits of flexibility which the company has. If the company is publicly held, such facts are usually presented in its annual report and in the summaries of investment counselors or stock brokers. The consultant can obtain such summaries from any stock broker. If the company is not publicly held, the consultant should get a summary for a publically held organization to use as a guide to the kind of information he should have from the organization under study. If he is unfamiliar with balance sheets and the meaning of financial summaries, the consultant should ask an accountant to explain what the summary means as far as the organization is concerned. He should be particularly alert to the facade the organization is trying to present in its financial reporting and the implications of its reporting practices for the way the management perceives itself, its competition, and its environment.

Finance and control procedures for nonprofit organizations — churches, colleges, and similar nonprofit organizations — are considerably different from those of business. In such cases the dues, contributions, or tax structure may be important as a reflection both of the organization's financial problems and who exerts control. This excerpt from a magazine article and the one that follows, from a case study, are illustrative:

The decade of dynamic thrust which the University of Pittsburgh enjoyed under the late Edward H. Litchfield hit a major roadblock in the summer of 1965 when it became apparent that the university had accumulated debts of more than $20 million and had run out of operating funds . . . One of the main points of contention between Litchfield and the trustees was the amount of money the trustees had to agree to raise to help build Pitt into a great university. At one point Litchfield mentioned the figure $125 million but the trustees always shied away from such specific figures . . . Litchfield, after suffering a mild heart attack left the University in July 1965 . . . there was a sense of urgency about picking the chancellor . . . [since the University] needed funds flowing back to the university from private sources . . . The University had hesitated to approach private givers until a decision on the chancellor had been made. [While the trustees were deciding upon a chancellor,] the Commonwealth [of Pennsylvania] provided about $20 million of Pitt's $70 million budget . . . [during the 1967 academic year] . . . However, the need for money was paramount at Pittsburgh. In light of this concern university officials were understandably joyous when the Richard King Mellon Trusts announced a gift of $3.23 million [in December 1966] for the creation of a department of neurology in the School of Medicine . . . But the Mellons and other private givers have tended to lavish most of their gifts to the University in the areas of medicine and public health. No doubt many faculty members and administrators who have remained loyal to the university during the financial crisis expect their own areas to be better funded in the future than they have been in the past . . . [On January 13, 1967, the University announced that it had found a new chancellor — Wesley W. Posvar.] Hired as an educator, the new university chancellor may soon conclude that his place in educational history will be largely determined by his skill in opening up the hearts and the coffers of the financial potentates of Pittsburgh. (*Science,* February 3, 1967, pp. 541–544.)

Wakefield Methodist Church is often referred to as "Cadillac Methodist Church" because the owners of the various furniture industries and textile mills are members of the congregation. Six millionaires have extended their empires into the church and run it with a paternalistic type of leadership. These men have built influential power structures within the congregation using their top management employees as the core of each group. The influence of these men is so great that during the labor strikes of the 1940's and 1950's, the labor voice was silenced within the congregration. Today labor is almost nonexistent in the church. The ministerial leadership has felt obligated to abide by the will of these powerful laymen lest there arise an overt contest of authority. Also, since these six men are generous not only to the church but to the Conference in which the church is the most influential member, their leadership is questioned neither by the ministers nor the bishop of the Conference.

The financial assessment of noncommercial institutions is more difficult than that of business organizations. Schools may be compared on a cost-per-pupil basis with other schools; on comparative square-foot cost of buildings; on amount of money spent on libraries, laboratories, and other specialized equipment. Journals and books on educational administration offer various yardsticks. The same is true for hospitals, churches, and other institutions. Every institution also has its equivalent of "profit," some accrual of the results of its effort. Every institutional form has some way of judging whether it is getting its money's worth out of what it is spending, however inadequate the yardsticks may be. Contemporary concern with social indicators for making alternative choices among possible governmental programs is one such yardstick. However, one must be careful in making interinstitutional comparisons because accounting systems may vary. There is considerable argument in the accountancy literature about the need for standardization. Before making comparisons within the same organization from one year to another, check to be sure there has been no change in accounting methods and also that adjustments have been made in actual figures for inflation and other forces which might alter the value of figures that are being compared. For example, if the cost of living is discussed in terms of 1949 dollars, a comparison can be made in absolute terms.

Three general comparisons may be helpful: intraorganizational over a span of years; interorganizational, within the same industry, field, or service; comparison with other (national) trends. A different inference will be made if the organization is doing poorly while others of its kind are doing well; while all of its kind are doing poorly; during an economic depression which affects everyone.

Accrediting agencies are good sources of criteria and comparative statistics. The Joint Commission on Accreditation of Hospitals, 645 N. Michigan Avenue, Chicago, Illinois and the North Central Association of Colleges and Secondary Schools, 5454 South Shore Drive, Chicago, Illinois are two such agencies.

5. Personnel

Personnel refers to both the people in the organization and the formal organization practices with respect to them as employees. The consultant, at this point, should determine who the people are in the cultural and behavioral sense and how the company or institution relates to them. The structure for formal personnel relationships, or "how it is done here" is based on implicit assumptions about human motivation, social responsibility, mutual obligations, and similar issues. Both the people and the practices should be described in sufficient detail that subsequently the consultant can validate the organization's assumptions by examining the practices and comparing those assumptions with the socioeconomic and cultural facts.

a. How many people are employed

The consultant would do well to break the personnel into different functional groupings. These excerpts are illustrative:

When the present chief of police assumed office in 1948, Garden City had a population of under 10,000, and its police force consisted of one sergeant, five patrolmen, and one clerk. Five years later the city had more than doubled in population, in part owing to annexations, and the police department kept pace. With the creation of the position of lieutenant and inspector, the force numbered 19 men. By 1960, the police department included 33 members, an increase of over 300 per cent during that 12-year period. Within the next five years it is expected that several new positions will be added, including a captaincy, another lieutenancy and several additional sergeants and inspector positions. (Robert L. Peabody, *Organizational Authority*. New York, Atherton Press, 1964, p. 64.)

In 1966 The Menninger Foundation had 900 employees, most of them in full-time service. There were 80 medical doctors; 35 psychologists; 35 social workers; 30 registered nurses; 5 clergymen; 25 adjunctive therapists; 70 nursing assistants; 60 child care workers. Supporting these persons were more than 500 others: administrators; food, maintenance, and housekeeping services; research assistants; secretaries; librarians; engineers. There were also 170 postgraduate students in courses ranging from one to five year; 67 graduated from their respective courses in June.

b. Where do they come from and what is their ethnic composition

The consultant should consider here certain aspects of the employees' background. For some employees it might be important to know their country or location of origin which will say something about their traditions and attitudes toward work. For example, a large group of German-descended machine tools specialists settled in Rockford, Illinois. They have a national tradition of mechanical skill, high mechanical standards, and compulsive personalities. These features are assets for certain industries while at the same time they might create problems when such men supervise others who do not share the same tradition. For other industries it might be more important to know that the employees come from the surrounding farm communities or that they have been born and reared in the city. "From" should refer to that locale which is likely to have significance for present behavior related to the organization.

Although St. Mark's began as a German community and remained, at least in part, a German-speaking community, even into the 1930's, the character of the community has become cosmopolitan. Among the fathers, national origins of several European countries are represented, in addition to China, Japan, Korea. Beginning in 1940, several Negro students from the South found that they received kind reception here. Since that time, 23 Negroes have been professed as monks of St. Mark's. (This figure does not include the brothers.) Since 1950, applicants have come from the four areas of missionary work: Japan, Mexico, Puerto Rico, and the Bahamas. Of the 54 clerics presently in the clericate, 44 were born in the U.S. Of the 54, 27 were born in Minnesota. Seventeen were born in 12 other states of the Union. (Three were born in the Bahamas, three from Mexico, two from Puerto Rico, one from Haiti, and one from Ireland.)

Almost all of the nonprofessional staff of The Menninger Foundation are drawn from nearby Kansas communities or from similar communities in surrounding states. They therefore tend to have a conscientious farm-born attitude toward work and a sense of obligation to others derived from "Bible-belt" philosophy. The professional staff, by contrast, is drawn from many parts of the world. Their sense of mission derives largely from their identification with their roles, their professional reference groups, and the treatment ideals of the organization.

c. What are the various educational levels

Here the consultant should determine if there are significant differences in education among people in the organization. Are such differences random or by skill; are they based on occupational responsibility or on some other basis? How many people are there at various educational levels and what are their occupational relationships to each other? Two examples follow.

Of the one male (the district director) and 22 females who make up the membership of the Ventura County welfare office, only 3 have had graduate training in social work, only the director holds a master of arts degree. Although a college degree is a job requirement, only 2 social workers had undergraduate majors in sociology or psychology. Three of the 6 clerical workers have had 1 or 2 years of college; the balance of the clerical staff, including the supervisor, graduated from high school. Only 6 of the 23-member staff belong to one or more professional organizations. (Robert L. Peabody, *Organizational Authority*. New York, Atherton Press, 1964, p. 69.)

There are 56 persons on the staff of St. Mary's High School. The staff includes members of three separate groups: priests, sisters, and lay teachers. All of the teaching faculty have received their bachelor of science degrees and teaching certificates. Fifteen have their master's degrees and six others are working toward it. Eight lay teachers have master's degrees while only four sisters have theirs: However, four other sisters are working toward theirs. The department heads are always nuns, regardless of education.

d. What is the average tenure

The consultant should discover how long people stay in this organization. Does tenure vary at different levels and in different parts of the organization? Has it changed over the years? These excerpts illustrate:

The northern branch office of the Ventura County Welfare Department, with its staff of 23, was created in the fall of 1959 to administer to the needs of several suburban communities. It is located 20 miles from the central office of the welfare department. Staff turnover per year, which ran as high as 25 per cent in the county, was almost nil in the branch office. (Robert L. Peabody, *Organizational Authority*. New York, Atherton Press, 1964, p. 69.)

Leary's Book Store, . . . doing business at the same old stand for 128 years is as much a 'Philadelphia tradition as the Art Museum and Bookbinder's restaurant . . . Its 31 salesmen are mellowed with an average of 20 years with the company (it takes that long to gain proficiency in the business. One of them, John Mears, has been there 40 years. (*Business Week*, September 12, 1964, p. 81.)

About 80 per cent of the employees at the Markley plant in Lawrence are women, mostly wives of students at the university. These women frequently leave after the graduation of their husbands. The average tenure is from 2 to 3 years. One plant manager said that only 15 per cent of the entire 400 employees had worked there for more than 2 years.

e. What is the range of skills

Here the consultant should ask: Do employees come to the organization unskilled and receive limited training? Do they arrive with a wide variety of educational and skill experiences as on a complex construction or engineering project? Are there a few at the top who have most of the knowledge and skill? Can the organization develop its own talent? These excerpts illustrate how these questions may be answered:

Many of those interviewed at Pioneer Ridge Lab mentioned that most of the employees, including the highly educated engineers, are typed when they are hired and. allowed only to do work appropriate to that type. This generally reduces the freedom of movement and variations in task processes. The organization offers the opportunity for collaboration and compliance on the part of its employees. Even though this is an organization that is creating new systems, there did not appear to be much opportunity within the scope of the individual for innovation and initiation. The engineering rooms did have small labs to the rear where the engineers could experiment, but this "experimentation" was in a literal sense for it was built into the well-defined task roles. Nonengineers, such as artists, draftsmen, checkers, and technicians, seemed to feel this constriction to one specialty or role even more strongly than did the engineers. The lack of a broad range of task roles from which to learn manifested itself in frustration and immersion in detail.

[At] the Circle Diamond [Ranch] . . . heifers are bred at 2 years of age, or 6 months earlier than usual . . . pregnant heifers are trucked for deliveries under the skilled hands of six male midwives [who deliver the pregnant heifers] and a staff of nutritionists who fatten the calves once they are weaned . . . employees also include cowhands with agricultural degrees and three hunters whose job it is to keep off all marauding bears, coyotes and wildcats. (*Time*, October 20, 1967, p. 96.)

The Third National Bank is largely a one-man operation. That one man, the president, has single-handedly been responsible for its remarkable growth. His major forte is political and public relations in which he wields tremendous skill. All of the other officers are technicians rather than managers. They go by the book; they are uncomfortable with power and aggressive behavior. None can really succeed the president. When he retires or dies, a new president will have to be recruited from outside the organization.

f. What is the absentee rate

The absentee rate is a significant indicator of morale. The rates are computed within industries and can be computed within an organization for different units. Like all other rates, they may be computed differently in various organizations, so comparisons must be made cautiously. Sick-leave statistics are one good indicator, but they do not include days taken without pay. Rates differ for men and women and for older versus newer employees. Some people consider the absentee rate to be an index of people's withdrawal from the organization. For churches and schools, attendance rates may serve a similar purpose. This rate may be described as in these excerpts:

The Weldon Pajama Company had a history of difficulty in maintaining balanced production lines. High absence rates (7 per cent daily) meant that there were many inexperienced operators who could not hold to the scheduled output pace. Each morning there were a number of vacancies to be filled by temporary transfer of people from their regular jobs. (Alfred Marrow et al., *Management by Participation,* New York, Harper & Row, 1967, pp. 18–19.)

In a New England telephone company it was found that in any one year, the heavy proportion of absences in the group of telephone operators was the product of a small number of employees. The relationship between absences in the first year of service and total absence throughout subsequent years of service showed a high positive correlation.

The absence rate is low among the instructors at St. Mary's High, but when an illness occurs, the absent teacher is readily helped by a substitute teacher from the staff or a part-time instructor. The priests and religious teachers are probably absent most frequently; in fact, one staff member reported that there is rarely a week that some priest is not absent from his class.

g. What is the turnover rate

The absentee rate is an indication of the rate at which people stay away from the job; the turnover rate tells in what numbers they leave it. Turnover rates are compiled by industry just as are absentee rates. A high turnover rate may suggest poor working conditions, inadequate selection efforts, or a change in the social value of given work. These excerpts reflect both rate and causes:

At the Carothers, Barrand & Swenson law firm, the turnover rate among the stenographers is extreme. One of the stenographers interviewed indicated that in the last 6 years between 40 and 50 girls have worked for the firm. The problems relate to the rate of pay and benefits, both of which are better in industry and state employment. The partners in the firm recognize this problem, but are not willing to solve it by paying higher salaries, although a benefit plan is being worked out for the stenographers.

For most of its century of life, Drew Theological School in Madison, New Jersey, has had a reputation as the nation's most intellectually adventurous and scholarly Methodist seminary. Within the past year, however, its dean has been dismissed, 6 of the 24 professors have quit for other jobs, and more resignations are expected in the near future.

   Cause of the uproar is an administrative civil war between the seminary and parent Drew University, to which it is attached. (*Time*, February 2, 1968, p. 37.)

h. What is the accident rate

   Accidents may be viewed psychologically as another form of withdrawal from what is unconsciously experienced as a painful and difficult situation from which there is no other escape. Accident rates are computed in varying ways. The generally accepted standard for computing this figure, and the comparative industry rates can be found in the *National Safety News*. Some organizations pride themselves on their low record of lost-time accidents. Such records should be reviewed carefully because they can often be facades; with pressure for a good record people may be carried to the job even if they cannot do much work. Some companies do not include certain accidents in their accident rate unless the employee has lost two days time. The accident rate may be less relevant to organizations where there are fewer opportunities for accidents (a university as contrasted with a steel mill). Here are two statements that describe accident rates:

In 1919 the accident rate in the Peoples Gas Light and Coke Company was slightly over 31.0. The same year the company established a safety department. In 1965 the accident frequency rate reached a low of 4.0. In 1966 the rate climbed slightly to 6.9. However, the severity rate was only 197 days lost per million man-hours.

At the Michael Manufacturing Company, there were 11 accidents in 1962; 9 accidents in 1963; 14 accidents in 1964; and in the first 7 months of 1965 there were 13 accidents. In a recent monthly newsletter the statement was made that the average for the Michael Company is 22.9 as compared with the National Safety Council average of 3.94. However, these figures do not reflect the fact that a "reportable accident," as defined by the Michael Company, is one of substantially less seriousness than that used by the national averages. In addition, "time lost" during the day of the accident makes it "reportable" while time must be lost on the day *after* the accident to classify it as "reportable" according to the National Safety Council.

6. Structure for handling personnel

All organizations have established practices, policies, and programs for their personnel. These range from highly sophisticated, professionally managed activities to informal practices derived from precedents. In this section the consultant should describe them in detail.

a. Recruitment

The consultant should investigate the methods the organization uses to get its personnel. Where does it look for what kinds of people, and what are its processes for bringing them into the organization? What success does it have with its methods? Two excerpts and a newspaper article illustrate the kind of information to be included here.

First National Bank uses its domestic loan officers and personnel staff to visit certain college campuses to interview prospective candidates for its officer training program. These people recruited basically at eastern colleges and universities, but they also visited Stanford, Chicago, Northwestern, and Berkeley to interview M.B.A. candidates, and Thunderbird Institute, for potential international banking officers. During 1967 they interviewd 442 students on campus and invited 93 to the home office for further interviews. Of this number, they offered positions to 77; only 9 accepted. However, 6 of these were from Thunderbird. The remaining 3 represent only .78 per cent of those interviewed on campus and only 4.9 per cent of those offered positions. Thirty-three others were employed who came for interviews as a result of advertising, personal contacts, and letters of inquiry those men wrote to the bank. Other local metropolitan banks estimate that half of their prospective management trainees come from college recruiting. First National therefore does not come close to that average.

Everett, Mass. (*UPI*) — There is a new kind of "campus recruiter" around, and he does not wait until his prospects get to the campus. He tries to capture their interest in the lower grades.

The Rev. Bede Ferrara of Mount Vernon, New York, career guidance director for the Franciscan Friars, was on hand when the aspiring youngsters of the Pop Warner Little League played the midget super bowl game in Everett Stadium.

Father Ferrara was passing out balloons inscribed "happiness is being a friar." "I'm trying to use modern means to attract the youth into the order," Father Ferrara said. (*New York Times,* December 21, 1969.)

Instead of recruiting people [at the Weldon Manufacturing Company] on a day-to-day basis and assigning them randomly to jobs, an effort was made to determine in advance the probable number of trainees that each key position would require. New people were assigned to training in a type of task for which their tests showed them to be suited. Every effort was made to assign them after preliminary training only to the jobs for which they were trained. The expected rate of recruitment was placed initially at about 16 new people per week, and plans were made for the training center to have 50 to 60 trainees at any one time. (Alfred Marrow, et al., *Management by Participation,* New York, Harper & Row, 1967, chap. 8.)

b. Orientation

Here the consultant should ask: In what ways does the organization help people learn about what they are expected to do? What the company stands for? What its range of activities is? He should determine what process there is for the new employee to become familiar with the setting, the people, the expectations, and the politics and if there is any procedure for defining the psychological contract. These two excerpts describe such activities:

When an individual is hired by Kenmar Products, a member of the personnel department goes through the entire Kenmar handbook with him. This procedure is repeated by the individual's immediate manager, so a new hire has two opportunities to understand Kenmar, to review its rules and regulations, and to have any of his questions answered. In addition, the new employee is taken on a tour of the facilities and an invitation is sent to the person's home, inviting his or her immediate family on a plant tour.

Upon arriving at St. Mary's High School, new teachers are briefly oriented in a faculty meeting, given their department assignments, and expected to do their jobs. Orientation may continue in some department meetings where the textbook and class assignments are decided. Through informal meetings with the older staff members and colleagues, questions and problems are discussed.

All the new teachers are overtly encouraged to visit Father Smithfield's office when they have a problem. But, it is difficult to see Father Smithfield because the teachers are kept busy every hour in the day except for a 1-hour break.

c. Training

Orientation is the attaching process. Training prepares the employee to perform the jobs expected of him. Here the consultant should ask: In what ways does the organization help the person develop the skills he will be required to use in performing assigned tasks? Training will vary with the degree of competence required of the person when he is employed. A nurse would get far less training than an unskilled person employed as an orderly. Some organizations have formal preassignment training programs. Others use on-the-job training programs in which the supervisor is expected to instruct the new employee. Apprenticeship is a form of on-the-job training. Still other organizations provide no training at all or expect the employee to learn his task from other employees. The kind of training program reflects the organization's assumptions about people and also something of the organization's self image, for example, "They won't stay anyway" or "There's no point in our having a training program. We're not very sophisticated here; anybody can do this kind of work."

The first excerpt, taken from a case study, illustrates one condition of training. The second, composed from newspaper reports, describes one practice in detail.

The oldest elite corps, the Jesuit Order, does not subject its men to training in advanced theology and philosophy until they have had many years of practical experience in the study of lay subjects, such as medicine, sociology, or meteorology, in teaching, and in administration. It has found that the most advanced, the really professional training for being a Jesuit, does not "take" until a man has acquired the actual experience in the work that his advanced studies organize, make meaningful, appraise, and focus.

The New Jersey association and a sister organization, the New York Sandy Hook [Harbor] Pilots Association, were formed in 1853. The two groups have their own presidents and separate membership rolls (51 New Jersey pilots and 92 New York pilots), but otherwise they operate as a single enterprise, sharing facilities, equipment, revenues, and expenses. New York and New Jersey state laws require every commercial vessel passing through the Atlantic approach to the harbor to have an association pilot aboard. Trainees must have at least two years of college. They begin their apprenticeships with the Sandy Hook groups by spending three months or more polishing brass, washing windows, swabbing decks, and doing other menial chores 40 hours a week aboard the associations' big 205-foot and 168-foot pilot boats. One of the pilot boats, anchored off Sandy Hook, a point of land jutting out from the New Jersey coast, serves as a way station for pilots waiting to take the helm of incoming ships and for others who are awaiting transportation back to shore after steering outgoing ships from the harbor. The second pilot boat cruises the harbor, checking locations of buoys, searching for floating debris, and watching for dangerous shifts in the harbor shoals. Later the trainees learn to operate the pilot boats and the small motor launches used to ferry pilots between the anchored pilot boat and incoming and outgoing ships. During the first seven years, they work six days on and three days off and are paid the federal minimum wage of $1.60 an hour. For the next seven years, they learn to pilot even bigger ships by accompanying regular pilots through the harbor. During this time, they are paid an average of $10,500 a year and gradually become proficient enough to start taking ships, even the biggest ships, through the harbor on their own. When they finally become full-fledged pilots, their salaries average $20,000 a year. (Exact source for this material is not certain.)

d. Growth on the job

The consultant should ascertain what provisions the organization has for planned horizontal and vertical job growth. Horizontal job growth refers to scheduled training and experiences which help a person learn more about and do better at what he is presently doing. How, for example, does a psychiatric aide become a better psychiatric aide? What provisions are there for talking over problems on the job? For encouraging staff members to write or lecture? For keeping abreast of technical changes? Planned vertical job growth refers to systematic preparation for higher levels jobs. The following brief excerpts exemplify the kind of information to be entered here.

The child-care workers in The Menninger Foundation's children's hospital participate in a weekly meeting at which video tapes and films are shown of troubled children in specific situations. Trained child psychologists, psychiatrists, and social workers lead discussions or explain the psychodynamics of the problem situation and encourage questions by the trained aides.

The Westinghouse Electric Corporation endeavors to have an integrated program for managers at all levels of the organization. This "career development" conception includes a "new plant startup" sequence for the entire management of a new plant; courses for local implementation for managers; supervisors of salaried personnel, supervisors of hourly personnel, and professional personnel; a general management program; a functional management program;

a business environment program; a technical professional program; a management skills program; a presupervisory program. Each of these individual programs is comprised of a series of interrelated courses under a systems concept that includes organization of the program, implementation, review, and feedback, leading in turn to planning the next step in career development. The entire effort is carried out by the Training and Development Department and makes use of university degree-oriented curricula as well as other extramural training in addition to intramural courses.

e. Promotion

Here the consultant should investigate what opportunities exist for upward mobility and to whom they are available. Does the company promote from within the organization or seek outsiders? Some companies have a covert NIH (not invented here) policy that precludes bringing in outsiders with different ideas. Others have a covert NHKA (nobody here knows anything) policy; preferred positions are offered to outsiders. How frequently are people promoted? Some companies have regular and predictable promotion steps; some, like the military or State Department, have an "upward or outward" policy: people are either promoted within a given period or they must leave. Still others promote erratically. Some promise rapid promotion but cannot deliver; others, without adequate criteria, just think they offer rapid promotion. Promotions in some organizations are on the basis of favoritism or nepotism. In others, there are panels of superiors who make choices. In the latter case, performance appraisals are usually the basis of choice. In some organizations, particularly for higher level jobs, psychological testing is the practice. The more farsighted the organization, the more likely it is to have anticipated its future staff needs, to have designed a program to assist potential candidates for roles of increased responsibility, and to remain informed of their human resources with some form of skill bank — a readily available record of who can do what. The more open, definitive, and objective the promotion policy, the more it contributes to trust and a sense of fairness. These magazine and newspaper excerpts describe promotion practices in three widely different organizations.

Freedom of expression is traditional at Reed College, but it has probably also been influenced by the institution's "benevolent" promotion practices. Reed is not a "publish or perish" college. Some of Reed's officials look with favor on research, but publishing research findings is not necessary for promotion. Although a Ph.D. is an important factor in determining whether an individual will be hired, especially in the natural sciences, it is not absolutely necessary for the initial appointment and it certainly is not a requisite for promotion if the individual proves himself a good teacher. (*Science,* September 15, 1967, p. 123.)

The U.S. Army has been looking for men to apply to the new Armor NCO Candidate School. Those accepted in a grade below E-4 will be promoted upon entry to the 12 week NCO training course. All graduates will be promoted to E-5 upon successful completion of the 12-week formal phase . . . Upon graduation from the 12-week formal phase, graduates will be sent in 16-man packets to an armor training unit for 9 weeks of on-the-job training. The army is permitting units to promote one additional man from each packet to E-6 upon completion of this final training phase. (*Army Times,* date uncertain.)

According to newspaper and magazine reports, General Motors follows the policy of choosing and promoting executives with the talents best fitted for dealing with its current problems. In the past half century, managers, engineers, salesmen, and financial experts have all taken a turn and applied their special abilities as needed. The company in 1967 needed fresh ideas in design and marketing to recapture the initiative in the fiercely competitive automobile world. It also needed an ability to anticipate social situations and devise corporate policies to deal with them. Edward N. Cole was promoted to the presidency partly because of his strong sales experience and partly because of his ability to serve as an articulate public spokesman.

f. Compensation

Compensation is sometimes a difficult area to delve into since some organizations prefer secrecy. That in itself says something. Closed salary practices are often rationalized on the basis that they avoid conflict. Usually they serve to suppress the conflict and to avoid dealing face to face with people. Also, compensation may be structured in such a way as to militate against productivity, for example, unit piece work that increases production of components but does not assure the quality of the whole. Some compensation is bargained for as in union contracts. Some is beneficent: the management bestows it upon employees in such a way as to communicate their kindness. Some is based on comparative salary structures in the community. Charitable organizations frequently scale their wages and salaries below profit-making organizations on the thesis that they provide more stimulating work environments or that they serve a cause and the employee therefore should accept a lower wage. Some organizations offer long-term financial security and therefore lower wages. Some view their employees as temporary and expendable while others anticipate a consistent relationship. Incentive systems indicate the organization's underlying conception of work motivation. The investigator should be interested in the internal, external and comparative aspects of the wage scale.

Questions the consultant should ask are: What are the wage rates and how do they compare with others in the community? What variations are there in the company? How do they compare with others in the same field? How are they established? who decides? who reviews the scales how and when? Who gets what increments? bonuses? stock options? overtime? These excerpts illustrate how such information may be noted:

Increase in salary comes with tenure and postgraduate hours received. The teachers at St. Mary's receive a $300–$500 lower base pay than do the teachers in public schools, but many of the men receive additional stipends from coaching assignments. The base salary for teachers is $4500 for those unmarried and $4700 for those married, but salary varies greatly. The salary for the laymen is based on a graduated scale considering their marital status, graduate hours, responsibility, and years of experience. Each 10 hours of graduate study entitles the teacher to a $100 raise and each 10 years experience deserves a $100 raise. The head football and basketball coaches both receive an additional $1000 a year, and their first assistants each receives an additional $600. The coaches of minor athletic events have a graded scale, and the events include track, wrestling, cross-country, golf and tennis. The sisters each receive $1000 a year which is paid to their order rather than to the sisters directly; priests are paid according to their time spent which is two hours a day, four days a week. Father Smithfield, the principal, receives a salary of $110 a month, whereas Father Drake, his assistant, receives a salary of $120 a month. Father Smithfield explained that the additional salary he receives for serving two parishes influences the difference in salaries between himself and Father Drake. They both receive mass stipends which help to increase their salaries. However, both have personal expenses and are expected to furnish their own automobiles.

There are no specific pay days for the partners of the Carothers, Barrand & Swenson law firm. The salaried people are paid monthly. The partners divide whatever is left after expenses on a point system ranging from 11 per cent to 15 per cent. The two senior partners receive 15 per cent; the youngest partner, 11 per cent, amounting to a salary range for this firm between $18,000 and $25,000. Fees are set at firm meetings; fees above $300 are considered by the group of partners as a whole. The result has been a 25 per cent increase in fees as compared to those set earlier by the lawyers individually.

g. Performance analysis

Performance analysis means a periodic evaluation of the employee's job performance. In some organizations it is not done at all; some have provisions for semiannual or annual performance reviews; a few ask subordinates to evaluate superiors. In some organizations standards or goals are formulated by the personnel department or with its help; in others, by a man's immediate superiors. The more detailed a man's job description, the more likely there is to be a performance analysis and the greater the likelihood that it will be used as a basis for promotion and compensation. More progressive organizations look upon performance appraisal as an opportunity for subordinate and superior to review their joint efforts and their working relationship. Some separate performance review from salary review so that the superior does not act simultaneously as teacher and judge.

Judgments are always being made about performance; the more open they are, the greater the opportunity for people to evaluate their own realities. Otherwise, they tend to find out how they are doing only by the "squawk index," this is complaints when they err. Sometimes there may be a formal system honored in the breach or applied only at middle management levels; some systems fail because those who must appraise and evaluate others usually have feelings of guilt about negative criticism and therefore do not really evaluate. If no one works with the guilt feelings of the superiors, the appraisal system then fails. The consultant should look carefully at the way the appraisal system actually works in practice. Here are some examples of appraisal practices:

The ministers within the Mid-Atlantic Conference of the Methodist Church were not conscious of effective evaluation of their work. Evaluation of work was explicitly made by the District Superintendent to the men if their work was not up to par. The most important criterion for advancement was the ability to get along with the members of the church.

In the Michael Manufacturing Company, performance analysis is informal; it is usually not written unless related to work of such an inferior nature that an item of equipment is rejected by one of the inspectors in the quality control department. In such a case a man is notified by a "pink slip" (a rejection slip) that the work must be done again. Most of the men feel that they are readily reprimanded for mistakes or inferior performance but seldom applauded for superior performance.

The performance appraisal system at the Nalor Stores includes three steps. Each manager prepares a prereview on each of the people reporting to him. Each subordinate also prepares a prereview on his own work. The two then meet to discuss their preliminary reviews of the subordinate's performance against previously determined goals. After the prereview session, both prepare formal final reviews according to an established form. They discuss these final reviews, including their percentage estimates of the degree to which goals were achieved. On the basis of these discussions, goals are set for the following year and recommendations for raises are made. There are no appraisals of superiors by subordinates nor does the process extend below the management trainee level.

h. Kind and intensity of supervision

Supervision is the key element in the support of a given employee or employee group, regardless of the level of the person in the organization. The consultant may make a subjective judgment based primarily on his interviews with the organization's employees, he may make inferences from a questionnaire (see examples in the appendixes), or he may have direct information from an attitude or morale survey. The consultant will want to know whether the supervision is directive, supportive, or autocratic; close or distant; regular or intermittent. Does the supervisor meet regularly with those who report to him or for whose work he is responsible? Is his supervision predictable or is it intermittently harsh and lenient? Do employees know what to expect? Are they comfortable turning to the supervisor for advice and guidance? What is the span of control or the ratio of supervisors to supervisees? How much time is the supervisor allotted for supervision as contrasted with having to take time from his other activities? How do the answers to these questions vary from level to level? Here are three excerpts which speak to these questions:

The supervisory philosophy of the staff of Fairfax Elementary School is to expect the teachers to do their job and to know what they should do. The principal presumes his teachers to be competent unless he notices otherwise, and he expects them to know when they need to ask for help. For new staff members there is a system of "indoctrination" by the principle to the rules, values, and expectations of the school. He then asks someone at the same level as the new teacher to spend extra time and be available to guide her on day-to-day affairs. The principal supervises the weekly lesson plans and frequently visits the classroom to see if there is any way he can help. As he feels that the teacher is gaining competence, he spends less and less time with her in the classroom and eventually (within 8 to 10 weeks) ceases his requests for lesson plans. The principal says that he is available for consultation whenever the need arises. The teaching staff feels free to approach the principal at will.

There is no formal and little or no informal supervision of a monk's tasks at St. Anthony's Abbey. This creates problems. A monk never knows where he stands. He himself must determine whether he is doing what is expected of him.

He has no supportive guidance from his superiors, no adequate assessment or areas he needs to improve and little consideration of his personal needs. Many of the men indicated that if they make a mistake they may be called on the carpet. Even so, a man is often unable to profit from his errors, since the monks are reluctant to criticize "members of the family."

Supervision constitutes a major problem at Ralston Savings and Loan. The supervisors of the tellers are new at their jobs and seem to have some potential capability but are so overwhelmed by the sheer amount of work, that they have been unable to develop their skills; they simply have no time for it. They, in turn, are supervised by three managers. One, Mr. Smith, is a hard-driving, production-oriented person who is insensitive to the needs of others. Among these higher echelon personnel, Mr. Clark, who is a thoughtful, patient, considerate person, provides a kind of helpful buffer. A third supervisor, Mr. Bell, is repeatedly described as being crude and tough. He appears to supervise in a disparaging rather than a helpful manner; he arouses a great deal of anger in the tellers. One supervisor was concerned with the fact that he might have to fire a secretary who worked directly under him who had been hired by Bell without his (the immediate supervisor's) consultation.

i. Rules and regulations for employees

Rules and regulations are the "laws" by which the organization seeks to control behavior. Many organizations have both written and verbal rules. The former usually are codified in the form of an orientation manual, a volume on rules and procedures, or a series of published memoranda. Verbal rules most often have to be elicited in interviews. Sometimes there are rules which are unverbalized but adopted by employees in reaction to a statement or reaction by a superior. We do not include here the terms of the labor contract. The consultant should note the form the rules are in, if written: book? pamphlet? How comprehensive and detailed are they? What matters do they cover? What rules are more important? Are the rules the organization's own or are they required by its customers or clients, for example, government contracts. If there are no formal rules, are there deeply ingrained traditions that cause people to behave as if they were rules?

Throughout this part of the outline, as already indicated, the consultant should be interested only in reporting and describing. This is a compilation of raw data from which conclusions will be drawn later. The question of how closely the rules are obeyed is reserved for Chapter 7. He should also reserve interpretations and inferences from the rules and regulations about the character of the organization. Here are some samples of how this topic has been handled:

Although there is no written rule in the Harding Company's research laboratory that the researchers must arrive at 8:30 each morning, and often there is no formal reason for doing so, the researchers do arrive at that time. Furthermore, there is no rule about dress, but should a female employee not wear hosiery, that omission will be mentioned either by her supervisor or fellow employees in a joking manner.

The monks at St. Anthony's Abbey found it extremely difficult to conceptualize the rules and regulations by which they live. However, they were able to come up with three general categories of rules: (1) required attendance at all communal exercises including worship and chapter meetings; (2) observance of silence at meals within the monastery and at specified times of the day; (3) the necessity of obtaining permission from the abbot or designated superior to leave the premises. It was generally felt that the last regulation is the only one universally followed and that the others are breached at one time or another by one or more persons.

In keeping with the autonomous policy of the Girondeau Foods Company, there are few rules. One implicit rule is that everyone try hard and be honest. To violate either of these is a serious sin. Otherwise, everyone seems almost heady with the freedom they enjoy. As long as there is achievement in the form of production and growth, a person's time is his own. There is no reason for executives not to take an afternoon off to play golf if the work is caught up. Expense accounts are to make life as pleasant as possible; everyone takes full advantage of them.

j. Medical program

We refer here not to an insurance program, but to actual medical services. The consultant should determine if there are such services in the organization. Is there a medical department with physical facilities? Are there physicians or nurses there regularly or on call? Is there a preventive medical program that includes regular examinations of personnel, inspection of the premises for toxic and other environmental hazards? How does the medical department compare with standards for an accredited medical department established by the Industrial Medical Association? What is the relationship of the medical department to management; that is, to what extent is the physician or nurse alert to the stresses created by managerial practice, and how is that awareness conveyed to the management? With what results? These two excerpts illustrate this information:

The Menninger Foundation offers the services of a complete health office without charge to its employees. The office is prepared to care for minor illness and injury that occur during working hours. Sick call is from 8:30 to 9:00 in the morning; any employee may consult one of the three doctors on duty at this time without an appointment. All full-time permanent employees are given a physical examination, including laboratory tests, at no expense to the employee. Most employees are given this examination at the end of three months of employment. Food handlers, child care workers, nurses, aides, and adjunctive therapists are examined at the time of their employment. The Foundation also gives individual periodic health appraisals. For the employees' benefit, mass inoculation programs for influenza epidemics, and so forth, are offered. In addition, an employee is allowed one free session with a psychiatrist; subsequent sessions are charged for at a reduced rate.

Johnston Elementary School uses the 8-by-12-foot faculty lounge as the medical office. A corner of the faculty lounge is supplied with a first aid kit, a stretcher, a few splints in a variety of sizes, and equipment for eye and hearing tests. The nurse is in attendance at the school on Mondays and Fridays from 8 A.M until 10 A.M. She services students, faculty, and staff. The faculty members are required to have passed a course in first aid so that, in the event of an emergency, they may take care of a situation in the nurse's absence. For a dire emergency, the nurse is called; however, since she is the only nurse serving the area, by the time she arrives at the school, the situation may already be out of hand. If the nurse cannot reach the school during an emergency, the sheriff's office is phoned to transport the injured person to the closest doctor's office. The nurse is not allowed to dispense any type of medication to either students or faculty with the exception of polio and smallpox vaccines.

k. Safety program

The consultant should determine what the organization's formal safety program is. In some organizations there is a safety director. He maintains a continuous inspection of the plant for hazards, often working in conjunction with the company physicians. If it is a large plant, or there are specific chemical hazards there are likely to be industrial hygienists and toxicologists as well. A well-run manufacturing plant will have hazards conspicuously painted and guarded. Paths will be demarcated with paint to avoid dangers. Safety glasses will be required of anyone going through the plant. There may be emergency drills, practice alerts, and similar training activities. Many companies have safety meetings, safety contests, first aid training, and other devices. Sometimes the safety program is just a gesture. The program may be the responsibility of the employees, the supervisors, or the professional director. It may be systematic or sporadic, rigidly enforced or lackadaisically ignored. The enforcement medium may be public exhibition of the offender as in placing his name on a public bulletin board, comparative statistics between departments, posters, inter-departmental competitions for lowest accident rates, pins and trophies for accident-free years. It is rare to find a safety program that takes into account the emotional climate of the organization as a precipitant of accidents and where there is a relationship between the safety officer and higher management to examine such forces. The following excerpts describe safety programs:

At the A & B Chemical Tecumseh plant there is an emphatic emphasis on safety. Numerous posters are displayed around the buildings congratulating the men for their low accident record. The plant has an injury rate of 0.3 million man hours. The average in the film industry is 3 to 6 per million man hours. To reinforce the safety campaign at the plant, there is a large marquee-type billboard visible from the parking lot that says: "Protect your eyes today and see tomorrow." In conjunction with the emphasis on safety is the concern with neatness and cleanliness. Everything in the entire building is maintained in perfect order. There are restricted smoking areas throughout the building. Visitors are not permitted to enter the plant proper without donning glasses and giving up their cigarette lighters.

The Pioneer Ridge Lab has a record of 3,750 days without lost time due to accidents. The record is 6,700 days. The company has an active safety program and promotes safety at work and at home. The company makes available some safety devices to the workers for home use at very low prices. However, when the consultant toured the plant, he noticed that some of the workers were not wearing their gloves, goggles, or masks although the majority of them were. The company does have a first aid room and trains people to handle minor injuries that occur.

l. Retirement program

Some organizations have a formal retirement policy; others do not. Those which do usually have a published statement of the policy together with a summary of the benefits to which the employee is entitled. Some have a preretirement program to prepare the employee for retirement. Some continue to furnish medical services; send the company newspaper;

invite the retired employee back to company functions; and provide legal, financial, and other counsel. Some companies permit retired executives to use their offices, even their secretaries, or to continue to be related to the company as consultants. Many companies retire employees with a gift and a handshake, abruptly severing the tie.

Retirement programs vary widely and the consultant must carefully examine the company's policies, particularly because the psychology of the work relationship is so deeply imbedded in the retirement program. A man may, for example, lose his retirement rights if he leaves the organization before a certain time. He may also be subject to early retirement, at lower income, at the whim of the company. The retirement program may bind the company and employee in such a way as to make their relationship inflexible. Another thing to determine is how often the retirement program is reviewed and from whose perspective. The paragraph from a case study and the following excerpt from a magazine illustrate:

The Ajax Pharmaceutical Company has an independent consultant review its retirement plan every 5 years. The consultant is instructed to consider the employee's needs first and to recommend what serves the employee best. Cost to the company is a secondary consideration.

To document the notion that the quest for security sometimes overruns its goals, we take you now to the main ballroom of the Castellano Hilton Hotel in Madrid where recently were gathered members of a class that might be called *nouveaux rentiers*. Ninety-three of those present were retired American seamen, mostly of Spanish or Portuguese origin, who had returned to their homelands; the ninety-fourth was the Spanish widow of a retired seaman; the ninety-fifth, the object of their gratitude and adulation, was Joe Curran, founder and head of the National Maritime Union. The retired mariners all received U.S. social security benefits. These range up to $116 a month, plus 50 per cent more for wives over the age of 65. In addition, they receive up to $100 a month in pension payments under a plan wrung from American shipowners by the National Maritime Union, which makes a total of $274. Social security also provides $56.50 a month for each minor child. In addition, moreover, the N.M.U. Welfare Plan pays medical benefits for the men and their families up to a total of $500. All these benefits combined would provide a livable income in the U.S. But in Spain, these old sea dogs are upper middle class. The N.M.U. has 355 such pensioned seamen living in forty countries around the world. They are conspicuous — and exaggerated — examples of U.S. living standards in countries where living standards are low. (*Fortune,* September 1960, p. 130.)

m. Recreation program

Some companies foster comprehensive recreation activities and facilities for their employees. IBM, for example, at one time provided country clubs for its employees in the New York area. Other organizations sponsor teams and leagues, paying for uniforms or operating expenses for activities engaged in off the premises. Many companies have no such teams, or those that carry their name may be voluntarily composed by employees. The consultant should ascertain: What is done in the organization he is studying. For what stated reasons? How many people participate? With what feelings on the part of the employees? Are trophies displayed? Is recreation played up in the company newspaper? Two illustrative paragraphs from case studies follow:

For students of St. Simon's College, the main community recreation consists of listening to music. They have a good collection of classical and popular records. The college also has its own movie projector and a very well designed auditorium. Movies are shown at least once a month during the school year and more frequently during vacation time. The students are not permitted to watch television except for special occasions — the World Series, political conventions, and so on. Frequently small groups will engage in heated discussions about politics, philosophy, theology. Some like to become involved in milder and friendlier conversations. For the priests and older brothers, recreation is usually low keyed. It is scheduled after the day's work is completed. Alcoholic drinks and snacks are usually available. Some play bridge, others read, watch television, converse.

Although Crane & Co. has no formal recreation program, employees are encouraged to form employee teams. There are such teams in local bowling, softball and basketball leagues. The company will buy the uniforms, pay league expenses, and even defray travel expenses if a team wins and must compete in tournaments out of town. The uniforms bear the name of the company; the teams are thought of as company teams. Winning trophies are displayed in large cabinets in the company's main lobby, together with pictures of the teams, year by year. The displays are reminiscent of those in a high school or college. The company also gives recognition in the company newspaper to employees who compete in bridge tournaments, art shows, and similar activities.

n. Other fringe benefits

The consultant should investigate what, if any, other special benefits and conveniences are provided by the organization. Some provide stock options; others give bonuses or extended vacations. Some employ the children of their employees during the summer months. Many universities pay for the college tuition of their professors' children. Other organizations pay for medical examinations outside the company. Some provide parking facilities, and for executives above a certain level, even cars. Others grant their employees a discount on company products. Some provide below-cost meals; others, club memberships; some allow for teaching in colleges if the employee is a specialist. A few even allow their specialists outside consultation if not with a competing firm. Some fringe benefits have a paternalistic tradition. Years ago the Kohler Company provided a smoking and reading room for the men to use during their lunch hour. A band concert was given every Monday afternoon for employees and their families. In addition, Walter J. Kohler, Sr. spent much time and effort Americanizing his German emigrant employees. He would escort them to the company courthouse in Sheboygan on company time to get their first and second citizenship papers. His support during this period of naturalization was considered a fringe benefit of the job.

Other fringe benefits may have a public relations motive, such as the provision in the Prudential Insurance Company home office cafeteria that employees may invite a given number of guests per month to join them for a free lunch. Still others, such as liberal severance pay and help in finding a new job, are intended to ease the process of moving people out of the organization with less friction and recrimination. These excerpts from magazine articles are illustrative.

As an employer, Olivetti is famed throughout Italy for its enlightened welfare program, which is the more remarkable in a country where the image of *il padrone* is about as *simpatico* as the mustachioed villain who foreclosed mortgages in the old dime novels. Near the Ivrea plant are clustered a library, an infirmary where employees get free medical attention, and rows of pastel-colored balconied workers' apartment houses. Fringe benefits add about 50 per cent to take-home pay — no one can say that Olivetti's success in selling abroad is based on cheap labor. Other companies have cast upon the waters expensive welfare programs without getting back any crumbs of employee gratitude. Olivetti gets the respectful and eager loyalty of its workers. (*Fortune,* September 1960, pp. 139–140.)

To instill the "Southern hospitality approach" in his salesmen, E. Claiborne Robins, president of the A. H. Robins Pharmaceutical firm, pursues a policy of intense paternalism. On his birthday each employee gets not only a birthday card but a $25 check as well. At Christmas, each gets a bonus, a Virginia ham, and a Christmas card. (*Forbes,* September 1967, p. 45.)

Like many large United States corporations operating in Latin America, United Fruit has been accused of economic imperialism . . . Present criticism of United Fruit's activity is based on past events. The company no longer wangles tax and tariff concessions; a typical United plantation now includes housing, schools, and recreation programs for employees. (*Business Week,* July 8, 1967, p. 94.)

o. Labor contract

If an organization has a contract with a labor union, the consultant should get a copy and append it to the case write up. He should examine the contract not only for its specific provisions but also for its tone. Some contracts will be highly militant; others, innocuous. There are likely to be reasons for either extreme. A bland contract may be a "sweetheart" agreement; that is, one in which the management has bought off the union leadership. An important question is who negotiates the contract: depending on the union, it may be done by a local committee or an international representative. A contract negotiated by an international representative is likely to be more in keeping with an industry-wide pattern than one negotiated by a local committee. How detailed is the contract? How rigidly interpreted?

If the institution is a school or a university, there may be individual contracts with individual teachers. A union of teachers or a chapter of the American Association of University Professors may represent the faculty beyond the individual contract. Usually there are college-wide or system-wide provisions for tenure and in universities, faculty senates or other consultative bodies. The relationships between employee-representative bodies and management or administration should be examined. An excerpt from a case and an illustration from a news article follow.

Because of the labor union contract, the Shawnee Rubber Company must maintain piece work rules and balance the hours throughout the factory. At the end of the year, the difference between the highest and the lowest number of hours worked must be no more than 18 for all employees throughout the plant. When overtime is necessary, those with the lowest number of overtime hours worked must be given the opportunity to work first. Sometimes the need for overtime arises immediately at the end of a work shift and the supervisor doesn't have the time to check the records to see who should be asked to work first. However, if the low hour rule is not followed and if a man who is entitled to work overtime is bypassed, a grievance is filed. Under the contract, the company must pay not only the man who actually worked overtime, but also the man who should have been asked to work.

The Naples Zoological Station, one of the oldest marine biology stations, is passing through a time of trouble, both financial and administrative. In a general way, the station is a casualty of the conflict between Italian academic traditions and new research modes, as well as of forces gathering momentum within modern biology. In May 1967 it became known unofficially that the Italian government would soon announce appointment of a commissioner to take over the functions of the station's governing body for a year and prepare the way for restructuring of the institution. The Italian General Labor Confederation has sought higher pay for station staff of The Naples Zoological Station — pay is low at the station and in Naples in general — and has also pushed for more tenured positions for the employees; about a third now hold permanent jobs. Tenure is an important matter in Italy where security of employment compensates for somewhat lower wages. In addition to economic demands, the union has also pushed for participation of the staff in the making of policy. Scientific staff members felt, for example, that they have not been consulted sufficiently on reconstruction plans. But the main point at issue is the staff's desire to have their right to conduct independent research formally recognized in the new statutes. (*Science,* May 26, 1967, pp. 1066–1068.)

7. Policies and procedures

The various ways in which an organization relates to its personnel have been described in the previous discussion. This section deals with an organization's efforts to maintain a common mode of operation. The more formal these efforts are, the greater their number, the more bureaucratic the organization. However, to label them bureaucratic is not the same as passing negative judgment because they may have to do with maintaining the quality of the product or service, with protecting the employee and the company from injury or suit, with assuring that the employee or customer is treated similarly in all branches or aspects of the operation. Policies and procedures are the methods by which the organization accomplishes its work economically and according to certain standards.

a. Scope

Here the consultant must learn how much of the organization the policies and procedures cover. They may have to do with emergencies, such as fires and accidents, or they may cover all aspects of the activity as do policies and procedures in the military. They may vary from section to section within a single organization. Here are three case illustrations:

Most of the policies and procedures of The Menninger Foundation fall into two categories, those having to do with patient care and those related to administration. For legal, professional, and functional reasons, the former are much more detailed than the latter. Thus, personnel in the departments of research, education and preventive psychiatry have greater flexibility in their professional activities.

Theoretically, the whole of life and work of a religious institution is governed by clear policies and uniform procedures, but in fact this is not so. When speaking of the Province of the Holy Trinity, rather than a particular house, the matter of policies and procedures is complex. There are many situations to be covered; the Province is engaged in a variety of work, and the work is in conjunction with many other institutions — colleges, dioceses, and so on, which have their own policies and procedures. Therefore, it is not always clear which are to be followed nor is there any codified information about them. Some are contained in the *Acta* of the Provincial Chapter, some by a letter from the Provincial's office, while others are only in the publications of other institutions. In some situations a man new on the job will find it difficult to find out about policies and procedures. They may be generally known to those with more experience; the new man will learn of them only as he asks questions about particular cases.

At Michael Manufacturing Co., because of the militant nature of handling employees, there are numerous rules and regulations which stipulate specific steps in the approved work procedures. However, these written instructions are usually corrective and arise as a reaction to a situation which the plant manager considers unfavorable. For example, it was noted that many of the cleaning rags were missing; the towel service, in supplying new rags to the dispensing machine, had to make an additional charge for the dirty rags that were not turned in. A written notice was published instructing the men on the proper procedure with regard to turning in one dirty rag for each clean one taken from the machine. In addition, it was suggested that, "You look around your house and garage for any that you might have taken home."

b. How they are communicated

Some companies bind their policies and procedures in massive loose-leaf books, while others frame them and hang them on the wall. Elsewhere they are communicated by word of mouth; some are ritualized. Some are stated on bulletin boards, in company newspapers, on public address systems. Those which are published in books are frequently revised and amended in some organizations, but ignored in others. The form in which the policies and procedures exist suggests something about how much attention the organization gives to their control. The consultant should investigate whether there is a systematic method for informing employees of the policies and procedures, or does the organization ignore the matter. If the policies and procedures are written, who has copies of them? Are they conveniently available to all or hidden on a shelf behind a supervisor's desk? Are copies given to new employees during their orientation? Do the employees have the opportunity to learn the "why's"? What is the tone of the material: helpful? forbidding? instructive? Are they covered with dust? Three paragraphs from case studies are examples.

In the Hardiman Company office, the office manager has compiled an extensive manual. This describes in detail many "standard procedures" to be followed: making or receiving a long distance call; answering correspondence; sending telegrams and speed letters; filling out an expense account, and so forth. The manual is available from the office manager's desk; there is only one copy.

At The Menninger Foundation, each member of the professional staff who works with patients has a loose-leaf book of policies and procedures having to do with patient care. Changes are routinely distributed. Specific nursing policies are part of each nursing station's information. Administratitve policies are also contained in loose-leaf notebooks which are updated as necessary. In addition to the formal administrative responsibility for policy formulation, ad hoc committees formulate policy recommendations on issues ranging from the use of the swimming pool to what to do about children who run away from the children's hospital.

At the Michael plant, most of the policies and procedures are determined by the plant manager, handed down verbally to those concerned (usually the foremen), and decided upon in keeping with the current needs of the production schedule. Except for the printed rules, which tend to be disciplinary in character, most written policies and procedures are limited to the union contract.

c. Who knows about them

In many organizations there are multitudes of policies and procedures of which many employees are woefully ignorant. People tend to forget even about such personal matters as insurance and retirement provisions if they are not immediately concerned. Sometimes there are specific policies for rare circumstances about which many supervisors may be unaware. Gaps in knowledge of policies and procedures can lead to poor customer relations and can give rise to communications difficulties, to manipulation, to projection and feelings of injustice. The consultant should check for this situation in the company he is studying. These case examples illustrate such problems.

Carlyle Transportation Company was in a difficult situation with the state Human Relations Commission. Its policies required new employees to be high school graduates. A newly employed Negro clerk was discharged when it was discovered that he had not graduated from high school. However, he did have a high school equivalency certificate and had completed his junior year in college. He filed a complaint alleging discrimination. The incident arose because a personnel clerk made a literal interpretation of an obsolete policy.

One taxi cab company makes no provision for charges for passengers in addition to the first one. There is no statement to that effect on the fare schedule posted in each cab, and drivers attempt to charge each airport passenger the same single fare. When the passengers complain that such charges are unfair, the drivers content there is no company policy prohibiting such action.

Charing Institute has a policy of paying $500 toward moving expenses for new staff members. This is nowhere publicly stated. As a result, most department heads are unaware of it, and only those new staff members who have specifically asked the business manager have received reimbursement. Those who had paid their own moving expenses became angry when they discovered that they could have been reimbursed and felt that they had been manipulated.

d. What discretion is left to lower supervisory levels

Here the investigator should ask: What degree of flexibility does the organization have with respect to its policies and procedures? To what extent must the employees follow the exact letter of the written policy or, conversely, use his own discretion? Discretion may be permitted voluntarily or by failure to enforce the stated policy. Where the discretion is voluntary, it may take the form of a specific statement from higher levels or be a general attitude which says that policies are only guides and are expected to be used as such. The following two case examples and an excerpt from a book are illustrative.

The Great Lakes Insurance Company employees, especially those below the supervisory level, are told exactly when to arrive; where to park; where, when, and how to smoke and eat; where to relax. The president is noncommunicative to the degree that the plans, policies, and procedures of management are known only to him. Nothing is left to the discretion of the employees; the president decides everything for the organization. The president demands total control over every aspect of the company. There is practically no division of responsibility.

The speech therapists in the Lawrence Public School System decided among themselves the structure of their work week. At the beginning of the school year, the four therapists agreed to divide the district according to individual preference. They also made up their own schedule of school visits. What they teach in their classes is at their own discretion. They report the progress of their students twice a year to the Lawrence Board of Education. If one of the therapists feels that a child needs more help, she may schedule more visits with him after consulting with the principal of his school and his teacher. In addition to conducting therapy lessons for lispers and stutterers, the therapists must also give hearing tests to every child and every teacher from kindergarten through the twelfth grade every year.

Staff members [at the Weldon Company] were discouraged from making decisions on their own and from suggesting innovations. Higher level managers were expected to — and did — intervene daily in the work of their subordinates, checking activities, passing judgments on routine matters, and often reversing actions taken under the pressure of the events. Managers and supervisors at all levels became accustomed to this arrangement even though they were all often frustrated by their inability to deal directly with matters well within their personal competence. (Alfred Marrow, et al., *Management by Participation*, New York, Harper & Row, 1967, p. 9.)

8. Time span and rhythm

Many organizations are time-bound, some by season, some by inventory or book-balancing tasks, some by fiscal or academic years, some by the weather, others by manufacturing processes. The consultant should first determine whether the company he is studying is time-bound. If it is, he then must determine the nature of the circumstances.

a. Seasonal cycles

If the company is bound by seasonal cycles, he should ask: Do the cycles, to some extent, control the periodic peaks and valleys of energy expenditure? Do they require forward planning? Here are examples from a magazine article and a case:

[Many married women find that working for a temporary-help service such as Kelly Girl is a great compromise between being a full-time housewife and having a full-time job] . . . Seasonal ups and downs in availability of the married women conform to the school year [however] . . . Thousands of mothers phone the services in June, when their children are let out of school for the summer, to report that they will be unable to accept assignments until autumn. At this point, the services go begging for help for a few weeks until another large group of women workers become available. These are the college coeds looking for summer employment. They troop into the offices in June and depart in late August or early September, when services again scrape the barrel bottom until the mothers begin showing up again after school starts. (*Fortune*, September 1960, p. 260.)

The workload at Michael Manufacturing varies with the season. Sometimes as early as the end of November, and always by January 1, production demands increase in response to anticipated sales. There are some advance orders from Bristol Machinery which builds up its inventory with a new line of spring equipment. The plant remains busy, and sometimes works an hour a day overtime, until approximately mid-July, when most of the new equipment has been purchased by consumers. However, the parts department remains busy because of requests for replacement of broken or worn parts. Production is shut down completely in August when the more senior people take either a two- or three-week vacation. Those not entitled to lengthy vacations spend their time cleaning, painting, and repairing equipment and preparing the plant for the following year of production. Production increases again early in September. At this time, the experimental and engineering division works at its peak refining new models. The fall production, while less extensive than that of the spring months, is in response to the continuing demands from Bristol. There is a drop in production in the fall coinciding with decline of the construction business. Some effort is made at this time to retool for spring. However, since Michael does not maintain an extensive inventory, it is continuously producing current items to fill orders.

b. Diurnal cycles

In some industries, such as newspapers, restaurants, banking, and the legitimate theatre, there are daily peaks of energy expenditure. The consultant should discover how diurnal cycles affect an organization, as in the following cases:

Mondays and Fridays are generally heavy days at the Ralston Savings & Loan Company, particularly near holidays and paydays. At the retail level, the peak period of the day corresponds roughly with the noon hour; at the commercial level, the rush is later in the afternoon. One of the main pressure periods among the tellers appears to be when they are balancing out their accounts at the end of each day and have to achieve some degree of correctness before they can leave. When this is accomplished smoothly, it appears to provide one of the major satisfactions of the job. In other departments there are frequent demands for immediate attention and demands that involve securing information immediately.

At Michael Manufacturing, there is some cyclic variation in the working day. There is less variation in the welding department than elsewhere. The welder works at a steady pace dictated by the work process itself — and cannot be hastened or slowed. Once he begins to weld a joint he must proceed at a certain speed determined by the melting point and flow of the metal. However, there is some opportunity for slowing down or speeding up while he is setting up and aligning the component parts to be welded on a jig. He also has some control over his speed during the process of chipping slag from the welded joint. In the machine shop the worker has similar control over the time he is changing the setup on his machine. Once he begins a certain operation (punching, sawing, milling, cutting, shaping or honing), the machine operates at its own rate. In the machine shop the men try to get "ahead of schedule" at the beginning of each day so that they can coast later on in the work shift. This is usually frowned upon by the foreman; a more steady work pace is looked upon with greater approval. Men do not stand idly waiting for materials in either department. The flow of raw and partially processed goods occurs in an orderly manner so that there is always work to do.

c. Planning spans

Here the consultant should determine the time units by which the organization plans its future. Some organizations have a 10-year plan for the organization as a whole, 5-year plans for major divisions, two-year plans for major divisions within a division, 1-year plans for subsidiary units, and 6-month plans for smaller units. Taken together, these comprise a consistent direction for the whole. Many organizations, however, do not have long-range plans and operate on a day-to-day basis. The more the latter condition is true, the more the organization lets fate determine its course. Some concerns must necessarily plan decades ahead, for example, lumber companies, which must have a stand of trees 50 years hence, replace the trees they harvest with saplings. A major plant investment which will take 40 years to amortize implies a commitment to a long-range plan. These magazine excerpts are examples:

As pressures for more radical solutions to the air pollution problem raised a threat to the internal combustion engine itself, the [automobile] industry shifted from the defensive to the offensive. Ford rushed out one weekend with the announcement of a three-year, seven million dollar joint research program with Mobil Oil, aimed at ensuring "early development of virtually emission-free, gasoline-powered vehicles." (*Fortune,* August 1967, p. 78.)

In 1962 The Travelers Insurance Company called Morrison H. Beach from his post as life insurance actuary and assigned him to create and direct a long-range planning function. Beach set up a working committee of 18 — consisting of high-ranking representatives from each department in the company — organized a technical staff, and began the preparation of a five-year forecast, updated annually. This planning group not only forecasts the national economy, projects the total United States insurance market, and estimates the Travelers' share of that market, area by area and line by line, but it also weighs in with its best judgments on the significant changes ahead in the social and political environment. And in these efforts it draws freely on the consulting services of several of the leading sociologists and political scientists of the academic world. (*Fortune,* August 1965, pp. 138–141ff.)

d. Degree activities are regulated by time

How much are people's daily activities regulated by time in the company being studied? There are two major ways this may happen: by a paced process, as in an assembly line which moves at a regular rate or a machine which operates in cycles; by piece work or other time-measured units of production. Such activities usually mean that the work regulates the people rather than vice versa and, often, that people feel subsidiary to the work process. People in executive ranks, though they may work from 8 A.M. to 5 P.M. are usually largely free of time regulation. Typically, executives are not really paid for their time but for their results or achievements. Here is a description from a case of how activities are regulated by time.

The definition of the task in the folding area of the Magnia Envelope Company is clear. The machine controls the rate of productivity and the day is outlined in advance. The orders are given and the actual procedures are specified. There is relatively little variation in the task flow, and the individual must work on the task assigned to him. The required investment and commitment to work is well defined within the work day. The worker punches in and punches out at the end of the work day. There are no problems to think through unless the individual is preoccupied with the relationships which may have been stressful during the day. Psychological energy demanded by the work setting is more in terms of keeping up with the speed, of sustaining the drive required to maintain a running machine. The work itself is comprehensive and fairly compelling because attention to the machine is always necessary as the possibility of a foul-up is likely.

e. Attitudes about punctuality

The consultant should find out how the organization feels about its employees coming to work on time. What, if any, are the penalties for tardiness? Is there a time clock?

At Ajax Pharmaceutical, the chairman and the president are both early risers and are at the office by 7:00 A.M. Although the workday does not officially begin until 8:00, at about 7:30 the president starts calling executive offices. Most of the executives have learned to come in by 7:30. There is great pressure on line employees to be on time. However, once there, both executives and line employees have ways of "goofing off" which are difficult to combat. It is said of the president that he is the only one in the company who can call a meeting for a given time, arrive 10 minutes early and still be late.

Punctuality is very much valued and demanded in almost all religious life. In particular, in monastic life when a large number of people have to come together for worship, meals, and various community exercises, it is a great inconvenience for someone not to be punctual. Also, the church in general demands punctuality for its religious services. Mass starts on the minute and any tardiness irritates the celebrant. The same would be true for educational work where classes are tightly scheduled and start and stop punctually. At St. Mark's punctuality is the way of life.

Michael Manufacturing values punctuality very highly, and disciplinary measures for tardiness are included in the union contract. Sterner measures are listed for anyone caught punching another's time card. Overtime does not seem to be valued positively either by management or the workers. Most prefer working an hour less to earning extra money, especially in the summer months. They did not like to work on Saturday.

f. Urgency

Some organizations permit their work to lag until the last possible minute. Then they put considerable pressure on their employees. Some carefully schedule their activities to avoid the pressures of rushing. The consultant should determine how much pressure there is to meet deadlines. How often do crises about deadlines occur? If there is a repetitive sense of urgency, why does it exist? In these case excerpts the sense of urgency is noted:

At Carothers, Barrand & Swenson law firm, there is always a sense of urgency and some pressing work to be done in the office. This pressure creates a problem since each stenographer works for all of the lawyers; at times, a stenographer finds herself in a conflicting situation with one attorney pressuring her to finish his work before she does another's. Such conflict occurs frequently and the problem is recognized. Nothing, however, has been done to resolve the problem. Often a stenographer finds herself having to make the decision of whose work is to be completed first. It is not uncommon for a stenographer to be taken off one job and put on another only to have the first person become angry that the girl has not finished his work.

Time is an important factor in Lincoln Heights High School because of the constant scheduling of the students. However, the teachers can, on occasion, step out of their classrooms to visit or to take care of some minor work while their students are busy studying. There is a tendency for the administrator to let things go to the last minute before final action is taken.

The tempo at the Sunflower Brick Products Company is leisurely and the atmosphere is casual in the office. The tempo of life in this part of the organization is such that one may go along from day to day performing one's job without tremendous expenditure of energy or emotional investment in the activities undertaken.

g. Concern about deliveries

Here the consultant needs to find out how strongly the organization feels its responsibility to finish its work on time. Do its delivery dates mean something or are they just there? Does it realize that if it fails to keep its commitments about time, others may be unable to meet deadlines? How much does this trouble them? For schools, churches, and hospitals, the issue relates to concern for the effects of nonpunctuality, a form of nondependability, on others. A school, for example, might be unconcerned about when it delivered requested transcripts, about returning papers to students, about examination reports. Church services may be notoriously delayed or punctual. This factor has a certain cultural bias; punctuality is something quite unimportant in Latin countries. At one point Iberia Airlines was contrasted unfavorably with Lufthansa; the former, it was said, rarely departed or arrived on time, the latter prided itself on its punctuality. These excerpts from published sources are examples:

So concerned was Henry Ford I about his delivery schedules being kept that in 1920 he bought the Detroit, Toledo, & Ironside Railroad. This expenditure gave Ford the opportunity to break his shipping bottleneck. Once he bought it, he routed it into the River Rouge plant to handle all the incoming and outgoing material. With the railroad, Ford was able to establish assembly points into the Chicago, St. Louis, Kansas City, Cincinnati, Pittsburgh and New York areas. (Charles Sorenson, *My Forty Years with Ford,* New York, Norton, 1946, pp. 180–183.)

Because fashion is, as it were, subject to fashion, it forced Penney['s] into new techniques of distribution to meet new time scales . . . In the pre-fashion days a manager picked his assortment of women's clothes from a giant internal seasonal price list (with photographs) . . . Under this system, the lead time from the buyer's purchase to sale in a store was three months. Under Penney's new system, the store manager specifies only a range of sizes, quantities and other general categories. The actual designs and colors are decided on by the buyers and distributed out of three centers. Stocks are controlled out of these centers by a staff of distributors, each of whom is responsible for the merchandise in a group of stores in collaboration with the store merchandise manager. Thus if the Penney buyer feels that the market is in trumpet sleeves, he commits the company, which then owns the merchandise. The distribution center then places the merchandise where it will sell. A control group in New York receiving computerized information on sales, governs the levels of fashion inventory for the whole company. Under this system, lead time for fashion merchandise is reduced to about six weeks and in special cases to two weeks. (*Fortune,* July 1967, p. 113.)

To achieve mass distribution, Bobbie Brooks [the sportswear firm] instituted a "vendor program." Under this program, a department store would guarantee to give Bobbie Brooks at least $100,000 worth of business a year. In return, Bobbie Brooks would guarantee deliveries. Deliveries are of the essence in the clothing business . . . If a fashion goes [is highly successful] in a store and the store can't keep the fashion in stock, the salesladies might as well take in a movie. (*Forbes,* October 15, 1967, pp. 28–29.)

B. Process Data

1. Communication systems

A vast amount of information is available to all organizations, most of which abstract only a small amount of it and utilize an even smaller fraction of that. The system for receiving, organizing and integrating information is usually not clear even to those who make the selections. However, such a process occurs whether the organization recognizes it or not. Observation and interview will quickly disclose that there is a regularity to information getting and information handling. The questions for the consultant are: What does the organization "pick up" from its environment? What from inside itself? How? To what particular kinds of communication is it especially sensitive? How is what it receives transmitted inwardly? At what point is the communication interpreted, organized, integrated, assimilated or rejected? Having accomplished that process, however inadvertently, how does the organization respond to the data it receives?

a. Incoming: reception and routing

How much of what kinds of information actually comes into the organization? Sometimes this is difficult to determine unless the consultant asks many different people within the organization and unless he observes, in his various visits, the kinds of information people have on their desks, the informal discussions after they return from professional or trade association meetings, and the themes of luncheon or coffee break discussions. Typically, specialists receive technical journals which are not shared with administrators. The latter may read general management publications to which specialists are oblivious. Typically, also, various departments within an organization do not share information from the publications they receive. It is not unusual for a president and several vice presidents to have regular meetings in which they discuss facets of personnel, finance, research, engineering, and marketing. However, it is rare for these men to bring routinely to each other, and their group as a whole, new information in their respective fields.

(1) *Amount and types of material*

Information may range widely from publications to which the organization subscribes to reports on local politics from branch managers. It may include confidential reports on competitors' market testing, informal notes on discussions at a scientific meeting, a list of good restaurants in a major city, lectures by future oriented thinkers, long-range weather reports and a wide variety of other data. Here are two descriptions of amount and type of material, one from a case and the other from a magazine article.

The Fanchon Fabricating Company subscribes to 59 periodicals which are distributed to 12 of its 16 departments. *Supervisory Management* is circulated to all foremen while *Business Week, Fortune, U. S. News and World Report* are found in the reception rooms. There are half a dozen trade journals that appear to be shared widely among the manufacturing units. These are largely "how to do it" publications, heavy with ads of equipment manufacturers. The more technical and professional levels get their own "trade" publications. For example, the personnel department gets the *Industrial Relations Newsletter* and *Personnel*; the medical department, the *Journal of Occupational Medicine*; the accounting department, the *Tax Reports of the Research Institute of America*; and so on. There are weekly bulletins from the local chamber of commerce and monthly bulletins from the state chamber. Most of the information about product performance comes from customer feedback at sales shows and from the reports of servicemen in the field. Professionals bring back reports from their meetings and occasionally send for reprints. Marketing people do an annual customer survey, an effort which is shared by the public relations department, which is interested in the corporate image. Personnel and public relations people share the informal responsibility for keeping up with local and state political events and chamber of commerce activity.

The daily operations that Cargill's present management oversees have an intriguing complexity. Cargill's executives strive to anticipate, detect, and counter the moves of rival forces around the world. Company experts watch huge blackboards that post the ever-shifting "futures" prices of wheat, corn, oats, rye, barley, flax and soybeans from the various commodity exchanges of Chicago, Minneapolis, Kansas City and Winnipeg. A stream of messages over a private communication network report not only prices but amounts of company sales and purchases, weather conditions, crop prospects, ship movements, trade gossip, [and] Washington fact and rumor. [This information flows directly into the offices of the chief executive and his executive vice president.] (*Fortune,* December 1965, p. 169.)

(2) *Modes of transmission*

How does the information get to the organization? By what means are the customer complaints, the information from sales shows, the reports from scientific meetings, the topics in a given periodical, the economic forecasts, projected market changes, technical inventions information, and so on, fed into the system? By noting how the organization gets its information, the consultant can begin to formulate some conception of the nature of the input, the form it takes, and the kinds of data the organization has to work with. There are various ways of viewing how the organization receives incoming information. The following breakdown is one simple classification:

(A) ORAL OR WRITTEN

Oral reports would range from a simple statement of a few sentences by a colleague of what went on in a trade show to a formal conference of invited participants who would be given a systematic summary of the trade show, followed by discussion and questions. A closed-circuit television broadcast such as a surgical demonstration could be considered an oral input. Written reports or inputs could be items from an abstracting service, an insider's newsletter on politics, as well as a marketing intelligence summary. Information that is written or printed is more likely to be considered to be authoritative, is more permanent, and can be more easily reviewed subsequently. Here are two such descriptions from cases:

Chetopa Power and Light gets much of its economic statistics in written form: bulletins, reports, and trends from official sources like the Federal Reserve Banks. Its political information comes from weekly written reports from local managers but more frequently from contacts by its executives with public officials and political leaders. During legislative sessions, the company's legislative representative phones in bits and pieces of information to the president of the company. Members of the corporate operating committee report orally on issues that were discussed at trade association meetings they have attended. Customer complaints may come in by phone or letter; the company prefers them to be oral so they can act quickly to avoid complaints to regulatory bodies.

Communication from the Board of Education to Shaker School usually consists of written instructions regarding policies or new methods. These are supplemented by verbal reports which the principal brings from the weekly principals' meetings and by comments from subject matter supervisors who come from the central administrative office. Parents' concerns usually are communicated directly by the parents to the teachers or principal; some come up in PTA meetings. Legislative information comes largely through the publications of the state teachers association and salary discussion information through monthly meetings of the local teachers association. New information on teaching techniques comes largely through individual refresher courses and education journals.

(B) FORMAL OR INFORMAL CHANNELS

Material which comes through formal channels and by formal means more often requires some direct or indirect response by the organization. Sometimes this response may be only acknowledgment in the form of initialing the message. Sometimes it may stimulate the organization to prepare some sort of response "just in case." Here are two case examples of how incoming information is channeled:

When the respective department heads of Ajax Pharmaceutical Corporation bring back informal reports from trade association or scientific meetings, these tend to be minimized by the president. However, when he reads an article on marketing, regardless of the publication in which it appears, he immediately circulates it to the marketing people with a request for their reactions to it. The same kind of thing happens with respect to authorities in given fields. He will pay little attention to what a specialist may have said unless the specialist is an invited speaker to the company and is paid a substantial fee.

Broch's Department Store gets its style information by sending buyers to overseas as well as domestic markets. These people are well aware of likely trends from their continuing study of fashion publications, art magazines, and perusal of tangential publications such as those that related to architecture, product design, community planning, and so on. The buyers are alert to what they call "flair" from whatever source. Therefore much of the external input they get is subtle. Each buyer manages his own department so he can put his hunches into practice. They communicate their hunches, observations, and conclusions to each other in formal biweekly buyers' conferences. Higher management contents itself with evaluating the financial results.

(3) *Timing, rhythm, and urgency*

The consultant should determine if the organization gets regular inputs of information suitable to its needs. Is the information timely for the organization's tasks? Or does the organization have a "squeaking wheel" philosophy about incoming information, getting information only when it has a problem? Does it do anything about regulating the pace and intensity of input or does it find itself from time to time overwhelmed because it did not anticipate or cannot assimilate what it is getting?

(A) ACCORDING TO PLAN

Some organizations have a regular plan for systematically obtaining information. They depend on regular reports on styles, trends, cycles, building starts, industry-wide sales, and so on, for their own planning. If such communications occur regularly and are comprehensive in their content they constitute a solid, dependable base for organizational action. Here are two case examples of the lack of a systematic plan and a third describing such a plan for getting information.

Clamore Products sells the bulk of its frozen packaged vegetables to the Allied Food chain. Allied tells Clamore after deliveries have been made what the market prices were on given dates, and Clamore must accept them as stated or give up Allied as a customer. Such after-the-fact information plays havoc with Clamore's financial planning; often it finds it has sold products below cost when it might more wisely have withheld them from the market.

During the legislative session, the Kansas Psychological Association receives a continuous flow of information from Commerce Clearinghouse. Much of this duplicates information already in newspapers and reported by legislative representatives, but the added system helps to insure that no important — however distantly related — issues will slip by.

Barford University simply had no way of "hearing" the discontent of the students until the riot broke out. Now the deans are particularly alert to changes on the horizon. At the president's weekly meeting each dean is expected to report to the others any trends and problems in his area from information he has gleaned from colleagues on other campuses as well as his conversations with students and faculty. Already, as a result, a faculty committee is looking into the establishment of student evaluations of faculty against the day when students will demand that privilege.

(B) ERRATICALLY OR SPONTANEOUSLY

Some organizations pay attention to incoming information or seek it out erratically or spontaneously, almost as if on whim or fad. Perhaps a crisis gives import to data they had or were getting all the time. Perhaps an officer was stimulated at a meeting or made to feel quilty at the country club or a speaker touched a sore organizational nerve. These two case examples illustrate input of isolated, unexpected information.

Gramercy Park Church is going through the throes of sensitivity training since the pastor returned from such a session in Asheville. The various youth and adult classes are not certain what this is to do for them, and some of the parents are concerned about what they hear. But the pastor is convinced that openness is next to godliness.

Computers are the thing. Recent managerial meetings have devoted much attention to data processing. So the executives of Chetopa Power and Light reported to their colleagues. Chetopa sent a man to computer school. Now Chetopa has a computer but no one is quite certain how to make effective use of it.

(4) *Source and audience*

With many kinds of incoming communication it will be important for the consultant to know where it comes from and for whom it is intended in the organization. With political, economic, and labor relations information this is particularly important because the origins of such information and the people who get it will have significant impact on the company's attitude on these matters. Following this communications route will help to indicate to the consultant who the influential person is on which matters. Discovery of who is subscribing to what publications and who is privy to what kinds of information will tell the consultant something about the informal power structure of the organization. A certain degree of power is inherent in possessing information which others do not have. Those who share such information form enclaves, the boundaries of which are often reflected by the routing slips on the material transmitted. Comparison of such routing slips will indicate the extent to which circles of formal information overlap and where the lapses occur. Here is a sample case example:

The president of Michael Manufacturing got all his information about the labor relations climate from the executive of the state manufacturers' association. As a result he took adamant stands which reflected the line of dominant figures controlling the association. His own industrial relations man could not persuade him to look at his own people and their feelings. Labor relations policy might just as well have been made in Cleveland.

b. Processing: integration and decision

Having assessed what information comes into the organizational system and by what means, the consultant should now seek to discover what happens to various types of material. Who processes it? How? For what emphases and what purposes? What material is given what treatment, by what means, and with what timing?

(1) *Amount and types of material*

Who does what to what types of material? Political data, for example, can be used as a basis for an essay by the president of the company in the company magazine. Morale studies can be muted in various ways to soften criticism of certain officials. A prospective merger may be presented in glowing terms to anticipate and avoid possible anxiety. The daily cash register tapes of a department store may provide accurate inventory or financial information for corporate management, but comparable information about supervisor-supervisee relationships may be suppressed at the store manager level. Some companies avoid public recognition assiduously and carefully guard public pronouncements. Hospitals are bound by the law and medical ethics to control information about patients. Until recently the Roman Catholic Church published no financial information about itself. An example of how one company discloses certain kinds of information to its employees follows:

For several years Kansas Gas and Electric Co., Wichita, has staged a series of employee information meetings early each January. The company's top officials spend an evening in each of the communities where KG&E has a sizable number of employees, and their wives and husbands are encouraged to attend as well. As part of the 1965 program, employees were given the opportunity to ask questions of a panel composed of three company vice presidents. The employee audiences were divided into groups of six. Each group elected a spokesman and, after six minutes of deliberation, composed its question and submitted it. Thus it was not possible to tell specifically the author of the question, and each group was more or less compelled to emerge with some kind of query. The company concedes that this may have resulted in a contrived question or two, but in general, the method brought many good questions into the open. Following these meetings, all questions and answers were assembled in an attractive booklet, which was mailed to each KG&E worker, along with the company's annual report to employees. The plus values of this follow-through have impressed the company. First, every employee has the opportunity to see all the questions, whether they were asked in the meeting he attended or not. Second, the booklet put the company permanently on record with the answers — substantial evidence of management forthrightness. Finally, it made it possible for the company to add more specific details to replies that might have been incomplete at the meeting. (From a newspaper clipping, now lost.)

(2) *Modes of processing*

Here the consultant is concerned about what actually is done to the information according to its mode of transmission.

(A) ORAL OR WRITTEN REPORTS

Are the reports from sales meetings translated into written form? With questions about their import? With suggestions about who should do what about problems? With action recommendations? Are the morale study reports secreted by top management or edited with glib generalities for the company newspaper? Are the stirring of labor organizers translated into alarm-ringing memoranda to all supervisors? Are critical statements about a product from the Federal Trade Commission shunted to the public relations and legal departments thus denying that the employees would have any interest in them? Are the figures about decreasing seminary enrollment withheld from denominational discussion? Is the bishop unwilling to hear complaints about his administration and therefore much more inclined to give emphasis to "identity crises" of the ministers in his synod? Do successive layers of management rewrite subordinates' reports in keeping with what they think higher management wants to hear? Two case examples and an excerpt from a magazine article are illustrative:

At Shaker School, the response by teachers to instructions from the Board of Education regarding policies or new methods may be varied by the principal's attitude and the method by which he presents them. For example, he could put the notice on the staff bulletin board without comment; he could send the notice around to each classroom with a note appended; he could discuss the contents of the communication with the teachers at the time he shows it to them. In this way, the teachers perceive his interpretation of the board's regulations. Information to the board is initiated from the school supervisors who visit the individual schools in their district from time to time. Also, once or twice a year each school principal reports orally to the Board of Education.

The weekly staff meeting at the Great Lakes Insurance Company is one mode of communication. This is paralleled by monthly information exchange meetings of all supervisors and selected specialists and technicians. By company policy, supervisors are required to summarize these meetings for their subordinates. An informal type of communication exists through use of the company bulletin boards. These are found in each department. The information tacked to them varied from a memo from the president concerning the presence of the consulting team to notices about bowling teams and the formation of other sports teams. Lost and found items are publicized on the bulletin boards as well as on the "trading post" — where people post notices about items they would like to buy, sell, or trade. The bulletin board is available to any employee for personal use of this type. Company memos are generated by company officials or supervisors.

For years Weston and Metcalf resourcefully protected the secrecy of their widespread operations. Documents from subsidiaries often were sent to Metcalf's home rather than to his office. The companies rarely volunteered information not required by the relatively lax disclosure laws of Canada and Europe; questions — even some from large minority shareholders — were ignored. Executives in Toronto, headquarters for North American operations, referred to subsidiaries by code names: British Columbia Packers Ltd., the fish processor, was known as "Phisch"; Power Supermarkets Ltd., a sizable Canadian chain, was "No. 1." Even chiefs of subsidiaries were not encouraged to take an interest in corporate family relationships. (*Fortune,* June 1967, p. 117.)

(B) FORMAL OR INFORMAL CHANNELS

Some organizations give heavy emphasis to controlling and directing the formal distribution of information as in company newspapers and magazines, paying no attention at all to informal channels of communication. Others deliberately try to plan information on the "grapevine." Those companies that are more technically interested and research oriented will organize and distribute abstracts of current literature and maintain a file of such abstracts in the company library.

The process of handling suggestions is a mode of handling formal communications, for suggestions usually require investigation and assessment by committee, decision about importance and relative value, and integration within organizational activities, as well as some statement to the person who made the suggestion. In some companies prizes are awarded, almost randomly, and suggestions rarely put to use. Others pay cash remuneration based on value and explain in detail to all employees which suggestions were given what awards and why.

In some organizations financial data is organized on a comparative monthly basis and trends are charted, but these data are limited to the top management personnel. Some organizations suppress inspection reports, taking the risk that explosion, collapse, or catastrophe will not occur. Some deliberately seek, as in long-range planning, to collate all kinds of information in such a way that it can be used meaningfully for decision making. With contemporary data processing equipment there is a tendency to concentrate heavily on such data as can easily be given numerical values. This means that the decision making process may be heavily weighted in one direction.

When material is formally distributed through regular channels, it has, in effect, been given official recognition and approval. Material which must be distributed through the informal power structure may, on the one hand, tend to undermine the established authority (or be seen that way) or else not be given the recognition and support it needs. If, for example, information that a rival company has a new product which might jeopardize the organization's survival is the subject of rumor and if that news is not dealt with officially by management, employees may panic. The contrast between the formal channels of information distribution and employee reports of where they get their information is an extremely important one because it reflects something of how much employees trust the formal information they get. Here are examples of three widely varied situations.

In the Ajax Pharmaceutical Corporation employees receive a company newspaper each month; a weekly announcement is posted on all bulletin boards indicating promotions, transfers, reorganizations, and similar matters; a separate weekly announcement is similarly posted indicating news about employees — who is sick, who won the bowling tournament, and so on, as well as informal classified ads. Each employee also receives a copy of the company's annual report. However, when asked how they find out what is going on in the organization, almost all respondents refer to rumor, grapevine, or going directly to people who are thought to be knowledgeable about a given subject.

Communications within the Weldon organization — upward and lateral, but particularly downward — were not always frank and honest. In many instances, the real and the apparent reasons for asking subordinates' opinions differed, and people had learned to be guarded in expressing their views. Supervisors and assistants were reluctant to express themselves openly and hesitated to share information or to coordinate efforts with each other. (Alfred Marrow, et al., *Management by Participation*, New York, Harper & Row, 1967, pp. 133–134.)

At the Acme Technical Laboratory, reports which collectively constitute a scientific journal in the sense that they provide a formal, public, and orderly means of communication within the company are selectively distributed internally by the Sage system. The Sage system was designed to get newly written papers into the hands of those who are interested in the field via high-speed computers. The system is based on the idea that journals must recognize the need for very rapid communication in certain fields. By distributing to each subscriber a personalized stream of papers, abstracts, and titles, this is more possible than ever before. The author of the paper codifies his subject matter; the computers send that paper to all of the subscribers who have noted that subject on their reader request forms. The readers may receive papers and abstracts separately as they come out or receive them at set intervals. Sage became operational at Acme in 1967. Prior to that time, internal technical reports were distributed exclusively to named individuals, usually only those known personally by the author. Others could order copies from a monthly list of titles. For most, this system provided high relevance but low coverage, although some who have chosen very few subjects get instead greater relevance with about the same coverage. In either case, there is a significant increase in the quality of communications occurring in the Laboratory.

(3) *Timing, rhythm, urgency*

Is there some sense of the importance of transmitting information of a routine kind at regular intervals? Of a crisis kind immediately? What is the degree of seriousness with which communications distribution is regarded? The pace of processing, integration, and decision making in many organizations is notoriously slow, partly because of procrastination, partly because of indecisive leadership, partly because of inadequate delegation of responsibility. Some have formal steps for dealing on a regular basis with information and decisions about information. Others go to great lengths to organize and integrate information which is then often ignored in favor of impulsive action. Some investigate and reinvestigate, only to enter a market or build a plant long after competition has a head start.

(A) ACCORDING TO PLAN

Some organizations have a regular plan for distributing incoming information. The employees know the plan and depend on it. If such communications occur regularly and are comprehensive in their content, people come to respect and to trust them. If information transmission is also flexible enough to be governed by the importance of the event and people's anxieties, then that, too, will increase trust. Does the organization hold a regular weekly or daily meeting for managers? Does the manager then inform his department of recent developments? Are these developments and matters the basis for some kind of decision making? Are responsibilities assigned, time schedules projected, the available information "squeezed dry" and allocated to areas of greatest relevance? If there are crisis situations, can the organization process information and make its decisions quickly? These two case excerpts illustrate such information distribution:

Holton Drug Company discovered from marketing information agencies that a competitor was market testing a new vitamin preparation. Holton's marketing information indicated that national advertising and distribution of this preparation would be forthcoming within a short period of time. This marketing intelligence transmitted through the marketing research director to the vice president of marketing in turn came immediately before the corporate policy committee which authorized the vice president of marketing to undertake a crash program to meet the competition. As a result, when the competition's distribution date arrived the Holton Company already had its product on pharmacists' shelves and pursued a sample-distribution technique for introducing its product to counteract the national ads which its competition had scheduled.

Information about The Menninger Foundation and its personnel, relevant to employees, is transmitted to them in four major forms: current announcements — a weekly bulletin of scheduled events, visitors, and ads; a monthly employee newspaper — TPR; a newsletter from the president, distributed as necessary, for reporting to employees on matters which should not await the monthly newspaper but are too long for the current announcements; a Monday Morning Report from the Developmental Office and another from the Director of Clinical Services. When the then president, Dr. William C. Menninger, became ill and was hospitalized at the Mayo Clinic, an immediate and detailed verbal report was made to all department heads on a Sunday morning followed by newsletter distribution to all employees the next day. Subsequently there were frequent newsletters detailing medical reports. The speed with which the information was transmitted and its comprehensiveness made the newsletter a trusted source of information. There were practically no rumors because the published information was too definitive to allow for gaps which could be filled by rumor. Instead each employee had solid information whose import was clear to him.

(B) ERRATICALLY OR SPONTANEOUSLY

In some organizations information is only occasionally or spontaneously organized and processed for the use of the organization as a whole. This may be due to a crisis situation or the sudden interest of a somebody in a high place or because of the pressure of the external environment. A company president, having attended a seminar on performance appraisal, an abbot having heard a lecture on communications, a personnel director having participated in sensitivity training may return to their organizations to subsequently prepare a survey of the literature or a brief for the introduction of a given program into the organization. Many organizations have fadlike phases of interest in given topics. There are styles and fads in management as there are in clothing. Some organizations provide information reactively. That is, they report to their people when there is a crisis or an eruption of some kind. For example, a company which is facing imminent unionization and only then takes the trouble to tell its employees of its economic circumstances can hardly expect to have its communications trusted by its employees. These excerpts from books illustrate erratic handling of information:

A major example in recent times was the late President Eisenhower's handling of the U-2 incident. When Khrushchev announced that an American plane had been shot down over Russian soil, spokesmen for the Department of State and the National Aeronautics and Space Agency agreed that it must have been a weather plane operating from a base in Turkey. Obviously, they reported, the pilot had lost consciousness owing to some failure in his oxygen supply, and the automatic device which took over the piloting moved the aircraft off its course. Khrushchev then shook the administration with the announcement that the pilot was alive and that his photographic equipmene was intact. Secretary of State Christian Herter thereupon made the embarrassing announcement that the plane was probably on an unauthorized reconnaissance mission. Then the nation was informed that the president had authorized the flights and that they had been going on for several years. Herter asserted that the government would be derelict in its duty if it did not take measures to safeguard the country against the possibility of surprise attack. Subsequently, Vice President Nixon appeared on a television program and said that the United States should not cease its protective surveillance just because a plane had been shot down. The next day the president announced that the flights would b discontinued, thus reversing in fact and in spirit both his vice president and the secretary of state. (Eugene E. Jennings, *The Executive: Autocrat, Bureaucrat, Democrat,* New York, Harper & Row, 1962, pp. 69–70.)

Weldon Manufacturing Company had a policy of closely guarding information about future plans. Only those in top echelons were ever alerted to impending events — and then only just before the events occurred. Lower level managers, floor supervisors, and employees were ordinarily given no advance notice about decisions to expand or contract volume, to close plants, to alter the organization or the operation. The news that Weldon had been sold to its major competitor produced mixed reactions. To most, it came as a complete surprise. To some, it came as a shock for they had great loyalty and commitment to Weldon and had not imagined such an event. To others it came as a relief, for they had feared that the plant would close down entirely, and the purchase opened the hope for continued operation. For all, the sense of anxiety and uncertainty was heightened. (Alfred Marrow, et al., *Management by Participation,* New York, Harper & Row, 1967, pp. 129–130.)

(4) *Source and audience*

Much of the information needed here will already have been gathered for the previous communications items. However, particularly with informal information, it will be important for the consultant to specify where such information arises and to whom it goes. This not only tells the investigator who talks to whom and about what but it also reveals something about who uses whom. Sometimes people communicate indirectly, knowing that information will eventually reach those to whom it was directed. It is also important to know where memos accumulate and on what subjects. Source and audience is equally relevant for formal inputs. For example, it is not unusual for the editor of the company magazine to draw on articles published by manufacturers associations and chambers of commerce which are then to be transmitted to employees as, in effect, endorsed by the company. The important point here is to find out who controls the formal communications channels within the organizations, to what audiences do they go, and for what purposes are they used.

This section will also say something about what aspects of the incoming communications are selected for processing, what information is given formal recognition by the organization, how is that information integrated, and for whom does it serve as a basis for decision making. Here, too, the consultant should be concerned about the possible audience outside the organization for whom such information is intended. Some company publications can be veiled statements of position and policy directed to political officials. Others, like IBM's publication *Think,* can serve both to increase the general knowledge of executives in the organization and a selected readership of influential persons outside it. A policy statement enunciated by the president of a company may influence the political views of his employees who serve on city councils, school boards, and similar public bodies. Two published excerpts and a case example illustrate the idea of source and audience in communications processing.

At Weldon Manufacturing Company the system of control required a reliable system for surveillance. Certain favored employees in different parts of the plant or office were encouraged to "report confidentially to the boss" any divergence from policies and procedure. Paperwork multiplied in response to work errors and in response to top management's need for detailed information. The reports, however, were not planned on any overall basis for economy or to get information quickly to the operative levels of management. Some records were deliberately falsified by people who feared the reactions of supervisors; there occurred deliberate collusion in keeping important information from the partners. The reports and records conveyed information of doubtful value to people who were in a poor position to react appropriately. All this meant that management costs rose with little effective management obtained for it. Expenses mounted, profits declined and no one could or would say why. Alfred Marrow, et. al., *Management by Participation,* New York, Harper & Row, 1967, p. 9.)

[John Kenneth] Galbraith's cables to the State Department were prized as titillating reading material. "Well, the President's policy has fallen on its face again," was a typical salutation. A postscript might be: "Now would somebody back there please get off his ass!" A little vulgarity, Galbraith found, assured a personal reading by President Kennedy. (*Time,* February 16, 1968, p. 28.)

At the Great Lakes Insurance Company, the grapevine related to the way the company's president was "connected" to it, according to the description of one of the appointed officers. The president was visualized as keeping his fingers on the pulse of the organization by means of a maiden lady who was a long-time and trusted employee of the company. Although theirs was an informal relationship, its function was visualized as being understood by both parties: the lady utilized her membership on middle management committees as a basis for grass roots information; the president accepted information gleaned via this means that he would not tolerate from appropriate hierarchical sources. The woman confirmed this when asked, "What happens when problems arise?" She replied that since she had been in the organization for a good length of time, she could usually figure the problems out as well as anyone. She said, "I make informal minutes of meetings and present them to the president, who had final approval of everything."

c. Outgoing: routing and response

Once the data have been received and processed how are they used? How is the integrated information and decisions based on it made part of the organization's functioning? What is distributed to whom and why?

(1) *Amount and types of material*

How much organized data and what kind are put into the organization's external communications distribution channels? Do regular publications go to a select audience or does the whole business community know how the company is faring? Does the organization publish information which might be helpful in health, welfare, or economic planning, for example, health statistics published by an insurance company, carloading figures published by a railroad? Does it exchange salary information with similar organizations? The answers to these and similar questions in this section will tell the consultant something about organizational secrets and will also serve to delineate the areas about which rumors are most likely to originate. The following two examples refer to amount and kind of material the respective organizations put out.

Ajax Pharmaceutical permits its scientists to publish papers on their research, providing the findings have no readily apparent commercial value or after patents have been obtained. It keeps the FDA continuously apprised of its findings on its products so that the FDA scientists can raise questions early, if they have any. If laboratory findings raise questions about a product, it will pull the product from the market, notifying physicians, distributors, and the press why it is doing so. It shares statistical information of many kinds with others in the Pharmaceutical Manufacturers' Association to establish industry norms, but salary information is shared only for overseas operations to prevent pirating of employees. Financial data are reported in the annual report and in meetings with security analysts. Recommendations about employees leaving for other jobs are uniformly positive. Negative judgments are not shared, nor is the public or business community informed about many of the reasons for frequent reorganization. Sales marketing information is closely guarded.

The Anti-Defamation League of B'nai Brith gathers a wide range of information on anti-Semitism, civil rights, and other forms of community human relations problems. This information consists of reports on antidemocratic movements, racial disturbances, employment discrimination; research results on intergroup relations and discrimination; methods and techniques for teaching human relations in the classroom, for teaching specific groups like teachers, ministers, policemen. Most of this is made available for public use, and the organization initiates programs for human relations. It exchanges information with other civil rights groups, government agencies, and Jewish organizations. It does not publicly discuss its differences with other Jewish agencies, its fund-raising efforts or governmental contacts. Such information is limited to internal policy making committees.

(2) Modes of distribution

Here the consultant should determine the specific ways in which the integrated information is distributed.

Once the data is integrated, is it transmitted by word of mouth or by some kind of written statement? The more an organization depends on oral communication, the more likely it is to be reluctant to express itself publicly and the more likely it is to minimize its public relations. These examples refer to modes of distribution of information:

The Central City-County Health Department makes periodic inspections of restaurants, inspecting not only cleanliness but the quality of the food (to avoid adulteration) as well. Some local hamburger stands have been told to put more meat in their hamburger, while others were found to serve high quality ground beef. Since no information is distributed, rumors substitute for fact. The inspector's judgments are not made public. There is much informal discussion by the public about the presumed findings and how they reflect on the various stands. Reputations are being deflated or established by word of mouth. The same problem exists for other types of health inspection.

The Anti-Defamation League of B'nai Brith disseminates most of its information in publications. The results of research are distributed in books, press releases, and lectures. It distributes pamphlets, books and visual aids on intergroup relations to teachers, ministers, adult educators and college instructors, and human relations commissions. Specialized material for given audiences is circulated to them, such as guidelines for police or ministers. The latter include reprints from magazines and newspapers. It distributes to its National Program Committee minutes of that committee's meetings, reports on conferences it has sponsored, projected programs, and professional activities in crisis situations. It publishes *Facts*, a periodic report on particular subjects, like the neo-Nazi movement in Germany, or the radical right and left, and the monthly *ADL Bulletin*, the latter devoted to feature stories on civil rights problems and activities. The printed material is public information. The communications to the National Program Committee are sometimes on a "not for publications" basis, often because the information is confidential or because it is either not yet ready for publication or is of insufficient public interest. Members of the National Program Committee are supplied with fact sheets, statements of information on given topics which are to be the basis for program planning. Special reports and memoranda are issued to inform commission members on crisis events like the Arab-Israeli conflict, race riots, and similar matters. The national chairman irregularly issues an informal four-page newsletter to the national committees of the organization. These are supplemented by regional reports. The general membership of B'nai Brith is kept informed through the *National Jewish Monthly* news items and feature stories. In addition, staff members lecture frequently to all kinds of audiences, and regional office staffs visit local communities both to gather and transmit information.

Some organizations have formal channels for the distribution of integrated data, some provide data for those who ask for it. Some crucial data are transmitted informally by prearranged telephone conference calls and individual telephone messages. The more informal the transmission, the more likely the data are to be limited to a select audience and the more power is shared by those who are privy to the privileged information. A magazine excerpt and an advertisement describe channels of information distribution.

Throughout his Indian tour — and ever since — Galbraith also waged a hot war with the State Department. Communications from Washington took too long to arrive, he complained, and communicated nothing when they did get there. His mistrust of the State Department was not altogether unfounded. Once, when he was away from New Delhi, an aide handed him a coded message from Washington. How was he to read it without a decoding machine? The practice, the aide said, was to call Washington — on the telephone — and ask what was in the message. (*Time,* February 16, 1968, p. 28.)

Responding to the complaints about delivery and quality control, Wheeling Steel revitalized its efforts and reported its new readiness to the business public in advertisements in business publications which read:

"Ready, Wheeling and Able."

"The growing pains are over at Wheeling Steel.
Our new facilities are humming.
Our new policies have become standard operating procedure. And I think the time has come for us to make this commitment to you:
You can depend on Wheeling Steel. You can depend on us for all-BOF hot rolled steel, delivered when you want it.
You can depend on us for all the galvanized steel you'll ever need. For all the pipe. You can depend on us for alert, responsive service.
We know just where we stand with you.
We know just how hard we'll have to work to earn your business. And we're willing."

D. C. Duvall, President

(*Business Week,* March 16, 1968.)

(3) *Timing, rhythm, urgency*

Some organizations provide a steady flow of processed information on the basis of which others can then take action — customers, the public, suppliers, and so on. Other organizations may provide information at regular intervals, depending on sales cycles or other time spans relevant to the organization. Still others report only when compelled to do so.

(a) ACCORDING TO PLAN

Does the organization operate on the thesis that all its publics need to know about its activities? Does it assume that they need to know well in advance of the execution of any plan or mode of operation? Does it give partial information, leaving people to fret about its implications? Does it think of how it wants to make maximum use of information distribution? These case examples describe both planned and unplanned modes of distribution of information:

When the county welfare department reported new regulations to mothers of dependent children, the mothers interpreted the regulations to mean that their allotments were to be cut. These regulations had not been adequately detailed and explained in simple language. Case workers were asked to explain individually to clients as they called in. However, the worry was so widespread, and the administrator not sufficiently aware of its impact, that a consultant firmly suggested that the mothers be brought together in groups for explanation and discussion.

When Sanford Electric was to close its Norville plant, it announced that fact to the community two years before the plant was to be phased out. It explained to the community the economics of its operations which required the closing and then joined with the community to find another company which might take the plant over. It guaranteed to take those supervisory personnel who wished to be transferred elsewhere, but it could not accommodate line employees. Sanford paid for advertising brochures, visits of city officials to prospective companies, and for a booth at electric manufacturing trade shows. The joint effort was successful, and Sanford left Norville with the esteem and affection of its populace.

(b) ERRATICALLY OR SPONTANEOUSLY

Does information sometimes burst upon the respective publics who are then surprised to be hearing it? Do they complain about sometimes being told, but not at other times? Do they learn systematically about some things but only occasionally and inadvertently about others? One case example illustrates spontaneous, but useful communication, the other erratic and misleading communication:

In January 1968, the top officers of Litton Industries were faced with the task of telling the world that the company was anticipating a decline in quarterly profits for the first time in its fourteen-year history. The top five men of the organization agreed it was essential for any statement to scotch rumors of a management crisis. They warned each other that a badly worded announcement could lead to such headlines as, "Litton's Earnings Drop Confirms Reports of Management Troubles." This fear in mind, they spent most of Sunday afternoon drafting a letter to stockholders. Released the next day, the letter acknowledged that profits in the second fiscal quarter, due to end on January 31, would be "substantially lower than planned for this period." It conceded that the decline "is, to a great extent, the result of certain earlier deficiencies of management personnel." . . . But, it added, "Organizational changes to correct this condition have been made."

Far from allaying any fears, the letter was taken to mean that Litton — the very symbol of all that is modern in U.S. management — was indeed subject to seriously inadequate management. (*Fortune,* April 1968, p. 139.)

Hints of trouble [within Europe's biggest enterprise, the House of Krupp,] began to spread in late 1963, after the London *Sunday Telegraph* reported that Krupp was in a [money] squeeze because it was overburdened with short-term debt which it could not convert into long-term loans·. . . . [The immediate reaction from the organization was "Ridiculous!" An official government spokesman in Bonn suggested that this was another example of the British "Krupp trauma" and that perhaps certain "special interests" were seeking to spread false rumors. Even the Deutsche Bank's Hermann Josef Abs, most respected eminence of Germany's financial community, called the report unfounded and irresponsible . . . But . . . the Germans learned the news about Krupp that sent a tremor of angst through the country . . . the firm was operating at a loss. It was so far in debt that its bankers would grant no new credits to finance its exports unless the credits were guaranteed by the federal government. After protracted negotiations, the guarantee was given, but only on severe conditions. No later than . . . 1968, Krupp would cease to be the private domain of one man and would become a publicly owned corporation. Until that conversion, the company had to accept the imposition of an administrative council which would pass on all major management decisions . . . [These were stringent and frightening conditions for a company that had once been the bellwether of the German economy]. (*Fortune,* August 1967, pp. 73–74.)

(4) Source and audience

Who actually gets which information in contrast with those for whom it is intended? These two case examples describe unintended consequences of information distribution:

The PTA Council sends many kinds of bulletins to the presidents of local PTA's. However, most of the information is intended for elementary school PTA's. Since it is largely irrelevant for junior high school PTA's, most of it winds up in the waste baskets of the junior high PTA presidents. Furthermore, even when appropriate information is transmitted to elementary school PTA's, it may or may not be used, depending on the initiative of committee chairmen.

As part of a savings bond campaign, the Treasury Department mailed to every household in a certain part of the country a pamphlet on bonds. A check on the effectiveness of the pamphlet was conducted by interviewing a sample of the recipients in the test area. Despite the fact that the pamphlet had been in every mailbox, two weeks later, only 17 percent of the people even recognized it when they were allowed to examine it, and 83 percent of the people could not remember having seen it two weeks before. Of the 17 percent who recognized it, one-third remembered having seen the cover and, consequently only about 10 percent were even exposed to the material within. This gloomy result is probably characteristic of the fate of information carried in many media of communication where a generalized negative evaluation has been made of the kind of facts that are apt to be found within.

2. Current and previous studies in and reports to organization

Most organizations have various kinds of reports in their files. Some are not called reports but staff studies, others are called reviews. The consultant should make a special effort to see these. They can serve as a check on his own findings, illuminate areas with which he is less familiar, and suggest considerations which may not previously have occurred to him.

a. Consultant reports

Practically any business organization of any size has used consultants; and often educational, religious, and other institutions have also done so. Consultants' reports seem to have two fates: (1) they are acted on precipitously and result in drastic reorganizations without much thinking; or (2) they are placed on an obscure shelf, there to gather dust. The usual reason for this is that most consultants do not know how to feed back their reports in such a way that they become the psychological property of the organization and a basis for concerted action. Often consultants' reports are simply digests of what the consultants have been told by people in the organization and are therefore regarded with contemptuous cynicism by those who have been interviewed. The latter feel exploited because they cannot give their views directly to their superiors and someone else is paid high fees to report as recommendations what they themselves have said.

Despite these problems a sensitive consultant can learn many things from such reports. He should try to discover why management approached a consultant in the first place. What problems did the company think it had? What kinds of consultants did management employ?

Why these particular consultants? For example, if the company had a morale problem and chose a communications expert, it might be inferred that the management expected to coax its people out of the problem by talking to them more effectively. However, if management employed an expert in organization, the consultant could at least hypothesize that the management sought to deal with this problem by compulsive control.

If the consultant discovers that the organization has had repetitive consulting reports, he might infer that management does not regard its own staff's capacities highly. He might also infer that management tends to regard people outside the organization in an idealized way.

While looking for and at previous consultant reports, the consultant can sense how the organization feels about the reports. Sometimes he will discover that nobody knows about such a report and that it lies untouched on the president's desk. Why?

Here is an example of how a company defined the nature of its own problems and chose a consultant who provided the management with easy answers that did not require much introspection or corrective effort. Yet a consultant with different training could glean much of greater importance from the same data.

Sonic Communications, concerned about threatened unionization of one of its plants, had a survey organization make an attitude survey of its supervision and management. The consultant reported that the respondents wanted better communications. Already flooded with communications from top management, it seemed hardly possible that they could want more. A clinically oriented consultant pointed out that the respondents could only reply to the questions they were asked. If the responses were understood at greater depth, it could be seen that the men did not want more communication, but closer relationships with higher management, particularly some indication that higher management cared about them.

The next case example illustrates *effective* reorganization based on competent consultation. Presumably there was a *good* definition of problems to be dealt with and a constructive mechanism for dealing with them. The consultant could learn much from such a report.

Drastic reorganization of the Wheat Process Company into six subsidiary companies has brought the top management closer to its operating heads; provided a clearer, faster picture of operations; and increased efficiency. This followed on the recommendations of an organizational consultant when profitability declined despite continued increase in sales. The new organization provides for greater autonomy of subsidiaries, and a more functional grouping of their activities. Most of the executives seem pleased with it.

b. Special staff reports

Special staff reports can tell the consultant the same kinds of things as do previous consultants' reports. Why were the staff reports undertaken? By whom? What became of them? With what attitude are they regarded by the rest of the organization? What use was made of them? When an organization has many staff reports which are used in decision-making, the consultant can know that top management leans heavily on its own people for gathering information and making judgments. Often such staff reports are a device for teaching staff to diagnose and make recommendations on problems. However, management can also use such reports as methods of keeping people busy or for procrastinating. This is particularly a problem in political and university circles. A special staff report can also say something about who has to please whom, how, and why. It will be important to assess the discrepancy between what is on paper and what is actually felt by those who composed the report.

If a staff report and a consulting report on the same subject are discovered, the reason for both reports should be carefully examined. Here are references from four cases to staff reports:

When Brach's Department Store decided to evaluate the book retailing business, top management designated a team of executives to study the field. These men evolved a comprehensive feasibility study which recommended that the firm enter the bookselling business, which it promptly proceeded to do with considerable success.

In 1965 six staff members of The Menninger Foundation were appointed, three by the president and three by the Professional Staff Organization, to study and recommend a new organizational structure. The committee met weekly for nearly six months, drafted its recommendations, and submitted them to open staff and administration discussion. The entire staff was divided into ten groups to critique the recommendations. The recommendations, together with the comments on them, were subsequently presented to a committee of the Board of Trustees. The committee and the board could not seriously consider the recommendations because their latent agenda was who was to be the president's successor? Besides, they wanted him to handle organization problems. This was further complicated by the death of the president, an eight-month interim period, and the accession of a new president. Meanwhile the Professional Staff Organization became less active. The recommendations remain unimplemented.

When the Topeka Board of Education had to undertake new construction and to delineate school service areas, its professional staff demarcated the attendance zones based on population statistics. However, the board feared complaints and criticisms of favoritism so it engaged a specialist from the University of Minnesota whose recommendations, it turned out, closely paralleled those of the administrative staff.

Ajax Pharmaceutical's top management rejected the study of its own staff which recommended that it enter further into the nutritional food business. Instead, it followed the recommendation of an outside management consultant that it strengthen its research department and become more expert in ethical drugs. The staff contends that the consultant did not understand research, particularly that he did not understand that Ajax' scientists were more congenial to product research than to basic research. And that, they say, is why basic findings have not been forthcoming.

c. Marketing studies

Here the consultant should ask: How does the organization look at its markets? How well does it define the business it is in? Does it have a broad generic concept of what it is doing? Does it know not only who and where its markets are, but also who is likely to be served by the competition? Is the organization looking for competition from unexpected sources? Marketing surveys, as contrasted with staff studies, and consultant reports, tend to be either continuous or repetitive. Consultants are called into an organization to advise on specific problems. Staff studies are usually also responses to specific problems. However, marketing surveys are asking the question, "Who are the customers and how are they reacting to what the organization is doing?" A school system is conducting a marketing survey when it makes its annual pupil census study. A church undertakes a marketing survey when it seeks to learn the age range, occupational status, interests, and so on, of its parishioners or of the people in a given neighborhood whom it wants to recruit to membership.

The firm chosen to conduct the market survey is of critical importance since that choice reflects the organization's degree of sophistication. For example, a management unsophisticated about psychological motivation but concerned about loyalty would more likely choose a survey firm that provided relatively quick and easy "yes" and "no" answers. As with the consultants' reports, the consultant must ask if the market survey is being used for its own sake or as a device to protect management jobs. Is its prime function to keep critics at a distance? Here are two published references to market studies:

A marketing survey reported to Gillette that its product Right Guard, a deodorant for men, was being widely used by women. So Gillette Chairman Vincent C. Ziegler decided both to beef up advertising and to change its emphasis: He began selling Right Guard as a *family* deodorant. Right Guard quickly took over the No. 1 spot with about one-fourth of the total deodorant market. In the process it helped to nearly triple Gillette's volume in men's toiletries in four years to an estimated $70 million last year. (*Business Week*, April 1, 1967, pp. 58, 65.)

Conventional market research never went into the Edsel. Instead, Ford used a type of motivational research called "imagery studies," based on the premise that a customer can describe what kind of a product will best reflect his image of himself — and be most acceptable to him. In the more conventional approach to market studies, economic and social factors are sifted to seek out a chink in the product line — a group of consumers inadequately served. Such an analysis, even in 1955, probably would have revealed no chink in the medium-priced auto field. This would have led to the conclusion that Edsel would have to wrest customers away from its well-established rivals. (*Business Week*, November 28, 1959, p. 27.)

d. Engineering studies

Engineering studies are technical in nature and deal with the questions of plant layout, product design, time and motion studies, work feasibility studies, work simplification procedures, and similar matters. They speak largely to the technical efficiency of the organization. Important questions for the consultant to ask are: What facets of the organization do these studies focus on? How often are such studies conducted? Have the studies brought innovations? What kind? What are the underlying assumptions about the motivation of people? These questions are important because some organizations seek to rationalize production by engineering methods so as to eliminate the effects of people's feelings. Some implicitly assume that human beings are simply another form of a machine. Management may undertake repetitive engineering studies in an effort to avoid the underlying, more complex human problems or out of a failure to recognize them. A typical example of the contradictory effects of such studies is the recommendation for super highways to be constructed in such a way as to funnel traffic into downtown areas and to divide the city into nonviable sections. To go to the other extreme, a management may be so preoccupied with other matters that it is unable to recognize the importance of mechanical efficiency. A published reference and two case study excerpts illustrate what is meant by engineering studies:

Ernest E. Roberts, President, Norris & Elliott, Inc., was given the job of surveying the Weldon manufacturing operations and suggesting a program for revitalizing the plant's performance, particularly reducing costs and upgrading quality. Two engineers were charged specifically with studying the following areas:

1. What can be done to increase employee's earnings within the piece-rate standards and wage rates prevailing in the industry?

2. What can be done to get a better job of meeting customer demands on both cost and delivery?

3. What plant layout changes are necessary to improve overall plant performance?

4. How adequate is the performance of the supervisory staff, and what is the potential for improvement?

5. What improvements in equipment and work method may aid overall plant performance?

Recommendations were prepared and discussed with the new Weldon owners and with the Weldon plant staff . . . We were asked to carry out the recommendations and agreed to do so.

Through the open discussion of collective shortcomings and strengths, a sense of team spirit was developed and changes and corrections were received in an atmosphere of cooperation. This modus operandi was applied plant-wide to everyone — from the operator at a machine up to and including the plant manager (Alfred Marrow et al., *Management by Participation.* New York, Harper & Row, 1967, pp. 76–77; 86–87.)

The president of the Acme Company, disturbed by conflicts between sales and production over inability to get products out on time, called in an industrial engineer who made sweeping recommendations about layout and managerial organization. The engineer told the president that unless such changes were made, the organization would inevitably suffer, particularly if the president did not delegate more responsibility. The president told the consultant not to take life so seriously, that he was having a lot of fun doing what he was doing. He did not implement the recommendations.

Despite careful acoustical design, the sound of music in the new Asbury Cathedral left much to be desired. After the building was completed, considerable additional engineering consultation was required to attain good sound quality. Meantime, soloists had already established a negative opinion of the auditorium and some were reluctant to perform there. No one seemed to be able to explain how such poor acoustical quality had occurred.

e. Accountants' reports and audits

Most organizations have annual accountants' reports and most do regular audits. Some are checked by outside sources such as banks, which are checked by state auditors. Accounting control systems have three purposes: (1) economic motivation, (2) evaluation, and (3) planning.

Here the consultant must ask: How well does this organization's control system serve these purposes? An important subsidiary question is: How are the accountants' reports used? Another is: What power do accountants have in the organization? Sometimes those who manage the organizational record keeping, because of their intimate knowledge of the organization's financial status, acquire extraordinary power. They are often the behind-the-scenes power figures and formulate policy, without being responsible for it, by recommending budget allocations. Often they are more likely to think of dollars first and the nonfinancial costs of financial decisions afterward, if at all. Across-the-board cuts in spending, regardless of how reasonable the reduction is, suggest that the budget has become all important and the accountants are actually running the organization. Thus, the auditing and accounting system can be used as a check, as a feedback for decision-making, or as a cudgel on programming.

Another form of accountants' reports is long-range planning reports. These are most often studies by economists that forecast long-term cost and pricing trends or that forecast average ages and incomes of employees, and their implications for an organizational pension plan or a medical payments plan. Here are two case examples of auditors' powers:

Per capita costs of the children's service of Portal State Hospital are three times those of the adult services. Fearful of the criticism of state officials and legislatures, although the costs are genuine, the administration does not publish separate figures for the two services. Rather, it publishes a per capita figure which includes them both. This means that state officials and legislators never come to appreciate the costs and complexity of dealing with psychotic children and, particularly, the implications of specific budget cuts.

When the projected expenses promised to be more than $200,000 over anticipated income, the Board of Regents told the president of Burnside University to cut expenses and bring the budget into balance. Instead, the president recommended a raise in tuition, saying that cutting expenses would destroy the academic program. The board turned the budget over to the controller who blue-penciled the required increase in tuition. This produced a great public hue and cry, so many of the cuts were restored. But some cuts were cuts only on paper because the money was not going to be expended if staff could not be obtained.

7

INTERPRETATIVE DATA

Portion of outline covered in chapter 7

III. INTERPRETATIVE DATA

A. Current Organizational Functioning

1. Organizational perceptions
   a. *Degree of alertness, accuracy, and vividness*
      (1) *To stimuli from within the organization*
         (A) FROM PERSONNEL
            i. Employees to management and vice versa
            ii. Supervisor to subordinate and vice versa
            iii. Departments to each other's needs
         (B) FROM PHYSICAL PLANT
      (2) *To stimuli from without*
         (A) PRIMARY EXTERNAL STIMULI
            i. Marketing conditions
            ii. Purchasing conditions
            iii. Labor conditions
         (B) SECONDARY EXTERNAL STIMULI
            i. Legislative (tariff and tax laws)
            ii. Transportation
            iii. Competitors
            iv. Research developments
            v. Economic, social, and political trends
   b. *Direction and span of attention (selectivity)*
      (1) *Dominant foci of interest*
         (A) LONG-TERM FRAMEWORK
         (B) SHORT-TERM FRAMEWORK
      (2) *Significant neglected foci*
   c. *Assessment of the discrepancy between reality and perceived reality*

(1) *Of reality within the organization*
(2) *Of reality outside the organization*

2. Organizational knowledge
   a. *Acquisition of knowledge*
      (1) *Methods of obtaining new knowledge*
         (A) RELATED TO PERSONNEL AND PLANT
         (B) RELATED TO PRODUCTS, SERVICES, OR COMPETITORS
         (C) RELATED TO FINANCIAL RESOURCES
         (D) RELATED TO FORCES AND TRENDS AFFECTING THE
             ORGANIZATION
         (E) BY WHOM (SOURCES WITHIN AND OUTSIDE THE
             ORGANIZATION)
         (F) RESERVOIR OF INTELLECTUAL SOURCES
             i.   Talents and skills within the organization
             ii. Consultants
             iii. Affiliations with specialized institutions or
                  universities
             iv. Library facilities and services
      (2) *Degree of receptivity to new knowledge*
         (A) BY WHOM
         (B) TO WHAT
      (3) *Level and range of knowledge*
         (A) CONCERNING THEMSELVES, THEIR PRODUCTS, THEIR
             SERVICES AND RELATED FACTORS
         (B) OUTSIDE THEIR IMMEDIATE AREA OF INTEREST
   b. *Use of knowledge*
      (1) *How is it brought together*
         (A) WHO THINKS ABOUT IT
         (B) LEVEL OF ABSTRACTION
      (2) *How is knowledge organized and systematized*
         (A) COMMITTEE SYSTEM
         (B) RECORDS AND STORAGE SYSTEM
         (C) OTHER MODES OF ORGANIZATION AND
             SYSTEMATIZATION
      (3) *Amount and kind of use (retrieval)*
      (4) *Organizational conditions affecting the use of*
            intellectual sources
         (A) ABILITY TO DEAL WITH ABSTRACT PROBLEMS
         (B) FLEXIBILITY
         (C) CHARACTERISTIC STYLE AND VARIATIONS
   c. *Dissemination of knowledge*

3. Organizational language
   a. *Themes and content of employee publications*
   b. *Organizational ideology*

    c. *Advertising themes*

    d. *Organizational symbols and slogans*

    e. *Language of policies as distinct from the policies themselves*

    f. *Language of customs, taboos, prohibitions, and constrictions: direct and implied*

4. Emotional atmosphere of the organization

    a. *Prevailing mood and range*

    b. *Overall stability or variability of mood*

       (1) *Intensity of reactions*

       (2) *Duration of reactions*

       (3) *Appropriateness to stimulating factors*

    c. *Intraorganizational variability*

       (1) *By hierarchical level*

       (2) *By department*

       (3) *Other (geographical location, profession)*

5. Organizational action

    a. *Energy level*

       (1) *Consistency or variability of application (rate of discharge of energy)*

       (2) *Points and periods of peak expenditure of energy*

    b. *Qualities of action*

       (1) *Degree of directness*

       (2) *Degree of flexibility*

       (3) *Planning and timing*

       (4) *Degree of persistence*

       (5) *Effectiveness*

       (6) *Constructiveness or destructiveness*

A. Current Organizational Functioning

The data gathered prior to this point have been almost wholly factual. It would be easy to obtain agreement about the data if several disinterested parties were to undertake the same search. Those inferences which may have had to be made at various points were but limited extrapolations from the data and could be made by most people without specialized training.

Now, however, the consultant must begin to exercise his professional judgment. Different consultants using this outline may arrive at different interpretations, depending upon their training, experience, and theoretical orientation. Regardless of these factors, every consultant should be aware that he is dealing with inference; he must be prepared to offer evidence for the interpretations he makes or the conclusions he reaches. Only by offering evidence to himself or to others can he indicate how well he has tested that hypothesis he advances, can he specify the sources of his knowledge, and can he identify speculation and opinion. There is nothing wrong with either speculation or opinion, intuitive hunches or global judgments. However, the consultant should keep facts separate from inferences. If he fails to do so, he not only defeats the value of the scientific attitude, but also fails to take advantage of the opportunity to teach himself consciously.

Current organizational functioning refers to how the organization learns, thinks, feels, and behaves, if it can be said that an organization does these things. In Chapter 6 we talked about its structure or the equivalent of its anatomy or sociology. In this section we will be talking about its functioning, the equivalent of its physiology and psychology.

1. Organizational perceptions

Organizational perceptions refer to how and what the organization senses, both within itself and in its outside environment. Perception is the active, interpretative, receiving system of the organization.

a. Degree of alertness, accuracy, and vividness

Here the consultant should be concerned with the extent to which, and with what effectiveness, the organization recognizes and uses that which is available to it. The bombardment of stimuli may range from newspaper reports stating that for the past five years summers have been arriving earlier and lasting longer to the most recent Supreme Court decisions affecting parochial schools or organizational mergers. An alert organization may realize quickly from weather and sales curves that it should have its fertilizer on the market earlier next year or, in the course of a law suit, that it may have to adopt different business practices. Conversely, an organization may be insensitive to the import of the data it is getting or may misinterpret or perceive them only dimly. Its actions will subsequently be governed by what it is able to perceive.

The consultant must make subjective judgment about "degree of alertness." An experienced consultant may be able to compare his organization with others or may be able to contrast the way people speak with the way they act. *Alertness* refers to the number of antennae the organization has out and the degree of sensitivity it has to their vibrations. It also has to do with the kind of antennae, since the organization cannot "hear" what its sensing instruments cannot resonate with.

Accuracy refers to the judgment about the correctness of the interpretation of the stimuli. For example, metropolitan city officials often heard early rumblings of a potential riot. However, just as often, they failed to interpret what those rumblings meant and frequently attributed the cause of the riots to outside agitators.

Vividness refers to the detail with which the stimuli are interpreted. Inadequate differentiation of detail results in a fuzzy conception of the input, which in turn culminates in shotgun responses. Such public programs as rehabilitation of the unemployed and efforts to deal with juvenile delinquency flounder for just such a reason.

It is theoretically possible to be alert without being either accurate or vivid. For example, many people could see new-fangled inventions like automobiles, airplanes, and electricity. Failing to perceive accurately their implications for social change, few felt such inventions would last. Even fewer differentiated special commercial possibilities.

(1) *To stimuli from within the organization*

How does the organization know what is happening within itself? Specifically, how alert is it to what is going on? How accurate and vivid are its perceptions?

(A) FROM PERSONNEL

By this time the consultant will know what the processes of communication are within the organization and what the structures are for relationships among personnel. He should be able to make a judgment about how internal communications are received by organization management. For example, management may conduct a morale study and receive a report that its employees want more communication. Does management hear this as "We must tell them more," "We must sell them more," or "This is an agitator-generated employee complaint"? Much of what management hears is determined by what it wants to hear. The consultant will have to judge how accurately and with what understanding management is listening to its personnel.

i. Employees to management and vice versa

Of the examples of perceptions which follow, two are excerpts from cases and the third is drawn from an article describing the relationships between a governor and state university administrators. The governor may be regarded as management and the administrators as employees.

The employees of the Arrowhead Tool and Die Manufacturing Co. are more perceptive of management than management is of them. This perception is one of alertness more than accuracy since the employees are not informed of what is happening in the organization in most cases. For example, many of the employees recognize the dependency relationship of the company on the Reardon Corp. Some feel it is only a matter of time before Reardon takes over the company. In addition, many employees are sensitive to the sales manager's tendency to respond quickly to sales demands. These create many small special orders necessitating "short runs" and interfere with routine production procedures.

The doctors, nurses, and aides of Dalton State Hospital feel that the management is insensitive to them. They feel that *things* happen; they have neither say in the matter nor knowledge that something is going to occur. They had repeatedly received the following message from the administration: "You are all important to your particular section individually and as a team to the hospital and to the patients of your section." After the administration had seduced them into believing how vital they were to their section, suddenly and without warning, all the staff members of one section were told that a decision had been made to close that section within six weeks. The administration told them they would be placed in other jobs within the hospital or that each staff member could find another job at another hospital.

[The year] 1968 is the centennial year of the University of California, and by the usual measures of academic girth and quality, there is much to celebrate. U.C., with nine campuses up and down the state, breaks or presses all records for enrollment, expenditures, Nobel prizes, membership in the National Academy of Sciences, Guggenheim awards, Woodrow Wilson fellowships, and numerous other marks of scholarly scope and achievement. Though money is unprecedentedly tight, great construction projects are under way on virtually every campus to accommodate an ever-growing student body. Nevertheless, against this background of achievement, and, in fact, because of it, the people responsible for the affairs of U.C. today comprise what is probably the gloomiest set of administrators in all of higher education. Their mood is not without cause, for relations between Governor Ronald Reagan and the university have now settled down to a condition of subdued hostility that is steadily eroding the margin of money, elan, and confidence that made U.C. the greatest system of public higher education in the nation. "There has never been more statewide hostility to the university than there is now, and it shows up in the way they treat us in Sacramento." A graduate dean of one of the university's major campuses frankly states, "I have a feeling of absolute futility. There's a general fatigue here. People are really afraid of Reagan. He's shown that he can hurt us, and that there's nothing much we can do about it." One chancellor remarked: "There's a sense of insecurity such as I've never seen before. There's an absence of trust that makes it very difficult for an institution to function. A lot of people simply don't trust anyone anymore. I'm not used to having people look me in the eye and say, 'I don't believe you.'" In response to charges of maltreatment of the university, Reagan has come back with the charges of "poor mouth talk," and statistics that purport to show that "U.C. has a greater increase in its support this year in relation to its enrollment than in the last 19 years." To which U.C. officials respond that this may be so when the proposed budget is measured against the pruned-down budget that is now in effect, but that when measured against both need and the long-term pre-Reagan trend, the proposed budget is at best a standstill budget. Says Berkeley's Heyns, ". . . Last year Reagan seemed to be remorseful about the budget problem, but now he's not. We attracted people here because we had a lot of spirit and an atmosphere that this was the place to come to. Now this spirit is being challenged. No one has hit the panic button — there's no mass exodus, but among the faculty there's a kind of anxiousness and sober reappraisal." (*Science*, March 29, 1968, pp. 1440–1441.)

ii. Supervisor to subordinate and vice versa

How well do supervisors perceive subordinates' feelings, wishes, and problems? And how do employees perceive those of their supervisors? These two excerpts, one from a magazine and the other from a book, illustrate this point:

Subordinates and executives at Ford complain that Henry Ford II exercises too much control from the top. He intervenes at too many organizational levels. He bypasses too many organizational lines. With no one to answer to, Ford can be arbitrary and ruthless in his selection of men for promotions, demotions, or dismissals. It's true that the upper level G.M. executives are better protected; however, at G.M., an outstanding man can't advance as rapidly as, say, Robert McNamara. (*Fortune*, January 1967, p. 106.)

". . . One of his ablest and most loyal supporters on Capitol Hill, Senator Styles Bridges, tried to tell Eisenhower about his concern for the weakness of the national defense program. Alsop describes the president as turning crimson, then white with fury and launching into a volcanic tirade against the presumptuous persons who dared to suggest that such weaknesses existed. On this subject Eisenhower repeatedly lost his composure toward those who dared to challenge his opinion. He vented his displeasures on overtly independent and outspoken military administrators and several left the service under high pressure from the president. Many used his rigidity as an excuse to leave, to stay, or to react strongly . . . The president, however, seemed to want to stand up and be counted on this issue. But on this issue he should have sat and listened. Much of the criticism he received from the military and Congressmen for his directed verdicts concerning the defense budget only ruffled him further. Because he chose to move against these criticisms rather than with them, his successor, Kennedy, made splendid political capital out of them during the 1960 presidential election. In this instance Eisenhower seemingly failed to realize that his powers of authority and prestige were more effective when placed in the service of the administrative needs and purposes of conscientious subordinates who depended upon him for help and guidance. Not even the president can arbitrarily command without serving the needs of those commanded." (Eugene E. Jennings, *The Executive: Autocrat, Bureaucrat, Democrat,* New York, Harper & Row, 1962, pp. 67–68.)

iii. Departments to each other's needs

Often there is insensitivity and even conflict between departments within the same organization. The most common conflict occurs between sales and production departments. Such conflict usually exists in direct proportion to the pressure on each from higher management. As a result of pressure from top management, communications between departments decreases, empires are guarded, one group refuses to assist another for fear of having trouble with higher management. Conflict also occurs because of differences in values or objectives. These three case excerpts illustrate insensitivity because of the latter kind of conflict.

The local campus minister in the Wesley Foundation is involved in a highly complex situation within the Methodist Church. Although he is a member of the Methodist Conference, he feels as if he is outside the conference. He also feels he is looked upon by other Methodist ministers as being an outsider. He is subject to appointment from one year to the next like his fellow ministers, but unlike his peers, his work on the campus does not seem to count in terms of moving up through the organization. In addition, there is much conflict between the local pastors and their churches with the campus ministry and campus ministers. Some express misgivings about campus ministry since they feel that the Wesley Foundation is a rebellious group; expressly, they can't see what they are getting for the money invested in it. This feeling is especially reflected in local churches situated near Wesley Foundation.

At Dalton State Hospital the outpatient services visualize the inpatient section as reactionary, rigid, conservative, and interested only in promoting their own aspect of the hospital's functioning. The inpatient department sees the outpatient services as superficial, getting all the attention and money from the administration and the state legislature, and stealing therapy cases from the doctors of the inpatient department. Inpatient services also feels that the core of the hospital's functioning is within its domain and therefore it should be regarded as the "favorite child." The struggle over who is in control of therapy cases is intense: inpatient says that all therapy cases should be referred to them; outpatient says that they are the experts in this field. Much of this conflict is due to the failure of the medical director to establish goals adequately and to involve the respective directors in decision-making. Part of it is because of two different treatment philosophies.

There seems to be an accurate alertness by individuals to the others' needs in the various departments of St. Mary's High School. The individuals within each department apparently work well together and appear to show more loyalty to each other than was evident between different departments. Each department is primarily concerned with its own needs and problems; each is apathetic about and insensitive to the problems in other departments within the school. A great number of people cross departmental lines, and, in a sense, they are responsible to two departments. Those faculty members seemed to be more alert to the problems of both departments in which they work but not to those of other departments in the school. On the questionnaire, three-quarters of the staff reported that the relations among the staff groups are cooperative but independent of one another.

(B) FROM PHYSICAL PLANT

People in the organization receive a variety of stimuli from the physical plant. Some are more easily identifiable than others. Smoke, heat, shabbiness, dirt are within everybody's purview. Lighting, decoration, quality of machinery, statistics of equipment breakdown say something. In Part II the consultant examined the plant and described and analyzed what he observed (see Chapter 6, A2). Here he interprets the effects of what he saw and the effects of things he did not notice then but has seen since or has had reported to him. He should begin by asking: How are such things experienced by those in the organization? Here are two examples, one from a case and the other from an article. In the latter, inferences about the effect of the plant are implicit in the comments quoted.

The personnel of the Dalton State Hospital frequently complain that the maintenance and janitorial service in the hospital is extremely poor. This is in evidence in the upkeep of the offices, many of which have not been painted in the last ten years. In many places, both in the patient areas and in the offices, plaster is falling off both walls and ceilings. Personnel have made no attempt to add a personal touch in their offices. Many of the offices are used daily but appear to be empty, as if they had not been used for years. The condition of the physical plant apparently communicates to employees that they are not worth much, that little worthwhile is expected of them, and they apparently withdraw from work by remaining out of their offices and giving little attention to them.

. . . The Mount Anthony Union High School in Bennington, Vermont, centers on a two-story library, has lounges for students who are likely to have frequent free periods and a flexible arrangement of twenty classrooms, seven science rooms, twelve vocational shops, offices, and a gymnasium . . . The school is an architectural essay in deliberately plain, blunt materials: brick and bare concrete block, quarry tile and asbestos vinyl floors, unhidden utility pipes, rugged tables, and benches made of laminated rock maple. But modern as the building is in conception, it fits faultlessly into the New England landscape.

A visitor to the new school quickly senses its success with both the students and teachers. Dr. Arthur S. Faris, a board member says, "The biggest difference is that these kids seem to enjoy going to school today, and I never began to enjoy it until I went to college. It is a kicky environment. The kids say, 'Here we belong.' " Says Elizabeth Dwyer, a local newspaperwoman, "You have the feeling that education is going on there." (*Fortune,* April 1968, pp. 144, 146.)

(2) *To stimuli from outside the organization*

(A) PRIMARY EXTERNAL STIMULI

Most factors which are basic to the organization's survival — where and how it buys and sells, what its labor sources are going to be, how markets are going to change, and so on — are conceived to be primary external stimuli. Some reference has been made to these earlier. Here the consultant must infer. How alert is the organization to the implications of these factors and the trends, pressures, and data which relate to them? The consultant must make judgments about the organization's response to nuances, its alertness to and accuracy and differentiation of subtle external stimuli.

i. Marketing conditions

The consultant will need some knowledge about the markets for the particular organization in order to judge its degree of alertness, accuracy, and vividness with respect to them. He can obtain such information from trade journals, from annual reviews in such publications as *Forbes* and *Fortune,* from summaries in *Business Week.* Population trend data, social class data, insurance data, and similar information will yield the same basis for judgment with respect to schools, churches, and hospitals. The first example, drawn from a magazine, shows alertness and effective response for marketing conditions. The second and third of these examples show that the same conceptions may be applied to both business and non-profit organizations.

Stouffer Foods Corporation, the coast-to-coast restaurant chain noted for Victorian decor, modest sized drinks, matronly clientele, and waitresses in puritan dresses . . . realized it had been appealing almost entirely to a market shrinking in numbers: those 40 years old and over. So it had begun a reach for the 21–40 crowd — where the action is, as well as a lot of today's money . . . There's a clutch of new Stouffer restaurants where waitresses wear miniskirts and lace garters, the drinks are oversized, and the whole place rocks with a contrived frenzy of group singing, and hot dancing. (*Business Week,* February 4, 1967, p. 63.)

In the Ionian Order, the House of Studies ought to be sensitive to the needs of the parish, the high school, and the ministry of Newman Clubs and college teaching. While there has been more alertness to these needs during the past few years, it is still not very great. The regent of the House of Studies stated that there was little communication between faculty and those in the active apostolate. Little attention is paid to external stimuli except to those which feed into their concern with the internal stimuli. The members of the order are overly sensitive to criticism and had a negative attitude about this part of their work.

. . . The American Cancer Society and others concerned about the [cigarette] problem are not abandoning their educational campaigns or their lobbying for legislation — for example, to limit cigarette advertising. But they are also taking a different, and some think more practical, approach. Since most people apparently aren't going to give up cigarettes, the idea now is to try to provide them with the next best thing — a cigarette that won't do as much damage. "The choice of 'Smoke ten cigarettes and live, or smoke twenty and die' didn't appeal to people" . . . "So, now we're [the National Cancer Institute] saying 'Smoke as many cigarettes as you want and we will take out everything that's bad for you and leave everything that's good for you.' " (*Fortune,* November 1967, p. 147.)

ii. Purchasing conditions

The ease or difficulty of buying supplies, obtaining raw materials or components will also affect an organization's chances for long-run survival. These two examples, one from a case study, reflect accurate alertness to purchasing conditions — both the availability and unavailability of supplies — and active adaptive efforts on the parts of the respective organizations.

Serious fluctuations in the cocoa market have forced the Hershey Foods Corp. to expand into other fields. With purchases of some 100,000 tons a year, Hershey is the largest U.S. buyer of cocoa; and in Ghana, the principal provider, supplies have pushed prices up 200 per cent in two years, to 30 cents a pound. To combat such price rises and increased wages for its employees, Hershey has already chopped one-eighth of an ounce off its popular 5 cent bars. Since 1966 the company has acquired two macaroni firms, a French Canadian banking company, and the Cory Corp. of Chicago, which makes coffee brewers, appliances, pens, and automatic pencils. Noncandy operations will soon account for 35 per cent of Hershey sales. (*Time,* February 9, 1968, pp. 90–92.)

The Trinity Lutheran Hospital laboratory sports a new 12-channel automatic blood analyzer, a marvelous machine of plastic tubes and dials and vials that can test just a few drops of blood from each of 30 patients for a dozen abnormalties — all in two minutes. And it's cheaper for the patient, too. Machine-run analysis costs $15 compared with $65 when the tests are done by technicians. The analyzer will enable the hospital to soon train its American Medical Association approved quota of ten medical technologists a year. In addition, a new heart-lung machine has also been recently purchased as part of an expanded cardiac surgery program, along with some new monitoring equipment for the expanded intensive care unit. Trinity's board does not quibble about buying equipment as contrasted with City Hospital, which is always fighting its budget ceilings.

iii. Labor conditions

Here the consultant should be concerned with the organization's sensitivity to the supply of potential employees, their preparation and training, their willingness to be employed, and the conditions under which they find employment acceptable. Two article excerpts illustrate different degrees of such sensitivity:

[The Cadillac] is tooled, fitted, and inspected by hands who have an exceptionally high average of experience on the job. The Cadillac's stability of employment is outstanding. Not once since World War II has there been a layoff for reasons of slack sales; and of the 10,400 Detroit employees, more than 1,500 have been on the job for 25 years or more. Former general manager Howard Warner says, "This continuity of its people is the most important asset — the one real competitive advantage — that Cadillac has. I could hand over a complete set of blueprints to any good competitor you might select, but they couldn't build a Cadillac." (*Fortune,* April 1968, p. 162.)

The increasing difficulty of attracting and retaining assistant professors and instructors is probably the most disruptive faculty problem which Harvard University administrators face, but that does not necessarily mean that it is the faculty problem that bothers them the most. The real blow to institutional pride is the rejection of tenured positions at Harvard by a sizable number of senior scholars. In a recent three-year period, nine out of forty people refused a formal offer of a tenured position at Harvard; this figure does not include the large number of informal soundings and refusals which have occurred. In some departments, such as biology and history, there have been a sizable number of refusals. A particularly galling point was mentioned by another scholar who said that professors in the social sciences and humanities at nearby MIT had turned down tenured Harvard positions, even though such a change would not have required a move in place of residence. Why the problem? There are more distinguished universities in the country than there were a few decades ago. In teaching at Harvard, a professor becomes just another distinguished scholar in his department. Harvard is not a place that breeds heroes. Salary is another factor. At Harvard salaries do not range widely within a given rank and seniority. The top salary is $28,000 annually: there are few men at Harvard who are earning more than $25,000. Another factor which diminishes the attraction of Harvard is a teaching load which is considered "heavy" by top professors at several universities. Harvard has the temerity to ask its professors to teach undergraduates, which offends some scholars. Some professors, especially scientists, complain about inadequate physical facilities. Another quibble made by faculty members is that Harvard is "stingy" with fringe benefits and supplemental aids, such as secretarial services, stamps, and even paper. Professors' children do not receive any tuition rebate at Harvard or at any other institution, unlike the children of faculty members at many universities. Except in a few isolated cases, Harvard has no university-owned faculty housing. Thus, economic necessity forces many faculty members to reside in Belmont and other suburbs to the west. The professor then becomes a 9-to-5 commuter, an especially upleasant prospect during the snowy Massachusetts winter. (*Science,* May 19, 1967, pp. 922–925.)

(B) SECONDARY EXTERNAL STIMULI

Here the consultant should ask: What are the organization's perception of other environmental factors that influence it but do not immediately and directly affect its survival? Often organizations react to secondary external stimuli as if they were primary. For example some businessmen spend much time and effort fighting the "communist menace." The consultant will want to interpret such a misinterpretation.

i. Legislative (tariff and tax laws)

How alert is the organization to what Congress, the state legislature, the city council, and various other regulatory bodies are doing? Some organizations exist by means of government protection — tariff, subsidy, or facilities. The rates others may charge are regulated. The operational standards of still others may be regulated by half a dozen different bodies. Some maintain powerful lobbies; some public utilities maintain continuous suits before regulatory bodies which enable them to adjust their rates at will "pending the outcome of the decision." Some pay minimal attention to government. Others are highly sensitive to advantages given to competitive businesses by means of governmental regulation, as, for example, savings and loan associations versus banks. The first of the following three examples indicates a keen sensitivity to potential government reaction; the second, a variable alertness; and the third, an aggressive stance toward manipulating governmental processes to serve an organization's own ends.

While Parke, Davis & Co. has aggressively promoted its product, Chloromycetin — a potent and valuable antibiotic that also has serious and fatal side effects — it has had to yield to demands from the Food and Drug Administration to temper its advertising with warnings. In a current ad, with one page of type, less than a quarter is devoted to recommending the drug, more than three-quarters to warnings about how not to use it. With every package goes a leaflet carrying the same warnings. They are reprinted in the manual that doctors keep on their desks. In addition, Parke, Davis representatives urge doctors to report any adverse reactions in patients taking Chloromycetin. Parke, Davis will not let itself knowingly get into difficulty with the FDA.

The principal of St. Katherine's High School tries to keep abreast of federal laws regarding aid to education, especially laws pertaining to parochial schools. He attempts to obtain supplementary funds or introduces new courses using whatever governmental aid is available. On some occasions, however, he has not taken full advantage of federal projects. However, he gets very much involved in such legislative issues as bussing parochial school students. He ignores more basic considerations, like the necessity of keeping up with the academic standards of the state's Department of Education.

Each year in Congress bills are written, and committee hearings are held, but . . . the National Rifle Association alerts its members and friends to man the barricades against any [gun legislation] proposals strong enough to be effective. The barrage of letters that the NRA can call down at short notice is probably unmatched by any other lobbying group. Since the 1930's, when Congress passed two bills — one aimed at eliminating the sawed-off shotguns and machine guns favored by gangsters of that era and the other an ineffectual dealer-registration law — no bill dealing with the regulation of guns has reached the floor of Congress. The NRA's record is particularly impressive considering that it was compiled over a period that saw the assassination of one president, an attempt on the life of another, and the shooting up of the House of Representatives by fanatical Puerto Rican nationalists in 1954. (*Life*, May 10, 1968, p. 4.)

ii. Transportation

Changes in transportation facilities, networks, schedules, and modes affect the use of all kinds of institutions and organizations. Some are alert to the implications of such changes, while others are oblivious until long after they occur, as this magazine excerpt and the following two case examples illustrate.

The automobile brought mass production and the $5-a-day wage to the United States. It ended rural isolation, gave a mighty impetus to the development of consumer credit. It also gave the working man something to do on his day off; the Sunday family automobile ride became the ancestor of today's traffic jam. The auto's detractors said it never would become a mass item: too few people could afford them. Besides, outside of the cities there weren't enough suitable roads over which they could travel. But the automobile carried its own logic. It got the roads built and helped expand the very purchasing power on which its own growth depended. The auto ended the railroad industry's virtual transportation monopoly. It was one of those great paradoxes that while investors were excited about what are now called "science" stock — radio, electrical equipment, aircraft — they failed to understand what the rise of one industry could do to other industries. Coalmen failed to understand that what was good for oil would be bad for coal. Investors failed to see that the railroads were going to be eclipsed by autos, trucks, and highways. The automobile also hurt the mail order business. The farmer could get into town easily to do his own shopping. *(Forbes,* September 15, 1967, p. 110.)

The Benevolent Order of the Wise Owl provided hospitalization for its members at the order's hospital in Denver. The promise of hospitalization helped the organization sell memberships. However, the order rarely had to redeem its hospitalization promises because people would not travel long distances for hospital care. When air transportation made quick trips possible, more members demanded their due. The hospital could not economically meet the demands. The order sold its hospital and provided insurance policies for members so they could get treatment closer to their homes. Not having anticipated this eventuality, though, the order was unprepared for it, lost members, and now is only a shadow of its former million-member self.

Oakland Methodist's parishioners scattered all over town as they became more affluent. The younger ones have affiliated themselves with newer churches closer to their homes. The older ones regularly drove back to the Oakland church to retain their old ties. Many took the bus. But the older ones drive less frequently now, and the bus no longer goes by the church's door. It did not see these changes coming; its congregation is now limited to those in Oakland who live within a few blocks of the church.

iii. Competitors

Does the organization maintain an awareness of what is happening in the rest of its industry or field? How does it understand what its competitors are doing? The issue of competition is just as important for churches, schools, hospitals, and other institutions as it is for businesses, since each competes for constituency, endowment, resources, staff, and so on. The following examples, one from a magazine article and the other from a case, contrast the difference between what would be interpreted to be a vivid and therefore important perception and an accurate one which does not move the perceiving organization.

The Italian tourist industry . . . does not want to go the way of France, Europe's one-time Queen of Tourism, now suffering a case of unbooked hotel space. Rudely awakened to the realities of competition in 1963 . . . Italian tourism officials first coaxed 35,000 of the nation's most important restaurants . . . into adopting fixed-price "tourist menus" and "all inclusive" hotel prices. At the same time, the government is promoting investments, in new hotels in the less crowded areas of the country such as Sardinia, Sicily, and the Gargano promontory . . . [They are] trying to overcome the communication problem by stepping up construction of big, new car ferries, such as the Canguro Rosso (Red Kangaroo) between the mainland and Sardinia, and encouraging "package holidays" and charter flights.

Three new highways have also been built: one down the Adriatic coast from Bologna to Bari; another over the Appennines between Naples and Bari; and the third down the Tyrrhenian coast from Salerno to the wild hills above Reggio Calabria. Hopefully, they will lure tourists . . . from the overcrowded resort centers of the north to the 1,000 miles of almost empty shoreline along the southern end of the Italian boot . . .

Officials have also embarked on a multipronged drive to make the crowded cities more pleasant for the travelers . . . This includes . . . measures to control and ensure clearer marking of prices in shops and restaurants, elimination of excessive noise, and a restriction on the activities of particularly bold "Latin lovers." . . . Italy has [also] joined with its new Adriatic competitors, Yugoslavia and Greece, in building up car ferry service between the two coasts.

The efforts are paying off. More than 25 million tourists swarmed into Italy . . . [in 1967], pumping a record sum into the Italian economy and helping it to maintain its prized position as the world's leading earner of the tourist dollars. (*Dun's Review*, May 1967, pp. 70–72.)

There are two main hospitals in Lawrence, Riverside General and St. Patrick's. The former solicits maternity cases through information supplied by the various practicing obstetricians in town. Upon learning of the pregnancy of some woman, Riverside General immediately sends her a questionnaire asking admission information. The hospital implies that the administering doctor has recommended Riverside General when in fact he has not. St. Patrick's realizes what Riverside General is doing, but feels that such "advertising" is beneath the dignity of a professional institution.

iv. Research developments

Some organizations are alert to what is being accomplished in universities and are aware of current financial trends. Others are not so attuned.

Some organizations do not use the fruits of their research, preferring to get patents on the discoveries and inventions of their laboratories solely to prohibit others from also discovering and using the ideas. Some relate their research to current research trends; other seem unaware of them. Some churches revise their authorized translations of the Bible in keeping with contemporary archeological findings; for others it is as if such findings did not exist. Many university psychology departments wish away psychoanalytic findings because the faculties are unsophisticated in the area and so many of the data are unmeasurable. It is important that the consultant learn his company's attitudes in this area. These two excerpts, one from a magazine and the other from a case, illustrate two extremes of alertness.

. . . The strategy that brought E. I. du Pont de Nemours & Co. to greatness was simple and brilliant. It enthroned scientific research and skillfully converted scientific discovery into highly salable new products and innovations, protected by patents that gave it "proprietary" positions in new markets long enough to ensure a return in its investment far superior to that enjoyed by less creative companies. Despite the colossal sums du Pont laid out for research and development, it managed, even while its investment was growing at a rate of more than 8 per cent a year, to generate all its capital out of cash flow. (*Fortune,* November 1967, p. 136.)

Dalton State Hospital actively supported and encouraged both pharmaceutical and social psychological research in its own wards. A major study demonstrated important innovations in ward care. However, the experimental ward was returned to its former status and nowhere in the institution are the innovations being employed. The findings are not rejected; in the eyes of the staff they seem not to exist. The hospital is relatively insensitive to recent research developments elsewhere. In fact, it is at last ten years behind in putting research developments into operation. The hospital does not keep up with current trends in the field of psychiatry. Dalton operates on a pragmatic basis with emphasis on patient oriented programs. The section chiefs and residents at the hospital are too busy working with those problems to investigate what is happening elsewhere. Within the organization, no articles are being written since the emphasis is on "good" case histories rather than aggressive, innovative research. The hospital is suffering from a lack of leadership in the research department.

v. Economic, social, and political trends

The United States is moving toward an increasingly middle-class, affluent, highly educated society where the unit of government will be the megalopolis. This means that its people are more sophisticated, want greater choice of product and service and want to be more fully informed about it. These are only a few gross social trends. There are many others. The consultant should determine to what extent the organization is aware of them and with what clarity. At the same time, the consultant should be aware that occurrences and trends in countries around the world can affect an organization. This is, naturally, especially important in organizations that operate in foreign countries. In the first examples from a published source, hotel keepers seem unalert to national trends while the school in the second is already responding to its perception of national currents:

Miami Beach innkeepers, who have been losing winter visitors to Puerto Rico, St. Croix, and other Caribbean isles, are facing fresh competition right in their own backyards. An increasing number of more affluent sunseekers along Florida's Gold Coast are abandoning glamorous hotels to lease space in one of a score or more posh high-rise apartment buildings that have leaped skyward in recent years. For about the same amount of money that it costs for a lengthy winter vacation at a leading resort hotel, guests can rent an apartment year-round that is fully as splendid. Herbert Robins, managing director of the Carillon, and president of the Southern Florida Hotel & Motel Association, estimates that the big ocean-front hotels have lost about 7½ per cent of their former room occupancy so far. (*Business Week,* October 14, 1967, p. 169.)

Today the 770 Mills College students are broadly drawn from 45 states and 24 countries. No longer interested in a protective, genteel education, the Mills girls plunge eagerly into such unsheltered activities as tutoring Negro youngsters in Oakland, and studying city government by taking part-time municipal jobs. [Mills teaching has shifted accordingly.] (*Time,* Oct. 27, 1967, p. 61.)

In these two published examples, neither company apparently was able to discern and anticipate political trends which had significant impact on its international market.

Part of Marathon's troubles . . . lies in the struggle going on within the company between an internationalist faction that wants to see it cover the bets in Europe, and another U.S. oriented group that wants to see more black ink in European operations. The new U.S. restrictions on dollar investments abroad apparently tipped the scales in favor of the U.S. oriented group. Marathon only recently decided to sell its German service stations, for example. Some of the stations were completed only in the last few months. (*Business Week,* March 16, 1968, p. 37.)

Green Giant Co., which built a $1.8 million food processing plant in Pozzaglio, Italy in 1963, is looking for a quick buyer for the plant after four years of losses. Green Giant can blame France's General Charles de Gaulle for its misfortune. It built the Pozzaglio plant to can corn for the British market in the expectation that Britain would soon join the Common Market. When de Gaulle rejected Britain's bid, Green Giant found it couldn't possibly clear the tariff hurdle into Britain from Italy. Nor could it sell canned corn on the Continent; most Europeans regard corn as animal fodder. It switched over to canning peas and beans, but these are low profit lines, and Green Giant couldn't get the volume to move into the black. (*Business Week,* February 24, 1968, p. 64.)

b. Direction and span of attention (selectivity)

Here the consultant should learn what, of all of the perceptions an organization has, it concentrates its attention on and how wide its focus is. To what stimuli does it give exquisite attention; in what direction is its organizational radar turned?

(1) *Dominant foci of interest*

(A) LONG-TERM FRAMEWORK

All organizations concentrate selectively year in, year out on some aspects of their environment. In some organizations this is formalized in the form of "organizational planners" or "consultants in long-range planning." These organizations typically evolve statistical trends, projected years into the future. Other organizations may not plan formally in this same sense, but because of the training and experience of the leadership, continuously concentrate on those issues that are important to that leadership. What are those foci in the consultants organization?

Two examples from published sources and a case excerpt illustrate three different foci.

Mobil has concentrated abroad on its marketing efforts in the highly industrialized countries of Western Europe, as well as Japan and Australia. The trouble is that the company's long-range plans in these areas, particularly in Western Europe, have been predicated on the idea that petroleum prices would remain stable. But European prices have eroded as more and more Libyan crude [oil] pours into the area, and the internationals have been forced to cut prices to prevent independents from gaining a larger share of the market. (*Fortune,* September 1967, p. 88.)

In December 1967, Yale announced a fund-raising drive of $338 million, the largest goal ever set by an American university. The campaign's significance lies not so much in its staggering target as in its time span, ten years. Nearly a decade ago, Yale's rival, Harvard, upset the conventional wisdom of university fundraisers by seeking and getting $82.5 million; up to that time no university had ever dared seek so much. The pattern established by Harvard was that of a mammoth, single, capital campaign of limited duration, usually 2 or 3 years — donors could be asked to give generously on the presumption that the drive was a unique event. The Yale announcement now explicitly says that this approach will not suffice; the gigantic fund-raising campaign is becoming permanent. (*Science,* December 29, 1967, p. 1658.)

The dominant foci of interest at Narragansett State Hospital are appropriations from the state government and concern with what the Burnside University Department of Psychiatry is doing. The hospital is most insensitive to the expectations of the legislature or the governing bodies or the community at large. For example, the legislative bodies and the community feel that the hospital should be offering short-term treatment to more children. However, the hospital refuses to hear this since it is preoccupied with the goal of long-term, intensive treatment of a few children. The hospital feels that if they had more funds to work with, they then could offer more services to more children. At the present time, the hospital has no long-range dominant focus of interest. In addition, there is no unified direction or focus, either. One reason for this condition is that Narragansett is moving in too many directions at one time and with varying amounts of energy to the point that the organization has no idea where it is going or how it is getting there.

(B) SHORT-TERM FRAMEWORK

Short-term framework may refer to those matters with which an organization concerns itself that are likely to be relevant within the next year or two. It may refer to the fact that the organization focuses only on short-term issues. An article and two case excerpts illustrate:

In seeking to reduce costs, [Dr. Austin Smith, chairman and chief executive officer of Parke, Davis & Co.,] has reached into the most remote corners of the company. Example: The company normally consumes about 1 million eggs a week in which to grow vaccines. Until now, the labs threw away the unused parts of the eggs. Now it peddles the yolks to mink breeders, and [it] is thinking of selling the shells as a source of lime for plant food. More significantly, hundreds of employees have been laid off, and research funds have been rechanneled into projects that are closest to producing marketable products . . . More basic research and less promising development projects are being put on the back burner . . . The stress will be on drugs near the "top of the ladder and on getting them over the top."

Parke, Davis' great need is for important new drugs that command fat profit margins. (The company has introduced only two new drugs over the past 5 years, considerably fewer than its main competitors.) One reason it hasn't had them in recent years may have been its overconcentration on research in areas such as cancer and heart disease where the odds of coming up with an immediately marketable product are toughest. Partly because of such emphasis, research more likely to yield a marketable drug was underplayed. The company spent no more than 7 per cent of sales on research and development while others were spending up to 10 per cent. (*Business Week,* March 2, 1968, p. 48.)

At Dalton State Hospital one segment of the staff would become enthusiastic about a special project using one theoretical approach. This approach would then be idealized as being the one way of reaching the organization's imagined goals. The unit would then maintain its excitement by walling itself off from the rest of the hospital onto which it would project feelings of worthlessness and inadequacy. The rest of the hospital became so angry at this treatment that they were not able to accept any information or findings that the special unit made available to them. Eventually, the special units would run into trouble because their goals were not congruent with those of the organization as a whole, even though the organization had no goal other than to do the best work possible. Therefore, the special projects would end abruptly with disappointment, discouragement, and anger.

In 1962 a new Presbyterian church was proposed as a mission of the First United Presbyterian Church. One of the elders in the Presbyterian Church was in the process of developing an area called Buena Vista; he offered property for the new church within the area. The new church moved into the area even though there already was a large Presbyterian church eight blocks from the site selected. It also did not find out from the city planners whether or not a full development — houses, schools, utility lines, sewers, roads — was to be built immediately. Now that the Buena Vista Presbyterian Church has been built, it finds the competition with the neighboring larger and well established Presbyterian church frightening; it is upset that projected housing developments have not materialized and are unlikely to unless new industry comes to the community. The Buena Vista Presbyterian Church was focusing only on the immediate issue of building a physical plant. It should have projected itself into the near future as well as concentrating on the here and now.

(2) Significant neglected foci

Having abstracted and interpreted to what the organization pays attention, now the consultant must make a judgment about those matters that seem to him relevant or that appear to be relevant in the eyes of others to which the organization is not attuned. Those things that an organization does not heed — if they are relevant to its survival — will ultimately be the source of its downfall. If an organization cannot recognize relevant stimuli, this suggests impairment or pathology in organizational functioning which must be further investigated. Two case excerpts and one from a magazine illustrate neglected foci.

Burnside University has mounted an aggressive campaign to get black students. The campaign is floundering because Burnside neglects to consider social realities, as reflected in this excerpt:

Over half of all college-bound Negroes now choose Negro colleges over Northern white colleges. There are two main reasons why this is likely to continue. One is economic — costs at Negro colleges are low, roughly half that of the national average. The other is cultural. There is a loneliness among Negroes who find themselves isolated in an overwhelmingly white college community. The Negro college is a social center and marrying place, as well as an occupational training center. And it will continue to reflect, in its racial character, the existence of a separate Negro community in the United States. (*Harper's,* May 1966, pp. 77–78.)

At the Great Lakes Insurance Company, there was only one allusion to the impact of automation on the industry and on the organization in general. Automated data processing was a neglected focus. It would seem to have great import from two viewpoints: (1) since many functions of the insurance company are clerical in nature, they could easily be mechanized; (2) the president of the organization prides himself on being knowledgeable about all aspects of the organization. However, neither has he the technical background for data processing nor does he avail himself of information in this area or even hire people who are knowledgeable in the data processing field.

The Buena Vista Presbyterian Church is totally unattentive to what is happening within the community in which the church is located. The primary focus of the church is internal. This is evidenced by the fact that some of the most difficult questions for those interviewed were: "What does the Buena Vista Church say it stands for?" and "What outside groups are paid attention to?" There was almost total inability to deal with these questions. Nor did the church seem to be conscious of what information it needs from the external world to provide for a more adequate program of evangelism and missionary work. The church must learn to master its environment by solving problems that have roots outside the congregation. The church must assess external reality. The church is unaware of whether or not there are growth factors in the community of which they should be aware or which they could influence by putting pressure in the proper places, such as the planning board.

c. Assessment of the discrepancy between reality and perceived reality

The consultant must now assess the organizational perceptions he has documented. Is there a difference between reality as the organization perceives it and as the consultant (or informants) sees it? An organization may be accurate in its perception of some stimuli but be incorrect in its interpretations of them. Sometimes an organization believes itself to be inept in a certain area; with new leadership, it may rise to unforeseen heights. The converse is also true. Sometimes an organization precipitates its own difficulties and then must live with self-fulfilling prophecies.

(1) *Of reality within the organization*

If an organization has trouble understanding itself, the consultant will know that he must subsequently use subtle therapeutic or quasi-therapeutic methods. Such will be necessary when the disparity between what goes on in the organization and what it perceives protrudes in bold relief to the consultant. The following examples drawn from a magazine article, a case, and a book, respectively, illustrate how organizations fail to perceive or how they inaccurately perceive their own internal realities.

First among a corporation's intangible assets is its sense of self — the knowledge, securely coiled away somewhere in the recesses of the corporate mind, of what the company is and where it is going. In the past, Ing. C. Olivetti & Co. was exceptionally strong in this respect: Olivetti always knew what it was. The company for years has led the world in its production of a wide range of office machines . . . Its great factories in northern Italy are complemented by plants in nine other countries; its network of distributors and agents sell Olivetti machines in more than a hundred nations . . . Olivetti's understanding of and belief in its own concepts powered the company to its present eminence. Its originality, shown mostly by its leadership in design, won worldwide celebrity. Purpose, creativity, imagination . . . were Olivetti's greatest products . . . It is just this invaluable, ineffable, and unassailable essence that is now in jeopardy. Three years ago a coalition of new owners bought into Olivetti, and by so doing probably saved the company from going under. But that coalition has yet to find a management capable of eliciting from the corporate entity the sustaining spirit, the sense of loyalty, and purpose that used to make up Olivetti's most durable strength. (*Fortune,* July 1967, p. 93.)

Within the Ionian Order the Superiors are usually aware of personality conflicts and conflicts of interest within their community. Their solution, however, tends to be to remove one or the other of the parties in conflict or to advise the use of spiritual values to avoid the conflict. It also seems that subjects are perceptive of the desires of their Superiors since so much of the style of management is dependent upon the Superior's personality, likes, and dislikes. They are less aware of the subject's difficulties. Since it is difficult to meet various needs, the provincial's office usually does not perceive the needs or denies their validity. Nor do the various groups or departments know much about other groups or departments. Not much attention is paid to the work they are doing, its significance for the province as a whole, or their particular needs.

According to the Fairfax Heights police department manual, the work of the police department consists of preservation of the public peace and order, the apprehension of offenders, the protection of persons and property under the laws of the state, and the enforcement of the ordinances of Fairfax Heights. However, whenever individual members of the force were questioned, the range of perceived goals was different. Although the preservation of peace and the protection of life and property were regarded as important, the men on the force emphasized patroling, law enforcement, and traffic control as the most vital organizationals goals. (Robert L. Peabody, *Organizational Authority*, New York, Atherton Press, 1964.)

(2) *Of reality outside the organization*

If an organization can perceive accurately what is going on inside itself, the most difficult kind of perception, but cannot see clearly what is happening outside, presumably the consultant can improve the situation by cognitive educational methods. Sometimes distortion of external reality is a matter of the personality orientation of the leader, as for example when Sewell Avery led Montgomery Ward in the post World War II years as if a depression was imminent, or Henry Ford in his later years failing to accept the reality of union organization; often it may be a matter of simply not having sufficient education, broad enough perspective, or specialized knowledge to gauge the situation. Whatever the case, the consultant will have to make a statement about his understanding of this issue.

If he finds an organization that has difficulties in perception both within and without, the consultant will have to raise serious questions about the kinds and quality of the assets available to the organization for its rejuvenation. Some problems cannot be solved, particularly if the same people remain in the organization. The following published examples and case illustration show how the perception of external reality may be inadequate for the judgments which must be made.

While Stuart T. Saunders, newly appointed chairman of the Pennsylvania New York Central Transportation Co., was maneuvering so skillfully toward merger of the two railroads, an unexpected problem arose: the New York Central began making noises about backing out of the deal. Elated by rising profits in 1966, New York Central's president, Alfred E. Perlman, announced that the Central appeared to be "recession-proof" and might not have to merge in order to prosper. Saunders paid calls on Central directors, and pointed out that their line, unlike the Pennsy, was not widely diversified; he warned that a dip in the general economy would cause the Central painful headaches . . . [The 1967] mini-recession proved Saunders right. While Pennsy earnings held up better

. . . Central's income for the nine months figured so far showed a $2,640,000 deficit. Suddenly the Central's merger enthusiasm revived. (*Time,* January 26, 1968, p. 71A.)

Sprawled across the east bank of Virginia's James River, the shipyard of Newport News Shipbuilding & Dry Dock Co., is bustling . . . For Newport News — the nation's biggest shipbuilder and one of the industry's few consistent money-makers — everything seems dandy as it [Newport News] whittles away at its hefty $477 million backlog. But to a large extent, the hustle and bustle is a facade behind which serious problems lie ahead for the company. There is a ferment in the industry that is undermining the way Newport News normally does business and is threatening the company's prolonged leadership in the industry. For one thing, aerospace companies are invading the business. They are attracted by the record $2.3 billion backlog of orders in shipbuilders' hands . . . [For another,] Defense Secretary Robert S. McNamara and Transportation Secretary Alan Boyd want to revamp the government's traditional relationship with the industry . . . McNamara . . . is plumping for construction of new private yards. U.S. shipyards, he charges, are "generally technically obsolescent compared to those of northern Europe and Japan." McNamara scoffs at shipbuilders' arguments that higher U.S. labor costs account for a cost difference of some 50 per cent and contends that other domestic industries can hold their own against foreign competition . . . Donald A. Holden [Newport News' president] is not turning his back on the new competition . . . Indeed he is joining with missile and electronics companies . . . Holden, though, has put limits on how broadly Newport News should branch out. "We should look first in the direction of activities that we know something about . . . as opposed to the conglomerate approach that is purely financial diversification." (*Business Week,* October 7, 1967, pp. 178, 179, 180, 186.)

Throughout the Lutheran American Merged Evangelical Church synod there is general agreement that the future of the church lies in the cities. Merger seems to be the only viable, concrete hope for many rural churches, particularly because the population within the state in which the synod functions has been rapidly declining during the past decade. Therefore, the synod emphasizes starting new churches in the cities and expanding those that are already there. However, the synod fails to understand the impact of the ecumenical movement and the trend to church mergers in the cities which may soon make its new churches superfluous.

2. Organizational knowledge

In Chapter 6 we spoke about organizational communications channels, modes, sources, and targets. In the preceding discussion of perceptions we were asking, in effect, what the organization's capacity for receiving stimulus input is. We then sought to make an assessment of the effectiveness of the organization's perceptions. In this section we are concerned about what the organization *knows*. What body of information does the organization possess upon which and with which it can act? Such a body of information is usually transmissable in the form of techniques, history, experience, specialized competence, research data, and project reports. How an organization acquires and makes use of knowledge is an indication of its adaptability. Here we must be careful to distinguish between that gross input called communication, which is a transmission of perceptions, and internalization, that which is organized, integrated, and anchored within the organization as one of its strengths. Perhaps an analogy might be helpful. A college student may take a wide variety of courses and achieve good grades in many. He may quickly forget what he has learned in most of his courses after he has taken the final examinations. However, he will usually remember and integrate into a systematic body what he has learned in his major courses and those which have had the greatest relevance to him. He has, then, perceived many things; indeed, he may have communicated at great length about them. However, his knowledge is the integrated crystallized residual of all those data, which he can draw on for problem-solving and adaptation. The task of the consultant at this point, then, is to interpret from the previously noted data what the organization learned and how.

a. Acquisition of knowledge

Here the consultant is concerned with how the organization learns.

(1) Methods of obtaining new knowledge

(A) RELATED TO PERSONNEL AND PLANT

How and where does the organization acquire knowledge about plant and personnel? Are there regular audits and reports that it makes use of, as contrasted with those which are made and filed? Does it have a personnel library, a personnel staff? Some personnel departments are continuously aware of what is occurring both within and without their own organizations. They maintain their own training programs into which they bring outside lecturers. They also participate in university seminars and other activities in related areas. There is usually a relationship between the size of the company and the elaborateness of its personnel department. Sometimes, however, one will find a small organization whose president recognizes the importance of personnel practices and will devote time and attention to them. If, however, the chief executive officer must be his own sales manager, he may not have the time or the interest to be a personnel manager as well. Another factor is the degree of stability of the organization. Construction companies which hire men from union hiring halls usually do not pay much attention to personnel practices.

The same methods that are used for learning about personnel considerations may also be used for learning about the plant. Supervisors; plant managers; office managers; and others who subscribe to journals, attend conferences and seminars, do considerable outside reading in their field, and who have to be sources of organizational guidance, will be far more alert to personnel and plant problems than those who do not. In addition, many equipment manufacturers have consultants who will help their customers learn the most effective ways to use their plants and equipment. Consultants are available through the American Management Association, the Small Business Administration, trade associations, and internal staff consultants in large organizations. The consultant's concern here is not merely with noting where information comes from but, more importantly, with interpreting its integration into a body of resource and practice. A published example and two case illustrations show how such knowledge is obtained:

Scientists and engineers engaged in research at Hughes Aircraft sometimes change roles in a way that is both unusual and rewarding. The company has long had a policy of translating its researchers' ideas into hardware by doing the manufacturing itself. This approach arose out of necessity when Hughes Aircraft was so far ahead in electronics that there weren't any suppliers of components in existence. Thus, in the late 1950's, Hughes Aircraft emerged for a time as the world's largest supplier of diodes. Today it is a major supplier of microwave tubes to other companies and expects to grow big in the sale of highly sophisticated integrated circuits. The men who lead theoretical investigations in such fields have the opportunity to move out of the laboratory and to run the new manufacturing operations, if they are so inclined. Once production is set firmly on course, they can return to the laboratory. (*Fortune*, April 1968, p. 176.)

In addition to its comprehensive education and training program, the Westinghouse Electric Corporation has a monthly "Meet the Author" program for its top management group. The management group first hears an hour-long presentation by the author, then has dinner during which the author's theses are discussed by small groups of executives as they eat. Each group poses a question for the author when discussion is resumed after dinner. Included among the authors are those concerned with both specific aspects of business, like personnel, finance, economics, emotional stress, as well as those who are more general in their view. The program helps to insure that the top management is aware of trends, issues, problems, and concepts which either are or will become part of what their subordinates are learning in more structured courses. It helps, further, to insure that the top management group has had an opportunity to talk about those topics together and thereby to enhance consideration and integration.

Members of the administrative staff of The Menninger Foundation attend meetings of hospital associations, personnel associations, housekeeping groups, controller's groups, and so on. They report their findings to a weekly administrative staff meeting. To these they add reports of their frequent visits to other institutions and the reports of consultants. However, these data are communicated to respective members of the professional staff *when* there are problems to be solved, ranging from planning a new building to salary schedules. Thus integration may occur long after the original data have been gathered, and then only on a limited basis.

(B) RELATED TO PRODUCTS, SERVICES, OR COMPETITORS

There are various ways of gathering information about products, services, and competitors. Some stores hire shoppers who compare competitors' prices. Others buy competitors' products and test them in their own laboratories. Some invent, test, and evolve their own products. Some discover what customers want and prepare products accordingly. Some employ marketing services and keep a careful check on competitors. Some are heavily involved in trade and professional associations.

The two examples from published sources illustrate how one company gets continuous information from its own efforts about its own product and another failed to obtain sufficient product knowledge to stay abreast of its competition. The excerpt from a case illustrates good knowledge about the competition, leading to effective action.

Over 23,000 inspection checks are made in the course of the subassembly and final assembly of a Cadillac. [After that, random selection of completed cars] — about 2 per cent of the total — undergo an exhaustive Final Car Audit by the independent Reliability Division, and on the shipping dock outgoing cars get still another check for functional performance and appearance. Nor are the pros the only people around the place who vote on Cadillac quality. Each night, 15 selected employees — from supervisors to top executives — are assigned new production cars, which they drive home, or anywhere they wish; they bring them back in the morning with a written report of their reaction. The program is taken very seriously at Cadillac. A few years ago, for example, it was an overnight driver who complained that the windshield wiper, as it swept to the left, would leave an unwiped triangular gap at eye level that bothered his vision. As a result, Cadillac re-engineered the mechanism, which now wipes almost to the pillar. (*Fortune,* April 1968, p. 162.)

The pittance [Underwood] spent on R. and D. was inadequate to develop new products. As competitors introduced more advanced equipment, . . . [Underwood's] Elliot Fisher and Sundstrand machines gradually lost their markets while the Underwood typewriter slipped behind the better designed rivals. Adverse to taking chances on anything daringly new, Underwood turned down an opportunity to manufacture the electric typewriter that went to IBM. By the time Underwood got around to making its own creditable machine, IBM had a stranglehold on the market. (*Fortune,* September 1960, p. 141.)

In Anglia, Ohio the two most successful churches belonged to the Christian and Episcopalian denominations. Both churches operated from large, well equipped physical plants and attracted the greatest numbers of people to them. The latter had achieved tremendous success with programs for teenagers. After the new Methodist minister moved into town, he analyzed the situation and began to direct his efforts into a comparable program for teens. Within three years, the Anglia Methodist church bolstered its sagging image and moved to the forefront of the town in church attendance. Today it is far ahead of its competitor.

(c) RELATED TO FINANCIAL RESOURCES

How does an organization discover what money sources are available to it? Can it turn innovation in funding to its own advantage? Three published examples illustrate:

In 1937 Underwood's sales ($31 million) were about equal to IBM's. From then on, IBM took off and increased in sales more than thirtyfold in twenty years, while Underwood's did not even triple. A look at the contrasting policies of the two corporations helps to explain why. Whereas IBM kept plowing back its earnings into growth, Underwood paid out over the years an average of 87 per cent of its net profits in dividends. (*Fortune,* September 1960, p. 65.)

Apart from the shrewdness of its purchases, Textron has generally been rated by Wall Street as an extremely keen judge of values. In large part, say most financial analysts, this is due to Chairman Rupert C. Thompson, Jr. And Thompson himself acknowledges that his banking background has proven invaluable. "As a loan officer for many years I was long accustomed to evaluating things," he says flatly. "Not many people have had the opportunity to be educated as I was." During his eight-year reign as chief executive, Thompson put his New England background and his banker's instincts to good use in building a sound financial base for Textron. In 1961 he found the company's debt tipping the scales at a lofty $92 million, nearly 42 per cent of its total capitalization. By 1967 it had been shrunk to $67 million, almost a pittance compared with Textron's $368 million of equity. Textron's debt-equity ratio thus stands in sharp contrast to the 70 per cent of Ling-Temco-Vought. Clearly, the company has "substantial unused borrowing power available to support future growth." In addition, Thompson has kept Textron from plunging deeply into stock dilution in the manner so common today. Its dilution factor is less than 2 per cent, a rarity among acquiring companies. Avnet, by contrast, faces a 30 per cent dilution of earnings when all its preferred stock becomes converted to common; Gulf & Western, 23 per cent; Bangor Punta, a dangerous 39 per cent; and Teledyne, 19 per cent. (*Dun's Review*, May 1968, pp. 21–24ff.)

While most Protestant denominations make it a standard practice to issue yearly statements of their financial assets, the Roman Catholic Church has not — a fact that had led to endless, and largely bootless, speculations about what it really does own. Now, the Most Rev. Robert E. Tracy of Baton Rouge has lifted the greenback curtain slightly by publishing the first detailed financial statement ever issued by a U.S. Roman Catholic diocese. The picture was impressive. Although one of the nation's smaller sees (membership: 491,434), Baton Rouge has boosted its net assets an average of $3.4 million a year since 1962, largely as the result of parish-based tithing programs and a successful diocesan development fund. Overall, Baton Rouge's assets total $44.2 million, of which $38.4 million consists of buildings and real estate. The diocesan debt is a modest $3.4 million, which is being retired at the rate of 11 per cent a year. (*Time*, September 22, 1967, p. 85.)

(D) RELATED TO FORCES AND TRENDS AFFECTING THE ORGANIZATION

Earlier the consultant was concerned with the various political, economic, and social forces that affect the organization. Here he is concerned about how this organization *learns* the various external political, social, and economic *trends* that might affect it, as contrasted with *learning about* them. Some organizations are constantly alert to government commissions of a tentative and exploratory nature, anticipating that in time they may become firmly established parts of government. Others "tap into" regulatory bodies to keep a constant check on changes. Some organizations extract their information from the newspapers. Others assign one man to the job of watching the state legislature. Some companies keep statistics about new housing developments, new light and water meter installations. Still others send their executives to monthly chamber of commerce luncheons. Others make it a practice to have their executives play golf regularly with selected people. Some subscribe to economic reports, labor relations reports, and similar services.

In these two examples there is a striking contrast between how one organization obtains knowledge about forces and trends affecting it while another fails to turn information into knowledge.

The *Washington Post* reporters, thanks to a generous travel budget, wing around the country to keep provincial Washington up-to-date . . . [Ben Nardlee, *Newsweek*'s Washington bureau chief,] is building the *Post*'s corps of foreign correspondents . . . Also he is adding some high powered specialists: Wolf von Eckhart . . . on city planning . . . George Wilson . . . [on] defense reporting; Hobart Rowen . . . on markets and finance . . . The *Post* has become a sort of Montparnasse for ambitious journalists, and there is a long waiting line [of applicants]. (*Business Week,* May 27, 1967, p. 164.)

Last year [1966] the average daily cost for hospital patients jumped 16.5 per cent, after years of rising at a comparatively slow annual rate of 6 per cent. The hospitals' total yearly expenses have risen dramatically, including the salaries of nurses, residents, interns, and nonprofessional workers. [Also,] a decade ago, hospitals employed about three workers for every two patients. Today they need at least two staff members per patient . . . Medicare has sent about 4 million more over-65 Americans to the hospitals, further burdening already overcrowded wards.

Population growth has also added another 3 per cent to the normal demand for beds. The electronic revolution, with its expensive computers and laboratory, diagnostic and treatment devices, have added to the burden of the spiraling hospital costs. (*Business Week,* July 15, 1967, p. 128.)

All this might just as well not be the case as far as St. Patrick's Hospital is concerned. The staff reads about the current hospital situation in journals and newspapers, but the information seems to go in one ear and out the other. The staff does not organize what it leases into considerations for advance planning. It does not seek to anticipate, understand and act on trend. Rather, it waits for external pressures to compel the hospital to do something about acute crisis.

(E) BY WHOM (SOURCES WITHIN AND OUTSIDE THE ORGANIZATION)

Here the consultant must determine who acquires the knowledge about the four items just delineated: personnel and plant; products, services, or competitors; financial resources; forces and trends affecting the organization. Is it done by individual specialists who then communicate it to others? Is it done by outside consultants who report regularly or on assignment? Does the organization attempt to utilize what its people at the operations level have learned about the most effective ways to do their tasks? These two case excerpts illustrate:

In Ajax Pharmaceutical the financial vice president works closely with the president on financial matters, and these in turn are discussed weekly with the operating committee. The president and financial vice president have the advice of two members of the board and an outside consultant from a major banking house, Smith, Barney & Co., to help. The personnel vice president is responsible for personnel information, which he draws together with the help of his six-man staff and brings to operating committee meetings. However, the operating committee pays little attention to these matters except for specifics like pension programs, so the personnel vice president remains the acquirer and depository of knowledge. Presumably the administrative vice president is responsible for plant knowledge, but the real authority is the plant superintendent. No one else gets involved unless there is a crisis, so no one else has paid much attention to technical processes. The vice president for long-range planning organizes knowledge about forces and trends which he, too, reports to the operating committee. Obviously this in turn is acquired by others on the committee for they talk about the projections with respect to the company's future. This kind of material is transmitted by staff meeting to the second level of management, and sometimes there are special feature stories in the company magazine about one or another prediction. The vice president for marketing is responsible for acquiring information about competitors and product performance. He has the help of marketing information services, marketing consultants, and public relations consultants. The vice president for research has much the same function, though the operating committee pays little heed to his statements unless he is announcing the development of a new product. It is assumed that new ideas come from managers and scientists, that the only ideas to come from employees have to do with their specific jobs, and such ideas are gathered by suggestion box.

It would be hard to say in Knollwood Presbyterian Church who acquires knowledge about personnel and plant, services and competitors, and so on. The Session (the elected management body) operates from month to month; it simply seems to exist, following a time-hallowed routine. If they need specialized help, they can turn to specialists on the denominational staff.

(F) RESERVOIR OF INTELLECTUAL SOURCES

What is the pool of intellectual sources for this organization? How much does the organization have to depend on? The consultant must make a judgment of quality and quantity at this point.

i. Talents and skills within the organization

Most organizations have many skills and talents among their employees not known to management. Often if they are known, management tends to ignore them. Some companies, conversely, will buy other organizations just to get some of their men. What exactly is available within the organization for its utilization? A published example and a case excerpt show how this point may be noted:

In the burgeoning computer field, making acquisitions may be an easier way to get qualified workers than running help wanted ads. That was one of the main reasons behind Control Data's recent purchase of SCM Corporation's Data Processing Systems division. Says William C. Norris, CD's president, "We need a considerable number of qualified computer personnel. The SCM division has many experienced and skilled sales, programming and customer engineering personnel who fortunately have become available to us through this purchase." (*Forbes*, February 15, 1968, p. 10.)

The talents and skills within the Mountain View Baptist Church were varied. The congregation was short on people who could think through the direction and planning for the church's life, and long on people who could serve at church suppers or put on a barbecue. There were several people who could call on other members for the church (church census, evangelism, canvas, and so on). The women's association, however, had some very talented leadership, and their level of functioning was distinctly superior to that of the rest of the church. The women had taken an interest in a local Baptist retirement home. Through this interaction, a lively interest developed between the two bodies, to the advantage of both. The Sunday School teacher was a dean at a nearby college. Through her efforts, the class developed to a remarkable degree and began community relations projects that had never before been attempted.

ii. Consultants

An organization will often use outside consultants when it does not have anyone within the organization who can solve a particular problem. In addition, it may use such consultants to reinforce the in-house specialists. How does the organization under study make use of such consultants and in what areas? Two published examples and a case excerpt illustrate the range of considerations about consultants.

Although Rollei's famed twin-lens reflex practically revolutionized photography when it was first introduced in 1929, business began to go stale in the late 1950's when its patents ran out, cheap imitations rolled in, and Rollei was caught without a new development of its own.

Rollei began to get back into the picture in 1963. Then, as head of the family heirs of cofounders, Paul Francke . . . asked for an outsider's assessment of the company. Called in for the job, Dr. Heinrich Peesel, a Hamburg physicist, submitted a frankly "insulting" report that rapped Rollei for feeble [research and development] efforts and outdated production methods. Far from being insulted, the company hired Peesel to put his recommendations into effect . . . Peesel started modernizing Rollei's gothic production line, and more than doubled the research budget to a current $875,000 a year. By telescoping Rollei's normal seven-year development period to two years, the company was ready with two new cameras in 1966, which now account for half its sales. . . .

In 1967 Rollei's 1,700 workers turned out 90,000 cameras. And they are constantly working on new products, including half a dozen strobe guns, projectors, and camera models. (*Time,* February 2, 1968, p. 70.)

In July 1962, following a consolidation of school districts in Bennington and two smaller nearby Vermont towns, a new union school board was elected. Almost its first action was to engage the management consultant firm of Booz, Allen & Hamilton to help it formulate an approach to secondary education equal to that offered by the country's most sophisticated urban and suburban schools. The concept finally devised by the board and its consultants was to give the students a unique amount of flexibility and freedom of movement. There were to be no assigned homerooms, no "study halls." And the class schedule would be based on a 25-minute teaching period called a module. A conventional class might be two "mods," but a student might spend one "mod" practicing French pronunciation on a playback tape recorder, then go on to spend four "mods" in the science lab. (*Fortune,* April 1968, p. 143.)

Only once in its history has Temple Beth Sholom called in a consultant from outside the denomination, and that was a fund-raising consultant who presumably was needed to help raise money for a new building. However, the congregation did not take well to using a consultant and he withdrew. From time to time, the religious school teachers are taken to Kansas City if a workshop on curriculum is being held by a visiting consultant from the Union of American Hebrew Congregations. Unless one considers the observations and comments of candidates for the pulpit to be a form of consultation, there is no other.

iii. Affiliations with specialized institutions or universities

Most organizations have their own particular field of university specialists to draw on if they so desire. Historically, farmers and farm bodies have drawn on land grant colleges and universities. Pharmaceutical companies have relationships with medical schools and chemistry departments; hotels, with hotel management schools. Such affiliations serve as sources of knowledge by sending relevant bulletins, offering refresher training and consultation on specialized problems, and similar things. These published excerpts illustrate what is to be entered here:

In order to avoid too ivory tower an approach to journalism, Northwestern University gives its students practical experience covering a newsbeat for Chicago's *American.* Similarly, some 15 students each quarter [term] go to Washington, D.C., where they work out of the National Press Building under the supervision of a professor in residence. The Missouri School of Journalism plans to send students to Brussels for a semester where they will report on EEC [European Economic Community], Euratom [European Atomic Energy Agency] and other European affairs. (*Time,* February 9, 1968, p. 63.)

The circuit of ideas, attitudes, and techniques which characterize the Newton, Massachusetts, school system are more likely to originate at Harvard, MIT, or

Tufts College than they are in the community, or even in the school committee. College professors work with teachers to develop curricula in history and the social sciences; materials such as those produced by the university-oriented physical sciences and mathematics committees are being used in Newton classes. The association between Newton public schools and the nearby graduate schools of education is of such long-standing that no one even bothers to mention it; Newton's first "joint" appointment with Harvard dates back some forty years (p. 100). In contrast, as far as the San Francisco school system is concerned, Berkeley — a thirty-minute ride across the Bay Bridge — might be on the east coast judging by its influence on the public schools (p. 221). However, in Southern California's Orange County public schools, a member of the faculty of Harvey Mudd College helped to draw up the physics course that Fullerton High School is now using (p. 207). (Peter Schrag, *Voices in the Classroom*, Boston, Beacon Press, 1965, pp. 100, 221, 207.)

Just after World War I when the Los Angeles area first felt the need to bring hydroelectric power from the Colorado River, California Institute of Technology and Southern California Edison Company set up a high-voltage laboratory to study the problem. Out of that project came much of the switching, insulation, and transformer technology that made long-distance transmission of power feasible.

Similarly, Caltech hydraulics engineers designed high-efficiency pumps that allowed water from the Colorado to be pumped into Los Angeles. Chemical engineers — in a project supported by the American Petroleum Institute — studied underground behavior of gas and oil, making valuable contributions to oilfield management. The pattern of these and other research efforts has been for Caltech to open up a frontier area, then back away when industry takes over the research. (*Business Week*, March 16, 1968, p. 58.)

iv. Library facilities and services

Is there a library in the organization? If so, is it and its related functions part of the resources of the organization? Is it well supplied, current, used? Is it staffed by professional librarians? Are the employees allowed to check out material for the usual duration? Is the library open throughout the day? Does it have a good interlibrary loan service? A library can truly serve as a repository of knowledge, or it can simply be a repository of books. These two case excerpts contrast the use of the library as an organizational resource:

The Menninger Foundation library contains 25,000 volumes and subscribes to the major journals in the various fields represented in the organization. The library is maintained for the professional staff of the foundation and is a viable, coordinated function of the organization. It is staffed by two professional librarians and one staff worker. The professional staff of the foundation is allowed to check out material for a two- or three-week period. The library is open during the weekdays from 8:30 A.M. until 5:00 P.M.; it is closed during weekends and on holidays. There is always at least one staff member on duty during the normal lunch hour. There is no limit to which the library staff will go to obtain material through interlibrary loan services. The library is in constant use although it is never crowded. The library staff takes great pride in the maintenance and operation of their facility.

Chetopa Power and Light has a library on the second floor of its administration building. This is largely management and electric utility oriented, and it consists of some 3,000 volumes. A list of the books is available in each branch office, and those employees who want to borrow a book may write to the personnel office for it. Only a few bother to do so.

(2) Degree of receptivity to new knowledge

It is one thing to have systematic methods for acquiring knowledge and another to want to integrate it for organizational action. For example, some managements deliberately, although unconsciously, refuse to make use of knowledge about new sources of money. They may fear loss of control, as, for example, in going public. A church may raise money simply by increasing its dues but may prefer to use a heavy mortgage as a device for binding people to the organization. Many managements are aware of sophisticated psychological knowledge about motivation but seem unwilling to translate it into organizational practice despite the costly, self-defeating consequences of continuing to manage as they are currently doing. An organization may know of ways to expand on its product-service mix but may be reluctant to do so because it requires expanding the organization or because management is spread too thin already or because it will mean bringing in new people with other identifications and values. Conversely, some organizations are always alert to new knowledge and try to use it before they have the experiential maturity to do so.

(A) BY WHOM

Here the consultant should determine who the people are who are stimulated by the new knowledge. How much do they want to know? Who does not want to know what? Why?

The Newton, Massachusetts, public school committee does its homework, not only in studying the problems of the system, but in keeping up with the latest critiques of American education and society. Committee members will quote you Conant or Reisman, or sections from *The American Melting Pot* by Daniel

Moynihan and Nathan Glazer. A school principal talks about *The Child Centered Society* and *Education and the New America,* and experienced public librarians explain that *Tom Swift* and the *Bobbsey Twins* have been removed from the shelves because "nowadays there are better things to read." (Peter Schrag, *Voices in the Classroom,* Boston, Beacon Press, 1965, p. 101.)

Inventor Charles Carlson worked for years on a better way to copy documents. He led the way to the xerographic process aided by scientists at Battelle Memorial Institute. In the end, it was tiny Haloid Co., which bought the rights to the process that giants like Eastman Kodak and International Business Machines had turned down. [In 1967], the Xerox Corp., boasted sales of $528 million vs. $27 million in 1958. (*Forbes,* September 15, 1967, p. 142.)

The Ionian Order has made very little use of the wide range of worship activities (in contrast to the standard mass) as encouraged by the Vatican II Council. In addition, almost no provision is made for continued growth in a priest's professional work once his academic education has been completed. Although much importance is placed upon the experiences a priest has had, especially in parochial work, little is done to enhance the quality of the experience. Upon completion of his studies, a man is almost "thrown into the job" with very little provision for a period of orientation and learning. Too often the beginner is exploited and given the more onerous and less desirable assignments. There is a natural growth that comes from this kind of experience, and there is a shifting of assignments so that one may be forced, several times in his lifetime, to learn an entirely new field.

(B) TO WHAT

What subject matters attract greater interest? Lesser interest? No interest? A magazine excerpt and two case illustrations exemplify modes of dealing with this topic:

Computers and the men necessary to run them have nourished a new breed of railroaders — management experts with wide-ranging interests. And they, in turn, have fueled the railroads' drive to diversity — if the government eases up — into related areas of transportation. The Missouri Pacific, which already owns two truck lines, extending 17,000 miles, applied recently to the CAB [Civil Aeronautics Board] for permission to start an air-freight service. The new railroaders have no interest in passengers; in fact, they are more interested in diversifying their railroads per se. (*Time,* January 26, 1968, p. 72.)

The principal of the Pocasset Elementary School aims to assist in the overall education, growth, and development of the child and to implement this with the means at his disposal, largely defined by the Board of Education. He expresses the concept of the total development of the child within a democratic framework as guiding his philosophy. Although other members talk of it, few formulate their philosophy as succinctly; in practice, principal and teachers seem tolerant of the individual differences among children to a degree greater than in many other school settings, for example, letting a child wear a knitted hat in school for three weeks without insisting he take it off. The teachers later found out the boy's father had shaved his head as punishment.

Chetopa Power and Light is particularly interested in developments in atomic energy. Such innovations attract great attention up and down the hierarchy. Fossil fuel generation and distribution are routine and regarded as such, as are collections. Almost no attention is given to learning about current developments in management philosophy or psychological understanding of personnel. These topics are buried under a paternalistic concern for employees. Political, economic, and social problems are rarely discussed except in gross generalities, and few people in executive ranks take any special interest in reading about them.

(3) *Level and range of knowledge*

How sophisticated is the organization and over what range of phenomena? An organization can be knowledgeable about one area and naive about another. For example, a bank may be ultrasophisticated about financial matters but impoverished in its thinking about personnel practices. A monastery may be erudite about theological matters and not have even a glimmering of managerial conceptions.

(A) CONCERNING THEMSELVES, THEIR PRODUCTS, THEIR SERVICES AND RELATED FACTORS

Some organizations are ignorant about themselves as organizations; in some, knowledge about products is limited to the specific people who make or market them, and the same is true with services. Others are informed about every aspect of their history and operation. Without a grasp of their organizational history and organizational image it is difficult for employees to adhere to a commonly shared set of values. Some understand their products but do not know their customers as well, a fact they discover when their customers turn to another company's products. College professors who know their subject matter very well may be poor teachers.

The following examples, two of them case excerpts, show the wide range of ways knowledge of self or lack thereof comes through.

Litton Industries has very fine quantitative reporting techniques but no qualitative techniques. They must rely on their divisional managers to tell them that they are taking care of things qualitatively — whether they are keeping up with the field, with their customers' needs, with the technology. But the whole point of Litton's system of constant, microscopic checking of the performance of its divisions is to see that corporate management quickly corrects any errors at lower levels. Operating managers submit monthly statements of their financial results and their progress toward previously agreed goals. In addition, at the beginning of each fiscal year, each division has to produce a detailed plan and forecast of results for the coming year. The manager has to justify and defend his plan not only to the head of his group, but also to what one former Litton man calls "the murder squad" of corporate executives, usually including Roy Ash [president of the organization]. Once accepted by top management, plans must still be revised and updated every three months. (*Fortune*, April 1968, p. 186.)

Barford University prides itself on its law school and claims to have one of the best in the west. The faculty points with pride to the fact that many students work full time and go to school too. To a reasonably intelligent observer, there is a naive quality to this self-image. Actually, there are many mediocre students in the law school, more attention is given to the practicalities of practicing law than to historic, philosophical and constitutional issues, and it is difficult for most students to work full time and give adequate attention to their studies. The law faculty simply does not know what the level of teaching is at such law schools as those at Harvard, Yale, Michigan, and Columbia.

Methodist Bishop James K. Mathews of Boston, writing in the April 18, 1968, issue of the *Christian Advocate,* denies that Episcopal power is the main cause of lowered ministerial morale. He argues that there are three major advantages of the appointive system as administered by bishops: It is a principal guarantee of freedom of the pulpit, for a bishop can provide effective support for a pastor. It provides a way to deal fairly with both pastor and congregation. And it can match pastor with congregation's needs. Anyone who has ever studied Methodist churches knows that all three issues are honored more in the breach than in practice, for there is no systematic support of pastors in any denomination; the pastor is almost invariably rejected in favor of pacifying the congregation. And there is no systematic, let alone scientific, way of matching pastor and congregation.

When H & K [Hill & Knowlton, the public relations firm] purchased Robinson-Hannagan Associates it acquired the account for the Bahamas and their tourist business. Publicizing the advantages of clear water, pure white beaches, and cloudless skies in an idyllic atmosphere seemed like a delightful assignment for any account executive, and the business was profitable as well . . . But during the 1960's, while H & K was trumpeting the beauties of the Bahamas, gambling was legalized there and it soon came under the control of gangster elements . . . While the links between . . . the island politicians and U.S. gangsters were widely rumored, there was no detailed evidence to support the reports.

Then one Allan W. Witwer . . . who had gone to work for the Ministry of Tourism and Finance news bureau (which meant he was on H & K's payroll) decided to write a book [about the alleged corruption in the Bahamas]. He wrote . . . seven chapters of a proposed twenty-one chapter book. . . .

[Turned down by a reputable agent as unpublishable by legitimate publishers] Witwer went to Hill & Knowlton with his manuscript and suggested that perhaps the Bahamian Minister of Tourism . . . might be interested to know about the book. . . . The firm then attempted to find a publisher to buy the manuscript on behalf of a "nongovernment figure." . . . [When] the sale [of the book to a subsidized publisher] was finally completed [including all the papers connected with it] . . . [Witwer] promised not to "discuss or comment upon the book with any person, firm, or corporation, or government authority, or otherwise." (Apparently the intention was to print copies but not to allow them to become public, thereby to silence Witwer. — ed.)

Some copies of the book got into the hands of the political opposition . . . [whose] platform included a promise to discharge H & K as the island's publicity agent.

There are really just two questions about H & K's conduct in this episode. The first is how such an informed, sophisticated organization could remain ignorant of what was happening on the islands. In early 1966, Peat, Marwick, Mitchell & Co., which had handled the auditing of the gambling receipts, resigned — a sure hint that there were problems. It couldn't have been easy to miss the gangster influence by that time.

The second question is how could H & K become involved, even indirectly, in the [Witwer book] episode. (*Fortune,* September 1967, p. 144.)

(B) OUTSIDE THEIR IMMEDIATE AREA OF INTEREST

The more enlightened and sophisticated the people in the organization are about the environment in which their organization operates, the more able they are to take advantage of that knowledge for adaptation. By widening the sources of input and gratification, employees have more resources for creativity, as illustrated in this case excerpt and published example:

The Ionian Order is paying considerable attention to its association with the Graduate Theological Union and is hoping that this association with other Protestant seminaries and with the state university may provide the opportunity for the Order to become involved in significant intellectual work.

Today the company's [Pan American World Airways] Aerospace Division has 6,500 people at Cape Kennedy doing everything from running the cafeterias and police and fire departments to systems design and evaluation . . . and for the Atomic Energy Commission's Nuclear Rocket Development Station at Jackass Flats, Nevada. And 256 are studying the upper atmosphere and northern phenomena such as the aurora borealis at the National Research Council of Canada near Ft. Churchill. The company got into all this early in the U.S. space program. Its first job was to build and operate island tracking stations in the Caribbean . . . , because the president asked . . . [them] to. Today the Aerospace Div. makes money on the deal . . . [In addition,] Aerospace Services

. . . [has created] a place for Pan Am's brightest scientists to extend their knowledge to the frontiers of space. And the company has gained vast experience in collecting, processing and evaluating huge amounts of information, which is a plus for any airline. (*Business Week,* February 17, 1968, p. 166.)

b. Use of knowledge

Here the consultant should try to discover how knowledge is translated into a basis for organizational action and usefulness and what happens to it after it has been so translated.

(1) *How is it brought together*

Knowledge may be formalized in the form of proposals, long-range planning projects, committee task-force reports, administrative decisions, and interpretations of annual reports. The consultant must determine what his organization does. The following excerpt and two case examples show how three different organizations bring or fail to bring knowledge together.

What is unusual about Harold Geneen [chairman and president of International Telephone and Telegraph] is the detail he demands. He demands monthly reports from all divisions. He discusses them at monthly meetings attended by his key staff people and his important line people. The monthly reports have to include not only major items on why a division is above or below quota, but items as minor as a lost order. To insure that the reports are made in such detail, Geneen has a staff that is constantly dropping in on operations to check on things. And line people know that if Geneen finds out anything negative about a man's operation, no matter how petty, from anyone else but the man himself, he explodes; so the reports are highly detailed.

Because Geneen might ask a dozen questions on even a minor item in a report, Geneen executives are forced to pay more attention to details than is the case in other companies. Each month Geneen reads all the monthly reports, which fill a book ten inches thick. He has a photographic memory and total recall — not just for numbers but for technical details. (*Forbes,* May 1, 1968, p. 29.)

St. Anselm's is in a muddle. For months the monks have been meeting in renewal sessions, trying to pool their knowledge and aspirations toward the formulation of long-range goals, policies, and programs. But no one factually knows what they are up against or how others have solved similar problems. Therefore nothing concrete evolves from the meetings.

A metropolitan area YMCA has organized three task forces comprised of its 26-man executive staff. One concentrates its efforts on organizational structure, a second on urban problems and a third on programming. Each task force is responsible for organizing all available information in its area, assessing the organization's own needs, and presenting recommendations to the executive staff as a whole. These are then debated, revised, and presented to both branch and central boards for further discussion, revision, and approval. By this time both executives and boards are intimately familiar with the issues and recommendations so, psychologically, the knowledge is integrated into program, policy, and goal formulation.

(A) WHO THINKS ABOUT IT

How is the knowledge considered for its import and usefulness? Does the executive appoint a committee? Does the chairman of the board expect a report? Where are the nodules of concern? Is all innovation left to the top? To the research laboratory? To changes in chief executive? In the following published example, one man did the thinking. In the second example, an executive committee thinks together with others. In the third example, knowledge is supplied to the point of action for consideration.

Members of the staff of . . . [Clark Kerr], [former chancellor of the Berkeley campus (1952–1958) and president of the University of California (1958–1967),] would prepare each day folders of material for his attention. These folders are gathered about 4:30 P.M. and taken to his home. Next morning the folders are back on the assistants' desks, adorned with Kerr's numerous and detailed reactions, comments, and suggestions written on the margins in green ink. He delegated, of course, but rather tentatively and usually on an ad hoc basis. He will assign a man to a certain immediate task rather than give him a free hand on the basis of a continuing responsibility for a defined area of the university's work. This method, obviously, threw a tremendous volume of decision and supervision on Kerr. Another result has been noted by one in a position to observe the operation: "The men around Clark Kerr do not bloom." (*Fortune,* September 1965, p. 198.)

[The Borden Company is run by a triumvirate system of management: chairman of the board, president, and executive president.] They keep their fingers on the pulse of the organization by frequent consultations and with the traditional "officers' luncheon." On the first Monday of every month, the Board of Officers, comprising the Big Three, division heads . . . and treasurer, gather at headquarters for food and discussion about business. Each of the regulars is invited to bring along two guests from within the company. The talk may occasionally get beyond the bounds of Borden business . . . but it affords each man in the room a feeling for every division's activities and problems. (*Dun's Review,* May 1967, p. 84.)

This past winter at their monastery near St. Louis, the Roman Catholic Redemptorist Fathers put into operation an electronic data processing service designed to provide a "71-facet view of each practicing Catholic." Pastors who want to make use of the service must distribute a questionnaire to their faithful and then wait for the Redemptorists to feed the answers into the IBM System 360 computer. The 180-page printout that the machine delivers gives the pastor a cybernetic summary of his parishioners' religious attitudes. In a Chicago parish the priests were about to start a public relations campaign to improve the image of their parochial school among the congregation. The computer reported that most parishioners already thought well of the school; it was the priests themselves who needed to refurbish their image. Parishioners felt that they were not getting enough personal attention from the clergy. The school PR campaign was dropped and the clergy made new efforts to meet with parishioners. (*Time,* March 29, 1968, p. 92.)

(B) LEVEL OF ABSTRACTION

Concrete knowledge usually goes hand in hand with short-term planning. Both in turn suggest reaction to external stimuli and forces rather than mastery of them. Concrete knowledge about elementary biology is relatively useless in high school courses today because in order to meet the demands of college entrance examinations, students must acquire higher levels of proficiency. Contemporary developments in communication have made it anachronistic for AT&T to think it was in the telephone business. Schools of business have increasingly had to shift from teaching business skills to teaching management conceptions. The following two published excerpts contrast an abstract conception of function with a more concrete one:

Walter Kidde & Co., a New Jersey based manufacturer of safety products, industrial equipment, and consumer goods, . . . [has recently merged] . . . with U.S. Lines . . . [the company that has] an obvious great edge in the race for the potentially huge North American container trade since its American Lancer, first of six giant containerships, goes into service in May 1968 . . . But [Fred R.] Sullivan's vision of what Kidde, is interested in buying . . . is not merely a shipping line but a transportation system — with U.S. Lines' worldwide container routes the cornerstone. The key to Kidde's scheme is in U.S. Lines' operations . . . First, U.S. Lines has invested heavily in the future of containerization . . . In 1964 it already had signed contracts with . . . [a shipbuilder] for five highly automated vessels . . . capable of carrying 1,200 containers each at 21 knots. Second . . . U.S. Lines has franchises for the Europe-to-U.S. transatlantic trade. It also has routes from Eastern U.S. ports to the Pacific via the Panama Canal . . . [Recently] U.S. Lines acquired a transpacific route from the East Coast via Panama . . . This would give U.S. Lines routes between Europe and the Far East. The only element missing is the "land bridge" of high-speed container trucks or trains across the North American continent — and that takes only the signing of a contract. For this reason U.S. Lines is anxious to continue its plans for coordinated operations with U.S. Freight Co. (*Business Week,* February 24, 1968, p. 158.)

Along with the majority of Los Angelenos, [former Chief of Police William] Parker had small regard for concepts of crime prevention through positive social action or for the preservation of human rights that sometimes interfere with the efficient apprehension of criminals. These notions were frills, expensive luxuries, which society could not afford if anarchy were to be avoided. Policemen were policemen, and social workers, social workers; the two performed different and totally unrelated functions. Parker's only concern with minority groups was with the high crime rates in ghetto areas: "The main source of crime in Los Angeles just happens to be in the areas populated heavily by Negroes, and Negroes just happen to be figuring in most of the city's crime," he pointed out. "This comes from the record." His job, and his only job, was to crack down on that crime with repressive police work. (*Atlantic Monthly,* December 1966, p. 96.)

(2) *How is knowledge organized and systematized*

The consultant should examine how the organization incorporates the knowledge into a viable condition. It can be "packaged" in the mind of an individual, a committee, a consultant, different committees having a variety of interests. It can be placed on computers and be given multivariate analyses. The way in which it is organized and systematized says something about how much it is "owned" by the organization as a whole and how rich a resource it is for the organization.

(A) COMMITTEE SYSTEM

Some organizations have transdepartmental committees. Others have specialized committees in given subject areas. Some use committees only to facilitate administration or to handle special projects. These three examples illustrate the uses of committees to organize knowledge:

In the United States, more than 280,000 Salvation Army soldiers are under the field command of four territorial commanders. Territorial commanders have autocratic power . . . But leadership in practice boils down to a series of committees, commissions, and consultation between top officers. Each week, 10 separate top level committees meet at territorial headquarters. The final responsibility . . . [belongs to the territorial commander, but actually decisions are made by the group.] (*Business Week,* June 19, 1965, p. 123.)

In 1920, fearing that the then chaotically organized General Motors Corporation was dangerously lacking in controls, Pierre du Pont (then head of GM) established an inventory allotment committee for the company. If not the first corporate committee having a specialized function in the history of American corporate organization, this was certainly the first to leave an enduring impress on the general form of business structure.

The inventory allotment committee set a policy for all divisions of the General Motors organization, covering the quantities and values of inventories which any division might accumulate for its immediate production program. That these instructions were disregarded is a matter of history, as is the loss of $85 million suffered by General Motors ($64 million of it in those divisions which disregarded the committee's instructions).

The actual details are less important than the theoretical concept which underlay Pierre du Pont's innovation in corporate organization. The creation of the committee was in itself a complete departure from the previous haphazard practices and structure of American business. Establishment of the committee was recognition that a giant corporation might be conducted in a uniform manner in all its departments. It therefore represented the first growth of concepts of statesmanship in business conduct. As such, it represented a distinct move toward control and away from the vague guesswork by which many companies, including General Motors, had been guided in earlier years. It is the pattern on which permanent committees have been modeled in American business over the past forty years. (Jackson Martindell, *The Appraisal of Management*, New York, Harper & Row, 1962, p. 30.)

The Menninger Foundation has a wide range of committees. Some, like the Medical Records Committee, the Library Committee, the Monograph Committee, and the Publications Committee, formulate policy and practice for those functions. Others serve to coordinate departmental activities, largely as consultants or cooperators. Many are ad hoc, appointed by the president to make recommendations on special problems. There seems to be no particular concept regarding the formation and function of committees. They come into being when there is a particular problem to be solved, or when a function transcends the work of any single department.

(B) RECORDS AND STORAGE SYSTEM

The consultant must separate the formal records *of* the business from the formal records *about* the business. The formal records of the business will include data used in Chapters 5 and 6. Those which are *about* the business will include reports on new techniques, discussions of innovation, current market surveys, changes in tax information. The consultant's concern here is with the functional usefulness of the acquired knowledge, using the following three points as guides:

Accuracy: How much of the knowledge is factual? How much of the detail can be trusted? How much is speculative?

Availability: Where is the information stored? How is it filed? Is it convenient to check out? To whom is it accessible? Can it be recalled for repetitive use?

Comprehensiveness: Does the knowledge represent thorough data or is it incomplete? Is it annotated? Does it contain errors, bias?

These examples are illustrative:

The marketing-service department of the [Hill & Knowlton public relations firm] makes design awards [for their client the American Iron & Steel Institute] every two years, and not only publicizes the winners, but builds up a backlog of informative stories on the use of steel in various projects. It publishes *Steel Developments Digest* and mails it to key people in industry and education. It puts the designs on slide films and sends them to engineering instructors, who may use the material in class, and to architectural firms. (*Fortune,* September 1967, p. 140.)

Medical records are stored in locked vaults at The Menninger Foundation and are available only to responsible professional personnel who are engaged in diagnosis and treatment of the given patient. Historical data, whether of personnel, practices, finances and so on, are preserved in the files of the respective offices and are ultimately stored in the archives. New information, such as research advances, is most likely to be found in professional publications in the library, which are available to all staff, but specific information in a given research area is most likely to be in the office of the person in charge of that project and may have to be sought out there if anyone else is interested.

(c) OTHER MODES OF ORGANIZATION AND SYSTEMATIZATION

Some companies make films of their products in action. Others make public announcement of the performance of their products. This happens when automobile companies recall cars. Some, as certain religious institutions, pass on much by word of mouth. Indian tribes and other primitive societies would pass knowledge from generation to generation through song. The following excerpts from case studies illustrate a range of modes of organizing and systematizing knowledge:

Magnia Envelope Co. presents its envelopes to the customer with a twenty-minute color-sound film which depicts the uses of envelopes. The film is geared to customer pleasure and satisfaction and is focused primarily on specialized types of envelopes to meet each customer's particular needs. The film stresses the concept of an "ever changing product" and the need for innovation. In telling its story, it shows the machinery by which envelopes are made but says little about the people involved. The film shifts from business uses of envelopes to family uses, perhaps reflecting the family type of business Magnia is. It also conveys to the customer "We are small enough to want you no matter how small you are." Quality control and kinds of customers both come in for careful attention; the latter are depicted as religious institutions. The art department and its special skills for design, which are at the service of the customer, is the single area in which there is a major focus — on people. I was amazed by the way in which many of the themes which emerged in our study — the focus on machines and envelopes to the relative exclusion of the people who did the task, emphasis on versatility in production methods and products and on the organization's fight for survival — were expressed in this film. We could have inferred from this film much that we learned without having to study the organization itself. I would expect from seeing this film that the key experience of people who work in such an organization is that they adapt to the machine and product demands in combination with customer demands, but are less likely to have the feeling of playing a significant role in it. Technically the movie is of good quality, fast-paced, and with harmony of presentation, music, and rhythm of the machines. It is exactly the kind of movie I would expect this company to produce: like its envelopes, neat, temporal, and straightforward.

Temple Beth Sholom has an annual congregational seder, or ceremonial dinner for the Passover, in addition to the customary family seders. At the seder the story of the Exodus is read, recalling the suffering of the Jews in Egypt and their flight from slavery. Components of the meal symbolize various events related to the Exodus — unleavened bread, which was the only bread that could be baked in the flight from Egypt; horseradish symbolizing the bitterness of the experience; green herbs and wine symbolizing God's gifts. In recapitulating this story publicly each year, the tradition of freedom, God's beneficence, and the longevity of Jewish experience is transmitted from parents to children, family by family and, as in this case, reaffirmed as a group experience.

The *Alumni News* of the University of Kansas devotes considerable space to the history of the university, its trials, tribulations, and successes. These, cumulatively, build up into a consistent story about the university with which all loyal alumni are familiar.

(3) *Amount and kind of use (retrieval)*

Who has access to the formalized knowledge? How does he (they) then inject it into organizational thinking? How much of the knowledge is confidential? How much is available in day-to-day awareness? Who can learn from it? These excerpts come from cases:

The formalized knowledge of Arrowhead Tool & Die is fully known only to the president. Not that he deliberately hides anything, but no one else is left in the organization who started with him. The early experiences and traditions have not been committed to paper. Although the operating committee discusses current production and marketing problems and is aware of the company's financial status from day to day, they are not privy to the details of the offer by

Reardon Corp. to buy Arrowhead. The technical designs for Arrowhead products and experiences with them are all filed in the engineering department and available to any of the operating committee who ask, but they are not summarized and discussed with the operating committee as the basis for thinking out new products. Rather, the engineering department is supposed to do this by itself. Only the stockholders are privy to historical financial information. The president informs the operating committee on an ad hoc basis about contemporary issues; each operating committee head does the same. However, none of this is systematically related to previous experiences to maintain a continuous thread and thrust within the awareness of the decision-makers.

There is repetition of the early experiences of treatment and development at The Menninger Foundation in annual meetings, papers, books, and other publications. Much of the professional experience is summarized in the *Bulletin of the Menninger Clinic*. This is available to any interested person in the library, the archives, and, if he is a professional person who has been cleared for access to confidential material, in the medical records library. Such material can be reinjected into the system in professional papers or historical documents, sometimes reenacted in the programs of the annual Old Timers' meetings. Confidential information is largely patient data, salary data, and specific contributions by individuals and groups to the work of the Foundation.

(4) *Organizational conditions affecting the use of intellectual sources*

Given knowledge, what circumstances enhance or interfere with its application by the organization?

(A) ABILITY TO DEAL WITH ABSTRACT PROBLEMS

The ability to deal with abstract problems is an increasing problem for many organizations, often posed by people who are using computers for the first time but do not know how to view their organizations more abstractly than they have in the past. Other organizations are highly abstract in their considerations. A component of the ability to deal with abstract problems is the facility with which the organization can contend with the selection of a problem on which to focus its efforts. This is a growing problem because of the plethora of new information and the need to have some basis for selection. Frequently the problem is not a matter of selection but, rather, one of organization of the information around a given core such as an enunciated organizational purpose. The following two case examples illustrate limitation in the ability to deal with abstract problems:

Three major events facilitated the transition of the Ionian Order's way of doing things. It had fallen into rather minimal functions — a few men taught in seminaries, some in high schools, and some served as parish priests. These functions had little of the stimulation, prestige, or color of the order's traditions. Enrollment began to fall off, then took a drastic downturn; seminary teaching became increasingly obsolete as compared with other college experiences; and the younger men began to rebel, rumbling about forming their own chapter. The parish priests were pulled back, the seminary turned into a liberal arts college, and monks are being sent to universities for advanced degrees. In fact, a priory has been established in Boston to serve as a local base for those enrolled in area graduate schools.

Greenbriar Hospital is not able to anticipate and meet changing patterns of hospital care. Doctors, nurses, and ancillary personnel are all technicians. They have been taught to do specific work and do it reasonably well. However, there is no nearby medical school to stimulate them nor do they have the conceptual tools or the time to think beyond their daily routine responsibilities. The hospital management sees its task as providing a direct service in response to community need. It waits to be asked.

(B) FLEXIBILITY

Can the organization change itself or open itself to new kinds of knowledge? For example, some engineering companies find it impossible to make use of contemporary advances in personality and organization theory because, both in terms of the personalities of the individuals in the organization and the nature of their work, they are psychologically unable to make use of anything other than formulas or to take into account people's feelings. Others are so entrapped with a "hard sell psychology" that though they may hear the words, they are unable to shift from their style of operation to apply new conceptions usefully. It has been common knowledge for many years that newborn infants are better off when cared for by their mothers, yet most hospitals still continue to maintain nurseries where the newborn are kept in isolation from their mothers. These two examples show flexibility in the use of knowledge making for more effective adaptation:

With [Carlton B.] Chapman at the head, the [Dartmouth] Medical School focused its planning . . . [on] the development of a new curriculum that would . . . lead to a full 4-year program . . . As he sees it, the medical school must devise a curriculum that is responsive to the nation's needs for practicing physicians, biomedical researchers, and medical and research administrators [in order to establish itself as a thriving basic research center] . . . One of Chapman's first steps was to ask the faculty to strive to cut nonessentials from classroom and laboratory courses. The working assumption was that the hours spent on such courses would be reduced by 50 per cent. Faculty members acknowledge that there were many howls, but the trimming process called for each department to justify its programs before members of other departments. Before the course cutting was completed, many of the faculty were ready to concede that habit, rather than rational design, accounted for the presence of a good deal of antiquated material in the curriculum. Thus, the biochemistry department concluded that it could slash its course hours by 60 per cent, eliminating, for example, fifteen hours that had been devoted to physiochemical principles, and cutting the hours alloted to the study of enzymes and kinetics from twelve to four. The rationale for these drastic cuts is spelled out in detail in a departmental paper, but basic to the reduction is the assumption that today's students are coming out of college with far better scientific training than was recognized by the current curriculum; that some of the biochemistry curriculum overlapped other courses; and finally that, by enrichment and better structuring of the subject matter retained, less will prove to be more. (*Science,* January 19, 1968, p. 285.)

William J. Levitt started out as a small but successful merchant builder in the 1930's and blossomed out after World War II with the huge tract developments and mass-produced techniques at Levittown. Now Levitt has gone abroad to Western Europe. His most important venture abroad is located 18 miles to the southwest of Paris in Le Mesnil-Saint Denis. There he opened a 700-unit project named Les Résidences du Château. Levitt's highest hurdle at Le Mesnil-Saint Denis was the cost of building. His houses in France are more expensive than those in the United States because French skilled labor, although paid only about one-third as much as its American counterpart, is far less productive. Some materials and all fabricated items are much more costly than in the United States. And there were restrictive building codes. The houses, priced between $22,000 and $33,700, reflect concessions to French tastes and building codes: stucco and brick exteriors, mansard roofs clad with slate, parquet floors, and two doors between the bathroom and bedroom. Yet the houses recall America's suburbia with their fully equipped kitchens, built-in closets, and garages.

(c) CHARACTERISTIC STYLE AND VARIATIONS

If an organization exhibits a characteristic style, it will often represent a hardening of the intellectual arteries into a psychological stance. A characteristic style can inhibit the use of new knowledge by circumscribing, distorting, or uncritically accepting new information. For example, many authoritarian leaders encourage the development of personnel and training staffs and the teaching of psychological knowledge in their organizations, provided it is focused on making lower level management more effective with line employees. Some organizations are comprised of dependent people who have difficulty when asked to assume initiative or to be amenable to ideas that will require them to act independently or that will stimulate conflict within the group. Some can be outwardly aggressive but passive and conforming within the organization as, for example, a police department. Some can be passive outwardly and aggressive inwardly as, for example, a college faculty torn by political bickering. Characteristic style and variations might be equated to the dominant mode of attack and the number of plays of a football team. Some teams are passing teams while others play a running game. Two published examples and a case excerpt illustrate what is meant by characteristic style:

In 1948–49, William Paley decided that CBS Radio should originate and produce more programs, instead of being a mere pipeline for advertisers' shows. Paley also foresaw that TV was about to become a big factor in the marketplace, and that some stars and shows could transfer to the new medium. Armed with money, tax advantages, and charm, Paley raided his opposition and captured a galaxy of network radio stars. The raids laid the foundation of CBS's success in TV. They also locked it into a star-based, high-cost formula that explains a great deal about the state of its prime-time programs. To get high ratings, CBS bought stars; to keep those stars, it has had constantly to pay them more. As a result, it cannot afford to be too adventurous in its programming, or to cater to any except the mass audience. To make the pilot for a series of one-hour drama shows costs up to $400,000. If the series is to amortize that, as well as continuing production costs — $175,000 to $200,000 for an episode — it has to attract a mass audience of some 20 million people, and hold them for a minimum of twenty-six weeks. Even then, the show might still lose money. (*Fortune,* May 1968, p. 227.)

The characteristic style with which The Menninger Foundation approaches new knowledge is based on the psychoanalytic conception of deriving understanding from face-to-face contact with patients and using that understanding in depth as the central device for treatment. This means careful and consistent attention to the individual, but it also means correspondingly less responsiveness to psychiatric fads and fancies. Some contemporary fields of psychiatric interest, like drugs, group methods, and brain studies play a secondary role.

Mr. Lois and other Papert-Koenig alumni say the slump was avoidable. Management says it wasn't. Mr. Lois tends to blame a great many of Papert-Koenig's problems on, of all people, huge Proctor & Gamble Co., some of whose advertising business Papert-Koenig acquired in 1964. "We had been a creative, crazy place until then," asserts Mr. Lois. "When P&G came in we got up tight. Everyone started mumbling about becoming more responsible, more businesslike. We swerved off the road. The agency lost its character." (*Wall Street Journal,* May 23, 1968, p. 26.)

c. Dissemination of knowledge

Having observed, described, and interpreted how and what kinds of knowledge are acquired by whom, the consultant must determine whether the information is used as an organizational asset. How is it dispersed? Does it serve the organization maximally? He should not be concerned with the communications network as outlined previously but, rather, with an identification network or some kind of capillarylike process. To illustrate how knowledge is disseminated by identification, in his book *On Aggression* (New York, Harcourt Brace & World, Inc., 1966), Konrad Lorenz reports an experiment in which one young chimpanzee was removed from a cage full of chimpanzees and trained to obtain bananas by following an elaborate number of steps to which he had been conditioned. When he was returned to the cage, the other chimpanzees saw him obtaining bananas as he was trained to, and even ate some of them, but did not learn how to obtain them by watching him. However, when an older chimpanzee was similarly trained and returned to the cage, the other chimpanzees observed him as they had observed the younger one, but they learned to follow the process.

Are authority figures consciously used as models in disseminating knowledge? Is new knowledge stated in memorandum or procedure form with the assumption that people will then apply it without the need for models or instruction? Are people formally trained to use new knowledge? If so, who does the training? How quickly and completely is it assimilated by what other parts of the organization? Two cases and a published example show varying ways of disseminating knowledge.

When the Royal Department Store president became convinced of the need for a more effective managerial process, he convened his operating committee for a two-day session with his consultant, followed that with a similar session with the next level of management, and, in turn, with presentation and discussion with 600 supervisory employees. This was followed by repeat sessions devoted to concepts and problems in implementation, questions, and discussion about interpretation and practice and further continued discussion with division heads and their staffs. A simple experiment was devised to contrast two store units, one with the new methods and one that continued the old to demonstrate within the store both the usefulness of the new ideas and the problems that followed on their introduction. The promotion department and the appliance service department were the first to try the new practices with groups within their department and reported the results to the operating committee. Members of the groups that had applied the new techniques then presented their work to the 600 supervisory personnel in panel fashion and answered questions about their practice.

The direct interpretation method of treating schizophrenics was presented to the Veterans Administration Hospital staff and trainees by Dr. John Rosen. Residents in training immediately began experimenting with the technique on their wards. For some months there was lively discussion about both method and concept and critical examination of some of the problems that followed upon the technique. When earlier the same kind of presentation had been made about prefrontal lobotomy, an experimental ward was set up and a staff council was formed to evaluate and recommend patients and to follow up on the results. Weekly staff conferences served to critically analyze what had been learned and to establish a body of experience with respect to the technique. Both events communicated an openness to learning in the context of careful evaluation of results.

The Newton, Massachusetts, teachers are wrestling with substantial problems of belief and technique, and with the matter of finding an effective means of discussing historical continuity and historical change. But in doing so they function with certain clear advantages; the enthusiasm of those who feel that, despite the difficulties, they are on to something better than what they did before; a sense of their own command of the profession; and the understanding that they have the help of professional university historians and the support of their own school administration. No interview with these teachers, however brief, leaves much doubt about their enthusiasm or about their refusal to shut the doors of perception and to cling to the certainties of an earlier age. (Peter Schrag, *Voices in the Classroom,* Boston, Beacon Press, 1965, p. 109.)

3. Organizational language

Organizational language tells people what is going on *in* the organization. It is therefore important to note and interpret the meaning of how the organization speaks. In this section, the consultant should analyze the style, content, syntax, figures of speech, attitudes, and values that appear in organization communications. He should be particularly interested in the feelings that are disguised by the language used, the degree to which the organizational language is a barrier to discourse within the organization or between the organization and others, and the degree to which it constitutes a cultural or industrial boundary. A published example and case excerpt illustrate:

The language in which Lyman C. Conger, Kohler Company attorney referred to the KWA [Kohler Workers' Association] leaders who had "defected" to the

[United Auto Workers] revealed the underlying psychological interactions which were at least as important as any economic factors in the Kohler strike. He accused them of trying to "become militant labor leaders" and trying to further their own ambitions; "they brought Kohler employees more trouble than benefits in the last two years," he said, and "have been aping typical abusive Congress of Industrial Organizations tactics for the last two years." (Walter H. Uphoff, *Kohler on Strike*, Boston, Beacon Press, 1966, p. 132.)

The themes of obedience and sacrifice of self for the community permeate the official statements of St. Bede's. These, presumably, are the ways of monks dedicated to God's will. Such language suggests that questioning is the same as rebellion; difference equals hostility; and that if a monk has doubts about where the monastery is going, he needs to expunge such thoughts with further contemplation and prayer. Involved circumlocutions are therefore necessary if anything at all is to be discussed, and discussion with anyone from outside is almost precluded.

a. Themes and content of employee publications

In many house organs the themes are: (1) produce more; (2) serve better; (3) look how good we are to you and our customers. The content abounds with personal data: births, deaths, unusual hobbies, and so on. There usually is very little news pertaining to policies and problems with which the organization must deal. Thus most house organs are quite "newsy"; however, they tend to hide the realities of the organization and place a smiling organizational facade before the readers, who most usually disregard it. Such propagandistic publications are usually disguises for paternalism that, in turn, veils underlying authoritarian attitudes.

Some employee publications are clearly political, intended to represent the viewpoint of the management or administration. Usually house organs are relegated to editors who are well controlled by several administrative layers above them. Dissent, debate, criticism therefore are rarely found. The consultant should be aware that while this need not necessarily be so, it is nevertheless commonplace. The following excerpt and two case examples illustrate what is meant by themes and content:

The management of creativity is a subject that frequently receives only token attention from either businessmen or educators.

Not so at Kaiser Aluminum & Chemical Corp., whose quarterly, *Kaiser Aluminum News,* is entirely devoted to the process of creativity and its management.

The issue called "You and Creativity" follows an earlier one labeled Corporation as a Creative Environment. While its lavish format is typical of many corporate internal publications, the issue untypically contains a bibliography of more than 20 books in the behavioral sciences for readers who desire to pursue the subject. (*Business Week,* February 24, 1968, p. 154.)

Blakely Methodist Church's *Messenger* tells its members repetitively of achievement, the need for money, the church's illustrious heritage, and how to be good Christians. Achievement refers to new members obtained, the work of various church groups and classes, missionary work, and community participation. Discussion of money revolves around campaigns, facilities to be built, and endowment needed or obtained. Stories of developmental crises of the past and how they were surmounted tell the parishioner he is part of a noble tradition. The application of Christian principles to daily problems is illustrated in brief human interest stories and discussions of ethical and moral concerns as well as editorial comments on holiday observance, racial problems, and a few legislative issues like crime, liquor, and gambling. Underlying all this is the theme, "You are part of an extended Christian family; do you part in making it bigger and better."

Mt. Pleasant Hospital tells its staff and contributors, "Look how good we are and how well we serve you." This is done in feature stories in its monthly publication, *Trends,* about individual staff members and their work; in reports about improvements in the hospital; discussions of volunteer activities; and statistics on the number of patients treated, nurses graduated, and accreditations attained or renewed.

b. Organizational ideology

The dominant set of beliefs of an organization is considered its ideology. The theme and content of employee publications reflects the organizational ideology. In general, the consultant will infer the organizational ideology from the forces or factors given attention or ignored. One can interpret from these the stance the organization assumes toward the outside world, what its conception is of its reason for being, what it sees itself to be, and who it perceives to be its opponents. Labor publications reflect the theme that management is the enemy. In much of the literature of investor-owned electric power companies, the foe is government regulation. Many industries share a political ideology of individual independence which is often at variance with their efforts to seek government support and regulation of the competition.

Organizational ideology can also be inferred from the kinds of public relations activities an organization will support or finance. For example, business organizations will often contribute to the support of economic education in high school and college courses but will not contribute to programs that might teach minority group members how to organize themselves to strengthen their own neighborhoods. Many leading church-men espouse an ideology of justice but feel their responsibility stops at acting upon that ideology.

Within the organization there is always a relatively congruent set of values. If there is a dichotomy, major steps will have to be taken to breach the schism. Two published examples and a case excerpt illustrate what is meant by ideology:

During the 1930's, as viewed by independent merchants, the ideology of the A&P was one of intense competitiveness regardless of social cost. Sometimes they temporarily set prices low enough to drive neighborhood competition out of business. They ran their stores from headquarters and disdained to advertise in local papers. They got business but they were cordially hated as murderers of the American dream of the little business of one's own. (Caroline Bird, *The Invisible Scar*, New York, McKay, 1966, p. 132.)

In its relentless search for money, the modern university has let concern for "image" replace aspiration for an ideal. Public relations with the outside world has often become more important than human relations within the university itself. . . . Marketability — not truth — has become the criterion of intellectual value. Almost no one in the status-conscious education industry has seriously challenged Clark Kerr's view (*The Uses of the University*, 1963) that the "really modern university" is simply "a mechanism . . . held together by administrative rules and powered by money"; that academic subjects will ultimately survive only if they earn their own money; and that "it only pays to produce knowledge if, through production, it can be put into use better and faster." (*Life*, May 24, 1968, p. 32.)

Dalton State Hospital identifies strongly with the tacit view that the best patient care arises from one-to-one relationships between staff and patients, that this is achieved when there is harmonious functioning of the professional team headed by the psychiatrist, and that its greatest enemy is the money-grubbing legislature and higher administrators who fail to identify with this concept. Between the emotional lines of this conception is another, namely, that staff members must relinquish aspirations for higher incomes, that they are misunderstood by the outside world, and that no one cares as much as they do about mental patients.

c. Advertising themes

Advertising themes are relatively self evident. They are as relevant to the understanding of colleges, monasteries, hospitals, labor unions, and churches as they are to businesses. Colleges advertise by their catalogues, recruiters, alumni associations, publications on overseas campuses. Denominational schools speak about their Christian atmosphere. Monasteries promote Christian vocations. Regardless of the particular kind of institution, advertising themes are public relations gambits that more often represent pretensions rather than facts.

Advertising themes often represent the organizational self-image as the members of the organization would ideally like it to be. Frequently they reiterate the dominant value the institution wishes the public to believe it to hold or to be striving toward. The consultant must be careful not to take a condescending attitude toward advertising themes as a result of his being able to observe the gap between fact and fiction. No human being fully lives up to the aspirations he holds for himself, nor does any organization of humans. However, this is not to say that the consultant should not make inferences about dominant values, organizational self-images, and aspirations. The consultant will want to be alert to elucidating, enunciating, and clarifying advertising themes sufficiently to be able to differentiate between illusion and reality because the greater the gap, the more the intraorganizational difficulty.

Many of the predominant features of an organization's self-concept result from the incorporation of values that originated from pretensions. Public utility companies, for example, had to identify themselves as service organizations to combat the residual hostility when holding companies were fractionated. The effort to live up to this concept of self has been a vital component of the organizational self-image of some public utilities for many years. The first example illustrates the advertising theme of a nation. The three case excerpts which follow it illustrate what is meant by advertising themes in other organizations.

Growth statistics, offered everywhere [in North Vietnam], on bicycle-ownership, irrigation, rice harvests, maternity clinics, literacy are the answer to "the war of destruction," which began February 7, 1965; a bombed oak putting out new leaves is a "reply" to the air pirates of the Air Force and the Seventh Fleet. All Communist countries are bent on furnishing growth statistics (it is their form of advertising), but with Hanoi this is something special, carrying a secondary meaning — defiance. On a big billboard in the city center, the number of U.S. planes shot down is revised forward almost daily in red paint — 2818, they claimed when I left, and the number keeps growing. In villages the score is kept on a blackboard. Everything they build is dated, down to the family wells in a hamlet — a means of visibly recording progress, like penciling the heights of children, with the dates opposite, on a door. And each date has a clear significance in the story of resistance: 1965 or 1966, stamped on a well, proclaims that it was built *in spite of* the air pirates. (*New York Review of Books,* May 23, 1968, p. 4.)

Chetopa Power and Light has had extensive and varied advertising since its organization in 1921. Ads have appeared in the newspaper, labor journals, government journals, and business magazines. This advertising is devoted to propagandizing the company's policies and is presented as part of the "trend of the times." There appear to be seven basic themes that are now and have been the foundation of the company's contact with the public. (1) Keeping up with industrial Pennsylvania: (the state): "The capacity of Chetopa's plants and distributing systems always have been kept well ahead of customer requirements." (2) Concerning military efforts: "No public funds need be spent to provide adequate power for the country's defense activities . . . farsighted growth policy has proved invaluable." (3) Concerning natural catastrophe: "We too have suffered damage . . . our crews are working around the clock to restore service." (4) Concerning individual welfare: "Household drudgery is a thing of the past in a home that makes full use of the many time- and laborsaving electrical appliances . . ." (5) Concerning cost: "Electricity is cheap and has remained so despite the rising cost of living." (6) Concerning the "common good": "One ideal — to serve all from the humblest home to the greatest industrial plan." (7) Concerning ownership: "Socialism, no matter how honestly administered, is essentially nonproductive, regimented, and does not have the basic ingredient of good management."

"We are a friendly, congenial church that stands firmly on the Word of God as propounded in the Bible," say the ads for Ardley Baptist Church. "Come hear preaching that will restore your faith, worship with others who are not swayed by worldly distortions of His Word." Put another way, the ads say, "Come and reaffirm your fundamentalist belief with people who share it."

The themes of the Antioch College catalog are: (1) we are good — we work continuously to develop new pathways to liberal education; our work is as large as life itself. (2) We are humanistic — we teach people how to live in a changing world with democratic values; to appreciate culture, beauty, intellectual matters; and to achieve personal fulfillment. (3) We are practical — our students alternate between adult work and school, including foreign experience. (4) We are effective — 80 per cent of our students go to graduate school, many decide to do so while here, changing their life purpose while here. (5) We are personal — our professors are good models. (6) We are nonmilitary — there is no ROTC on the campus, students do get deferments until they finish their academic work.

d. Organizational symbols and slogans

Here the consultant should ask: What is the organizational symbol and why has the organization chosen this particular one, maintaining and nurturing it? Symbols range from abstract designs, to animate objects, to animal images. The symbol of an organization says something about the relative strength and mode of handling aggression as viewed by the people in it. The University of California Golden Bear and the Princeton University Tiger are different from the Hornet of Kansas State Teachers College of Emporia. Antioch College has no such symbol. These excerpts illustrate:

Reddy Kilowatt, the symbol of investor-owned utilities, is a bright, captivating little fellow who is "at your service." He combats the image of a powerful ogre, an image more characteristic of the electric utility during holding company days. He is a harmless lad, always ready to help, who presumably has no selfish interest. Investor-owned public utilities would prefer to be viewed as service oriented organizations rather than as money grubbing companies that maintain effective lobbies in state legislatures.

The silver pin with its Confederate battle flag unfurled inside a capital C, for Confederacy, with the one word beneath it: "survivor," is a simple symbol of a cause at Wade Hampton Academy in Orangeburg, South Carolina. Confederate veterans in South Carolina wore the pin to show that they had survived the disaster of the Civil War and the ignominy of Reconstruction. Today's "survivors," wear the pin to symbolize their survival of public-school desegregation. The pins are worn today by students in private, all-white Southern schools chartered since the 1964 Civil Rights Act began forcing segregated Southern public schools to admit Negroes. Rather than submit to what they regarded as Federal meddling and "social experimentation," parents in many towns put their money and their children into newly organized private schools. (*The National Observer,* March 25, 1968.)

Compared to [Elsie the cow], Betty Crocker might be counted among the kitchen help. From Ann Page to Ann Pillsbury, no other female corporate personality is more celebrated, more beloved, or more fawned over than the fawn colored, pure bred Jersey heifer known as Elsie the Cow. In thirty years as the bovine symbol and spokeswoman ("Penny for penny, your best food buy is milk") for Borden's milk and dairy products, her daisy garlanded, contented countenance has appeared in thousands of ads, on billions of containers, cartons, and packages, and even grace the company's annual report . . . Yet, so diverse has Borden grown that while Elsie is still a fitting symbol for milk and ice cream, President Marusi wonders: "How can you put a cow on a drum of formaldehyde?" Still, Borden is not about to abandon a character who once proved more recognizable in a public poll than Dwight Eisenhower and Jane Russell. As a Russian critic writing in the Soviet publication *Minimag* once observed, "A cow named Elsie is alluded to frequently in the advertisements of a milk company named Borden. I am sorry that in Russia we have no advertising of this type." (*Dun's Review,* May 1967, p. 44.)

Chrysler Corp. assembles [d] a new identity . . . by employing a program with the Pentastar as its symbol . . . Townsend [chief executive officer] wanted the identity program to:

Tell Chrysler's public . . . that it was a large, progressive company making a variety of important quality products; . . .

Establish that Chrysler was a cohesive, viable and understandable organization with which an individual could easily deal . . . [and]

Increase the effectiveness of advertising and marketing by providing continuity through a "memorable corporate signature." . . . The company thinks that Pentastar provides an image of precision, strength, integrity, and unity. It chose a symbol without words because the corporate name was the name of a car line, and because an emblem provides greater flexibility and would represent the company regardless of changes in direction, personnel, or fortune. [The symbol surmounts language barriers, too.] (*Business Week*, April 29, 1967, pp. 59, 62, 64.)

The organizational slogan tells the consultant what the company feels itself compelled to be or what it sees itself as being. The slogan is the way a company projects its image to the outside world. The consultant should note the extent of that projection: How far does the company push this slogan and into what areas? For example, does it say the same thing to a scientific audience as to a lay audience? To physicians as to patients? To wholesalers as to retailers? If not, why not, and what difference does it make? Unofficial slogans should also be included in this section. Sometimes slogans are used like security blankets, some people feel secure as long as they can mouth a certain set of words:

> *Comprehensive four-year liberal arts college*
> *E Pluribus Unum*
> *People are our most important products*
> *Live better electrically*
> *None may enter who can pay; none may pay who enter*
> *Research for Life*
> *Maximum benefits at minimum cost — with the best possible service*
> *Avis tries harder*
> *So we may better serve*
> *To the stars through difficulties*
> *A city in motion*

e. Language of policies as distinct from the policies themselves

Pursuing organizational language, the consultant should review the way in which organizational policies are stated. The tone of directions given inwardly more often conveys the true feelings predominating in the organization than those words that are spoken outwardly. The contrast between the language of policies and the manner in which the company speaks to its respective public reflects a gap that may have important psychological significance. The greater the emotional distance between the language of policies, as opposed to the language of advertising, ideology, and themes of employee publications, the more likely the latter is to be a facade and the greater the likelihood of internal conflict. The language of policies informs the investigator about the manner in which the organization envisions its employees. How does it look upon them? Is the language condescending, forbidding, commanding, reasonable, obtuse, pretentious? Does the language address the employees as human beings? Is it so complex that the employees will not look at the message unless they absolutely have to? Must explanations be followed verbatim? Some organizations make their policy statements in a superficial manner, as if to say, "You won't feel this if we gild it." This is the "orange juice and castor oil" treatment.

Policies often vary in their tone from institution to institution. For example, hospital policies are likely to be formal and specific because of the relationship to legal obligations and the treatment program. However, even under such circumstances there might be variation in policy that would indicate the flexibility of the institution according to the requirements of the situation. It would indeed be a flexible hospital that would say, "If you are the nurse in charge of this section, the visiting hours are 2 P.M. to 4 P.M. At times, when the patient needs extra support or when the patient is a child and would profit from having his mother close, use your own judgment." Another policy statement might say: "Do not use any bottle in which ether has been stored. Break and destroy. Failure to adhere to this rule will result in immediate dismissal." In some organizations all policies carry the same forbidding quality whether they concern minor or major matters. The following case excerpts indicate how the language of policies has been discussed.

The policies of the Veterans Administration Hospital are stated in formal, official governmentese. They say in no uncertain terms what must be done, how it must be done and with what sanctions. There is no room for people or feelings in these statements, and there is a rule for almost everything. All this is in basic conflict with the theme of affectionate warmth that must characterize a good psychiatric hospital, for it presumes that the hospital will run as a social machine according to plan.

The policies of the First National Bank make two things clear: that only the economic growth of the bank counts and that people who work there are to do as they are told. After pages of discussion about how the bank has grown, how consistent its dividends have been, the annual report touches on local race riots that got international attention only by mentioning that they affected the economy of the community during that period. Nothing is said about the bank's responsibility for helping to do something about the issues that gave rise to the riots. The policy statement clearly indicates it is the function of top management to make policy and for all other employees to effectuate it. This philosophy is in conflict with efforts to develop more responsible middle management, greater initiative, and more concern among employees with the future of the bank.

There are not many policies at St. Mary's, and those few which are on paper are vague and of little help. For example, presumably a student who fails to attend regularly or who is a disciplinary problem will be expelled from the school. But the teachers do not know from incident to incident what will happen to any given pupil. Almost all decisions depend on the whim of the principal.

f. Language of customs, taboos, prohibitions, and constrictions: direct and implied

The language of custom refers to the wording of special events, methods of worship, modes of behavior. The language of address in some churches is "sister" and "brother." Priests address each other as "father." The custom of Yom Kippur is self-abasement and atonement. The "language" of this custom would be "If you cry enough, father will forgive." In the military, the company commander is referred to as "the old man" by his subordinates. Some companies require employees to address each other as Mr. and Mrs. Some require them to dress in certain ways because the dress has certain implications to the customers, patients, parishioners, others. Here the consultant is interested in what the customs, taboos, prohibitions, and constrictions say about the organization. Does the emphasis on dress, for example, reflect a pretentiousness or a facade on the part of the organization? Does it deal with the realities of the organization's situation? Is smoking prohibited because it will contaminate the product or because the senior officer believes it to be hazardous? Are women not promoted because custom says in effect, "woman are less competent and less adequate and therefore cannot accede to these roles." What do the customs, taboos, prohibitions, constrictions say about the fears, concerns, myths, and problems of the organization?

It will be more difficult to deal with taboos because they are implicit. A taboo is proscribed verbalization or behavior. There are no written rules governing it, but it simply does not happen, at least in most instances. For example, in the armed forces, officers do not socialize with the enlisted men; in the business world, a subordinate does not invite his superior to his home for informal social purposes. For many years at IBM, there was a taboo against drinking alcoholic beverages. Even today, while there were no written rules about it, there is no liquor at IBM training centers. Here are some other examples of taboos:

An Ionian monk will not go into an expensive restaurant because the monks have vowed to live simply. Furthermore, the money for their needs must be raised by service or contribution. Therefore his conscience will not let a monk squander money in a frivolous manner. This constitutes a forceful prohibition although there are no written prohibitions to that effect. Such a taboo says, "Don't indulge yourself."

Friendship between [a professional employment agency] counselor and applicant is, of course, taboo. "Friendship breeds compassion," and compassion has no home in the private employment agency. A counselor who is a friend could cater to an applicant's wishes — and might even reverse the relationship, becoming the buyer instead of the seller. (*Trans-action,* March 1968, p. 23.)

The architecture, furnishings, and liturgy of First Presbyterian bespeak quiet dignity: uncontrolled, loud noise is prohibited here. Even the pastor presents his sermon in a tone of quiet urgency: soft, gentle, inspirational, and loving of gentle people. The parlors of the church are decorated in conservative greens and browns. The meetings and weddings held there are equally conservative. There are no "No Smoking" signs, but neither are there ash trays. The Calvinist ethic of overcontrol is everywhere silently apparent.

Only black, grey, or blue suits may be worn by Soy Co. executives. Behind that unwritten law is the implication that a man who does not dress in a conservative way is not to be trusted with money. The implicit target of the taboo is the investment analyst and the banking fraternity. The taboo extends to the wives of executives, too. They must exude dignity, elegance, and position; good taste in dress means never calling attention to yourself. The taboo is enforced by asides and casual remarks. After years of success, and with an international reputation, Soy Co. need not fear the financial community. The taboo reflects the underlying striving and insecurity of executives who have come from lower socioeconomic origins.

4. Emotional atmosphere of the organization

The emotional atmosphere of an organization refers to its tone. Characteristically, dress factories on Seventh Avenue in New York are hurried and harassed in emotional tone. There people work quickly. They speak loudly and use their hands and other body movements to facilitate communication. By contrast, the emotional tone of the Metropolitan Museum of Art is more reserved. The emotional atmosphere can be hectic but congenial, noisy and joyous, or loud and hostile. It may, in effect, say to people, "Be on your guard and control yourself," or "Enjoy, enjoy," or "One slip and you're out." In other words, the consultant wants to find out how it feels to work in the organization. Is it warm, pleasant, and supportive? Is it rejecting, hostile, and threatening?

a. Prevailing mood and range

What is the dominant emotional theme? What is more characteristic of this organization and how widely does its emotional tone vary? The range of emotionality is narrow in an undertaking establishment. There is little occasion for laughter. In the case of a newspaper editorial office, the mood may vary from excitement on election night to sadness on the eve of war. Reporters and editors in a news room are freer to swear and have less consideration for women who may hear them than might be the case with government officials in a state office building. Here the consultant is interested in the tone of the dominant emotional theme or feeling and how widely it fluctuates. These published examples illustrate:

The Jean Baptiste Point Du Sable High School, which occupies a long ugly block of South Wabash Avenue, looks, and sometimes feels, like a prison. Its long locker-lined halls are constantly patrolled by teachers stationed in such a manner that they are always in sight of each other; reinforcing them are two uniformed policemen. Wherever one goes in the school there are locked doors, keys, and patrols. The school's administration emphasize that these precautions are designed mainly to control pilfering and disturbances generated by outsiders, most of them former Du Sable students who have dropped out, but they also concede that places like the cafeteria could be powderkegs without the cops, and that the teachers' desks are likely to be cleaned out if they are left unlocked or unguarded. At the same time Du Sable is almost hopelessly overcrowded; it lacks adequate gymnasium facilities and laboratories, and although its ninth graders have been forced into other buildings, it must still conduct classes on the gymnasium floor — sometimes several going on side by side — because all the classrooms are filled. The self-contempt and the corresponding lack of motivation is the school's paramount concern and its most contagious disease. "My friends told me not to come here," said a young teacher with barely a year's experience. "Some people here are discouraged. They come to class late, sit and smoke during half the period, and dawdle over lunch. You have trouble getting books — usually they arrive late — and sometimes you suspect that they're the culls from other schools." The brighter and more ambitious students — and some are very bright and very ambitious — concur. "Sure we get the worst books," one of them said. "They say we don't take care of the books, but that's a lot of baloney. Most people do. Many of the good teachers don't use the books much; they try to get you to work with other materials." The students also agree that some of the teachers have lost interest, that they appear late for class, and that other schools "try to bribe the good teachers away." The better teachers, one of the boys said, are strict. "At Du Sable," he added, "caring and being strict go hand in hand . . . There are some teachers who don't care, and some who tell you 'I'm not here because I like it — as soon as I can I'll transfer to a white school." (Peter Schrag, *Voices in the Classroom*, Boston, Beacon Press, 1965, pp. 59, 60, 61.)

Lawrence A. Hyland explains Hughes Aircraft's ability to attract and hold onto brilliant men in terms of "a certain atmosphere, a certain environment, the measure of scientific and technological understanding within the company. It's an atmosphere, he says, that he can best characterize as having "an *élan vital*, which is something that you can't put into an organization chart or into rules and procedures. It has something to do with honesty and integrity in the way you pursue your business. I wouldn't say that there are no politics in the company. We have plenty of politics, but not quite as vicious as you find it elsewhere. We try to create an environment where this elusive *élan vital* isn't smothered, where imagination and innovation survive." (*Fortune*, April 1968, p. 174.)

b. Overall stability or variability of mood

What is the level of intensity of emotion in the organization? How rapidly and how widely does it shift? For example, how "hot under the collar" can people safely become? How free or constricted are they to say what they feel? How *strongly*, how *much*, in what *direction*, under what *circumstances*, and for what *duration*, can the people within the organization express the range of their feelings? These factors may be difficult to judge. Perhaps the best subjective yardstick for the consultant is the question, "How appropriate is this expression of feeling?" Three case excerpts are illustrative:

Linemen in the Kansas Power and Light Company work quietly and seriously while they are high on the poles. There is little direct communication among them except in soft, quiet tones, more loudly when they yell to the groundman for a piece of equipment. They are carefully guarded and concentrate intensely on what they do because of the danger from hot wires. When they descend the pole, however, they immediately start kidding each other and razzing the ground man. When they get back in the truck they will start playing cards. It is not unusual for them to curse each other in a half-joking way. Both the highly controlled behavior on the poles and the more relaxed behavior on the ground is appropriate for these men because each is a response to the situation and circumstances in which they find themselves. After periods of being overcontrolled, they must relax and discharge the pent up aggression. The continuous banter when they are on the ground is a manifestation that all is well. On the other hand, if one of the executives were to curse at an employee as the men swear at each other, that would be such an abrupt departure from his normal behavior and so inappropriate that one might suspect the executive was losing control of himself.

The atmosphere of the Pocasset School is one of activity, cheerfulness and verve. The staff is interested in each other in an open, casual way. Members are on a first name basis and there is quite a bit of kidding, especially with the principal. One gets the feeling of freedom and lack of oppression. They regard themselves as a group and enjoy each other's company. However, the two older teachers do not mix as much with the group, and one rather worried looking female teacher and a male teacher do not seem closely knit in the main group. Personal problems are expected to be contained within oneself, especially the resultant anger generated in others by personal problems and "bad feelings" within a faculty member. The atmosphere is consistently the same. Rarely is there a crisis with increased tension, and that usually occurs when a teacher's contract is not going to be renewed.

The mood at the Dalton State Hospital can be characterized by chronic depression, apathy, helplessness, and inadequacy. Lately morale has dipped to an all time low. Some years ago the hospital was much more lively, but the staff seems to have lost hope in the last few years that anyone cares about them, will lead them, or do anything for them.

(1) *Intensity of reactions*

The adjective "intensity" speaks for itself. The consultant should be interested here in the strength of the feeling. Is the hostility jocular or is it deadly serious? Does the joking serve as a basis for relationship; is the laughter in response overexaggerated and suggestive of something else? These examples speak to the point of intensity:

After years of bitter hostility between them, the union directed the following advertisement in the Sheboygan, Wisconsin newspaper to the Kohler Company: "Let's wash the ring out of the bathtub! For years we made good bathroom fixtures at Kohler Company. The basins and bowls were as good as any in the industry. The wages and working conditions were not. Into each tub we made went a lot of workmanship, and little invisible rings of resentment — resentment against the atmosphere of fear . . . against second-class contracts we got for making a first-class product. The layers of that resentment kept piling up . . . Why are our ranks still intact in the tenth week of the strike? The answer is easy, those rings of resentment were piled pretty thick." (Walter H. Uphoff, *Kohler on Strike*, Boston, Beacon Press, 1966, pp. 176–177.)

The cat that hangs around a certain Israeli restaurant must be a Jewish cat, for it has real *chutzpah* (impudence, audacity, élan). One day last summer it leaped from the floor and pulled a piece of boiled chicken into the lap of a lady. As she was dabbing ineffectually at her dress, a waiter sauntered over, looked reproachfully at the cat and said, "She does that all the time. We've tried to kill her, but it doesn't work. We threw a piano at her once, but nothing happened to the cat, and the piano got broken. He shrugged, smiled, and walked off . . . [The woman] shrugged and smiled herself. "Nowadays, we all behave in a nice Jewish hysterical way," she said.

After their triumph in the Six Days' War, many Israelis became tolerant of minor disasters. They could afford to be gracious about losing small skirmishes to restaurant cats. They were not smug or arrogant, but they radiated self-confidence. A visitor felt almost as it he were in the midst of a society composed exclusively of manic depressivess — all of them riding the crest of a manic cycle. (*Holiday*, December 1967, p. 64.)

The monks at St. Ignatius are bitter in their frustration. The conservatives in the majority resent what they take to be the disloyalty of the liberals; the liberals look upon the conservatives as frayed and psuedo religious. They tear at each other in chapter meetings and then withdraw into cliques to berate the enemy. The atmosphere is similar to a hot civil war.

(2) *Duration of reactions*

How long do these reactions last? If people are happy, do they stay reasonably happy or are they quickly disillusioned? If they are hostile, are there lasting residuals of hostility or is the hostility dissipated quickly as it might be among rival partisans in the audience of a football game? If feelings last a long time, they may on the one hand reflect stability of mood, basic solidity, or a positive quality. On the other hand, if minor provocations precipitate feelings of great intensity that last long periods of time, the consultant might suspect continued aggravations and chronic hostility as reflected in the union advertisement cited above. A published example and two case excerpts illustrate duration:

The departure of Mr. Lois climaxed a year or more of internal strife, resulting in two administrative reorganizations, one of which is still under way, and enlivened by rumors, at least partially confirmed, of executive suite — donnybrooks, usually involving the volatile Mr. Lois . . . The agency's present management contends most of these stories have been spread by unhappy former employees and that they're all vastly exaggerated. (*Wall Street Journal*, May 23, 1968, p. 34.)

Once the fifteen-year-old breach between businessman members of the congregation and the academic-professional group was healed, reactions of the congregation at Temple Beth Sholom, though intense, passed quickly. There was agitation about not renewing the rabbi's contract, but there was no name calling or bitterness. When it became apparent that the board was making every effort to meet both its legal and moral obligations to the departing rabbi and considering his interests in a gentlemanly way, argument disappeared. By the end of the annual congregational meeting, though, this issue had been in process for five months, the members were congratulating each other on what a good job they had done and how much better it would be for the rabbi to find a new post. Now, differences flare but quickly die out. Congregational cohesion has never been stronger.

For the first five years after its revolutionary change, nothing could daunt the staff of Dalton State Hospital. No problem, even schizophrenia, was too big to conquer; no other hospital was half as good; no institution was more loved by the press or the community. Budget difficulties were only temporary hurdles to be surmounted. Gradually, the spirit declined. Now, the reverse is true. Only once in a while does hospital spirit perk up — usually when a new clinical director is appointed or a new building erected.

(3) *Appropriateness to stimulating factors*

Are people appropriately pleased and happy because their accomplishments and achievements lend themselves to such feelings or because they are whipped up into a false sense of achievement? If the latter is the case, then they will again and again have to be whipped up to that level, and ultimately the effectiveness of that kind of motivation will decline. If they can take many minor frustrations without becoming disillusioned in their leadership, then this speaks well for the kind of affectional bond and trust existing between the leaders and their subordinates. If reactions are disproportionate to the events that precipitate them, then the consultant must ask their source for they are then likely to be displacements from discontents that cannot be discussed for conscious or unconscious reasons. These two case excerpts are illustrative:

The Central YMCA executives lose their sense of achievement with each new accomplishment, and they then have to be fanned into enthusiastic pursuit of the next goal. This is partially because quotas for membership, building campaigns, annual budgets, and special projects are always set far above what is possible to attain. The specific attainments themselves have consistently exceeded previous levels, but because they are so distant from the quotas, the men repeatedly experience failure rather than success. So their negative feelings are really not appropriate to their record. Their anger at the executive secretary and the laymen who set the quotas is appropriate because they are deprived of satisfaction and live continually with feelings of failure.

The girls who assemble the greeting cards at Phoenix Card have reason to be pleasantly satisfied. The work proceeds routinely, the plant is bright and clean, they are able to visit freely with each other and they are paid comparatively well. No other demands are made upon them except for their work during working hours. They are free to devote their major psychological energies to their homes; they are uninvolved and untroubled by marketing, manufacturing, distribution, or profit problems. If they did not perceive the job as temporary but, rather, invested years and feelings in the organization, perhaps the story would be different.

c. Intraorganizational variability

Different parts of an organization often will have different emotional tones. Some parts may feel discriminated against by others. Some may feel they are the favorites. Some may feel oppressed. Some parts of an organization are laconic in their pace and conservative in their mood. Others are frenetic. The consultant must determine how the emotional atmosphere varies in the organization.

(1) By hierarchical level

Variability by hierarchical level refers to the nuances in feelings and attitudes from level to level. People in top management may know that the organization is going to disintegrate and feel depressed; people at the bottom are not concerned with this because either they do not know about the situation or they are aware of the ease of getting other jobs. In a merger, top management may want to get its money and get out; middle management may be frightened of the change because of the effect it could have on their jobs; laborers may be unconcerned because they can get a job anyplace. This case excerpt describes differences in mood by hierarchical level:

At lower levels in the Great Lakes Insurance Company hierarchy the prevailing atmosphere seemed to be one of goodwill and general satisfaction with the working conditions. People and work companions were generally described as "friendly" and the common allusion was made to "one big happy family." As one progressed up the managerial hierarchy, a shift in attitudes was evident. The old-guard employees idolized the president. They praised his extensive knowledge of the insurance business and frequently mentioned the wide range of important or influential people that he knew and associated with. In some manner, they felt that such acquaintances lent an added air of prestige to the organization. The middle management level of employees with decision-making positions had a different attitude toward the president. They were concerned about the difficulties that arise from the paternalistic attitude of the major executives, extending downward from the president. This attitude has a tendency to squelch initiative all the way down the line. The president often reversed decisions that were not to his liking. In addition, he frequently shortcut all channels of communication and authority to reverse a procedure or decision made by someone responsible for a particular area of operation. This resulted in a general disregard for established operating norms. There was also some expression of hostility by newer employees at the middle management level toward the old-guard supervisory personnel, exemplified by comments such as, "Some jobs have grown beyond the capability of the individual who started out in the job."

(2) By department

In addition to varying by hierarchical level, the emotional atmosphere within an organization will often vary widely from one department or one unit to another. This may have to do with the leadership of that unit, with the pressure on a particular unit, with the partiality shown toward one unit or another, with particular problems in a given unit, and many other factors, as these examples show:

Of all the departments in Ajax Pharmaceutical, the research department has the lowest morale. Almost since its inception, the research department has been a product research service whose work has been to produce variations on a theme — different forms of the same two or three basic products with which the organization deals. However, two things have been happening. The chronological age of the researchers has been advancing, no newer, younger people have joined the staff, and there has been a resulting decline in product ideas. Simultaneous with a shift in company focus there has been increasing pressure to evolve more basic drugs, but these researchers are not prepared to do it. Top management maintains its pressure on the marketing department as well as the research department so that the marketing department, in turn, criticizes the research department. As a result, the researchers feel themselves to be in a tenuous position and accuse top management of not understanding that research takes a long time and includes setbacks.

As far as the consultants in other medical disciplines go, there is talk about integrating psychiatry with medicine at Dalton State, but no action. The consultants feel they are window dressing and have little contact with the psychiatric staff. Were it not for good consulting fees, few would have any interest in the hospital. Next to them, the lowest morale is to be found on the night shift where the aides feel they have no part in the treatment program and rarely see the doctors, let alone the administrators. The mood in both settings is one of angry disappointment and routine boredom. "We don't matter much," they seem to be saying.

(3) Other (geographic location, profession)

Emotional tone or mood will also vary from place to place within the same organization, or it may vary widely depending on skill level, competence, and things of that kind, as reflected in these case examples:

Of the five electric generating plants in the Chetopa Power and Light Company, one is a newly automated plant and the other an older station. In the new plant, which is farthest away from the metropolitan area, the men are younger, more recently in from the farm, more highly educated, and more comfortable with electronic controls. They reject union membership, are more frequently Republican in their political outlook, are more conservative and highly identified with management. As a corollary, they are more concerned about the way their bosses regard them and with the human relations attitude of the boss than are the men in the older plant. The latter are themselves chronologically older. They learned many years ago not to expect very much interest in them as people from their superiors. They are all unionized. They are primarily Democratics and expect, not personal interest, but technical competence from their superiors. With the younger men in the newer plant, human relations competence was valued more highly than technical competence.

The pastors in the small rural churches of the Mid-Atlantic conference feel correspondingly that they have no support, no stimulation, no one to talk to. They do not dare to call on the superintendent to air their views because he will be judging them. So they are out there in the sticks. The young ones may yet move into the towns; the middle aged ones have had it, and they know it. They exhibit a restless disquiet. They would escape if only they could, but to where and how?

5. Organizational action

Here the consultant is concerned with how the organization acts, its characteristic style of behavior. Sometimes organizations are described as fast moving, lean and hungry, bumbling, and so on. Each of these words or phrases captures a nuance of what we mean by organizational action.

a. Energy level

What is the pace of the organization? With what degree of enthusiasm or lethargy does it pursue new products, different markets, innovative technology? How aggressive is it in its competitive efforts? In speaking of the degree of "vigor" of an organization, the consultant will be making a value judgment. Implicitly or overtly he will be comparing this organization to another, in the same or in a different field. For clarity's sake, he may want to state his yardstick, as in this excerpt:

Craig Elementary School is bright, shiny, colorful, and well-equipped. The teachers exude pleasure and vitality. Benson, by contrast, is almost the extreme opposite. There are few books in its dingy library. The walls need paint. The children are shabbily dressed, the teachers seem dull and frowsy. There is an air of lethargy about the place that does not bode well for the children. It's hard to believe both schools are in the same system.

(1) *Consistency or variability of application*
   (rate of discharge of energy)

Here the consultant is concerned with whether the organization applies itself continuously and diligently to whatever it perceives to be its tasks, whether it operates from crisis to crisis or in response to some form of pressure. Some organizations operate continuously at high pressure and fast tempos, others are very quiet and sedate. Two case examples and a published excerpt illustrate:

The Erio Gas Distribution Company goes quietly about its daily business. Its gas is fed through its major pipelines to local city distribution systems. Prices are fixed by the state regulatory board and the major work on rates is therefore done by the company attorney. Apart from routine maintenance of lines, compressor stations, and offices, there is little actual management work to do. Meters are read, bills distributed, collections made — all this is handled routinely. Even the sale of gas appliances is carried on in an unspectacular way. As a result, most of the executives are easily able to take considerable time for golf, public relations, and community affairs.

If anything, the Ionian order has been consistently passive. It has not sought to learn from others about such matters as new ways of ministering to the various needs of parishioners, the management of retreat houses, new models of theological education in seminaries and colleges, or even to consider its basic theology in the light of contemporary developments. Its fund-raising efforts have yielded only half of what was expected and that goal was comparatively modest.

A visitor to the new school [Mount Anthony Union School] quickly senses its success with both students and teachers . . . a board member says, "The biggest difference is that these kids seem to enjoy going to school today, and I never began to enjoy it until I went to college. It is a kicky environment. The kids say, 'Here we belong.' " (*Fortune,* April 1968, p. 146.)

(2) *Points and periods of peak expenditure of energy*

For some organizations, there are particular times when they must be especially vigorous. They may be deliberately slow-paced at other times to allow sufficient reserve to cope with the peak periods. How and when they do so says something about the organization's capacity for adaptation and also its point of great vulnerability. These are case examples describing peak energy expenditure:

The point of peak energy expenditure for the Central Telephone Co. is following a natural disaster. For example, following the 1965 tornado that devastated much of Middletown, repair and reconstruction crews were mobilized from surrounding states. They worked around the clock for several weeks restoring service. Operators worked extra shifts. Executives, too, worked overtime to support and coordinate the reconstruction in this and similar catastrophes. Telephone company employees must work long hours at points distant from their homes under dangerous and difficult conditions, sometimes in freezing temperatures. Because they anticipate having to call on their people for such herculean effort from time to time, the company is satisfied with a reasonably steady day's work without exerting too much pressure for speedup.

Christmas and Easter are the times of peak energy expenditure for Oakdale Methodist. All efforts are focused on those two holiday observances for at least six weeks preceding each holiday. Other activities are simply pushed into the background or delayed until after the holiday seasons. Summer is a time of recuperation. Church attendance drops sharply after school graduation and remains erratic through Labor Day.

b. Qualities of action

If by "energy level" we mean *intensity*, by "qualities of action" we mean the *form and consequence of the behavior.*

(1) *Degree of directness*

To what extent does the organization confront problems head-on? Does it attack the real problem or create substitute targets on which to focus its energy? The degree of directness with which an organization deals with its problems is contingent upon the sophistication available to it for recognizing problems and being able to confront them. If the organization has sophisticated resources available to it which enable it to delve into the core of a problem rather than by attacking the superficial aspects of that issue, the consultant must raise a question about the reasons for blind spots. These examples illustrate varying degrees of directness.

In the 1940's, John Deere and Company spotted early the exodus of labor from the farms to the metropolitan areas and the shift to bigger, more efficient and more highly mechanized farms . . . It aimed its research, design, and development mainly toward meeting the needs of the top . . . 20 percent of the farmers . . . In developing new machines in response to these farmers' changing need, Deere moved boldly where competitors hesitated. (*Fortune,* December 1966, p. 148.)

The solution of today's most urgent problems need not await the transformation of the whole pattern of British life . . . The nation's resources are more than adequate for such a task. The trouble is that those resources have not been properly put to work. Rarely has an economy been so overmanaged, and performed less well in response. In the land of Keynes, Keynesianism has gone slightly mad.

In order to support defense spending, to preserve the role of sterling as a reserve currency, and to keep up expensive welfare programs, British governments have constantly spun the wheels and valves of the economy. Dogged alternatively by the fear of inflation and by the fear of unemployment, they were forever heating things up or dampening them down. When the threat was inflation, they would raise taxes and curb private investment, but would leave the public sector untouched. Higher taxes would confront trade unions with the prospect of a rise in the cost of living, and so touch off demands for higher wages. Employers, certain that the government's policy would presently change and that stimulus would soon be applied once more, would hoard labor rather than risk being caught short later on. So employment stayed high, while levels of productivity lagged. The natural corrective consequences of unemployment on an economy were virtually never felt. The market was not given a chance to make its own adjustments. (*Fortune,* February 1968, pp. 108–109.)

The Salvation Army . . . [has a program that] constantly . . . [reviews] practices, goals, and procedures to make sure that they are getting the most for their money. But it also means coming up with new services — such as the residential program for narcotic addicts — as the need arises. Throughout the Army, there is a great push for new methods and techniques. Part of the new stress is on education. (*Business Week,* June 19, 1965, p. 116.)

(2) *Degree of flexibility*

Some organizations respond to any problem with a predictable pattern. Others have a more task oriented focus and will respond in different ways, depending on the problem. Here the consultant should be concerned about flexibility of action or modulation of organizational behavior. Such flexibility or lack of it is shown in these excerpts:

Like most hospitals, St. Agnes' thinks it can solve all its problems if only it has enough money. There is indeed a perennial shortage of funds, but by overconcentration on that problem, the administration fails to see a host of other problems. Much could be done by way of internal reorganization, airing of problems, and more adequate supervisory support. Instead, most energy goes into continuous fund-raising efforts.

There is a simple beauty about the way Central Presbyterian distributes its energy. Once an activity is functioning well, the pastor selects those people on that committee who are most responsive to new challenges and suggests a new approach. They then investigate that possibility. If it seems possible, they look about the congregation for someone who would also be interested but who is not yet invested in a project. Momentum increaes until there is an active attack on a problem; the amount of effort varies with the number of people required on a project and its relative importance. Members of the congregation can choose not only what areas they want to work in, but the degree to which they want to invest themselves.

The [New York Stock] Exchange's decision to close at 2:00 P.M. points up some of the industry's underlying problems. In effect, this move was an admission that the industry simply could not handle all the business it could expect to get in a normal working day. Other businesses, of course, sometimes become unable to fill all their orders, but usually their problems involve a shortage of plant capacity or possibly of materials. The Street's difficulty involves the mechanics of its business, and particularly its paperwork. In this age of automation, the Street has conspicuously failed to keep peace . . . it completely misjudged future trading volume. In the 1967 market there were no high peaks or deep valleys in trading, just heavy, sustained volume, day after day. In a way, this unrelieved pressure just made the back-office problems that much more difficult to handle. (*Fortune*, May 1968, pp. 150–151.)

(3) *Planning and timing*

Some organizations let events happen to them. Others make things happen, master their own worlds, and compete aggressively to survive. Planning refers to how the organization uses itself as a mastery device. It refers not only to scheduling, but to anticipating change, mobilizing resources, and applying resources with maximum thrust at optimum moments. Planning and timing is the focus of these excerpts:

Perhaps the most important decision Alan Fish will have to make as chief executive officer at Preston Publishing will be one of timing. Fish will have to time Preston's entry into the field of educational electronics. So far the company has held back. But it cannot stall indefinitely, because the education market is very important to Preston, which has some 11 per cent of the U.S. textbook market. Needless to say, the coming of electronic computers to the education field could change things drastically for textbooks. Right timing is going to be very important to Preston. The education market figures prominently in its plan to reach $1 billion by 1976 — triple its present size.

The Topeka School Board realized that it could not delay in establishing adequate educational facilities. To wait until the schools were overcrowded before building new ones would be unfair to students and teachers, cost more for land and construction, and inhibit community development. In 1960 the board confronted the community with these realities, proposed a $6 million bond issue, and set about building new schools as well as acquiring land for future ones. There was criticism for building schools in empty pastures while abandoning old ones, but the board has been vindicated. There are few temporary classrooms in Topeka; there never have been double sessions, and housing developments soon grew around what appeared to be isolated sites.

(4) *Degree of persistence*

Here the consultant should be concerned with whether the organization finishes the tasks it sets for itself or abruptly leaves them in order to pursue other objectives. If a project is unsuccessful, does the organization readily disband it? Persistence can be either useful or costly. Three brief examples illustrate degree of persistence:

So eager was Henry Ford II to enjoy the fruits of government contracts that he purchased Philco Corporation whose electronic transistors were used in vehicles for the space program. He aggressively took over the organization and within a few years had fired the majority of top management. During the first few years under Ford's direction, Philco sunk into the red. He persevered until Philco pulled itself into an enviable profit picture. (*Fortune,* February 1966, p. 117.)

The congregation of Temple Beth Sholom is doggedly persistent. It struggled for nearly 15 years, through the tenures of three rabbis, to build a new sanctuary. Despite the small size of the congregation, various rifts, rising costs, and an abortive fund-raising campaign, the new sanctuary was ultimately built. Its maintenance taxes the resources of the congregation; nevertheless, the members have responded to increased costs and have even raised the salary of the rabbi to a commendable level.

Dalton State Hospital becomes excited about one project, then another. There is a fadlike quality to this activity. Committees are born and die; no one misses them; they just peter out. Part of this is due to staff turnover; more, to a lack of consistent direction and urgent demand from the administration.

(5) *Effectiveness*

Here the consultant is concerned with how well the action works. It may be effective though stereotyped as, for example, when a management threatens to move its plant everytime it appears that unionization might be successful. Effectiveness has to be judged in financial terms, in terms of the reputation of the organization and its position in its field, in terms

of its stability and capacity for long-term survival, and in terms of meeting its own goals. The question of effectiveness throws into relief the issue
of whether the organization knows what its goals are. The consultant,
however, will have to be careful not to misjudge temporary achievement
for long-rang effectiveness. These examples refer to effectiveness:

Nathan's Famous, a crowded, cluttered hot dog stand and short-order eatery at
the corner of Surf and Stillwell Avenues in Brooklyn's Coney Island that looks
like a Duncan Hines reject, has grown to become the world's biggest small business with a volume of $8 million annually. In 52 years as a gastronomical institu-
tion, the red-hot restauranteur who owns Nathan's Famous, Nathan Handwerker,
reckons that he has sold more than 200 million hot dogs. But to say that Nathan's
sells franks is to suggest that Tiffany peddles baubles. For Nathan's Famous
frankfurters are a triumph of the sausage maker's art. Prepared specially for
Nathan's, primarily by Detroit's Hygrade Food Products, the franks are made of
lean, high-protein beef free of fillers or starches and contain Nathan's special
blend of spices. Their quality is constantly spot-checked by an independent testing laboratory. The kitchens of Nathan's are so efficiently geared to fast food
service that Nedick's once sent an engineering team down to see how Nathan's
makes its orange drink. (*Dun's Review,* May 1968, pp. 87–92.)

Central Presbyterian Hospital is an effective organization. It is financially stable;
accredited by appropriate agencies; has the respect of physicians, community and
staff; and has less trouble than any other attracting personnel. No fund-raising
effort has ever failed. It has never been overcrowded or accused of giving sloppy
care.

Millard G. Roberts' 12-year effort to combine cost accounting and higher education at Parsons College, Fairfield, Iowa, ended abruptly when Parsons' trustees
fired him. Many of Roberts' ideas were imaginative: 12-month operation of classrooms and high salaries for top professors . . . [and] admission of any high-
school graduates regardless of grades and limited curriculum. During Roberts'
tenure, Parsons grew from some 200 students to 4,900 . . . But Parsons also became known, among other things, as Dropout U . . . the North Central association of Colleges and Secondary Schools . . . revoked Parson's accreditation; the
trustees, in turn, removed Roberts. (*Fortune,* August 1967, p. 32.)

(6) *Constructiveness or destructiveness*

Here the consultant may want to make a value judgment about the
organization's actions vis-à-vis its goals. In what ways does the organization's action undermine its long-run purposes? How does it hurt or support the community? How does it entrench itself firmly in the social
fabric? These issues may well have been fully covered by information
gathered for the preceding item ("effectiveness"). If not, the consultant

should examine the organization's actions in detail here. These excerpts emphasize the constructiveness or destructiveness of action:

St. Catherine's complains about state-set educational standards and maintains a running battle with accreditation authorities. It claims it is giving superior education, and many of its supporting parents believe that. As a matter of fact, the quality of education is inferior. Thus the school does its students a disservice and provokes unnecessary hostility with secular authorities. Its posture is self-defeating.

The NASA contractors have played a part, too, in helping Huntsville [Alabama] adjust to the space age. The Association of Huntsville Area Contractors (AHAC) was formed in 1963 for progress in race relations . . . AHAC realized that few Negroes would ever qualify for good jobs in the space and missile field unless the public schools did better at teaching and motivating the large number who grow up in culturally deprived homes. Accordingly, the association joined with Huntsville area school systems in persuading the Ford Foundation to finance, by a $2.7 million grant, nursery school and kindergarten instruction and a program for home improvement. Also, AHAC is cooperating with Alabama A&M College, a Negro institution, in a work-study program for students. (*Science,* March 10, 1967, p. 1228.)

In this chapter, the consultant has begun to give meaning to the factual data he has gathered. He has begun to define subtleties of process, nuances of difference, in preparation for developing an understanding of those forces and factors which distinguish the organization under study from others, no matter how similar it may seem to others. It is these sutble distinctions which allow him to feed back to the organization the kind of information about itself that the organization can use. The inferences he has made in this chapter constitute the bases for the interpretations he will make in the next.

8

INTERPRETATIVE
DATA

Portion of outline covered in chapter 8

B. Attitudes and Relationships

1. Contemporary attitudes toward, and relationships with, others

   a. *Range, diversification, depth, and constancy*
      - *(1) Customers*
      - *(2) Competition*
      - *(3) Employees*
      - *(4) Occupational associations and representatives*
      - *(5) Stockholders*
      - *(6) Legislative bodies*
      - *(7) Executive and regulatory bodies (governmental)*
      - *(8) Control bodies (internal)*
      - *(9) Suppliers*
      - *(10) Financial community*
      - *(11) Host community*
      - *(12) Dealer organizations*
      - *(13) Plant builders*
      - *(14) Consultants*
      - *(15) Others*

   b. Major attachments
      - *(1) Positive*
      - *(2) Negative*

   c. Masculine-feminine orientation
      - *(1) Of organization*
        - (A) MASCULINE
        - (B) FEMININE

(C) DEGREE OF ACHIEVEMENT

(D) HOW PERVASIVE

(2) *In relation to the industry*

d. Transference phenomena

(1) *Related to the consultant*

(2) *Related to the organization*

(3) *Related to each other*

2. Relations to things and ideas

a. Quality and intensity of relations to plant, equipment, raw material or supplies, product, and services

(1) *Symbolization*

(2) *Unconscious personification*

b. Time: how is it regarded

(1) *Past, present, future orientation*

(2) *How is future planned for*

(3) *Is time valued as an investable commodity*

(4) *View of work cycles*

c. Space: how is it conceptualized

(1) *As a local concern*

(2) *As a cosmopolitan concern*

d. Meaning of work for the organization

(1) *As a device for coping with the environment*

(A) IN ECONOMIC TERMS

(B) IN TERMS OF SKILL

(C) IN TERMS OF THINKING

(D) IN TERMS OF PSYCHOLOGICAL DEFENSE

(2) *As a device for fulfilling psychological contract*

(3) *As a device for channeling energy*

(A) CONSTRUCTIVELY

(B) DESTRUCTIVELY

(C) AS A PROCESS OF REGRESSION

    i. Within the work setting

    ii. In nonwork activities

e. Authority, power, and responsibility

(1) *How does the organization regard power*

(A) THE POWER OF OTHERS

(B) THEIR OWN POWER VIS-À-VIS THE WORLD OUTSIDE

(C) POWER INTERNALLY

    i. Generally

    ii. By ranks

(2) *How does the organization handle authority*

(3) *How does the organization handle responsibility*

(A) OUTSIDE THE ORGANIZATION
(B) INSIDE THE ORGANIZATION

f. *Positions on social, ethical, and political issues*

3. Attitudes about self
   a. *Who do they think they are and how do they feel about it*
   b. *Where do they think they are headed and how do they feel about it*
   c. *What are their common aspirations*
   d. *How do they look to themselves*

4. Intraorganizational relationships
   a. *Key people in the organization*
   b. *Significant groups within the organization*
   c. *Implications of a and b*

B. Attitudes and Relationships

In Chapter 7, we discussed the organization's perceptions, attention, knowledge, language, emotional level and modes of action. When these aspects of the organization are integrated, they result in characteristic attitudes and relationships. We speak of these characteristic attitudes and relationships as the organization's psychological stance. Having made inferences from the factual data about the many ways in which the organization is functioning currently, the consultant now must synthesize his inferences into statements about an organization's psychological stance. What feelings lie behind the ways the organization functions? The focus here is on enduring psychological postures or perspectives that give unity, cohesion, and consistent direction to organizational behavior or, conversely, that may be detrimental to it. These are reflected in attitudes toward major dimensions of existence: attitudes toward self and others, toward time, work, and authority. Although the consultant has already referred to attitudes in many of his examples, here he must give them explicit attention. It is imperative to understand attitudes and relationships since they represent ways of coping with enduring implicit or explicit problems. Also, any attempt at organizational intervention or change will necessarily involve an alteration in the configuration of the organization's attitudes and relationships. It is this configuration, rather than isolated variables, that must be dealt with if changes are to be

effected and effective. In Chapter 9 we will consider the systematic inter-
relationship of many factors and the configurations into which they fall
in the concept of organizational integrative patterns.

1. Contemporary attitudes toward, and relationships with, others

What is the organization's conception of and relationships to those
persons, forces, and institutions outside itself? Toward some it may be
truculent; toward others, supportive; toward still others, hostile. An
organization may build permanent working relationships with other organizations. It may be transient in its relationships. It may be expedient:
now friendly, now hostile, depending on the problems. If the consultant
examines these attitudes and relationships, he will learn what the organization perceives to be the source of its problems, upon whom it is more
likely to project blame, how it regards the emotional quality of its environment and, ultimately, its style of behavior.

a. Range, diversification, depth, and constancy

The range of its attitudes and relationships reflects the complexity of
the organization. The greater the number of attachments, the more secure
the organization will feel. The wider the scope of gratification, the greater
is the likelihood that the organization receives stimulation from many
different sources and the more energetic it is likely to be.

Diversification in this context refers to varied relationships. Some organizations insulate themselves from the economic and political world,
limiting their activities to suppliers and customers; others invest themselves heavily in trade associations, a range of specialized publics, educational institutions, and community activities.

Depth refers to the degree to which the organization becomes involved
in its relationships. For example, some organizations, like an air terminal
news stand, can be casual in their relationships with their customers;
others, like hospitals, must become deeply involved, literally in life and
death matters. All become more deeply involved with, or related to, some
persons, institutions, or activities than others. Depth of involvement will
tell which relationships are more important to the organization.

Constancy is the other side of the coin of dependability. Constancy of attitude characterizes the stability of the organization's perceptions and stance and the enduring nature of its relationships. It also says something about the degree to which the organization can be counted on and by which other persons, organizations, or publics.

(1) *Customers*

There is a business axiom that the customer is king. In some organizations he may be regarded as almost a nuisance. A customer (patient, client, parishioner, student) is presumably the person for whom the organization is in business. The organization's relationship to its customers is a vital index to the kinds of problems it has or is likely to have. In the following case example and published excerpt we glimpse organizational stands toward customers.

The attitude of the faculty of St. Mary's High School toward the students, and the relationships with the students, were generally positive. Many of the students do well scholastically. The teachers spend long hours in extracurricular activities on behalf of the students. They delegate some positions of trust to students. They make a concerted effort to combat self-segregation among the Mexican-Americans. Students with low IQ's are integrated in the classrooms with those with high IQ's; the teacher evolves his own arrangements for the differential rates of learning. The faculty was split on the matter of discipline: the lay teachers thought there was enough and the nuns felt that there should be more.

Rich's forte, and the despair of other merchants, is the lavish credit and exchange policy that has made it as much an Atlanta institution as Scarlett O'Hara. "The customer is never wrong" is a Rich's policy, and on that friendly basis the store goes to the improbable length of accepting any merchandise returns — even if they were bought at another store. Once . . . Rich's exchanged hundreds of pairs of defective nylons of a brand it did not stock . . . A bride's mother, who complained that a Rich's wedding cake came with yellow layers instead of white, got another cake even though her guests had already consumed the first . . . Rich's seldom duns . . . "Our theory," explains Rich . . . "is that 95 per cent of the people are honest, and we're not going to discommode 95 people to root out the other 5" . . . Rich's credit department patiently lets people pay when they can [and] never tacks on service charges . . . When Atlanta had to pay its schoolteachers in script during the Depression, Rich's exchanged the script for money. When the Winecoff hotel burned in 1946, . . . Rich's handed out free clothes to the survivors and provided shrouds for the dead. (*Time,* June 23, 1967, pp. 89, 90.)

(2) *Competition*

Competition between organizations, as between individuals, arouses rivalry, hostility and, more covertly, fear. The manner in which an organization relates to its competitors, competes with them, and reacts to their competitive behavior relates to the stability and security of the organization. There can be a range of diversified relationships with the competition, depending on the history of the relationship and the behavior of the competitor. These diverse relationships will reflect some of the values of the organization being studied. Here are two different stances toward competitors:

The Lakeview Baptist Church feels that it is in direct competition with the highly prestigious and well established First Baptist Church, which is four times its size and located about nineteen blocks away from it. The Lakeview Church is about six years old and is in an area of town which is attracting young married couples. Because the Lakeview membership has not swelled noticeably in the six years since its founding, the congregation is disappointed and feels hostile toward First Baptist.

Two years ago Mercy Hospital at Benton Harbor, Michigan and Memorial Hospital at St. Joseph, Michigan decided to stop competing against each other. So that their trustees might gain a new perspective, the two hospitals simply exchanged them. They launched a joint fund-raising campaign — collecting $1.7 million more than the $3 million they were aiming for — and drew up a combined pension plan. Their next project is a psychiatric unit. While the American hospital will continue to be the center of medical services, planners see it also as the center of giant medical complexes — a trend that can already be seen developing around the nation's 87 medical schools. The prime value of such facilities is that they would cut down on duplication of services, equipment and personnel. (*Business Week,* July 15, 1967, p. 132.)

(3) *Employees*

Attitudes toward, and relationships with, employees may vary with hierarchical level, geographical dispersion, history of the plant, and so on. Much of the time a consultant would be tempted to assume these to be constant, just as he would assume parents to act in exactly the same manner toward each of their children. At this point in the analysis, differentiation is important. Some companies are paternalistic with respect to their line employees but exert severe pressure on their executives. In some, the customer is always right and the employee always wrong. In still others, there is a latent attitude that the employee could not be very

good or he would not be working in the organization. These two case
excerpts and a published example illustrate stances toward employees:

The management of Pioneer Ridge Laboratory recognizes that the organization's
effectiveness depends on its engineers' satisfaction and caters to this group in an
attempt to give it the status recognition demanded by professional personnel.
This policy creates conflicts between the engineers and their supporting personnel. Technicians, draftsmen, and shop workers resent the special privileges given
to engineers: advantageous parking spaces, no time clocks, freedom to arrive at
work later than other groups of employees.

The university has long had a "repressive" atmosphere, with students and faculty chafing at what they regard as "unreasonable" restrictions. Students are not
allowed to drink on campus (nor are faculty for that matter); most are not allowed to possess cars; and, until recently, they were not allowed to live off campus, except in university approved housing. They also feel they have little voice in
university affairs. A 1967 survey of Delaware seniors, conducted by the university, revealed that a surprising 55 per cent strongly agreed that "the college
administration here generally treats students more like children than adults" as
compared to only 13 per cent who expressed this belief in a 1963 national sample of undergraduates. At the faculty level, a reporter visiting the campus is
struck by the fact that many faculty members are critical of the administration's
"heavy handedness" but are afraid or reluctant to voice their complaints publicly. "Who wants to be a martyr?" explained one full professor. The campus is
full of stories of faculty members, even department heads, who were allegedly
"bawled out" for incurring the administration's displeasure. And a resolution
adopted last December by the faculty of arts and science refers to a "long-standing cleavage between the university's faculty and [the] administration." (Science, May 10, 1968, p. 630.)

Relationships between the synod staff and the pastors of the Lutheran American
Merged Evangelical Church are distant, and pastors believe the staff expects
them to be "good boys." There seems to be a tacit understanding that conflict
and disagreement should not arise between them. Two members of the interviewing team attended the synod convention and found it to be quiet and
peaceful with little debate or controversy. One pastor said, "The district staff
said they welcome debate and difference of opinion, but everyone knows that's
not true." "If I challenge any synod actions," declared another, "it will only
cause me to lose status."

(4) Occupational associations and representatives

Occupational associations range from trade associations and professional societies to labor unions. Here the consultant should infer whether
the organization looks upon such associations as allies who can help with

recruitment, maintenance of internal standards, and similar needs, or views them as competing for employee loyalty. Are there varying attitudes toward different groups? What is the degree of accommodation in union-management relations? How well does the grievance arbitration process function? What is the character and degree of union challenge and management response? Such attitudes are illustrated in two case examples and a published excerpt:

The Ajax Pharmaceutical Company encourages its managerial and scientific personnel to join their professional and trade associations. It pays their dues and their transportation to meetings. The company offers awards for scientific achievement to academic scientists to keep its name prominent in appropriate scientific circles. Scientists therefore view the organization as seriously interested in science and a good place for scientists to work. Because of its attitude and actions, the company obtains a constant flow of scientific, industrial, and marketing intelligence. The company is more interested in its historic ethical drug field, so fewer of its staff are to be found in those trade associations and activities having to do with proprietary products. The company will mobilize its resources to help professional associations with which it is allied, for example, medicine. However, it is hostile to any implication that the employees might want to organize. There is a vigorous antiunion sentiment throughout the managerial hierarchy and great reluctance to have an association of employees that might serve as a mutual benefit society.

During the merger talks between the Pennsylvania and New York Central railroads, a railroad spokesman glowingly boasted that the merger would enable the lines to get rid of some 7,800 employees. Officials and members of the 24 railroad brotherhoods reacted to this statement with understandable concern. In an industry where management and labor rarely meet except in the hostile environment of the bargaining room, Stuart Saunders, chairman of the Pennsy, began seeking out union leaders for informal talks. "I knew I had to change labor's position," he says. "My argument with the leaders was: 'This is really in the interest of your people. Merger means better earnings, which means better savings, more business and more jobs. I can only get these savings with your cooperation.'" As a more practical matter, Saunders also promised the unions that no one would be fired because of the merger; only as jobs became vacant because of retirement or death will the Penn Central cut down on employees. (*Time*, January 26, 1968, p. 71A.)

While most of the membership of Temple Beth Sholom have little knowledge or understanding of the Union of American Hebrew Congregations, the Board of Directors, committee chairman, and rabbi depend heavily on it. The membership would just as soon not pay dues to the union, but the board depends on its placement service and policy guidance papers. Without the texts and educational materials, the religious school would be impoverished. The Temple therefore supports the rabbi's expenses to meetings both of the union and the Central Conference of American Rabbis as well as to regional conferences.

(5) *Stockholders*

Stockholders are to be equated with owners at this point in the outline. They may be literally stockholders or members of a cooperative, the citizens who own a community's schools, the religious denomination that supports a hospital, or the contributors to a charitable agency. Here the consultant should ask: Does the organization feel answerable to its "owners"? If so, how? Is it open and straightforward? Does it manipulate them? Does it exploit them? Some organizations go to elaborate lengths to inform their stockholders of exactly what is happening within the company. They conduct their annual meetings in convenient places and send stockholders detailed information. Others are almost cavalier in their attitude, holding their annual meetings in inconvenient locations, furnishing a minimum of information, and using annual reports as window dressing. This is an area that the consultant must scrutinize because many organizations consciously or unconsciously try to deceive the "owners" so that the management will be freer to run the organization. For example, in one organization's annual report, an increase in profit and decrease in dividends was reported; however, the organization never stated why this condition existed. One had to presume that the increased profits were diverted back into the organization. Another organization heralded its employee pension plan. What was not mentioned was that the pension fund owns a controlling interest in the company's stock; the company executives are the officials of the pension fund and therefore, for all practical purposes, are free agents. This case excerpt and a published example illustrate attitudes toward "owners" from which depth and constancy of relationship may be inferred:

At St. Catherine's High School, little attention is given to the parents except through contacts made by the secretary on a specific student oriented problem, contacts indirectly through the parish priest, and contacts made during social and athletic events with the parents.

Late in 1964, Yale, a New York based trucker and freight forwarder, reported nine months' net earnings of $904,000, a figure somewhat disappointing to the creditors and stockholders. It indicated that Yale, after a year and a half, still was not enjoying the promised high return on its very ambitious acquisition of Republic Carloading & Distributing Co., a leading freight forwarder twice as large as the parent company. But the figure was routinely accepted as fact by some observers who could, and certainly should, have taken the trouble to look behind it. If they had, they would have found that the "profit" was pure fiction, and that Yale was out of control and headed for bankruptcy.

Unfortunately, no outsiders, except the auditors, Peat, Marwick, Mitchell & Co., looked closely at what was going on inside Yale until it was much too late. Yale's distress was disclosed early last March [1965] when the company announced that its interim reports of profits during the previous year were incorrect "in the light of errors discovered in the 1964 accounts." Instead of the anticipated year-end profit, which the senior lenders had privately been told might be as much as $1,800,000, Yale announced that it would suffer a loss estimated at $3,300,000. This was merely the first shock. Next came the stunning disclosure that the $1,140,000 profit shown in the audited 1963 financial statement was also incorrect. The figure had been restated, and it was now a loss estimated at $1,880,000. (*Fortune*, November 1965, p. 144.)

U.S. colleges and universities have begun to regard the reunion as a chance for the alumni to catch up on their education. Easing out the cocktail parties are lectures and seminars. Gone are the days of the four-day binge. Harvard, MIT, Amherst, Vanderbilt, Yale and the University of Minnesota are already conducting education-oriented reunions. (*Time*, June 16, 1967, p. 76.)

(6) *Legislative bodies*

Most organizations of any size must necessarily have relationships with legislative bodies because they are so easily affected by what city, county, state, and federal legislative bodies do. Some organizations maintain formidable lobbying efforts through trade associations or public relations counsel; some have direct relationships with specific legislators; others mobilize a significant number of voices whenever necessary. Earlier the consultant examined the *attention* given to external legislative and regulatory bodies. Here he is concerned about *attitudes* toward them. Are they held in esteem, fear, respect? Treated forthrightly or maneuvered? In the case excerpt that follows, the company's attitude toward the legislature is clearly inferred. In the subsequent published examples are the bases for making inferences:

The Delaware and Hudson Insurance Company views its relationship to the state legislature as being of prime importance because of the legislature's vast potential for regulating insurance companies. Implicitly they see the legislature as a bunch of patsies, stacked in their favor. The company feels that their president, by appointing a distinguished group of men to the board, has assured the company of the best possible lobbying influence on the legislature. Each one of these men is widely known in the state and is likely to be listened to in his own right. That people were appointed to the board for this reason is apparent because the board has little influence over the direct operations of the company, and the president retains all operating power.

The university is an unusual blend of public and private characteristics. National surveys often lump it in the "public institution" or "state university" category, but Delaware generally refers to itself as a "state-related" or "state-assisted" university. It is a land-grant institution; it admits all qualified residents of the state; it performs various service functions for the state; and it draws about 35 per cent of its operating budget from state sources. Yet the ultimate authority is vested in a thirty-two-man board of trustees which is largely self-perpetuating and thus not directly controlled by the state. And within that unwieldy board, power tends to reside with the du Ponts. (*Science,* May 10, 1968, p. 628.)

Squeezed by rising costs of the Vietnam war, still troubled by the fatal Apollo fire, and influenced by polls reporting slipping public interest in space flight, congressional economizers have been slicing away at NASA's space budget. Their efforts have been so successful that the U.S., while still committed to landing men on the moon by 1970, has virtually scrapped its once ambitious planetary exploration program. NASA Administrator James Webb has been unsuccessful in getting Congress to allot the space program any more money; indeed, President Johnson requested the smallest civilian space budget in six years in 1968. In a signed editorial in *Science,* University of Iowa physicist James Van Allen contrasted the "ambitious and increasingly competent" Soviet planetary program to U.S. plans, which now include only two more flights to the planets: a pair of photographic flybys of Mars in 1969. Criticizing both Congress and the reluctance of NASA "to forcefully request adequate funding," Van Allen also warned that the U.S. "is now allowing its own high competence in planetary exploration to decay." (*Time,* January 5, 1968, p. 64.)

(7) *Executive and regulatory bodies* (*governmental*)

Banks, savings and loan associations, transportation businesses, public utilities, drug companies, schools, hospitals, colleges, and many other organizations are immediately and almost continuously involved with governmental executive and regulatory bodies. Such bodies often set rates, standards, performance requirements, make inspections, renew licenses, award franchises, and, in fact, hold almost life and death power over the organizations they regulate. In the following case example the company's attitude is one of accommodation. In the subsequent published example, the attitude is more direct and aggressive:

The Ajax Pharmaceutical Company is attuned to the Food and Drug Administration. It not only submits reports as required by that body but also its scientists maintain informal contacts with scientists representing that body. The company must keep the FDA apprised of the directions in which it is going; keep itself informed about conditions, criteria, and problems; and avoid the possibility of unfavorable decisions by keeping in the good graces of the agency. When it discovered that one of its products that was being sold overseas was producing untoward reactions, it immediately notified the FDA and voluntarily withheld that product from the domestic market. As it happened, the difficulty was with the method of operation in the overseas plant rather than with the drug itself or with domestic production. When the FDA summarily ordered one of its products off the market, the company responded with alacrity even though it felt that FDA's judgment was premature and unnecessarily negative. In the safety of their own offices, both management and scientists complain about the conservatism of the FDA, or what they view as inordinate procrastination and bureaucratic delay. They feel they are considered guilty until they can prove themselves innocent, and this inhibits product development.

In 1958 Garfield Weston's plan to start a supermarket chain in West Germany [similar to those in Canada and the United States] created near panic among German grocers. Some 24,000 of them petitioned the government to keep him out. Weston went to Bonn to meet with Ludwig Erhart, then Economic Minister. "You need a man like me," he told Erhart. "I'm a specialist in keeping down the cost of living." Discovering that none of the ministry men present at the meeting knew the cost of food distribution in Germany, he said: "I'll tell you. Your retail grocers are making 5 percent while in the U.S. and Canada we operate on 1½ to 2 per cent. I think food can be distributed for less in Germany and I'm willing to put in my own money to prove it. If I'm right, it will improve Germany's competitive industrial position in world markets." Weston currently owns 45 per cent of Deutscher Supermarket whose 100 stores have estimated sales of nearly $80 million [per year]. (*Fortune*, June 1967, p. 120.)

(8) Control bodies (internal)

A control body regulates and restrains an organization. It may be either a board of directors, a board of governors, or a group of trustees. It is usually differentiated from the executive group which runs the organization and from the public regulatory bodies which enforce public controls on the organization. Control bodies range from those that exercise little control to those that are intimately involved in the organization's management. These two case excerpts illustrate stances toward internal control bodies:

The Northeast Valley Church is a part of the Northern District Conference of the Mennonite Church. The conference represents the control body for the church. The members of the church regard the conference as being too conservative. The congregation feels that the conference does not know "what the score is in a new city church." Yet the church is dependent upon the conference, grateful for the relationship with it, and therefore loyal to it.

The board of the Burnett Ship Building Company was carefully chosen by the president to represent important areas of managerial knowledge. One member of the board is widely known as an authority in data processing, another in finance, another in education. At each meeting the president and his staff report to the board in detail about what they are doing, and particularly what they are doing in the areas of specialty represented by the board. In fact, in the eyes of some of the management, the board is "snowed" with detail. The president says that his task is to please the board and do what they require of him. However, those among his management who are uncomfortable with this kind of a relationship to the board assert that he uses the board to disguise and give legitimacy to his underlying unilateral control of the organization. They point out that he has chosen as members of the board men who run their own organizations as he runs his.

(9) Suppliers

Suppliers may provide goods and services, personnel, students. They may refer patients, provide data, or manufacture complementary or component units. Some organizations are heavily dependent upon suppliers. Others organize themselves and shape their activities in order that they will not be so dependent, such as having captive suppliers (ones which they own). Some organizations have a wide range of suppliers so they will not be at the mercy of any one. Some exploit their suppliers. Others build enduring relationships. The more the organization dominates a given market and the more it controls a given product, the greater is the dependency of the suppliers on the goodwill of the organization. Two case excerpts and a published reference illustrate attitudes toward suppliers:

Food Basket Supermarkets sets its own wholesale prices on a day-by-day basis. Its suppliers cannot bargain. The supplier either accepts the price Food Basket has set or withdraws from that relationship altogether. The supplier usually does not know from day-to-day what the price is going to be and must take his chances with his own suppliers and costs. With increasing retail competition, Food Basket is exerting more price pressure on its suppliers, and as a result, the suppliers are less able to remain profitable. However, because Food Basket has held them captive for so long, it is difficult for them to find other markets, especially among food chains who also have captive suppliers.

Temple Beth Sholom must maintain a continuing relationship with the Union of American Hebrew Congregations and with Hebrew Union College, the seminary for that body. To be cut off from that body and its seminary would cost the congregation its source of replacement rabbis and educational materials in reformed Judaism. Its pulpit would be less attractive, and its religious school would ultimately suffer. The congregation therefore pays its assessment to the union, however grudgingly, sends delegates to the biennial conference and to regional conferences and maintains a direct if distant relationship. The distance arises because neither the union nor the college can do much about the shortage of rabbis, and the services otherwise rendered are mostly by means of publications. There is therefore little vitality in the relationship, although even this relationship is better than none at all. For most of the congregation, the union and the college are distant bodies.

In 1968 Neiman-Marcus President Stanley Marcus announced that henceforth civil rights will be as important a factor as price, quality or delivery time in what his six Texas department stores will buy. Specifically, Neiman-Marcus intends to deal as much as possible with firms who hire and train more people from minorities. "We would rather do business with a company which is actually and sincerely pursuing a policy of equal opportunity than to continue to do business with one which is not," he said. "The Federal Government requires that every one of its suppliers of goods and services certifies that it is an equal-opportunity employer. We believe a private company should do no less." (*Time,* January 19, 1968, p. 83.)

(10) *Financial community*

The financial community contains official sources of funds. These may be banks, brokerage houses, fund raising agencies, insurance companies, and similar groups. A case excerpt and a published example reflect attitudes toward the financial community:

Sewell Manufacturing takes pride in not having missed a dividend in its 78-year history. The president is particularly concerned that this record be maintained so that in the eyes of the financial community his company will be recognized as a well-managed, conservative, stable organization in which people can invest for income. The president maintains a line of credit with the International Bank in New York and seeks the advice of the officials of that bank in decisions about raising money by stocks, bonds, debentures, and loans. The president makes an annual appearance before the security analysts' meeting in New York. The company's cash is maintained in local banks, and one local banker serves on the board. The president feels that the banking community is his greatest source of support: their willingness for the company to remain the stable organization it is enables him to maintain control, avoid the possibility of manipulation of the company stock and vulnerability to economic pirates, and be secure in his conservative political position. In effect, this company is run to please the International Bank and its colleagues in the financial community.

When Norton Simon bought into Wheeling Steel he looked at the company's balance sheet and decided that he could handle the company's modernization program and turn Wheeling into a really profitable operation. As soon as he bought into the organization, he kicked out the steel executives and proceeded to denounce publicly what they had been doing wrong. That brought into play something that had never shown up on the Wheeling balance sheet: the resentment of the old-time steelmen who make up what Simon calls the "steel establishment." "The trouble with not being a part of the 'steel establishment,' " Simon said, "gets into the intangibles of borrowing money. The people you have to go to get money from are a lot more inclined to give it to you, in the steel business, if you have a steelman running the company, instead of some interloper from a west coast food company." Lenders would not give Wheeling Steel the money it needed for modernization, thereby wrecking Simon's whole plan. Now the steel establishment has taken Wheeling back to its breast. It wasn't that Simon hadn't looked before he leaped; it was simply that he failed to look beyond the figures. (*Fortune,* July 1967, pp. 105–109.)

(11) *Host community*

The relationship of an organization to its host community can vary from one in which the organization is the single dominant force and controls the host community to one in which it is isolated from it. Some organizations are intimately related to a community politic; others are involved in town-gown debates. The manner in which an organization relates to the community contributes to the growth, sophistication, responsibility, and integration of the community or the stifling of it. Attitudes toward host communities are indicated in these excerpts:

Over the years, one very large national department store chain has concentrated heavily on being a good citizen in the communities in which it has stores. It has sponsored scholarships and supported charitable activities. Its managers have taken a leading role on voluntary boards, agencies, and on chambers of commerce. In recent years, it has worked to upgrade and support minority group neighborhoods, particularly those which surround its Chicago headquarters. As a result, during the Chicago riots of 1966 and 1967, the store's property in that city was untouched.

St. Matthew's Church sponsors a "housing clinic" for beleaguered residents in the ghetto area. This program is interdenominational and is intended to help the ghetto residents find adequate housing, exert pressure on slum landlords to improve and maintain their property, and to stimulate city inspection and control authorities to fulfill their obligations. The church also provides a remedial reading program and study hall on specified afternoons to help remedy the academic deficiencies of the Negro young people and provides a quiet place for them to do their homework. The church also works closely with other churches, with civic and reform bodies, and with city officials toward solving ghetto problems, finding people jobs, redressing grievances, and organizing neighborhood concern for the sick and handicapped.

Apart from buying supplies and drawing on a few community services, St. Peter's Abbey has almost no contact with members of its host community. Its monks are trained to serve missionary functions in distant lands; the priests trained in its seminary return to their respective dioceses.

(12) *Dealer organizations*

Dealer organizations are the middle men between the manufacturers and those who actually sell the product to the public. For example, a Ford agency is a dealer organization. The salesman who sells a Ford car represents the agency rather than the company. Some companies go to great lengths to build up and support their dealer organizations; others manipulate them; still others control them rigidly. The dealer organization, in effect if not literally, holds a franchise to represent the manufacturing organization. The equivalent groups for colleges are departments or schools; for a diocese or synod, the local church; for a school system, the individual school. There is an implication here that the dealer organization has a degree of autonomy from the larger organization of which it is a part and which may be the subject of study here. If this is not the case, as often it is not with respect to schools or branch stores, the individual unit must be viewed as part of the whole and not be regarded as "dealer organizations." Four case excerpts illustrate a variety of attitudes toward "dealer organizations":

The Arrowhead Tool and Die Manufacturing Co. tried to court its dealers' favor. Sales meetings were conducted, complete with a variety of drinks and a cold buffet at the end of the day. During the sales meetings and equipment orientation meetings the upper echelon Arrowhead people were almost obsequious to the distributors. The Arrowhead organization is dependent on salesmen and distributors and is constantly trying to motivate them to sell more Arrowhead products. Some conflict arises about these meetings among the employees who see the maneuver as one of seducing the distributor who can "freeload booze and steak" that might better be given to the employees.

The State Department of Mental Hygiene looks upon the respective state hospitals more as troublesome satellites than integrated components of a state system. They view the hospitals, not as units that they are to serve by means of their relationships with the governor and legislature, but as theirs to command and direct. The respective hospital superintendents are given a relatively free hand in patient care, providing there are no complaints from families, local officials, or legislators. If a conflict arises, however, the state director tries to make the hospitals conform to the political pressures, rarely examines in depth what the hospital needs to do its job, and resents the fact that it has "made trouble." The hospital administrations not only feel that they are unsupported but, more important, that they are exploited and abused.

The United Fund is presumably the joint fund raising agency for all local serv-ice organizations. Because of its function, however, it passes in detail on the budgets of all of the agencies, thus becoming a "superboard" for them. Its atti-tude toward them is cautiously guarded because the United Funds assumes that the local organization always want more money, that they are continuously en-gaged in empire building, and that they manipulate their budget requests to avoid United Fund control. Relationships between the United Fund and the respective agencies are therefore uneasy and in many cases, hostile.

Relationships between the administration and the respective schools of Barford University are marked by a cooperative spirit. The president was the choice of the deans. He meets with them regularly, seeks to compromise their differences, and presents them continuously with the problems of the entire university. The administration's point of view, with which the trustees agree, is that *they*, the schools, are the university; the function of administration is to facilitate their operation.

(13) *Plant builders*

Growing organizations do much building and rebuilding of their phys-ical plant. Some have continuing relationships with architects, contrac-tors, land planners, and others. Other organizations have no consistent relationships with such people. Obviously, in the former case, those who plan and build the organization's facilities can be intimately knowledge-able about the organization's business, personnel, and problems. They can be working partners. Those who operate more casually and expedi-ently will not have the advantage of such a partnership. Working-partner attitudes are reported in this excerpt and published example:

Berghof Refining maintains a continuing liaison with the Ludwig Corporation. Ludwig has engineered and constructed seven refineries for Berghof and the relationship between them is an optimum one for both organizations. Rather than having a range of engineering firms bid to construct plants, Berghof and Ludwig work out the details of construction and establish a cost-plus-fixed-fee arrangement. The goal for both is the best, most modern refining plant with the highest quality engineering. In the long run, this is less expensive for Berghof because of the overhead saved in nonremunerative bidding on the part of en-gineering firms, because of the engineering firm's intimate knowledge of the petroleum company's needs, and because they can plan together to allocate their respective resources to systematically meet expansion needs.

Irvine, California is a small town rushing headlong to become a big city. It was deliberately planned to be a city, and this is what sets it apart from other totally planned new towns that have been built from scratch in recent years. Irvine's quality has all along been the main concern of the man who drew up the master plan in 1961, Los Angeles architect-planner William L. Pereira. He

. . . [has] the conviction that they [cities] should be "man's greatest work of art" and ideal places for enjoying life. First as planner and more recently as consultant with some say as to how the city will evolve, Pereira has attempted to imbue Irvine with a unique character. Prominent in his plans are the elements that give Southern California its vitality: preoccupation with research and higher education, avidity for culture, and a love of outdoor living. Pereira's distinctive contribution was to provide Irvine at birth with a brain and a soul in the form of a new university. Convinced that a great university is an essential resource for a modern city, and vice versa, he served two clients by marrying their interests. He recommended Irvine to the University of California regents, who were seeking a campus site. And he helped persuade the corporation developing the Irvine Ranch to donate the land, one of the requirements of the university. His master plan calls for the campus to grow by extending spokes so that city and university will remain in intimate contact. One of Pereira's precautions is to choose clients who intend to retain ownership of their land and manage its development. Whenever possible, he also likes to stay on as consultant after the planning stage, do enough architecture to set a standard, and review the proposals of other architects. He has had such an arrangement at Irvine with both the university and the landowners. He explains: "When we do this we are like a corporation lawyer who helps to put together a new company, then carries through as counsel." (*Think*, January–February 1968, pp. 3, 5.)

(14) *Consultants*

Consultants are literally helpers from outside the organization. Some organizations will treat consultants as aliens, to be used and discarded as quickly as possible; others will see them as threats; still others will use a range of consultants who are specialists in various areas to compensate for the organization's limitations. Some will go so far as to use consultants repetitively so that, for all practical purposes, the consultants make the major organizational decisions. Three case excerpts illustrate various attitudes toward consultants:

Petro Chemicals makes extensive use of Hammond and Associates, a consulting firm, for all of its problems. This developed because the president of the company has a close relationship with one of the partners at Hammond and apparently believes in keeping his organization alive by continuously shaking it up. The consulting firm has been instrumental in three corporate reorganizations and has organized the employee benefit plans, the personnel program, office lay-out, public relations, and a range of other corporate functions. The consultants had even designed the new quarters of the medical department without consulting the medical staff. All other consultants that the company uses are retained by Hammond. The only effective employee communication to the president is through the Hammond interviewers. However, while the president is enamored of the consulting relationship, the rest of the organization resents the power of the consultants and the concomitant depreciation of their competence.

As far as the Los Almas school administration is concerned, no one knows as much about their business as they do. They therefore make no use of consultants except when they need to reinforce a point with their board or their community. Therefore consultants are expected to do what they are told and to reinforce the administration's position. Few consultants are willing to do that; and those who are, are not esteemed in their fields. For all practical purposes, the administration has hostile, distant, and contemptuous relationships with consultants.

As part of the arrangement made by the State Department of Mental Hygiene to upgrade its state hospitals and maintain their effectiveness, consultant panels were set up for each state hospital, following the model of the VA (Veterans Administration). These consultants are professionals from nearby communities and are, particularly, members of medical school psychiatry faculties. Northeastern State Hospital takes and pays for its quota of consultants. They participate in case conferences, lectures, and otherwise follow a program evolved by the hospital. Most of this arrangement, however, is a professional confidence game. Unknown to the hospital superintendent, the state director, or the consultants themselves, the hospital staff regards the consultants as interlopers who do not know state hospital practice or problems. The staff therefore sits politely in consultant sessions, knowing that if it does so, it will then be free to do just what it wants.

(15) *Others*

If there are other outside groups with which the organization has relationships, the consultant should discuss the nature of those relationships here. Some organizations, for example, are frequently involved in consortia. These are associations of companies to do together what no single one could do alone. Petroleum companies who form joint ventures for overseas projects are an example. Other organizations are involved in joint experimental ventures like various electric power companies that build atomic energy generating units or railroads that jointly operate a terminal. Some organizations, like the military, have relationships with employees' families. Hospitals, schools, colleges, and other institutions often have to deal with accrediting bodies that have no official (governmental) status. Two published examples illustrate other kinds of relationships an organization may have and its attitude toward them:

When a Minnesota company engaged in developing diagnostic equipment for testing automobile engines recently was looking for a new way to analyze exhaust fumes, it took its problem to Marshall W. Keith of the University of Minnesota — and got an offbeat but practical solution. Keith put the company in touch with the university's hospital, which had built an analyzer that sorts out the components of human breath. With a little modification, the machine is now analyzing exhaust gases. It may prove useful in upgrading engine efficiency and, theoretically, measuring output of pollutants. As director of the university's technology utilization program, Keith represents a new academic breed — the industrial extension specialist. His responsibilities are analogous to the agricultural extension services that are the pride of land-grant universities. These schools have discovered that the states they serve have an industrial constituency, as well as an agricultural one. In recent months they have been pushing hard to build a closer relationship between campus and business. As Keith puts it: "The university realizes that it has a very definite responsibility to industry as well as to agriculture." The technology utilization program approach is to foster statewide and regional industrialization with tailor-made programs at the state university. (*Business Week,* November 25, 1967, p. 64.)

Consumer Union [CU], the biggest, probably the most influential and certainly the most vocal adviser to the American consumer, sometimes makes it seem that the emptor who does not damn well caveat every minute will be scandalously swindled, if he is not electrocuted or mutilated by one or another of the machines or appliances he may be tempted to buy. CU's influence on sales is hard to measure across the board. However, there have been isolated instances in which its impact was traceable and tremendous. One of the most spectacular instances developed out of a December 1959 rating of dishwashers. Two RCA Whirlpool models were said to be "superior by a clear margin." What happened after that, according to Charles Reinbolt, manager of the Whirlpool Specialty Products Division, was so fantastic that "every morning when I wake up I shake myself wondering how long it can keep up." At the beginning of that December, Whirlpool had what it assumed was a 27-week supply of the highly rated dishwashers. Within a month, 80 percent of this stock was gone. Two months later the two models that Consumers Union liked so well were on 60 to 90 days' back order . . . [The Whirlpool people] are convinced that CU's rating is largely responsible for this big jump. (*Fortune,* September 1960, p. 157.)

b. Major attachments

Here the consultant is still concerned with the relationships in the preceding discussion. But now his attention should focus on which of the relationships the organization has the strongest connections to and feelings about. That is, in the eyes of the organization, which of these is the most important to it? The following case excerpts illustrate:

(1) *Positive*

The major attachments of the Menorah Medical Center are to patient and reputation. Staff and employees alike talk about the need to serve the patient, their wish to do so, their dependence on him, and the need to increase their effectiveness and reputation. Almost in the same breath they speak of community relations. They assume top level proficiency to be that which is expected of the hospital as a public service institution and as they, as individuals, must carry the same responsibility. All else seems to recede in importance.

The employees of the Hopkins plant of the Phoenix Card Co. are proud of the imaginative cards they produce and of the company president whose creations the cards are. In the minds of the employees, the president is practically a demigod, having built the company almost literally with his own ideas and business wizardry. They see their product as "the Cadillac of the greeting card business." When talking about their work they rarely mention any other single individual or group of individuals. This reflects a close psychological relationship between the employees and the president and heavy identification with the president's creations.

Ajax Pharmaceutical gives detailed attention to what, in effect, amounts to its dealer organizations. Actually, the people who buy its products do as customers in drug stores. But the people to whom the company caters, whom it woos with great affection, for whom it renders all kinds of support services are physicians. Wanting to remain within the ethical image, the company depends on physicians to recommend its products.

(2) *Negative*

The major negative attachment of the Pawnee and Southwestern Railway is the Interstate Commerce Commission (ICC), followed closely by the railroad unions. The management of P&SR feels that the ICC unduly constricts its managerial activities, keeps it from expanding into nonrailroad operations, insists that it maintain unprofitable passenger lines, and that its (P&SR) job is to serve the public. The management feels that the days of railroads as public servants are long since past and railroads now have to be concerned with making a profit and staying out of the financial morass. The railroad unions are seen to be similarly constricting forces, as economic barnacles dragging down a management struggling to keep its head above water.

For the employed staff and the board of the Lawton Hospital, the major negative attachment is to the local medical society. While the board and staff recognize that their purpose is to provide a medium through which local physicians can treat sick people, and although many of the physicians are individually held in great esteem, the board and staff believe that the progress of the hospital is limited because it will not become a comprehensive teaching institution or affiliate with such an institution. The stated reason is that nobody is particularly interested in following through. Privately, members of the board and staff indicate that they believe the physicians do not want the institution to organize an intern program or to become affiliated with the university medical school. They think the physicians oppose these efforts because they might lose some of their power and autonomy and that some might even lose hospital privileges if standards are raised. The physicians deny these allegations and insist that there is no need for interns because emergencies are adequately covered, welfare patients are now paid for by Medicare and other protection programs, and the community neither needs nor can support a teaching hospital.

As far as the administration and the parents' advisory committee of Bishop Pringle Junior College is concerned, the most painful craw in their organizational throat is the community of teaching nuns. The nuns, while comprising only one-third of the faculty, have had a long-term attachment to the junior college from the days when it was a high school. In fact, they have a great deal of psychological and financial investment in the school. Before the diocesan administrator assumed the role, a nun was the president. However, the nuns have two obligations — to the school and to their order — but they are more identified with the order than with the school. Following the rules of the order, they are so rigidly scheduled that they cannot remain at the school afternoons to talk with the other members of the faculty; they cannot easily associate with the parents of students, let alone the students themselves in informal after-school relationships; and, because of their tenure, as well as their status as members of a religious order, they preempt administrative positions even though they are often less qualified than the lay teachers. The college does not have the money to pay a faculty of lay teachers alone; it must make expedient use of the nuns, even though the latter are not viewed as being aware of or attuned to contemporary social educational problems of late adolescents and young adults.

c. Masculine-feminine orientation

Organizations evolve orientations and styles of behavior, some of which have already been discussed. Here the consultant should view these on a masculine-feminine continuum.

(1) Of organization

(A) MASCULINE

C. Northcote Parkinson points out in *In-Laws and Out-Laws*: "A male corporation is to be identified first of all by its rough exterior. The lay-out is more practical than pleasing, the machinery unconcealed, and the paint more conservative and drab. Combined with this rugged appearance is an assertiveness in advertising, a rather crude claim to offer what is at once the cheapest and the best. The organization is extrovert, outgoing and inquisitive." The more masculine the organization, the more it will tolerate its own aggressive behavior and that of others, the more militant its posture is, the less sensitive it is likely to be to the feelings of its customers and employees. Two case excerpts and a published example illustrate:

The Pawnee and Southwestern Railroad shops are obviously a man's bailiwicks. The tools and equipment are large. There is much pounding, smashing, shaping, welding, forging. A man needs considerable strength just to lift the massive wrenches let alone use them. The men in the shops become grimy and sweaty early in the day. In the summertime they must withstand the internal heat of the shop in addition to the external temperature. In the wintertime the big shops are cold and drafty. The yards outside the shops are a combination junk yard, parts supply area, and parking lot. Apparently it has not dawned on anybody that a coat of fresh paint would brighten the place and that trees and bushes would screen the ugliness of the buildings from the nearby residential area.

The Cigar Institute of America has been trying to win female acceptance of cigars by launching a campaign that suggests that female cigar smoking is permissible as long as she confines herself to any of the long slender shapes or many cigarillo types on the market. However, the Institute is flirting with the destruction of an equally important marketing concept — the image of the cigar as a symbol of masculinity. "A cigar asserts a virile personality," contends Dr. Ernest Dichter, a specialist in motivational research. "Cigar smokers are likely to be direct-action, no-nonsense people. A cigar makes a man feel independent. That's good. Women, naturally, will resent this." (*Fortune,* May, 1968, p. 30.)

In the interviews, Great Lakes Insurance Company was always viewed as a man who was generally well educated and who almost always exhibited some degree of benevolence. An old time employee said, "I see it [the company] as a wise and astute father — and I don't mean paternalism by that — who wants to provide and give the best to his children. However, he makes certain rules so that there is a contribution on the part of the child as well. He's not philanthropic; he engages in a mutual giving and taking."

(B) FEMININE

Despite the denials of contemporary feminists, there are psychological consequences of sex differences. Those are reinforced by cultural role definitions. And they influence organizational behavior. The more feminine in style and orientation an institution or organization is, the more its control is modulated, the more sensitive it is to feelings, and the more concern it manifests for people. Feminine organizations are more caring, more considerate of their employees and customers. These are case excerpts:

The decorator designed offices of Contemporary Advertising Inc. explode in an array of vibrant colors. The executive offices look more like living rooms than offices. There are no desks — only work tables. Filing cabinets are cleverly disguised in the book cases against the walls. There are many pictures, plants, curios, and other feminine touches in the offices. One would never guess these offices were the same modular units as the law offices across the hall.

The Holy Trinity Abbey is called the "mother house" although the members of the community are monks. While many religious orders also use the same term for their headquarters, this order is relatively nonaggressive. Its membership is declining; its program seems to be falling by the wayside with little effective spontaneous effort to recover; its functions are largely caring functions. Its orientation is fundamentally feminine.

Elm Street School is primarily feminine in identification. All the teachers are women, though the principal is a man. The emphasis in school is on being neat and orderly. Children are urged not to fight if attacked, but to report the attacker to the teacher.

St. Agnes' Hospital is clearly feminine. There is a vagueness about financial matters, job definition, supervision, and management as a whole. Relationships with the physicians are poor because the physicians have no definitive role in the hospital's programming and feel the nuns interfere too much in medical controls in a nagging, prying way. In supervisory sessions, the nuns will talk about religious matters instead of focusing on the problems to be solved. The atmosphere is one of "Be reliable, do a good job, sacrifice and don't create any problems." Money matters are "dirty" and to be avoided.

(c) DEGREE OF ACHIEVEMENT

Here the consultant should ask: How well does the organization achieve its apparent sexual orientation? How much conflict is there between a masculine and feminine orientation? How well is the conflict between the two orientations compromised? These two case excerpts indicate how this topic is discussed:

The Republic Service Gas Corporation portrays itself to its customers and to the public as a utility that wants only to serve them. It talks in its ads and to its employees from this stance. However, in interviews, the management portrays itself as an alert, virile, aggressive, competitive force that must remain on the offensive and grow in order to survive. It identifies itself with innovation, change, pursuit of the customer and of the market. In practice, aggressive young executives cannot be tolerated in the organization because they are too competitive and are not challenged enough. If an aggressive man has been recruited accidentally or if a young man should be stimulated by a managerial training program to want to innovate, the company will generally help him find a job in a more competitive atmosphere. Thus there is a dichotomy in orientations. It is difficult for the company to accept itself as having a passive orientation and to shift its recruiting from its efforts to compete with other organizations for aggressive leadership.

Because of its focus, the nature of its work, and its community nurturing function, the Lawton Hospital has a strong feminine orientation. "Consideration of others" might be its underlying motto. However, it is aggressive in its pursuit of first place among the several hospitals in its community. It is more competitive than the others, more achievement oriented and likely to get its own way, that is, to be first. There is a fusion of masculine and feminine orientations in that the masculine orientation is in the pursuit of better facilities and services for carrying out the caring function, the feminine orientation. There is no conflict between the two orientations; rather, one complements the other. Thus, the basic cohesion of the organization in the pursuit of its functions is maintained.

(D) HOW PERVASIVE

The achievement of the underlying masculine-feminine orientation may be highly developed in one part of the organization, less so in another. If the two functions are in competition, conflict may develop, as in these three case excerpts:

Universal Sales sees itself as a dynamically competitive sales organization whose job it is to sell products in great volume. This often means pushing salesmen hard. Department managers pressure the buyers; the buyers pressure the salesmen; and the salesmen, who work on a salary-plus-commission basis, have no compunction about manipulating the customers. However, the personnel department, having become oriented to some modern concepts of personnel management, is now appealing to management to give greater consideration to personnel. The president of the company accepts this idea and is trying to implement it by having training programs for various managerial personnel. However, he is unaware of the incompatibility between pressuring his subordinates to sell, with resulting displacement of pressure downward, and urging them to care more about and for their subordinates. Thus, the merchandisers see the personnel department as "long haired," "idealistic," "do-gooder."

When Dalton State Hospital was reformed several years ago, the new administration tried to make the hospital patient-centered. The orientation of the hospital shifted from merely keeping patients locked up to treating them. Accustomed to being authoritarian, many of the older aides had to leave, and more sensitive aides were recruited. However, the old maintenance crew was maintained. The patients assigned to the maintenance crew were treated by them much as they had been before. When the conflict between the therapeutic orientation and the custodial orientation was discussed, the psychiatric staff felt powerless to curtail the activities of the maintenance men because they were all long-term civil service employees under the direction of a business manager who thought those crazy patients were being coddled anyway. The maintenance assignments were needed for vocational retraining and for rehabilitation of ward patients, yet the therapeutic possibilities were vitiated by the attitudes of the maintenance personnel.

Like many other universities, Barford struggles with the historic liberal arts tradition of learning for learning's sake and the pressure to get involved in solving the now-pressing community problems of industrialization, minority dicontent, and education. The "pure scholars" are fearful that the university will dissipate its scholarly functions with empirical problems that will not contribute to knowledge. Yet if the university does not take some responsibility for resolving social problems, it may lose support from industries as well as prospective donors.

(2) *In relation to the industry*

The orientation achieved by a particular organization has meaning for the organization's role within the industry. It has implications for organizational survival, for industry-wide leadership, and similar issues, as in these case excerpts:

Historically, bookstores have been operated by people who like books but who were not astute businessmen. When the Terhune chain decided to open a series of competitive bookstores, they entered a field in which 200 stores per year were becoming defunct. With an emphasis on merchandising, they effectively began to compete with mail order houses and set a new pattern for book merchandising. The introduction of a competitive, masculine orientation to a field that was otherwise "old maidish" offered a model for rejuvenating the industry.

Already the Holy Trinity Province suffers when compared to the Jesuits and other orders that have acquired more prestige, property, and recruits. To be inconspicuous and inactive means that fewer people know about the order, fewer young people want to identify with it, and other orders will preempt its functions.

While Barford has not grown nearly as rapidly as some of the major state universities, it has been carefully attentive to possible student discontent. Some faculty, alumni and community people feel this "soft" attitude plays into the hands of the radicals, but Barford has been singularly free of rioting, picketing, and other forms of activist rebellion. Others, who before used to disdain the Barford administration, are now asking how they keep the peace without force.

d. Transference phenomena

Transference means unconsciously bringing past attitudes into present situations. Transference phenomena are symbolic recapitulations of earlier relationships within the family. By unconsciously assuming that a superior will be hostile, caring, punitive, or supporting in the current working relationship, a man transfers attitudes that he established with his parents to his superior. At the peer level, transference occurs when a man assumes that his peer is a competitive rival, or the psychological equivalent of his brothers and sisters. Sometimes a hospital staff will treat patients as if they were naughty children, or the manager of a company will behave as if his employees were delinquent, unappreciative children. Conversely, the employees can regard the president as a good or bad parent.

(1) *Related to the consultant*

The attitudes of interviewees toward interviewers are frequently metaphors for how the interviewees perceive authority. They may look upon the consultant and his staff as spies, friends, allies, saviors. The more irrational the expectations behind such images, the more difficulty the consultant is likely to have and the more easily disappointed the organization will be. These case excerpts illustrate a range of transference reactions to consultants:

The older but still active and influential monks in St. Peter's Abbey reacted suspiciously to the consultant's questions. They would often echo the questions before attempting to answer; then the answer was usually stereotyped. They were negative to the idea of a self-study and asserted they could not understand what "all the fuss was about." They resisted any idea of change and seemed to be fixated on the past where their principal task had been to build the local cathedral and the seminary. They revelled in ancient memories and viewed the consultant as threatening that idyllic image.

When we approached the factory manager with a request to be allowed to interview the top management group and the line personnel, he responded first with hesitation and then with obvious disapproval. He indicated that talking to supervisors would not be helpful since it would not provide the type of information we were interested in. Allowing the consultant to interview within the plant would begin an unwanted precedent. He said, also, that the consultants might just happen upon a disgruntled employee and "might just get the wrong impression." He viewed the consultant's initial visit as a kind of espionage. During the course of the interview, he emphatically expressed the desire to control undesirable influences and unwanted outcomes. Whatever it was that the consultants wanted, they were up to no good and were obviously an enemy of management.

The Lawton employees, below the level of nurses, looked upon the consultants as agents of the hospital's executive director. It was inconceivable to them that anyone would approach them with an eye toward improving their lot, the functioning of the hospital, or patient care. There could be no reason other than spying; and who would want to spy but the boss himself, particularly since he was new to his post and would want to tap into sources of information?

Ambivalence about our coming was evident in several events we noted upon our arrival. The bulletin announcement read: *"A Team of Ministers* from Menniger [sic] Foundation, Division of Psychitry [sic] and Religion are beginning interviews this afternoon and evening in a study in Parkdale Church. The Pastoral Relations Committee, through a random selection, have chosen and contacted the persons to be interviewed." Rooms for interviewing had not been decided upon, although some idea had been given to using the various pastors' offices. We eventually used them. On the second Sunday, one of these was locked when we returned from lunch, and a key had to be found. We noted also that although February 12 and 19 had been scheduled for interviews, all the interviews were arranged for the nineteenth.

(2) *Related to the organization*

Members of an organization implicitly or explicitly have transference images of the organization. These take many forms. Most often the images are parental. They look upon the organization as carrying out maternal or paternal functions with respect to them, sometimes "big brother" functions; they also characterize the organization as benevolent or malevolent in referring to the way it behaves toward them. These transference phenomena relate to what people need psychologically from the organization, to what degree they get it, and how they perceive themselves vis-à-vis the organization. For example, telephone company employees will frequently speak of "Mother Bell," and refer to the benevolent supportive qualities of the organization. In these case excerpts are examples of a range of transference images:

When asked how they would use personal terms to describe the Winfield Methodist Church, a young couples' class said that they looked upon the church as a grandfather who was kind, but decrepit and slow, and even somewhat stuffy. The senior pastor, however, personified the church as a person who has reached out toward new things, who carried with him many ambivalences, mainly his fears about leaving home and not being too sure what his new home will be like.

The Tilton, Davis and Rossi lawyers view their firm as *ruling* their lives: demanding that they be in their offices at a particular time; demanding that they be subservient to special clients; demanding that they be concerned with the community they live in; demanding that they maintain their contacts; demanding that they be well informed. The firm has become their master. However, the lawyers feel that the firm is good. Through the firm they become personified as the good, ethical, practicing lawyers hard at work.

Within Dalton State Hospital there is a helpless dependency on the higher levels of administration that are idealized but at the same time feared and felt to be withholding needed support. It is as if the administration and the hospital itself, which in the minds of the employees are intertwined, constitute an unkind, unappreciative mother, who promises, urges, demands, but does not love.

The managerial staff of Great Lakes Insurance Co. characterize their company as "middle-aged, of distinguished appearance, now somewhat on the conservative side, friendly, helpful, and stable." Notice the distance, the lack of relationship between the men and the organization. The response is uninvolved, almost as though they were describing a not well-known acquaintance. Little was said by the interviewees about the interest of higher management in them or their futures or their investment in the organization.

(3) *Related to each other*

In addition to the transference reactions from the employees to the organization, there is frequently the reverse. This is most often reflected in the competition between the older and younger employees. The older ones will frequently speak of the inadequacy and incompetence of the younger, complain that they are not interested or do not care or are unwilling to uphold old values or that they simply are not experienced enough. The greater the gap in competence or power between the ruling clique of an organization and those who carry out its functions, the more vividly will the countertransference phenomena be seen. The more members of a family who are involved in a given organization, particularly if they are father and sons, the more frequently will ancient family rivalries continue to be pursued. In some organizations there is a "splitting" phenomenon: certain people are good and others are bad; certain divisions or departments may be good while others are troublesome. When such splitting occurs, the group usually will idealize its leader and project its hostility upon another leader or group or on distant malevolent forces.

These reactions are illustrated in two case excerpts and a published example:

Pastors of traditional Methodist churches tend to look upon the campus ministers of the Wesley Foundation as rebellious boys. The pastors, in addition, can't see what they're getting for the money that is invested in the Foundation. This feeling is reflected in churches located near campus ministries. Therefore, Wesley Foundation directors are lonely, estranged from a hostile parental church, and in conflict with it. They are often considered "the outsiders" by students, faculty, administration, and other Methodist pastors.

The attitude of the nuns at St. Agnes' toward the hospital employees is best characterized as matriarchal self-centeredness. The nuns have no questions about their mission to serve God in this way, nor do they question their right to demand that others do as they do and be subservient to their wishes. As a result, the feeling conveyed to employees is that they are privileged to be hard-working, reliable, underpaid and unheard in the context of an institution built on love and service. In short, they are lucky kids.

One of the factors which made industrial relations at Kohler [plumbing fixtures manufacturer] different from those of most firms was the difficulty its management had in understanding that some of their workers actually desired to have a voice in shaping their destiny. Management's paternalism satisfied some of the workers, but by no means all of them. The inability or unwillingness to understand this fact led the Kohler Company to assume, or at least to charge, that "outside agitators" had stirred up trouble. That practically all of the leadership and two-thirds of the membership of the company-controlled Kohler Workers Association had voted to affiliate with the UAW-CIO did not seem to provide any clue that the union had taken a strike vote and this justified the preparations that were made for the "defense" of the plant. The statement by the Kohler management representatives before the Wisconsin Employment Relations Board, the NLRB [National Labor Relations Board] and the McClellan Committee indicate that they believed a strike vote was tantamount to a strike and acted accordingly. The union leaders' counterclaim was that the company was determined not to bargain in good faith because it felt it could "break" the union.

The family-owned Kohler Company had been operated for three-quarters of a century on a paternalistic, we-know-what-is-best-for-you-and-what-is-best-for-us basis. The managerial staff was comprised of men who shared the attitudes and outlook of the Kohler's under the militant leadership of Lyman C. Conger, attorney for the company and chairman of the negotiating committee. No one, the management was convinced, should or could tell the owner of a company how to run it. They knew how much they could afford to pay and how much in work an employee could be expected to do safely. They had successfully staved off an "outside" union in the thirties and had established a close relationship from 1933–9 with their own Kohler Workers Association.

The language in which Conger referred to the KWA leaders who had "defected" to the UAW revealed the underlying psychological interactions which were at least as important as any economic factors in the strike. (Walter H. Uphoff, *Kohler on Strike*, Boston, Beacon, 1965, p. 132.)

2. Relations to things and ideas

In the preceding discussion of attitudes, attachments, orientation, and transference, the consultant was concerned with human relationships and with psychological stances toward other humans and toward the personification of the organization. Here he is concerned with relationships to concrete objects versus abstract ideas, nonpersonal versus interpersonal issues. That is, in what things and ideas does the organization invest itself psychologically? What differences are there in investment or attachment to objects and ideas within the organization? Do these complement or conflict with each other? Do attachments to objects or ideas transcend attachments to people? What psychological purposes do such investments serve? Beyond ideals, what other abstractions have meaning for the organization and how?

a. Quality and intensity of relations to plant, equipment, raw material or supplies, product, and services

(1) Symbolization

Plant, equipment, product, and service can symbolize a variety of things to the people who are involved with them. A product may be viewed as the "baby" of the man who created it. A piece of equipment may be seen by one man as an extension of himself; by another, as his master. A building may be a haven or a prison. For a man who distributes supplies, these may be his devices for purchasing affection. For one minister, the service that he renders his parishioners may be just that; for another, part of a crusade. These case and published excerpts illustrate what is meant by symbolization:

Lawton Hospital, as a set of buildings, is viewed by its staff as an instrumentality for service. For them "hospital" means this building and what goes on in it. It symbolizes their mission and is an arena for their dedication.

When Fraser Hall at the University of Kansas was to be demolished to make way for replacement, there was a great hue and cry among the students, alumni, and faculty. Ostensibly, they did not want it destroyed because of its architecture. However, for many, the building symbolized the university itself: the alma mater. As one of the oldest buildings on campus, it was a familiar locale. Those alumni who visited the campus repeatedly felt increasingly strange with newer and larger buildings which altered the skyline and their cognitive maps of the campus. Only old Fraser Hall seemed to stay the same. It was their touchstone to their academic past.

A motorcar is a functional piece of machinery that periodically has to be serviced, traded in, and replaced, and status does not forever adhere to it as it does, say, to the family silver. However much circumstances and showmanship may have accounted for the early establishment of Cadillac's status, it is the division's intensely concentrated effort to provide substance to the symbol — in design, engineering, manufacturing, and service — that keeps Cadillac in front. If there is indeed a Cadillac mystique, it lies not in some strange spell the car casts over the public, but in the dominance that the car, as if it were some kind of living organism, exerts over the thinking of the men who design, and build, and market it. At Cadillac, there is a firm belief that the car itself should dictate its requirements. Perhaps this philosophy is common to other carmakers, but at Cadillac it is a near fetish. When its people gather to discuss a problem or policy, one question that someone is bound to ask is "What does the car tell us?" (*Fortune*, April 1968, pp. 118–119.)

Today in Russia the name with the magic is Lenin. His presence is everywhere — the great mausoleum in Red Square to the gigantic three-story-high portraits adorning apartment blocks and factories . . . What counts in Russia is not the current leader, but a dogma — a set of Communist principles, articulated and propagandized by Lenin. (*Business Week*, April 29, 1967, pp. 81–82.)

(2) *Unconscious personification*

Transference is the tendency to look upon the organization as a contemporary representative of ancient power figures in the life of the individual. Here the consultant is concerned with what kinds of human qualities are attributed to plant, equipment, and so on. Sometimes a building or a piece of equipment is even given a sexual identification — "he" or "she." A service can also be personified, for in rendering it one can view himself as acting in the image of someone else. A priest, for example, may see himself as the vicar of Christ on earth. In the following two published examples two different kinds of personification are illustrated:

The first serious attempt at containerization of ocean cargo began in 1956 with four old tankers, a couple of hundred boxes and an unsentimental trucker's idea. The trucker was Malcolm McLean, then president of McLean Trucking Co. Unlike most shipowners, to whom a ship is a *she,* and a very special thing, McLean viewed it functionally, as a floating bridge between land masses or as a moving warehouse. His idea was to develop a closed system of transportation in which trucks would pick up individual containers packed by shippers and deliver the boxes to a vessel for carriage to the port of destination. There the containers would again be placed on truck-trailer chasis and hauled to the consignees' doors . . . [Thus] McLean foresaw the economic advantage that could be obtained by combining the flexibility of trucks, which can gather freight in relatively small lots anywhere, with the efficiencies of ships, which can carry hugh tonnages for long distances at a very low cost per ton-mile. (*Fortune,* November 1967, p. 153).

A decade ago the Chicago and North Western commuter line was like an alcoholic duchess expiring on Skid Row, still attired in silks and tiara. Riders with a taste for the antique loved the ancient intercity cars. The comfortable plush seats were stuffed with real horsehair, and through crazed, glass-thick varnish one could still see faintly the original walls, an exquisite mosaic of inlaid woods. Up ahead, a venerable coal-burner huffed and puffed grandly through the suburbs. But most commuters were not nostalgic rail fans, and the old lady was dying ignominiously. Over the generations the car interiors had absorbed a hopeless quantity of soot and cinders. The windows were broken and the doors came off in your hand. The sheet-metal roofs were cracked. On a rainy day passengers sat under umbrellas — or if they had none, huddled miserably in the wet green velvet. Timetables were a gallant fiction. The first snowfall each year was enough to cause operations to collapse into a snarl. But in any weather, scheduled runs would simply be scratched because the engines could not be repaired in time. Nor did departure guarantee return. The leaking locomotives ("Old Soaks" the crew called them) would fall apart so regularly that the enginemen carried baling wire to hold the machinery together. On one famous day the cab fell off, leaving the engineer and fireman naked to the world. (*Harper's,* January 1966, p. 66.)

b. Time: how is it regarded

In Chapter 6 (Part II), the consultant was concerned with the time span and rhythm that governed work. There he saw time as an external force that had its controlling effects on behavior. Here he is concerned with how people implicitly regard time. For some, only the past has any meaning and the present is merely an appendage to it. For others, neither yesterday nor tomorrow have significance. For still others, only the future has meaning.

(1) *Past, present, future orientation*

When people talk about the organization spontaneously, what is the implicit time focus of their conversation? Do they talk about its glorious history or refer to tradition as the basis for their perceptions? Do they talk about what the organization is planning for the future? Or do they talk about right now? Those who revere the past will tend to cling to it and have difficulty anticipating the future. Conversely, those for whom the past is irrelevant will lose whatever value there is for the organization in its history; they will be oblivious to the momentum from the past and the effects of organizational experience on present and future activities. These case excerpts illustrate:

As the men at Arrowhead Tool & Die talk, there is little reference to the past unless they are specifically asked about it. There are pictures of some of the company's more notable products on the walls of the offices, reflecting earlier product development, but there is no nostalgia about them. Future time is conceived of in terms of getting out contemporary orders or, at most, next year's problems. The present or near present are the major orientation points with respect to the job and the company. The possibility of merger with a large company crops up in comments occasionally, but that is in the indefinite future.

Much of the talk at Dalton State Hospital is in terms of past glory. People date the hospital's illustrious history not from its beginning but from the 1949 hospital revolution. Old timers recall the changes and newer employees pick up the aura of the past from them. The present, by contrast, is not as good; the future holds some promise but no one talks about regaining the glory of old, only about trying to live up to an idealized reputation.

Having transformed its style of insurance business to a more competitive effort, followed by rapid growth, Great Lakes Insurance has two time themes. The oldtimers feel that they were left out when the new trends were evolved and that the problems attendant on the change were "just pushed aside," and they reflect longingly on the old days. The newer people, particularly in managerial ranks, focus on the future, "Where we are going to be in the next 10, 15 years." Charts in the lobby point to the spiraling possibilities and trumpet the company's increasingly stronger competitive position.

(2) How is the future planned for

Some organizations engage in formal long-range planning; many do not. Even those who do not formally plan are, in effect, planning for the future by making no plans. Implicitly, they allow themselves to be governed by external and accidental forces and to that extent are less the masters of their own fate. Planning has been mentioned before. Here the consultant is concerned about attitudes toward it, as illustrated in these case excerpts:

Long-range planning at Ajax Pharmaceutical is a formal task, and a vice president is assigned to it. He has made many economic projections, tried to look toward long-term sociocultural changes, and given careful attention to trends in medical practice and care. His reports, summaries, and predictions are heard by his colleagues, and they frequently refer to what is coming "down the road." Coupled with these plans are projections of manpower needs, financial resources, and plant possibilities. These are offered as long-term goals toward which to strive and as a target at which the organization is aiming. However, there is a significant gap between the planning and the execution because of the rapid turnover of executives. It is impossible to proceed in step-by-step fashion when people leave or are moved before they can complete intermediate steps. One would have to say that the future is planned for in an abstract, on-paper fashion that is more in keeping with fantasy than reality. No one in the organization really feels it to be important.

As far as St. Andrew's is concerned, the future hinges on whoever becomes pastor. To its parishoners, it is a "house of cards." They describe it as fumbling, struggling, fighting for survival, distracted by his own problems, just standing still, expecting others to come to his aid, floundering, plodding, and feeling insecure. The majority of replies indicated that the church will never be big or powerful, but can have a good future "if we get the right minister full-time."

Long-range planning at Barford has two major components. The university had engaged a consultant to plan campus development and building needs. The consultant made long-term population, neighborhood, industrial, and similar projections as the basis for the plan he submitted. The university is following the consultant's plan, with periodic consultations for revision and updating. The second component is the academic rethinking of university purposes, goals, and functions. This involves planning by a faculty committee, by a trustee committee, and by the administration. These separate groups meet individually as their own work dictates and together quarterly over a two-year period. They take their task seriously. The students, with short-range views, couldn't care less.

(3) Is time valued as an investable commodity

Some organizations regard time as a commodity, which is investable and therefore valuable. Because time per se is seen as a resource, blocks of it are purposely invested with the expectation that they will yield benefit to the organization. Case excerpts illustrate views of time:

To the lawyers in the Tilton, Davis and Rossi firm, time is the most valued commodity because the lawyer sells his services on the basis of time. Deadlines, therefore, have not only their intrinsic importance but also importance as measures of income. The meaning of time and the meaning of work in this particular law firm are interchangeable.

To military commanders who operate the specialized professional orientation and training program, time seems to be unimportant. The course consists of rote didactic instructions from manuals having to do with the specialty subject as well as military regulations. The 100 men enrolled in the course have 45-minute lectures followed by a 20- to 25-minute coffee break before the next lecture. This pattern continued daily for three months. The specialists, having come from training and practice in which the matching of one's skills and talents against the racing clock was all important, were disconcerted and angered by the disregard of the importance of time by the faculty of the training center.

For the chaplain's section at McNevitt Airforce Base, the program revolves around regularly scheduled events like worship, religious education, counseling, public relations, pastoral visiting, and specific helping efforts. The attitude toward time is interesting. A general feeling exists (particularly among the enlisted men working in the office) that time is merely something to be put in; there is very little, if any, sense of time as being of any value in relation to the way it is used in the program. Rather, time is thought of as something to be spent, to be dispensed with as quickly as possible. This is true with respect to one's working day and his period in military service. This occurs in a context of anticipating future changes that may make the program better and the wish that such changes will occur, particularly in leadership.

Time is the measure of progress at Kosti, a construction company. Each contract has a time deadline. Each day costs money, each project is carefully planned to fit within a time schedule. Penalty clauses, overtime for employees, resources that cannot be used on other projects, all militate against loss of time. When there are unforeseen delays or problems, expediters are mobilized to break the bottlenecks. This, in turn, calls for innovative, flexible managers who are good at resolving crises as well as in planning. It also makes for special problems on construction projects in countries where time has little or no meaning to indigenous workers, politicians, or suppliers.

(4) View of work cycles

Are work cycles seen as problems or opportunities? Does the organization consider deadlines oppressive barriers to be overcome, or does it view work cycles as providing opportunities alternately for rest and for intensive activity? Some organizations appear harried and hurried, while others are relaxed and confident that the work will be done. These illustrations came from cases:

For the twelve men who operate the Public Service Gas Compressor Station, summertime is the period of rejuvenation: they take the large compressors apart, repair them, lubricate them, rebuild them if necessary. The station is repainted inside and out. There is a leisurely pace to this summertime activity as men go to and return from their vacations. With the compressors disengaged, the repetitive, pulsating beat, which is part of daily life in the station in the colder season, is absent. The men take advantage of this time to do all the things that cannot so easily be done when they have to devote their attention to making sure that the compressors are operating properly.

Although to the outsider it would seem that rush periods, particularly the Christmas rush weeks, are the bane of the department store business, they are, in fact, welcomed at Paramus Stores. In the six weeks preceding Christmas, nothing else is allowed to intrude into moving the stock out of the store. There are no meetings, supervisors have no time to check people carefully, and trivial irritations are forgotten. The days are so busy that by nightfall everyone is exhausted. There is a sense of collectively surmounting one enormous problem. The employees dread the end of the rush, although glad to be relieved of the pressure, because they will have more time on their hands, have to take inventory, and cope with the myriad frustrations of working with others. The sense of urgency, importance, and fun will be gone. Easter promotion, the next big date, does not provide nearly the same sense of excitement.

c. Space: how is it conceptualized

In Chapter 5, the consultant was concerned with the use of space and its direct impact on the individual. Here he is more concerned with what and how the organization implicitly thinks about space as an abstraction. For example, to some organizations space has no meaning at all. If the staff is increased, more partitions are erected or more machines are added or new buildings are constructed close to existing ones. To such organizations, space is not something to be lived in, mastered, controlled, or used to serve. Space simply exists. For other companies, space is a part of its thinking, whether it is a church board that plans the design of a new building to have a vaulted arch symbolic of the ascent to heaven or a community park department that seeks to utilize every inch of available ground within the city limits for a recreation area.

(1) As a local concern

How much attention is paid to the use of space in the buildings and grounds of the organization under study? Is it something to be capitalized on or economized on? The consultant can discuss the economic aspect by asking questions such as, "Does the organization deem it worthwhile to spend money just for space, or does it limit itself to the bare minimum needed?" "How expansive are the grounds?" "What effects are sought?"

Real estate values and the scarcity of space in given locations would not appear to be pertinent here because organizations that value space highly reflect that fact in the way they manage their space resources. One of the underlying psychological issues is the degree of freedom or constriction in the organizational atmosphere as reflected in its thinking about space. Two case excerpts and a published example discuss this issue:

The Burlingame Memorial Methodist Church building epitomizes the worst of spatial conceptions. It gives the impression that whoever designed it had contempt for its functions and the people who had to use it. The basement has a low ceiling impairing its usefulness for Sunday school classrooms. The kitchen is inefficient. A disproportionate amount of space is given to the gymnasium, and little or no formal office space exists in the building. The Sunday School Department is scattered all over the complex — in the attic, in the basement. There are miles (it seems) of dead space — hallways, closets, and similar features. The only attractive room in the entire complex is the women's parlor. The building itself is bounded by the sidewalks surrounding it. There is no greenery; there is no sense of beauty.

At Delaware and Hudson Insurance there is much unused space. The building is calculated to create an imposing atmosphere of dignity and opulence. The individual feels small in comparison; indeed, in the sense of having any effective impact on the organization, he is.

Since space is the greatest architectural luxury of all, most new hotel lobbies are mean and cramped — areas designed primarily to handle arriving and departing guests efficiently, but certainly not space to linger in. Now there is a notable exception: Atlanta's new $18 million, 800-room Regency Hyatt House, the city's first high-rise hotel in 40 years and the biggest in the South outside of Miami. The hotel was designed around a great skylit courtyard that rises 21-stories and is big enough, according to the hotel's ads, to contain the Statue of Liberty. Wrapped around this shaft of air on four sides is the hotel proper, layer after layer of rooms opening onto continuous interior balconies that take the place of traditional corridors. (*Time,* June 2, 1967, p. 50.)

(2) As a cosmopolitan concern

Space may be conceived of not only as an immediate setting within which an organization operates, but also in terms of how the organization views itself with respect to the broader world. Some organizations perceive the entire world to be their "oyster." They view themselves as having legitimate interests in all or various parts of the world and see their activities as being international or cosmopolitan. National boundaries for such organizations have as little meaning as state and county boundaries or even city boundaries for other organizations. Some organizations may be international in their operations but do not think in terms of international complexities. The consultant should determine how the organization under study relates itself to its space possibilities and what it conceives its life space to be, as in these case excerpts:

Although St. Mary's High School is a component of a large international religious organization, worldwide in its scope, it thinks of itself in purely local terms. It is in the single community to serve the children of that community.

Menorah Medical Center is closely identified with Kansas City and its geographical environs. Although the hospital aspires to be one of the best in the country and its staff speaks freely of that aspiration, nothing in the interviews suggested that the hospital can see itself as carrying on projects in distant countries as, for example, does the Harvard Medical School.

Although Ajax Pharmaceutical has operations in a number of countries and its management talks about its wish to have products everywhere bearing the company's name, there is a chasm between the company's expansive view of its economic possibilities and the way in which it thinks about such operations. "Tunnel vision" exists with respect to international operations: the management thinks of specific component countries and specific marketing possibilities; little mention is made of varying national politics, cultural differences, social trends, and similar matters. The company is not yet internationally minded in the deep psychological sense and would, at this point in time, still have to be understood as an American company with overseas operations rather than as an international organization.

d. Meaning of work for the organization

Work has different kinds of psychological meanings for individuals. These are described in considerable detail in the references. Suffice it to say here, for some it is a means of attack on the external world; for others it is a means of justifying their existence; for still others it is a means of maintaining a place in the social community or acquiring power. For all, it serves deep-seated psychological and cultural needs. Since people tend to affiliate themselves in and with organizations that serve their psychological needs, work will come to have meanings for the organization. One or more such meanings may be more prominent than others.

(1) As a device for coping with the environment

Work as a way to cope with the environment is particularly evident in highly competitive business organizations. Their race to be first bespeaks a wish to be on top. To be other than big or the biggest can seem to threaten them with ultimate annihilation.

(A) IN ECONOMIC TERMS

Growth and size are equated with power and stability, and compel the attention of the outside world. Such large and expanding organizations see their strength in either their monetary resources or control of raw materials, which enable them to deal with governments as if they were equals. The following two case excerpts indicate the economic meaning of work to individuals. The third, an extract from a publication, illustrates its concerns to an organization.

The employees of Arrowhead Tool and Die look upon work as a way to make a living rather than as a means of becoming powerful. In psychological terms, work is seen as mastery of a skill for most of the workers and also as a springboard to a better paying job as more skill is acquired. Young men come to the organization from local farms and begin as laborers at Arrowhead. Gradually they learn a skill, such as welding, and after they master the cruder types of welding needed at the company, they seek employment in the aircraft industry where welding skills are in great demand.

The ministers of the Lutheran synod indicate they do not work for profit or power but rather for the welfare of their people in the church. However, the synod can legitimately seek power and growth. The synod can ask for money for increase in membership, and the men can strive to achieve these things for the synod. This is over and against the reality that there are legitimate reasons for a pastor and his congregation to seek money or power. However, the pastors cannot admit this. It is interesting to note that few pastors ever voluntarily move down the scale of staus or income.

In 1965, three industrial corporations, General Motors, Standard Oil of New Jersey, and Ford Motor Company, had more gross income than all of the farms in the country . . . The gross revenues of each of the three corporations . . . far exceed those of any single state. The revenues of General Motors in 1963 were fifty times those of Nevada, eight times those of Nevada, eight times those of New York, and slightly less than one-fifth those of the Federal Government. (John K. Galbraith, *The New Industrial State*, Boston, Houghton Mifflin, 1967, pp. 75–76.)

(B) IN TERMS OF SKILL

Some organizations implicitly experience work as a way of mastering the external environment by means of the special skills they have. They talk about what they can do, how they are going to improve their competence, what contribution that competence may make to society, as in these published extracts and case excerpts:

As a company, IBM is probably more pervasive in its influence on the way business is done than any in history. Its products, preceded by squads of salesmen and flanked by corps of educators, are changing the whole fabric of management structure in business and altering basic methods used in science and engineering . . . "Our biggest benefit," says [IBM head] Thomas J. Watson, Jr., "was that we did have some knowledge of how to design, install and service systems." Because IBM's sales staff had that experience, it turned out to be a gold mine of executive talent; . . . this step from record keeping to handling current operating events is the most significant market trend. It puts IBM in a position to increase productivity not just in handling historical data, but in "almost all aspects of business" — in a position, that is, to offer its services to production, sales, and management, or, as Albert L. Williams [president] puts it, "the other six out of every seven employed people." (*Business Week*, February 2, 1963, pp. 92, 94, 95.)

The famous glassworks of Murano, where craftsmen puff their cheeks to create some of the world's finest chandeliers and glass objects, have entered a gloomy period of depression. "I guess we just industrialized and commercialized too fast," sighed glassblower Estevan Rossetto, as he looked out from the island over the swampy lagoon at the neighboring city of Venice. "We gave the modern-day mirror to the world, we hung the European palaces with all their chandeliers, we provided filigree glassware for the kings but suddenly some of us thought it would be more profitable to make toilets and test tubes. This was a mistake." Four centuries ago, the Venetian Doge would have dispatched emissaries of the state to murder any glassblower who emigrated with his secrets. Today, he is labeled "a traitor" by the islanders and the matter is dropped. "We must preserve our craftsmen's heritage," urges Angelo Barovler, director of the oldest factory on Murano, Barovler-Toso. "Our only hope is to appeal to people's tastes and forget about churning out cheap cups, bottles and mirrors." (*Topeka Capital-Journal*, May 19, 1968.)

Asbury Methodist has developed an amazing skill in holding its congregation. It encompasses a wide socioeconomic range in its membership. At one end of the scale are people from the highly educated middle- to upper-middle-class; at the other are the uneducated, sometimes unemployed of the immediate neighborhood. In between are a large number of teachers, social workers, and civil servants. Those at the top include several engineers, lawyers (but no doctors), real estate men, and office administrators. There has been a tendency for families who have been successful to move to outlying parts of the city. There has been a surprising loyalty on the part of these persons in returning to Asbury rather than affiliating with a local church. Even in Manhattan, the church draws persons from great distances, some coming from the luxury apartments on the lower East Side and in Queens. The congregation is widely dispersed, both socially and geographically. In spite of this, there are many families and members of long standing in the church, and continuity and memory are valuable assets to the unity of the group.

(c) IN TERMS OF THINKING

For some organizations, thinking is a way of coping with the environment. Ideas are the roots of power; concepts are devices for mastery, as reflected in the following extracts:

Had IBM and other companies decided just to sell computers and let customers do all the work of programming them, they would live in a much simpler world. But the market for computers would have lagged until there were enough people around who knew how to program them. So IBM, which has had a long tradition of educating its customers, took on the job of educating their computers, too. Right now, in the view of many IBM executives, it's programming — or "software," in industry parlance — rather than new developments in electronic hardware, that has become one of the major limitations of computer applications. IBM therefore is shifting much of its efforts and money toward breaking through that roadblock. So important is the software problem . . . that to make sure top management can make knowledgeable policy decisions about programming . . . the entire Corporate Management Committee [was invited] to spend three days in Vermont recently working on everything from binary and octal numbers to FORTRAN and COBOL. (*Business Week,* February 2, 1963, pp. 97–98.)

On the Smothers Brothers opening television show on the CBS network in September 1967, the network approved the guest appearance of folk singer Pete Seeger, who had been blackballed by the networks since he refused to testify before the House Un-American Activities Committee in 1955. But then CBS turned right around and banned one of Seeger's songs, "Waist Deep in the Big Muddy," because of its obvious reference to President Johnson's handling of the Viet Nam war . . . On another occasion the censors censored a skit on censoring . . .

The overriding problem, as far as the brothers are concerned, is that CBS, with its large commitment to the blandest sort of family shows, is out of tune with the times and with its audiences. "The whole country's in trouble," exclaims Tommy, "and we've started getting a kind of renaissance, in the arts, in living. Painters can reflect their society. And writers can. Why can't TV comedians?" (*Time,* February 2, 1968, p. 57.)

(d) IN TERMS OF PSYCHOLOGICAL DEFENSE

Work is not only a means of coping with the external environment, but it is also a means of dealing with feelings. Sometimes it is disproportionately a mode of managing feelings as, for example, when one is a work addict. Then work is seen to be a defense against the discomfort which would otherwise arise. Under such circumstances it is likely to be too intense or unremitting or in conflict with what the person says he wants to do. Organizations can give primacy to work as a defense. The question then is what behaviors the organization undertakes that seem to conflict with what it says it is trying to do and what behaviors it cannot give up even though they are no longer functional. For example, an organization may keep compulsive time schedules even though they serve no economic function. Thus, time is being used for a defensive function. It has been demonstrated that some management styles are less efficient for certain kinds of businesses than others. Yet some organizations cannot make changes that economics dictate. They are imprisoned by their own style of doing things. It is when an organization insists on continuing to operate in ineffective and inefficient ways, to deny the realities of the information it has about its own performance, that we speak of work as a defense.

Some dimensions of defense are illustrated in these excerpts:

In the Lutheran synod, work for one's own benefit or personal enjoyment is denied, as is the idea that a man might work to cope with his environment. Rather, one works for the Lord because one has already successfully coped with his own problems. The leader of the synod has suggested that a man's vocational commitment should take care of his problems; the pastors' apparent assumption that they should be self-sufficient confirms the president's viewpoint. To consider a man coping with his environment by way of his work suggests to most that his commitment to his vocation is tenuous.

The employees of the Arrowhead Tool and Die use work as a defense for channeling aggression. The work process is heavily mechanized: energy is discharged against primitive raw material, which is refined into something acceptable and beneficial, which, in turn, does hard work. In a sense, the product personifies the people — good, solid, hard-working, dependable — and an organization, with strong consciences. It also personifies the company in its relationships to its customers and community. Arrowhead cannot be housed in a "pretty" building; it cannot be exploitative. Its collective powerful conscience will not allow either.

For the clinical staff of St. Agnes' hospital, work is, presumably, a way of service. But from the controlling nature of the hospital's way of doing things, this is a rationalization. Taking care of people may be one way of gratifying the staff's own dependency needs, but it is also a way of being "one up" on the patient. Because the patient depends on the hospital, the hospital is stronger and more powerful than he, no matter how powerful the patient may be outside. This, in turn, may be seen as a defense against helplessness: this institution can act effectively in the face of critical and painful life and death problems.

(2) *As a device for fulfilling psychological contract*

The psychological contract is a set of mutual obligations and expectations between employees and organization that arises out of the needs of both. Some aspects of the contract are conscious, for example, the return of loyalty and service for guaranteed employment; some are unconscious, for example, the expectation that a manager will be able to move up and achieve rank and the expectation of the company that the manager will defend and protect it. There are a number of dimensions to the psychological contract. Here the consultant should determine the degree to which work serves as a device for meeting the organization's expectations of what it, ideally, ought to be. These are most often stated in the form of mission, obligations, purpose, or, put another way, in terms of values, rules, aspirations, and self-judgment.

These case excerpts show what is meant by the psychological contract:

The stated purpose of Midland Utilities is to generate electrical current, to return a profit on the investment, and to render service to customers. The underlying psychological contract that Midland makes with its respective publics is that it will be a good company to each of them, in return, it wants to be liked. Nothing pleases its management more than to be recognized as a responsible management that provides good return on investment and good service. The people in the organization, management and employees alike, hold this to be important as reflected in their wish to be good citizens in the community, rescuers during emergencies, and people who become increasingly efficient while lowering the costs of their services.

Grant College has as its purpose to equip college students both to live effectively in a complex and changing world and to help meet society's changing needs. These require more than intellectual knowledge; textbooks and classes, important as they are, cannot alone teach people how to live. Therefore Grant sends students back and forth between theory and practice, thought and action, books and life. Implicit in these purposes is the concept that the college will serve as an example of integrity, scholarship, flexibility, and humanistic service. Also implicit is the understanding that the student will act independently and will change himself into a more mature, dedicated person in the process. Students, in turn, see Grant as being highly intellectual. The atmosphere is both esthetically expressive and appreciative, contemplative and idealistic. Abstract and theoretical matters are more strongly emphasized than concrete, applied, practical considerations. Procedures, personal status, and practical benefits are not important. Students find a friendly, cohesive, group-oriented campus, with a strong sense of loyalty and group welfare. The students also expect, and find, something that is not in the catalog, namely, their personal lives are free of academic surveillance. The college "contracts" for students who can live with relatively limited structure and organizational support. Those who cannot fend for themselves in this way drop out.

Ostensibly, the purpose of Buena Vista Presbyterian and the contract it holds out to its members is the propagation of Christianity: to teach people to lead Christian lives. This, too, is ostensibly the purpose of the members. The church has almost no external focus, no interest in outside affairs through actions or giving of funds. But the contract of the members has specific connotations: those who have been in the church for some time seem fiercely attached to the church and to each other. They desperately want to band together around the institution, and they feel that their contract is being violated by a pastor who pushes them to exert pressure on each other to reduce the mortgage, pay the debt to the National Board of Missions, and become involved with the Presbytery and other church institutions.

(3) As a device for channeling energy

Some organizations are comprised of people who are compelled to go places and do things without thinking too clearly about where, why, and what for. This is particularly true of young, ebullient organizations that are expanding rapidly and acting on many fronts at once. It is also true of organizations that have been involved with some kind of internal revolution and have neither crystallized an organizational structure nor tied their activity to well defined purposes, tasks, or objectives.

(A) CONSTRUCTIVELY

For some organizations there is pressure to do something good, useful, or important immediately, if not sooner. Some are compelled to demonstrate what they are and can do well. Two extracts from published material and a case excerpt are illustrative:

. . . of course Geneen has not changed in his ambition or the pace he sets. The more he succeeds, the more ambitious he gets. "ITT will continue to earn 10 per cent more annually. That is my promise to stockholders, that is my pressure, my goal. We want it every year." Geneen did not accidentally create this environment. He had a dream, he fulfilled it. "I remember being way down in a highly structured one-industry company long ago," he says. "I couldn't get anyone to listen to my ideas. Now I wasn't asking anyone to make me president overnight. I just wanted to get some action on my ideas. I felt so frustrated, I resolved that someday I'd create an environment where a man would get a chance to contribute, and I did." (*Forbes,* May 1, 1968, pp. 30–31.)

When Dalton State Hospital was reorganized in 1948, there was little staff and almost no administrative structure. As a result, many untrained people had to undertake many different activities. There was almost a feverish intent on the part of the hospital staff to evolve programs. This extended to public relations efforts with the community and the legislature.

"The favorite word around the offices of the Xerox Corp. is 'momentum.' It's almost tangible, this 'momentum,'" says Xerox Number Two man, Executive Vice President for Operations C. Peter McColough. "People feel it and get terribly excited about it. It is an elan, a sense of vigor and confidence. It makes work harder and accomplishes more!" (*Forbes,* October 15, 1965, p. 32.)

(B) DESTRUCTIVELY

Some organizations and some organization activities seem disproportionately to serve the purpose of discharging aggressive or destructive energy, as in these examples:

The Hercules Wrecking Company is in the wrecking and salvage business. Its primary work is destroying buildings. Its equipment consists largely of cranes, scrapers, welding torches and other devices for tearing down buildings. Its work force is largely unskilled.

In the back room of a stucco house in the hills of Amman, a grave young Palestinian university student squatted on the floor and told eleven friends that he had just joined a guerrilla unit to fight the Israelis. "Any age, any size, and sex," he said. "It makes no difference. They are on my land, and I shall kill them." In his shell-shattered villa overlooking the River Jordan, citrus grower Raouf Halabi, a graduate of Beirut's American University, reported proudly that his riverfront groves have become a nightly jumping-off place for raiding parties into Israel: " 'Welcome,' I say to them. They are fighting for us. Is anyone else?" Such is Jordan's mood toward the men it calls *fedayeen* — the Arabic word for freedom fighters. (*Time,* March 29, 1968, p. 29.)

(C) AS A PROCESS OF REGRESSION

In some organizations work is a means of "letting go," of acting, at least temporarily, in less than mature ways. Some organizations are in the business of providing regressive opportunities, such as bars, night clubs, and similar entertainment activities. Others foster regression as a part of their function, such as trade associations and football teams.

i. Within the work setting

Regression within the work setting is a phase or activity of work which permits a socially acceptable return to a more childlike form of behavior, either as a part of the work process or in conjunction with it, as illustrated in these case excerpts:

In the Bel Aire candy factory, the girls sit around a large table packing boxes of chocolate. They are free to indulge themselves in the chocolate if they wish. They gossip, joke, laugh with each other. The work setting is like one large mock tea party, and the women are like little girls once more. This provides a striking alternative to the responsibility they must assume when they leave the factory: they must take care of their families, meet the demands of their husbands, and grapple with the realities of limited incomes.

The M. J. Sloan Department Store — all eight floors of it — is gaily decorated. There is a premium on color and style. People are encouraged to indulge themselves in fantasy, to give vent to impulse, for impulse buying is the heart of the store's business. And the employees, particularly those who pride themselves on being creative, dress in costumes that might seem outlandish in other contexts. The whole atmosphere of the store says, "Live, indulge, enjoy." This atmosphere is necessary to the creativity in styling, merchandizing, and publicizing that makes the store successful. There are no stern visages here.

ii. In nonwork activities

For some people, work is a means to an end, not an end in itself. It is something they have to endure in order to have certain pleasures. The job is more important for what goes on in relation to it than for what goes on, on it, as shown in these case excerpts:

When the day is over and the five o'clock whistle blows, the men rush as quickly as they can from their work benches. Most head to the nearby bars. There they will have several beers together, swap stories, recount exploits, complain about their wives, worry about the threat of automation, and fortify themselves for the journey home. Having had their evening meal, many will return once more to their favorite bars. These are, in effect, the living rooms of the community for these men.

Anybody who is anybody belongs to the Kettridge Country Club. There one finds most of the executive group in the community playing cards, drinking, having a good time. Some nights are stag nights; some afternoons, football afternoons. The locker rooms are the most informal places of all, and they are free of any feminine influence.

e. Authority, power, and responsibility

Authority is the potential for action, or capacity to act. *Power* is the degree of force of the action. *Responsibility* is derived from both authority and power, for any attempt to grasp responsibility without power is difficult, if not impossible. An organization's right to exercise initiative, to exert power in its self-interest must be recognized by the corporate self, by those who are in the organization, and by those who are outside it. Where there are conflicts about power, the organization may be inhibited in its actions. Where power is used without concern for its effects, there will be negative consequences sooner or later.

(1) *How does the organization regard power*

Within the organization power may be glossed over, denied, or shunned. It may be something to be undermined, controlled, feared, or used, as in these case excerpts:

(A) THE POWER OF OTHERS

How does the organization look upon the power of others

Dalton State Hospital feels that it itself has no power and is helpless and bound by both the State Department of Mental Hygiene and the legislature. The only ways it can obtain needed funds are by manipulating the budget for the Department by asking for more than they know they are going to get, by falsifying the number of aides' positions needed, by instilling guilt in the community through newspaper articles and speeches, and by withholding skills and facilities when an outside local agency seeks admission of a patient.

The gravest threat to the Barstow Chemical Company is that of unionization. Some of the plants are organized, but others are not. The management does not want any more to become organized. It is frightened that if more become organized, the union will become militant, and the company will be at the mercy of that union. Even the employees are apprehensive about the possibility, although some would like to see unionization. They fear the militant types who are approaching them to become union members.

The pastor of the St. Thomas' Lutheran Church and his congregation feel themselves powerless to act. The synod offices have considerable power over the property and buildings within the synod. The title for the land and buildings for each congregation is vested in the congregation, but that congregation cannot disband or move to another location without the approval of the synod. This gives considerable power to the synod. Pastor and congregation must step gingerly with respect to it. On the other hand, the church feels that it should act only to prevent evil. There seems to be no concept of the positive use of power. The feeling of the pastor seems to be: "If I help one person, I will have to help all of them." Thus he refrains from meeting personal needs to avoid being overwhelmed.

(B) THEIR OWN POWER VIS-À-VIS THE WORLD OUTSIDE

It was the British character that led . . . [that] country into its present [economic] predicament. Some nations do too little and give themselves credit for too much — one thinks of the French in this connection. But only the British have undertaken to do so much, from a relatively shrinking economic base. Lacking the muscle of natural resources, they have put their shoulders to pushing up the living standards and social benefits, and to carrying with honor their world responsibilities, and to investing abroad in the interests of their own future. At the same time, they have lost the assured markets of empire and the psychological strength that empire gave them. World prices have gone up since the last war. New industrial nations freshly equipped with modern plants have emerged as competitors. Plenty of British ingenuity still shows itself around London, especially in the City, London's Wall Street, where new buildings glitter with glass and steel against the old shadow of St. Paul's. But no amount of ingenuity could have warded off the consequence of those facts, over which the British had very little control, and which meant ineluctable erosion of their position of primacy in the world's economy. With the erosion, every crack showed up. The revealed deficiencies cannot be repaired over night. Some changes have got under way already in the field of education. Others will come when British institutions undergo the shock of entry into the Common Market, a moment not postponed by French intransigence. Still, the root changes will take a long time to mature. Renascences require lengthy periods of gestation. (*Fortune*, February 1968, p. 108.)

Today . . . mighty du Pont is no longer able to make as much of its proprietary positions as it once did. Rival chemical companies began to gain on it a decade ago, and are now giving it the fight of its life. The new competitive realities were blurred until last year; in the booming early Sixties, business was lush for everyone in the industry. Du Pont itself was so optimistic that in 1966 a whole platoon of its usually reticent top executives, sticking their necks out for the first time in recent history, descanted on the company's shining prospects before the national convention of the Financial Analysts Federation. Less than a month later, however, the blow fell. In a classic example of what happens when competition speeds up and the economy slows down, du Pont's sales began to taper off and prices began to drop. Du Pont no longer enjoys the clear advantage it once had as an innovator. Its competitors have become technically sophisticated too. They have cut du Pont's lead time on new products; they they have sold very aggressively; they have expanded right and left both by internal growth and by acquisition. Du Pont seems to have entered a new competitive era that may no longer allow it to grow at an exemplary rate, to finance that growth out of its own cash flow, and still pay out a generous average of 70 per cent of its profits as dividends. (*Fortune,* November 1967, p. 136.)

(c) POWER INTERNALLY

How do people in the organization view the power that is exercised within its boundaries? Is it benign, paternalistic, inhibited? Is it taken for granted, feared, benevolent? A case excerpt and a published extract illustrate:

i. Generally

In the Delaware and Hudson Insurance Company, the effects of the president's iron grip are felt throughout the ranks of the company, executives, and lower level employees alike. The president conceives of his power as being absolute. The employees recognize that he will not tolerate overt dissent. Since there is little division of responsibility, it is difficult for many people to know what their tasks are and how they are supposed to carry them out. There are frequent differences that must be either ignored, submerged, or settled clandestinely.

Like most American volunteer associations, the formal charter of the WCTU [Woman's Christian Temperance Union] enunciates a system of representation and diffusion of power in which the rank and file possess great influence in making policy. The WCTU had in addition developed an informal structure which placed power in the hands of an "active minority" and acts to perpetuate incumbents in office. One factor in explaining the power of the incumbents on the national level is the scarcity of the skills and resources requisite for holding office in a woman's reform organization. Those who operate the organization in its day-to-day routine must be able to live near the national headquarters. In a woman's organization, availability of leaders is influenced by the husband's occupation. In addition, the relatively low salary ($3600 for the national president in 1952) further restricted the jobs to wealthy members. Leadership in the day-to-day operation of an organization is of crucial importance in regulating control of policies. In the WCTU this fact makes the role of the national president immensely important. She reads the WCTU journal before it is printed each week and exercises considerable editorial power. The literature printed by the WCTU is chiefly made up at headquarters. Even the librarians pointed out that the library is run differently under different administrations. The "headquarters gang" thus has responsibility for the communications received by the local leaders and members. Further, the "headquarters people" travel among the local and state WCTU's frequently, working as speakers at WCTU events. Consequently they are in communication with local areas. In these ways, the official positions are not nominal but really entail power. One of the most significant ways in which the incumbent remains in power, however, is through the manipulation of the formal charter. This is most apparent in the incumbent's ability to be reelected to office. The nomination and election of officers takes place at the annual convention, but the group at the top of the organization controls the selection and succession of officers. Once in office, the incumbent has the power to make the rules. Her power is established by the sentiments involved in breaking her rule. One of the most significant of these sentiments operative in the WCTU is that against inflicting aggression. (Joseph R. Gusfield, "The Woman's Christian Temperance Union," in William A. Glaser and David L. Sills, (ed.), *The Government of Associations*, Totowa, N.J., Bedminster, 1966, pp. 231–237.)

ii. By ranks

Reactions to and concern about power may vary from one level to another in the organization, as shown in these case excerpts:

In the Automatic Display Machine Company the line employees are relatively immune to the exercise of power by management. They are on salary in a company that prides itself on its beneficence. The company takes frequent polls of the employees' feelings about supervision; the president has an open door policy and looks upon his employees as retainers to be loved and protected. For the managerial group, power is not so benevolent but, rather, something to be feared. Should a subordinate complain to a higher authority, the manager, by definition, is always wrong. If he fails to meet his required goals by the deadline, regardless of the reason, he is demoted. He is expected to give his all for the company, to compete all of the time. Indeed, he is driven to do so under threat of disapproval from the angry "father."

The employees of the Prairie View Bank accept the power of superiors as given. As relatively passive people who see no possibility of acceding to power themselves, their general reaction to authority and power is one of submission. However, the officers regard power ambivalently. There is no question that things will be done according to policies and procedures set down by the superiors and by the regulatory bodies. But, when it comes to aggressive disciplinary action, the reaction of the officers is likely to be relatively passive. This is exemplified by their feelings about firing somebody. They evade the issue as long as possible and then act abruptly and arbitrarily.

(2) *How does the organization handle authority*

We have differentiated power from authority: authority being the potential for action; power, the exercise of that potentiality. However, authority can be used in ways other than for direct action to compel somebody else to do something. For example, when a highly respected educational center makes a pronouncement about methods of education, it speaks as an authority. It has *social influence*. When a medical center calls attention to clinical hazards, it, too, speaks as an authority. Those who accept that authority will guide their own actions accordingly. With this in mind, the consultant should investigate how the organization thinks in respect to itself: Does it recognize its own authority? Does it act as if it has a certain authority? How comfortable is it in such actions? Two case excerpts and an extract from a published source are examples:

The senior council of St. Olaf's Monastery is face-to-face with the authority problem. No longer do they feel comfortable speaking with the same single forceful voice they once used. There are too many new ideas, new concepts, now permeating the environment which cause them to question their own authority. The younger men, those still in training or those who have recently completed the training, have learned to question authority, to be skeptical. They want another mode of relationship with the church than the acceptance of and restatement of authority.

The Menninger Foundation, as a prestigious institution among psychiatric centers, handles its authority with restraint and dignity. When public communications media approach the organization for feature stories or television shows, they are referred to the public relations committees of the American Medical Association and the American Psychiatric Association for clearance. When staff members write papers or books, they ask colleagues informally for comments; if a publication represents the work of the organization, it must be cleared by the respective department head. So gingerly is the institution's authority handled, that some critics feel it does not use itself with sufficient vigor in its relationships with its consultees and that it does not make sufficiently imperative demands on the public agencies to whom it renders services.

Authority is generously delegated all down the line at the newspapers owned by John S. Knight . . . Reporters are free to pursue a story as long as they think it is worth it. This has produced some memorable series, including the [Detroit] *Free Press'* Pulitzer-winning analysis of the summer ghetto riots of 1967 . . . Knight encourages all his papers to take a strong position on political issues. They are free to disagree with him and among themselves. In the 1962 Ohio gubernatorial campaign, the *Beacon Journal* supported Democratic candidate Michael Di Salle. Editor Maidenburg, who dissented, was permitted to run his own signed editorials backing Republican James Rhodes, the eventual winner. (*Time,* May 17, 1968, p. 71.)

(3) *How does the organization handle responsibility*

Here the consultant should ask: Does the organization carry responsibilities commensurate with its powers? Is responsibility avoided, rejected, unrecognized? Two case excerpts and a published extract refer to this issue:

(A) OUTSIDE THE ORGANIZATION

The Corcoran Community Mental Health Center offers individual and group therapy services to middle- and low-income people. It is subsidized by the

United Fund for just that purpose. However, the center is located on the west side of town, away from low-income housing areas and distant from the bus lines that low-income patients would perforce have to use. Furthermore, the center operates on an 8:00 A.M. to 5:00 P.M. schedule, which precludes its use by working people who work during the same hours.

The Cooperative Chemical Corporation noisily upholds its responsibility to its farmer owners and customers. However, the plant itself spews heavy orange yellow, sulphur laden smoke, which then settles over the surrounding area and contributes to air polution.

The Singer Co. phased out its industrial sewing-machines plant out of Bridge-port, Connecticut at the same time that it moved in a new instrumentation and control product line (Singer-Metrics). "We felt we had committed ourselves to maintain our employment level in Bridgeport," explains a Singer executive, "so we altered our phasing-out operation to correspond to the buildup of our new product line." (*Dun's Review*, March 1966, p. 158.)

(B) INSIDE THE ORGANIZATION

The Blaine International Company moves its employees abruptly and at will. They may be in Chicago today and Tokyo tomorrow. The company assumes no responsibility for the employees' losses on housing; the disruption of the lives of his family; the problems of adaptation of his family to climates, geographical areas, cultures, and circumstances or even for responsible assignment. The company has no ready retrieval system that would enable it to examine the training and experience of the wide range of men who work for it or their eligibility for a particular post. Rather, men tend to be picked because somebody knows them or of them. This means that not everyone has an equal opportunity for the same job, that some are more arbitrarily buffeted than others, and that the company is not cognizant of what it is doing to people.

Within the Province of the Holy Trinity, the organization has not adequately assumed responsibility for its members. It has not paid attention to the chronic and long-standing dissatisfaction among the students with their various student masters and many of their professors. It has not set up ways of systematically developing the talents of its priests, some of whom have subsequently become burdens when they have failed, nor of preparing men for the assignments they may have to assume. Assignments themselves are arbitrary. For example, a man may have taught in a House of Studies for a number of years and then have been sent to a parish; or a man who has been a parish priest may be assigned as a chaplain to a mental or penal institution. Adequate recognition is not given the monks for their individual achievements, thereby derogating con-structive effort. There is practically no supportive supervision.

f. Positions on social, ethical, and political issues

Sometimes explicitly, but more often implicitly, organizations take a stand on contemporary social, economic, and political issues. Some companies invest a tremendous amount of time and effort in economic education, while others actively promote concepts of democratic management. Still others are concerned about industry's responsibility to the community. The consultant should determine what stance the organization takes on specific issues and, particularly, in what *manner* it does so. This is especially important if the organization takes a tacit stand but works behind the scenes, because that activity then becomes a skeleton in the organization's closet. Two published paragraphs and a case reference to this issue exemplify:

John F. Merriam, chairman of the board of Northern Natural Gas Company, has called for a nationwide network of "learning pools" operated by business and industry. "If business and industry had earlier assumed the responsibility for training the unemployed and the not-yet-employed," he said, "they would have created an image that is vital for survival." (*Industrial Relations News*, July 17, 1965, pp. 3–4.)

Numerous references to high ethical principles were made at the County National Bank by all the people interviewed. The organization wishes to be helpful, serve and aid others, and make a profit. In general, it takes a conservative, probusiness, antilabor stand. Its responsible executives claim that they are all for what is good for the community. However, there is only one Negro clerical employee, and she works in the balancing office where she is not seen by customers. It takes little scratching of the surface to discover that the executive group is contemptuous toward those who are not white Anglo-Saxon Protestants of high social status.

Although Methodism has been slow to involve itself in contemporary social issues, in recent years politically-minded activists have attained increasing influence in both the Methodist church and the EUB [Evangelical United Brethren]. Delegates to the uniting conference approved a resolution to raise $20,000,000 during the next year for aid to the poor. Said the newly elected bishop of the United Methodist Church Association, Eugene M. Frank: "This *is* a new church . . . the old churches were patronizing at their best as concerns the racial issue. The new church is energetically and sacrificially dedicated to making Christlike brotherhood real. There will be foot-dragging and agonized cries from those who are backing into the future, but it *is* a new church." (*Time*, May 3, 1968, pp. 62–63.)

3. Attitudes about self

The self-concept of a company, as that of an individual, does not suddenly materialize. It is a result of years of interaction with others and with the environment in which it develops. The self-concept relates to how the members of the organization see themselves collectively, how they see themselves in relationship to other organizations, to their host community, and in their multiplicity of interactions and relationships.

a. Who do they think they are and how do they feel about it

These are illustrative case excerpts:

The inevitability of growth seems to vary the attitudes of the employees of Delaware and Hudson Insurance, from the clerical workers on up. "It's a strong company. It ranks high in insurance companies, top 10 per cent, I think . . . It's the largest company in Pennsylvania. They talk much about future growth . . . The company wants to do business with a company that's growing . . . We're branching out . . . The company wields considerable community influence."

There is a certain snobbishness within the Johnson & Johnson law firm. The members feel that the firm is better than most others, and they tend to be contemptuous of other firms and individual practitioners. They have due respect for the business community and do not use their power to manipulate it as they do to smaller, and perhaps less successful, firms. While the members of Johnson & Johnson want to see themselves as being independent, they are, in fact, dependent on a few clients in a symbiotic relationship. Realizing that they are dispensable, creates a tendency for the members to cater to some of the larger clients.

At St. Anselm's the most common attitude is one of self-depreciation. The clerics expressed feelings of worthlessness or uselessness or emphasized the "ordinary" ability required in the monastic life. Most thought that those outside the clericate did not know the clericate existed or what it was or that there was a general lack of concern for the clericate. This attitude was coupled with an unusually high ego ideal or self-expectation. The clerics perceived themselves as hopelessly far from their ideals. The structure of the clericate tends to emphasize the dichotomy rather than support constructive solutions to the problem.

One member of the Pineland Presbyterian Church said to the interviewer: "The Presbyterian image is that of the upper middle class. However, the congregation of Pineland is of the lower middle class. Naturally we all have a feeling of inferiority and a great deal of anxiety about our lowly status."

b. Where do they think they are headed, and how do they feel about it

An organization's feelings about the future have much to do with its present motivation. Those who see the realities as forbidding and overwhelming are likely to be depressed; those who see them as advantageous may be naively optimistic. However, realities can serve as solid bases of motivation and hope. Such feelings are reflected in these case excerpts:

The employees of Menorah Medical Center were optimistic about the organization's expansion program in particular and the future in general. They expressed pride in the advancement in education and research that will help the hospital move closer to its primary goal of patient care. The center is constantly striving to become comparable to the University of Kansas Medical Center. Menorah is not comfortable with being second best.

Several years ago the Dominican Order was urged by the Pope to start a St. Thomas Aquinas Foundation whose principal job would be to produce critical editions of the *Omni Opera* of St. Thomas. The foundation was also to establish centers where interdisciplinary research and philosophy would be done. The Americans of the order were commissioned to raise $2.5 million to support this worldwide foundation. In a recent announcement by the American branch, it was reported that $1 million had been raised and that the critical edition of one of St. Thomas' works had been completed. The Dominican Order sees this as an opportunity to become increasingly involved in significant intellectual work.

There is no question that Great Lakes Insurance Company feels itself to be a dynamic, growing organization and takes pride in its rapid pace of growth. As one of the executives put it, "We wouldn't have built that new building if we didn't think the company was going to grow and grow fast; in fact, I wouldn't be here if I didn't think so."

c. What are their common aspirations

Here the consultant is concerned about shared values and modes of achieving the goals implied by those values, together with people's feelings about their own aspirations and values, as illustrated in these three case excerpts:

Both officers and employees resent the fact that Farmers' National is the number two bank in Dubuque. Officers try to minimize this by emphasizing the soundness of the bank. Employees are more frankly resentful. They apparently feel that this lessens their own worth and self-esteem. Rather than apologize for being second, they prefer to concentrate on publicizing their quality. Despite expressions of cynicism, there appears to be a general feeling of pride in and loyalty to the bank and its principles of integrity, service, and soundness.

Numerous members of St. Anselm's Monastery indicated that the monastery does not adequately meet their spiritual aspirations. The monks felt that it was the responsibility of each person to seek the help he might need and to grapple with his own religious development. Both students and fathers stated there were inadequate provisions for the spiritual direction of those in the process of formation. They are disappointed in being unable to achieve the inspired effectiveness that they set as their goal.

Common aspirations at Arrowhead Tool and Die are in doing good work, assuming responsibility, and "carrying their share of the load." These deeply held values are prevalent throughout the organization and reflect subcultural standards in the rural area from which employees and management come. Building a bigger, better organization seems less relevant than quality of work.

d. How do they look to themselves

Here the consultant is concerned with self-image, or perception of self. The consultant must infer the information from the way people personify the organization and from what they say about the kind of people who would join the organization and why they would join. It incorporates, but goes beyond, the earlier masculine-feminine orientation. These case excerpts illustrate:

When asked the type of person the interviewee would select for life at St. Anselm's, the reply was: "The kind of person who was 'effective,' a good organizer, steady, efficient . . ." At the same time, the general tone was one of self-depreciation with frequent expression of inadequacy. The clerics personified the monastery in this way: "He is more than likely dissatisfied with the way things are run around here and he is afraid of the Abbot . . . He tries to tolerate those that he does not like as best he can . . . He is sometimes nervous. He gets mad. He still looks to authority for guidance and is probably worried about whether he is liked or not." On one level there seemed to be a consciousness of the transitional nature of the clericate, which may be related to the absence of deep commitment. There seemed to be a consciousness of the community but little feeling of incorporation within it. The men looked structurally and physically to the community to solve their problems of identity and feelings of inadequacy.

Both faculty and students at Grant College look upon themselves and their institution as highly intellectual, reflective, dedicated, critical, realistic, and identified with the highest human values but below average in propriety. Students say they are expected not only to develop ideals but to express them in action; at the same time, they also say they do not always ask permission before deviating from common practices and policies.

4. Intraorganizational relationships

Previously we have discussed the key people, different work group levels, and other bases for classifying people and units. Here we must interpret specifically the emotional relationships among these people.

a. Key people in the organization

By who, we mean psychologically who are they? The consultant must write a brief historical character sketch of the individual which will summarize a statement of (1) character defenses, (2) transference paradigm, (3) style of handling individuals and conflicts in the organization, (4) preoccupation in the organization, and (5) methods of communication, as in these illustrations:

Vice President, Engineering. One immediately feels warmth toward this man. I saw him once working in the shop, a quiet, large, resigned, dispirited looking middle-aged man working alone on a huge machine. He was trying to solve one of the technical problems by going directly to the manufacturing process. He is overconscientious and overconcerned with the welfare of others outside of his direct job responsibility. He appears to be unassuming to the extent of being retiring. He is, in fact, the key to the development of new products, the heart of the company. Yet, he says, "I don't think of things. Someone tells me what is needed, I just develop them." One is impressed by the responsibility he shows toward the product and other members of the company. He seems to think problems through. He is interested in his work and derives enormous satisfaction from mastering his product and from the financial return it produces for the company. Could it be he is the "mother" of the company? Without him, who would create, coordinate, and sustain? Without him the company would die. His two superiors do not seem to appreciate this fact and I find myself becoming angry with them because of the way they seem to regard him.

President. It is hard to speak of this man except in terms of negatives. The overall impression is of a rather dull person running busily around with a self-sustaining, barrage of words that lacks conviction. He is reluctant to talk of himself. Sometimes it seems this is because he has nothing to say; other times because he is shy in the presence of consultants. It is as if he is afraid that he is not worthy of speaking of himself. He seems content to derive satisfaction from his own work. These characteristics would lead one to think that he is likely to resist situations he disapproves of by being passive. This is illustrated in the interviews. During the unstructured interviews he spoke freely; his responses to the formal questionnaire were terse, uncommunicative, and lifeless. When speaking of a bank loan, he presumed that the bank would refuse him, which it did not, leaving the impression that he feels he is not worth assisting, that he questions what he contributes to the company. Perhaps he feels inadequate to the task. These are questions which recurred to me. I had the impression that he was using a formula to answer questions. I kept hearing about "a good product" but was never told what the characteristics of a good product were. Throughout I was impressed with his relative vagueness about the business. He did not answer the question, "How much do people know about the business?" Perhaps it had the implication that others knew something about the business that he did not. He did not seem to have an order of priorities. He is here because he owns the business. When asked what his function was, he replied, "I run the business as it should be run." In effect he said, "I don't know what I do." I asked: "What gives you the most headaches?" He replied, "I don't know." Is it that he does not have responsibilities? He doesn't know his priorities? What should he be concerned with? He was inclined to gloss over difficulties as, for example, in discussing labor relationships and strikes. He did not identify with the product or with sales but, rather, with the financial picture. There is a condescending perception of others reflected in the way he refers to "some of these people" or, in speaking of the vice president of engineering, "We put him to work." His relationship to the vice president of engineering is one of "He's only the man who works ideas up." I was struck by the number of times he used evasion as a technique for solving situations presented to him. This was more obvious when he did not answer a question, less so when the answers were tangential. I felt he was saying, "I'm a good guy; don't press me." He frequently resorted to reiterating statements, which may have been a response to anxiety or an effort to bolster weak arguments. He also gave the impression of rationalizing problems and situations out of existence rather than attempting to realistically work them through.

Chairman of the Board. He is a well preserved, active, alert man in his late sixties. He presents a picture of the hard driving executive with ideas, energy, and initiative who motivates others to realize them and is content to let others effectuate them. His farm background contributes significantly to his present role [in a farm machine company]. He was born in a farming community and raised on a farm, the eldest of six children. His father was a hard working blacksmith-farmer. He worked with his father at the smithy and on the farm. He acquired his knowledge of mechanics working as an engineer at steam plants in his early twenties, where he also started organizing the installation of several steam plants. Later he bought his own automobile garage, where he also sold farm machinery. At age 33, he moved to Canton where, with a partner, he bought the bankrupt stock of a farm machine company. Four years later, he took over the whole organization. This was the beginning of a series of operations which led to the present company. The original plant now produces items for the present main manufacturing operation. He enjoys being preoccupied with new product ideas, being on the shop floor, and leaving the actual management of the business to his operating executives, nevertheless he is always in the background. If he doesn't like a decision, he feels free to comment. He views the employees as hired hands who should be treated paternalistically. However, he almost closed the business rather than negotiate with them when they became organized. His relationship with his president is almost one of father to son. He perceives others on the executive staff as extensions of himself, and he suppresses and controls conflict by telling people what to do.

b. Significant groups within the organization

Here the consultant should specify what he thinks are the most significant groups in the organization and what the relationships are between or among them. There might, for example, be a technical group on the one hand and a marketing group on the other. They may be hostile to each other or may cooperate cohesively. In a church the most significant groups might be conservatives versus liberals; in a community, three or four ethnic groups; and so on. Community groups frequently fall into social class categories. In business, they may be according to management levels.

In specifying the groups he thinks important and delineating their relationship, the consultant should look particularly into their points of difference and conflict in an effort to understand why they differ. In some cases, groups will differ because of their geographical origins, as in the case of Kentucky hillfolk who have difficulty with lower middle class ethnic supervisors in Detroit plants. In other cases, they will differ because of varying value systems, divergences in goals and aspirations. Often groups with power, such as managers, will be contemptuous of those without power, such as their subordinates, and act accordingly. Conversely, highly unionized and cohesive work groups may well be contemptuous of management.

In assessing the relationships between important groups, the consultant will want to look at how they communicate with each other, what nonwork activities they undertake together, and under what conditions they mobilize against a common outside threat. His understanding of the significant groups in the organization will be crucial for his subsequent recommendations and change efforts. The following is an illustrative case excerpt:

The top management group at Arrowhead Tool and Die respects President Henry Allison and also Plant Manager Ralph Zeitz. They relate to plant personnel through Zeitz. Although the latter portrays a more naked kind of power in the way he handles men, he tends to handle authority openly, militantly, and, at times, almost brutally while Allison tends to deny his authority and projects himself as a benign "nice guy." Allison does not use his power to curb Zeitz within the organization but makes better use of it outside the organization in working with his distributors. This has resulted in a subtle abandonment of the men and in various strained relationships. For example, there was a "splitting" phenomenon in the feelings of the workers toward Allison and Zeitz. All their positive feelings were directed to Allison, despite the fact that in some ways he was letting them down, and all their negative feelings, toward Zeitz, though he ran a tight ship and was a bug on safety. Both Allison and Zeitz perpetuated these images. Employees frequently appealed to the consultants to act as intermediaries in their strained relationships with Zeitz. One consequence of this mode of behavior was that it undermined the foremen. There were three. Blair Cledsoe, the oldest, behaved in a benign, fatherly way with his men. They responded positively to him, though they knew he had no power to protect them from Zeitz. Owen Rockford was looked upon as "cocky and adolescent," someone to be avoided. Ken Franklin was seen as more "action oriented" but not to be trusted; he evidently has been known to leave his workers out on a limb by approving certain parts and then denying he had done so when the quality of the parts was questioned. The foremen functioned largely as distributors of work. Unable to support their men, they withdrew at break time and lunch. The men themselves come from rural areas surrounding the community. Most have limited education — high school at best. They usually farm part-time and use the job as a steady income source. They and their foremen come from the same working class and ethnic background. Their general attitudes are much the same as those of management. Management reflects traditional and conservative attitudes on political, ethical, and social issues. While 60 per cent of the employees are unionized — a departure from management values — and reflect many of the attitudes of union members (many vote Democratic), they pay particular attention to "Paul Harvey News," an ultra-conservative newscast, during their lunch break. This may be because they come from farm backgrounds and have a midwestern conservatism. The bulk of the workers see themselves as fairly "low type" people, limited in education, coming from lower socioeconomic levels. They are self-depreciating in many ways. This is related to the work they do, which is considered crude because it does not require exceptional skill or fine tolerances. They share the value of good work and fine products. All this serves to build emotional walls between the three levels. The men talk to each other at coffee breaks; they talk to management only in monthly meetings between stewards and plant manager; they talk to top management once every two years at negotiating time. Top management talks to the men occasionally when calling them together to report something. Only small cliques of men socialize together.

c. Implications of a and b

What difference in terms of organizational functioning do these relationships make? This might be summarized in the form of a paradigmatic statement like the following example:

The Stemble Company was formed by one man. It is a product of his own drive for the propagation and extension of himself by organizing a group of people concentrated on and specialized in a product with a limited market. The market is limited partly because other companies manufacture similar products and partly because the product must be used in conjunction with other equipment. The company is carried on by his son, who is still struggling with his own problems of resolving his dependency on his father. The son is not particularly equipped to run the business. His power derives from owning the assets and thus being able to direct or persuade others that something should be done. In addition, the son has the support of his father who also is able to persuade others to move in certain directions. As an extension of the son's struggle, there is no concise policy for the continuation of problem-solving: the company must grapple with each crisis on an ad hoc basis. There is a tendency for the subparts of the company to be isolated from each other; people identify with their own unit rather than with the company as a whole. The dealers who sell the products are uncertain about whether to commit themselves to the company and its products. There is a pervasive air of pessimism in the organization. It is as if the company is saying, "We have men and machines. We build, or will build, something for you. However, we can't sell it ourselves; we don't have patents, and we don't have brilliant innovators. We depend on others. We do not know what to do about this." The son depends on the father and the chief accountant. The company is wrestling with the questions. "Can it depend on the son? Who is running the company? Who is innovating now? Can the accountant? Can the son?"

9

ANALYSES AND
CONCLUSIONS

Portion of outline covered in chapter 9

IV. ANALYSES AND CONCLUSIONS

A. Organizational Integrative Patterns

1. Appraisal of the effect of the environment on the organization
   a. *Historical*
      (1) *Beneficial*
      (2) *Harmful*
   b. Contemporary
      (1) *Beneficial*
      (2) *Harmful*
   c. *Anticipated*
      (1) *Beneficial*
      (2) *Harmful*

2. Appraisal of the effect of the organization on the environment
   a. *Historical*
      (1) *Beneficial*
      (2) *Harmful*
   b. Contemporary
      (1) *Beneficial*
      (2) *Harmful*
   c. *Anticipated*
      (1) *Beneficial*
      (2) *Harmful*

3. Reactions
    a. *Of the environment*
        (1) To the injury
        (2) Toward source of the injury
    b. *Secondary reaction from the organization*

4. Appraisal of the organization
    a. *Special assets*
        (1) Material or tangible (financial, patents, physical plant, equipment, geographical distribution, transportation, communication, personnel)
        (2) Functional (including leadership and mental set, or attitude)
            (A) REALITY ORIENTATION
                i. To external environment
                ii. To internal environment
            (B) VALUES AND IDEALS
                i. Degree of institutionalization
                ii. Congruence with reality
            (C) TASK MASTERY
                i.   Psychological contract fulfillment
                ii. Growth and survival
                iii. Task-directed behavior
    b. *Impairments*
        (1) Material or tangible (financial, patents, physical plant, equipment, geographical distribution, transportation, communication, personnel)
        (2) Functional (including leadership and mental set, or attitude)
            (A) REALITY ORIENTATION
                i. To external environment
                ii. To internal environment
            (B) VALUES AND IDEALS
                i. Degree of institutionalization
                ii. Disparity from reality
            (C) TASK MASTERY
                i.   Psychological contract unfulfillment
                ii. Growth and survival
                iii. Task-directed behavior
    c. *Level of integration*
        (1) Normal adaptive activities
        (2) First-order adaptive activities
        (3) Second-order adaptive activities
        (4) Third- and fourth-order adaptive activities
    d. *Overall effectiveness and facade*

B. Summary and Recommendations

1. Present status
2. Explanatory formulation
   a. *Genetic*
   b. *Dynamic*
3. Prognostic conclusions
4. Recommendations

This chapter provides a framework for the consultant to selectively interpret the identifying, historical, and examinational data he has collected. The conclusions he arrives at will establish a basis for his understanding of, and intervention in the affairs of the organization. Since there is no consensus on established criteria for either assessing an organization or defining various modes of intervention, the consultant's conclusions and recommendations will necessarily be based on subjective interpretations and selections. They will reflect his professional orientation and, as such, will be that part of the case study in which there will be the greatest diversity of interpretation. Because of the variety of theoretical orientations, the consultant must approach the selection and understanding of these data open-mindedly and yet with firm conviction about the way *he* interprets the data based on *his* professional orientation.

With these qualifications, this organizational case study method provides guidelines for obtaining data from which interpretations can be made by practitioners of various disciplines. The validity of these interpretations will depend on their consistency within the particular frame of reference of a specific discipline. As previously stated, this organizational case study method was conceptualized and developed from a psychoanalytic orientation with a view toward consultative intervention. Psychoanalytic understanding therefore provides a basis for the recommendations considered here. For consultants trained in this particular discipline, the organizational case study is valid as a tool for understanding, learning, and the sharpening of professional skills only if it is approached from the viewpoint of its ultimate application. For other disciplines with different consultative goals, this need not be the case.

The distillation and extraction process necessary for a useful body of conclusions is analogous to the making of wine. Just as the vintner selects and processes the grapes, presses them, and filters out the extraneous matter and opacities to produce wine of brilliant clarity, so the consultant, from his accumulated data, must select and condense those which will reveal the essence of the organization's vitality. He must comprehensively describe the dynamic organizational processes, taking into account both internal and external interactions, in order to delineate and clarify the multiple determinants that bring about the organization's current adaptive behaviors. The dynamic processes that this organizational case study elicits are a reflection of the conflicts with which the organization contends in its effort to survive. From this study, therefore, the consultant can assess the various organizational strengths and weaknesses as they enhance or interfere with its ability to cope with stress.

This chapter first considers the data in terms of the ecology of the organization, the interaction of the organization with the forces external to it. It then considers the data in terms of the internal structure and processes of the organization itself.

The question always before the consultant is: "How does this organization hurt?" How do I interpret what the key people cite as their main problem? How do I interpret what other employees speak of as their main problem? The pain may be literally what the informants say it is or it may be symptomatic of something more deeply seated. How does the organization experience its problems? That is, how severe do the problems appear to be to the organization. And how well does the organization relate them to basic causes? This is a vital question because the degree to which the organization experiences pain is one measure of how ready the organization is to accept help. Here are case examples of how pain is described and defined:

There is a bland placidity at Kaw Novelties. No one has any problems related to work or to its organization. The girls on the assembly lines do their work efficiently and effectively for both personal and organizational reasons. They are called upon for only superficial emotions and are expected to look attractive. The work is compulsively organized. Because it must be done within severe time limits and because the girls have only a limited investment in their work, it is possible for them to keep their feelings about their work out of their private lives. The type of work and their kind of concern with it gives the employees an outlet for their moralistic, punitive superegos; yet the work also provides controls, distance, and satisfaction for their dependency needs. Their aspirations are limited, as are the company's aspirations for them; the employees do strive for high quality products and they meet this requirement well. In short there is little pain.

The point of most acute pain for the Southeast Conference of the Congregational Christian Church is the recent dramatic decline in its school membership.

There is open concern about this issue. Almost as painful is the church's concern about the number of men who are leaving the ministry. Three years ago the conference established a position of conference counselor to work with the pastors who were finding their pastoral roles difficult. The conference still does not understand how to deal with this issue and is casting about frantically for answers that will keep the church alive.

High Plains Chemicals has lost a significant part of its market because a new plastic wrap was developed by a rival organization. The complaint of the executive group concerns this issue. However, it is apparent to the consultant that this is only a symptom of the underlying problem. Plastic wrap stole a march on this oragnization, as it did on many other companies, because the executives here could not see beyond the ends of their manufacturing noses. They are not alert to what is happening in the marketplaces. They have not supported their research staff. They have not heard the younger men who are calling their attention to new inventions. They were not aware of the deceleration in the chemical business until it was upon them. So far, they still see their pain as externally caused and therefore likely to be remedied only by changes in the marketplace.

A. Organizational Integrative Patterns

In this section of the outline the consultant must continue to exercise his professional judgment. He must be particularly careful to indicate where and how, in his judgment, the organization is not integrating effectively. In making his observations and judgments, the consultant must not assume a pejorative attitude. His concern is not to seek out evil or to find the person who is wrong; he must, rather, seek out failure and potential failure (as well as strength and potential strength) for the purpose of helping to remedy those situations. There is a tendency on the part of diagnosticians and consultants to look for culprits — the cause or the person — and to substitute invective for consideration. Such actions can only blind the consultant to the realities with which he and the organization must deal. We continue our emphasis on being aware of the fact that the consultant is dealing with inference, that he must be prepared to offer evidence for his interpretations and conclusions, and that he must regard his statements as hypotheses to be tested.

As we review organizational integrative efforts, we are talking about the manner in which the organization is functioning cohesively and effectively as well as where it is disjointed, where it stumbles, where it falls, where it errs repetitively, where it dissipates energies.

1. Appraisal of the effect of the environment on the organization

The consultant cannot understand and appraise an organization in a vacuum; he can do so only in the dynamic setting in which it functions. In this section the consultant should appraise the relationship and interaction between the organization and forces external to it. He should take into account what the host environment has done to and for the organization, both in terms of the environment's response to the organization and the organization's response to the environment. Of course, he will be making a somewhat arbitrary distinction by separating the effect of the environment on the organization and vice versa, but doing so will help him to analyze the operating forces.

The consultant's first step in this section should be an attempt to elicit and describe the significant points and sequences in the organization's past interactions with its environment so that he can state, "These things have happened; this is true of the organization today." To do this requires knowledge of the historical external influences on the organization, both real and as perceived by the organization. Although the way in which the environment is perceived by the organization is an integral part of this section and since this phenomenon will always influence the interaction, the particular psychological needs determining both quantitative and qualitative dimensions of the organization's perception of its environment must also be discussed. And they will be taken up in the section of the conclusions that deals with the organization's internal functioning. Making this appraisal also necessitates inferences drawn from past behavior and functioning, much as one infers from the rings of a tree those periods of drought, freezing, fertilization, and so on, which influence the growth of that tree.

In order to avoid biased selections that would lead the consultant astray, he must be as comprehensive as possible in making this assessment. A parallel pitfall that would lead to erroneous or misleading conclusions would be to accept too easily seemingly obvious explanations of cause and effect. This would ignore the principle of multiple causation and result in overly glib, one-to-one, causal explanations, rather than recognize that the same outcome may be possible from multiple and different determinants (for example, ascribing the decline of the railroad passenger business *completely* to economic and competitive factors, ignoring the influences of long-standing railroad management attitudes that neglected the necessary service functions, those having to do with taking care of people, an attitude rooted in the hypermasculine origins of the railroad industry).

This retrospective view of the organization's development and change in response to environmental influences must consider both immediate and long-term effects if the consultant is to be able to assess what changes produced stable steps in the organization's evolutionary process. War, for example, may increase a particular market; a specific demand for a new product may bring an immediate growth. In these instances, however, the short-term success may be dangerous for organizational survival if the organization's response to it is at the expense of long-term growth and diversification. Conversely, what might appear, at first, to be harmful environmental stresses may, at the same time, open onto avenues that will foster organizational growth. The demise of the trolley car, for example, forced the utility companies to become involved in, and actually to develop, new community and public uses for electricity. At the same time, the government attacks on public utility holding companies in the 1930's allowed the birth and development of independent utility companies.

The ongoing and reciprocal nature of the organization's relationship to its environment involves both past and present considerations and can produce an attitudinal climate among the public which is often a stimulus of strong potential force. An illustration is the neglectful misuse of natural resources that may go unnoticed for a long time. When the exploitation is finally brought to public attention, the enormity of such contemptuous behavior, together with its chronicity, may evoke strong feelings and unduly restrictive countervailing legislation. A similar example might be the way the public reacted to its perception that the automobile industry disregarded safety features in cars. Here again, however, there is the danger of ascribing an overly glib, one-to-one, cause and effect relationship when other facets of the industry's image and interaction with the public influenced public attitude and response. To take this illustration a step further, if the consultant were to try to assess a contemporary environmental response, he might not yet be able to say whether a given ecological phenomenon will foster or hamper the survival of any given organization.

Another example involving attitudinal climate but eliciting a positive rather than negative environmental response is the protective alliance stockholders form with those large, stable companies with outstanding and reliable dividend performance. Many stockholders of American Telephone and Telegraph rise in righteous indignation in response to antitrust investigations or attempts at restrictive legislation.

The following section of the formal outline divides the ecology into three main historical groups — past, present, and predicted future — with subgroups for qualitative assessment in terms of beneficial and harmful aspects, that is, those that may foster and promote organizational survival versus those that may be destructive to the achievement of these goals. There are, necessarily, overlapping and interrelated classifications. It becomes necessary, therefore, for the consultant to be flexible in the formulation of this part of his appraisal so that, at this juncture, the accuracy and validity of those interrelationships are not hidden by a rigid need to "split hairs" regarding time and qualitative judgments. The focus should be on the genetic forces that have resulted in the current state of the organization and those that will determine its future.

The items to be considered, as covered in the outline (geographical and natural resources; economy; market — long- and short-term; manpower; labor movements; legislation and regulatory agencies; supplies and suppliers; competition; and cultural forces), are similarly exemplary rather than all-inclusive. The limitations of these items will be more accurately determined by the data that are included in the body of the case study. The examples are taken from case studies, and, where indicated, from published sources:

a. Historical

(1) Beneficial

Following its emergence as a major university at the turn of the century, McGill acquired two identities. One was its international identity as an institution emphasizing scientific studies and research, where such luminaries as Ernest Rutherford, in physics, and Sir William Osler, in medicine, did their early work. The other was its local identity as the cultural symbol and financial beneficiary of Montreal's economically dominant English-Canadian community. This dual identity has persisted. Moreover, McGill still enjoys a good reputation, even though its relative importance in Canada has declined as the University of Toronto, the University of British Columbia, and other Canadian universities have come into their own. McGill . . . enjoyed relative affluence during the University of Montreal's years of financial misery. McGill traces its origins to 1813, when a Montreal fur trader and civic leader, James McGill, died and left £10,000 and some land for the establishment of an institution to bear his name. Favored by good leadership and its location at Canada's commercial gateway, McGill began to thrive during the latter half of the nineteenth century. Benefactions from Montreal's wealthy English-speaking commercial and financial elite gave the university a depth of resources unique for a Canadian institution.

McGill's ties to this elite were intimate, for it was from this group that members of its board of governors invariably were drawn. (*Science,* May 31, 1968, pp. 974–975.)

The prevailing anti-Catholic climate in 1912 and subsequent years compelled the Catholic community to found a Catholic hospital, which ultimately became St. Clare's. The external pressure, hostile at the time, compelled the Catholic community to organize itself around its parish and its hospital. Thus the hospital became a pivotal institution, deeply imbedded in its host community and strongly supported by it. It also became a symbol to the Protestant community of the care and concern of the Catholic community, and provided a device through which both the Catholic and Protestant communities could unite to provide necessary medical service.

(2) *Harmful*

On August 26, 1935, the Public Utility Holding Company Act was passed by the Congress. This act, bitterly opposed by representatives of the utility industries, essentially provided for the dissolution of holding companies. Section 11 of the Act was termed the "death clause" because it gave the Securities and Exchange Commission the power to investigate the various utility groups and then, after 1938, to dissolve those units it deemed superfluous to the efficient operation of any company. By 1938, holding companies had to limit their operations to single integrated systems *directly* connected with the supply of power service to consumers. The impact of this act on the future of Kansas Power and Light was neither immediate nor direct, for KPL was at that time a part of the system controlled by North American Light and Power Company. However, subsequently KPL and all other companies formerly held by the larger company found themselves in a new and less secure, though independent, position. Although the company continued to grow and remained profitable, the effect of legal constrictions and the limitation of its business to that of providing direct consumer service, narrowed its business confines. The company thereby lost a certain freedom and flexibility.

Dalton State Hospital shares with most such state mental hospitals in this country a common developmental history. It was conceived, not out of nurturing love, but from desperate necessity. Its early sustenance was granted, not from love, but from duty, although great efforts were made to provide it with an acceptable and even an attractive physical facade. However, this could not overcome the feelings of revulsion it aroused in its parents, the citizenry. It was isolated both physically and emotionally from its closest natural kin, the medical profession. In general it was looked upon with disinterest, distaste, and detachment. The paternal attitudes went further than the late nineteenth-century view toward children — it should not be heard, and if possible, not seen. It was placed "out in the country"; in fact, a city ordinance was passed prohibiting a mental hospital within city limits. There followed decades of relative neglect of the hospital, except for political patronage. Even now, twenty years after the reform of the hospital, it retains a self-image of being inadequate and unloved, despite its notable achievements and new buildings.

b. Contemporary

(1) Beneficial

To an increasing degree, United States aerospace companies are beginning to profit from the research and technology spin-off accruing from the vast quantities of federal contracts in recent years. The industry is determined to parlay the knowledge it has acquired — not only in technology but in the managerial techniques of coordinating complex programs. From the industry's standpoint, the developments in the past months have dovetailed neatly. In 1966, just as sales to NASA were beginning to flatten out, Defense Dept. demands for Vietnam were rising and commercial jet aircraft sales started to zoom. [In 1967] as military orders started peaking out, the nation was becoming increasingly aware of the need for such things as air and water pollution control, urban planning and transportation, and the unexplored underwater world — commercial as well as military. The industry sees vast potential in these and a number of other fields. Among them are medicine, communications, meteorology, and topography. One recent listing of the significant product and technological developments that United States aerospace companies have realized as a result of the U.S. government spending in space research was made by some European space companies. It included: several dozen electronic components, instrumentation and controls, communications, power sources, structural and mechanical engineering bearings (particularly stress measurements and fail-safe devices), servo-mechanisms, metallic and non-metallic materials, finishes, matching techniques, vacuum engineering and chemical and electronic propellants. (*Business Week*, December 9, 1967, pp. 150–153.)

Until recently, most urban universities tended to stand aloofly apart from the cities in which they lived. But the school's hunger for more land, the traffic and housing problems they create, have sharpened old town-gown tensions — and also have made administrators more conscious of the fact that their institutions may possess the intellectual resources to help create what New York University President James M. Hester calls "a renaissance in urban life." Universities are now creating new interdisciplinary departments for academic investigation of urban problems and they are setting up field agencies that plunge into practical action to help ease those problems. The two usually mesh. UCLA's Institute of Government and Public Affairs . . . is studying the feasibility of subways for freeway-clogged Los Angeles, electric cars to ease smog. It also set up an "urban observatory" two days after the Watts riots to probe the causes of the violence. (*Time*, January 6, 1967), p. 59.)

Not too long ago, a herd of 150 cattle could be grazed economically; today 400 represent the lowest economical unit . . . [On Robert O. Anderson's Circle

Diamond ranch near Roswell, New Mexico] heifers are bred at two years of age, or six months earlier than usual. This spots the non-breeders and shy breeders, who eat up feed without producing offspring, also guarantees that good breeders will have .8 of a calf more in their eight- to ten-year breeding span. "That .8 calf is often the difference between a profitable producer and just an expensive cow. This is a precision business with no margin for errors," he says. The results of [his careful breeding] and the carefully integrated operation is cattle that reach markets in Kansas City or Chicago at 16 months instead of 24, and with a live weight of 1000 pounds to 1040 pounds, will dress down to 600 pounds when slaughtered. (*Time,* October 20, 1967, p. 96.)

(2) *Harmful*

McGill University, once preeminent among Canadian institutions, is now finding its peculiar situation as an English-speaking institution in a predominantly French province an uneasy one. The uneasiness arises primarily from the circumstance that, while McGill grows increasingly dependent on the Province of Quebec for financial support, the province is caught up in nationalist ferment and is pressing the development of its French-language institutions. Now, however, McGill suffers because many French-Canadians seem not to regard it as a *Quebec* institution. Indeed, McGill's most urgent task is somehow to convince French Quebecers that the province should, in its own interests, generously support and maintain a strong, internationally respected English-language university. In considering McGill's present complaints, it is well to remember that about 60 per cent of the university's operating funds next year will come from the province, whereas 10 years ago support from that source was insignificant. (*Science,* May 31, 1968, pp. 974–975.)

The reasons why these great Andrew Carnegie–vintage libraries are in trouble are known to every public librarian: the changing composition of our city-centers; the popularity of TV and paperbacks; the increase in street crime, which keeps users away from the library; too little parking space; too much prosperity, which means more money for flashier entertainment; and better school libraries, which have been improved with Federal funds. One librarian, writing in that outspoken spokesman of the trade, *Library Journal,* even cited uneasiness over Vietnam as a cause. Certainly these factors contribute to the general malaise of public libraries in center-city. But most librarians, entombed behind card files, refuse to confront the one cause that is central to all others: themselves. By and large, librarians — white, middle class, patient, and dedicated — are still dishing up service for a white middle class which long ago fled to the suburbs and has been replaced by Puerto Ricans, poor whites, Negroes from the rural South, and Mexican-Americans. Unlike the Eastern Europeans who flocked to this country and its public libraries at the turn of the century, these new emigres have no tradition of book-learning and few of them aspire to the values of the white majority, which the librarian stands so ready, by training and tradition, to inculcate. (*The Reporter,* June 13, 1968, p. 34.)

Small signs are already beginning to appear that the era of seemingly limitless expansion in suburban retailing is nearing its end. Heavy traffic and inadequate parking space originally helped repel the shopper from the downtown store. Now the growth of the suburbs and of the two-, three- and four-car family has often made it nearly impossible around any but the best planned shopping centers. The population explosion can jam the check-out counter in a suburban supermarket even faster than in a downtown one, since there is more room in which a suburban population can explode. Already the day is past when just about any kind of suburban shopping center could make money. For example, Woolworth is finding that a surprising number of its problem stores are located not in a decaying downtown business area but in a smaller suburban shopping district. They now suffer from the competition of larger, newer and more elaborately designed regional centers. (*Forbes*, October 15, 1967, p. 15.)

c. Anticipated

(1) Beneficial

According to a report in *Science* (September 8, 1967, pp. 1151–1154): During the last several years, the need for a fully developed university in Portland, Oregon, has been the topic of special study and discussion. The City Fathers feel that Portland has been lagging far behind other metropolitan areas in the west, especially since employment in the state's main industries — agriculture and timber — has substantially declined in recent years and because the rate of income growth in the state has been well below the national average. A committee studied the situation and concluded that Oregon has a great need for the science-based industry which only a university with graduate programs in most scientific disciplines would help stimulate. Therefore, in order to attract new industries to the Portland area, Portland tried to establish a local university. The efforts failed for a variety of reasons: the unwillingness of many Oregon taxpayers to increase the amounts spent on higher education; the desire of some backers of the state's two major universities to preserve their institution's prerogatives and existing piece of the state financial pie; and the desire of some Portlanders to make Portland State College into a full-scale university rather than to create a separate graduate center. Senator Mark Hatfield later arranged for the incorporation of a new Graduate Center as a nonprofit organization in 1963. Research and devolopment organizations have begun to show an interest in the area. The Center has attracted some high quality scientists and students. The question now is whether the Oregon Graduate Center can become a first-rate educational institution, and whether it will achieve the long-range objective for Portland: science-based industry.

There are several major trends that can enhance the effectiveness and position of Menorah Medical Center. With increasing insurance, reliable income from patient care is assured. The trend to establish networks of hospitals around a basic teaching hospital where major diagnostic and treatment resources are centered will work in Menorah's favor for it has already developed a research program and kept itself in the forefront of technical medical advances. Although there is a trend away from religious adherence as such, Jewish identification with charitable causes, particularly medical ones, ensures a stable supportive constituency that will take the hospital's needs seriously, that will identify with its ambition to be the best, and that will continually demonstrate to the staff that "someone cares" when public hospials are buffeted by their distance from their political and community base. All this is apart from population growth in the city, and the rising numbers of middle-class people who will value high quality hospital care.

(2) Harmful

[The Travelers Insurance Company feels that] more serious in its ultimate implications if not in dollars and cents, . . . the new Medicare legislation . . . is bound to take business away from the Travelers . . . and . . . stifle significant progress the company has been making in efforts to care for the health-insurance needs of the elderly. When Chairman Wilbur Mills' bill was passed by the House, Travelers President Sterling T. Tooker protested that it had a threatening impact on well over a quarter of a billion dollars of Travelers' premium income. But what concerns the Travelers even more is that medicare benefits, once linked to social security, may not stay fixed at age 65, and will in time come to apply at age 60, or even lower. Medicare is a prime example of how social change, translated into political action, can ride roughshod over an important area of the insurance business, and in this instance, practically carve it out of the private sector entirely. (*Fortune*, August 1965, p. 140.)

Ralph W. Conant, associate director of the Lemberg Center for the Study of Violence at Brandeis University, has painted a bleak picture for the future. Writing in the May 15 issue of *Library Journal*, he predicted: "Black political leaders of the future will aggressively reorient public schools, libraries, and the other lesser institutions toward black history, culture, art, and politics . . . The whites cannot help in this future effort and the blacks know it, even if the whites do not." To support his thesis, he submitted a timetable for the coming black political leadership in U.S. cities: by 1975, Newark, Detroit, and Philadelphia; by 1980, Chicago, Atlanta, Baltimore, and St. Louis; by 1985, Memphis and New Orleans. While Conant may be extremist in his predictions, it is evident that a constructive course of action for center-city libraries is desperately needed. (*The Reporter*, June 13, 1968, p. 34.)

2. Appraisal of the effect of the organization on the environment

One of the ways a consultant can note that organizational integrative efforts are failing is to observe how the organization thrashes about. As a result of its pain, the organization can injure its environment by withdrawal, assault, aggression in its relationships with others, and random adaptive patterns. To resolve its discomforts, it may first do one thing and then another. Another way the consultant can note failing integrative efforts is to observe how little difference the organization makes in a community. An organization may fail to assume its share of responsibility for community planning or attack its environment by political manipulation aimed at self-satisfaction. Failing to benefit a community may be just as harmful as denuding mountains of trees or polluting the air or water. To make a judgment about the failure of integrative efforts, the consultant must also have as a context the beneficial effects of the organization. Examples not otherwise identified are drawn from case studies:

a. Historical

(1) Beneficial

The Menninger Foundation has trained 8 per cent of the psychiatrists now practicing in the United States beside a number in foreign countries. Since the inception of the Menninger hospital in 1925, it has set a high standard for psychiatric hospital and psychotherapeutic care that has earned it an enviable reputation. Beginning with the work of David Rapaport, it also set an exemplary model for diagnostic psychological testing and research. Its training efforts and hospital rejuvenation programs contributed many trained personnel of varied disciplines to the nation's professional manpower pool and established creative models for hospital operation. It did pioneering work in juvenile delinquency and rehabilitation of criminals through its association with the Kansas Boys' Industrial School and the Kansas Reception and Diagnostic Center. Its consultative efforts with other states have also had positive ramifications for improvement of patient care, and it has spoken with an influential voice toward positive, progressive goals in professional associations, government agencies, and its community.

In addition to educating Catholic students for 53 years, St. Clare's school has served as an identification device for the Roman Catholic community, a public relations medium, and an instrument of upward social mobility. Students and families alike obtained a sense of Catholic solidarity in times of discrimination; they took collective pride in the achievements of their fellows and sought to emulate them. Through athletic and other competition with public schools, they had a medium of interchange and fellowship with Protestants in the community. Thus, the net effect of the school was to facilitate the integration of the Catholic community and to surmount prejudice with less conflict than would have occurred without it.

From its organization in 1888, Central Congregational Church had an unusual impact on its environment. Its first pastor, Dr. Charles Sheldon opened a kindergarten in 1893 primarily for children from a Negro ghetto, Tennessee Town, which was not far from the church. This was the first of its kind, Negro or white, in the community and by 1897 it had become a laboratory for training kindergarten teachers. *In His Steps,* Sheldon's most famous religious novel, was published in 1896. By 1946 this best seller was second only to the Bible; 25 million copies were sold, and translations were made into 27 languages. In addition to novels and plays about individual piety, the pastor had a passion for temperance and peace. During his first pastorate, more than 30 young people were commissioned as missionaries, ordained as ministers, or inspired to go into YMCA foreign service. The members found a vicarious model in the writings of Sheldon and pursued his community contribution concept. Central Congregational Church was therefore an important force in the community.

(2) *Harmful*

In its small community, the elite status of the First Congregational Church and its pronouncements on all kinds of issues gave the rest of the community the impression that it was a place for self-righteous goody-goodies who thought they were better than other people. This resentment was directed toward the insiders who for years had run the church as a "closed shop." The effect of having created such resentment was to make it difficult to have cooperative ventures in the community, to take a common stand on community improvement, and to evolve genuine participation across social class and denominational lines. Another injury to the environment was the continual round of money-making activities that preyed on the community. All local merchants were squeezed for ads in anniversary books, space for bazaars, memorial donations, and so on. Since most of the power figures in the community belonged to the church, they could ill afford not to respond.

When the franchise renewal time drew near for General Gas Distribution Corp., several citizens of the community, including two college professors, publicly campaigned for changes in the franchise which would lower rates and increase the pressure under which gas was delivered to the consumer. The protesting citizens were never large in number or influential in effect. Ultimately General got the franchise it wanted. However, when it came time for contract renewal at the college, one of the professors was told he could not continue teaching what he had been because he was not qualified and the other had his department reorganized from under him. Both left the college. Rumor had it that a General vice president had called a member of the Board of Regents who in turn had called the college president. The rumor was later confirmed in the course of this study. The same tactics were used in other communities, with the addition of the scare word "socialist," if there were those who wanted community ownership of distribution. Thus the company, mobilizing its powerful advertising and political resources, made it impossible for the communities it served to discuss intelligently and calmly common problems and come to reasonable solutions. This destructiveness later plagued general when it sought community cohesion to attract new business or make community improvements. The officials themselves never saw the connection between the history of their relationships with their environments and the later community behavior. They could only say that local people did not care.

b. Contemporary

(1) Beneficial

From the standpoint of Hillsdale United Presbyterian Church's impact on the environment, we perceived both positive and negative aspects. Fundamentally, it sees itself as making constructive effort on interracial problems, easing local tensions, providing avenues for social action, and mobilizing its congregation toward problem-solving rather than conflict. In general it has a positive beneficial effect on its environment. In response to the change in its neighborhood, the church has opened its gym to the children of the area without attaching any condition of membership. In the near future a youth lounge will be opened, likewise available to all. Also planned is a tutorial program for nearby junior high school students. These efforts can be classified under the general positive heading of the church's willingness to stay in the area and as part of its general contribution to constructively resolving some of the racial issues which it, as a church, must confront. On the negative side, the church has not been successful to any extent in attracting students from a nearby college or in drawing neighborhood newcomers into the membership.

In the months since *Harper's* published Johnie Scott's "My Home Is Watts" some of the teachers at Jordan High School have been analyzing our recollections of the students who have been graduated from this predominately Negro school in our time. We remember that *Time* magazine in its November 21, 1960, issue selected Jordan as an example of a senior high that enabled many of its graduates to go on to college — even if it meant buying them everything from socks to study lamps, and getting them jobs in the summer. Nevertheless we know that many of our boys and girls are starved educationally, for a myriad of reasons, as Johnie implied, and that those who go on to a four-year college and make the grade are the exceptions. However, the number of these [students] is steadily increasing . . . who have received their education in Watts, who have known many successes in many areas and are now making contributions of which they have reason to be proud. In addition, Jordan graduates are at present attending Antioch, Oberlin, Redlands, Whittier, Occidental, Carleton, Knoxville, Seattle University, Pacific University, Stanford, Lewis and Clark, UCLA, and the University of Utah. (*Harper's*, May 1967, p. 38).

(2) Harmful

The Union Pacific's train No. 6 leaves Los Angeles at 11:15 P.M. for Omaha, a 43-hour journey. It has no sleeping cars (a pillow can be had for 35 cents). It has no dining or refreshment cars. At 7:30 A.M. on the first day, when the train stops at Las Vegas, passengers are given 25 minutes to grab a bite in the station. For lunch they get 15 minutes at Milford, Utah. Dinner is more leisurely — 35 minutes at Ogden, Utah, close to where the Golden Spike marked the linking of East and West by rail just 99 years ago. The service was better then. The trip today, in the words of a recent passenger, is "a nightmare." True, No. 6 at its best was never an outstanding train. But it is an outstanding example of the reduced service that many railroads have resorted to in an attempt to drive passengers away and abolish their money-losing trains. Such tactics have helped bring about the demise of some 500 long-distance passenger trains in the past decade. By the end of 1967, only 650 regularly scheduled intercity trains were left in the U.S., compared with 20,000 in 1929. (*Newsweek*, May 6, 1968, p. 79.)

One has to say that the Mid-Atlantic Conference does more damage by its existence than it does good. One of the pastors stated that he feels like the tail on a dog. Everyone waits until it grows up to see if it will be useful. If it gets in the way, they cut it off. The pastors are lonely, depressed, lacking a sense of competence, uncertain as to their future, and feel unloved. This is at a time when they should be leading the way in civil rights, helping to ease community tensions, holding up enduring values for confused youth and troubled parents, and serving as stable organizing points for changing communities and neighborhoods. The conference is not helping the pastors, which in turn diminishes the help the pastors can give to their congregations, and deprives the community of the leadership it has a right to expect of one of its major religious denominations.

c. Anticipated

(1) Beneficial

The committee concluded that, while salary is important to scholars, it is "apparently less important in recruiting and retaining senior personnel than some of us had thought. Housing and schooling are presumably of more concern to a man pondering a move to Cambridge." Noting that housing is difficult to find in Cambridge, the committee urged [Harvard] to undertake large-scale faculty housing programs. The committee dismissed he idea of having Harvard run a school for faculty children and of providing tuition assistance at the primary level, arguing that the case for tuition assistance in secondary schools for faculty children is "distinctly more persuasive." The committe put great stress on the argument that improvement of the "quality of life" in Cambridge was of utmost importance in recruiting faculty, at both the junior and senior levels. Efforts to improve public services and housing, the committee said, would require that Harvard become much more involved with the Cambridge city government and "our sister institution M.I.T." than it has been in the past. (*Science,* May 31, 1968, p. 978.)

When St. Agnes' hospital shifts its facilities over to convalescent care, it will fill a void in the community. Presently there are only scattered nursing homes of varying quality, almost all of which have minimal medical facilities. St. Agnes' could establish a high-level standard of convalescent care, serve as a pivot for the other nursing homes, train their personnel, work out complementary relationships, and free the resources of City Hospital for intensive care. Equally important, the end of rivalry between St. Agnes' and City Hospital could permit the whole community to unite behind a comprehensive hospital and medical care program, now often bogged down because the conflicting interests of the two hospitals must be compromised.

(2) *Harmful*

. . . to what extent does a giant corporation have an obligation to serve the public interest as well as its own executives and stockholders? This question is being posed in dramatic form in a remote roadless area of Washington's North Cascade Mountains, often known as the American Alps. The corporation is Kennecott Copper. Kennecott has announced plans for a huge open pit mine at the heart of the Glacier Peak Wilderness: a region which, because of its unique natural beauty, is already a part of our national wilderness preservation system. Recently, it has assumed a new significance because of its close association with the proposed North Cascades National Park. If the company's plans go through, a priceless scenic treasure will be destroyed. And a shattering precedent will have been created. Unlike the earlier exploitation of the public domain by other companies through fraud and corruption, Kennecott's proposed action is strictly within the law. The issue is therefore more far-reaching and more complex than that of mere law enforcement. Kennecott does not, of course, own these forested ridges and snow-clad mountains; they are public property, administered by the U.S. Forest Service of the Department of Agriculture. Kennecott does, however, own 300 acres, and has unpatented mining claims on another 3000. These claims were staked out under our free-and-easy mining laws at the turn of the century, and taken over by a Kennecott subsidiary some 10 years ago. Under the Wilderness Act of 1964, areas officially designated as wilderness are protected from lumbering, road-building, mechanized travel, or from any other use incompatible with their pristine character. But prospecting is still allowed until 1984 and previously existing mining claims can be exploited. Like a buried bomb that hasn't been defused, this situation has haunted conservationists, who have wondered when and where the bomb might go off. Now they know. (*Harper's,* September 1967, p. 48.)

An aspect of the report that disturbs the outside observer (in this era of student revolt) is the absence of discussion of ways in which student-faculty

328 ANALYSES AND CONCLUSIONS

relations might be improved so as to make [Harvard] more attractive to concerned faculty members and to students. Of course, one could reply that it was not the Dunlop committee's job to examine relationships with students, that faculty-student relations are better at Harvard than at many other universities, and that the committee members are concerned about such relations even if they did not discuss them in the report. Perhaps so, but faculty members should be aware that the picture which increasingly emerges when professors discuss their condition is one of men who are interested in using the universities primarily as bases for their own activities, research, and well-being, and only secondarily as places to teach students. On the other hand, most people outside the university (as well as most students) believe that universities should be primarily teaching institutions. As universities become progressively more dependent on federal and state governments for support, the opinions of those on the outside will have to be considered more seriously. Those universities which are truly interested in encouraging their professors to teach students would do well to work harder at making that interest clear to those outside the university's walls. (*Science,* May 31, 1965, p. 978.)

3. Reactions

a. *Of the environment*

Whenever an organization injures its environment by withdrawal, assault, aggressive relationships, or random adaptation efforts, inevitably the environment must react. This process of stimulation and reaction tells the consultant something about the organization's characteristic mode of adaptation, at what point it is likely to be in conflict with its host environment, and the need for the organization to observe this pattern of provocation and reaction. Examples from published sources are identified; others are from case studies:

(1) *To the injury*

The news of this impending disaster [Kennecott's plan for a mine pit in Glacier Peak Wilderness] broke late last year. Protest was immediate. The Sierra Club and the North Cascades Conservation Council, long aware of the threat, went into action. The Governor of Washington, speaking officially for his state, and the Secretary of Agriculture came out against the project. This is a case, said Secretary Freeman, "of balancing a priceless, yet intangible, national treasure against ledger sheets and profits . . . The scenic values of this area are as well known to the company as they are to you and me. The company can, if it so chooses, ignore these values; gouge out its road and begin operations . . . But I cannot really believe that such an application will ever reach my desk" . . . The final, unanswerable opinion comes — amazingly — from the Department of Defense. Assistant Secretary Paul R. Ignatius has written to Senator Henry M. Jackson, Chairman of the Committee on Interior and Insular Affairs, who conducted hearings on the bill for a North Cascades National Park: "Because of the length of time necessary to bring the mine into production and the relatively small amount of additional copper that would result therefrom" it is doubtful that its contribution would be "sufficient to outweigh other important considerations, such as the inevitable damage to the natural beauty of the wilderness area." (*Harper's*, September 1967, p. 50.)

If West Hills Mennonite Church had any harmful effect on the environment it would be only in the form of withdrawal which deprived those who might have been helped by what the church had to offer. The reaction of the community was largely one of indifference: not many people knew about West Hills Mennonite and even fewer cared anything about it. Some of the other pastors wondered why West Hills did not enter into their joint activities more, and a few of the worshippers of other churches were disappointed that they did not get greater response when they invited West Hills parishoners to visit their services. But that was the end of it.

(2) *Toward the source of the injury*

For [air] passengers from California's suburban Orange County, the frustration of an hour's drive to Los Angeles International Airport to catch an hour's flight to San Francisco seemed particularly ridiculous. County officials pleaded in vain with major airlines for direct service from Santa Ana to upstate points. Then, where the established carriers feared — or at least failed — to go, five young men with no aviation experience dared to start an airline of their own. With only two planes — (Lockheed Turboprop Electras) about 160 employees and the San Francisco-Orange County route that nobody wanted, Air California has snared an impressive and rapidly growing volume of business. (*Time*, June 9, 1967, p. 105.)

The community's reaction to First Congregational's condescension was one of angry resentment toward every idea advanced from the church. When funeral guidelines were established, the local undertakers cried out against interference. If First Congregational undertook the leadership of an interchurch activity, it was sure to fall flat. Had it not been for the pattern of ecumenical activity everywhere else, First Congregational would have been left out entirely.

b. Secondary reaction from the organization

How does the organization react to the environment's reaction? Do they understand it? Do they recognize their contribution to precipitating conflict in the first place?

Historically, the American Medical Association failed to recognize the mounting discontent with medical services as being a product of a genuine feeling of anger and deprivation. As a result, they directed their public relations and political efforts to countering movements toward better health care, including the expansion of medical schools. They attributed such movements to discontent aroused by political agitators and left-wing politicians. They did not recognize the extent to which they had aroused antipathy toward themselves by failing to recognize the underlying problems and directing their counterattack to denying the need for services that people acutely felt.

Since the January 27, 1967 fire that killed three astronauts in a ground test of an Apollo space capsule, North American, the Apollo prime contractor, has been faulted for "poor workmanship," "carelessness" and "negligence" . . . Reaction to these charges range from anger among employees who feel too much blame is being piled on the company to a supercaution about quality that sometimes slows production unnecessarily. Immediately after the fire, some North American employees went so far as to light matches to components to test their own theories on flammability. And at least some departments were hit with a raft of resignations by hourly workers fearful that the disaster would lead to a major internal upheaval at North American . . . The post-fire controversy has brought some shift in key management personnel, along with changes in management attitudes and methods. The company raised work standards and created trouble-shooting groups on both the technical and middle management levels to bolster quality. One of these new teams proposed irradiating tools so that a Geiger counter could insure none were left behind in completed Apollo vehicles, as some investigators charge has happened in the past . . . The changes were intended to serve the practical purpose of restoring confidence in Apollo workmanship both inside and outside the company. Without question, they intensified the attention to detail. (*Wall Street Journal,* June 23, 1967, p. 1.)

4. Appraisal of the organization

The consultant must recognize, at the outset, that any "appraisal" is just that — an estimate, a value judgment that is made in terms of the appraiser's professional orientation and that is influenced by certain biasing factors unique to both the discipline and the individual.

For example, business oriented consultants would think in terms of "assets" and "impairments" — positive and negative factors, strengths and weaknesses, pluses and minuses. From the standpoint of survival and growth, what one consultant might see as an organizational impairment — such as the *inability* to function without federal support, as in the aerospace industry — another consultant might view as an asset — such as the long-established tradition in the aerospace industry of interdependency with the federal government.

In the fields of psychiatry and clinical psychology (here seen as part of the field of the healing arts), the orientation is traditionally "pathological." The focus of interest is heavily on the impairments (the "disease," if you will), sometimes to such an extent that the assets are not always accurately recognized. Since this organizational case study method has been extrapolated from a clinical case study method, the consultant using it must constantly recognize the need to guard against overemphasizing the impairments at the expense of the assets — and thereby skewing, or distorting, his appraisal.

In this section of the outline the consultant will succinctly evaluate the organization. He should do so in terms of survival and growth, how the organization has functioned in the past and how it will be able to continue to function in the future. In making such an appraisal he will necessarily have to make positive and negative value judgments with regard to the organization's assets and impairments and, in doing so from a clinical orientation, what he chooses to call "assets" and "impairments" will be related to the proposed "treatment" to follow, *that is, consultative intervention.* Consequently, he will pay special attention to such organizational qualities as points of vulnerability, points of necessary intervention, and points of therapeutic usefulness. Consultants from other disciplines may adhere to different principles in their appraisal of the organization.

A second difference, that is usually more apparent than real, is that the consultant will think of assets and impairments in both *material* and *functional* terms.

a. Special assets

(1) *Material or tangible (financial, patents, physical plant, equipment, geographical distribution, transportation, communication, personnel)*

Material assets and impairments are definable quasi-permanent elements that form a relatively enduring part of the organizational matrix; they are, or are treated as, nonhuman elements. In the 1930's and early 1940's, the dark green delivery trucks operated by Marshall Field and Company of Chicago, Illinois, were perceived by the community as sources of help in emergencies. During their regularly scheduled delivery rounds, the drivers often became sidetracked on errands of mercy — getting a kitten out of a tree, returning a lost dog to his home, hastening a mother-to-be to the nearest hospital, putting out a fire. These events occurred so often, and the drivers of the dark green trucks became so well known for their humanitarian qualities, that it was as if these qualities resided in the *trucks themselves*, rather than in the men who drove them. It was the *truck* that was sought for in times of emergency.

Items to be considered, as listed in the outline, are examples, not a complete list: financial status, patents held, physical plants and equipment, geographical distribution, transportation facilities, communications, personnel (that is, their particular talents — such as the *number* of engineers in a construction firm). Illustrations come from both case and published sources:

At its inception Arrowhead Tool and Die was minimally capitalized; since then it has improved its financial position and has a flexible line of credit. The physical plant has been expanded on an ad hoc basis to meet the growing needs of increased production. Adequate acreage still exists for further building expansion. Competition for labor is not particularly intense in the area so there is an adequate number of unskilled and semiskilled workers. The equipment is obsolescent but adequate for the demands made upon it.

The Hillsdale United Presbyterian Church has 1,000 communicant members, a budget of over $100,000 which increases steadily, and an adequate church plant whose value is listed as $275,000. It is located at an intersection of several distinct areas, giving it a good drawing potential, and is within range of the community's major activities and institutions. Its membership is largely middle class; it has a history of stable leadership.

The Menninger Foundation has two campuses, one of 40 acres and the other of some 800 acres. The buildings, for the most part, are relatively modern. Both the adult and the children's hospitals are well designed and attractively decorated. Buildings and grounds have a warm, peaceful air about them. The staff of some 900 people, including a third who are professionals, are highly competent and widely recognized for their effective work. Drawn from many parts of the world, the professional staff is cosmopolitan in its outlook. The clinical activities are self-supporting. One-third of the $9 million budget is supported by contributions and grants. Research grants have a history of renewal and continued support making long-term research possible. Both trainees and staff members are avidly sought by other institutions.

The Mount Anthony Union High School in Bennington, Vermont, is an architectural essay in deliberate, plain, blunt materials: brick and concrete block, quarry tile and asbestos vinyl floors, unhidden utility pipes, rugged tables and benches made of laminated rock maple. But modern as the building is in conception, it fits faultlessly into the New England landscape. The concept finally devised was to give the students a unique amount of flexibility and freedom of movement. The school centers on a two-story library, has lounges for students who are likely to have frequent free periods and a flexible arrangement of twenty classrooms, seven science rooms, twelve vocational shops, offices and a gymnasium. In all, the school has 156,000 square feet of floor area, large enough to accommodate as many as 1,200 students. (*Fortune*, April 1968, pp. 143–146.)

(2) *Functional (including leadership and mental set or attitude)*

The qualities the consultant looks for in the functional assets of the organization are human in nature. They are dynamic; at this point he should think in terms of the organization "being alive" — "being able to respond." In appraising "functional" assets and impairments, it becomes impossible to exclude an assessment of organizational key figures, and it is difficult to separate the assessment of such figures in their own right from the assessment of the organization as an entity. However difficult such an appraisal may be, it must be made. What is an asset to the individual may well be an impairment to the organization; the reverse is also true. In differentiating the positive and negative qualities of the *key figures'* behavior, the consultant might ask, "What is the cost to the *organization* of this individual's behavior?"

(A) REALITY ORIENTATION

One dimension of a functional asset (or impairment) is seen in terms of the organization's orientation to reality (or lack thereof). Here again the distinction must be made between the organization's ability to perceive and judge the world around it as opposed to its perceiving and judging the organizational self. Robert Burns' famous lines about the importance of being able to see oneself are as germane for organizations as they are for individuals.

i. To external environment

In 1950 IBM was, as it is now, the dominant company in the data processing industry. But then it was dominant in electro-mechanical equipment, based on the Hollerith type punched cards known as unit record systems — with only a smattering of electronic equipment attached to the punch card sorters. The company had its first warning of the coming electronic transformation of the industry in 1948, when the Bureau of the Census in Washington ordered a UNIVAC electronic computer from a new and struggling company called Eckert Mauchly Computer Co. later bought by Remington Rand). The warning had little immediate effect; IBM went its electro-mechanical way and did not grasp the chance to get in early by embarking on all-out computer development. The younger Watson blames the oversight of his own and others' complacency . . . Once he had full authority, Thomas Watson, Jr. wasted little time in making changes in IBM. In the spring of 1956 he began a series of meetings with

Albert L. Williams, now president, and Louis H. LaMotte, now chairman of the executive and finance committee. The three redesigned the corporation between the spring and the fall . . . IBM, in fact, has become almost a phenomenon as well as a company. It has installed more than three-fourths of the computers in the world — an estimated 13,000 to 14,000 — or more than 10 times the tally of its nearest competitor, Univac Div. of Sperry Rand Corp. It has over 19,000 data-processing customers, more than 125,000 employees. Though some five decades old, its stock has been one of the darlings of the growth stock fanciers of the past decade. (*Business Week,* February 2, 1963, p. 93.)

Menorah Medical Center knows its constituency as well as the current medical trends. It is knowledgeable about quality of professional care; the importance of research, funding, the state of other hospitals all over the country; and its place in its community. More than that, it seeks to adapt to reality, that is master it, rather than adjust to it or conform.

ii. To internal environment

The pastor (of Hillsdale United Presbyterian Church) knows his constituents. When he was called by the congregation, he was asked to "be a challenging voice from the pulpit, improve communications, and attract young people." He has emphasized worship, stewardship, communication, and leadership enlistment. The church has attracted and held members by a diversified approach that, in the main, concentrates its attention on those deeply involved but offers enough to retain those who are largely uncommitted. The pastor divides his congregation into 20 per cent dedicated, 20 per cent indifferent, and 60 per cent marginal. He sees his success as having attracted this last group, interesting them to work for the church, and using the dedicated group to approach the uncommitted. He sees his own role as that of interpreter and prompter who helps and guides the laity to perform their various functions as members of the church. He understands the middle-class values of his congregation; he feels that they are more often "hearers" rather than "doers" and are, therefore, slow to implement ideas and need his support to do so.

A recent report in a news magazine told of a foundation, that was dedicated, among other things, to promoting the realization of individual human dignity and worth. The organization gives away $300 million a year, much of it for urban studies and for the arts. The foundation recently moved to the center of a large city into a new building that would symbolize its aesthetic preoccupations and, according to the president, provide the best urban environment for working people. The new $16 million headquarters, into which over 350 executives, technicians, and secretaries moved, is a 12-story work of art, as exciting and refreshing to look at from the outside as it is exciting to work in. What is unique about the building is the 12-story center of greenery and light occupying the southeastern corner of its plot. Employees in the L-shaped office floors encircling the western and northern sides of the building can look either across the court through a 120-foot-high "glass wall" into each other's offices or down at a cool and fragrant garden, landscaped with very high magnolia trees, a water-lily pool, and almost 100 varieties of shrub. Besides providing an all-year whiff of nature, the courtyard is essential, say the architects, because it provides the staff with a sense of community. According to the architects, the worker takes an elevator up to his floor in a conventional building, and goes into his office. He has to depend on memos to make him aware of the fact that he is a member of a group.

(B) VALUES AND IDEALS

Another dimension for assessing the functional assets and impairments of an organization concerns its values and ideals and the degree to which they are institutionalized or have become part of the organization itself (rather than remaining solely those of the individuals within the organization). In other words, how deeply imbedded in the organization are they? How much are they part of the organization itself? This is difficult to define and detect, but the consultant should think in terms of the perpetuation of something that the organization stands for — something that is adhered to regardless of changes in personnel, economic and marketing conditions, world events, and so on. In addition, he must ask, "How congruent are these values and ideals with the organization's internal and external reality?" (as an indication that they are an asset) or, "How great is their disparity with the organization's internal and external reality?" (as an indication that they are an impairment). Examples are from both case and published sources:

i. Degree of institutionalization

The Thomism is still there [Notre Dame] and, though the split-T has given way to flanker formations invented by the professionals, so is the football. But Notre Dame, driven by new currents of scholarships and the winds from Vatican II, is trying to become what has never existed before in America: a major Catholic university. Although a fourth of Notre Dame's students are enrolled in an ROTC unit and expect to become commissioned officers, more than half the seniors go on to professional or graduate training, the best of them at Berkeley, Chicago, or Yale. The total number of Rhodes Scholarships (5) and Woodrow Wilson Fellowships (122) earned by Notre Dame men to date, while not impressive by Harvard standards, has climbed steadily, and far exceeds the record of any other Catholic college. The mean College Board scores for entering freshmen now stand around 570 on the verbal tests, and 630 on the mathematical — equivalent to the average Ivy League freshman class a decade ago. The Notre Dame brand of undergraduate impudence is rather tame. The students — many of them children of middle-class, college-educated parents —

are fiercely proud, not only of their football team but of the fact that Notre Dame is not Berkeley. Under their sloppy sweaters and levis, many tend to be social moralists and political prudes. Some 400 are involved in tutoring programs in South Bend, a few have tried to picket the annual ROTC review, protesting American involvement in Vietnam, but only a handful are engaged in any serious political activities. Sitting in the Huddle, an undergraduate snack bar decorated with murals of football players, a student says that "everybody is pretty normal around here. We get a few longhairs — the longhairs get jumped sometimes. Last fall one got jumped by some jocks and shaved. But there's no demonstrations — no LSD and all that. If McNamara comes here — well he's an important guy. It doesn't matter whether you agree with him, you feel for him." Early in 1967, the senior class overwhelmingly elected General William Westmoreland, U.S. Commander in Vietnam, as its Patriot of the Year. Men with a strong religious commitment or a keen interest in problems of value find the South Bend academic community more congenial than the secular institutions where they previously taught. "Notre Dame's concern about values," said [President Theodore] Hesburgh, "is probably an asset for the kind of people I'm trying to get. If a man feels that this quality is not relevant to an institution, then I'm not sure he ought to come." Hesburgh's own prestige in American life — what one teacher called "his clout on the outside" — apparently gives him almost total freedom from Church interference. (*Harper's*, May 1967, pp. 41–49.)

The values and ideals of Menorah Medical Center are deeply institutionalized. Many employees know the history of the hospital. They speak frequently of "giving the best care" and the aspiration to be first; they already believe they are giving the best patient care in the city. They believe the hospital to be selective in its recruiting. They are proud of their achievements and look forward to even greater effectiveness.

ii. Congruence with reality

The values and ideals at Hillsdale United Presbyterian Church are eminently congruent with reality. The development of lay leadership is in keeping with Presbyterian polity. The social-action orientation, which is not at the expense of worship, and the attraction of younger members to service meet both the needs of the organization and those of the community. The focus on racial and neighborhood problems, simultaneously "front door" (because they occur just outside the church) and community problems, is congruent with congregational concerns, community needs, and national issues to which the church is expected to speak. Furthermore, the manner in which the pastor leads his flock is congruent with their middle-class status, their business and professional interests.

Menorah Medical Center has the resources, skills, reputation, and experience to support its value system. Furthermore, it is precisely that deeply held and widely shared value orientation that makes the hospital so attractive to staff and patients alike. When it comes to a matter of life and death, people do indeed want the best, to be cared for by those who want to be "first."

The service value at Kansas Power and Light has many implications beyond the satisfaction of those who work for the company. Effective service, community support, and pride in service achievement are money in the organizational bank when it comes time to have franchises renewed in the respective communities, when legislative or regulatory bodies raise questions or threaten controls. It also fits the cultural and religious ethos of the employees who come from a rural, helping tradition.

(c) TASK MASTERY

The consultant can look at task mastery as an additional dimension of a functional asset or impairment.

i. Psychological contract fulfillment

What is the psychological contract in the organization? To what degree is it recognized and fulfilled? For a complete explanation of the concept of the psychological contract, the reader is referred to *Men, Management, and Mental Health* by H. Levinson et al. (Cambridge, Mass.: Harvard University Press, 1962, Ch. 3). Briefly, the psychological contract is comprised of those unspoken, and often unconscious, expectations that both man and organization bring to their relationship. Two such expectations are the mutual dependency of man and organization and a concern for the extremes of this dependency and the amount of psychological distance needed to function optimally. A third expectation has to do with the way organizational change is handled by both parties. Finally it is postulated that when these three issues are effectively dealt with the reciprocal relationship between the man and the organization tends to be such that it promotes mental health and more effective individual and organizational functioning.

For the most part the psychological contract at Menorah Medical Center is reasonably well fulfilled. People come to the hospital to give service both to relieve superego pressure and out of identification with ideal caring figures. They deal with their dependency needs by having stability of employment while at the same time caring for others. They seek to master by increasing their skills and to control the environment by being best. Their common pursuit of the ideal brings them psychologically close to each other, and the demands of the task require the sublimation of aggression. The administration is increasingly trying to involve the staff in making their own changes.

Employees of Kansas Power and Light expected to be able to "get ahead" in the company, by which they meant to have long-term employment security. They expected the company to provide them with some opportunity for occupational growth, to use their skills, to "fit in" with their fellows, and to be assigned to work in keeping with their psychological needs for closeness or distance from others. They also wanted to render service and be "good citizens." The company expected its employees to render service, particularly in emergencies; to be attuned to community social and political realities; to assume increasing responsibility with experience; and to be dedicated to the free enterprise system. The company wanted orderly people who would not be militant or demanding and who sought rapid promotion and high wages in an organization whose income was controlled by governmental regulation. That the psychological contract was largely fulfilled was reflected in low turnover and the high percentage of long-term employees.

The contract between the teachers and Curtis Elementary School is viable and reflected in the teachers' feeling that it is a desirable school in which to teach. They come from the same cultural backgrounds as their pupils: the emphasis is on denial of aggression, being considerate and polite, and attaining a respectable position in the community through their occupational roles. With tenure the teachers have job security; with the pressure to upgrade themselves, they have the feeling of improving their skills. They want protection from intrusion by the administration, which the principal gives them by sensitive application of his control, support and interpretation of the many conflicting roles with which their work confronts them. Being isolated from each other in their own classrooms enables them to regulate their distance from each other and from the principal. Changes occur slowly, which is the way they want it. The fact that they have been chosen to teach in this school indicates that they have already met the expectations of the system as a whole about how teachers should operate.

ii. Growth and survival

What has been the past history of organizational survival and growth? What are future prospects along this line?

Menorah Medical Center was opened in 1931 with a staff of 16 doctors and 50 nurses. From 1931 to 1948 patient admissions increased over 3 times to 6,300 and the hospital was operating at 30 per cent over capacity. Menorah completed a $2 million expansion during 1948. The hospital expanded again in 1962, bringing its capacity to its present level of 341 beds. Eight hundred and fifty employees handle more than 10,000 admissions and 18,400 outpatients annually with a $7 million budget. Menorah is in the middle of a $5 million expansion program that will increase existing facilities by two-thirds.

Last week, IBM took another leap forward with the announcement in its annual report that worldwide sales for 1962 passed the $2.5-billion mark ($2,578,

337,070, to be exact) — more than three and a half times what they were when Thomas J. Watson, Jr. took full command seven years ago. Its growth pattern — a threefold increase in assets, 3.6-fold increase in sales, and more than four-fold increase in net since 1955 to this year's $241-million — is more typical of a new company in a growing industry than of one that has been a bona fide member of the billion-dollar-a-year sales club for half a decade. And it keeps pushing along at a 12½ per cent per year increase in domestic sales, a 25 per cent increase in foreign revenues . . . applications for data processing are still growing by leaps and bounds in many new fields. IBM isn't an "old" company any more. It's vastly different from what it was in 1955. There are many outward signs of the change. Eyebrows of some veterans of the sales division, with its tradition of sartorial neatness, still rise at the sight of a mathematician in checked shirt and baggy pants. But the transformation goes deep down, too — the company is vastly different today in product mix, in production technology, in management structure. With all these fast-moving changes in both software and hardware, IBM executives look forward confidently to an exciting future of continued growth. For 1963, total sales will approach $3-billion. And IBM World Trade's sales are growing so fast that Pres. Williams predicts they'll exceed domestic revenues "In a reasonable number of years." If, as a mathematical exercise, you project IBM's current growth rates for foreign and domestic revenues, the two sales curves cross in 1973 at about $6-billion each. But IBM management itself refuses comment on such projections. (*Business Week*, February 2, 1963, pp. 92, 98.)

iii. Task-directed behavior

Finally, to what extent has, and does, this organization demonstrate the ability to consistently direct its behavior toward task performance and problem solution? Or, conversely, to what extent *must* this organization resort to defensive maneuvers and regressive behavior?

It wasn't just that IBM had grown up under a single dominant founder. With the computer advance, its whole technological base was out of balance. It had to make the leap from electro-mechanical equipment — basically, the slowly changing world of the machine shop — to the galloping technology of electronics . . . So, for the big reorganization, Watson decided to stick to an old IBM tradition — promotion from within. The new setup was worked out in a series of meetings between Watson, Williams, and La Motte, together with John L. Burns, then with Booz, Allen & Hamilton, Inc., management consultants . . . IBM Pres. Williams tells the results of the planning sessions: "We ended up with about 110 empty boxes in a new line-and-staff-structured management chart. And Tom decided to go ahead and do the whole thing at once" . . . Necessarily, men were put into jobs they weren't thoroughly prepared for; the switch from an operating job to a staff position is a difficult one at best. A number of executives had to become experts in a hurry, says Williams: "Quite a few were stretched, and found out that they could do." For six months, things were pretty confused, he adds, then started to get better. "I think we've been improving ever since" . . . As Williams describes it, the business IBM is in has undergone just as drastic a change as IBM itself. That means new goals for the company, new sophistication in its products, a new place for IBM in the U.S. business picture . . . IBM is making a lot of money in the computer business. Its competitors, on the other hand, are having a hard time. It has something like 70 per cent or 80 per cent of the market — only the company itself knows for sure. (*Business Week*, February 2, 1963, pp. 94–98.)

Hillsdale United Presbyterian Church is a task-oriented church. The task is to minister to its own and then to extend into the community. The church has a sense of identity and stability and a mission in the community. Specifically, the deacons minister to needs within the church and Front Door (a church neighborhood service organization) serves those outside. It is a solid, well-organized church that is performing well and is satisfied with itself. The ability to identify with the pastor or church has fostered pride and spurred the members on to new goals.

b. Impairments

(1) *Material or tangible (financial, patents, physical plant, equipment, geographical distribution, transportation, communication, personnel)*

Profitless prosperity is what seems to be afflicting Chicago's Sunbeam Corp. these days. What went wrong? In a sense, Sunbeam probably tripped over its own optimism. Seeing a future even rosier than the past, President Robert P. Gwinn decided to expand and improve Sunbeam's somewhat scattered (26 different plants) manufacturing setup. Instead of simply expanding its existing plants, Sunbeam decided to capitalize on the economies of mass production by concentrating the production of each of its major appliances at a single plant and then compounding the advantage by building those plants in the South where labor was cheaper. Since 1962 Sunbeam has spent over $67 million on five major plants and some smaller projects. According to former Sunbeam executives (of whom there are many these days), the whole program has been a mess. Some of these new plants cost 50 per cent to 100 per cent more than Sunbeam had projected. When the new plants got into operation, the expected savings didn't materialize. Sunbeam didn't have enough experienced production people to manage a plant expansion program of such magnitude. "Many of the production people were second rate," says another former executive, "and there weren't enough to go around. We even had merchandising people running our plants." In early 1967 Sunbeam had to borrow $50 million in long-term money at 5½ per cent to finance these short-term commitments. That meant an after-tax bite from earnings of nearly 20 cents a share — without any resulting profits to counterbalance it. As Sunbeam's problems mounted, Gwinn began to lose key personnel. In the last year and a half, two vice presidents (sales and shaver operations), the heads of the appliance division and of research and engineering took off for more agreeable positions. Sunbeam's production chief took an early retirement. (*Forbes*, June 15, 1968, pp. 20–21.)

West Hills Presbyterian Church is located in a marginal area, bounded by railroad shops, a Mexican-American enclave, the river, and a superhighway. Its people feel themselves to be confined and cut off. Geographically they are. The socioeconomic level of the community is declining; the average age of the parishioners is increasing. The congregation does not want to change. The church has had a series of interim pastors; no permanent pastor is in the offing. The small wooden church building severely limits the church's potential activities. While there has been some increase in donors and donations, the percentages are more impressive than the actual numbers. The number of pledges is up 35 per cent, 69 vs. 51; the actual amount of money is up 45 per cent, $10,403 vs. $7,163; the total number of donors is up 16 per cent, 80 vs. 69. The church is a poor relation in the Presbytery.

(2) *Functional (including leadership and mental set, or attitude)*

(A) REALITY ORIENTATION

i. To external environment

Perhaps the most serious impairment in reality orientation of St. Anselm Seminary is its failure to grasp the fact that the theology of St. Thomas is not meaningful to the modern Catholic intellectual. This is true not only for this seminary, but also for others as well. For example, when the Dominican order published a translation of one of St. Thomas' works, there was appended this statement: "Contemporary students feel that these commentaries often relied on allegory, on mystical and moralizing explanation, and that artificial, logical minutiae were overstressed. It is for this reason that the *Exposito Super Job* deserves to be returned from oblivion; for in this work St. Thomas showed himself to be an authentic precursor to the spirit of modern exegesis." Members of the faculty quote this statement. St. Thomas might very well be a precursor, but his works are so far behind current scriptural scholarship that they are only of historical interest.

Some authorities trace the start of the [*Saturday Evening*] *Post*'s decline to the early 1930's when it opposed Franklin D. Roosevelt's Administration and appeared to lose touch with the mood of the American people. More important, outmoded headline type, antiquated layouts and often stuffy stories during this era contrasted unfavorably with the lively makeup and content of the new *Life* magazine founded in 1936. The *Post* faced competition from other general-interest weeklies, notably *Collier's* and *Liberty*, before *Life* entered the field. But it was *Life* that cut deepest into the *Post*'s vital ad revenue. *Look*, first published in 1937, started more slowly than *Life*, but came on fast in the 1950's

and passed the *Post* in ad pages in 1962. As general-interest magazines with
large circulations, all three were more vulnerable than special-interest periodicals to competition from television. TV's ascendancy hastened the end of such
well-known publications as *Collier's, Woman's Home Companion* and the
American. As the *Post*'s circulation and costs rose, it boosted its ad rates beyond
the budget of many advertisers, who drifted away to publications with lower
rates. Curtis [the publishers of the *Post*] started losing money in 1961, and decided something had to be done. Its solution was to abruptly redesign the *Post*
to make it faster paced, unpredictable and controversial. The innovations star-
tled and displeased many old subscribers and advertisers, while others who always had looked on the magazine as unsophisticated were slow to change their
opinion. After the 1961 revolution scared off many advertisers, a rash of libel
suits tarnished the magazine's image. The *Post* changed editors four times between late 1961 and late 1964. Since then, under Editor William A. Emerson,
Jr., the magazine has kept out of serious libel trouble, but it hasn't developed
a cohesive editorial formula or a strong and unmistakable personality of its own.
(*Wall Street Journal*, May 17, 1968, p. 6.)

ii. To internal environment

The management is relatively unaware of the problems of the staff and employees of Dalton State Hospital, as reflected in the quality of memos, shifts in
organization and administration without prior warning or preparation, and
failure to adequately delegate or set up mechanisms for problem solving. Even
janitorial and mail service are often inadequate. The aides have responded to
the feeling of "just hanging, not knowing where they fit in the organization"
and to their distrust of a distant "they" on whom their fate depends by organizing a union and militantly pursuing negotiations with the state director of
mental health, the governor, and the legislature.

While student unrest has been much on the minds of academic administrators
ever since the upheavals at Berkeley in late 1964, the events of this past school
year have given the problem new urgency. Scores of institutions have experienced sit-ins, mill-ins, or worse, and at Columbia the conflict between student
demonstrators and constituted authority attained an unprecedented savagery.
Faced with this upsurge of student discontent, college and university officials
and many faculty people are asking: How can disruptive protests be avoided
and how can they best be dealt with if they occur? Mounting student demands
for greater participation in institutional governance and for changes that would
make curricula and student living conditions more relevant to student needs
were seen as inevitable. Treating students as responsible adults and giving them
a major voice in policy through their student government will be a half measure, however, unless the student government itself truly represents student interests. Often it does not. The development of effective student constituencies
on a large campus is a problem closely related to that of finding ways to help
the student escape anonymity. But while new or developing institutions such as

SUNY at Buffalo or the University of California at Santa Cruz may provide mass education in a small-college atmosphere, there is not much evidence yet that large established institutions are going to accomplish this . . . [the] acting chancellor at Berkeley in 1965 . . . advocated dividing the College of Letters and Science into four separate colleges. This proposal, while still under consideration, has gained little momentum. (*Science*, June 14, 1968, pp. 1205–1207.)

(B) VALUES AND IDEALS

i. Degree of institutionalization

Reviewing the questionnaires and the interviews, I conclude that much of the unrest at St. Ignatius High School comes from the fact that a concise philosophy of education for a Catholic high school has not been worked out. Reasons for justifying the existence of a parochial school in 1966 are much harder to define than in 1911. Because of this confusion, lay teachers, sisters, and priests are not sure what they are trying to accomplish. The final query on the questionnaire asked for suggestions for improvement; to only three teachers the improvement of religious instruction was important. All this is further complicated by conflicts among the nuns about philosophy of education versus philosophy of religious life, and about vocational struggles related to whether they should live a monastic or active life.

After the war the management [of a foundry] decided that its costs in . . . [the grinding department] were not competitive. As a means of increasing productivity, the industrial engineers worked out a system whereby one operator could run several fine-grinding machines. When the union claimed this change in work method was in direct violation of the contract, and succeeded in proving its case through arbitration, the company turned to incentives. The union resisted these just as vehemently as it had resisted the increased work loads, and again the case went into arbitration and again the union was victorious. To spur acceptance [of the incentive plan] by the fine-grinders, the company officers threatened to move the entire grinding operation to another plant if the union continued to refuse to negotiate an incentive plan. [The pressure put on the workers was tremendous. They were constantly involved in meetings] . . . The union couldn't assure them that the company wasn't bluffing about moving out of town if they didn't accept some plan. The union wanted to be sure they wouldn't be blamed for what happened . . . To intensify the situation, the company's labor relations director issued a statement that the company was looking over new sites for the mill. Then they brought some new machines into the plant, and didn't even unpack them — They said it would be easier to ship them the way they were . . . [The] men became alarmed. Their futures were at stake: their homes were in the town; their jobs were important to them.] In the next contract there was a provision that the company would develop incentives. (Leonard Sayles, "Intergroup Conflict," in William F. Whyte, (ed.), *Money and Motivation*, New York, Harper & Row, 1955, pp. 68–69.)

ii. Disparity from reality

The poorly defined ideals and values of St. Ignatius High School are hardly congruent with reality. For what other purpose would a Catholic parent pay tuition to send his child to a Catholic high school if not for a religious education? The parochial school previously survived in its competition with the public school largely because of external discrimination and for defensive reasons. With those gone, the school must have a positive, attractive ideal or it will lose its constituency.

Obviously the values and ideals of the nuns of St. Agnes' Hospital need to be modified considerably to serve as a motivating device for employees and doctors. They are simply no longer the reasons people go to work in hospitals. The value of professional achievement in the context of religious service, however, is a functional ideal and, under the right circumstances, could unite the hospital behind a common purpose.

In the examples in the preceding discussion on degree of institutionalism, from Sayles, *Money and Motivation,* there were two sets of values. Both were incongruent with reality. Management's values did not take into account workers' feelings; the workers' values did not accommodate to management's need to become more competitive. Even though management compelled the acceptance of its values, their failure to have them congruent with the employees' reality created a situation in which there will be continuous battle about the incentive issue.

(c) TASK MASTERY

i. Psychological contract unfulfillment

There are two different kinds of psychological contracts at Great Lakes Insurance Co. The clerical employees, largely women, seek support and affection — meaning regularity and continuity of employment, interested and helpful supervision, and no demands that would interfere with their home and family lives. The type of work supports their compulsive defenses; the environment excludes the dirty, unmannerly, impulsive person besides suppressing like thoughts in those who are there. For the women, the contract is reasonably well fulfilled. However, for upper-middle management and those at the officer level, the story is different. These are educated men with professional skills who chafe at the authoritarian, arbitrary way they are managed. Neither individually nor collectively do they make any major decisions. They have no stability of employment if they differ with the president. Thus they are made overdependent; the psychological distance between themselves and the president is distorted into father-child arrangements and they are not masters of their own destiny and therefore subject to the whims of fate. Their anger reverberates through management ranks, making them guarded with each other, self-critical, uninvested in their tasks and results in short tenure for the newest and potentially most capable young executives. The president unconsciously contracts for bright obedient children; the executives contract for adult, male managerial roles.

The membership of South Hills Presbyterian Church has contracted for a *small church* — the church of rural America — for a *community church* — the institution that gives identity to the community in which most of the members live — for a *middle-class church* — "Our kind of people," those who have almost made it in our society. The contract now is only minimally fulfilled. The church is small; it provides an identity point geographically but not yet psychologically. The people are a homogeneous group of white-collar workers with a sprinkling of skilled craftsmen. The internal struggle mobilizes aggression that has to be repressed, thus threatening these controlled people. They are related to the church more out of wish and obligation than identification.

ii. Growth and survival

Chicago's National Tea Co. has the unenviable distinction of being a below-average company in an industry with below-average growth prospects. For example: 1967 profits. They dropped 9 per cent to $1.18 a share. This in itself wasn't unusual in a year when severe price competition made things difficult for all food retailers. But National's earnings were lower than the $1.33 a share it earned in 1958 and were based on 9 per cent fewer shares outstanding than in 1966. National's 1967 net profit margin of 0.8 per cent (on sales of $1.15 billion) was low even for a low-margin industry. It compared with Winn-Dixie's 2.3 per cent, Safeway's 1.5 per cent and archrival Jewel's 1.4 per cent. The company's average sales increase in the past five years has only been 3.2 per cent, compared with Jewel's 12 per cent and Kroger's 7.6 per cent. National's recent stock price of $15.50 a share is just about book value and well down from a ten-year peak of $25 in 1959. This problem, like National's others, can be blamed on past management, but Stapleton has been the chief executive for seven years and he hasn't been able to get profits up yet. If he has the answers, he hasn't yet shown what they are. (*Forbes,* June 15, 1968, p. 34.)

When a housewife arrives at the Carroll Park branch of the Brooklyn Public Library, she is confronted with an iron-spiked fence that encloses a two-story brick imitation Greek revival building of the Victorian era. When she climbs a flight of six steps she will find taped to the door a sign that reads: "No pets allowed. No shopping carts or baby carriages. There will be no Saturday hours at any branch library June 1 through September 8." Inside, a uniformed guard keeps order, which does not seem hard to do. The shelves are half-empty, as is the library itself. The golden oak mission furniture is brown with age. Why has this representative of that great private institution of the nineteenth century, the public library, fallen on such seedy times? At the Carroll Park branch, circulation has dropped slowly over the past half dozen years, setting in motion an inevitable cycle. With fewer book withdrawals and fewer registrations, the budget was cut. This in turn curtailed hours, staff, and services. Finally, in 1963, the Carroll Park branch was downgraded to the status of "reading center," and the librarian was replaced by a library "aide." The slow decline of the public library is not unique to Carroll Park. Despite rising literacy rates, unparalleled leisure time and money, expanding book budgets, and Federal assistance programs, circulation, registration, and usage of center-city libraries across the country are dropping. The library, out of tune and out of date, is no longer relevant to the problems of center city and its new residents. And no matter how noble its goals, an unused library each year becomes a weaker competitor for scarce municipal funds. (*The Reporter*, June 13, 1968, p. 34.)

iii. Task-directed behavior

The South Hills church at the present time has no concise goal or agreed upon function. Individuals and groups in the church operate on the level of meeting necessities, but there is no planning or work for the future because there is no sense of direction. The lack of communication is particularly relevant here. Since no one has a sense of where the church ought to go, the members tend to hide or disguise what they do or hope, since it might not fit with what others want. This problem also reduces the quality of their work as individuals. An individual is threatened if he invests too much of himself in his job, since that would indicate he knows where the church ought to go. With no agreement on goal, and no way to make the agreement, others tend to criticize and destroy the incentive of the individual.

Not long ago W. R. Grace & Co. was one of the darlings of Wall Street. But Grace has fallen from grace. Today its stock sells at only about 15 times last year's earnings and is down 40 per cent from its 1966 high in a stock market that is up more than 16 per cent. What happened? A number of things. Grace originally went into chemicals as a means of reducing its dependence on Latin America. But in the early sixties, Chief Executive Officer J. Peter Grace, grandson of the founder, shifted gears. He launched a major reinvestment program in the company's original Latin American stronghold . . . At a time when Grace was struggling with local plant start-up problems, there were devaluations in Peru, Colombia and Argentina where Grace had invested heavily . . . But Latin America is only part of the problem. The on-again, off-again attitude that Peter Grace displays toward Latin America shows up in other Grace ventures. Since 1960, for instance, Grace has acquired some 31 companies and in the same period, has sold in whole or part 12 companies or divisions. The company has come a long way since Peter Grace took over the running of the family business in 1945 . . . More so than it is in most companies, the responsibility for such a record is the CEO's [chief executive officer] own. As one former Grace executive puts it, "Peter Grace *is* W. R. Grace & Co". . . . Even so the record has its flaws. If Grace knows precisely *what* he wants to accomplish, he is far less certain of just how to go about doing it. In assessing a prospective acquisition, he has tended to rely too heavily on historical financial data, paying only scant attention to the broader movements within an industry or to whether Grace itself has the management talents to cope with the companies it acquires. This problem has grown increasingly serious as Grace has advanced into consumer products where marketing rather than technical talents are required. Grace's defense is nothing ventured, nothing gained; and Grace executives point out that none of their mistaken acquisitions has cost them money. Over the past five years, in fact, they have produced some $35 million in capital gains. But measured against the drain in executive time, it is by no means clear whether Grace has come out ahead. (*Forbes,* June 15, 1968, pp. 36–41.)

c. Level of integration

When organizational integrative efforts fail, emergency activities are instituted in proportion to the severity of the threat to the organizational equilibrium. These activities are attempts to maintain the organization's equilibrium. All coping activities "cost" energy. As the organization's equilibrium becomes progressively more precarious, the organization will apply increasing energy to shoré itself up.

The level of integration is reflected in the adaptive coping efforts or emergency activities that the organization expends. These can be catalogued according to their effectiveness and the amount of energy they require. However, it is difficult to distinguish levels, so such labeling will necessarily be arbitrary. In *The Vital Balance* (New York: Viking Press, 1963), Dr. Karl Menninger categorizes coping devices for maintaining individual equilibrium according to similar considerations of effectiveness and energy requirements. A comprehensive list of organization adaptive activities, modeled on that list, is contained in the appendixes of this volume.

When increasing amounts of energy must be devoted to coping activity, this energy is deflected from its potential discharge in the forward motion of the organization. In a sense, an organization is like a space capsule that maintains its equilibrium by using jets of gas. If it uses most of its fuel in maintaining its equilibrium, it loses forward momentum. Furthermore, the greater its use of the jets, the more likely the capsule is to be deflected from its forward course. The same is true with individuals and organizations. Thus, the very nature of these coping activities is such that too frequent use impairs the organization's relationship to reality beside demanding greater investment in the coping mechanism. As the organization becomes increasingly disordered, it acts less successfully on its problems. It also achieves less return for its investments in its coping activities. Companies are reorganized again and again without showing notable success in either profit or survivability, for example. Each effort, however, has the advantage of being better than the next effort the organization would have to undertake if this one is not effective.

The decreasing efficiency of these counterbalancing activities is characterized by increasing amounts of energy invested, increasingly less successful coping efforts that provide fewer results and less gratification.

Once the organization goes beyond the normal adaptive activities it is headed for danger. Each time an organization moves to a more severe degree of dysfunction, it becomes easier for it to regress to that level. It is as if a psychic path were being worn in a field. There is a commonly used analogy in physical medicine: When a person dislocates his shoulder it is easier for him to sustain the same injury another time. Each succeeding dislocation makes the person more susceptible to a future dislocation under *less* stress. Another factor in this phenomenon is the frequency with which the person dislocates his shoulder: if the second dislocation occurs relatively soon after the first, the chance for a subsequent dislocation is further increased. All the ligaments and muscle bands in the injured shoulder become stretched and never fully recover and, therefore, cannot protect against a future dislocation.

This analogy applies to considering the organization's use of various orders of defense. Repeated stress leads to the greater use of more expensive coping activities. Since stress is not quantitatively and qualitatively the same at all times, the organization does not operate on any one level of defense at all times. Rather, it has to "dip down" in its level of functioning to meet increasing stress. Therefore, an organization operates mainly with normal activities; frequently with first-order activities; sometimes with second-order activities; occasionally, third-order ones. Keep in mind that with coping activities, the emphasis is on the *discharge of aggression*. In keeping with clinical observation, the discharge of the creative or constructive drive, fused with the aggressive drive, seldom embroils the person in difficulty. In most instances it is the inappropriate discharge of aggression as a defense that provokes difficulty.

(1) *Normal adaptive activities*

Normal adaptive activities permit some discharge of energy toward problem resolution and, concurrently, offer some provision for gratification to compensate for the threat the organization experiences. In addition to helping to deal with whatever arouses anxiety, they also serve to assuage the anxiety.

(2) *First-order adaptive activities*

First-order adaptive devices are more intensive versions of the normal activities an organization will undertake to set things right when it is hurting just a bit. These are *exaggerations* of the normal regulatory coping activities of the organization's everyday life. They are temporary and are used only when needed to meet a given situation. They offer some provision for gratification to compensate for the sense of threat and for guilt feelings. Often first-order activities seem to reflect a feeling in the organization that it is under attack by hostile forces and must therefore become either more guarded or more self-centered. Hostility in this sense serves either to whip the organization into shape or to attack the purported enemy. Self-centeredness serves to diminish in importance the external information that is threatening to the organization. Nothing is allowed to prick the organization's balloon, as it were.

(3) *Second-order adaptive activities*

Second-order devices are usually a means of coping with chronic stress. They tend to be a massive focusing of energy on some particular task or problem at the expense of the ongoing activities of the organization. For example, immediately after both Kennedy assassinations, Congress was intensely preoccupied with firearms legislation. Such preoccupation, however justified, was disproportionate to the problem and to the attention that the problem normally would generate. These two case excerpts illustrate what is meant by orders of coping activities.

The normal adaptive activities of everyday adjustment that are utilized at Arrowhead Tool and Die are: daily reports, nagging (especially by the plant manager), periodic expansion, shared fantasies and dreams of increased production, participation in professional trade associations, manipulation of organizational structure, an accent on selling and advertising, quality control, new-product development, self-laudatory advertising, organizational moratorium periods (summer cleanup sessions during vacations of more senior people), development of a proving grounds, pilot studies on new models, sales promotion and sales indoctrination, absenteeism. First-order coping activities utilized are: revision of tasks, increased turnover of personnel, more frequent pep talks, increased absenteeism, increased travel. Second-order coping activities are restricted to one category, namely, aggression turned upon the organizational self. This is seen most blatantly in: increased accident rate, scapegoating, excessive rigidity of routine, and increased self-blaming activities. There is a general tendency to "take the blame" to an unreasonable degree. When the recent bankruptcy of a distributor cost the company approximately $50,000, the president himself assumed complete responsibility for having extended credit to the distributor and apologized to the board. As a matter of fact, there was no reason, on the basis of previous experience with that distributor and others, not to extend the credit. The plant manager's militant methods reinforce the employees' tendency to depreciate themselves and assume blame. When certain parts are rejected by the quality control department, the workers see the cause as being their own inadequacies, failing to give due weight to the obsolescent equipment with which they must work. To date, the organization has not utilized third- or fourth-order coping activities.

The level of integration of West Hill Church is primarily of the first order, although there are some second-order characteristics. In the first order would be included such things as: unrealistic optimism, minimizing the threat, ignoring own history, reduction of intake of information from the outside, increased stereotyping, restriction of outreach into the community, and increased absenteeism. In the second order would be: withdrawal from some community activities, intense chronic preoccupation with internal concern, the making of the pastor and the session into scapegoats, and reduction of ideas of presentation of new program suggestions.

(4) Third- and fourth-order adaptive activities

The difference between third- and fourth-order activities is that those of the third order tend to be intermittent or episodic in nature while those of the fourth order have a chronic or continuous quality. These excerpts from published articles are examples of third-order activities:

But student demonstrations are a familiar story in Louvain [France]. As soon as the procession [of students] was safely in the square, paddy wagons loaded with police and gendarmes sealed it off. Then they disgorged helmeted, baton-wielding troops who converged on the student mass. A score of students were seized and escorted to the trucks, laughing and shouting. This seemed to be all in good fun, but other student activities, before and after, were not so playful. One group of activists . . . invaded high-ranking university officials' offices, stripped them of furnishings, books, and papers, and carted off the spoils to feed a bonfire at the edge of town. Molotov cocktails were tossed into the fortunately empty corridors of some buildings, fire extinguishers were sprayed in halls and classrooms, and gangs of Flemish students roamed academic halls and disrupted classes being conducted in French. In the meantime, Flemish student organizations had instituted a boycott of classes, and soon the university's Flemish Professors Association voted to support the students by joining the boycott. Such was the pressure for solidarity that academic functions in the Flemish half of the university came quickly to a virtual standstill. Recognizing this, the Flemish academic council announced a week's suspension of classes, whereupon students and professors decided to continue their strike another week. In all, three weeks of classes were lost through strikes and suspensions. (*The Reporter,* June 13, 1968, p. 31.)

The departure of Mr. Lois climaxed a year or more of internal strife, resulting in two administrative reorganizations, one of which is still under way, and enlivened by rumors, at least partially confirmed, of executive-suite donnybrooks, usually involving the volatile Mr. Lois. One account executive, William Casey, quit because, as he said in a letter to Mr. Koenig, "I am very much afraid of Lois and (former vice president Robert) Fiore. If I see either of them on the street I will run to the nearest cop." Mr. Lois admits vaulting a desk toward Mr. Casey during an argument, but he adds the classic disclaimer: "I never laid a hand on him." Another Papert-Koenig alumnus recalls a 1965 brawl in which one executive, an ex-boxer, broke up a fight between two others by knocking one of them out. "It took an hour to mop up the blood," he says. The agency's present management contends most of these stories have been spread by unhappy former employees and that they're all vastly exaggerated. (*Wall Street Journal,* May 23, 1968, p. 34.)

In considering coping activities, an organization can go from second order to fourth order without touching third order. The first episode can lead to a chronic, continuous fourth-order level of integration.

d. Overall effectiveness and facade

Some types of disorganization or discomfort will not be manifested in markedly lower competence. The facade that prevents inner problems from becoming noticeable may be a great asset or a great liability. There should be some attempt to appraise this facade, as in these case excerpts:

Curtis Elementary School, as a subgroup of a larger organization, being composed of relatively homogeneous members, seems able to function effectively largely through mutual support and the principal's ability to interpret the multiple demands placed on the members. Psychological withdrawal, projections of hostility, resorting to rigidity, and acting-out of aggression are thus minimized.

St. Agnes' Hospital presents a facade of innocent, self-sacrificing dedication, an institution struggling against sickness, death and economic odds and, therefore, deserving of adherence and support. This serves simultaneously as a bulwark for its activities and to mask the underlying, gradual disintegration of the institution. Had economic and social circumstances outside the hospital not changed, it could have continued its work effectively for that mode of adaptation served it well for many years. But that virtuous stance toward the outside, a reflection of deeply held values, makes it impossible for the organization to look at what is now transpiring and to change its modes of action to deal with the fractionation of its three major components: employees, medical staff, and nuns.

Arrowhead Tool and Die, to itself and the outside world, is a hardworking, conscientious, slowly growing organization that "makes it" because its products are good and its people are both interested and competent. Fighting a hard competitive environment of organizations bigger and more powerful, it has achieved its present position by determination and quality. This facade has been, indeed still is, a tremendous advantage, particularly because larger organizations have greater difficulty changing their product lines and maintaining quality control. The facade has also been helpful because it presents mighty Goliaths for this David to fight, and this battle makes it necessary for internal issues to be subordinated. The disadvantage of the facade is that such a narrow continuing battle makes it difficult for the organization to view other possible dimensions of competition, to adapt flexibly to other modes of behavior, and to recognize and deal with rising internal tension. The last is reflected in rising accidents and uneasiness in the ranks, which are functions of the hostility displaced by people whose consciences do not permit them to express hostility more openly and directly, particularly when there are no managerial mechanisms for doing so constructively.

B. Summary and Recommendations

The summary and recommendations section considers the data first in terms of the ecology of the organization, that is, the interaction of the organization with the forces external to it, then in terms of the internal structure and processes of the organization itself.

The data the consultant has gathered and interpreted thus far have provided him with the material he needs for viewing the organization and its external and internal environments from both a longitudinal and a cross-sectional point of view. From this dual perspective, he can make a definitive statement of the present status of the organization. Finally, an explanatory formulation will provide him with the dynamic and genetic understanding of the organization's present status. Based on perspective, present status, and explanatory formulation, prognostic conclusions are stated. Case examples follow:

Arrowhead Tool and Die was started at the end of World War II in Burlingame, Iowa, at a time when the population was 43,000. Since then, the city has grown slowly. Located in midwestern United States, Burlingame had several small war-generated heavy industries that were being converted to peacetime activity. The environs were, and still are rural in character. This midwestern area has been termed a "Bible belt" whose subcultural values are honesty; diligence; a sense of responsibility; self-control to avoid any outward display of anger; respect for one's superiors; and, above all, hard work. In this context, the company began modestly, largely due to the efforts of its founder, Henry Allison, Sr., assisted by his son Henry, Jr. and his son-in-law Marvin Schultz. The postwar need for machine tools and dies provided an immediate market for their first products, drill bits and reamers. An early but significant event occurred in the late 1940's when another local concern, the Travis Company, developed an automatic stamper and contracted with Arrowhead to manufacture certain parts for this product. After an initial overture to join forces with Travis, Arrowhead decided to design, produce, and distribute its own stamper, a move that was feasible since Travis held no basic patent on the stamper. This required the employment of an engineer to design the product and led to the development of a small research and design department which was able to engineer variations of the stamper and enabled it to become the company's major product. The company was able to weather a 1952 tornado despite significant financial damage, to win a patent infringement suit in 1956, and to resolve a major labor organizing crisis in 1958. The last involved a strike for recognition, increases in wages, and fringe benefits, which cost the company $375,000 in lost sales.

In 1961, the Reardon Company offered to buy Arrowhead. Arrowhead decided not to sell but agreed to manufacture equipment under the Reardon name. This agreement is still in existence and has been responsible for the major part of each year's production since. It has also been responsible for Arrowhead's continued expansion. However, this arrangement has created problems for Arrowhead with its franchised distributors. The Reardon and Arrowhead lines are differently painted but otherwise identical and the distributors therefore have been lethargic in promoting Arrowhead products. They would prefer to sell a product different from and competitive with Reardon's, not the same product with a different coat of paint which has no unique selling points. This lethargy threatens Arrowhead because it cannot afford its own distribution system and is dependent on the distributors for whatever independence it has from Reardon. This problem is still a critical one for Arrowhead. In 1963 the company was able to obtain long-term financing at $5\frac{1}{2}$ per cent which improved and stablized its financial position and provided for further expansion and the support of inventories. In the same year a new long-term contract (5 years) was negotiated with the union. Recognizing the need for developing more effective cohesion, innovation, and managerial competence, the president arranged for this consultation the following year. Currently, competition remains a constant threat to the organization, as does the possibility of being absorbed by Reardon. Arrowhead responds to both of these threats by placing heavy emphasis on routine innovation and trying to remain sufficiently flexible to tool up for short runs of immediately needed items, a method by which it can compete with larger organizations and manage with minimum capitalization.

Curtis Elementary School was established in 1956 after some years of heated controversy about its location, which was the product of a community split about school policies and administration. As one of nine such schools in the city, it is in a largely middle-class neighborhood of a slowly growing, conservative north central midwest community of 72,000, which places a heavy emphasis on pleasant conformity. Its building is reasonably modern, clean, and uncluttered, but it is becoming crowded as its students gradually increase in number. The library has already been displaced for classroom needs. There are now 340 pupils, twelve teachers, and a principal. The playground is half the size set by the state. The first principal, who was there for 2 years, was selected for his diplomacy to smooth community discord. The present principal and two teachers remain from the original staff. Teachers are employed from a community pool, with some unofficial string-pulling by the principal for suitable teachers, a leverage derived from the need to maintain good community relations. The teachers are academically highly qualified; seven have master's degrees. The history of the school since the initial storm surrounding its founding has been relatively uneventful. It has a casually efficient, friendly atmosphere, marked by self-discipline of pupils and staff. It is neither experimental nor innovative, following the major guidelines of the larger system of which it is a part. The school is a social catalyst, a resource center where boys and girls come together to learn a democratic way of life, where the individual can discover his basic worth and talents and can develop them to full capacity. For the teachers it is a pleasant, even desirable, setting in which to carry on their professional activities in largely routine ways and in the context of social respect and acceptance. There are no major threats on the horizon.

In 1917 a $250,000 bequest was earmarked for the destitute sufferers in the city. And from this grew the idea for Menorah Medical Center. The sum was not enough to build a hospital, but it served as the impetus for a 1926 fund raising campaign that produced more than $1,000,000 and the beginning of the Jewish Memorial Hospital Association. In 1930 the name was changed to Menorah Hospital, since it was to be operated as a nonsectarian institution. The hospital was opened in 1931 with a staff of 16 doctors and 50 nurses. From 1931 to 1948 patient admissions increased over 3 times to 6,300, and the hospital was operating at 30 per cent over capacity. Menorah completed a $2,000,000 expansion during 1948, adding four stories, laboratory facilities, operating rooms, chronically ill units, and outpatient clinics. The name was changed to Menorah Medical Center in 1952 to emphasize the ideals of patient care, education, and research. The center expanded again in 1962 bringing its capacity to its present level of 341 beds. Eight hundred and fifty people are presently employed at the center, handling over 10,000 admissions and 18,400 outpatients annually. The employees and patients come largely from the city and surrounding areas. Average tenure is three years; absenteeism is low. Dedication is high. Menorah is a nonprofit organization with revenues of $7,000,000 to meet its annual expenses of $7,000,000. A large number of federal and private grants contribute to research and educational functions and activities. The center also maintains library and auditorium facilities for educational and research purposes. Educational relationships are maintained with several universities and professional societies to provide training and continued education programs. Menorah is in the middle of a $5,000,000 expansion program that will increase existing facilities by two thirds. Menorah has a solid, successful history, is well established and well regarded in its community, and has high aspirations that are supported by devoted contributors and staff. It has great energy, strives competitively, and is sustained in a growing community by its ideal. Its major potential threat is rising costs, and its major adaptive problem is its evolving relationship to governmentally financed hospital care.

1. Present status

In this section of the outline the consultant makes a statement that conveys a cross-sectional description of the organization in its environment and at one point on the time spectrum — the present. This statement should be a summary and integration of the material discussed in the first section of this chapter, "Organizational Integrative Patterns." While it need not be lengthy, the statement should contain those pertinent facts and inferences needed to capture the essence of the current situation in which the organization finds itself. This statement, diagnostic in nature, should contain a complex set of conclusions: descriptive, analytic, and evaluative. It should describe an organization, an environment, and their interaction; it should pay particular attention to those aspects of the interaction that seem to be unsatisfactory, costly, inefficient, painful, or full of conflict. Such a statement will always be polydimensional, multidescriptive, and continuous. Theoretically, such a statement cannot be recorded, because no sooner has it been written than it begins to be out of date. Therefore, the quality of continuous change must be recognized and the statement of "present status" must be recognized to be *dated*.

Questions the consultant should ask himself when composing the statement of "present status" include:

1. To what degree does the present level of integration represent an attempt to relieve pain *or* an effort to salvage the present situation and prevent further disorganization?
2. To what degree does the present status represent downhill progression, a maintaining of the status quo, or evidence of improvement?

Case excerpts illustrate:

The South Hills United Presbyterian Church is a small, young, relatively power-less institution in continuing conflict in a poorly developed lower middle-class neighborhood, burdened financially and without cohesive identity. It is at present functioning as a marriage that is not going well. The members of the church are aware of problems and difficulties with each other, but not knowing how to solve these problems, they have ceased communicating effectively. They continue to live together and carry on essential functions, but there is little joy in the marriage. Each participant is afraid to make an unexpected move for fear it will upset some delicate balance and destroy that which does remain.

Arrowhead Tool and Die, a 20-year-old midwestern manufacturing firm of 140 employees is in a position of tenuous economic stability despite its gradual growth. There is a rising accident rate, increasing restlessness among the employ-ees, and difficulty in maintaining a consistent profit picture. It has a good record, produces fine products, and enjoys the confidence of its customers and employ-ees. It is caught between its dependence on its major customer and its ina-bility to evolve effective relationships with independent distributors to enhance its own independence. Management is increasing the pressure on itself and its employees largely to hold present gains together.

Menorah Medical Center is a well-established, eminently successful medical institution striving hard to maintain an innovative atmosphere and a sensi-tive patient care function while, at the same time, continuing to expand in major steps. The intensive task-directed effort, with its high achievement goals and aspirations, tends to direct attention from considerations of what is going on inside the organization, for example, personnel problems, and override them in the pursuit of the ideal. The needs of the environment and the dependence on the hospital to meet them exacerbate this tendency.

Curtis Elementary School is a middle-class neighborhood school. It functions well in a symbiotic relationship with its constituency. It maintains a stable equi-librium at the cost of certain aspects of growth of both teachers and students. It is quiet, steady, conforming, and conscientious. It is both embedded and en-meshed in its larger system and its community and, therefore, not subject to stress so long as system and community do not change radically. Psychologically, its task and its effort is to hold firmly to the status quo.

2. Explanatory formulation

Once the consultant has described the present status, he should offer an explanation of how that status was reached; that is, the explanatory formulation. It is in this section of the outline that the consultant is called upon to demonstrate the consistency and validity of his particular discipline and the theory of motivation he assumes.

a. Genetic

For the consultant who has a psychoanalytic orientation, the explanatory formulation must have a genetic dimension. It must explain the present status in terms of the entire life process of the organization. Such a longitudinal explanation will take into account those significant events in the organization's life span that have molded, shaped, and influenced its present state, as in these case excerpts:

South Hills United Presbyterian is a poorly planned mission church. The construction of the building was cheap, and the congregation began with a large debt. The church had a poor start. The area did not grow as expected. A problem with sewage delayed development. A shopping center planned for the area 10 years ago is just now being built. The church is a bastard offshoot of the central church, which never really cared for it. It has been exploited by a dominant widow and led by ineffectual pastors who could not establish an identity for it among lower middle-class parishioners of limited perspective.

Arrowhead Tool and Die arose from the needs and skills of its founder, in an ethos of hard work. Although management and employees still share that compulsive hard-working tradition and the organization has surmounted developmental and crisis problems because of it, it is now being managed by a second-generation president who, though mild mannered, is without the inventive skills of the founder and sees his role as primarily in sales. In keeping with the hard-work ethos, the president has named a plant manager who is militant in his handling of the men. The men view the president's lack of intraorganizational involvement as evidence that he does not hold them in esteem. They are also deprived of an important identification figure. This reinforces their own culturally determined feelings of inadequacy and makes them increasingly angry. Furthermore, the hard-work ethos is followed at the expense of imaginative flexibility that makes success increasingly hard to come by with more intensive competition from larger, more efficient companies.

Organized to fulfill an ideal contained in a bequest, together with a community service need and a strong religious tradition, from the beginning Menorah Medical Center has had both a permanent, never-to-be-reached goal and an external requirement to meet it. The drive of its medical tradition, coupled with the drive of its religious tradition, and the esteem in which it holds its work and it is held became the impelling forces for dynamic growth. When these drives could be organized around specific skills that continually needed to be improved to live up to the aspirations, solid structural growth was assured, which, in turn, established its own momentum.

Curtis Elementary School achieved its present status largely by the established definition of professional and social roles, reinforced by the community and school system. It can hardly be said that it grew. What can be said is that in addition to its teaching functions, it was asked to be a peacemaker and people were chosen to fulfill that task. It did not "get that way"; that's the way it was to start with; that's how it is now.

b. Dynamic

In addition to the genetic dimension, the explanation must have a dynamic dimension for the psychoanalytically oriented consultant. It must explain organizational behavior and the environmental response in terms of energy systems, defensive maneuvers, conscious and unconscious conflicts, and multiple causation and motivation. It must see the organization as being moved by forces of which it is often unaware and continually making compromises and adjustments in order to achieve the best level of functioning in light of the forces coming from within itself and from the environment, as in these case examples:

South Hills United Presbyterian Church seems to be in a state of depression. Characteristics of depression seen in the organization are a loss of self-esteem, self-directed hostility with feelings of inferiority, a loss of interest in the organization, a reduction in programs, and a vagueness about life in the institution. It muddles in its environment.

Arrowhead Tool and Die is an organization that has introjected the subcultural value of self-control to the service of avoiding open display of anger, particularly toward parental figures. The lack of intraorganizational involvement of the president, together with the militant modes of the plant manager, stimulate anger that cannot be expressed directly. Unable to be openly hostile to the organization or to sabotage the product because of their strong superegos, the men redirect their anger toward themselves in the form of increasing accidents. The same constriction of aggression and the hard-work ethos which inhibits imaginative problem solution engenders more and more self-drivenness to solve problems and more and more guilt about not solving them.

There is a simple, benign blandness to Curtis Elementary School. This is evident in the way teachers learn and accept the teaching role in middle-class conservative terms and learn and accept it in this structure. They feel they do a good job as teachers and as responsible adults; they manage situations well; they have a good school; they try to please others on the staff, the parents, and the children and are upset when they do not. As a result, the teachers' feelings and consideration of the children's feelings are largely repressed and, therefore displaced. There is, therefore, a tendency to avoid issues, to be guarded, which inhibits the development of trust and mutual support in more than superficial terms. This, in turn, makes for a static situation rather than for growth; dependence and superficiality, rather than deeply meaningful investment in teaching children.

Menorah Medical Center is to be understood largely in ego and superego terms: skills, identifications, and models as well as self-demands, aspirations, and ideal goals. It earns its way with goodness, achievement, and service. It could not live with itself as a mediocre hospital, nor could its supporters. It is a device for their ideals of service as well as those of the staff. It is this drive that makes Menorah impatient with itself and its progress and never satisfied with its achievements.

3. Prognostic conclusions

Here the consultant must weigh those factors that help the organization, help the consultant help the organization (if that is his goal), or help the consultant help the organization help itself against those factors working against it.

He must first consider those forces or circumstances that seem to work *against* improvement and ask himself such questions as:

1. Are the prospects for improvement limited beforehand by unalterable factors; for example, the advent of the automobile to a company that can make *nothing* but buggy whips or the loss of financial resources or of a dominant leader?
2. Are the prospects for improvement impaired by conditions *unlikely* to be altered; for example, the advent of a "throw-away" society to a company that makes equipment for repairing shoes, hats, and so on?
3. Does the organization's life history indicate that its aggressive impulses are difficult to deflect, modify, placate, or direct into task performance and problem solution; for example, the history of militant labor relationships in some heavy industries?
4. Is the organization's self-centeredness so extreme as to preclude the capacity for establishing new, gratifying relationships; for example, the investment of a maternal organization in "taking care of her own flock?"
5. Are the indirect satisfactions from the present level of integration in excess of the price paid for them; for example, the aerospace industry being "on government teat?"

6. Is there apparent acceptance of self-destructive behavior within the organization; for example, the failure of organized medicine to recognize and deal with increasing demands for better distribution of medical services?
7. Is the environment within which the organization must function frustrating, corrupting, or otherwise harmful; for example, county governments and the patronage system?

Likewise, the consultant must consider those forces or circumstances that seem to work toward improvement that are capable of being exploited in this direction.

1. How much does the organization's discomfort motivate it to seek a more favorable compromise?
2. How painfully does the organization sense the loss of satisfaction?
3. How well endowed is this organization with competence? How accessible is it to reason, reeducation, and counsel?
4. Does the organization show some propensity for acquiring and utilizing relationships with other individuals, groups, or organizations?
5. Are there latent capacities for diversification or consolidation from which gratification can be achieved?
6. Is self-punitiveness such a marked feature that substitution of other forms of penance or realistic restitution are impossible, as in some religious orders?
7. Are there undeveloped potentialities for creativity and innovation within the organization?
8. Are there "ultimate environments" within which the organization can function that are attractive and health-promoting?
9. Is the organization's basic temperament essentially optimistic or pessimistic?

The consultant must also recognize that any prognostic statement must be expressed in terms of degree of probability. Since no one actually *knows* about the future, one can only say what the trend seems to be.

And finally, it must again be emphasized that even the prognostic conclusions of this organizational case study are made from the consultant's point of view, primarily as precursors to consultative intervention.

Both published and case excerpts illustrate:

There is little indication that under present conditions South Hills United Presbyterian Church will experience a marked change. Some factors that might effect change are:

1. A realistic appraisal of the church's situation.
   a. An effort to deal with the organizational depression with the help of a consultant.
   b. A turning from the self to increased concern for others.
   c. Planning that could make hopes and dreams into realistic goals that could be met.
2. Better leadership. New or more effective pastoral leadership that could effect a working relationship with the session and with the church leadership in general.
3. Sociological factors.
   a. Continued development of the community such as the building of homes across the major highway and the growth of the shopping center in the area.
   b. An effective ministry of the church to the community with consideration of how the church could take advantage of its being the South Hills community church.

What can McGill do to increase its share of provincial operating grants? It may well be true, as some McGill people believe, that no real solution to the university's problem will be found until French Quebec accepts, ungrudgingly, the English-speaking minority as a partner whose institutions must be supported on the same basis as French institutions. Such acceptance may come, but, for the moment, the temper of French-Canadian opinion is hard to judge. Quebec nationalist sentiment is expressed in a variety of ways, ranging from separatist demands for an independent Quebec to demands for revisions of the Canadian constitution allowing varying degrees of provincial autonomy. Extreme separatists would have McGill either become a French-speaking institution or lose its public financial support. Separatism has not, however, had much of a following in the past, and its present devotees may be more vocal than they are numerous. Being in a largely French milieu and charging fees which are quite low by comparison with those of many American universities, McGill hopes to attract increasing numbers of able French-Quebecers, some of whom will be seeking a convenient "bridge" to predominant North American culture. But McGill surely will fail in this unless it has the resources to keep its strength in those fields in which it excels, such as medicine and psychology, and to build strength in fields where it has been weak or mediocre, such as in most of the humanities and social sciences. A plebescite of sorts will soon be held on the issue of whether there should be "one Canada," with the federal government relinquishing no more of its power to Quebec or other provinces. The outcome may, indirectly, affect McGill and every other English-speaking institution in Quebec that depends on the goodwill of French-Canadians for continued success. (*Science,* May 31, 1968, pp. 975–976.)

The prospects for significant changes within Arrowhead Tool and Die are moderately favorable. The president is receptive to new ideas as evidenced by his willingness to seek consultation. He welcomes consultative help, provided it is available at his pace. The men themselves welcome the opportunities for working with the professional staff with enthusiasm. They feel sufficiently painfully oppressed by the authoritarian plant manager to want a change. The plant manager himself is already looking for another job. There is the possibility of merger with the company's largest customer, which should mobilize new resources for further change and new demands for increased effectiveness. The major countervailing force is the organization's style of repressing hostility, its passively aggressive acceptance of authority, and its reluctance, therefore, to openly face hostility once the displaced target, the plant manager, is removed. There will be too great a tendency to accept the prospective change in plant managers as the solution to all problems.

There seems to be no alternative to St. Agnes' Hospital becoming an adjunct to City Hospital as a wing for chronic and convalescent cases. The nuns simply cannot manage, in the modern sense of the word, because of their own psychology. The same reasons that require them to be "too nice" to everyone also distort and disrupt their relationships with both the lay and medical staffs. They do not have the money or the skills to obtain high level support. To employ professional management, or to overcontrol a professional manager, is in effect to give up the hospital. Besides, with fewer nuns entering the order, a rising average age (now in the forties), they simply cannot maintain the hospital burden.

4. Recommendations

Recommendations are part of the study proper. They are not the report to the client, which is discussed in Chapter 11. These recommendations are intended to be a summary of proposed modes of intervention, based on a review of all the previously integrated data. Ideally, the consultant should be able to point to a series of reasons as the basis for each sentence in this section and to reject alternative actions on the same basis. If his reasoning is tentative, he should so indicate. If his proposed actions are trial efforts, that should be indicated, too. Recommendations are still part of the consultant's road map. If he errs, they permit him to retrace his steps and reexamine his actions, to formulate and try out alternative hypotheses. The more detailed the recommendations, the more hypotheses the investigator has to test. In fact, for researchers, this section should constitute a rich source of formal experimental topics.

The first step at Arrowhead Tool and Die must be to establish a working relationship with the president to strengthen his self-esteem, to help him recognize and accept some of the psychological implications of his role and the psychology of the people who work for him. This should be followed by formal learning experiences that reinforce his managerial knowledge and enhance his competence. Both of these steps can come about after he has gotten feedback of the results of the study, which will pinpoint some of the problem areas to be tackled. Once there is a working relationship with the president and he begins to feel his own strength, individual interviews and group discussion of the findings should be undertaken with the top management group. These group meetings should be task-oriented, and matters of psychological dynamics, both group and individual, should be taken up only as they derive from task problems. If the group wishes, seminars and other learning experiences may follow. Only after this base is established can the third step be undertaken, which would be to develop, with the top management group, other modes of internal organization that would make it more possible for employees to contribute their thoughts, ideas, and wishes. This, in turn, could lead to joint development with the employees of more effective modes of mutual problem solving. Thus the anger could be funnelled into the task rather than into symptoms. These steps would require careful support from the consultant, particularly with respect to the threat to management and employees alike of opening themselves up emotionally in a cultural context that prohibits such expression. The consultant must be sensitive to the additional stresses that will be created, and he must be certain to proceed in slow, gentle steps. He must also be alert to the concreteness of thinking of many of the unskilled men at lower levels, their difficulty in verbalizing their thoughts and feelings, and their dependence on their leadership. We are talking here about what is likely to be at least a two-year process, even if undertaken on a weekly basis.

The consultant at Curtis Elementary School, meeting regularly with the staff and, separately, with the principal, could assist the organization by helping the teachers to focus on their anxieties and dissatisfactions rather than repress and displace them. Lowering of defensiveness would enhance mutual support and thereby the concept of a working team. However, unless the consultant simultaneously works with higher authority, these efforts might be nullified by changes in staff and by reactions from superiors. The consultant should recognize that his efforts will be limited by the realities of the teachers, their environment, and the system, but he can help to make more effective allies of teachers and parents by helping them to learn together more of their own feelings about the children and the frustrations of their roles. This will never be an innovative, experimental school, but it can be a freer, more stimulating one for everyone involved.

In presenting the report to Menorah Medical Center, it will be important to show how the organization's strengths make it easy to overlook the feelings of lower level people on whom, in the last analysis, care of the patients depends. Particularly, attention should be called to the tendency to praise less and criticize more than is optimal and to fail to adequately support lower level personnel. Also it is important to help them recognize how easy it is for a hospital to become fractured into autonomous noncommunicating units at the expense of the whole. If the administration and staff agree that these are problems to which they want to devote attention, then plans should be made to submit the report for more critical discussion by departments and service units. These discussions could lay issues on the collective table for further examination and, with the help of the consultant, for the development of mechanisms for problem solution. The word "mechanisms" is used here advisedly because it seems that the primary need is for building in modes of managerial practice as well as in managerial skill, that will capture more effectively the ideals and energy of the employees. This may require additional training for many on the staff, but hopefully they will see the need for such training as they discuss organizational problems and ask for such help themselves. The organization is sufficiently stable and open, and the consultant need not fear stating the issues.

Two major things need to be done at South Hills United Presbyterian Church. First the congregation needs to look at itself in an effort to find more effective ways of serving its members. The members need to know publicly what their frustrations, disappointments, hopes, and wishes are with, and from, this institution and each other. This should lead to the development of ways of meeting these needs and statements of attainable goals. The church should plan activities that the members can talk about and take pleasure in. These, too, can arise from opening the floor for a discussion of the real, but hidden, feelings. Once such statements and goals are forthcoming, it will be possible to define expectations for a new pastor. Obviously, the current pastor cannot survive in the present situation. Another need is to mobilize the church's resources to master its environment by solving problems that have roots outside the congregation. The members must more carefully assess their external reality. Two matters need careful investigation. One is the growth potential of the church. Are there growth factors in the community of which they should be aware? Are there changes in services, like sewage facilities, that might be effected by organized pressure in the right places? The second matter for investigation should be the presumed competition from other churches in the area. How many people who were prospective members of South Hills joined other churches and why? This report should be presented to the congregation at a congregational meeting. If the congregation, after discussion, feels there is enough merit in it to investigate further, the session should conduct personal interviews with the parishioners to validate the findings, provided that the members of the session can be trained in nondirective interviewing by one of the consultants. Once the data are collected from the session's interviews, the consultant can help the session analyze them, interpret them, and present them to the congregation. The session need not wait for the completion of the interviews to take action. While this process is going on it can appoint a committee to investigate the external realities, to act as the eyes and ears of the church. This committee could ask why people in the community are not coming, why they have joined other churches, how many Presbyterians did so. They could check with city and county planning offices, with the school board, with area developers to determine what growth is expected in the area and when. They can raise the question of what the church can do to expedite such growth. Then, and only then, should the issue of finances be raised again, this time as something facilitating rather than burdensome.

Part III

ORGANIZATIONAL
CASE STUDY

10

CLAYPOOL
FURNITURE AND
APPLIANCES

The following case is an example of how a case study is written according to the outline. This particular case is a composite to obscure detail sufficiently to insure confidentiality. It also deals with a relatively small organization, which has the advantage of focusing the analysis on a limited number of issues. That limited focus facilitates learning but, of course, at the expense of that complexity which would be characteristic of a larger organization.

Although the case follows the outline, not every heading and subheading in the outline is indicated in the case. In the process of writing a case it is frequently simpler and more economic to combine information called for by several headings. Sometimes there is insufficient depth of information to discuss a topic in detail; sometimes that information has already been discussed in some detail under a different heading. The headings call the reader's attention to dimensions which must be covered, but they are not intended to compel rote discussion. There should be enough references to the outline in any write-up to help organize the material for any reader, but not every item need be designated.

There is necessarily some repetition in every case write-up. This results from reviewing the same material from different angles and from the need to digest and summarize the material while at the same time being able to retrace one's steps when that becomes necessary.

I. GENETIC DATA

A. Identifying Information

Claypool Furniture and Appliances in Atlanta and Macon, Georgia, is a retailer of moderately priced furniture and household appliances. Claypool is controlled by the Claypool family under the direction of Robert D. Claypool III, the president. The Claypool family holds 93 per cent of the stock. The remaining 7 per cent is split among the board of directors and a treasury fund held in escrow for employees' pensions.

Claypool currently has one store in Atlanta and another in Macon, with approximately 600,000 square feet of usable space. Revenues for the past six years were:

1964	$19,663,160
1965	21,373,794
1966	23,283,784
1967	25,336,710
1968	27,510,237
1969	30,048,432

After-tax profits for the six years were:

1964	$ 1,398,700
1965	1,498,000
1966	1,700,900
1967	1,543,300
1968	1,127,500
1969	780,000

The main store is located in an older part of Atlanta, near an industrial district, close to lower- and middle-class housing areas. The Macon store is located on the outskirts of town in a shopping center near affluent suburban areas. The breakdown of employees is:

	Atlanta	Macon	Total
Sales	170	130	300
Stock	190	160	350
Clerical	75	10	85
Staff	15	5	20
Maint. & Security	50	10	60
Management	80	25	105
	580	340	920

Claypool is noted in the furniture industry for its successful selling approach. It has employed massive advertising campaigns and extensive promotions on its moderately priced furniture and appliances to attract the average family buyer. Newspaper, radio, and television advertisements repeatedly tell the customer that brand-name merchandise cannot be purchased at a lower price in the Atlanta and Macon areas. The organization has kept its overhead expenses to a minimum. These two factors have contributed, according to Robert Claypool, to Claypool's being able to carve out a 35 per cent share of the moderately priced furniture and appliances market in the Atlanta and Macon areas. It does not offer a broad range of merchandise but concentrates on conservatively styled furniture and big-ticket appliances (refrigerators, washers, televisions, radios, and stereos). It has small departments for kitchen appliances, such as blenders, mixers, toasters, electric frying pans, and irons, and for other household items. There is a rug department that sells medium priced rugs under the "Claypool" brand name.

6. Situation of the initial contact

The study was undertaken in 1970 by a consulting institute at the request of Robert Claypool. He had attended one of the executive siminars offered by the institute and had asked the director for guidance in applying contemporary concepts of motivation to his organization. The director suggested that a comprehensive study might be a starting point for both groups. This suggestion was accepted by Robert Claypool and the Claypool management.

The major reason Mr. Claypool had for undertaking the study was to strengthen the company in anticipation of expansion. Because of the success of the Claypool operation, he wanted to expand Claypool Furniture and Appliances into a regional organization. By utilizing the firm's demonstrated merchandising and marketing skills, he felt expansion could be a financial success.

However, part of Robert Claypool's motivation for a study arose from some slippage in profit margin about which he was concerned. While sales were continuing to grow at an acceptable rate, profit was not.

7. Circumstances of the study

It was agreed that a task force would spend approximately six weeks in the Claypool organization collecting data. These data would be compiled into a summary report and reported back to the Claypool management. The summary report, it was agreed, would also be given to all members of the organization. The data to be collected would be derived from a short questionnaire completed by each employee, individual interviews with a sample of employees, observations of the work process, and analysis of financial and published information. The task force team consisted of two consultants and three research assistants.

The expressed purpose of the study was, therefore, to assess, evaluate, and understand the operations of the organization as a unit, to obtain a comprehensive view of its functioning, and to learn how the members of the organization saw themselves and the total unit as an operating entity.

The first week of the study was spent in orienting all employees in both the Altanta and Macon locations and having them each complete the short questionnaire. This was done in ten sessions in each store in large rooms used for promotional displays. One of the consultants read a prepared statement describing the study process, emphasizing the confidentiality of the information. After the short speech, employees were invited to ask about the procedure, purpose, method, and results of the study. Each person was then asked to complete the questionnaire. The next five weeks were spent interviewing individuals, attending group meetings, and observing the work process throughout the organization.

After the demographic data were summarized by the computer, 100 individuals were selected to be interviewed, on the basis of the following determinants: (1) part- or full-time employment; (2) male or female; (3) education; (4) department; (5) hourly wage or salary; (6) length of employment; and (7) promotions. The demographic distribution of the personnel is discussed in a later section of the outline. Suffice it to say here, the people who were randomly chosen from these categories fairly represented that distribution.

Each task force member spent an average of one and a half to two hours a day in observation and on-the-job interviews with people at work in the various departments. The task force observed salesmen selling, stock personnel handling merchandise, clerical workers completing monthly reports and daily billings, and so on. The task force conducted an average of three on-the-job interviews in each working area. This represented a total of 300 hours of observation and 78 on-the-job interviews. In the latter, employees were asked what their jobs were, how they did their jobs, what were their on-the-job problems, and what kind of supervision they had. The task force observed the attitudes, feelings, communications, and interactions among supervisors and employees. Each team member acted briefly, for periods of an hour to an hour and a half, as cashiers, stockmen, buyers, clerks, and salesmen. They were allowed to sell small kitchen appliances, kitchen ensembles, living room furniture, and rugs. They ran credit balances on credit customers and sat with the key punch operators. They handled cash transactions and sat in on the planning of an advertising campaign for a holiday sale. They unloaded furniture, stacked small kitchen appliances in the warehouse, and distributed merchandise at the pick-up stations. They met with several buyers as the latter decided on merchandise for the coming season. And they operated one of the switchboards for an afternoon. They attended the representative council twice, (a group of six employees who meet with the president and vice president of personnel once a month to discuss problems of the employees); the executive committee meeting once (a group composed of the president, executive vice president, and vice presidents of merchandising, marketing, distribution and security-maintenance, who meet weekly to discuss pricing, promotions, and deliveries); and the Wednesday coffee session three times (a group composed of the executive vice president, two store managers, four department managers, the controller, the vice presidents of personnel, and the vice president of finance who meet each Wednesday morning to discuss store operations).

One month after the data gathering was completed, two and a half months after the study was started, the task force reported back to the organization. One of the consultants spent one afternoon with the president presenting the report; the next morning, he further discussed the findings, implications, interpretations, and recommendations with him. The same process was followed with the executive committee meeting and the Wednesday coffee session. The consultant then held 15 meetings at both stores to present the report to the rest of the organization, managerial levels first. Each presentation, was followed by discussion of the findings, implications, interpretations, and recommendations. Both management and employees received the same report.

8. Special conditions affecting validity of the study

Several special conditions may have affected the outcome of the study. During the early part of 1970, most retail operations were feeling the consequences of the nationwide economic slowdown. As a result, the morale of the management of Claypool was somewhat depressed. There was much discussion about the effects of the "recession." The economic slowdown followed several strikes by manufacturers of major appliances which resulted in several "stock outs" of major lines in the Claypool stores. The combination of these two factors caused the projected sales volume to be overestimated for the fiscal year 1970. Major expansion plans were having to be revised, and Mr. Claypool was uncertain about the outcome.

In addition, Claypool had recently hired several new executives in key positions. These included a controller, vice president of personnel, legal counsel, and two store managers.

Another factor was the reluctance of the management to disclose any historical financial data to the consultants. After a lengthy discussion with the president, records for the previous 6 years were made available, but they proved to be incomplete, inadequate, and sketchy. It was also difficult to determine much personnel data since those records were also incomplete and inadequate.

9. First overall impressions

The first impression of the main store is the surrounding neighborhood. The store is located in an older section of Atlanta and is surrounded by large warehouses and manufacturing concerns. The inhabitants of the area are working class people who live in row houses, usually duplexes or triplexes. The streets had not been cleaned recently. There were broken bottles and beer cans in the gutters, loose papers in the streets and on the sidewalks, and piles of rubbish on street corners. The traffic in the area was heavily snarled in the narrow streets, and several cars were double-parked or broken down. Children darted in and out of the slow moving traffic while adults sat on the porch steps. The men wore work clothes; some were drinking beer.

Several semitrailers were negotiating the narrow streets, loading and unloading merchandise at the warehouses and factories. These trucks often stopped traffic for several minutes while they maneuvered in and out of the loading docks.

Claypool's main store, a converted brick warehouse, is three stories high and covers approximately one half of a city block. A large parking lot encompasses three sides of the store. The building is old and has several coats of peeling paint. The original color was white, but the building now has a surface color of pale yellow. There are no display windows in the building, but there are large signs advertising the specials of the week. On the second and third floor there are rows of 3' x 5' metal windows.

Robert Claypool had distributed a letter to the personnel of both stores describing the purpose of the study prior to the arrival of the task force. The letter listed the names of the task force, stated how long the study would last, and gave a brief description of the study process. He also asked for the cooperation of all the personnel in this study, and he stressed the confidentiality of all information gathered.

The study team was taken on a tour of the Atlanta store and premises the morning of its arrival. The tour was conducted by the president's secretary, Miss Maggie Featherbee. Miss Maggie, as she is called by most of the employees, is a tall, slender, middle-aged woman with gray hair, blue eyes, and a smooth, white complexion. She was dressed in a tailored dark blue suit and she wore no jewelry. Her manner was efficient and proper and she seemed the personification of the prim secretary. She spoke with authority and was well respected (we later learned that, in truth, she was feared) by everyone the team met on the tour. She had typed an itinerary for the team, which was annotated for every fifteen minutes of the morning.

Upon entering the building from the street entrance, the task force was immediately met with the sight of two and one-half acres of furniture spread out on the first floor. There were hanging signs from the twenty-foot-high ceilings, pointing the way to the different departments. These large, bright yellow guides were distributed every half acre. While the vastness of the first floor was overwhelming to the task force, the process of getting from one department to the next was tedious and confusing. The narrow aisles and the end-of-aisle displays created a labyrinthlike experience for the visitor or new customer. The task force, only half jokingly, asked if people were ever stranded in the middle of the floor for any great length of time. Miss Maggie replied with a straight face, "Once you are here for awhile, you get to know your way around."

The floors were uniformly dirty, and the furniture was covered with a thin film of dust. Miss Maggie, apparently embarrassed and angered by the dust, repeated that her boss, Robert Claypool, always complained about it when he walked through the store. She explained that the local factories created the dirt and Claypool could never seem to stay ahead of the settling dust.

Miss Maggie explained that the store was divided into four selling departments: furniture, major appliances, small kitchen appliances, and rugs. She went on to say that there were ten major areas on the first floor: bedroom, living room, dining room, recreation, home-office, bath, outdoor furniture, rugs, exchange and complaint section, cash register–pick-up stations, and the catalogue station. These areas were not partitioned off from each other but were merely separated by slightly wider aisles. The task force would be able to meet the managers of the furniture, major appliances, and small kitchen appliances departments, but the fourth was in Macon, she said.

We were first introduced to Henry McDanielson, the manager of the furniture department. Mr. McDanielson is a large rotund man in his late fifties. He spoke with a strong Southern accent and in a loud and firm voice. His red face was topped by short red hair, and he was dressed in a business suit without the coat. His sleeves were rolled up and his tie and collar were open. Mr. McDanielson accompanied the group as we threaded our way through the various furniture areas. He explained that the purpose behind the various groupings was to show how ensembles would look in the customer's home. "Most of our customers have difficulty picturing how one piece of a complete set would look in their own room at home. We try to help them by suggesting complementary pieces and arrangement patterns," Mr. McDanielson said as he took us through the various living room ensembles. He introduced us to all of the store personnel we met in his department. He greeted each by his first name and said, "Here's the group from Boston who's going to straighten us out." He stopped to ask a question of one of the salesmen about his sick son, joked with one of the area supervisors, and usually slapped all of the people on the back when he met them.

The predominant styling of the furniture was conservative, heavily colonial. Comparatively few pieces of Danish modern, contemporary, or period items could be seen. When the task force asked Mr. McDanielson about the sameness in styling, he responded that the customers didn't get too excited about fancy furniture. "They're just plain hard working folks."

Miss Maggie next directed us to the rug department, which is located against one wall with the rug samples arranged along the wall in a checkerboard fashion. Most of the samples carried the Claypool name; only a few carried names familiar to the task force. Most of the samples were plain and subdued. Since the department manager was not present, Miss

Maggie introduced us to the three salesmen in the department. Each man was in his early to mid fifties, quiet, and reserved. They greeted us cordially but were silent unless spoken to.

Miss Maggie then took us to the other end of the store to the exchange and complaint department. This area was situated against a side wall and separated from the customers by a long low counter which ran two-thirds of the width of the store. Near the counter were two large double doors that led to the parking area. Behind the exchange and complaint counter were several younger girls, each one chewing gum. Miss Maggie explained that the girls had the authority to make exchanges and refunds. The counter was busy so we did not have a chance to meet the girls.

At right angles to the exchange and complaint department was the catalogue station. Miss Maggie told the task force, that if a customer could not find appropriate furniture on display, he could order it through one of the manufacturers represented by the store. She said this department was really just a service to the customer and that Claypool did not make enough money on it to keep it open.

We were then directed to the cash register–pick-up station in the center of the floor. Miss Maggie explained that all merchandise sold on the first floor was recorded here. If the sale was cash, the clerks handled the transaction. If the sale was on credit, the clerks checked with the credit department and processed the sales ticket. Miss Maggie also explained that all merchandise weighing less than 40 pounds was delivered at this station to the customer. The merchandise was being distributed in its original shipping cartons and was being checked by the clerks as it was conveyed to the first floor from the third floor warehouse by a dumb waiter. When a sale was made, the salesman would send one copy of the sales ticket to the third floor via a pneumatic tube from the selling area while the customer went to the cash registers to have the ticket processed. The stock people would retrieve the merchandise from stock and send it down to the pick-up station. The task force watched the operation for about thirty minutes, noting that it took about fifteen minutes for each customer to get his package. Sometimes there was a mistake and the process was repeated by having the clerk call the stock room over the phone.

The task force proceeded to the second floor where the major appliance and the small kitchen appliance departments were located.

As we got off the elevator, we were greeted by the department manager of the major appliances, Sheldon Jennings. Mr. Jennings was a tall well-built man in his early forties. He was conservatively dressed in a navy blue blazer, gray trousers, white button-down shirt, and regimental striped tie. When he was introduced to us by Miss Maggie, he offered to show us his department. Miss Maggie excused herself, and Mr. Jennings started us through the major appliances.

The major appliances are divided into two areas: white goods (refrigerators, dishwashers, clothes washers, stoves, and kitchen appliances) and brown goods (stereos, televisions, radios, air conditioners, and other large electrical appliances). The second floor was similar to the first except for the merchandise. Row after row of refrigerators, washers, and other kitchen appliances stood in bright, gleaming uniform order. Along two of the walls were the brown goods. Mr. Jennings was also responsible for complete kitchen ensembles, which were located along a third wall. As we walked through the white goods area, the task force noted that 95 per cent of the appliances were white. Mr. Jennings explained that they offered all the standard colors, but displayed only the white merchandise.

They all had the same film of dust as the furniture. The salesmen to whom we were introduced were middle-aged and were very courteous. When one of the salesmen asked the task force if we were going to fire anyone, Mr. Jennings responded that we were only there to learn about the organization. He said we had no authority to run the organization. The salesman was somewhat relieved. Throughout the tour of his area, Mr. Jennings was calm, informative, and displayed a vast amount of knowledge about the products. He mentioned that he had been with one of the manufacturers before joining Claypool and that he enjoyed selling his merchandise.

When Miss Maggie returned, she escorted us to the small appliance department where we met Phillip Anderson, the department manager. Mr. Anderson explained that his department was composed of smaller kitchen appliances such as blenders, toasters, mixers, and electric irons. His department was located in the center of the floor and was arranged in neat rows of showcases about seven feet high. The merchandise was neatly arranged but had the same film of dust as the furniture and major appliances. Mr. Anderson introduced us to the saleswomen in his department. This was the only department that had women selling. Of the four we met, three were middle-aged, while one was a high school student working part-time. They were friendly and seemed eager to talk with us about their department. One of the women told us she was glad someone was finally going to listen to the people in the organization. She spoke about the low salaries she and her peers were receiving and asked if we could do something about that. When we told her we could not raise wages, she seemed upset and left the floor.

The sales personnel that the task force met on the tour were strikingly similar in many ways. The men uniformly wore dress slacks, dress shirts, and ties. They were neat in appearance and conservatively groomed. They were polite and relatively silent when Miss Maggie was around. They seemed generally eager to help us in our work, but several were skeptical about the outcome of a study. One of the salesmen in the furniture department said, "Hell, nothing around here is going to change." He was given a stern look by Miss Maggie and the matter was quickly dropped. The women we met were also friendly and conservatively groomed. Their hair was stylishly short, combed, and neat. They wore very little makeup and little jewelry. They were dressed in simple cotton or blended dresses and most wore low-heeled shoes. All of the sales force wore bright yellow vests or jackets. They kept pens and sales books in the pockets and could be easily spotted on the floor.

The credit counter was near the back of the second floor. Miss Maggie informed us that most of the store's sales were to credit customers and that the store encouraged people to open credit accounts. The credit counter was very busy with people opening accounts and paying on their accounts. The counter was staffed by several women who were all in their early to middle twenties. They appeared to be efficient and polite but harried.

The task force then proceeded to the third floor. This floor was divided into three sections. The largest section (about 50 percent of the floor) was devoted to inventory for the pick-up counter. The rest of the space was devoted to clerical and managerial offices.

Miss Maggie introduced us to Larry Stuart, the supervisor of the third floor inventory. Mr. Stuart was in his early sixties, dressed in casual slacks with a sport shirt, and appeared very busy. He seemed hesitant when Miss Maggie asked him to show the task force through the warehouse. He responded by saying, "All we have up here is the merchandise in the cartons. What do you want to see?" All the merchandise was in the original shipping cartons and was neatly stacked in high rows throughout the floor. Down the middle of each aisle was a conveyor system that carried the merchandise to the dumb waiters to be sent down to the pick-up stations. Mr. Stuart said the merchandise was arranged by manufacturer throughout the floor. When we asked him if it was difficult for someone to learn where everything was, he said, "If you stick it out long enough, you find out where everything belongs." We asked him where the rest of the store's inventory was stored, and he told us that it was across the street in the warehouse. When the task force asked Miss Maggie if we could go there next, she said it was just like this only with bigger merchandise. She did not offer to show us where it was or to take us.

The stock personnel on the third floor were either young boys recently out of high school, or older men, many of whom looked ready for retirement. They were all dressed in cotton work trousers with shirts to match. Their clothes were dirty from the dusty cartons and the dirty floors, and many were soaked with perspiration. They were noncommunicative and many tried to ignore the task force as we walked by. As we were walking down one of the aisles, one of the older men yelled at us to get out of the way as he had work to do. We obliged him and left the area.

Miss Maggie then escorted us to the executive offices. They are located along one wall of the third floor overlooking Claypool Avenue. The executive suite was partitioned off from the warehouse and was completely enclosed by a lowered accoustical tile ceiling. The offices are all on a central hallway leading from a small reception area near the elevator. A name tag hung above each door and perpendicular to it. The floors were tile simulating linoleum and the wood paneling was a simulation of stained mahogany. Each office was small and confining. There were no windows in the 10' x 10' work spaces. The offices were furnished with damaged merchandise from the furniture floor. Most of it was cheap looking, with scratches and chips on the corners. The desks were metal with painted wood grain. The two chairs in each office were unattractive, and many were beginning to fall apart. In addition to the desk and chairs, there was usually a four-drawer, gray, metal filing cabinet. The offices were cluttered, papers were strewn about the desks and chairs, stacks of catalogues and magazines were on the floors, and there was an odor of cigar smoke throughout. Several of the files were open as the task force passed by, and the files were in disarray. The drawers were overflowing, and the papers were jammed into place with little regard for orderliness. On the wall in each office hung a plaque with the motto, "If we don't treat the customer right the first time, we won't have to treat the customer at all the second time." Miss Maggie said that the motto was the favorite saying of Robert Claypool.

As we walked down the hall to Robert Claypool's office, executives were hurrying from one office to the next. Many were in shirt sleeves with loose or undone ties. We asked Miss Maggie if an important meeting was about to take place. She looked surprised and said this was the usual state of affairs.

The president's office was in sharp contrast to the rest of the store. It was considerably larger and more spacious. It was a model for the furniture industry. The walls were paneled in a dark rough cut New England pine. There was a heavy pile carpet on the floor. The large walnut double desk had leather inserts on the top in deep maroon. There were four leather easy chairs and a leather couch. Two prints depicting Civil War scenes hung on the wall behind the desk. The opposite wall had book shelves which held several hundred volumes primarily on the Civil War. The office reflected manliness. Soft, dark, and strong tones were used effectively.

A small conference room adjoined the president's office. Since the entrance was only through the office, the task force assumed that permission had to be granted by Robert Claypool before anyone else could use it. The paneling there was bleached walnut, and the floor was covered with a dark brown carpet. The conference table was a white oak ellipse surrounded by eight white oak swivel chairs. The president had a private washroom, complete with shower and sauna.

After the brief discussion with Robert Claypool, he invited us to lunch with him in the employees' cafeteria in the basement. The cafeteria is a collection of vending machines serving sandwiches, coffee, and soda. The area was filled with employees. About half of them had brought their own lunches. The area was sparsely furnished with odds and ends of furniture from the sales floor. The task force felt uncomfortable in the spartan environment. We noted that most of the employees left as soon as they had eaten. Adjoining the cafeteria is a small room used as a lounge. It has several couches, a Ping-pong table and a television that did not work. Only three people were in the lounge, two were sleeping and the other was reading.

The same afternoon the task force drove to Macon to visit the other Claypool store. This store is the largest one in a shopping center financed by the Claypool family. The shopping center is surrounded by several affluent suburban communities. The Claypool store projects above the other attached stores like a mother hen above her brood. The store is three stories high and covers the same floor space as the Atlanta store. Show windows on both sides attractively displayed furniture and white and brown appliances. Two stories high and running through the center of the store is the central mall. The store opens freely onto the mall, and pedestrians pass back and forth between the two selling areas. Two glassed walkways above the mall connect the two second floors.

The interior of the store was well lighted and spacious. The primary yellow motif used throughout the store served to maintain a bright atmosphere. The furniture display on the first level was arranged in a fashion similar to the Atlanta store, which made it difficult to travel from the front to the back of the store.

The store manager's office was on the third floor, and that was where we met Maurice Lightner, the Macon manager. Mr. Lightner was in his late fifties. He moved slowly, had gray thinning hair, and walked with slightly stooped shoulders. He looked older than his actual age. He had been the assistant store manager in Atlanta and had been transferred to Macon to open the new store in 1959. He spoke with a soft Southern accent as he escorted us through the store, and several times it was difficult to hear him. He took us first to the third floor where merchandise for the pick-up counter was stored and where the clerical and accounting offices were. Mr. Lightner introduced us to Rudy Wilson, the third floor inventory supervisor. Mr. Wilson, in his early forties, was pleased we were able to make the trip, and was anxious to show us his store room. As we walked through the narrow aisles, we noticed that the floors were spotless and that the merchandise was neatly stacked with hand-written descriptions on all of the cartons. When we asked him about the descriptions, he responded that this helped the stock boys and the customers identify merchandise in the unopened cartons. The stock boys who were working were silent as we passed through and afterwards gathered in groups to talk.

Mr. Lightner then directed us to the back part of the third floor where the clerical and accounting offices were located. These were small cubicles partitioned from the rest of the storeroom with wallboard. Mr. Lightner explained that since most of the paper work is done in Atlanta, the only need for office help or accounting personnel was for daily transactions and correspondence. All of the women were busy and did not look up as we passed through their area. The women were young, in their late teens and twenties, and wore simple clothing and little jewelry.

Mr. Lightner took us to the second floor where the white and brown goods and the small kitchen appliances were sold. The layout of the floor was the same as the Atlanta store except for the dirt, which was missing here. Even the personnel looked the same. The sales force wore the same bright yellow vests and jackets and were of a similar age range. As we walked through the second floor, Mr. Lightner was greeted by all of the sales force, and he stopped to chat with most of them. He did not introduce us to any of them.

The task force then proceeded to the first floor, where we met John Recker, the rug department manager. Mr. Recker, in his middle forties, was small in stature but had a booming voice. He was busy explaining a projected sale to his employees but took a couple of minutes to introduce us to his people. He explained that most of the merchandise in his department carried the Claypool name since they had been able to negotiate a favorable deal with a nearby textile manufacturer. Mr. Recker said that they carried a few other lines only for the convenience of their customers. Usually, the customer would buy the Claypool carpet because of similar quality at lower cost.

As we walked through the rest of the areas on the first floor, the sales force was busy and Mr. Lightner did not bother with introductions. When we returned to his office, the task force asked him about eating and lounge facilities for the personnel. Mr. Lightner responded that since there were two cafeterias in the shopping center, Claypool had not installed one for employees. Employees were expected to use facilities in the shopping mall. He mentioned that this sometimes caused inconvenience for the personnel because they had to schedule their meals at somewhat inappropriate hours since the cafeterias were usually busy during the normal lunch and dinner hours.

The offices for the Macon store were similar to those in Atlanta. There were only three private offices. These were occupied by Mr. Lightner, his assistant, and the personnel director. A large room adjoined the personnel office, which was used for training purposes and for promotional displays.

The task force agreed among themselves that Claypool had kept overhead at a minimum in the Macon store by using simple fixtures, inexpensive or damaged furniture from the sales floor, and simple decor throughout the store. The only difference between the two stores was the newer lighting, the openness of the mall, and the location of the store. The mood in both stores was similar. People were courteous, polite, but somewhat sullen. They seemed to be without vitality, except for the department managers. The sameness of the personnel, sameness of merchandise, and sameness of the facilities was somewhat depressing to the task force.

B. Historical Data

1. Chief complaint

The chief complaint leading to the study was Robert Claypool's concern about establishing a solid base for expansion of the Claypool organization. Obviously, he did not yet feel comfortable about the capacity of Claypool's management to successfully carry the larger burden. Profits had been down and the projected forecast for the present fiscal year was lower than expected. When one of the executives was asked why the profits were not increasing steadily, he hesitated and then said, "I don't know, people just aren't as committed to retailing as they used to be. One of the ladies in the small kitchen appliance department quit yesterday. She had been here ten years and her reason for leaving was that she was just tired. I don't know; it just doesn't make sense."

2. Problems of Claypool as stated by key figures

Robert Claypool III was also concerned with the daily affairs of the organization and about the impact on his employees of any action that he might take. He talked frequently about his pride in the employee benefit programs. He also mentioned his fear of losing contact with the older employees who had been with the organization for many years. The fact that Claypool was becoming larger and, therefore, more impersonal, was causing Robert Claypool to be more distant from the employees. He recalled past Christmas seasons when both he and his wife would work on the sales floor with the employees during the evenings and when he knew 95 per cent of the employees by their first names. Now he had little time for that kind of fraternizing, but he still sent birthday cards to all employees. The loss of closeness with the employees was giving him second thoughts about the plans for expansion.

The vice presidents and subordinates were much more business oriented in their worries about, and their verbalization of, the problems confronting the organization. The vice president of marketing, Peter Jackson, felt that the organization was drifting from one year to the next. He spoke about the lack of long-range planning in the executive group and the "additive" and "ad hoc" nature of all the actions in the company. Whenever a decision had to be made concerning a new or untried line of merchandise or concept, the usual process was to ignore the problem and let it resolve itself, he said. He used as an example, Claypool's entry into the low-priced kitchen utensil market. When other stores in the area were capitalizing on this market, the Claypool management decided to follow suit. They opened a "Pot Boutique" in one corner of the second floor and bought out a line of utensils from an eastern distributor. There was little planning. Consequently, the department ran into several problems and was eventually forced to close. The net result was a loss of $73,000 and a drop in the morale of the executive team and employees.

Mr. Jackson also mentioned that he did not know who he really reported to and what his responsibility was. According to the organization chart, he was to report directly to the executive vice president, Michael Samson. In fact, he took orders from both Robert Claypool and Mr. Samson, and many times the directives were contradictory and confusing. As a result, he usually cleared any projected action through both men.

The vice president of personnel, John DuLawrence, spoke about the problems of hiring, training, and keeping good sales personnel for the two stores. There was no formalized training program for new employees, and therefore they were "thrown to the lions" the first day. He also mentioned that the annual turnover was approximately two and a half times the total number of employees. He felt the major reason for this problem was salary inequities. Beginning sales people, while starting at comparatively low salaries, were usually paid more than present employees. Part-time people were paid the same as full-time people on an hourly basis, and the compensation from area to area differed considerably. He cited the example of the major appliance department which started its salesmen at $3.05 an hour while the small kitchen appliance department usually started people at $1.43 an hour. While the salary schedule was not public information in the stores, he said that most employees knew each other's take-home pay.

Mr. DuLawrence also voiced concern about Claypool's inability to attract young potential managers to the organization. Claypool had attempted to train its own managers from within the organization, but this effort had not proven successful. As a result, he said, most of the department managers and supervisors were older men who had been with the store for many years, and there was virtually no one who could be called upon to replace any of them. Recently one of the department managers died, and the company had to hire someone from outside the organization to replace him. In the past, the organization tried to hire young college graduates as assistant managers, but usually they quit within one year. The reasons given for quitting, according to Mr. DuLawrence, were inadequate money, lack of opportunity to advance, being looked upon by the managers as young "whippersnappers," and the offer of better jobs elsewhere.

The consensus throughout the management ranks was that Claypool had been unable to obtain and keep young potential managers. The executive vice president, Michael Samson, was quite concerned about this. He laid the blame on the department managers for not teaching the younger men what retailing was and about how they could advance. Mr. Samson was also concerned about the apathy in the company. He reported that when he first came to the organization after World War II, people were happy to have any job and were willing to work a full day for a full day's wage. This was not true of today's younger employees, and the result was "almost complete passiveness and apathy throughout the operation."

3. Background of Claypool

a. Key developmental phases

Claypool was started by Colonel Robert DuLawrence Claypool during the early Reconstruction days after the Civil War. He opened a general store on the outskirts of Atlanta in 1868 and his customers were primarily farmers from the surrounding area. It was a typical general store that sold everything, but the emphasis was on practical items: plows, harness gear, staple foods, and bolts of cloth. The store was the gathering place for the surrounding area, and all of the local gossip was either started or disproved around its cracker and pickle barrels.

Since Colonel Claypool owned approximately 17,000 acres of farm land in the area and since he derived considerable income from the cash crops, his textile mills and his horse stables, he was not particularly concerned about the profits of the general store. He had a messianic zeal about him. His parents had taught him that all people were equal in their rights and privileges. Since the Claypools were fortunate to be wealthy, "they should do their part to help those who were less fortunate." The Civil War had pretty well destroyed the farms around Atlanta, and the smaller farmers were having great difficulty getting started again. They needed credit and they needed supplies. Colonel Claypool gave them both.

The eldest son of the colonel, Robert II, followed in the philosophical footsteps of his father. The colonel had not attempted to expand the general store but had kept it more as a service for the farmers than as a profit-oriented business. However, thirty years after the store opened its doors, Robert II, foresaw the rapid expansion of Atlanta and the opportunity for a furniture store. In 1916, two years after the Colonel died, Robert II purchased land in Atlanta and opened Claypool Furniture Co. The philosophy was still the same: give the customer plenty of credit and the best value possible. Because of the Claypool family name and the close business contacts the colonel had established, Robert II was eventually able to buy furniture at the lowest possible cost and to pass the savings on to the customer. Overhead was kept to a minimum.

However, during World War I, Claypool Furniture was only modestly successful. Expansion costs were expensive, personnel was scarce, and furniture was difficult to buy because of retooling for the war effort by the furniture manufacturers. Robert Claypool II was called into the cavalry, and the store was operated on a stand-by basis by the employees. After his return in 1919, he gathered the reins of the operation and ran the store until his unexpected death in 1936. The presidency of the organization was passed to the eldest son of Robert II, Robert III, who was then only 23 years old.

In 1946 Robert III added a line of brand-name appliances to the store and changed the name to the present one, Claypool Furniture and Appliances. The store continued to prosper, and in 1948 Claypool brand-name rugs were introduced. It was felt that the Claypool name connoted value to the consumer and that rugs with the Claypool name on them could be sold successfully.

In 1958, Claypool and his top management group began to discuss opening a new store. Part of the original estate was sold, and the money was used to build a new store in Macon about 60 miles south of Atlanta. The Claypool family helped to finance a large shopping center and the central store was to be Claypool Furniture and Appliances. The store opened in the spring of 1959 and was immediately profitable. The problem of staffing the new store was met by dividing the personnel from the original store between both.

There were no major changes in the stores' operations, policies, or success until the early part of 1968. Volume started to drop, profits were being squeezed, and management was worried. The practice of establishing credit for all customers was starting to be questioned as the receivables were growing at a rapid rate. Merchandise costs were rising, and competition was trying to match or surpass Claypool's pricing policies. This competitive-cost-profit squeeze threatened plans for expansion and forced Robert Claypool to look for help outside of his own organization.

b. Major crises experienced by the organization

There have been four major crisis periods in the history of Claypool. The first was the change from a general store to a furniture store. This was prompted by two forces. The first was the decline in the general store's volume due to growth of the city and the growing number of competitive stores. The second was the close relationships the Claypools had with nearby furniture manufacturers. Robert II was able to purchase moderately priced furniture at considerably lower cost than other retailers in the area, and he gladly passed these savings on to customers. It is legendary in the organization that Claypool could have been selling two-legged chairs and customers would have continued to buy them. Customer loyalty was at its peak prior to World War I. However, the risks of switching from one kind of merchandise to another are always high, and it was some years before Robert Claypool II felt secure in the furniture business.

The second period of crisis was the unexpected death of Robert II in 1936 at the age of 56. Robert III had only recently graduated from Georgia Tech and had entered the Claypool organization as a furniture salesman. When he assumed control, with the unanimous approval of the board of directors, the employees mobilized behind him and helped him through the next three difficult years. The ability of Claypool to survive this critical period has been credited to sustained customer loyalty to the Claypool organization and to the employees' dedication to the Claypool family.

The third critical time was the introduction of appliances into the furniture store. After World War II, while appliances were still rationed, Robert III realized the potential in the appliance business. More people had disposable income for large-ticket items, the national morale was high, and Claypool had considerable financial flexibility. Appliances were difficult to get from the manufacturers and Claypool had no experience in, or knowledge about, marketing them. However, customer loyalty prevailed. It is the consensus of the older employees that the customers trusted Claypool to protect them from poor merchandise and service.

The fourth crisis, the current one, is the lack of managerial depth in the organization, combined with declining profit margins. As was pointed

out by both DuLawrence and Samson, Claypool has been unable to train
or hire potential managers. If this issue is not resolved, expansion will be
difficult, and the survival of Claypool will be strongly tested.

d. Organizational folklore

The Claypool family is well respected throughout the city of Atlanta
and the state of Georgia. Colonel Claypool donated considerable money
to local colleges and had been the chairman of several fund-raising drives.
The state presented him with an honorary colonel's commission because
of his philanthropic work throughout the state. His son, Robert II, also
a community leader, was influential in Atlanta in reassessing and equaliz-
ing tax assessments throughout the city during the Depression. The result
was a much higher tax rate for the Claypool family but a lower tax rate
for the lower income residents of the city. He served as the president of
several local organizations and was active in various trade associations
related to Claypool Furniture.

Robert III established the Colonel Robert Claypool scholarship fund
at two local Negro colleges for deserving students in 1939. Throughout
his tenure at Claypool, Robert III has continued his drive for equal rights
throughout the South. He has been a major contributor to several civil
rights movements and has appeared before the state legislature on several
occasions to urge quiet integration of school systems.

It is generally felt throughout the city that the Claypool family is un-
selfish and has given generously of its time and money for the benefit of
the community and state. Many newspaper articles read by the task force
in the public library described the family in glowing terms and talked
about the contributions to Georgia and Atlanta as a result of the efforts
of the Claypool family. There are constant reminders throughout the city
of gifts from the family: the Colonel Robert Claypool Memorial Park in
downtown Atlanta, the Claypool Zoo, the new addition to the Claypool
Institute for Child Health (a nonprofit organization devoted to research
into learning disabilities), the Claypool Library at one local college, and
Claypool Avenue on which the Atlanta store is located. There is no doubt
that the family has had an impact on the community and that the community appreciates it. When the colonel died, state officials attended his
memorial service and local merchants closed their stores for one day in
solemn observance.

From its original position of giving credit to the farmers after the Civil

War, Claypool has continued to place the customer first and the organizational profit second. On the wall of Robert III's office is the following quote, "If we can give the customer fair value at only a marginal profit to us, both of us will be happier, as we will have retained a friend for life." The quote is attributed to Robert II.

During the Depression, families who had shopped at Claypool for years were given unlimited credit and little effort was made to get repayment. In the early fifties, when the store discovered that there had been a bad shipment of air conditioners, the store replaced all the models sold with more expensive units and gave coupons worth $25 to all the families who had purchased the faulty models.

Each year, Claypool sponsors a debutante ball at considerable cost, where any 18-year-old girl is able to have her "coming out" party at the expense of the store. The store will supply the gowns at half price to the girls and then rent a ballroom and cater the party.

II. DESCRIPTION AND ANALYSIS OF CURRENT ORGANIZATION AS A WHOLE

A. Structural Data

1. Formal Organization

a. Chart

The Claypool organization is divided into the three major retail functions: sales, distribution, and support. These three functions are further divided into eleven subfunctions. All eleven are headed by vice presidents. (See Figure 1 for organizational chart.) Robert Claypool and Michael Samson are responsible for the operation, administration, and growth of the three major areas. The sales function is divided between the merchandising vice president, and the marketing vice president. Warner Lambert, merchandising vice president, is responsible for the buyers and their assistants. At the time of the study, Claypool had 12 buyers and 5 assistants. This group of men have their offices in the warehouse across the street from the Atlanta store. They are responsible for maintaining a continuous flow of merchandise into the stores to meet the requirements of the marketing department. The most effective tool they possess, accord-

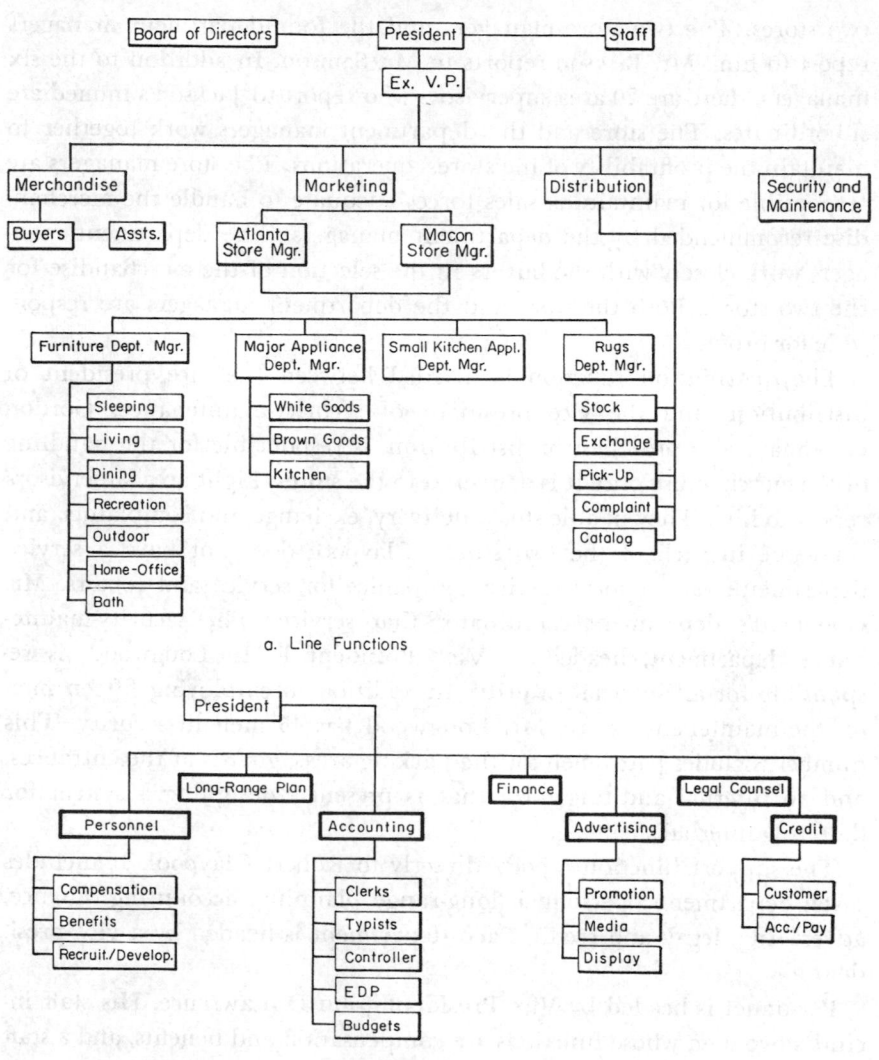

a. Line Functions

b. Staff Functions

Figure 1. Organizational Chart

ing to Mr. Lambert, is the personal contacts each of the buyers has with colleagues, manufacturers, distributors, and salesmen throughout the country. They usually purchase merchandise six or seven months before delivery.

The other half of the sales function is headed by Peter Jackson, marketing vice president. Mr. Jackson is responsible for the sales activities in the two stores. The two store managers and the four department managers report to him. Mr. Jackson reports to Mr. Samson. In addition to the six managers, there are 20 area supervisors who report to Jackson's immediate subordinates. The store and the department managers work together to maintain the profitability of the stores' operations. The store managers are responsible for maintaining sales forces adequate to handle the merchandise recommended by the department managers. The department managers work closely with the buyers in the selection of the merchandise for the two stores. Both the store and the department managers are responsible for profit.

The distribution function is divided between the vice president of distribution, and the vice president of security-maintenance. Gordon Goodman, vice president of distribution, is responsible for the handling of the merchandise once it is delivered to the stores. Eight area supervisors report to him. They handle stock, delivery, exchange and complaints, and catalogue in each of the two stores. Claypool does not have a service department. It uses local service companies for service and repairs. Mr. Goodman's department coordinates that service. The security-maintenance department, headed by Vice President F. L. Longwood, is responsible for all internal security. In addition to employing fifteen men on the maintenance force, Mr. Longwood has 45 men in security. This number includes patrolmen for the parking areas, guards at the entrances, and an internal auditing force that is presently designing a system for detecting internal shrinkage.

The support function reports directly to Robert Claypool. It includes seven departments: personnel, long-range planning, accounting, finance, advertising, legal, and credit. Each department is headed by a vice president.

Personnel is headed by Vice President John DuLawrence. His staff includes two men whose functions are compensation and benefits, and a staff of people who are responsible for recruiting, hiring, orientation, and training new employees.

The long-range planning department is composed of three men who have the responsibility of coordinating strategies directed toward the long-range viability of the organization. They help Robert Claypool plan for the future utilization of the resources of the organization. Currently they are examining sites in Georgia for future expansion.

The accounting department is headed by Anthony Robertson, the controller. The functions of the department are four: it employs and manages all clerks and typists in the organization; manages the cash position; manages the data processing and information systems; prepares, manages, and administers the budgets. There are approximately 100 people in the department. Most are clerks, typists, and keypunch operators.

The finance department is responsible for two aspects of the organization. Its major function is to determine the need for and to arrange for sufficient short-term financing to allow for flexibility in planning and buying. The second function is to conduct and administer financial analyses. The vice president in charge of the finance department is Scott Gordon.

The advertising department is headed by Vice President Murray Kneeland. Mr. Kneeland is responsible for coordinating the activities of the advertising agency handling the Claypool account with the marketing needs of the organization. Display work, signs, and other art work used in the two stores are coordinated by Mr. Kneeland and his three-man staff.

The legal department is composed of one lawyer and two secretaries. Richard Morrison, the attorney, reviews all contracts, delivery schedules, and other legal details.

The credit department is headed by Vice President Philip Soucy. There are two major functions for this department. They receive all customer credit data from the data processing of the accounting department and are responsible for the collection of accounts. They also are responsible for all of the accounts payable, excluding payroll, which is under the accounting department. All checks must be signed by both Mr. Soucy and Mr. Robertson.

b. Systems concept

Claypool Furniture and Appliance revolves around the successful interplay of three major systems: merchandise, customers, and market information. Each of these systems affect each individual employee in some way.

After products are ordered, they are delivered to one of four warehouse locations. If the merchandise is heavier than 40 pounds, it is delivered to the separate warehouses at the two stores, if it is lighter than 40 pounds, it is delivered to the third floor of each store. When the merchandise is delivered to the appropriate warehouse, a clerk accepts the merchandise and checks it against the shipping order. Copies of the shipping order are sent to Gordon Goodman, vice president of distribution and to the accounts payable area in the credit department. Goodman notifies the marketing department of the arrival of merchandise and the date when samples may be placed on the selling floor. When the invoice is received, accounts payable checks the invoice against the shipping order and the buyer's order form and, assuming that all agree, the bill is paid. If there is a discrepancy, information is requested from Gordon Goodman.

Once a customer has purchased an article, he may pick it up at the cash register if it is lighter than 40 pounds or have the store deliver to his residence. Claypool does not have its own fleet of delivery trucks. According to Goodman, the cost of maintaining a fleet is prohibitive. Consequently, the stores rent trucks from a local dealer and use Claypool distribution personnel to deliver the merchandise. There is a standard charge of $5.00 for each individual delivery within 25 miles of either the Atlanta or Macon store. Deliveries are not made out of these trade areas, and customers must make their own delivery arrangements if they live elsewhere.

Most of the customers now have only a casual relationship with the organization. (They are less loyal for reasons to be discussed later.) If a customer pays cash for his merchandise, he either picks it up at the cash register or has the merchandise delivered. If the sale is a credit sale, the customer's credit is checked, and, if okayed, the customer takes the merchandise. Each month statements are mailed to credit customers, and payments are received. The checks are sent to the accounting department, and the receipt is forwarded to the credit department. If the customer has a complaint about the merchandise, he is directed to the complaint department. If he does not receive satisfaction there, he may see the store manager. If there is a problem with the customer's statement, he is directed to the credit department. When the customer makes a purchase on the selling floor, it is noted in the area's inventory control book. At the end of each day, the salesman reconciles his salesbook with the inventory control book, indicating the amount of inventory on hand. This information is collected by the store manager daily and rechecked against the sales tickets and invoices to determine individual and area sales and inventory levels.

Market information is collected from three sources: trade shows, personal contacts by the buyers and executive team, and manufacturers. This information is analyzed by the buyers to select merchandise for forthcoming seasons. When an order is submitted, it is checked against the department budget by the accounting and finance departments. The buyers give copies of the various orders to Mr. Samson, and he in turn forwards them to the accounting and finance departments. The buyers also send copies of these orders to the president, and he distributes the information to the advertising, legal, and credit departments. Copies are also sent to the marketing department and routed through the various department managers and store managers. Copies go to the vice president of distribution and are routed through the stock and the catalogue departments. From these order copies, Murray Kneeland can tell the ad agency to design advertising for the coming merchandise, Richard Morrison can check the legal terms of the contracts, and credit can file the necessary information until the invoices are received.

The only additional input into this system is the information collected by Mr. Samson from the professional shoppers. He weighs information about the competition and the buyers' selections and then determines the exact orders to be processed. If there are changes in the original orders, these are referred back to the buyers and then must pass through the whole system again. Other information collected by Claypool has limited distribution and impact. For example, Robert Claypool attends conferences conducted by the National Retail Furniture Association, but he fails to relate information he learns there to his subordinates.

2. Plant and equipment

Claypool Furniture and Appliances owns and operates four buildings. There are two buildings in Atlanta and two in Macon (a store and warehouse each). These four buildings carried a depreciated value of $12,432,-669 in the 1969 annual report. The land owned by the company is the land on which the buildings stand plus the adjacent parking lots. The value of this land is listed in purchase price dollars. The land in Atlanta is recorded at $200,000 while the land in Macon is listed at $500,000. The value of both of these properties is understated. Land in the Atlanta area has at least tripled, and land in the Macon area has at least doubled since the respective purchases.

Inventory is listed in the annual report at $4,217,535. This is the value of the inventory at the end of the fiscal year, January 31, 1969. According to Warner Lambert, this is an understatement of the inventory carried throughout the year. He said the inventory may fluctuate 40 percent from the end of the fiscal year to the Christmas rush. He said that the inventory frequently approached $6,000,000 during the November–December selling season.

Most of the office furniture (desks, tables, chairs, filing cabinets, and so forth) is damaged merchandise from the sales floor. The value of this furniture is minimal since most of it was written off the books as being worthless. The fixtures in the Atlanta store are relatively old. The lighting fixtures are standard three-bulb fluorescent fixtures hung about 15 feet above the floor. Display and work counters are made of formica-covered plywood, which shows signs of wear. In the Macon store, the fixtures are new (installed in 1965 when the store opened). While the counters are made of the same formica-covered material, they do not yet show wear. The office machines (typewriters, adding machines, duplicators, and so forth) in both stores are relatively new. The task force noticed that clerks had considerable difficulty using the Atlanta cash registers. Manufacturer dates indicate that some of the cash registers were 20 years old or older. The cash registers in the Macon stores were all uniformly new (circa 1965).

The credit department recently put all customers' charges on punch cards that are fed into an IBM 1401 that produces the monthly bills. The computer is owned by a time-sharing facility in Atlanta, and Claypool leases time. The accounting department also uses the 1401 to process the payroll and to keep cash balances current. Very little is done with the information other than mere processing.

The practice of storing all of the lighter merchandise above the sales floor and distributing it only when sold via a dumb waiter to the cash registers has proved highly successful. All small merchandise (under 40 pounds) is stored unpacked in the stock rooms. Merchandise is stacked according to manufacturer and product. When a sale is made on the floor, the customer takes the sales ticket to the cash registers and waits for the merchandise to be delivered to him. The salesman, meanwhile, has put one copy of the sales slip into a pneumatic tube connected to the third floor storage area. The product is taken from stock and delivered to the appropriate cash register and given to the customer. If there are several customers at the cash registers, sometimes there is confusion and merchandise can be lost in the shuffle; if the wrong merchandise is delivered, the wait for the exchange is usually between 20 to 30 minutes. According to interviews with the sales and stock personnel, sometimes the inventory control book does not agree with the physical count on the third floor. If this happens, and the third floor is out of stock, the customer must return to the salesman, who either gives the customer the floor model or refunds the price of the product. This situation was frequently mentioned as a problem by those interviewed in both stores.

There are basically four different settings in the Claypool organization: Sales floor, warehouses, staff department, and executive offices. The sales floor is the most obvious and the largest. The two sales floors in both stores are usually busy with customers milling about the merchandise. It is difficult for the sales force to tell a buying customer from one who is only browsing or one who has already purchased an item because few carry packages. This has resulted in two kinds of behavior by the sales force. Most of the salesmen, the task force observed on the floor, did not actively meet or engage customers in conversation to determine if they wanted to buy or if the sales force could be of any help. They stood in their areas and waited for the customer to ask a question or to make a purchase. Many of the salesmen told us that the customer is familiar with the merchandise he wants to buy and often can give the salesman the product number and color. Customers usually have done considerable comparison shopping before coming to Claypool. Therefore, many of the salesmen said that they were not really "salesmen" but merely "order-takers."

The settings in the two stores are similar. Merchandise is arranged in similar selling areas (however, in the Macon store, the aisles are clearer and wider), traffic flow is similar, and the uniformity of the sales force has already been mentioned. The distinctive difference between the two stores is their location and age. The spaciousness of the shopping center contrasts sharply with the warehouse location of the Atlanta store. The Macon store is newer, with brighter lighting, more modern fixtures, and more efficient cash registers. However, the task force felt that the atmosphere in both stores was strikingly similar.

Figures 2–8 are representative floor plans of both the Atlanta and Macon stores. Each selling area has a different setting. In the Atlanta and Macon stores, the rug department is most isolated from the customer flow through the store. The rug salesmen have contact with customers only when the latter have negotiated the paths back to their department. Their view is also reduced because of large display racks running the length of the department separating it from the rest of the store. This physical separation results in separation from most of the customer traffic and also from the rest of the sales personnel. Since the freight elevator is in their depart-

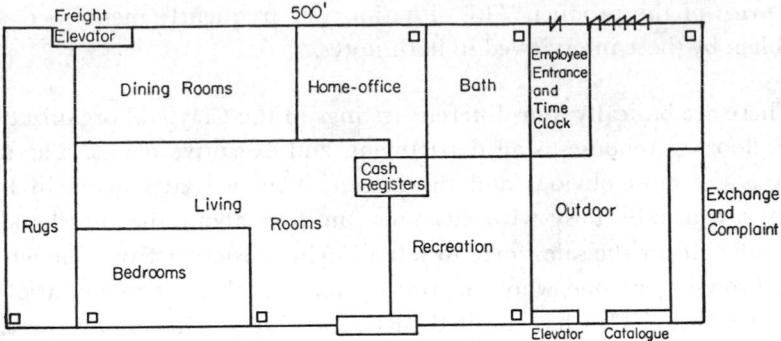

Figure 2. Atlanta Store, First Floor

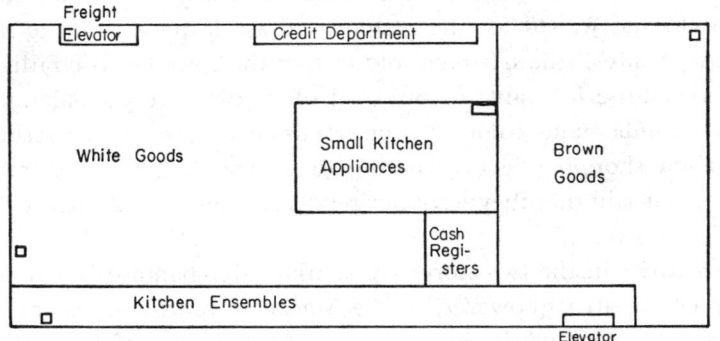

Figure 3. Atlanta Store, Second Floor

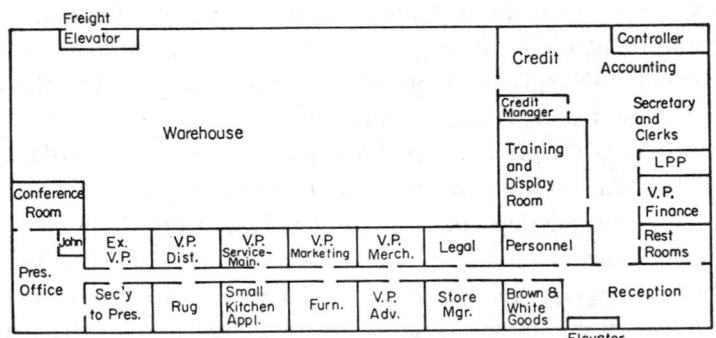

Figure 4. Atlanta Store, Third Floor

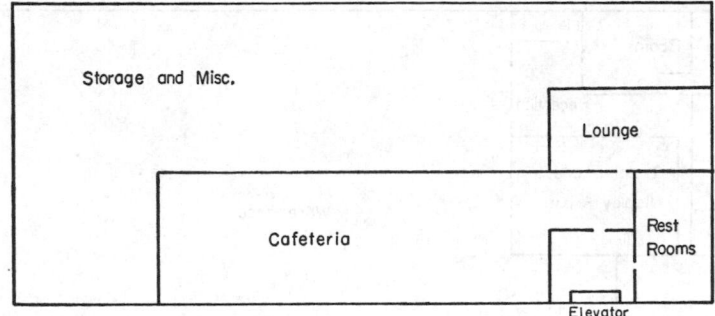

Figure 5. Atlanta Store, Basement

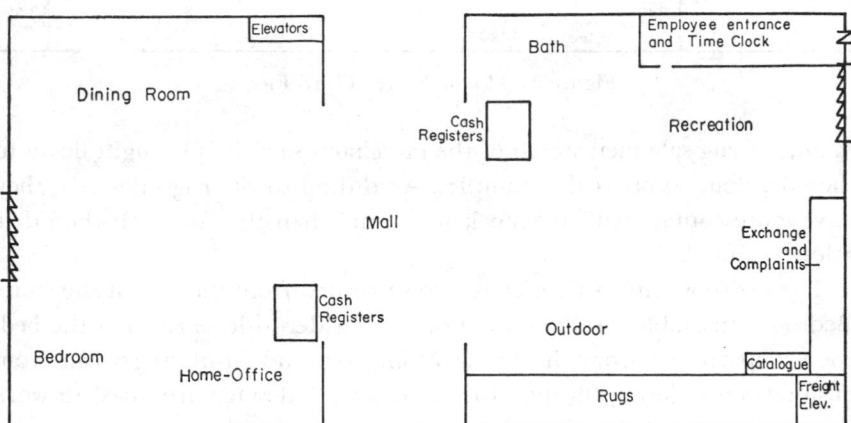

Figure 6. Macon Store, First Floor

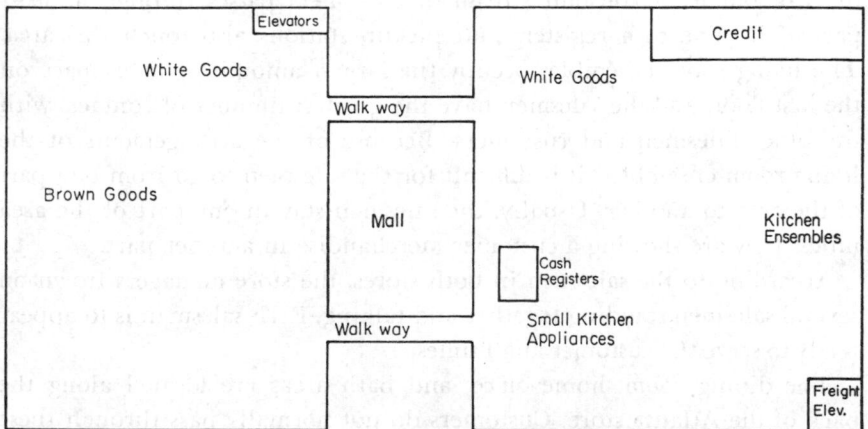

Figure 7. Macon Store, Second Floor

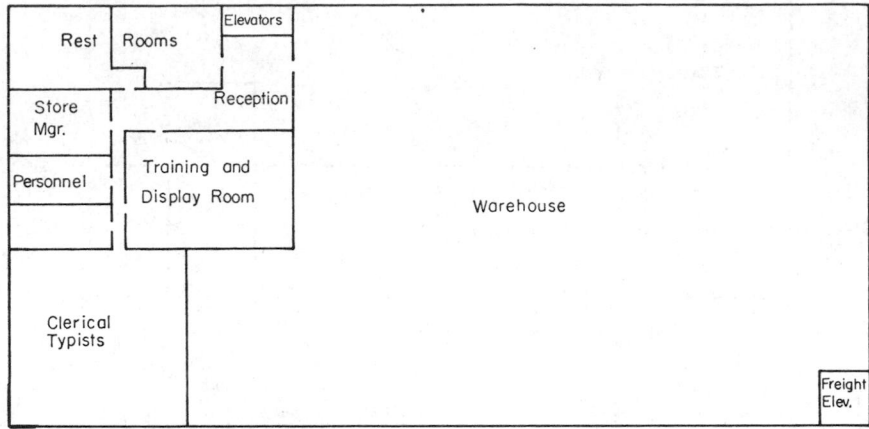

Figure 8. Macon Store, Third Floor

ment, the rug salesmen see all of the merchandise as it is brought down to the sales floor to be used as samples. According to the rug salesmen, they have more contact with the stock personnel than they do with the other sales personnel.

The bedroom furniture area is also separated from the rest of the store. Bedroom ensembles are laid out along the wider aisle separating the bedroom department from the living room area and insulating them from customers wandering through the store. Since salesmen are hired to work in only one area, these salesmen have little contact with others.

The living room area is perhaps the busiest. Part of it is located near the front door. A constant stream of customers passes through at least part of it. The cash registers and pickup stations also touch this area. The living room ensembles occupy the largest amount of floor space on the first floor, and the salesmen have the greatest number of contacts with the other salesmen and customers. Because of the arrangements of the living room ensembles, it is difficult for the salesmen to go from one part of the area to another. Usually, the salesmen stay in one part of the area unless they are showing a customer merchandise in another part.

According to the salesmen in both stores, the store managers frown on several salesmen standing together and talking. Each salesman is to appear ready to serve the customer at all times.

The dining room, home office, and bath areas are located along the back of the Atlanta store. Customers do not normally pass through these areas unless they are interested in the merchandise. These three areas are isolated from each other by wide aisles. There is little opportunity for the salesmen to pass from one department to another. In the Macon store, these three areas are all located adjacent to the mall entrances. Consequently, people usually wander through the areas "window shopping." Also, because of the two cash register and pickup stations located in these areas, they have become gathering points for all customers on the first floor.

Personnel assigned to the first floor enter through the employees' entrance near the rear doors at the parking lot. There are places for them to hang their coats and leave personal items. The time clock is in this room. Since the employees' schedules vary so much, it is rare for more than 10 or 12 people to be in the room at the same time. After punching the time clock they proceed to their respective areas where they spend the remainder of the work day. There are no toilet facilities on the first floor in Atlanta. All of the personnel must use facilities either in the basement or on the third floor. In Macon the only facilities are located on the third floor.

The recreation and outdoor areas are more congested with customers because of their proximity to doors, elevators, the catalogue department, and the exchange and complaint department. All of the personnel must pass through these areas going from the employees' entrance to their assigned stations. The task force observed that the salesmen in these areas were constantly talking with other personnel if they were not serving customers.

The personnel in the catalogue and exchange and complaint departments usually deal with customers who have not been satisfied with how they have been treated. People use the catalogue department, according to the personnel, to find merchandise not offered by the store. The exchange and complaint department continually faces customers who have purchased faulty products or products they do not want (often gifts). The girls in these two departments have very little contact with other store personnel. If there is a problem that cannot be handled in this department, the customer is sent to an area supervisor or to the store manager.

The cash register area is always busy. The girls behind the counters not only check credit limits and handle cash purchases, but also distribute merchandise delivered from the third floor. The task force noted that people usually stood two or three deep around these counters waiting for service. Because of the traffic and location, the clerks have little time to talk with each other.

The second floor settings are less differentiated. The credit counter is located at the back in both stores and is the place to open new accounts and pay on current ones. While the clerks are harried, they still have sufficient opportunity to talk with each other.

On either side of the small kitchen appliances and the cash registers are the white and brown goods areas. In the white goods area, because of the row by row arrangement of the merchandise, the various salesmen have little contact with each other. The same is true of brown goods, except that the customers can view the entire area because of the relative height of the merchandise. However, it is difficult for the customer to get from one aisle to another without having to go from one end of the store to the other. As their names imply, there is a marked difference between the white and the brown goods. Since most of the televisions are turned on during the day, the lighting in this area is considerably darker. The wood cabinets exude a warmth and the area is noisy with music from the stereos and radios. Because many televisions were turned on, the task force had the feeling of being in a television studio with many monitors all tuned to the same picture. In contrast to this atmosphere, the white goods are stark, cold, and brightly awash with fluorescent lighting. There is less noise in this area, except for that from the occasional demonstration models of washing machines. The uniform rows of refrigerators created an image for the task force of white death and cemeteries.

The kitchen ensembles are located against one wall. The white goods salesmen sell in this area, which is separated from white goods by a wide aisle.

The small kitchen appliance area is separated from the rest of the floor by 7-foot–high display counters. The women in this department seldom leave their area.

The third floor in both stores is composed of three basic settings: small merchandise warehouse, staff functions, and the executive offices. Since all of the top management is located in Atlanta, the only offices in Macon are for the store manager, his assistant, and the personnel director.

The stock people rarely see or are seen by the customers. The activity on the third floor in both stores is based on two major forces: stacking incoming merchandise and distributing merchandise via the dumb waiters. Both third floors are cavernous. The ceilings are high, and the racks holding the merchandise are 8 to 10 feet in height. The task force members felt small standing in the narrow aisle, crowded against the conveyor system, surrounded by brown cardboard boxes. Each time an order is received through the pneumatic tubes, a stock boy goes to the point of storage and loads the merchandise on the conveyor system, which relays it to the dumb waiters. This results in the stock personnel gathering around the pneumatic tube terminal to wait for requests from the selling floors. Usually they have time to talk with each other, and a few times, the task force noticed, they had time to play gin rummy at the central desk and receiving station.

There is a difference in the atmosphere in the third floor warehouses. The lights are not as bright as they are on the selling floors, there is less noise, and there is a greater difference in temperature. In the summer, it is hotter on the third floor; in the winter, it is stuffier. Since the third floor is completely separated from the rest of the store physically, seldom is there anyone in the area except for the stock personnel.

The credit and accounting departments and the clerks and typists on the third floor in Atlanta are located in a large pool. In various rows throughout the area are desks and work tables where the men and women work on the financial data. A high noise level from the office machines makes most conversation difficult except with the next person. Along the far wall of the credit area is the central credit file. In front of the file is a long desk with a dozen phones connected to selling areas in Atlanta and Macon. When a request is made, the credit clerk goes to the file to check the customer's standing and to authorize the purchase. In the other areas, people are busy working on cash balances, auditing sales tickets, preparing statements, and entering credit sale information on punch cards. The majority of the employees in these three areas are women (mostly young girls recently out of high school). In the Atlanta store, the warehouse personnel must go through this area to get to the third floor stock room. This results in frequent conversations between the younger girls near the aisle and the young men in the stock department.

The executive area and the reception area are different from the staff areas. Each office along the executive row is small and confining. It is difficult for more than three men to meet together in one of the smaller offices, so conferences frequently spill out onto the hallway. The executives are continually running up and down the halls yelling for each other and bursting into offices, looking for information or people. There is little individual privacy in the offices, and executives frequently leave the floor if they have private engagements or appointments.

The reception area is constantly busy with customers waiting to see the store manager, salesmen waiting to see various personnel, and employee applicants waiting to see someone in the personnel department. There is a consistent stream of sales people coming from the elevator to the toilet facilities. Several times the task force noted that the reception area served as a staff meeting place.

The setting in the two warehouses that handle the larger merchandise is considerably slower and more relaxed. Seldom can the customer pick up the larger merchandise, so there is not a direct relationship between the activity on the sales floor and that in the warehouses. Because of lack of customer contact, both warehouses are dark, dirty, and seemingly empty of people. In one corner of each warehouse, there is an area where the supervisor has a desk and where the stock personnel gather when they are not busy. Merchandise is stacked on the floors in uniform order, by manufacturer and product. The lighting is poor, and it is difficult to read many of the labels on the shipping cartons.

3. Ecology of Claypool: spatial distribution

As previously noted, people, functions, and activities in both stores are distributed in ways that sometime encouraged and sometime prevented contact among them. The sales force has little contact with the stock people and neither have any opportunity to see the problems in each other's department. The same is true of the relationship between sales people and the staff personnel on the third floor. Some departments are relatively isolated from customer flow (especially the rug, dining room, bath, and bedroom areas in Atlanta). Others, like the warehousemen, see little of the fundamental selling process.

There is little interaction among the functional groups throughout the day. This results in a "we-against-them" attitude. An example is the conflict that centered around out-of-stock merchandise. When merchandise begins to approach a predetermined reorder point, the area supervisor is supposed to notify the buyers who then place another order. However, many of the sales and stock people reported that the inventory control book often did not agree with the physical inventory on the third floor or in the warehouse. The only communication between the two departments is by sales tickets sucked through the pneumatic tubes. When a mistake is made or when a product is out of stock, each department usually blames the other.

The hostility between these groups is rather severe, as reflected in the comments by members of both groups. One stock person said (and he seemed to speak for all the stock people), "They [sales people] don't understand or don't want to work with us on these problems [stock outs]. All they're concerned about is selling the customer. They don't realize that we are pretty important around here too." The feelings from the sales floor were rather intense, too, as expressed by one saleswoman, "Hell, those damned idiots up there [stock people] won't tell us if something is getting low or if something is out of stock. We have to find out from the customer who is pretty irate if we have sold her something which we don't have. It makes us look pretty foolish to stand there and tell the customer that according to our books there are so many items in stock."

Segregation by function was also evident during the orientation sessions of the study. Sales people sat in certain areas separate from the stock people.

This conflict is also reflected in the attitudes of the support personnel. They continually complained about the lack of consideration shown them by the stock and sales people. One clerk complained about the poor handwriting of the sales people, which caused them difficulty in translating sales tickets to punch cards. One of the women in the credit department commented, "Those damned salesmen put us in rather embarrassing positions when they guarantee credit to someone and we have to refuse the customer because they haven't paid their bills in over two years. Usually the customer comes screaming to us about how unreasonable we are and how they will never shop here again. It's probably best for the store to lose their account, but it's bad for the store's image." The ecology of both the Atlanta and Macon stores alone contributes significantly to hostility, lack of cooperation, frustration, inefficiency, and poor morale.

4. Financial structure

The past three years have been difficult for the organization because of the slipping profit margins. Michael Samson said this was the result of several factors: "rising costs of merchandise, not all of which can be passed on to the customer because of increased competition; inadequate advertising in the Atlanta-Macon trade area to compete with more aggressive competition; larger numbers of bad debts on credit accounts; the increasing number of staff people; and the inflationary rise in salaries and compensation." The profit-to-sales ratio has fallen from a high of 7.3 per cent in 1966 to a low of 2.6 per cent in 1969.

From interviews with various vice presidents, the task force learned that inventories had been increasing in the past several years because of the need to have more and varied styles in each line of merchandise; collection periods had risen because of the reluctance of customers to prepay credit accounts; bad debt expenses had risen because of the increasing number of poor credit risks accepted by the two stores; and interest rates on short-term financing had risen steadily from 6 per cent to a high in the spring of 1969 of 9.25 per cent plus the requirement of a large compensating balance.

The financial structure of the Claypool organization reflects the conservative attitude toward debt. The only long-term debt is the mortgage note due in 1980 for the Macon store. This note is held by the Claypool Family Trust.

When we asked Robert Claypool about the absence of long-term debt, he said that this allowed more flexibility in the financial structure. "With plans for rapid expansion in the future, we need to stay loose and ready to go. By having the capability to borrow up to 40 per cent of our net worth, we can expand without having to drain our cash assets." He also said that the firm had never had long-term debt. He said he was reluctant to break that tradition.

Current liabilities include a $500,000 note with a local bank for short-term financing of inventories and $3,600,000 in accounts payable, representing carry-over inventories to the next year. According to Scott Gordon, Claypool usually had accounts payable to manufacturers of approximately $3.5 million at any one time.

The common stock is "false stock," in that the value is fixed at $1.00 per share. Since 93 per cent of the stock is owned by one trust fund (Claypool Family Trust), the value of the stock is the value of the company. The remainder of the stock is split among the board of directors and the local institution responsible for investing the pension fund. (See the income statement and balance sheet.)

5. Personnel

Currently 920 people are employed in the Claypool organization. Of these 920 approximately 400 are full-time employees; the others, part-time. A large number of part-time employees is required because of the long hours the stores are open. Each store is open 72 hours a week. Consequently, there are several shifts in each department with people working various 4- to 6-hour periods. Many part-time people who work

INCOME STATEMENT 1969*

Net Retail Sales		$30,048,432
Cost of goods sold and other expenses	$20,038,745	
Salaries and compensation	5,402,522	
Depreciation	578,037	
Taxes other than federal	408,725	
Maintenance-security	236,981	
Interest and debt expense	1,803,423	$28,468,432
Profit before taxes		1,580,000
Taxes		800,000
Profit after taxes		$ 780,000

* Because of space and the fact that this is a composite of several cases, detailed financial information is not given. Ordinarily, detailed information and an annual report would be appended to the study.

BALANCE SHEET 1969*

Assets	
Cash	$ 468,000
Accounts receivable	6,083,728
Inventories	4,217,535
Supplies and prepaid expenses	185,418
Total current assets	10,954,681
Fixed assets	
Land	900,000
Building (less depreciation)	12,432,669
Equipment (less depreciation)	297,431
Total assets	$24,584,781
Liabilities	
Note payable	$ 500,000
Accounts payable	3,689,734
Total current liabilities	4,189,734
Long-term debt	
6 percent mortgage	5,638,097
Total liabilities	9,827,831
Capital	
Common stock	100,000
Retained earnings	14,556,950
Total capital	14,656,950
Total liabilities and net worth	$24,584,781

* Because of space and the fact that this is a composite of several cases, detailed financial information is not given. Ordinarily, detailed information and an annual report would be appended to the study.

during the evening come from full-time jobs elsewhere. These moon-lighters comprise a large portion of the evening work force (about 22 per-cent). They are usually teachers, housewives, students, and lower and middle management from local manufacturing companies.

When we scanned the demographic distribution on the length of em-ployment, the task force noted that full-time employees were composed of two major groups: one group had worked at Claypool for less than 3 years; the other had worked for more than 10. The former group can be further subdivided. A large percentage (35 percent) were housewives supplementing family income. The rest were younger people in their first job. The older people who had less than 3 years of employment were in the sales and accounting-credit area, while the younger people were pri-marily in the stock and clerical areas.

Those who had worked at Claypool for more than ten years were pri-marily men in the selling areas and in management. The average age of these people was about 55.

Part-time employees fell into four major groups: students, housewives, middle and lower management from local companies, and retired people. Students said they were working to help defray school expenses; house-wives were supplementing family incomes, lower and middle management were both supplementing incomes and taking advantage of employee dis-counts; and the retired people were supplementing their Social Security payments.

Approximately 60 percent of the employees are men. They predomi-nate in sales and distribution. The women hold largely office-clerical positions. Most of the female employees are part-time.

Most of the employees are recruited from the surrounding neighbor-hood. Therefore, the Atlanta store employees are mostly middle- and lower-class people with limited education, while the Macon store has a larger number of people who have attended college. Most of the employees are from southern families and were reared in the Atlanta-Macon area. Although blacks comprise 30 percent of the people in the Atlanta trade area, there is a decided preponderance of white Anglo-Saxon personnel. The task force saw only 10 blacks, and they were in clerical or stock posi-tions.

Most of the employees have limited education: 8 percent have not completed grammar school; 36 percent have not finished high school; 34 percent have a high school diploma; 14 percent have attended some college, and 8 percent have a college degree. The percentages are even more striking when the management and the nonmanagement employees are separated. Most of the management have had some college or have a college degree.

More than 60 percent of the Claypool employees have been with the organization less than 5 years. More than 25 percent of the employees have been with the organization less than 6 months. From past personnel records and interviews, this figure is fairly representative of the Claypool organization. The vice president of personnel, said that at least one-fourth of the organization was always new and inexperienced. About 15 percent of the employees have been with Claypool for more than 10 years.

Skills in the organization are rather limited. The clerical staff are required to have higher level skills than salesmen or stock people. The accounting clerks are required to be exacting and compulsive. They have no margin for error. Their work is tedious and time consuming. Their department usually has the highest turnover.

Since the customer most often tells the sales clerk what item is wanted, there is little need for the sales force to be "salesmen." Salesmen report that they lack knowledge about products and techniques to sell those products. Only those in the major appliance department have any sales skill. These men are aggressive, competent, and take great pride in their sales records. The skill level required in the stock department is limited to knowledge of the location of products.

The skill level of the management group is difficult to determine. While many are familiar with newer, sophisticated management techniques, Claypool's management generally felt that retail success was not based on these techniques. They questioned using elaborate management information systems, decision theory, newer cash-flow analyses, and smoothing techniques of inventory control. Robert Claypool said that management's major skill was its association with distributors and manufacturers. The task force felt that skills possessed by the management were a combination of personal associations, experience in retailing, and a sixth sense about merchandising. During an interview with an older and highly successful buyer, he was asked how he made merchandising decisions. He responded, "After I've gone to the trade shows, I talk with my friends around the country to see what they thought of the new lines. I always get a lot of conflicting and confusing views, but from these talks and from my retail 'touch' I order a season's line of merchandise." An additional factor is the amount of advertising in local media. It is difficult for the task force to determine whether the results are a function of the advertising or of the massiveness of the campaigns.

Absenteeism is difficult to determine from the payroll statistics because of the wide variety of work schedules. Area supervisors also mentioned that it was difficult for them to say definitively whether someone was absent or if the work schedule was merely confused. However, during the periods of observation, the task force heard considerable talk each morning about how employees were going to cover for those absent.

The turnover figure is elusive. Each year about one hundred extra employees are hired for the Christmas season. These people are put into a special "Seasonal" department and are not recorded as full-status employees. However, Mr. DuLawrence said that several of these seasonal employees were given regular payroll part-time positions after the Christmas rush.

Figures for the last three years indicate that Claypool hires an annual average in these departments:

sales	480
stock	800
clerical	210
management	8
security-maintenance	105
staff	45
	1648

This makes the annual turnover for the organization about 1.75. This figure is somewhat misleading because the number for management does not reflect the earlier problem mentioned, key personnel. The inability of Claypool to attract young management is shown not in the turnover figures but in their having disbanded the apprenticeship program in which younger men were made assistants to the area supervisors, buyers, and department managers. Mr. DuLawrence said that while that program was in existence, about 40 young men were hired each year, and in 15 months all had left for other positions. This program lasted about $3\frac{1}{2}$ years. Therefore, if the management figures are discounted, the turnover for the rest of the personnel is approximately 2.0.

Claypool has the lowest rating given by the Workmen's Compensation schedule. This rating is somewhat misleading, however; several of the stock people told us about hiding injuries from supervisors by using their own hidden first aid kits. The personnel department records only accidents that cause the employee to lose more than a day of work. During the last 5 years, this figure has averaged about one work day lost each month. The majority of these accidents occurred in the stock departments.

6. Structure for handling people

There is virtually no active recruitment of personnel. When there are openings in the various hourly positions, an ad is run in the local newspapers. The hiring policy is largely a matter of the personal preference of the department managers and area supervisors. There are no set standards for any job, and usually the person has had little experience in the type of work for which he is hired. The only exceptions are in the major appliance area and the accounting department. A large number of men in the major appliance department had their own stores before coming to Claypool. These men are affectionately known in the organization as "losers." The accounting department usually tries to hire girls who have graduated from business college and have some knowledge of accounting techniques and principles.

A person who is related to or knows someone already in the company has an advantage in gaining employment. There are many father-and-son and mother-and-son teams and cousins and near relatives working in the same department.

There is no orientation for new employees. Members of the sales force are given an introductory lecture on company policies and benefits by a member of the personnel department and then shown how to make out a sales slip. They are assigned to a department and turned loose. The department manager is supposed to assign one of the older employees to the newer member to show him around, but this is seldom done. The person has to discover on his own where the toilets are, where the cafeteria is, and what time he may take his breaks. Sometimes the outcome is embarrassing. One salesman reported that once a customer asked where the nearest restroom was and he could not answer. He had to refer the gentleman to another salesman. A new employee in the stock room is given a quick tour by the supervisor to obtain a general impression where the merchandise is located. Then he is on his own. From our observation of the stock room setting, many new stock people seem to wander for days through the maze of stock before someone takes them in hand and shows them where the merchandise is located.

According to our interviews, there is little training about products for the sales force. Each person is expected to acquire the necessary information from his peers and to learn on his own. Occasionally, product representatives come to the store and give demonstrations on the merits of their products. However, there is no concerted effort by the store to teach the employees the merits of each product.

Promotion is infrequent in the organization. Only 13 percent of the employees indicated on their questionnaires that they had had a promotion in the last 3 years. The vice president of personnel says that a normal progression would be: sales, assistant buyer, assistant area supervisor, area supervisor, buyer, and department manager. However, this progression is not fixed. One of the salesmen in the bedroom area was chosen as the area supervisor when the new store opened. He told us during an interview that he was a first cousin to one of the older buyers.

According to a recent survey conducted by the National Retail Furniture Association, compensation in the Southeast was below the national average. According to the employees and John DuLawrence, compensation in the Claypool organization is below the average of the NRFA survey. Employees who mentioned their wages in the individual interviews were usually most unhappy about how poorly they felt they were paid. John DuLawrence told the task force that the organization attempted to hire people at the lowest possible starting salary and then to give merit raises annually. When we asked how much the merit increases usually were, he replied, "about 5 percent." The NRFA survey pointed out that starting salaries for retail furniture stores were usually about 25 percent above the federal minimum wage requirements, and annual raises were usually 10–15 percent of gross salary.

Salary information for the top 13 executives was compared with comparable positions in the NRFA survey. The regional figures indicated that Claypool executives were paid an average of from 30 to 60 percent more than their peers in other companies. Several of the newer executives mentioned that they were offered salaries 50 percent higher than they had received in their previous position. They (the newer executives) mentioned that they had talked with friends in the furniture and appliance industry and discovered that Claypool paid considerably more for management talent than did other regional retail operations.

The area supervisors told the task force that they were paid only about 15 percent more than the hourly people in their departments. They mentioned that on the basis of hours worked, they were actually paid less than many salespeople in their areas.

The sales force were compensated only with salary. When the task force asked the reason for not giving commissions to salesmen, Michael Samson said, "It isn't too unusual in this business to have everyone on a straight salary basis. It simplifies the payroll procedures, and we don't have too many complaints."

Stock people were the lowest paid in the organization. Several stock men reported that they were hired at less than the minimum wage and told that they could take the job or look elsewhere. Since they needed the work badly, they had never questioned the legality of such action.

The top 13 Claypool executives enjoy many perquisites. Robert Claypool and Michael Samson both have company-leased Cadillacs. The vice presidents of merchandising, marketing, distribution, and security-maintenance all drive company-leased Buicks, while the remainder of the vice presidents drive company-leased Pontiacs or Chevrolets. Each executive receives special discounts on merchandise (usually half of the cost to the store), and many manufacturers send seasonal gifts to executives and their families. Each executive receives 6 to 8 weeks of vacation (half of which may be at the company's expense. Last year Robert Claypool spent four weeks in Hawaii and the organization paid for the trip, according to John DuLawrence). Key-man insurance policies are carried on each executive ranging in value from $2,000,000 on Robert Claypool to $300,000 on each staff vice president. A matching life insurance policy with the executive's family named as beneficiary is also part of the package. Claypool has a retirement plan for each executive that allows him to retire at 50 percent of his base salary after working at Claypool for 20 years. His retirement income lasts until the executive is 75 years old. Executives also have the option of participating in an investment program sponsored by the company. Each executive may deposit 15 percent of his gross salary, which is matched by the company and which is invested by a local fund manager. The return on this fund has been about 10 percent each year for the past 5 years. This means that an executive can create an endowment fund of approximately twice his salary every 5 years while contributing only 25 percent of it himself. The money can be withdrawn only when the executive retires.

Performance appraisals in the organization are used only for the area supervisors and those above them. During the latter part of January, Robert Claypool and Michael Samson begin talking with the vice presidents. According to the vice presidents we interviewed, these sessions are devoted to the variances in the different departments ("variances" are the differences between budgeted performance in a department and the department's actual performance).

The discussion is usually centered around the faults of the individual and the steps which need to be taken to correct the mistakes. As one vice president said, "There is little give and take. Michael and Robert do all of the talking and I do all of the nodding." At the end of the sessions, the vice presidents are told what their salary increases are. The vice presidents then meet with their subordinates and tell them what they have done wrong throughout the year. Second-level management (store managers and area supervisors) said in interviews that a similar situation occurred with them. The vice presidents did most of the talking about "variances" and individual problems and the subordinates did the listening. Pay increases were discussed at the end of the sessions. Most of the employees interviewed said they knew where they stood only from day-to-day. While they had been told by the personnel department when they were hired that they would have annual reviews, most said this had never happened. Whenever they received a raise, they were called into the office of the store manager and told about it by the store manager and area supervisor. Only six people we talked with said this had happened, the others said they had not received a raise yet.

The intensity and style of supervision varies from location to location. During the observations and on-the-job interviews, the different members of the task force noted that the area supervisors on the sales floor kept a close watch on the activities of their people. Task force members saw area supervisors reprimand salesmen for taking a smoke break without permission or for getting back from lunch too late. We also observed supervisors finding fault with daily sales performance of same sales personnel. When we asked the salesmen about the criticism, they replied that it was not too unusual. One said, "They (the area supervisors) can never seem to remember what we did last week. We may have had a good week, but they are always griping about yesterday's totals." These supervisors were new. Supervision by Michael Samson is especially intense. During one 3-day period, the task force noted that he called the store managers 74 times to ask about certain sales figures, delivery dates, personnel shortages, and so on. One of the task force members asked him about this frequency of telephone calls, and he responded, "I wish I didn't have to keep such close tabs on him, but if I don't, the whole store will go to hell in a bread basket." Throughout the study, Mr. Samson was observed constantly talking with department managers, vice presidents, and store managers about daily results, monthly variances, and "shoddy" performance.

Supervision in the distribution departments is considerably less close than on the selling floors. Larry Stuart, the third-floor supervisor for the Atlanta store, was the only distribution supervisor the task force noted who kept a close watch on personnel. The other supervisors allowed the personnel to pace themselves. Breaks were usually taken whenever it was convenient, the lunch periods sometimes ran overtime without reprimand.

Supervision in the staff departments varied from department to department. The accounting, credit, and finance supervisors keep close tabs on the work of their people. There were constant checks on work. The task force observed that Anthony Robertson had his entire department working late for two days to locate an error of $300 in cash transactions. When the error was finally discovered, he had a long talk with the clerk who was apparently responsible for the mistake. She left the room crying.

Supervision in the personnel department is relaxed. John DuLawrence allows his people considerable freedom. We observed one informal meeting of his people where a compensation problem was discussed. A policy had recently been initiated to allow the sales force the option of working 4 hours of overtime a week if they desired. People were confused about the implications of this new program. The problem had been assigned to one of the personnel staff, and he was reporting his suggestions and recommendations. Throughout the presentation, Mr. DuLawrence was silent, but nodded affirmatively at certain intervals. After the presentation of the report, DuLawrence made several positive comments and suggested that the group meet on their own to resolve some of the remaining issues in the report recommendations

Rules and regulations are not contained in a formal policy manual, but the task force observed and heard about a wide variety of rules personnel have to follow. These included being at work on time (which was not rigidly enforced); being neatly and cleanly dressed; not smoking on the selling floors; punching only one's own time card; being courteous to customers; parking in employees' spaces (at the risk of being towed if parked in customers' spaces); not stealing; buying merchandise (at the employees' discount) only for individual or immediate family use. (When the Atlanta manager discovered that one of the sales women purchased a color television for an aunt, she was fired.) Most of the rules that were readily apparent to the task force were general business rules, methods of handling cash, checking on credit, distributing merchandise, and handling returned merchandise.

No formal medical program or station exists. There are first aid kits in the stock rooms, at the employees' entrance, and in the personnel department. If any other than a minor injury occurs on the job, the employee must be taken to a hospital (the closest is 3 miles in Atlanta and 4, in Macon). No one is accredited by the Red Cross to administer first aid. There did not seem to be any worry about the lack of medical facilities.

There is no formal safety program. In the employees' entrances, a couple of posters are hung emphasizing the importance of safety. The supervisors in the stock areas are quite strict about behavior around and on the conveyor system. This was the only safety consciousness the task force saw.

The company has established a retirement plan that is tied to the organization's profit. Approximately 15 percent of the yearly profit after taxes is reserved to be shared with those employees who have been with the organization more than 3 years. The employees are to match the contribution made by the company (about 8 percent of the individual's gross salary), and the combined money is invested with a local trust fund to be used for pensions. Because of the length-of-employment clause, only about 45 percent of the employees are eligible for the program according to Scott Gordon, vice president of finance; and only about 28 percent of the store's employees are currently enrolled in the plan. If an employee wishes to withdraw the money prior to retirement, there is a formula for doing so. Basically, the person must wait 3 years and then may draw 10 percent of his share of the fund annually. A request must be submitted to the personnel department and a reason given for wishing to do so. Scott Gordon said that only four people had done this since he had been there (2 years).

Claypool does not sponsor organized recreation programs for employees. Several of the Atlanta salesmen mentioned that they had organized a bowling team which competed in a city league, but Claypool did not contribute money for it or give it formal recognition. The organization sponsors a local Little League team and a Pop Warner football team in each community. It furnishes the equipment and uniforms and contributes $500 a year to the leagues.

The task force was surprised to learn after the comments by Robert Claypool about the benefit program, that there were virtually no employee benefits. Employees have the opportunity to take part in a group

Blue Cross-Blue Shield plan, paid for entirely by them. Employees may purchase merchandise from the store at cost less shipping cost, and they receive one week's vacation for every 2 years worked, up to 12 years.

7. Policies and procedures

Policies and procedures deal with basically two factors: customers and merchandise. Claypool's purpose, according to Michael Samson, is to satisfy the customer. Virtually all of the verbal directives given by the area supervisors to the sales force were couched in terms of the customer's wishes, desires, and wants. One member of the task force heard one area supervisor tell his subordinates, "If that is what the customer wants, that's what we'll give her." This attitude was frequently heard and observed by the task force on the selling floor. A policy which has created a great deal of trouble for the sales force is the unwritten statement by the president that all merchandise can be exchanged for cash. One story which was told us by several of the female sales personnel exemplified this problem. A woman brought a blender to the store and asked for a cash refund from the exchange counter. The blender was not a brand carried by the store. In fact, it still carried a competitor's price tag. The exchange department refused to give the customer cash and referred her to the area supervisor. The area supervisor also refused and referred her to the store manager. The store manager gave her the money. Employees said this was not an unusual practice.

Merchandise policies and procedures deal more with security and merchandise safety. There are strict rules about internal theft and safety procedures. To control what Michael Samson feels is an extraordinarily large amount of internal theft (they do not have actual figures on the shrinkage) Michael Samson and F. L. Longwood are establishing an elaborate system of internal checks and audits. All of the stock supervisors told the task force that there were rigid rules in their department about behavior around the conveyor system.

According to the stock employees, in neither of these two areas are the policies closely enforced. One of the stock people said, "If the bosses knew how much was stolen out from under their noses, they would fire everyone in the store." The stock people frequently told about hidden first aid kits and the practice of not reporting minor accidents. One of the stock personnel said that a peer had broken an ankle by walking on the conveyor system and catching his foot in the belts. He told the supervisor that a carton had fallen on him. According to the stock people, the individual would have been fired if he had told the truth.

In the president's office there is a small loose-leaf notebook enunciating company policies and procedures. However, we found no employee who knew of the existence of this written policy statement. Policies and procedures are passed from manager to subordinate verbally. For example, in one session of the Wednesday coffee session, Michael Samson announced that every full-time employee now had the option of working 4 hours a week overtime. He was to be paid at the same rate as his regular salary. There was no written statement about this new policy. At the end of two weeks, the task force noted that only about 40 per cent of those we asked knew about it, and few of them repeated the same directive. Versions ranged from "anyone (part-time or full-time) would be allowed to work as many overtime hours as he pleased at time and a half pay" to "only those in the major appliance department would be allowed to work overtime, at no pay."

Responsibility for implementing policies and procedures is left to the area supervisors. However, if the policy deals with customers, Michael Samson and Robert Claypool frequently by-pass the store managers by calling the area supervisors in to discuss a specific problem. For example, the executive committee decided to change the policy of accepting personal checks for merchandise, to accepting only those which were accompanied by sufficient identification. Robert Claypool told the area supervisor in the accounting department about the change and asked him to relay the message to the clerks at the cash registers. One month later, the Macon store manager discovered that two of the cash register clerks were observing the new rule, but the third had not been aware of the change and was accepting all checks without the necessary identification. According to the controller, there had been no attempt to check on the directive by the area supervisor who had been notified of the change.

8. Time span and rhythm

The buying habits of the consumer force members of the retail industry (especially those who sell large-ticket items) into seasonal cycles. There are two peaks of revenue. Christmas season is by far the best time of the year for Claypool. It does approximately 40 percent of its volume for the year from the middle of November until the middle of January. The other major revenue period is the start of spring which sees the sale of air conditioners and outdoor furniture. The additional impetus of Father's Day, Mother's Day, anniversaries, and wedding gifts make this season account for approximately 35 percent of the annual volume. The two seasons combined, representing about 16 weeks of the year, account for approximately 75 percent of the Claypool volume.

However, expenses remain relatively constant. Payroll (about 20 percent of the yearly expenses) varies approximately 10 percent from month to month. Merchandise is paid for one month after delivery, usually before it is sold.

The two peaks in sales precipitate several corollary problems for other departments. Merchandise must be ordered several months in advance (buyers usually order in June and July for Christmas merchandise to be delivered in October), and provisions must be made for handling, storage, and financing of the large volume of goods. Most large orders are financed by a local bank which accepts 80 percent of the book value of the merchandise as collateral. Beside these preparatory steps, additional personnel must be hired for these peak periods. The seasonal employees must be oriented, superficially trained, and eventually paid through a separate accounting system.

The peak periods also have an effect on the clerical departments. The accounting department must be geared to handle three times the number of requests for credit clearances, which puts severe pressure on the clerks in that department. Not only is the volume increased, but also during these times there is an increase in the renewal of old accounts. This requires the clerks to check "dead files" and to update credit information. The process is time-consuming and tedious.

The first of January is also an important time. This is the start of the period for complete inventory. Once the inventory is taken, the balance sheet can be constructed and the profit or loss can be determined and the variances among the different departments can be seen. The issuance of the "report card" for the stores is a critical period for the executives (but not for the other personnel) since the yearly results determine pay increases for the supervisors and management.

Daily cycles for Claypool vary from department to department. The sales areas are busiest during the evenings and on Saturdays. Evenings and Saturdays are when families shop for major appliances and furniture. This cycle affects both the clerical and the stock departments. Clerical departments try to schedule their work so that they will be able to handle the increased credit requests and information from the sales floors. During the mornings and afternoons, the accounting department handles the more routine matters (preparing management reports, handling correspondence, and preparing statements). The stock department uses mornings in which to load merchandise on delivery trucks and to unload merchandise from the manufacturers. During the evenings, most of the time on the third floor stock rooms is devoted to handling requests from the sales floors. During the evenings at the major item warehouses, a skeleton crew handles requests from customers who have made arrangements to pick up their own merchandise.

The daily cycles for the buyers, supervisors, and other managers are not affected by the traffic flow on the sales floors. When buyers are in Atlanta or Macon, their day is spent in office work centered around the next season's purchases and the current season's deliveries. Executives are busy throughout the day. It is a practice for the older executives to stay at the stores until they close.

Planning spans vary from department to department with virtually no participation by the nonmanagement employees. The most detailed planning is done by the merchandising department. The process of getting merchandise onto the selling floor is started 6 months before a season by attending trade shows, discussing trends and prices with other buyers, and finally placing the orders and waiting for deliveries.

The long-range planning department, which is responsible for the corporate planning function, places its major emphasis, according to Vice President Edwin Stotts on plant expansion and real estate acquisition. Mr. Stotts said that with the economic slowdown and Claypool's consequent reluctance to expand rapidly, his department had little to do. He said that he had no connection with total corporate planning, except to supply Robert Claypool with projections of fixed assets for the forthcoming year.

The rest of the staff departments (personnel, finance, accounting, credit, and legal) do not submit future plans. According to interviews, most of the vice presidents said they had little time for "blue-skying" and were more concerned with daily problems. Of these departments, only the finance department worked with Robert Claypool on future expectations and projected problems. This department's concern was with Claypool's short-term borrowing capabilities.

The executive committee spends part of its weekly sessions talking

about future events (sales, promotions, delivery schedules, and speculations about competition). The horizon for this group is usually 6 to 8
months.

Robert Claypool is responsible for the coordination of all planning.
The task force observed that Mr. Claypool spent a considerable amount
of his time dealing with future events. During one week, he spent 6 hours
discussing a forthcoming sale with Peter Jackson, 4 hours listening to a
progress report on the internal auditing system devised by F. L. Longwood and Michael Samson, and 10 hours meeting with various other vice
presidents to hear their thoughts about the next season.

Claypool people are regulated by time in various ways. Each employee
has a work schedule to follow (ranging from 10 to 44 hours a week) and
is expected to adhere to that schedule. Most of the employees have fairly
regular hours (working the same time schedules each day), but about 75
of the sales force work swing shifts. They may work 4 hours one evening,
4 the next morning, and not work at all the next day.

Supervisors are expected to work a regular 9 A.M. to 5 P.M. schedule 5
days a week, and to spend a couple of nights a week at the store. Others
in management usually work about 50 to 60 hours a week. During the
interviews, most of the older executives mentioned the habit of working
long hours 6 days a week. While in the past they had been required to
be on the floors during the evenings, now they need not. They occupy
their evening time by reading magazines in their offices. They are still
expected to be in their offices at least 3 nights a week.

Claypool says it is concerned with the punctuality of its employees.
They are required to punch a time clock and to be on their jobs promptly
each day. However, during the interviews, the employees mentioned that
the area supervisors and the department managers were lax about enforc-
ing punctuality. Fifteen minutes is the point of excusable time for the
stores. After that, employees are docked, but usually there are no other
penalties. The area supervisors said it was difficult to enforce the time
schedules because of the variety of work schedules.

Testimony to Claypool's time pressures is the regularity with which
the executives were late for their interviews. While this tardiness could
be attributed to hostility and anger directed toward the task force for
"prying," it is more likely due to chronic time pressures. Members of
the task force were not the only ones treated this way. The reception

area was always full of product representatives, salesmen, and others who were waiting to keep their appointments. The rest of the personnel were always on time for their interviews. They seemed to be more relaxed and less pressured than the executives.

Management meetings that the task force attended always started late and continually ran later than scheduled. We also noticed that several executives missed appointments out of the stores because of time pressures at work and that scheduled reports and statements were usually one or two days late.

There is a continual sense of urgency among the top management. Vice presidents seem to be continually running from one office to another to solve urgent crises. One such crisis was an approaching sale. The task force observed that the vice presidents of marketing and merchandising had been aware of the sale for several weeks and had readied their subordinates. They had planned to hold the sale in the parking lot but had failed to notify the security-maintenance department about it; therefore, Security-Maintenance would not allow the merchandise to be moved out at the last minute until the premises could be secured. The merchandise was not ready for sale until 1:30 P.M., after the advertising had promoted a 9 A.M.–9 P.M. sale.

There are two types of deliveries at Claypool. Merchandise which is delivered to them and merchandise which is delivered to the customers.

Management is constantly concerned about the former delivery schedules. If merchandise is delivered to the stores too early, increased inventory costs and storage problems result. If the merchandise is late, there is danger of being out-of-stock and losing customers. Robert Claypool and Michael Samson both mentioned that the loss of the primary sale to customer (selling the customer the product he originally came for) was not as important as the loss of the secondary sales (additional merchandise sold to the customer on the same or subsequent visits). Because of the importance Robert Claypool and Michael Samson place on the delivery schedules, the buyers are frequently in touch with the manufacturers to insure prompt delivery.

Deliveries to the customer do not have the same importance to the management as do the manufacturer's deliveries. Gordon Goodman, vice president of distribution, told the task force that customers are not usually much concerned about a couple of days' difference between the time they buy an item and the time it is delivered. There is no consistent pressure on the warehouses to expedite delivery the same day or the next day after it is purchased. Mr. Goodman said that all merchandise was delivered within seven days of the purchase.

B. Process Data

1. Communication systems

a. Incoming

Claypool Furniture and Appliances does not subscribe to magazines or journals. The journals seen in the executives' offices were paid for by the executives themselves. Michael Samson said that the organization did not have the money for each one of the vice presidents to subscribe to the journals of his choice. The task force noted that each functional vice president (distribution, merchandising, marketing and security-maintenance) all had copies of the trade journals on their desks. Staff vice presidents usually had occupational journals in their offices, but most mentioned that they had little time to read them consistently. Robert Claypool subscribes to a wide variety of magazines and journals including *Time, Esquire, Harvard Business Review, Fortune, Forbes, National Furniture Retailer*. When asked if he had time to read these journals, he said that usually he only thumbed through them.

Claypool has three other sources of outside information. (1) Customer reactions to products are gathered from post cards sent to credit customers after they have made major purchases. This survey may be biased since only credit customers are solicited and, according to Robert Claypool, only about 10 per cent of the cards are returned. (2) A local consumer panel composed of twelve women is run by a local television station. The women regularly test new products and gauge the image and quality of stores in the Atlanta trade area. Michael Samson receives reports from this panel twice a year (July and January). (3) Four female professional shoppers are used by Michael Samson to check daily on competitors' products, prices, and promotions. Reports are sent to Mr. Samson three times a week.

In addition to these sources of information, the older executives have many contacts throughout the country in other retail concerns with whom they exchange prices, trends, and product knowledge. These contacts are used primarily during the buying seasons by the buyers, by Robert Claypool, and by Michael Samson.

Area supervisors, department managers, store managers and other executives notice the traffic on the sales floor. Task force members frequently heard these men say, for example, "Today looks like a better day than yesterday. There's been more traffic through my area, and the people look like they're buying." This traffic is mentally translated into sales dollars, dollar volume, and dollar sale per customer. The task force heard such comments as: "It looks like a $10,000 day. Traffic has been good and the salesmen have been writing a lot of tickets." "There isn't the volume of goods moving today, but the sales dollar is good. The larger items are moving pretty well." "Everyone seems to be a 'looker' today. No one is buying." Actual data are collected on a daily basis from the ticket slips in each department, and these figures are compiled and distributed to all departments and store managers on a weekly basis. These figures are compared to previous week, previous month, and year-to-date figures.

Robert Claypool attends many of the seminars sponsored by the local colleges and universities. He said they deal with management techniques like inventory control, cash analysis, forecasting, environmental analysis, and distribution. He mentioned that he did not understand all of the techniques, but he felt it was his duty to attend the meetings.

b. Processing: integration, decision

Most of the information coming into the organization is written: reports from the customers, consumer panel, professional shoppers, journals, and eventually sales data. Verbal information comes largely from the personal conversations of the buyers, of Robert Claypool, and of Michael Samson with others throughout the country. Some information is observation, such as the traffic noted on the sales floors.

Formal channels for sales data are the most complex. Data are recorded on the sales tickets which are sent to the accounting, distribution, and merchandising departments. These data are then compiled, summarized, recirculated. When buyers gather information from trade shows, this information is is passed on to Warner Lambert and Michael Samson. All other external information (information gathered by Robert Claypool at seminars, articles in trade journals, and reports received by Michael Samson) usually are not passed on, unless a crisis develops from the information. An example is a report from one of the professional shoppers about a competitor who drastically reduced prices on brown goods. This information was immediately related to Robert Claypool, and a meeting of functional vice presidents was called to discuss the implications and possible strategies.

Most information received by the organization, other than that previously mentioned, is transmitted through informal channels. An example was a letter received by Robert Claypool from an irate customer complaining about a salesman's attitude. Robert Claypool called the salesman into his office and threatened to fire him if his attitude did not improve. Articles of general interest in the trade journals are passed informally through the executive suite.

Merchandise orders must be placed at least four months prior to a selling season. For this reason, buyers are never sure of the trends in a particular line or style and must use their intuition. They also rely on their personal contacts to make an assessment of the market. Most of this information is systematically obtained, but only after the buyers have attended the trade shows. Most of the other information is routinely gathered but acted upon spontaneously and erratically. The reaction to the professional shopper's report is an example.

Robert Claypool and Michael Samson are the only two individuals in the organization who have an opportunity to see all incoming information. They give only partial information to the other executives. These two, together, with the controller and vice president of finance, are the only ones who know what the annual profit is for the entire organization.

Financial information about the success or failure of a product, area or department is systematically transmitted to the appropriate people through two committees, the executive committee and the Wednesday coffee session. Sales data, inventory levels, pricing, and promotions are the topics of these meetings. The executive committee, composed of Robert Claypool, Michael Samson, Peter Jackson, Warner Lambert, and Gordon Goodman, meets weekly to discuss competition, sales, and pricing. Promotional campaigns are usually initiated in these meetings and subsequently passed to Murray Kneeland to coordinate. During one of these meetings which members of the task force attended, the pricing of a line of outdoor furniture for the spring season was discussed for about an hour. An hour of each meeting that we observed was used to review past performance with an emphasis on finding reasons for failing to meet or surpassing objectives. An example was a discussion about the poor results of a special lamp promotion. It was finally decided that the buyer was at fault for purchasing a poor line of lamps.

However, information which is not routinely gathered by the organization is erratically handled in this meeting. During a strike by one of the furniture manufacturers, there was little discussion until Claypool could no longer get merchandise. Warner Lambert had known about the possibility of the strike for several months through a personal contact, but he had failed to tell anyone else in Claypool. Not until the strike was public knowledge did the subject come up in the executive committee and not until merchandise could not be purchased did a strategy emerge.

The Wednesday coffee session is composed of Michael Samson; the two store managers, Anthony Robertson and Scott Gordon; F. L. Longwood; and John DuLawrence. These weekly sessions are devoted to the variances in the stores and departments. The weekly figures are published on Monday and reviewed by Michael Samson and Robert Claypool Monday evening. If a particular department has had a poorer week than anticipated the store manager is notified and action is expected. As a result, these sessions usually are a rehash of information already possessed by the vice presidents and the store managers. The sessions the task force attended were used to attack the two store managers on a poor week. They were given little opportunity for debate, discussion, or defense.

Another committee is the representative council. This group is composed of Robert Claypool, John DuLawrence, and six employees (three from each store). The council meets once a month to discuss issues which are "important" to the employees. Robert Claypool described the intent of these sessions: "What I want to do is to allow the management and the employees to meet together to work on problems which are bothering the employees. These could be anything from salaries to work hours, to conditions, to employees' discounts, to future parties sponsored by Claypool." A task force member attended one of these meetings and observed the following: a short reading of the previous meeting's minutes by an employee; a one-hour discussion about a spring party to be sponsored by Claypool; several questions from the employees about salaries; management's reply that "everything is being done to give everyone more money." During the meeting, Robert Claypool and John DuLawrence did most of the talking while the employees merely nodded their heads in approval.

The area supervisors and department managers meet each Friday evening to be informed about the next week's promotions. This meeting is conducted by Michael Samson. He makes a few initial remarks about the sales volume of different selling areas and then turns the meeting over to Murray Kneeland who explains what the specials and promotions will be for the next week. During the two meetings task force members attended, Mr. Kneeland played tapes of radio spots, showed pictures from television spots, and passed around proofs of newspaper advertisements. Several supervisors asked how much inventory was in stock, and various procedural problems were discussed. The area supervisors were supposed to tell the sales force about the meetings. However, the task force found that the sales force lacked complete knowledge about the meetings. If a promotion was going to affect their area, the employees were aware of it. If, however, the sale was in another department, many times the employees did not know of it until the day of the sale or until they heard or saw the advertisements.

Information gathered by Michael Samson tends to be distorted when it finally is passed on to the various vice presidents. For example, the local consumer panel made a comment about the attitude of a few of the Claypool salesmen. The panel said that sometimes people were not treated in a courteous manner at Claypool especially if there was a sale, or during the Christmas season. Michael Samson called the store managers into his office for a half-day session to find out the causes for this "defamatory" (his word) report. When we talked with the store managers afterwards, they were under the impression that the report said that all of the salesmen were rude, callous, and impolite to the customers. They were uncertain about what they were to do to correct actions which they had not observed.

Some information is stopped by its recipient. One vice president commented, "Mr. Claypool must attend those sessions (at local colleges) for their social value since he certainly didn't offer any information to us." Similar blockage of information occurred with the reports of the buyers to Warner Lambert and Michael Samson. No one else interviewed knew what the buyers had seen at the trade shows, or what the basic themes would be in the next season. Several of the salesmen in the recreation area mentioned that they were usually unaware of arriving merchandise until it had been placed on the floors. One salesman reported that once some merchandise was delivered to the floor and no one knew what it was or if it belonged in that department. Only after checking with Michael Samson, could the area supervisor tell the sales force what the merchandise was and some of its features.

Claypool publishes an internal monthly bulletin entitled, "Thoughts from the Colonel." It contains items about people at Claypool and some of the happenings in the retail industry. It is written by Maggie Featherbee and edited by Robert Claypool. The major news items are about retirements, marriages, new employees, and new children. We found few people who read the bulletin.

The task force discovered that rumor and gossip were the most frequent sources of information. We were continually asked to verify the "facts" about nation-wide expansion; a 40 percent lay-off; an across-the-board pay increase of $1.00; the addition of a line of clothing; the poor health of Robert Claypool; the fight between Warner Lambert and Peter Jackson; and the move to unionize the sales force. The task force could find no basis for any of these rumors, which were persistent in both stores and were told to us by area supervisors and their subordinates.

Comprehensive financial data are not made available to anyone other than Michael Samson and Robert Claypool. Reports which are sent to the store managers, department managers, and area supervisors are brief, consolidated, and sometimes sketchy. The weekly report consists of a department's sales, a comparison with last week's sales, with sales for the month, and with year-to-date figures. Store managers receive information only about their store, and department managers receive information only about their respective departments. Each salesman is given a record of his weekly sales with his paycheck. Budgets for the different departments are not consolidated to show either relative comparisons or the relation of a department to the total organization. Neither profit figures nor gross sales figures have ever been announced to the employees. The only two people other than Robert Claypool and Michael Samson who have this information are the controller and the vice president of finance. During interviews with these two men, they were very reluctant to disclose any figures not approved of by either of the two others. They said they had been told they would lose their jobs if this information were released.

The only information systematically dealt with are the financial data in the executive committee and the Wednesday coffee session. Other information is dealt with erratically. When information is received, one of two things happens: either it is buried in the executive's desk or it is passed to those directly concerned for immediate action.

Other examples of a breakdown in transmitting information to various executives are: the failure to notify the security-maintenance department prior to an outdoor sale and the poor results connected with the opening of the "Pot Boutique." In that instance, Michael Samson had received information about the move toward smaller units in retailing and the success of kitchen utensils in an appliance store. However, the erratic manner of planning for the boutique left many people out and included people who had little connection with the operation. The poor planning apparently was the result of Michael Samson's erratic handling of the information he had.

A part of the information flow at Claypool is the manner in which information is gathered by Maggie Featherbee for the "Thoughts from the Colonel." She told us she repeatedly asked for information from the employees on what was happening in the stores, but she usually did not receive replies. Several employees told us that Miss Maggie was the "ear" for Robert Claypool and Michael Samson. When she came to employees to find out what was happening, many felt she was spying on them for the president and executive vice president. A few gave examples of personal situations which Robert Claypool had inquired about directly. These people felt that Miss Maggie was the only one who would have told Robert Claypool about them. As a result, Miss Maggie collected her information from the personnel department, from trade journals subscribed to by Michael Samson, from local hearsay and gossip.

c. Outgoing

All financial data are held within Claypool. The company has not published an annual report since it was incorporated. Neither does it publish salary information. All salaries are individual matters between the superior and the subordinate. The personnel department is the only place where complete salary information is compiled.

The employees have little idea about Claypool's relative success. Their comments were, "We must be successful, they opened a new store in Macon 5 years ago and are planning to open more." A saleswoman in the small appliance area said, "Don't let them fool you, the bosses are making plenty good money." According to Robert Claypool, Claypool does not take part in regional or national surveys about salaries, profit margins, share of market, volume of sales, or any other indicator which might tell people what the condition of Claypool is.

Judgments about the success of an area are based entirely upon the financial data. Supervisors frequently said if sales figures did not come out well, there was nothing else that could be said in their behalf. Also, sales employees receive only negative evaluations from the management. If a complaint is made against one of the employees, that employee is guaranteed an audience with the store manager, with Michael Samson, or with Robert Claypool. Many of the salespeople said that if they did a good job, "that is what is expected and we receive no compliments." Therefore, the emphasis placed on customer satisfaction is partially the result of this unidimensional evaluation system.

The marketing strategy is a reflection of the method used by Claypool for processing information from outside the organization. As previously mentioned, market information is gathered by the buyers from trade shows and from personal contacts in the retail industry. These data are processed by Warner Lambert, Michael Samson, and Robert Claypool. After a decision has been made about the merchandising mix, a strategy is developed to market the merchandise.

In the earlier days of retailing, promotion was limited to "price down" sales; however, with the pressures of competition, Claypool has reacted with various creative sales and promotions. Examples are: Giving Georgia peaches with the purchase of a certain amount of merchandise; the Debutantes' Ball now sponsored by Claypool; giving small birthday cakes and special prices to people whose birthday occurred in the same month as the store was founded (April); holding a "sidewalk bazaar," complete with tents and appropriate costumes, to sell old merchandise at lower-than-cost prices; month-long offerings of loss leaders in certain departments; giving a special discount to customers who had the four letters c-l-a-y somewhere in their last name; stretching a piece of Claypool Carpet across the street to show its endurance; staging a "sleep-in" on a new line of bedroom furniture; and, having various well-known personalities appear at the store to sign autographs.

The practice of "purchase" first and "strategy" second is not always followed because the merchandising mix is always being altered by the relative success of products and the reports gathered from the competition. The purchase-strategy relationship is of little importance to the organization, though, because once a decision has been made, the problem is to sell the merchandise.

There are three major factors in Claypool's marketing mix: price, advertising, and distribution. Price is determined by two factors: competition and cost of merchandise. Claypool's philosophy of giving the customer the best possible price means, to Michael Samson, that Claypool must always be either the lowest in the trade area or very near the lowest on most merchandise. Sometimes merchandise is purchased because Claypool is able to make special arrangements for large volumes or because it takes certain items at less than standard cost to reduce the manufacturer's inventory. If this is done, the merchandise is usually used as a loss leader with special promotion. Robert Claypool explained the rationale behind this as follows: "If we can continually offer some type of loss leader, we can get the family in the stores. Once we get them coming to the stores and show them that we do care about them and that we will give them better service, then we can get the secondary purchases from them on items with a profitable mark-up. We don't think that the consumer is so sophisticated as to purchase only loss leaders. The historical evidence shows otherwise. People will continue to return to the store if they received good merchandise at a fair price the first time. It seems that the habit of shopping at one store is hard to break. However, the habit must be continually reinforced. And that is the philosophy behind our advertising."

Claypool advertising is of two types: hard sell–price advertising and institutional advertising. The major emphasis in its advertising is the connection between quality merchandise and the lowest possible prices. Hard sell–price advertising was ten times more frequent than institutional advertising in those ads we saw. Claypool used extensive advertising in the local media, usually six to a dozen daily spots on all eight radio stations in the Atlanta-Macon trade area. Claypool also ran an average of 25 minutes of daily ads on the three television stations. Newspaper advertising was the principal focus for the advertising agency handling the Claypool account. Claypool used three daily and two weekly papers in the Atlanta-Macon trade area to great advantage. In reviewing the advertising columns in these papers, we found an average of 7 full pages out of a total advertising lineage of 105 pages. According to the advertising agency, Claypool was the largest advertiser in the trade area. Most of the ads had a central theme: brown goods from one manufacturer, dishwashers at a reduced price, living room ensembles, or some loss leader. Within each of these hard sell–price advertisements, the prices were the most conspicuous feature on the page. Pictures of the merchandise were second with possibly two inches devoted to the theme "Claypool Cares. Easy Prices, Easy Credit."

Institutional advertisements dealt with the respectability and quality of the merchandise and with the service and friendliness of Claypool people. Specific products were never mentioned in these ads, but the customer was reminded of the variety of merchandise and the low prices. One of the central themes in the institutional ads was the emphasis on distribution and delivery of products.

Claypool said that it was able to offer lower prices partially because of the lower costs in delivery. The one delivery charge ($5.00) for all merchandise simplified the charges to the customer, and he was assured of having his merchandise within 7 days. The internal distribution of lighter merchandise also lowered the price of products, which saving, advertisements said, was passed on to the customers.

2. Previous studies at Claypool

Numerous studies and reports have been done in and about Claypool. These studies have been largely in three functional areas: finance, marketing, and inventory control.

In 1964, Claypool retained the services of a local CPA firm to help analyze various policies and procedures in the accounting and credit departments. It was recommended that Claypool:

(1) eliminate all credit accounts from the files which were over three years old
(2) eliminate the 10 per cent slowest paying accounts from the current files
(3) institute a service charge on unpaid balances of .75 per cent each month
(4) place all credit information on magnetic tape for the time-shared IBM 1401
(5) use a series of "canned" computer programs to help analyze the credit accounts
(6) set up minimum criteria for issuance of credit to customers
(7) sell all unpaid accounts over 90 days old to a collection agency
(8) institute a daily cash balance statement
(9) attempt to establish easier terms than 2/10 net 30 with manufacturers
(10) attempt to establish short-term credit lines with manufacturers lasting from one season to the next with the accounts being cleared every 120 days

The report was submitted to Robert Claypool and he in turn issued a written statement to the controller and the vice president of finance, telling them to adopt recommendations 4, 6, 8, 9 and 10. Robert Claypool said that the other recommendations would tend to hurt the image of Claypool with the customers. These recommendations were filed in Robert Claypool's desk for "future reference."

During the past 5 years Robert Claypool has retained various other financial consultants. One report was concerned with the financing of future expansion (the central recommendation was to issue stock to raise the necessary capital). Another considered the consolidation of accounts payable (the central recommendation was similar to No. 10 of the CPA report). Still another report considered, and recommended, eliminating all cash sales and giving credit to all customers. Robert Claypool acted on one of these reports and none were circulated among the vice presidents.

Various marketing studies have been done in the past ten years. One, conducted by the marketing department of a local television station, recommended supporting the consumer panel sponsored by that station. This recommendation was accepted. Two market research studies were done to determine the demographic features of the Claypool customer. Both studies revealed that the average customer was "white, middle to lower income, had more than four children, was politically conservative, and placed a great deal of faith in the Claypool family name." Both of these market research studies were done by sampling the current credit files. One study was conducted to determine the geographic distribution of customers. That study disclosed that a 25-mile radius from each store included 85 per cent of all the credit customers at that store. This finding prompted the current policy on delivery costs and range. An extensive study was conducted prior to locating the second store in 1963. After spending 6 months in the field and 4 months back in the office, the consultants recommended:

(1) establishing a second store close enough for management to stay in touch with operations
(2) financing the store through the Claypool Family Trust
(3) locating the store in Macon

Two inventory control studies were done within the past 10 years. The first recommended the current method of distributing merchandise to the customer via the dumb waiters. The second dealt with the problem of reorder levels. The consultant recommended tying in with the IBM 1401 and using punch cards for each product, which would determine the frequency of purchase and the daily level of inventory. Cost estimates for installing this system were from $30,000 to $50,000. The report was given to Robert Claypool and nothing was heard of it again.

Two central themes emerged from a review of these studies. The first was that a report had to recommend a direct cost saving to Claypool if it were to be accepted and acted upon. Second, the direct cost saving could not directly affect the customer's image of the stores. All of the studies seen by the task force were done for Robert Claypool personally, and he was the only one in the organization to get a final copy and a set of recommendations.

III. INTERPRETATIVE DATA

A. Current Organizational Functioning

1. Organizational perceptions

a. Degree of alertness, accuracy, vividness

In order to ascertain the level of perception of the Claypool employees, the Levinson Reciprocation Scale was administered to 880 of them. The results indicated they have significantly greater expectations of the organization than are currently being met. There was statistically little difference between work areas, departments, stores, or other breakdowns of the stores' personnel. This indicated that the feelings reflected on the questionnaire are widely shared throughout the organization. (See Figure 9.)

More than 90 percent of the employees sampled thought that working at Claypool should allow them to have "a lot of self respect." However, more than 60 percent felt this happened either "occasionally" or less frequently. Responding to the statement, "People like themselves because of the kind of work they are doing," more than 75 percent said that only "occasionally" or less frequently did they do so. By way of contrast, 87 percent felt they should either "quite often" or "often" be able to like themselves. Responses to a similar statement, "You keep your identity as an individual," indicate that this does not happen as frequently as

Total Claypool personnel, 920
Number responding to questionnaire, 880 (96 percent)

	Number	Percent
Part-time	480	55
Full-time	400	45
Male	528	69
Female	352	40
Single	281	32
Widowed	35	4
Divorced	44	5
Married	520	59
Length of Employment		
0–6 months	105	12
7–12 months	123	14
1–3 years	343	39
3–5 years	61	7
5–10 years	116	13
10 or more years	132	15
Education level (highest level attained)		
Grammar school	70	8
Some High school	317	36
High school graduate	299	34
Some college	123	14
College graduate	71	8
Age		
Under 21	266	29
21–25	94	11
26–30	72	8
31–40	150	17
41–50	63	7
51–60	93	11
61 or older	152	17
Number of promotions in last three years		
None	803	91
One	69	8
Two	6	0.7
Three	2	0.3

Figure 9. Personnel Demographic Data (supplement to questionnaire)

employees would like. Also dealing with self-perception was the statement, "You get the feeling here that you really never know whether you're going to be fired or promoted." Claypool employees felt that they should know where they stood and how well they were doing, but more than half felt they did not.

Another area measured in the questionnaire was the employee's attitude toward the style of management, guidance and leadership at Claypool. To the question "People were put under stress in order to get them to do better work," more than 75 percent said "occasionally" or more often, while more than 60 percent felt it should happen "seldom" or "never." All employees felt that people should be treated in a fair manner, but 68 percent felt this happened "occasionally" or less often. In addition to not being treated fairly, employees feel that management does not care about their problems as much as they would like. Ninety-seven percent said management should "always" or "frequently" care, while more than 65 percent said that only "occasionally" or less often did this happen. Eighty-five percent of employees felt that supervisors did not listen to people as often as they should. Also reflecting employees' attitudes about management's lack of support were the responses to the statement, "Someone else gets the credit": more than 65 percent felt this happened either "frequently" or "occasionally," while more than 80 percent felt it should happen only "seldom" or "never." Similar responses were recorded for the statement, "You get credit for what you know." A very large number, 92 percent felt that "unusual or exciting ideas" were not encouraged, while the same group felt they should be. Most (70 percent) felt that "standards set by management were difficult to achieve," while only 40 percent felt they should be. Taken as a whole, these responses indicate employees' feelings that management is not providing the support, guidance, or leadership the employees desired.

With respect to employees' behavior, more than 90 percent felt that people are "expected to look and act right," and a similar percentage felt that they should. However, more than 90 percent felt that people tried to "get around the rules here," while almost 80 percent felt they should not. Most employees felt that people could only "occasionally" show their feelings openly, while, at the same time, they said they would like to be more open more often. There was general agreement that "What you do after working hours is considered your own business," indicating that the organization did not intrude into personal lives. Only 22 percent, said that "People ask permission before deviating from established policies or practices," but 61 percent said that this should "always" be so, suggesting widespread deviation despite attempts to control behavior. The only statement which indicated a difference between the two stores was, "People mind their own business": 80 percent of the Atlanta employees felt this happened only "occasionally" or less, while 38 percent of the Macon employees concurred. We interpreted this to mean that Atlanta employees felt more intrusion from the executive group because of their proximity. Employees in both stores agreed overwhelmingly (95 percent) that people should "always" or "frequently" mind their own business.

These statements, taken together, indicate employees' feelings that their behavior is restricted more than they would like and that there are managerial efforts to closely regulate and discipline their behavior.

Employees also said they did not know as much about Claypool as they would like to. The responses to the statement, "Management policy, goals, and objectives are carefully explained to everyone" indicated that 90 percent would like to know about them but that only 31 percent felt they were carefully explained. However, employees' confidence in management's ability to make decisions was supported by their responses to the statement, "People are efficient at making decisions": 95 percent felt that decisions were made efficiently at least "occasionally" or more often. Though efficiency was praised, effectiveness was wanting. Even though employees felt that decisions were made efficiently, they did not think that "the ability to plan ahead was highly valued": more than half (57 percent) felt that only "occasionally" or less was it true, while more than 90 percent felt that the ability should "always" be highly valued. These statements suggest that employees would like to become more involved in Claypool's decision-making process.

The large number of people (80 percent) who said they do not prefer working at Claypool over other organizations reflects the number who hold other jobs. It also indicates how far Claypool has to go to repair employee relations. Eighty-five percent said people should "get so absorbed in their work they lose the sense of time"; 75 percent said they rarely do. A lack of adequate orientation was indicated by the responses to the statement, "New people quickly learn that they are wanted": 64 percent felt that "seldom" or "never" did this happen, while 94 percent said it should be so either "always" or "frequently."

Two statements were directed toward employees' attitudes about the physical facilities. While 99 percent of the sample said that "The physical facilities" should be "neat and clean," few (13 percent) said they were.

More than 90 percent felt that "Everything should have its place," but only 45 percent said this was true. These two statements reflect our observations about the poor layout, the dirt, and the outward confusion of the two stores.

Considering the responses to the entire questionnaire, employees were clearly expecting more guidance, greater responsibility, more inclusion, more support, better working conditions, more participative leadership, and more care by the organization and the management than is currently true. In effect, the employees' part of the psychological contract was far from being fulfilled.

The questionnaire taps how well the organization meets the individual's ministration, maturation, and mastery needs, as he sees it. Ministration refers to legitimate dependency needs — for supervision, guidance, orientation, and so on. Maturation refers to the need for growth and development in a particular position. Mastery refers to increasing independence and competence. The degree to which the organization meets these needs as reflected in the expectations of its employees is the degree to which the organization's part of the psychological contract is being fulfilled.

According to these responses, ministration needs are being met minimally; maturation and mastery needs, for all practical purposes, not at all.

Management's perceptions were another thing. Michael Samson and Robert Claypool said that they were aware of several complaints from their employees which they listed in the order of the frequency of response. They had compiled this list from various talks with employees and through the representative council.

  (1) low salary structure
  (2) no training prior to assignment
  (3) no orientation about responsibility
  (4) poor or absent lunch facilities
  (5) poor or absent toilet facilities
  (6) salary not based on performance (no commissions)
  (7) inequitable treatment by the area supervisors
  (8) lack of product knowledge
  (9) Claypool placed the employee at the mercy of the customer
(10) employees did not know what was happening in the organization
(11) management basically not concerned about employees' problems

(12) very poor benefit program

(13) full-time personnel said part-time personnel were given preferential treatment, and vice versa

(14) employees did not know where they stood in comparison with others

Robert Claypool's comment on the long list was, "Some people have to have something to complain about or they aren't happy. I don't think things are as bad as they [the employees] say they are. We try to do all we can. I know we aren't perfect, and that's the reason you're here."

Michael Samson was more upset about the complaints than Robert Claypool. "People just don't know when they're well-off. We give them a steady job with a steady income and they expect us to treat them like they own the store. I don't think we are in the business to make our employees happy, only to pay them an adequate wage and in turn to get a loyal commitment from them."

However slightly treated by management, these issues are important to Claypool personnel. The salary structure is lower than the regional average, and frequently people leave Claypool to work for a competitor. Ninety-six per cent of the personnel responding to the questionnaire and interviews said they had received no training for their specific jobs and 85 percent said they wanted to know what Claypool expected from them.

Most of the sales people we talked with said they did not have a thorough knowledge about the products they were selling. More than 70 percent of the sales force said they would like to know more about the individual products because they were embarrassed when they could not tell the customer what advantages one product had over another.

No commissions are given on sales in either store. One comment we frequently heard from the sales force was, "How do they [management] expect us to break our backs and sell more when there isn't any difference in the money if we sell plenty or nothing." Robert Claypool was correct when he said many furniture and appliance stores did not give commissions, but in a short, random survey (we talked informally with 15 employees in competing stores in the area), we found that if a salesman was on a straight salary, he usually received a bonus of cash or merchandise at the end of the year which reflected his contribution.

Toilet and lunchroom facilities were spontaneously mentioned by 89 percent of the work force as being inadequate or missing, and this same group felt that Claypool should offer better facilities.

Many of the personnel, 84 percent of those interviewed, felt that Claypool cared more about, and would do more for, the customer than it would for its own personnel. The emphasis that Claypool puts on satisfying the customer, the advertisements telling the customer he is special, the liberal exchange policies and credit plans, the catalogue department, and the statement of the area supervisors that personnel should do anything to please the customers, all confirm the concept of "customer first."

We also observed that the employee did not know what was happening in the various departments beyond his own. Previously mentioned examples include sales personnel not knowing what was on special sale in other departments before the day of the sale, not knowing how profitable the organization was, not knowing the policies, and the secrecy of salary schedules.

Claypool's benefit program is considerably less than that of other furniture and appliance stores in the region according to the NFRA study previously quoted. In questionnaire and interview responses, most of the employees felt that Claypool should pay for part of the medical insurance, and that there were other fringes which it could offer to employees. Sick leave, maternity leave, college tuition payments, life insurance, recreation programs, and medical facilities were all mentioned as possible additions to the present program.

Most of the personnel interviewed talked about the different treatment given to part- and full-time people. The full-time people felt that part-timers were given preferential treatment since they were paid the same hourly wage as the full-time people. One stock boy said, "Why should they get as much money as I do when they are only working here as a second job? Their loyalty isn't to Claypool, it's to whoever they work for on a full-time basis." The part-time people felt that the full-time people were given preferential treatment because part-time people were not allowed to take part in the benefit program.

When we asked people how they knew where they stood in the organization and how they found out how well they were doing, the interviewees usually said they did not know how they stood in comparison with others and only by making mistakes did they knew what they were doing wrong. Virtually all of the people we talked with said they would like to have some way of finding out how well they were doing their jobs. Many mentioned they would like to have performance review sessions as the management did. Many said they would like to be ranked by their supervisors, and several of the salesmen said they would like to see a chart which showed daily individual sales figures.

We also noticed that area supervisors would reprimand certain employees for being late, missing sales, smoking on the floors, and making mistakes, but would not reprimand other employees for the same actions.

From these examples, interviews, and observations it is clear that management has an accurate perception of employees' feelings but not of their intensity. Many people were angry as they spoke about the low pay, the inequitable treatment, the lack of product knowledge, and the insecurity they felt in their jobs.

Few of the employees have any knowledge about the problems which face the management of Claypool. Their perceptions of management centered around the rules and regulations passed down to them. According to the employees, management is continually telling them:

(1) the customer must always come first
(2) employees must obey all of the rules we establish
(3) employees have security at Claypool
(4) it is the responsibility of the employees to do an excellent job; we will tell the employee when he is not living up to his responsibility

It was apparent to us that management was also telling the personnel other things which the employees could not readily verbalize but were aware of. The clearest was the implicit message from management that they expected the employees to give a full day's work for what they assumed to be an adequate salary and to not question the authority of management. In effect, management tells the employees that they (management) are interested only in "buying warm bodies" for the stores. Michael Samson's comment illustrates this point: "They think they should be running this company and they expect us to let them." Employees did not verbalize this attitude, but we felt that they sensed it. Indicators of their awareness are the high turnover figures (with many people going to work for competitors), the increasing internal shrinkage problems, a reluctance of the Representative Council to force employees' problems on Robert Claypool and John DuLawrence, and the obvious anger directed at Claypool for not fulfilling employee expectations.

Area supervisors, store managers, department managers, and vice presidents all see their immediate supervisors as having little ability to influence events in the stores. The area supervisors told us that the department managers were superfluous and had little to do. One of the area supervisors in the Atlanta store said, "I suppose there is a need for someone to coordinate the different selling areas into four major parts (furniture, major appliances, small appliances, and rugs), but these guys can't do anything without clearing it through the store manager, the vice presidents, Michael Samson, and Robert Claypool. They can't buy merchandise, that's the job of the buyers; they can't run the area, that's the job of the store managers and the area supervisors; and they can't hire and fire anyone; no one seems to do that." Most of the department managers were older men who had been with Claypool for many years. Several of them had personal contacts with manufacturers, factory representatives, and supervisors in local competitors' stores.

The area supervisors also said that they were not always sure who their immediate supervisor was. According to the organization chart, they reported directly to the store managers, but in fact they received orders from department managers, buyers, store managers, vice presidents, Michael Samson, and Robert Claypool. Most of the area supervisors felt that either Claypool or Samson made all of the policy decisions affecting each store and the store manager was there to implement the policy and not to help devise it. However, the area supervisors also see Claypool and Samson by-passing several levels to implement the decisions arbitrarily.

The store managers see their supervisor, Peter Jackson, as having very little authority to control his area. As one of the store managers said, "We can't rely on what Jackson tells us about some policy, because we know that if Mr. Claypool or Samson decides to do it differently, they will tell us themselves. A lot of times we have problems which we need help with, but going to Jackson doesn't do any good. He has to get clearance from Samson, and usually Samson calls us and tells us what to do."

The interference referred to by both the area supervisors and the store managers was also mentioned by the functional vice presidents. They have accurately perceived that Samson and Claypool both interfere in the actions of managers several levels below them. However, they do not see what Claypool and Samson are telling them (the vice presidents). The same message of "You don't matter," that management unwittingly communicates to the employees is the essence of what Claypool and Samson are telling the rest of the management team. The inability of the lower management to act on their own, combined with Claypool's and Samson's condescending attitude, is shown in the stock-out problem. The employees are not able to resolve the problem by themselves since there are no direct and formal (or even informal) lines of communication between the third floor stock personnel and the sales force on the sales floor. When a stock-out occurs, the sales force complains to the area supervisors and the stock personnel report to their supervisors. However, the area supervisors in both functions are unable to make a mutually satisfying decision because they must have clearance from their supervisors. Even Warner Lambert and Peter Jackson are not able to make a decision without the expressed consent of Michael Samson. Samson told us that a new inventory system (which was recommended by a consultant and which Samson has concluded is the only solution to the inventory problem) would cost more money than the investment is worth. He tells the vice presidents that they will just have to get their people to work together and keep better records on the floor. If, however, a customer complains to Michael Samson about an out-of-stock item, he will usually call the area supervisor to his office to "find out what the trouble is." Frequently he will call the area supervisor for the third-floor stock room and suggest that he teach his men where merchandise is and to inform the buyers when merchandise is getting low.

Departments are not sensitive to the needs of other departments or personnel within other departments. The security-maintenance department is not sensitive to the parking problem experienced by the employees. Employees told us about two kinds of parking problems; poorly lighted and unattended parking areas, which allowed for possible attacks and thefts, and the inequities in parking permits. F. L. Longwood said that these were really not very important issues since the number of cars stolen from the Claypool parking lots was less than the inner-city average for similar parking lots. He also said that since most of the employees left at the same time each night, there was little need for security men to patrol the parking lots. Mr. Longwood said there was more need for his men to be inside, checking employees' packages and personal belongings.

As previously mentioned, John DuLawrence was aware of the employees' discontent about orientation and training. However, he saw little value in instituting a program to resolve the discontent because of the high turnover and cost. The personnel department has not accurately perceived the intensity of the employees' feelings about this problem. The policy of not bothering about training because it is too expensive may be short sighted; it is probably a major reason for the high turnover. While the personnel department does not have the authority to implement personnel programs without the consent of Michael Samson and Robert Claypool (which is seldom given), we saw no instance in which that department studied a problem to prepare a report for the management's education. According to John DuLawrence, the personnel department is responsible for carrying out the personnel aspects of policy at Claypool. This does not include listening to the employees.

There is little formal interdepartmental communication. This is especially true among the three major functions; sales, stock, and clerical-staff. The communication which does result is based on problems which overlap functions. The stock-out, or out-of-stock, issue is a good example of a problem overlapping the sales and stock functions. Presently the customer tells the sales force that an item is out of stock, which the sales people feel puts them in the uncomfortable position of knowing less than the customers do about the store. When a product is unaccountably out of stock, the sales force accuses the stock people of either stealing the merchandise or losing it, and the stock people accuse the sales force of not keeping accurate records. The perceptions of both the sales and stock personnel are partially valid, but we discovered that the fault was not unilateral. Sometimes merchandise was stolen (as admitted by the stock personnel), and sometimes merchandise was misplaced or could not be found (as admitted by the stock people, especially the newer workers), and sometimes the sales force did not keep accurate records (we observed the sales personnel in the small appliance department making sales without recording them in the inventory control book). This problem existed mainly between the small appliance department and the third floor stock rooms, as the most frequent items out of stock were smaller appliances. However, there were also occasions when smaller radios, tape sets, lamps, and accessories were unaccountably out of stock. The salesmen in the major appliance and furniture areas said this was not as severe a problem in their areas although it occasionally did happen.

Another area where problems overlap functions is in handling credit sales. The problem usually arises when a salesman guarantees credit to a customer and then the credit people refuse to approve it because of the individual's credit history. The philosophy of granting credit to all customers is reinforced by Robert Claypool and the sales management, while the selectivity of customer credit is emphasized by Anthony Robertson and Phil Soucy. The credit department has the final word on a customer's credit, and his rating must be checked before a large purchase is made. The sales force often tells the customer that the credit standing is irrelevant and that Claypool will give credit to all. This is supported by the advertising campaigns which also emphasized the ease of establishing credit.

The Claypool management is not sensitive to the possible effects the physical plant and surrounding environment might have on customers and employees. As was mentioned earlier, the dust and dirt on the merchandise is a thorn in the side of Robert Claypool, but viable solutions have not been found. Employees in the Atlanta store usually commented on the dirt in an apologetic manner, but we seldom saw them dusting or sweeping. While the advertising tells the consumer about the quality of the products and service, the Atlanta store atmosphere tells the customer about the "cheapness and indifference" of Claypool. The dirt, noise, clutter, and poorly designed floor plans all indicate an effort to control costs by not giving the customer shopping comforts. This effect is reinforced by the large gaudy price tags on all of the merchandise. The large tags seem to tell the customer that price, not quality, really matters. The conflicting image resulting from the physical atmosphere of the Atlanta store is subtle, but we think important.

Neither store is designed for the employee's comfort. The employees' lounge and lunchroom in Atlanta is shabby, the restrooms are small and inadequate, and the parking stalls for the employees are in the more remote sections of the parking lots. (One of the clerical women talked about her fear of going to the dimly lit area at night after the store had closed. She said the security force was usually not outside and that anything might happen.) In Macon there is no lunchroom and only one restroom on the third floor, and there are no designated places for the employees to take a short break and have a smoke if they wish. The image projected to the employees is that the management does not care about them and is more interested in making money and satisfying the customers' needs.

Claypool is very sensitive to internal data generated from sales. Daily reports of each salesman are recorded and reviewed by the area supervisor. Daily area sales are collected and reviewed by the store manager, and detailed store reports are collected and reviewed by Peter Jackson, Robert Claypool, and Michael Samson. When daily figures are lower than expected, Michael Samson contacts the store manager or the area supervisors to determine the cause. As previously indicated, weekly sales figures are distributed to each store manager and area supervisor. The Wednesday coffee session spends most of its time reviewing the sales figures in great detail. The controller composes various ratios for this session: sales per customer; sales per credit customer; dollar sales per item; total volume of products; and comparison with figures from the previous week, previous month, and previous year. The controller also collects year-to-date information for the Wednesday coffee session. The information is distributed to Michael Samson and Robert Claypool on Monday; if the variances are significant, they meet with the area supervisors or the store manager prior to the Wednesday coffee session.

Claypool is also sensitive to the inventory levels and data associated with the distribution of merchandise. There is a daily computation on the inventory level according to sales and product. The buyers get this information from Warner Lambert; from this information, they decide when to reorder merchandise.

Robert Claypool and Michael Samson are also quite sensitive to direct and indirect costs. They get cost figures weekly from the controller and usually a full day is spent reviewing these data. There is a stronger reaction when costs are out of line than when sales are too low. Area supervisors are required to explain the reasons why certain costs are higher than expected. While few people are fired, allowing direct costs to get out of control is sufficient justification for discharge. We were told about the discharge of the previous controller for this reason. According to Michael Samson, the former controller continually exceeded his departmental budget approximately 15 percent annually. After 6 months in succession at this annual rate, Robert Claypool dismissed him with one week's notice.

The management visualized the Claypool customer as the family who is in the market for either furniture or a major appliance. According to the customer analysis referred to earlier, the average customer is, "white, middle to lower income, has more than four children, is politically conservative, and places a great deal of faith in the Claypool family name." It is to this market that Claypool directs its advertising and merchandising. The effect is a self-fulfilling prophecy: Claypool wants to cater to that customer, and an analysis of its credit customers indicates that it is he who buys at Claypool.

While Claypool's perception of its customer may be clear, there is reason to doubt its accuracy. It is generally accepted that today's customer is more demanding and more sophisticated than a generation ago. This implies that the conservative consumer who is the backbone of Claypool may now be a smaller percentage of the buying public. The focus of the marketing concept disregards most of the younger families whose spending comprises a much larger percentage of their discretionary income. Claypool's reluctance to move into higher fashion items is the result of the older buyers' conviction that conservatively designed and moderately priced merchandise will continue to be profitable for Claypool. Both Robert Claypool and Michael Samson agree. While Claypool was successful with this marketing approach 10 years ago, the continued success of this concept should be questioned. Management has neither redefined its customers nor identified separate marketing segments in the Atlanta-Macon trade area which might easily be captured. While it was difficult for us to measure the difference between the Claypool marketing strategy and that of other furniture and appliance retailers in the area, it was apparent to us that others were placing more emphasis on higher fashion and more expensive items, which appeal to the younger and more discriminating buyer.

Claypool has been plagued with purchasing difficulties during the past several years. The early personal contacts with manufacturers and the resulting favorable contracts have diminished as manufacturers have become larger and more impersonal. Claypool now has less leverage with manufacturers about delivery dates, prices, and reorder flexibility than it had 15 years ago. This circumstance combined with increasing prices has caused Claypool to work with smaller profit margins than is desirable. There is greater uncertainty about the merchandise available, and there is greater difficulty in getting special shipments of loss leaders. As manufacturers are able to produce more products at a single production run, the quantity to be purchased to get special discounts has also risen. In many cases, that quantity has become larger than Claypool could successfully order for a season. For example, the quantity needed to get a discount on a certain line of washing machines has risen from 100 to 500 in the past 3 years. Claypool cannot sell more than 300 of these washers in a year and consequently has had to forego the option of the quantity discount. The quantity discount on a brand name of dining room ensembles has risen from 25 to 100 in the past 3 years. One year ago, Claypool decided to purchase 100 sets in one style to get the discount and at the time of the study had sold only 65 of them. The inventory costs of storing the extra sets had evaporated the quantity discount.

The highly unstable work force has not caused management a great deal of concern. John DuLawrence explained that, "We can continue to hire young girls, married women, and retired men. Since there isn't any cost involved in training, we can benefit by always paying people the minimum wage and having a larger turnover." Robert Claypool felt that people wanted to work at Claypool since they were given discounts on merchandise and were paid "as much as is possible in this area."

Claypool is aware of legislative action only when it has a direct effect on the operation of the stores. An example was the new procedure for reporting and paying state sales tax. The plan was announced in the early part of the 1966 state legislature, passed, and announced to the public in the latter part of the session. Claypool took account of it only when the new directives and forms arrived at the stores. Claypool has taken no initiative regarding recent consumer legislation. They have instead left it to the manufacturers to keep them posted on events which will affect the stores. An example was the recall of certain color television sets last year. When the federal government announced that these sets would be taken off of the market, Claypool waited one week until the manufacturer notified them and arranged for their return. Michael Samson said rather proudly that during that one week Claypool sold four sets. "If we had taken them off the floor and sent them back to the manufacturer we would have been given credit, but this way we made a profit on each set."

Transportation issues which might affect Claypool are also left to the manufacturer. While Claypool might profit from the trend to containerization, piggy-back transports, direct rail service, and other newer transportation methods, it has done nothing about investigating them. Claypool's only concern with transportation is that merchandise is in the warehouse on the date specified. Claypool was more aware of the deliveries to the customer because, as Gordon Goodman said, "That is a direct expense for us and I have control over, and responsibility for, it." At the recommendation of the previously mentioned consultant, the $5 delivery charge was instituted. Gordon Goodman has kept close figures on the comparative cost of renting the delivery trucks versus maintaining a separate fleet. He said that if rental costs increase 18 percent while maintenance costs remain stable, Claypool will change its current policy.

Claypool is acutely aware of competition in the Atlanta-Macon area. Claypool defines its competition as furniture and appliance stores selling similar items. It has not used the broader concept of defining competition as any service or product which competes for the consumers' discretionary dollar. Michael Samson constantly receives information from the professional shoppers about the trends in local furniture and appliance stores. He reviews this information daily, comparing it with current prices and products in the two Claypool stores. When he notices a significant difference in pricing, there is immediate retaliation. For example, one of the competitors lowered its prices on a line of refrigerators on Monday morning and by Monday afternoon Claypool had followed suit. It was intent on "beating" the competition. The price-cut initiative fluctuated back and forth from the competition to Claypool for more than a week, until everyone in Atlanta was selling those refrigerators at less than cost. Finally, the manufacturer threatened to remove the line from the area unless the price war was stopped. Claypool claimed it had "won the war and defeated the enemy."

Buyers also gather information about the competition during the buying seasons. Seldom has Claypool introduced a new style, product, or merchandise without first checking with local competition and personal contacts among buyers in other stores. This awareness of the competition's moves and strategies results in Claypool being a "me-too" store.

The most important foci for Claypool are customers, competition, merchandise, internal sales and financial data, and direct and indirect costs. None of these factors are considered in terms of their long-range implications or in long-range planning. Even though there is a separate department devoted to long-range planning, we could not discover what this department was planning for. According to Edwin Stotts, vice president of long-range planning, his department is currently looking at sites in the Georgia area for a third store. We asked what criteria were being used in finding the site. He said they were just investigating possible sites for Robert Claypool.

Claypool has not initiated new techniques for the past several years. In fact the introduction of the dumbwaiter system of distributing lighter merchandise and the use of a time-sharing system to handle payroll and credit accounts were the only significant innovations in the past 10 years. Meanwhile, there have been a number of new developments in the retailing industry, like public financing of working capital by issuing non-voting stock, establishing computer programs to determine re-order levels in inventory, central distribution centers for merchandise, analysis of financial data from computerized cash register tapes, and so on.

Seldom has Claypool been the first to introduce new merchandise in the Atlanta-Macon trade area. Three years after cartridge tape players became economical to produce and a market was identified, and eighteen months after they had been introduced by other local stores, Claypool included them in the brown goods area. The same slow response was true of infrared ovens, portable color televisions, and color coordinated kitchens. New developments in the furniture industry have been accepted slowly. The most recent development is the use of synthetic materials to replace wood. Since most of the furniture produced with synthetics is more expensive and used in contemporary styles, this advance has had little effect on the merchandising of Claypool furniture.

b. Direction and span of attention (selectivity)

When we asked the employees what Claypool should be doing in the next 5 years, most (72 percent) said that it should be offering more stylish merchandise for the more discriminating buyer. Many times, the employees related, a customer would pass up a product because it was not in the latest style. The area supervisor in the Atlanta small appliance department said that he could, "sell plenty of French related cooking utensils if the store stocked them." He felt that women were more willing to try new cooking techniques which required different utensils. The buyers for his department said there was no profit in selling specialized merchandise because Claypool could not get discount rates on the products.

Energy at Claypool is marshalled into one promotion at a time. Attention is always directed toward the next sale with little attention to a broader conceptual scheme. This constant attention to daily matters may be the result of the lack of planning. Most of the top 13 executives seemed to be going from one crisis to the next. Many times, it appeared to us, these crises could have been avoided if there had been conceptual planning. An example is the failure of the Pot Boutique.

Several foci have been significantly neglected. Of central importance is the lack of awareness and the translation into action of broader marketing trends. The contemporary consumer is more selective, more demanding, more price- and service-conscious, more mobile, less loyal, less willing to accept poor treatment, and less sensitive to advertising claims than the consumer of the past. This has forced the retailer of consumer goods to constantly upgrade his merchandise and to train his employees to handle the more sophisticated customer. Claypool buyers, however, have interpreted these changes in the consumer's behavior to mean that the customer is more interested in bargains than value. As a result, the store has adopted a stance emphasizing many and varied promotions, easy credit, a nonchalant attitude about employees' merchandise knowledge, and the "me-too" merchandising philosophy.

Another important neglected focus is the employees' discontent with conditions at Claypool. Robert Claypool's inability to understand the intensity of the employees' wishes contributes to the high turnover and wide-spread discontent.

Claypool is not aware of the influence that the surrounding neighborhood may have on the success of the Atlanta store. A generation ago customers did not feel as comfortable going into downtown stores in work or casual clothes as they do now, but they did feel comfortable going to Claypool. Now they can go equally comfortably to downtown stores, increasing Claypool's competition. In addition, middle-income families who have moved to the suburbs, are reluctant to come back to the city, and to industrial areas, to shop. The success of the shopping centers and the decay of the inner city attests to this phenomenon. Claypool is located in an industrial section of Atlanta close to the downtown area. The dirt, noise, clutter, and drab surroundings are no longer unimportant factors in consumer behavior. While the environmental signals are subtle, they were sufficiently strong to us to suggest the possibility that the declining profits of the Atlanta store may in part be the result of its location. We can only surmise that the management is not attuned to these stimuli. They did not mention the location of the Atlanta store as a factor in any of their considerations.

In effect, the management of Claypool still believes that an organization which has been run successfully for the past 130 years can continue to be run on those same principles. It has failed to see the significant differences between operating a general store in the early 1900's and operating a large furniture and appliance store in a large metropolitan area in the 1970's. When Colonel Claypool first opened the doors of his general store, he had a captive market. The farmers needed supplies and credit, and he was the only one who would give them both. Subsequently, his name and reputation carried the store. The retail industry in Atlanta has changed significantly, particularly in the past 30 years. There are now numerous merchants who will gladly do for the customer what once only Claypool did, and this will challenge Claypool's position with increasing intensity.

2. Organizational knowledge

a. Acquisition of knowledge

Talents and skills at Claypool are limited. Only a small number of employees have been with the organization long enough to gain knowledge about retailing. The younger members all admit their lack of skills and of knowledge needed to become an integral part of Claypool. Most of the personnel saw themselves as filling slots and doing jobs rather than contributing to Claypool's growth. One woman succinctly verbalized this feeling when she said, "Claypool will continue to grow and expand, but I do not see myself growing with it. My job is to check credit references. No one asks me how I think it can be done better, and I have little idea about what is done with the information once I pass it on."

The largest concentration of talent within the organization is among the buyers. Their long experience and personal contacts create a sense of stability in Claypool merchandising. Their reluctance to explore new products, styles, or trends without their competitors' initial acceptance does not negate the ability of the buyers to judge carefully the profitability of products offered at trade shows. The personal contacts of the buyers and the vice presidents definitely enhance Claypool's marketing talents.

Consultants offer the opportunity for Claypool to also enhance the scope of corporate knowledge. However, the manner in which the consultants are used does not allow for the specialized information they possess to be transmitted through the organization. Because the consultants report directly to Robert Claypool and give their recommendations only to him, the consultants' input is kept from becoming organizational knowledge which can be applied broadly.

The only reservoir of intellectual talent through affiliations with universities is the seminars Robert Claypool attends at the local colleges. However, this opportunity is not fully utilized since the information and skills Robert Claypool gains are not transmitted to others. There are no library facilities at Claypool.

The management does not see knowledge as something which can be used in the management of a retail organization. This results in an implicit norm forbidding the use of textbook knowledge. The people who do use what is available to Claypool are the buyers and Robert Claypool and Michael Samson. They are always aware of the actions of the local competition, and they try to understand the implications of these actions to determine what possible course Claypool should take. Employees were uncomfortable about their own lack of knowledge. The sales force is easily stimulated by new knowledge, as indicated by their attendance at area meetings in the stores conducted infrequently by product representatives. While we were at the Macon store, one of the product representatives for a major furniture line held a short session explaining the positive features of the new fabrics being used in the furniture. For the next week, we observed salespeople telling almost every customer who would listen about the positive features of the newly introduced fabrics. According to the area supervisor in the living room ensembles, sales for that particular line of furniture during the ensuing week were 40 per cent higher than the previous week.

Much of Claypool's success can be traced to the astute merchandising skills of Robert Claypool II and Robert Claypool III. However, this appeared to be the only depth of knowledge at Claypool. The level and range of organizational knowledge is severely limited. Cost control is not systematized, personnel practices are elementary, marketing and financial sophistication is lacking, and environmental awareness is limited to credit customers and competition. While Gordon Goodman has a firm grasp of the economics of owning or leasing a fleet of delivery trucks, this expense is minuscule in comparison with the rest of the income statement. The level of knowledge is virtually the same among all of the 11 vice presidents. Because they are frequently talking together about specific problems, there is a cross-fertilization of experience, but it is limited to current problems, with little emphasis on balancing the situation against historical perspectives. As a result, all the vice presidents know a little about everyone's problems, and none of them know much about any one particular problem or area.

Claypool executives do not think much about new concepts. The norm of not using textbook knowledge suppresses most creative thought and innovative action. Since the greatest component of organizational knowledge is the experience and historical perspective of specific individuals and since there are no formal mechanisms for distributing this individualized information to others, each person becomes self-centered in his conceptualization and use of information and knowledge. One of the greater strengths is the vast experience that the buyers, vice presidents, and department managers possess. However, this experience is used for pragmatic solutions to everyday crises and to stifle the introduction of other possibilities or alternative modes of action.

b. Use of knowledge

Claypool has no process for using concrete knowledge and information from which to abstract more conceptual alternatives. After having to close the Pot Boutique the executives did not consider the implications of the failure nor did they attempt to understand why it failed. The customary reactions to such events reported to us by the executives were, "It was _____'s fault. If he would have done something else it would not have happened." The person at fault on different occasions was seldom the same one, and the "something" he "should have done" changed with each person interviewed.

The three formalized committees, the representative council, the executive committee and the Wednesday coffee session are designed to pass information from Robert Claypool and Michael Samson to others in the most expedient fashion. Seldom is there discussion, however; usually there are presentations of reports by various vice presidents and of decisions by Claypool and Samson. The executive committee meeting is the only place where there could be some integration of corporate knowledge about merchandise, pricing policy, promotions, and profitability, but it is not used for that purpose.

Factual information is hard to obtain. Financial information is closely guarded by Anthony Robertson and Scott Gordon, at Robert Claypool's direction. The only information available to an employee is that for which he is responsible. Individual salesmen know their own sales totals, area supervisors in the sales areas know their own area sales, area supervisors in the distribution sections know what they alone handled. The same is true of salary schedules. Each person is told only his own salary. Supervisors do not know the salaries of specific people in their department but know the level of pay within the department. Only three people have access to the total salary schedule: John DuLawrence, Robert Claypool, and Michael Samson.

Accuracy in three areas — sales inventory, salaries, and profits-expenses — are of vital importance to Claypool and Samson. Most people, however, did not know what the total sales were and could not even give a "ball park" figure. The same was true of inventory, profits, and expenses. People were, however, well aware of the salary schedule and were usually quite accurate in their assumptions about others' salaries.

There are areas where no accurate information exists. Internal shrinkage, personnel records, promotions, noncredit customer demographics, and environmental data are examples of areas in which Claypool either lacks data or uses insufficient and inaccurate data.

A potential medium for communicating knowledge is the "Thoughts from the Colonel." The shallow treatment of the employees (reporting only new employees, marriages, births, and retirements) and the shallow articles on industry happenings, as contrasted with the systematic accuracy of financial data, reflect the relative importance of these two matters to the management. Making money is the central concern of Claypool and Samson.

What little formalized knowledge there is at Claypool is centered within individuals. Only Robert Claypool and Michael Samson have a total view of the corporate history, and they seemed unwilling to communicate it to others. When we asked Samson to describe the history of Claypool and to tell us how it got to the point it was at the time of the study, he said, "What do you need to know that for? Bob's grandfather started the company in 1868, and with a lot of hard work here we are." When we asked him to elaborate on this he said, "The Colonel started with farm equipment and now we sell furniture and appliances. Don't you have any more important questions?" Robert Claypool was the only person who provided any sense of the historical development of Claypool, as others had little knowledge about the past.

Claypool's ability to deal with abstract problems is the ability of Robert Claypool and Michael Samson to deal with abstract problems. The Claypool management is composed of men with long histories of retailing experience. They are accustomed to dealing with problems pragmatically and concretely and not stopping to conceptualize issues or problems. The result of many years of such "hard-nosed" thinking has limited the ability of the management to step back and contemplate the position of Claypool among its competitors, in Atlanta, in Georgia, and in the nation. They are further prevented from this exercise by the limits placed on them by Claypool and Samson. Even if they were capable of conceptualizing their work, the company, and the issues, potential action would be tightly constrained by the management style.

Flexibility is limited to merchandising and promotions. As indicated in their responses to market conditions, Michael Samson and Robert Claypool have shown considerable flexibility in merchandising and promotions during the last 15 years. Because of the narrow scope of their jobs, employees have little flexibility in the manner in which they perform them. Salespeople must be on the floor to sell, and they must follow established rules and procedures. Stock people have simple jobs and therefore have little flexibility in their performance. Support people usually have work in such detail that flexibility is circumscribed by necessity. Area supervisors, department managers, buyers, and store managers have little flexibility because of the insecurity resulting from the vague procedures and policies.

In summary then, Samson and Claypool are alert, quick, intelligent and aggressive. Both men have college degrees and have proven themselves to be effective retailers. Both have the capacity to conceptualize and the flexibility to adapt to many competitive situations. They tend to ignore the former capacity and to concentrate on action. Under stress, both men intensify their characteristic controlling ways of behaving. As previously indicated, when one of the departments was steadily losing significant volume without adequate explanation, Samson virtually took over the department and pushed the area supervisors aside until the problem could be located.

Both men are highly secretive about information and knowledge. They are concerned more with making money than with how they make money or where their money-making efforts lead the organization. Both men are factual and pragmatic and are obsessed with performance and results.

The characteristic style of management does not allow for kinds of thoughts which might not produce an immediate profit. Their orientation is therefore short term.

c. Dissemination of knowledge

There are no formal mechanisms for integrating knowledge into the Claypool organization. Minutes of meetings are not written, distributed, or filed. Verbal agreement is reached on a plan of action with frequent checking and rechecking by Claypool and Samson. Most knowledge is distributed orally to those who need the information.

The previously mentioned method of passing information from the buyers to the proper executives is an example of the inadequate dissemination of knowledge. Once the buyer translates the order into product numbers and prices, those symbols are used subsequently. Consequently, only the buyers, Warner Lambert, and Michael Samson have a complete knowledge of what styles are being purchased.

The only formalized reports deal with sales data, inventory levels, and direct and indirect costs. Robert Claypool and Michael Samson are the only ones who see the complete reports; only specific portions of each report are sent to the various vice presidents and departments. For example, the area supervisor will receive a weekly report on the sales in his area. There is no mention of costs or profits. The area supervisor for the third-floor stock room will receive a weekly report on the merchandise he should have and the amount of merchandise that passed through his department.

3. Organizational language

Because there is not much written material in the organization, it is difficult to speak about organizational language. Written materials available to the employees are: "Thoughts from the Colonel," occasional memos from Robert Claypool about policy in an unusual situation (major illness while on the job, natural catastrophe, inappropriate behavior of customers), and letters explaining special situations (for example, for the purpose of explaining about this study and giving the names of the task-force members).

A memo spelling out Claypool's policy about natural catastrophe was representative of others we read. The opening sentences were, "Claypool must remember that the customer always comes first no matter what is happening to the stores. Therefore, this memo will describe what employees will do if a natural catastrophe occurs. The employees must follow these directives if Claypool is to remain first in the thoughts of the customer (our bread and butter)."

In effect, Claypool was telling the employees that what is most important to Robert Claypool and Michael Samson, that is, the organization, is making money. The language of the memo conveys to the employees the concepts that they must sacrifice for the customers and that Claypool considers the employees to be less important than the customers. It indicates further that the Claypool management manipulates its employees' guilt feelings to do "what is right." The language also suggests that Claypool rationalizes its self-interest in profit by continually referring to the desires of the customers rather than to the needs of the organization.

There is another dimension to Claypool's organizational language. Retailing has a special language, Claypool is no exception. Words such as "discounts," "mark-ups," "mark-downs," "margins," "variances," "year-to-date figures," "promotions," "credit terms," and so forth, are commonly used terms outside of retailing but carry important impact within the industry. The special language revolves around definiteness, numbers, performance, measurements, and nonpersonal attributes. At Claypool customers are referred to in general and in sweeping terms, markets are never clearly defined, and merchandise is usually referred to by product number and price rather than description. Products, by themselves, do not have a separate identity. Neither do the customers or employees. While the "verbal shorthand" is useful to the executives when discussing merchandise, it illustrates the lack of depth, range, and feeling about the essence of retailing, "customer differentiated products sold by people to people." Such differentiation cannot be made in the usual mass volume discount store, but Claypool tries to maintain it by product identification and personal service. Therein lies an important conflict: to be a traditional retailer or a discounter.

Claypool's advertising philosophy is the antithesis of Teddy Roosevelt's dictum: "Speak loudly enough and you don't have to carry a stick at all." As was previously mentioned, most of the advertising is hard-sell–price advertising. The two major advertising themes are: (1) The consumer will save more money and will get brand name merchandise if he shops at Claypool; (2) Claypool really cares about the customer and will do anything for him. Claypool is not doing either very well. Prices were not the lowest in the Atlanta-Macon area, and customer service is less than advertised. In addition, these two themes are contradictory. While it is to be expected that advertising will present an image of the store as the management would like to see it, Claypool's advertising themes lead to the conclusion that there is a distinct difference between what it says it is and what it actually is.

The tone of the advertising implies that the consumer is not sensitive to price or quality unless he shops at Claypool. This tone is a distortion of Colonel Claypool's original theme: "This is the only place in Atlanta where you can buy your tools on credit." While the Colonel's statement was true, using the same tone today suggests that the customer knows no better.

The subtle manipulation in the advertising themes is reflected in Claypool's slogan and symbol. The slogan, "Claypool Cares — Easy Credit, Easy Prices," suggests that Claypool can be equally generous to all people. This manipulative paternalism is carried through in the symbol, a pen and ink drawing of the Colonel. The gentle mein of the Colonel implies that whatever the customer's problems, the store will be able to accommodate him.

4. Emotional atmosphere of the organization

There are two levels to the emotional atmosphere of the organization. While top management dash from crisis to crisis in a hyperactive manner, the rest of the personnel were rather depressed. The range of feelings among the personnel is limited. There is little humor, laughter, or relief from the problems as seen by the personnel. The prevailing mood seemed to be a combination of anger, apathy, confusion, and depression. The emotional range of the top management is also limited as they flit from one urgent problem to the next. There is little time for laughter, contemplation, or supporting each other. There is time only to answer the phone, meet with representatives, solve current problems, order merchandise, keep in touch with the competition, and remain on top of customer complaints.

We observed the anger of the personnel when they spoke about low wages, lack of opportunity for advancement, lack of training, and the occasionally capricious manner of supervisors. Employees were apathetic when they talked about their chances to learn and grow with Claypool. They were apathetic as they described the probability of change. They were most apathetic when they implied that there was nothing they could do except stay or leave. One of the clerks in the accounting department said, "It really doesn't make any difference whether I get involved in my job and the department, Claypool is not going to change its way of treating employees. I guess that leaves me with two choices: I can stay and try to live with the situation, or I can leave and find another job."

We observed the employees' confusion in two ways. People were not sure what to do, how to do it, and how they should behave while they did it. Policies and procedures appeared to them to be the whims of Robert Claypool or Michael Samson. There was nothing the immediate area supervisor could do to help or clarify. Another form of confusion was the disorientation described by the newer employees. Even if there were no questions about policies and procedures, the newer employees talked about the confusion of starting a job with little guidance about what to expect and what was expected of them. One of the stock personnel on the third floor in Atlanta said, "For the first week I walked around in a daze just looking at all of those brown boxes with no names on them. It wasn't until one of the guys started to show me where things were that I knew what I was supposed to be doing."

Depression was reflected in comments like, "When I came here I was all jazzed up to do a good job. Now it doesn't make much difference." "How can I get excited about selling more brown goods when I can't even find out if I'm doing a good job?" "Maybe we [the sales force] aren't as good as we think we are. I'm sure that if we were any good, we would be paid more." "I tried to talk with my supervisor [the Atlanta third-floor stock room] about a better way of handling lamps, and he told me that he couldn't do anything about it. Maybe the idea wasn't any good, maybe he didn't care about listening to me, maybe he couldn't do anything about it; I don't know."

The depression of the employees has been misinterpreted by Robert Claypool and Michael Samson. While they were aware of these feelings, they said this was the reaction they wanted. As long as the employees did not know about the organization or where they stood, they could not be considered a problem. The implication is if the employees are kept in ignorance, they can be controlled.

The atmosphere in the executive suite is considerably different from that of the other personnel. The climate of frenzied activity changes very little from day-to-day: there did not seem to be any relief.

Employee dissatisfaction is of long standing. In interviews, people said that "things have gotten worse in the last 5 years." Since the opening of the Macon store and the increase in number of personnel, the individual treatment by superiors which used to characterize Claypool is no longer present. The same 5-year span is cited by the executives as the time when they became overworked and harried.

As competition has increased and prices have risen and margins have declined and demands for more sophistication and knowledge about merchandise have increased, the loyalty of the personnel has decreased. While Claypool's pressures and problems seem to be on an upward crest, the morale, loyalty, attitudes, and devotion of the employee is the lowest it has ever been, according to most of the vice presidents.

These feelings are appropriate to the Claypool management style and the actions of Robert Claypool and Michael Samson. As they continue to overcontrol and operate the entire organization, the pressures they face increase. This causes them to put more pressure on their subordinates (the vice presidents) for performance and results while not delegating the authority to manage performance responsibly. This mode of operation is passed down through the hierarchical structure until the employees are faced with insurmountable problems with little support or guidance from the area supervisors, department managers, store managers, or vice presidents.

The moods and tones vary from department to department. The amount of confusion, we found, was directly related to the amount of customer contact and the length of employment. The newer members of the sales force were most confused, followed by the newer people working at the cash register stand. People in the credit department who have only occasional contacts with the customers showed less confusion about their jobs and about Claypool than did the sales force. The least confusion shown was in the warehouses where customer contact is minimal. The same intensity of anger and apathy was observed in all departments. The depression was pervasive.

5. Organizational action

The energy of the Claypool management is channeled in four directions: (1) staying alert to what the immediate competition is doing; (2) adjusting internal merchandising structure to reflect competitive trends; (3) controlling the personnel; and (4) continuing to tell the customers about the virtues of Claypool. These four directions require constant monitoring by Robert Claypool and Michael Samson and go on at a level pace throughout the year. For the employees as a whole, as previously mentioned, the peak expenditure of energy is during the Christmas season. Extra sales and support people are hired for this season, and the warehouses and stock rooms are filled with merchandise. Other than that, there is little to distinguish this season from the rest in terms of energy expenditure. People continue to work their normal schedules, accounts are processed at the same rate, and other procedures are kept constant.

The lack of management sophistication and conceptualization results in an inability to confront issues directly and with precision. Three examples previously cited are: (1) the inability to fully understand the recommendations of the CPA firm which examined the organization's credit posture; (2) the indirect and imprecise manner in which Claypool and DuLawrence talk with the representative council; (3) the lack of precision in the definition of competition and the strategies which could be utilized in attacking the various segments of the marketplace. When indirectness and imprecision is combined with the management style of daily crisis resolution, the depth, range, consistency, and scope of a problem are never examined. Therefore, it is difficult for the organization to confront industry, local, and internal problems rationally and realistically.

Indications of future problems became apparent 5 years ago with the opening of the Macon store. The personnel was increased but the management team was kept constant; the sales increased but the methods of handling the paper flow were not changed; products were becoming more sophisticated and difficult to differentiate and customers were becoming more demanding of the retail industry, yet Claypool made no specific plans to meet these issues. Claypool keeps plodding along at the industry pace or slower, while customer demands are increasing exponentially. While the recent decline in profits is representative of the entire retail industry, the steeper decline of Claypool is considerably more than the regional averages.

Claypool's inability to keep in step with the increasing number of issues is, also, in part, a reflection of its lack of planning and timing. Claypool is in the position of having things happen to it rather than acting upon them. The basis for action is prodding — perhaps, the discovery that the competition is doing something different or that manufacturers are producing something different. Salaries are changed only under pressure from the competition. Benefits are offered only when others offer them first. Procedures are instituted only when they are tried and found true in other organizations. Promotions are usually granted only when the person threatens to leave and work for the competition. Perhaps the only recent organizational initiative was the installation of the dumbwaiter system of delivering goods. Although none of the other furniture and appliance stores in the Atlanta-Macon area are using the system, the task force was familiar with other companies which used similar devices to transport merchandise.

Claypool's plodding nature suggests a persistency in its action. However, the persistence in adhering to more conservative styles of merchandise, antiquated methods of handling the paper flow, and the simplistic method of dealing with employees is likely to be destructive.

Historically, Claypool has been a very effective retailer. It took bold, initiative, and aggressive action to grow from a small general store into the million dollar operation of 1969. However, recent events, trends, and issues have begun to take their toll. Claypool's reputation probably has carried it for the past several years, but the present performance is starting to erode customer loyalty and employee satisfaction.

Considered in the context of the past 5 years, Claypool's actions have had a short-term holding effect with longer range destructive effects. The failure to train employees, the continual emphasis on conservatively styled merchandise, and the disregard of consumer trends, is starting to have negative effects and will become increasingly destructive unless reversed.

B. Attitudes and Relationships

1. Contemporary attitudes toward, and relationships with, others

a. Range, diversification, depth, and constancy

Claypool management directs almost all of its manifest affection toward the customer, especially the credit customer. While it would seem normal for a retail organization to cherish its clientele, Claypool extends itself at the expense of other relationships. The philosophy of placing the customer first was one of the major components of its earlier success; however, that same philosophy now has another implication. The employees are angry about the management-forced attention toward the customer without concomitant attention to, and support for, the employees.

The anger was apparent when we asked the employees about the relationship of the store to its customers. The immediate reply was usually, "The store will go out of its way to please the customers." When we asked them how this made them feel, there was usually a hesitation, and then the reply, "Well, sometimes I think they pay too much attention to the customers and not enough to us." Several employees volunteered that the preferential treatment made them angry.

There is a significant difference between the treatment accorded the credit customer and that to the cash customer. Credit customers are sampled periodically to determine their feelings about purchased merchandise. They also receive information about special sales and forthcoming promotions before cash customers do. Cash customers are relatively neglected. While the stores are equally considerate of them when they are shopping, once the purchase is made, there is no method of tapping them for market data or to maintain communications with them.

Relationships with the competition are the obverse of those with the customer. Claypool (especially Robert Claypool and Michael Samson) sees the local furniture and appliance dealers as a hostile force in the marketplace threatening Claypool's survival. Several times either Claypool or Samson referred to the local competition as "setting their prices to directly attack and destroy us." Samson continually monitors the competition via the professional shoppers. He has an obsession about the competition's operations in the Atlanta-Macon area. Claypool reacts to competition quickly. The best example was the price war over refrigerators referred to earlier. The feelings about the "enemy" run deep and are intense.

Claypool sees its employees as being hired to do a specific job for a specific amount of money. Employees are not supposed to make demands on the organization because the organization is, "doing everything we can to raise salaries, improve conditions, and solve problems."

The employees are seen by the management as being thieves, capricious, noncaring, and petulant. Most of the top management believe that the employees must be controlled and forced to work. Both Robert III and Samson believe that the supervisors can be trusted to carry out the directives, policies, and procedures without tight control from the top. However, the supervisors are not to be trusted with formulation of the above. Michael Samson said, "If we let them decide what they want to do, they will start to build empires, and we will lose the cohesiveness of the organization." Claypool people are seen as being basically ignorant ("If they aren't, why are they working here?" asked John DuLawrence) and incapable of holding another job without considerable training and education.

Robert III and Samson see the middle management (department managers, store managers, and buyers) as being faithful, loyal, and sincere in their desires to work effectively for Claypool. However, this is tempered in that both men believe that the middle management needs constant guidance and direction in order to function. They do not allow middle managers to make individual decisions which might affect the profits of the organization. All such decisions must be cleared through either Claypool or Samson.

The Claypool attitude toward trade associations and representatives is to believe that by not noticing them they might go away. This is especially true of unions for the sales force, the stock personnel, and the clerks. It was difficult for the task force to understand why a union had not organized the sales force at Claypool. John DuLawrence said that the people did not want a union and had never even voted on the question. Because of the strong dissatisfactions voiced by the employees, we did not understand DuLawrence's reasoning. Robert Claypool expressed his feelings about trade associations when he said, "I really don't think they can help us. They don't know the problems we face, and I don't want someone from the outside telling me how to run my business."

Since Robert Claypool controls 93 percent of the Claypool stock, he is answerable only to himself. Members of the board of directors own about 2 percent of the outstanding stock. They are a rubber-stamp board composed of members of the Claypool family and close personal friends. The remaining 5 percent is held by the pension fund, which is controlled by Robert Claypool. While this has allowed him the freedom to act as he wished, it has not provided him checks and balances which might have been useful. The board of directors does not have full access to the records. Reports of the final consolidated figures are submitted to the board annually. And, according to Robert Claypool, it agrees that the year was the best, given the circumstances. There is seldom any question about the operations of the stores or the management philosophy voiced by the board.

The same attitude was expressed about legislative and regulatory bodies. Samson felt that Claypool should not be encumbered with governmental agencies regulating and legislating about the retail industry.

An important factor in Claypool's development was the close personal relationships the successive Claypools had with local furniture manufacturers. In later years the organization evolved the technique of polling retailers across the country to arrive at the best prices and then manipulating the manufacturers to match them. This strategy has become less effective because many of the manufacturers are demanding larger orders before granting discounts; and the number of personal contacts is declining as individuals retire, die, or otherwise leave their companies. Claypool has been able to maintain a close personal tie with two local manufacturers (one of rugs and the other of furniture). The other relationships vary from personal contacts who are not able to offer better prices, to impersonal, strictly business relationships. Claypool management sees the suppliers as the key to the success of the stores. It continues to pressure the manufacturers about prices, delivery dates, and special promotions.

The manipulative methods used previously are still being attempted, however, with little success. Most of the suppliers Claypool deals with are not closely dependent upon the Claypool outlets for distribution and therefore can afford not to be manipulated into unfavorable and unprofitable contracts.

Claypool's relationship with the financial community has been limited. The line of credit which is used to carry inventory balances is financed with a local bank. Claypool visualizes this relationship as one-sided ("The bank lends us money when we need it"). Robert Claypool or Scott Gordon have not utilized the special knowledge and skills of the local banker to determine cash requirements, payment procedures, or any fiduciary activities. Claypool has tried to remain independent.

In past years, Atlanta looked quite favorably on Claypool Furniture and Appliances as the logical extension of the Claypool family. At times it was difficult to separate the two entities. The family originally staged the Debutantes' Ball, and it was later run by the store. The activities of the colonel and his son were closely related to the position they held in the store and in the community. The gifts, legacies, and guidance they generously offered to the community were needed and appreciated. In the past 5 years, Robert Claypool III has been less active in the Atlanta-Macon communities than he had previously been. During the early 1960's, he was an active spokesman for fair and equitable integration in the South. While he still contributes money, he no longer devotes himself to the movements as he once did.

The Claypool organization now does very little for the communities it serves. Only support of the Little League was apparent. Few of the management (3) belong to local civic groups, and they are not active. Seldom has anyone from the stores spoken out on issues confronting the communities. In effect, Claypool has become an island in the midst of Atlanta and Macon, drawing on the consumer but not reciprocating in the community.

Employees see consultants with a jaundiced eye. Each time a consultant is employed, employees are led to expect that conditions will improve for them and they have been disillusioned several times. Therefore, during the orientation phase of this study, there were many questions about the actions management would take after the study was finished. Many of the employees viewed us as hatchet men for Robert Claypool, many viewed us as spies, and many viewed us as irrelevant because we were not retailers.

Robert Claypool uses consultants to gain information about methods of cutting costs and increasing profits. Seldom is the exercise seen as an educational one in which both management and consultants can learn from the association. Rather it is viewed as a "milking" process to cull the secrets from the consultant. Seldom is a consultant retained to implement recommendations or called for further consultation.

b. Major attachments

The major attachment for Claypool is the customer. Catering to the customer's wishes is the central focus of management activity. Just as the competition is an obsession with Michael Samson, so the customer is with Robert Claypool. Claypool continues to feel that if the customer is able to buy merchandise at competitive prices on easy credit terms, the success of the organization is assured.

The major negative attachment is the competition. While alertness to competition is necessary, we felt that Claypool devoted too much energy to the competition (they frequently know more about another store than they do about their own). The result is the "me-too" stance and the inability of Claypool to act until the competition makes a move.

c. Masculine-feminine orientation

Claypool is a hard, assertive organization. It asserts in its advertisements that it can offer lowest prices and quality service. It manipulates its employees for the satisfaction of the management and customers. It is housed in large, functional buildings, with relatively unattractive floor plans and few services for employees. It competes aggressively. Claypool's secrecy about financial and other details is consistent with the masculine emphasis on control. [Correspondingly, the vagueness about job definition, product knowledge, responsibility, and supervision reflect the lack of consideration for employees.]

d. Transference phenomena

The quiet attitude we first observed in the employees during the initial visit was not the Southern reserve we first thought. As the study progressed, the task force noted that the employees were silent for other reasons: doubt, fear, distrust. The employees didn't trust us to report their feelings to management because, "They won't believe you." Most felt we were there to judge them and their company. A common statement was, "You're going to tell us how bad we are, aren't you?"

Michael Samson, Robert Claypool, and the vice presidents also saw us as judges. They tried to withhold information and to evade questions, as evidenced by our difficulty in obtaining accurate financial data and Michael Samson's sketchy historical information. Only after confronting each person with the necessity of having valid information did they yield. Many of the executives also mentioned that they were afraid we would find out how incompetent they really were.

The silence, the fear of being judged incompetent, the mistrust, and the withholding of critical information all suggest that the Claypool people saw us in the image of an authoritarian father demanding too much from his children, who are unable to produce and can only passively object.

2. Relations to things and ideas

a. Quality and intensity of relations to plant, equipment, raw materials or supplies, product, and services

As noted earlier, employees see the management as not caring, as being unconcerned about personnel problems, and as being unwilling to teach and to minister to their needs. These reflect a perception of the management akin to a child's view of a bad, unloving parent.

The management sees the employees, as we have mentioned, as lazy, stupid, and basically ignorant. They see the employees as taking advantage of the company, as thieves, as threats to the survival of the organization. These all suggest a parent's view of a hostile, delinquent child.

The "children" are not much involved with each other. Many times an employee would say, "We're [all the employees] in this together." However, this perceived togetherness refers to having to band together to defend against the "bad parent," rather than banding together for a common purpose. Whenever there is criticism of one of the children, the child usually blames another child for the mistake. The issue of the stock-out problem and the manner in which it is resolved is a good example of this displacement.

The organization is afraid of being exposed (clearly seen in the manner in which they related to the consultant), afraid of outsiders viewing them critically, and afraid of the competition.

Most of the employees view the buildings as "functional." There were no psychological attachments to the buildings, not even the one in Atlanta with its historical significance to Claypool. The vice presidents see the buildings as something to be "used," and little attention is paid to design, form, style, or aesthestics.

The employees are not identified with the products or with the services. Since so few of them have a good working knowledge of the products, it is difficult for them to see themselves as masters of the products. As far as the stores are concerned, products are merely means to make money. There is nothing in the products themselves which distinguishes them meaningfully from each other for the management except their ability to produce revenues for the organization.

The Claypool management unconsciously sees Claypool in the image of the colonel as an aggressive businessman. The reluctance to change, the effort to maintain the status quo in procedures and attitudes is evidence of this feeling.

When we asked the employees to personify Claypool, only a few were able to do so. The responses ranged from, "a kindly old gentleman who tries to please his children, but can't" to "a young kid showing the other kids how tough he is." They have no clearly defined image, reflecting their minimal attachment to the organization.

b. Time: how is it regarded

The older employees live in the past, when relationships were simpler, customers easier to please, and demands more manageable. Most of the older employees spoke about the "good old days" when the store managers knew everyone by his first name and spent considerable time on the floor talking with employees. The newer employees were not concerned with the past and had little vision about the future. They were oriented to the daily work cycle.

Executives spoke of the past only when they mentioned past sales, promotions, and certain lines of merchandise. They see the past as a reservoir out of which to draw previous accomplishments for gratification. The future is seen only in terms of what to offer the customer in the next six months. As one of the older executives told us, "Yesterday and tomorrow don't mean anything to us; today is where the action is. If we don't please the customer today, she won't be here tomorrow to worry about."

As was previously mentioned, Claypool does not systematically plan for the future. Budgets are estimated for 1 year in advance, but the 6 months' figures are the ones used; projections for merchandise are 6 months in advance; manpower planning is nonexistent except for the daily operations; and capital expansion is disregarded until the need is urgent. This lack of emphasis on the future has resulted in Claypool having to deal with problems on a day-to-day basis, which might have been avoided if some contingency or formal plans were formulated.

Time is not seen as an investable commodity. Most of the people at Claypool see themselves as waiting for the customer to come to them (this is even true of those not directly associated with the customer, like the stock people and the support people). As a result, time is to be spent or put in. We frequently heard, "I put in my 8 hours today, what else do they expect of me?" Or, "I spent 4 hours looking for that mistake and my supervisor didn't even thank me for the time."

c. Space: how is it conceptualized

Space is of local concern. Space is translated into dollars in the form of amount of merchandise per foot. The more merchandise that can be stacked on the floors, the more that can possibly be sold. The "supermarket" syndrome is apparent. There is little concern for the use of space aesthetically. Employee and customer comfort or convenience are not considered in the floor plans. Only the absolute minimum amount of nonselling and nonstorage space is available. Individual needs for space are subordinated to the organizational needs for profit.

d. Meaning of work for the organization

Claypool's employees see their work as a means of subsistence, not as a device for growth, development, power, authority, or respect. A large percentage (almost half) of the employees work part time, and many of these have other full-time jobs. Their reasons for working are: to supplement the basic family income; to pay for extraordinary expenses like medical bills, college expense, and newer cars; or to take advantage of the employees' discount. Part-time people who do not have full-time jobs talked about working to pay for their schooling, to supplement their husbands' income, or to earn their own pocket money. Few people we talked with came to Claypool to learn a skill, a trade, or to prepare themselves for other jobs. Only a few of the younger employees mentioned coming to Claypool for the retail experience they would gain which could be used after they had graduated from school. Those people who work full-time for Claypool also see their jobs as a device for making a living.

The employees do not see themselves as being a part of Claypool. The earlier mentioned comment by one of the employees about not growing with Claypool is indicative of this feeling. While they do not see themselves becoming an integral part of Claypool, the results of the questionnaire indicate that they expect the organization to allow them to learn, to grow, to develop, to master their job and environment, and to gain respect. However, because of the limited scope of each job, it is difficult for an individual to aspire to or realize a future with Claypool. Therefore, work has little meaning to employees with regard to the mastery of their environment. The employees have many expectations about Claypool's responsibilities to them, but they do not anticipate that their expectations will be fulfilled.

The executives see their work in two economic ways. Most of them mentioned the enjoyment they received from being associated with the largest furniture-appliance retailer in the Atlanta-Macon area. There were many references to the largest volume sales, the largest amount of advertising, the most floor space devoted to selling, and other comparisons with the competition.

The second part of the economic meaning of work for the executives is the large salaries and generous fringe benefits they enjoy. Most of the newer executives mentioned that they were initially attracted to Claypool because of the compensation.

While Robert Claypool senses the civic responsibility which accompanies his company's position, few of the other executives see Claypool as having a debt to, or being responsible to, the community.

Work has little meaning to the people of Claypool in terms of thinking. Claypool does not value thinking as a manner of enriching the organization or increasing its ability to operate efficiently in the environment.

Because so few Claypool people have an investment in the organization, it is difficult for them to use the work as a defense against the environment or against their own feelings. However, working on the sales floor allows them to meet customers, which might be a defense against loneliness or the provocation to aggression at home because several said they came to work to "get out of the house."

Presumably, employees come to retail organizations because of the wish to satisfy other people's wants and desires for material things, in short the need to please. Management talks about "serving" the customer, "taking care of the customer's wishes," the customer "always being right," and "we're here to please the customers." Selling and pleasing customers is an effective way for many to channel aggression into socially necessary tasks, to gratify dependency needs and, at least for executives, to fulfill ego ideals of competence and mastery in a competitive world.

The Claypool psychological contract is composed of management's sense of obligation to its employees and the employees' expectations about management and the organization. Implicitly management assumes employees will do as they are told, willingly and with gratitude for the pay check. Management also expects the employees to satisfy the customers' wishes while at the same time making money for the organization. They expect the employee to follow the rules, regulations, policies and procedures management has established. In short, they expect the employees to be good children, that is, seen but not heard.

Employees' expectations relate more to the supportive and nurturant functions of the organization. The questionnaire results pointed out the gap between how the people see the organization and how they would like it to be. They clearly felt that Claypool should, and does not, more completely support them and help them grow in stature and become more competent. They expect the organization to take care of them, as many other organizations care for their employees; they expect the organization to help them master their own environments and their jobs, and they expect the organization to help them become increasingly useful to Claypool. In effect, the employees feel that Claypool should be a better "father." The "father" should love, care for, nurture, teach, guide, direct, and counsel his children. However, as previously cited, while the employees have these expectations of Claypool they also do not expect Claypool to respond to the implicit demands. This makes for chronic disappointment.

Both Robert Claypool and Michael Samson talk about directing the organizational energy to capturing a larger share of the furniture and appliance market in the Atlanta-Macon area. They also talk about becoming more important retailers (which to them means becoming more profitable). They say the only way to increase their market share is by decreasing the competition's share. When they talk about share of market, most of the time they mean "more customers," rather than a percentage of the customers in the Atlanta-Macon trade area. They conceive of the furniture and appliance market as static, growing only with the increase in population. Therefore, the finite numbers of customers to be had must be divided among the local merchants. Since Robert Claypool and Michael Samson do not see the furniture and appliance market as a segment of the disposable income market, that blind spot interferes with their thinking about alternatives. For example, when there are discussions about reorder quantities of certain lines of furniture, the attitude is, "How do we get the competition's customers to buy this item but at our store?" rather than one of, "How can we get the customer who has the extra money, and who may spend it on something else, to come to Claypool and buy our merchandise?" We have already discussed the dissipation of employee energy. In short energy is not fully utilized.

We did not observe regression at the work place on the part of either employees or management. This is true, we believe, partly because the atmosphere dampens humor, teasing, witticisms, and other forms of play. As we saw them, the employees were deadly serious people.

e. Authority, power, and responsibility

Claypool does not see others as having inordinate power over their operations. Although a union could be disruptive, manufacturers could affect its survival, and loss of financial backing would be disastrous, Claypool fears none of these possibilities with the intensity with which it fears competition.

Power within the organization, as previously mentioned, rests with Michael Samson and Robert Claypool. Others have power to direct operations only with the explicit consent of either Claypool or Samson. Their power is total and complete as they answer to no one except themselves and are responsible only to the weak Board of Directors.

Claypool does not project any authority in the retail industry. Rather, the reverse is true. By continually checking with others throughout the industry prior to making a merchandising move, Claypool has vitiated any authority inherent in its being the largest furniture-appliance retailer in the Atlanta-Macon area. Claypool is not sought out for ideas, leadership, or consensus about issues facing the retail industry. However, because of its sheer size, it does exert considerable pressure on the retail prices of furniture and appliances in its trade area. Claypool sees its power-authority as being severely regulated by the manufacturers who will withdraw merchandise if "improperly" handled. Therefore, the one stick which they could wield most effectively and comfortably, has been whittled down to an unusable size by those who hold the ultimate power over them. Its power over its employees is limited, its power over the competition is regulated, and its power over the manufacturer is diminishing.

3. Attitudes about self

Claypool's employees see themselves as being underpaid, oversupervised, locked into position with no room for growth, visibly ignorant about their job requirements and products, unheard, and considered to be second-class citizens in relationship to customers. Many think of themselves as pawns for the management and as having little or no control over their circumstances. Most do not enjoy the self-image they conjure up, but they accept their lot because they need the money. As one of the stock personnel said, "Even though I'm treated like a dog, this job pays more than welfare, and that's all I had before." Many said that they had not realized what the situation was really like until they had come to work, and many are looking around for other jobs. Some felt resigned to their positions. They realized that things were not good but said, "I don't know if I could expect any better anywhere else."

Most of the supervisors, department managers, store managers, and buyers saw themselves as being in a business which had passed them by. They said that without an adequate education, without training, and without guidance they were being asked to do their jobs in a climate entirely different from that in which they had started. Several of these supervisory people reported that it was only a matter of time before Robert Claypool and Michael Samson would become dissatisfied with their work and ask them to leave. Many of the supervisory people were upset that they were underpaid, oversupervised, and unheard. Several spoke about giving the best years of their careers to Claypool, only to receive very little in return. They talked about their career expectations and anticipations when they first came to Claypool and their present feeling that they had no chance to make the grade.

Michael Samson, Robert Claypool, and the vice presidents, see themselves as being overburdened with the demands of the stores. Several of the newer vice presidents talked about their dissatisfactions and confessed that they would like to leave the organization. According to them, the only thing holding them was money. Many of the older executives questioned their own retailing abilities in today's industry. One man talked poignantly about feeling worthless when compared with the younger and more educated men.

Although most of the people we talked with did not appear happy with their self-images and were not very comfortable with the realities they saw around them, most thought Claypool was a strong company with a good future: "What's Claypool's future? Claypool is going to make it. A lot of people think this is the only place to shop. The company is as old as Atlanta is; it won't fail." "The other day, a customer told me she felt Claypool was bright and alive. She was impressed with a promotion and the number of customers in the store. I wish I had her optimism about the store, but as long as there are people who think that way, Claypool has a good future."

Robert Claypool and Michael Samson both agreed that the future for Claypool was unlimited. They spoke in glowing terms about the possibilities — more stores, more people, more merchandise, and, implicitly, more money. They tempered their comments with reservations about the general economic decline, rising wages and merchandise costs, and declining margins. They both seemed to have a blind faith that Claypool would continue to grow and be an integral part of the retail industry in the Southeast.

4. Intraorganizational relationships

Only two people in the Claypool organization have any power or control over activities or exert influence in the policies, strategies, and decisions: Claypool and Samson.

Robert D. Claypool III is a driven man. When he became president, he did so more out of responsibility and obligation, according to his account, than out of a burning desire to be in the retail business. His grandfather, the colonel, had started the store; his father had carried it forward; and it was his responsibility to "pick up the fallen banner and carry it onward." Until recently he had carried the banner very successfully; the last 5 years were not as overwhelmingly successful as he would have liked. The current pressures have given him pause and caused him to reconsider his position in reference to his father and the colonel. During our talks with him, he mentioned several times the difficulty of living up to the challenge of his ancestors. He said that his father and the colonel lived in different times: "They could be good merchants just by knowing all of the manufacturers, employees, and customers. Their personal associations were able to carry them through situations where merchandising skills would have been better. Now it's different. There are too many people working here for me to know personally, we have over 200,000 active accounts, and the manufacturers aren't as impressed with the Claypool name as they previously were." Robert Claypool has tried to remain relevant in a world where he is not too sure he belongs. He attends various seminars in management techniques, he goes to conventions and trade shows, he talks with friends in the retail industry across the country, and he cares a great deal about the future of Claypool Furniture and Appliances.

He sees his role at Claypool as being the major force, the thrust behind the growth and future of the organization. He interprets this as meaning that he must be involved in all decisions which will affect the profitability and growth, that he must have the final word in all decisions. During one interview he offered the analogy of the shepherd and the flock. "The shepherd must lead, control, and govern the actions of his sheep. They can't do it themselves. They are more concerned with feeding themselves and taking care of their own, rather than having an investment in the success of the flock. I must make sure that the flock survives." Therefore, he reasons, he must handle all conflicts, problems, issues, and decisions since he is the one who understands the "entire flock." Obviously he sees himself as a father figure for his "family," and a father who has the authoritarian control to arbitrarily minister to the needs of each individual and the family as a whole.

His view of Michael Samson is: "Michael is literally my right-hand man. I don't have time or energy for the daily details of each store, and he does. It's his responsibility to see that the policies and strategies that we agree upon are carried out. He also has to act as my buffer. If I get involved with too many problems in the operation of the company, then I don't have time for the planning and more important details. He has to make the decisions about what I should be involved in and what he can handle himself."

Robert Claypool's way of dividing the responsibility between the two men indicates that, despite his expressed wishes to know employees personally, he wants to avoid personal contacts. It is difficult to make an appointment with him because he is always busy. Miss Maggie effectively shields him from the rest of the organization. He readily admitted that he would rather make policies and have Michael Samson carry them out than get involved in administering them. Even though he said, "My door is always open to talk with the employees about their problems," we observed that anyone who wanted to see him had to have permission from Miss Maggie and then probably would have to wait at least a week before being able to talk with him for 15 minutes.

Robert Claypool, we feel, is torn between two ideals. On the one hand, he identifies strongly with the models offered by his father and grandfather. He has a keen sense of his family and personal leadership role in his community, which is basically constructive despite all of its paternalistic overtones. He wants to be recognized and appreciated for carrying that role out and to have others benefit from his doing so. On the other hand, he also wants to demonstrate his competence as a businessman. In his eyes these two roles conflict. In the former role he could see himself as kindly, helpful, protective, and benevolent. In the latter he must see himself as cool, logical, and rational; aggressively competitive and demanding. In the final analysis the latter role must prevail or the business will fail, but it does so at the cost of the former. He misses his previous contacts and feels guilty about deserting his people, who are essentially his extended family, yet he is angry with them for not appreciating his efforts on their behalf and for not doing as he wishes and instructs them. He copes with his ambivalence by withdrawing from them and turning over the control and discipline functions to Samson. He thereby remains the "good father" in his eyes and in the eyes of many of his employees, while Samson becomes the "bad uncle."

Michael Samson is a hard man. He works hard, he thinks hard, and he acts hard. He assumes that his subordinates are not capable of making decisions by themselves and that he must make decisions for them. This bespeaks a powerful conscience that makes heavy demands on the man to control and drive himself. His efforts to cope with his own hostility by perfectionistic overcontrol spill over and create the same kinds of demands on the whole organization. He is obsessed with his mission and his responsibility to Claypool. He works at both from 10 to 14 hours a day and expects others to work equally hard and loyally. But such a powerful conscience implies that he does not think that he is very good as a person and, by extension, that others are even worse, thus his contempt for subordinates. In some ways he feels that he is the real leader of Claypool and that its fate rests on his shoulders.

Michael Samson is concrete and pragmatic. He measures performance and ability by the results of the income statement. People and individuality have little impact on him. If something fails, someone must be at fault.

When we asked Samson to describe his job, he said, "It's my responsibility to carry out the policies and strategies Bob [Robert Claypool] formulates. He and I decide what must be done to maintain our position in the marketplace, and then it's up to me to see that it happens. In effect, I'm held responsible for the profit or the loss at the end of the year." He continued by saying, "I suppose that's why I'm so tough on people. I have a multimillion-dollar investment to protect for the Claypools, and I won't see it go down the drain because someone doesn't know enough to come in out of the rain."

Samson lacks the flexibility to cope with his managerial problems in other than controlling ways. As a result, his job is becoming harder. It now demands flexible adaptation to a changing market place because the market can no longer be successfully mastered by intensity of effort and detailed control, nor can he possibly stretch himself to control several stores in the same way he could control one. He responds to the increasing pressure by driving harder and trying to control ever more tightly.

IV. ANALYSES AND CONCLUSIONS

A. Organizational Integrative Patterns

1. Appraisal of the effect of the environment on the organization

Atlanta needed Colonel Robert D. Claypool during the Reconstruction days after the Civil War. The area economy was greatly depressed because of the severe damage that had been done to both the farm lands and the urban area of Atlanta. Leaders had to emerge, money had to be generated, and individual faith had to be restored. In this climate, Colonel Claypool found a fertile area of development which would yield two major benefits. First, because of the lack of credit and machinery, Claypool was able to prime the economic pump with liberal credit and good tools. The farmers could once again begin to contribute to the economic stability of the South. While this messianic drive was an important motive in itself for Colonel Claypool, there was the second benefit of regaining the wealth that had been depleted during the war. Here was a chance to start afresh, to build something different, to contribute to the surrounding environment, and, ultimately, to gain profitably from doing so.

The growth of Claypool's General Store was slow during the early years under the colonel's leadership. The reason for starting the store was to provide a service for the surrounding area farmers, not personal gain for the Claypools. Therefore, profits were kept to a minimum, with most of the returns being passed on to customers in the form of lower prices and better merchandise.

Not until Robert Claypool II took the leadership from his father in 1914 did the store begin to expand. After the turn of the century, Atlanta seemed to regain her feet and to make substantial progress. Industry was beginning to develop in diversified fields, people were starting to get better wages, and Robert II saw that Claypool's future would be severely limited if it remained a general store. The Claypool textile mill sold cloth to a local furniture manufacturer who was a close friend of the Claypool family. Through this personal contact, Robert II was able to secure furniture at a better price than other retailers. This prompted the switch to a furniture store.

The external environment from that point until the early 1960's was congenial to Claypool Furniture (eventually Claypool Furniture and Appliances). The people of Atlanta looked upon the Claypool organization as an honest company. The community supported the store as the Claypool family supported the community. There was mutual respect, admiration, and trust. If there was any negative effect on the organization because of this climate, it was that Claypool was falling into the habit of believing that Atlanta would always be grateful, trusting, loyal, and respectful.

However, the early 1960's brought new developments. More retailers were beginning to compete actively with Claypool. They saw the Atlanta market as being able to support many retailers, and they intended to take advantage of this fertile market. The success of the competition jolted Claypool. Claypool was also receiving signals from manufacturers that relationships were going to change. Manufacturers were demanding larger order quantities for discounts, and they were not responding to pressures to lower prices for special customers.

2. Appraisal of the effect of the organization on the environment

In its early years, Claypool had a powerful positive effect on the environment. It supported farmers in their recovery efforts and it provided commercial leadership in the community, a trustworthy base for purchases, and yardstick by which customers could measure other stores. It provided jobs and stability for many people. In recent years, it has had little effect on the environment, except as another competitor to help keep prices down and as a shopping center developer.

3. Reactions

By the middle of the 1960's, Claypool was facing pressures from three forces: competition, customers, and manufacturers. It became harder for the store to develop consistent profit margins, to maintain customer loyalty, and to obtain quality merchandise at lower than general cost. To these forces a fourth was added: rising employee dissatisfaction with a traditional paternalistic management style whose underlying carrot-and-stick assumptions became clearer as the pressure for profitability increased. The company reacted to deteriorating customer loyalty by exerting pressure on the employees to work harder at pleasing the customer while failing to meet the employees' needs for more adequate income, training, and organizational support of their work. This made the employees feel that they were being sacrificed to the customer. Indeed, when they knew they were being paid less than other companies paid, had fewer benefits, and received no training, they could only feel that in the management's eyes they were worthless, except as instruments for profit; and that feeling was compounded by Claypool's limited facilities for employee comfort. Expansion to two stores led to more strenuous efforts at control by the two major executives while, at the same time, they increased the distance between themselves and the employees, and heightened the sense of helplessness and futility of middle management.

Robert Claypool III's ambivalence — the conflict over whether to be a good father or a successful businessman — and his consequent withdrawal from his people, abandoning them to the control of Michael Samson, has made it almost impossible for the organization to adopt new methods and strategies to cope with changing circumstances. Its single response is to control ever more rigidly and to drive harder. His withdrawal from the community and the organization's failure to participate more actively deprives him of much of the community's loyalty to the organization. Together these make for a colder, more impersonal, more exploitative, expedient organization which depends for its survival on only one issue, price, an advantage it can no longer sustain.

The pressures and issues confronting Claypool will not disappear. Although the economy will eventually turn itself around, which will alleviate some of the pressure on the profit margins, such an advantageous economic situation will not alleviate the environmental and internal pressure on the organization. Claypool will probably lose even more of the retailing impact it enjoyed during its first 70 years of business. If Claypool is to regain the dominant position it once held in the Atlanta area, then Robert III must be willing to face the realities of the interaction of the environment and the organization. He must be willing to work on these problems and issues, and he must become more introspective.

4. Appraisal of the organization

a. *Special assets*

Claypool's most tangible assets are the buildings and land it owns: two stores and two adjoining warehouses. While the Atlanta store is functional, it is not in prime condition. The Macon store is new, and little of its cost has been depreciated. The value of this real estate allows the organization greater flexibility in creating leverage and financing further expansion, which is also shown in the small amount of debt assumed by the company. Claypool could easily increase its capitalization by another $5 million–$7 million without endangering its liquidity. In effect, if a third store is needed, it could easily be financed through long-term debt without handicapping the financial structure of the organization.

The current number of active credit customers is also a positive, tangible asset. The 200,000 accounts represent an adequate base for flexibility and expansion. It also represents a large enough share of the

Atlanta-Macon market to encourage innovation of products, services, promotions, and customer communications. The credit accounts also offer an adequate base for further research into the reasons for customer satisfaction and dissatisfaction.

Another important asset is the Claypool's location, the booming Southeast. This region has shown a more than average growth pattern in the past 10 years with an emphasis on diversification away from textiles and agriculture-related industries. This change usually brings more people into the area who will be earning increasingly more money and, therefore, have more disposable income to spend on furniture and appliances.

Still another important asset is the relationship Claypool has with the advertising agency handling its account. The creativity, innovation, and persistence of that agency has enabled Claypool to sponsor many award-winning promotions. These promotions frequently have created huge crowds at the stores, resulting in many new customer contacts and credit accounts.

Claypool's special strength is the buyers' merchandising ability. They have bought profitable, however conservatively styled, merchandise for 15 years. Because of their personal contacts with their peers throughout the country and their long tenure as buyers, they have amassed an enormous amount of acumen about retail furniture and appliances. They are conscious of what is happening in the retail industry, and they have understood both the trends and their implications.

The drive, devotion, ability, and determinaton of both Robert Claypool and Michael Samson and their dedication to keeping Claypool an integral factor in the Atlanta market is also an important asset. These qualities, coupled with their intense competitive talent, constitute strong resources with which to work.

Of central importance to Claypool is the satisfaction of its customers. Despite the limitations of service, customer satisfaction has remained constant throughout the history of the company and is the cornerstone of the company's marketing concept. Though competitors now attract many of the same customers, they have not deserted Claypool. They return to the store when it offers them something they need at what appears to be a good price. Furthermore, although the employees are unhappy about being exploited for the customers' sake, they are identified with the need to serve. That value is already held by the older employees and could be developed easily in the newer ones. Therefore the twin drives — "always please the customer" and "always beat the competition" — have the potential of becoming sufficiently introjected by employees to become a mutual goal for them and management alike.

b. Impairments

There are many impairments to effective operation at Claypool. Of prime concern are the decreasing margins. The company is simply not as effective as it used to be. It seems to be faced with the dilemma of "the more we sell, the more we lose." The reasons for this are varied: the higher costs of merchandise (without compensating price increases), overhead, and promotions; the increasing number of people needed to handle the paper flow; the decreasing ability to successfully manipulate manufacturers for more advantageous prices; the successful introduction by competition of other styles of furniture; the increase in accounts receivable and accounts payable (both costly to Claypool); the increase in the cost of short-term financing of inventories; and the increasing cost of inventory storage. These impairments limit expansion through internally generated income.

Another important financial impairment is the Atlanta store. The physical environment detracts from the presentation of merchandise. The store is dirty, poorly located, and suffers from comparison with the competition in Atlanta.

Claypool personnel may also be considered to be an impairment. Few have had education beyond high school, most had little retail training or experience prior to coming to Claypool (and have received none since), turnover and absenteeism are high, morale is low, and the personnel have little knowledge about their specific tasks or responsibilities.

While Robert Claypool and Michael Samson may believe they save money by not training people and permitting high turnover, the cost is actually very great. Since there are too few management personnel to carry on expansion, lower level people must carry a more responsible load. Furthermore, the sales personnel want to sell and apparently can do so with training, thus increasing sales and profitability. In addition, it becomes increasingly difficult to sustain service with uncommitted personnel.

There are two severe functional impairments in Claypool's reality orientation. The first is the lack of authority and responsibility given to Claypool's and Samson's subordinates. The second is the lack of a clear definition of a viable market. The inability of Claypool and Samson to delegate authority has had two negative effects. Subordinates' growth and development have been suppressed. There is little opportunity for them to explore their functions critically and to look for alternative methods of managing. If they are to stay with Claypool, they must think and act in the manner prescribed by Claypool and Samson. They must remain subordinates (that is, without the knowledge or power to make an important contribution to the organization) and not question their superiors' authority or decisions. This limits organizational adaptive flexibility. The second effect of concentrating power and authority is the loss of opportunity for testing and evaluating their own decisions and actions. Because they are not questioned, they themselves lose the opportunity to grow.

Another impairment is the management's inability to hear the employees because of the condescending, paternalistic attitude toward them. The value of customer service is widely shared but easily becomes a rationalization for exploitation of employees. This blindness to employees' feelings about their own importance creates an atmosphere of distrust, apathy, and low self-esteem. Apart from any other considerations, these feelings are the opposite of the enthusiastic loyalty management is seeking. They also reflect the fact that the psychological contract is not being fulfilled. As a result, management and employees talk past each other and operate on different value assumptions. They have no devices to bridge their psychological separation.

c. Level of integration

Claypool's normal coping activities for daily adjustment include the wealth of reports on sales (store, department, individual), inventory levels, and professional shopping. Other coping activities include continual advertising and promotional activities, addition and elimination of merchandise to product lines, management's wishes for further expansion, weekly meetings of the executive committee and the Wednesday morning coffee session, and Friday meetings with department and store managers.

The organization's first-order coping activities include its emphasis on measurable employee performance, increased personnel turnover, authoritarian management of subordinates, and lashing out at the competition.

The second-order coping activities center largely around Claypool's heroic control efforts, particularly on the part of Samson, but largely as an organizational style. Much energy is dissipated in attempts to control employees, policies, procedures, and practices. These efforts are only partially successful and often do more damage than good. This results in management's seeking out individuals for blame and making scapegoats of them and in pressing each employee to be "good" rather than permitting each to cope more flexibly with the realities of his primary job, be it customers or stock or accounts. Secondary to the intensified control efforts, and largely a product of the time and effort they require, is the withdrawal of Robert Claypool from community activities and the noninvolvement of the other executives in the community.

The Claypool facade is one of service and savings — a store dedicated to serving the customers' needs and desires better than anyone else. By continually telling the customers that they purchase the highest quality merchandise at the lowest prices and that it is backed by the best service, Claypool presents itself in a kindly, helpful, beneficent role — the old colonel personified and still thriving. This facade is slowly being eroded by the internal strife and turmoil, conflict which results from displaced hostility, inadequate definition of tasks and responsibilities, and inadequate support of employees.

B. Summary and Recommendations

1. Present status

Claypool Furniture and Appliances is now in a tenuous position both financially and psychologically. Profits have fallen steadily during the last 3 years while sales have continued to grow. Because of the falling profits and their aversion to long-term debt, their expansion plans cannot be financed through retained earnings. Their choice is either to forego the plans for expansion or to give up part of the financial control to get the necessary money. The employees have lost confidence (if they had any) in their role in, and impact on, the organization. They see themselves as mere observers of a process that is slowing passing them by. They are angry at the organization and the management for not including them in the plans for growth, either by informing them of the plans or by training them to be an important part of them. They feel that the organization exploits them for its customers. Conversely, management feels that it is losing control of those factors which, in the past, were responsible for the success of the company. The personal relationships with the manufacturers and the other retailers are disappearing. The confidence of the line management is deteriorating because many see themselves as being unable to handle their positions. Robert Claypool and Michael Samson see themselves as being required to assume more of the managerial responsibilities, even though they are already overburdened. Management also feels that it is losing control over the employees. No longer can they manipulate employees freely. As a result, management places more pressure on itself to resolve the apparent conflicts by refusing to delegate responsibility, tightening its control, and increasing its competitive effort.

Claypool has discovered that its once greatest strength has now become its greatest liability. During the early growth periods of the organization, a controlling leader was important. The store was small enough so that one person could realistically assess issues and make decisions. Now the organization has moved beyond the scope of even two men's ability to maintain complete control. The historical lack of employee development, the lack of sensitivity to the employees' needs, and the continued one-man view of the furniture and appliance market have resulted in the current conflicts.

The decay of the area surrounding the store in Atlanta has also contributed to Claypool's decline. When the store was first opened, the location was most opportune. However, with the decay of the inner city and the migration of the middle and upper classes to the suburbs, Claypool's immediate market has shrunk. A greater proportion of its customers is now coming from lower middle and lower socioeconomic classes. This is not what Robert Claypool or Michael Samson want, yet they are constrained from moving by their inability to generate internal cash support for plant expansion.

Another consequence of the deteriorating location is the kind of people who will work at Claypool. They have limited education. Almost half have taken their jobs to supplement other work, and few have retailing experience.

The Claypool organization may be thought of as being in a depression as a result of the ambivalence of its leader and the compulsive drive of his deputy in the context of radical environmental changes that have heightened the ambivalence of the former and intensified the controlling dominance of the latter. Employees have little direction, low self-esteem, and are growing apathetic. Much of their aggression is directed toward each other in the form of interdepartmental conflicts, criticism, blame, and projection. Many of the middle managers feel incompetent and unable to handle their responsibilities, as do the personnel on the sales floor. Neither group has been formally trained for their jobs. All feel pressured, manipulated, and stifled; they tend to view themselves with the same negative feeling about their adequacy as do their bosses. The managers are fearful about what may happen to them; the employees in general see little future for themselves in the organization.

In addition to the inwardly directed aggression, there is some inappropriate hostility toward the competition. Samson blames much of the decline in profitability on other retailers. "Don't those other guys [retailers] realize that the market just can't bear any more stores in this area? We're all going to suffer." Robert Claypool has withdrawn from many of his previous community responsibilities and few others in the organization interact in community organizations. Claypool as an organization experiences pressure and pain, but the leadership's view of the sources of this pain is incomplete, leaving out, as it does, the conflicts of the two men and being limited in its grasp of the combination of forces operating on the organization. Efforts to cope with the pain are largely misdirected and serve only to increase it.

2. Explanatory formulation

Claypool Furniture and Appliances is the outgrowth of Colonel Robert Claypool's general store, which opened its doors in Atlanta in 1868. The store was the result of a semiphilanthropic attitude, a reflection of Claypool family values. In the Atlanta area the Claypool name was associated with the rare combination of wealth and generosity; from the beginning, the store attracted farmers from a large trading area. They trusted the Claypools to offer the best merchandise at the lowest possible prices, and they could purchase goods on the promise of forthcoming crops.

The store remained basically the same size, enlarging only to meet the needs of farmers, until Robert Claypool II replaced his father. In 1916, Robert II recognized the future potential of Atlanta as a commercial area. He purchased land to open what became Claypool Furniture. Because of his close relationships with the local and nearby furniture manufacturers, he was able to purchase furniture at lower prices than others. He passed this saving on to the customers in the form of lower prices. The philosophy of the store remained the same — give the customer the best possible merchandise at the lowest possible prices and gave him the credit to enjoy the goods. Farmers were already loyal customers, and Claypool subsequently was able to earn the loyalty of the townspeople. Customer satisfaction was a major concern from the beginning. Success resulted for three major reasons: the close relationships with the furniture manufacturers; the willingness to pass on to the customers the savings gained from these relationships; and the widely respected and admired name of the Claypool family.

After the untimely death of Robert Claypool II, control of the company was assumed by his eldest son, Robert Claypool III. Soon after World War II, he realized the growth potential in the appliance market. The Claypools had continued to foster the close relationships with manufacturers, and Robert III was able to purchase appliances at a better price than other retailers. The store's philosophy remained the same — these savings were passed on to the customers. As the organization began to develop, its physical structure was purposely designed to keep overhead and indirect expenses to a minimum to maintain the established philosophy. To insure continued family control, all of the expansion was financed either by cash generated internally or, when the Macon store was built, by family funds. Long-term debt was avoided.

Growth became important to Robert III. In order to survive, the company had to buy larger volumes to obtain discounts. This required more outlets. He visualized Claypool expanding into a national chain. The first step in this direction was the opening of a second store in Macon. However, soon after the Macon store opened, the effects of a highly centralized organization and the tight control by the two highest executives began to be felt. The two men could not adequately control what was now going on, yet they continued to intrude (particularly Samson) into all levels of operation, thus infantilizing subordinates and paralyzing initiative. As a reflection of this management style, personnel were seldom trained for their jobs, salaries were kept as low as possible, and employees were manipulated (in much the same way as Claypool handled manufacturers) to obtain the most work for the least money.

However, the growth of the operation has exacerbated Robert Claypool's ambivalence about his role as a kindly, paternalistic, helping figure, cast in the image of his grandfather, and his other role as a competent executive who is responsible for the survival of his business. His ambivalence has inhibited him from taking the managerial actions which would have helped the organization to cope with such problems as increased competition, declining customer loyalty, changing customer tastes, and advances in management practices and techniques that make many of his practices obsolete. This ambivalence has also resulted in inconsistent control efforts by management: they are tight on money matters and compulsive but inadequate in store arrangement and housekeeping.

Because of the desire for expansion and the increasing pressures from internal and external sources, Claypool sought consultation. The company has been responding to these pressures by intensifying its battle with the competition through increased promotions, sales, and media advertising. It had responded to the internal pressures by largely ignoring them.

3. Prognostic conclusions

The prognosis for the organization hinges on the resolution of Robert Claypool's ambivalence. He is obviously capable of making use of modern business techniques if he can resolve his conflict and accept the role of businessman. This role need not be as hard or impersonal as he perceives it is likely to be, for there are many ways in which he can guide the people in his organization to grow in competence and stature. Some of these ways will become apparent through consultation. Once he begins to resolve his conflict, he can be helped to withdraw some of the burden he has placed on Samson, relieving Samson's conscience, and diminishing his pressure. With the support of the consultant, both Claypool and Samson can begin to delegate — to encourage their subordinates to act more independently — and to undertake group problem-solving efforts which will modify the pressures on, and increase the effectiveness of, the whole company. In turn, this should alter their perceptions of the problems they face and bring into their view a wider range of alternative strategies. At minimum, this turn-around process, which must include planning and initiating training to increase several kinds of competence — managerial, interpersonal, sales — should take about 2 years. Initial consultations should be on a weekly basis for the first 6 months, biweekly for the next 6, and scheduled according to the joint judgment of the management and the consultant thereafter (but not less frequently than once a month). Probably the most difficult aspect of the consultation process will be to help Samson relax some of his controls by a "therapeutic" alliance with him, the consultant will have to help him to understand that there are more adaptive ways of controlling a threatening environment than by merely tightening the screws on his people and himself.

Specifically, the consultant should help Samson ease his demands on himself, suggest ways to guide and support his subordinates, encourage his efforts to delegate authority, and teach him skills of listening. Support from the consultant should make it possible for Samson to be less angrily impulsive and more thoughtful about alternative courses of action.

The report to the employees, and indeed to Claypool and Samson, should be brief and succinct or it will be overwhelming. Its recommendations should deal specifically with those first steps that will serve the dual purpose of bringing management and employees together around common problems while modulating Samson's overcontrolling behavior without undermining the control process. Specifically, it should suggest those standardized personnel practices widely adopted elsewhere which would not come as either a great surprise or an innovative (and therefore frightening) departure from ther current techniques. The process of working out these practices in detail will enable both Claypool and Samson to become familiar with them as well as with the principles of delegation of authority and the responsibility those principles imply. It will also open modes of communication as the details and implications of practices are discussed in employee groups and with the management. The consultant can play an important supportive role to both management and employees as they begin to learn to work with each other in different terms.

For the employees' part, moving in this rather simple direction will give them direct indication of management's wish to meet their needs, which should have a direct effect on morale. Then, as they begin to work on the process of defining their roles and interrelationships, they will begin to acquire skills in working together and confidence in their ability to do so.

Once these initial personnel steps are underway and people have evolved more comfortable ways of working with each other, other issues may then be raised, one at a time, which can become the subject of task force study. Probably the most relevant and immediately pressing is that of marketing conception, followed by those of finance and local location.

4. Recommendations

The recommendations to be made, following the logic expressed in the last discussion, are as follows:

Personnel Practices The company should establish descriptions and standards and objectives for all positions. It should develop orientation and training programs to properly prepare people for their jobs and provide appraisal devices by which personnel and their superiors can assess progress and training needs. Positions and training in supervision and management are to be included in this process. A procedure for identifying prospective managerial talent should be evolved. The representative council should be abolished, and it should be replaced by employee task forces appointed to solve specific intraorganizational problems. Such groups, to include stock personnel, would end the isolation of the stock people and contribute to organizational identification and group cohesion.

A continuous and open evaluation of the wage and salary structure below the managerial levels should be undertaken, with the intention of creating and maintaining an equitable and competitive salary structure. The salary plan should include return for individual performance, group or department performance, store performance, and total organizational performance. This effort should be supported by a mechanism through which people can get information about their positions and salaries, as well as accurate information on how their department and store are doing in terms of inventory, profitability, costs, and operations (but only to the extent that this can be done without harming the organization).

More personal facilities for the employees should be developed immediately: a cafeteria in Macon and better lounge, rest room, and first-aid facilities in both stores. Petty annoyances like parking lot issues should be resolved through the personnel department as such complaints arise through work-group meetings. Learning facilities, such as a managerial library and classrooms, should be created to support the training process.

Financial Practices The management should reconsider the option of obtaining capital for expansion from the outside. A possible alternative is to borrow the money from the Claypool Family Trust. This would require examining the costs of obtaining working capital as opposed to generating it from the inside.

Technical Practices An electronic data processing system needs to be developed to handle inventory control, sales data, and cost figures. This system should also handle credit statements for both customers and suppliers.

Distribution Practices Claypool should consider closing the Atlanta store and build a new one in a better location with a more esthetically pleasing and functional layout. Neither esthetics nor functionality need cost so much as to impair the limitations on overhead. The functions of the check-out stations and inventory distribution system should be separated so that customers can pay for their merchandise in one place and pick it up in another. The executive committee should clearly delineate the viable market segments and alternative methods for reaching those segments. Meanwhile, the confusion in the buying system can be reduced by eliminating Michael Samson's option of halting a buying process once it is in motion.

Managerial Practices The executive committee must create time for long-range planning and educate itself to consider both long-range and short-range views. It will have to understand that all short-range actions have long-range implications, and much of the committee's effort will have to be spent in developing its organization. In this it can be aided by the consultant.

Consideration should be given to moving the executive offices from the Atlanta store to free the store personnel from the surveillance of the corporate executives and their possible influence on selling operations.

Part IV

THE CLOSURE PROCESS

11

FEEDBACK

Having completed and written up the study, the next task is to begin the closure process by feeding back the results. This involves two steps: preparing a report to the client, and presenting the report to the client system.

However, these are only the mechanical steps. The closure process is a complex and subtle end-phase negotiating process. The way in which it is handled will be the most significant influence determining whether the client will proceed to work further on the issues discerned.

Preparing the Report

The report to the client should be a summary of those findings abstracted from the analysis and conclusions section of the study together with recommendations for action. It should be no longer than what can be read aloud in an hour. The summary should describe what the consultant did, how he got his information, and the period of time covered by his study. This will enable the client to put the report in perspective and to understand its sources and its limits. It should then state what in the judgment of the consultant are the essential findings. These should be couched in such a way that those hearing the report can say, "Yes, that's the way it is here. You have reported our feelings and experiences accu-

rately and with empathic understanding. You appreciate our struggles."
That is, the consultant should consider carefully the education, level of
understanding, degree of interest, and opportunities for action his audience has and, therefore, what they can hear. While being factual and
empathic, the report must not be dishonest at one extreme or an indictment on the other. The report must be carefully tailored to those who
will hear it and have to deal with its consequences. The consultant
should be careful not to overwhelm the client with negative findings
that leave him with disproportionate feelings of helplessness and therefore unable to act. For example, in one situation, the consultant was told
a great deal about an executive's aloofness and authoritarian manner by
his subordinates. Some of their feelings about his authoritarian role
stemmed from his aloofness from them. The consultant recognized that
the executive could not significantly change his personality and that part
of his aloofness resulted from not knowing how to get closer to his people. The consultant reported to the executive that his subordinates
looked to him for leadership and support and wanted to see more of him.
He recommended regular meetings with the subordinates about the
common problems they faced. Had the consultant merely told the executive he was authoritarian, the executive would have been left with criticism, which he could only reject because he saw himself not as authoritarian but fatherly. Once he rejected the consultant's findings, there
would have been no way for the consultant to help him further. In this
particular instance, the consultant was in a position to help him learn
to relate more effectively to his people and to mobilize them toward their
mutual tasks.

The consultant should be guided by the questions: How much of what
kind of information can the client (executive and organization) accept?
How must he be told?

The findings should give appropriate emphasis to the strengths of the
organization and its assets for coping with its problems. They should
provide a balanced picture of the organization and its problem-solving
efforts. They should be stated in such a way that organization members,
by following the same process the consultant followed, would return the
same findings. In technical jargon, the findings should have "face validity."

A statement of recommendations should follow the presentation of the
findings. The recommendations should offer *specific* avenues for confronting the problems disclosed in the findings, and they should be in

keeping with the strengths and assets in the organization. There is little point in making recommendations that are beyond the capacity of the organization to undertake. Too often consultants assume that the organization can readily use the strengths it has. Most, however, will need help in utilizing strengths — help in the form of delineated steps toward more effective functioning, together with support from the consultant or someone else in taking those steps. Often organization leadership will be fully aware of its problems but not know how to go about beginning to cope with them. And often the consultant's recommendations are too general to be useful.

An example of a report to an organization follows later in this chapter. This model has proved to be an effective one.

Presenting the Report

Once the report has been prepared, the actual feedback process can begin. And the first step is to present the report to the executive who was responsible for the consultant's entering the organization. It is important for the consultant to recognize that the client has the right to be in charge of what is happening to him. Therefore, I prefer to read the report to the client executive. I ask him to set aside two hours to meet with me alone. I indicate to him that I would like him to listen to me read the report, to make whatever notes he wishes while I am doing so, and to consider how the report will sound to the others in his organization when they hear it. I want him to be particularly alert to my use of words, to be sure that I do not convey meanings I do not intend, and to see that I do not inadvertently become trapped in organizational politics. I want him to be sensitive to the way I present matters so that he does not find himself in embarrassing or difficult circumstances because of the way I have phrased things. I make it clear that I cannot change the substance of my findings, but I emphasize my need to have his help in stating what I have to say in the most advantageous way.

I then read the report aloud, slowly. When I have finished reading it, the client executive is then free to ask whatever questions he wants, to discuss any items or implications, and to advise me on language. I also seek his advice on the next steps in presentation.

Ordinarily I prefer to present the report to others in the organization in the same sequence I followed when entering the organization. However, sometimes it is politically wiser to alter course. For example, in one study of an organization that was scattered in several communities, it was important to take the second step in the feedback process in a community other than the headquarters because the group there was more closely related to decision making than those at lower levels in headquarters. The chief executive's advice on this matter saved us both considerable difficulty.

After the initial two-hour session with the client executive, I give him the typewritten report that I have read and that we have discussed. I ask him to read it that evening and to meet with me again for two hours the next morning to review the report and discuss it further. *It is extremely important to follow this arrangement exactly.* Any such report is likely to have some disturbing implications for the executive no matter how much he needs the consultant's help or how willing he is to seek constructive diagnosis. He will tend to perceive definitions of problems as criticism of himself and to magnify that criticism in his own mind. He will therefore have many hostile feelings about the report and the consultant, particularly when he has had an opportunity to read the report by himself and think about it. Unless the discussion is resumed *immediately* the next morning, these feelings will fester, and could result in hostile rejection with possibly devastating consequences. The client may decide that the report is no good or that he does not want to go any further with the project or that the consultant has been unduly critical. When such feelings are talked out immediately, the client has the opportunity to reestablish a more accurate perspective and to assist the consultant in planning the next steps in the feedback process. *This phase is so critical the consultant should not undertake feedback to the executive client until an afternoon-evening-morning schedule can be arranged.*

For the next steps in the report feedback the consultant should provide mimeographed copies of the report for each of the listeners to have as he reads it aloud. Charts and graphs will complement the presentation. Such a concrete reference point can counteract the distortions that are likely to occur in listening to this kind of verbal presentation. It also facilitates questions and discussion. Each group to whom the consultant reports should have the opportunity to suggest changes in the wording, but not the substance, and offer suggestions about presentation to those who will next hear the report.

Usually the feedback process follows a consistent psychological course. At first the listeners tend to be tense and hostile, as if fearing the worst.

Then they become more attentive. Once they become more relaxed, they will frequently voice approval during the reading. Finally, the questions which follow, directly or indirectly, say, "Are we really going to do something about it?"

The discussion that follows the reading also tends to take a predictable course. During the first stage there is criticism of the report, and even of the consultant; sometimes, argument with the consultant about the validity of his information. Often there will be debate within the group about the findings and implications as well as about the recommendations. Such debate is frequently a form of intellectualization, which constitutes the second stage. People will then begin to talk in the abstract about the problems, using cliches from the literature or their particular field. This third stage is projection, the tendency to seek scapegoats or someone or something to blame for the problems. This is followed by rationalization: "things are that way because . . ." Next, the group usually wants to know how their organization compares with others as a way of assuaging their feelings of guilt and inadequacy. This is followed by an expression of feelings that problems are the inevitable lot of being human; they "own" these problems and they should take steps to correct them. Statements of acceptance of the report and support for its recommendations usually then follow. The last stage often includes remarks directed to the consultant indicating greater openness on the part of the group and sometimes comments intended to appease him for earlier hostile remarks.

Seen another way, there is usually an initial defensive, hostile phase that includes efforts to escape psychologically; a discussion of feelings and issues stage; and a stage of consolidation behind the report.

The consultant should let his report stand on its merits. By this I mean he should make certain his method of gathering information is understood with all its limitations and that his interpretations and inferences are clearly recognized as his and subject to critical examination. He must be sure it is understood that his recommendations are matters for the group or organization to consider. There may be many alternative ways of solving the perceived problems; his recommendations are only one. They are to serve as an impetus to the organization's problem-solving efforts, a way of getting problems and possibilities out on the table for organizational consideration. The consultant should make it clear that he is not there to tell them how to run their organization. His job is to gather and organize information; to summarize that information; to offer recommendations based on his experience derived from that information to facilitate action.

The feedback procedure will be the scene for the mobilization of powerful feelings within the groups to whom the consultant is reporting. Some will feel chagrined that he has discovered organizational secrets; others will gloat in their satisfaction. Some will feel guilty for having "squealed" for what they now feel is an indictment of their superiors. Some will feel attacked, some deserted by the consultant from whom they had expected much more. Some will complain that the inferences drawn from their statements were over exaggerated, that the issues raised are not that important. Some will want to know if top management has heard the report and what they will do about it.

Struggles over these and many other feelings will come to the fore during and after the feedback presentation. Sometimes they appear in the form of dead silence. Sometimes factions within a group will argue with each other. Frequently the attack is directed at the consultant.

The consultant should not become defensive. He has put forth what he has learned and how he understands it together with what ideas he has for dealing with the problems. It is now the job of the groups to whom he is reporting to work with that material and with him to define its usefulness to them and what they want to do about it.

If some are chagrined or guilty the consultant can raise the question whether such feelings are appropriate to the situation. If some feel attacked or indicted, he can help them express their resentment and then ask what aspects of the presentation seem to constitute the attack or indictment. If some feel their point of view to be inadequately represented or the conclusions to be inadequate or distorted, they have the opportunity to counterbalance the findings by the corrections they have been asked to make. Those who are concerned about whether top management has seen the report need to be reassured. The groups should be told what top management plans to be the next steps, if there are such.

Throughout the presentation, the behavior of the consultant should be a model for how he wants the organization to go about its problem-solving activity: *by joint engagement with authoritative leadership around open examination of mutual problems for collective solutions toward more effective organizational functioning.* He must demonstrate that he does not fear hostility; that he stands confidently for his findings despite differences, that he is willing to be cross-examined about what he has learned and how he has learned it, together with the assumptions he has made; that he is willing to be appropriately corrected and to have his conclusions modified by new data.

Sometimes the information he brings will be at a level never before considered by these groups. They will be uncomfortable. They may believe such information inappropriate for their level. They need to know they have top management's "permission" to hear and to think about these issues.

It is often helpful for the same groups to have a follow-up session with the company personnel director or someone in the same relative position. He can then ask, with the consultant no longer present, what they now think of the report. If they still believe it to be valid, then the company man might ask them what problems should be taken up and in what order. I prefer to have organizational groups assume responsibility for defining priorities rather than having management assume the responsibility for solving all problems indiscriminately. First, no management can do that, let alone do it well. Second, to do so contradicts the principle that people who share problems together should be responsible for helping to solve them. Third, it is self-defeating paternalism. Once problem priorities have been defined, then management, with the help of the consultant, can evolve mechanisms for their solution.

Sometimes the chief executive feels too threatened by the report to open up the possibility of discussion at lower levels. The consultant will have to work with him at some length on the problems that trouble him — fear, rigidity, anger that his people do not love him, helplessness, lack of knowledge about what to do and how to do it. Only when he is more comfortable and feels supported by the consultant will he be able to take the necessary steps. Some will need additional support from their boards, who will then also have to hear the report.

Some chief executives who want to deny they have problems out of helplessness or fear do so by avoiding the issues. They assume that once the feedback has occurred, that in itself should solve their problems. And, they conclude, people should be talking better with each other and everyone will love everyone else. Usually such men are afraid to take authoritative action and are uncomfortable with confrontation. Most often they need greater direction from the consultant about where to begin and they need support from him when hostility arises from their subordinates.

Some executives need restraint, particularly if their subordinates do not immediately become deeply involved in responding to the feedback.

The executive may want to force them to respond. The consultant should ask the executive to agree before entering the feedback situation that he will take no action during the feedback but simply let the participants speak as they will. If they do not participate, then executive and consultant together should try to ascertain why, perhaps even by additional consultant interviews with some of the participants, and plan the subsequent steps accordingly. The same restraint will be necessary if the executive wants to proceed immediately and unilaterally to implement the recommendations. No matter how good they may be, in such circumstances, the recommendations are bound to be rejected in subtle, if not open, ways.

When the consultant is finished, he should review all of his diary notes on the feedback process, together with those of the whole study, specify on paper for himself what he thinks he has learned, what mistakes he has made, and what he would want to do differently next time. Unless the consultant is himself always a learner, he will quickly become obsolete.

Of course there are many more possible psychological issues and problems in the closure and feedback process. Since they all cannot be elaborated here, I can only point out that the closure task is also psychologically an opening task. If the consultant will recognize the critical nature of this process, observe the phenomena of the process carefully, and consciously crystallize his own experiences, he will find himself increasing his own proficiency with time.

Report to
Claypool Furniture and Appliances
April 20, 1971

Introduction

This study of Claypool Furniture and Appliances was undertaken for three basic reasons:

(1) Robert Claypool's wish to expand the organization in order to remain competitive.
(2) The need to more fully understand this company so that growth could be accomplished with minimum stress.
(3) Despite increasing sales, profits have been declining.

It was agreed that a task force would conduct the study during October, November, and December 1970; and January, February, and March 1971. This report summarizes the task force's findings.

Statement of Problems

The chief concern leading to the study was that of establishing a solid base for future expansion, including a consideration of the need for greater depth of management. Decrease in profits, increase in competition from other retailers, greater consumer sophistication, and less flexible product costs raise serious questions about expansion.

Mr. Claypool was also concerned about the impact expansion would have on employees. As the company has grown, it has become more difficult for him to be as closely in touch with the employees and their problems as he used to be. Additional growth would inevitably diminish contact further, thereby threatening to make the company an even more impersonal place to work.

In interviews, members of the management also expressed the need for effective planning and more clearly fixed responsibilities. They saw inadequate long-range direction and managerial guidance as handicaps to the plans for expansion and the ability to quickly react to a changing environment. In addition, they expressed concern about recruiting and keeping good personnel.

Method

The study was undertaken in four steps. The initial phase was the orientation of the employees to the study and the completion of the questionnaires. This took two weeks in the two stores. The questionnaire was completed by 855 Claypool employees, representing approximately 96 per cent of the total number employed. The responses were programmed into a computer and summarized.

The second step involved interviewing and observing the work process throughout the organization. One hundred people were selected to be interviewed representing the following seven categories:

(1) part- or full-time
(2) male or female

(3) education levels
(4) departments
(5) hourly wage or salaried
(6) length of employment
(7) number of promotions

We feel that the people who were randomly chosen from these categories would fairly represent the personnel. Each task force member spent an average of one and a half to two hours a day in observation and on-the-job interviews. Each observed salesmen selling, stock personnel handling merchandise, clerical workers completing monthly reports and daily billings. This represented a total of 300 hours of observation and 78 on-the-job interviews. In the latter, employees were asked what their jobs were, how they did their jobs, and what were their on-the-job problems. We observed communications and interactions among supervisors and employees, from which we made inferences about attitudes and feelings. We also acted briefly, for periods of an hour to an hour and a half, as cashiers, stockmen, buyers, clerks and salesmen. We attended the representative council meetings twice, the executive committee three times, and the Wednesday coffee session three times. The interviews and questionnaires were undertaken with the mutual understanding that the information would be treated confidentially, so we believe the information given us to be honest.

The third stage involved the interpretation and analysis of the information. This report comprises our best understanding and interpretation of the data.

The fourth stage is the process of reporting our findings to you and discussing them with you.

The validity of our interpretations and inferences depends on the validity of the information you gave us and the degree to which this information is truly representative of the organization. We must leave it to you to judge whether these findings fairly represent your feelings and to point out where they do not. These interpretations and inferences should not be considered to be iron-clad conclusions but only our best understanding of your organization. Hopefully our understanding of Claypool will serve as a basis for further discussion toward solving Claypool's organizational problems.

History

Claypool was started by Colonel Robert DuLawrence Claypool during the early reconstruction days after the Civil War. He opened a general store on the outskirts of Atlanta in 1868, and his customers were primarily farmers from the surrounding area. It was a typical general store which sold everything, but the emphasis was on the practical items: plows, harness gear, staple foods and bolts of cloth. The store was the gathering place for the surrounding area, and all of the local gossip was either started or disproved around its cracker and pickle barrels.

Since Colonel Claypool owned approximately 17,000 acres of farm land in the area and since he derived considerable income from the cash crops, his textile mills, and his horse stables, he was not particularly concerned about the profits of the general store. He had a messianic zeal. His parents had taught him that all people were equal in their rights and privileges. Since the Claypools were fortunate to be wealthy, "they should do their part to help those who were less fortunate." The Civil War had pretty well destroyed the farms around Atlanta, and the smaller farmers were having great difficulty getting started again. They needed credit and supplies. Colonel Claypool gave them both.

The eldest son of the colonel, Robert II, followed in the philosophical footsteps of his father. The colonel had not attempted to expand the general store but had kept it more as a service for farmers than as a profit-oriented business. However, 30 years after the store opened its doors, Robert II foresaw the rapid expansion of Atlanta and the opportunity for a furniture store. In 1916, two years after the colonel died, Robert II purchased land in Atlanta and opened Claypool Furniture. The philosophy was still the same: give the customer plenty of credit and the best value possible. Because of the Claypool family name and the close business contacts the colonel had established, Robert II eventually was able to buy furniture at prices lower than others could and to pass the savings on to the customer. Overhead was kept to a minimum.

However, during World War I, Claypool Furniture was only modestly successful. Expansion costs were high, personnel were scarce, and the furniture was difficult to buy because manufacturers were devoting their facilities to the war effort. Robert Claypool II was called into the Cavalry, and the store was operated on a stand-by basis by the employees.

After his return in 1919, he gathered the reins of the operation and ran the store until his unexpected death in 1936. The presidency of the organization was passed to Robert III, who was then only 23 years old.

In 1946 Robert III added a line of brand name appliances to the store and changed the name to the present one. In 1948 Claypool brand name rugs were introduced. Claypool continued to prosper. Customers felt that the Claypool name connoted value.

In 1958, Robert Claypool and his top management group began to discuss the opening of a new store. Part of the original estate was sold, and the money was used to build a new store in Macon. The Claypool family helped to finance a large shopping center, and the central store became Claypool Furniture and Appliances. The store opened in the spring of 1959 and immediately became profitable. Some of the personnel in the Atlanta store became the nucleus of the staff for the new one.

There were no major changes in the stores' operations, policies, or success until the early part of 1968. At that time volume started to drop, profits were being squeezed, and management began to be concerned. The practice of giving credit to all customers was starting to be questioned as people paid their bills more slowly and many did not pay at all. Merchandise costs were rising, and competition was trying to beat Claypool's prices. This competitive–cost–profit squeeze forced Robert Claypool to look for help outside of his organization.

There have been four major crisis periods in Claypool's history. The first was the change from a general store to a furniture store. This was prompted by the decline in the general store's volume because of the growth of the city and other stores and by the close relationships the Claypools had with nearby furniture manufacturers. Robert II was able to purchase furniture at considerably lower cost than other retailers in the area, and he gladly passed these savings on to customers. While the risks of switching merchandise appeared to be high, it is legendary in the organization that Claypool could have ·been selling two legged chairs and customers would have continued to buy them. Customer loyalty was at its peak prior to World War I.

The second period of crisis was the unexpected death of Robert II in 1936. When Robert III assumed control, the employees mobilized behind him and helped him through the next three difficult years. The ability of Claypool to survive this critical period has been credited to sustained customer loyalty and employee dedication.

The third crisis was the introduction of appliances into the furniture store. After World War II, while appliances were still rationed, Robert III realized the potential in the appliance business. More people had disposable income for large-ticket items, the national morale was high, and Claypool had considerable financial flexibility. Appliances were difficult to get, and Robert Claypool had no experience in or knowledge about marketing them. However, customer loyalty prevailed. It was the consensus of the older employees we interviewed that the customers trusted Claypool to protect them from poor merchandise and service.

The fourth crisis, the current one, is the threat to necessary expansion posed by the forces mentioned earlier. In addition, the need for potential managers and a stable, loyal work force is fundamental for growth.

The Claypool family is well respected in Atlanta and Georgia for its philanthropic and community interests. There is a Claypool tradition of social responsibility.

From its original policy of giving easy credit to farmers until now, Claypool has continued to emphasize customer satisfaction. Through all of the changes and crises this emphasis has been consistent.

Now, we turn to our findings:

Questionnaire Results

The questionnaire was composed of two parts: general information about employees and questions related to their feelings and wishes about Claypool Furniture and Appliances.

General Information

Currently 920 people are employed in the Claypool organization. The breakdown of employees is:

	Atlanta	Macon	Total
Sales	170	130	300
Stock	190	160	350
Clerical	75	10	85
Staff	15	5	20
Maint. & Security	50	10	60
Management	80	25	105
	580	340	920

Of these 920, approximately 400 work full-time and the others half- or part-time. Many of the part-time people work during the evenings, coming from full-time jobs elsewhere.

The data on the length of employment indicated that two clusters of employees existed. The larger cluster contains those employees who have worked less than 3 years (65 percent); the second cluster includes those who have worked more than 10 years (15 percent). The former group can be further subdivided. A large percentage (35 percent) are housewives supplementing family income. The rest are younger people in their first jobs. The older people who had less than 3 years of employment were in the sales and accounting-credit area, while the younger people were primarily in the stock and clerical areas. Those who had worked for more than 10 years were primarily men in the selling area and in management. The average age of these people was about 55.

Part-time employees fell into four major groups: students, housewives, middle and lower management from local companies, and retired people.

Approximately 60 percent of the employees are men. They predominate in sales and distribution. Women are largely in the office-clerical areas.

Most of the Atlanta employees come from the neighborhood surrounding the store. They have less education, on the average, than those in the Macon store. The percentage breakdown in Macon is as follows: 8 percent have not completed grammar school; 36 percent have not finished high school; 34 percent have a high school diploma; 14 percent have attended some college; and 8 percent have a college degree. Most of the management people have had some college or a college degree.

There are relatively few promotions. Only 9 percent said they had received a promotion (a change in job title and not merely an increase in salary) in the past 3 years.

Feelings of Personnel

The questionnaire is designed to measure three aspects of employees' feelings about the organization. It touches on ministration needs, or how well the individual thinks the organization takes care of him; maturation needs, or how well the individual thinks the organization helps him to grow in it; and mastery needs, or how well the individual thinks the organization helps him to become increasingly effective and indehe sees the organization and how he thinks it ought to be. There was pendent in his work. The questionnaire asks the individual both how statistically little difference between the responses at the two stores, between departments, and between hourly and salaried employees. Therefore, we feel that the feelings and opinions reported are shared throughout the organization.

More than half of the employees said only "occasionally" or less frequently did they feel working at Claypool allows them to have a lot of self-respect. More than 90 percent felt that this should be the rule rather than the exception it is now. Other questions evoked similar responses. To the statement, "People are put under stress in order to get them to do better work," employees responded in much the same way. The implication is that Claypool employees feel they are pressured when they should not be. To a similar but more direct statement, "Management cares about our problems," more than 65 percent responded only "occasionally" or less frequently, while 97 percent felt that it should "always" or "frequently" be so. Another statement, "Unusual or exciting ideas are encouraged," points to the same conclusion. More than 90 percent felt that only "occasionally" or less was this so, while more than 95 percent felt this should be the standard practice. Similarly, more than half of the employees felt that only "occasionally" did superiors listen to people as well as direct them.

There seems to be a universal confidence in the management: 80 percent felt that "People are efficient at making decisions" either "often" or "occasionally." However, employees would like to become more a part of the decision-making process. Responses to the statement, "Management goals, policies, and objectives are carefully explained to everyone," indicate that this happens infrequently and that employees would like to see it happen "frequently."

What does the individual think about and how does he feel about how well the organization helps him to grow? More than half of those who answered said that they do not know if they are going to be fired or promoted. More than 90 percent felt that they should have this knowledge. While most (58 percent) felt that either "frequently" or "occasionally" people were treated fairly, more than 98 percent felt this should "always" be true.

The only variation between the stores was in response to the statement, "People mind their own business." A greater percentage of people in the Atlanta store (70 percent) felt that people did not mind their own business as compared to the Macon store, where the majority felt that they did. This may indicate that the Atlanta personnel feel more intrusion from the executives because of their proximity.

Claypool employees do not find their work as interesting as they would like it to be. This was indicated by the responses to the statement, "People get so absorbed in their work that they lose track of time." More than 75 percent felt that this "seldom" happened, while more than 60 percent felt that it should happen "frequently" or "always." Few people in either store felt that the "facilities were neat and clean," while the majority felt they should be.

It was a general consensus that the employees did not get deserved credit for what they did and were not made to feel welcome. Most employees felt that Claypool did not plan ahead as much or as often as it should, and many felt that things were not as well organized as they could be. Claypool employees would like to prefer Claypool to other places of work, but most did not have that feeling. This may reflect the large number who work at Claypool as second jobs or in part-time positions.

The consistency of these responses and feelings indicates that Claypool employees have greater expectations of the organization than are currently being met. The gap between what employees experience and what they expect in terms of opportunity to grow in competence, to become more proficient at their work, and to be better supported by the organization, is a severe one.

Interview and Observation Results

The most frequently mentioned problem in the interviews was salary. All of the employees we talked with said their salaries were too low or did not reflect their contribution to the store or that there was no incentive to do a better job.

The second most frequently mentioned problems dealt with product knowledge, store information, and the lack of promotions. It is a fact that most of the sales force has not had intensive product training and that most are not familiar with the advantages and disadvantages of a given product or of a departments' merchandise. This was especially true with those departments other than major appliances (white goods). Employees mentioned at the same time that they had little information about the store, its policies, procedures, and strategies, let alone its history. Most said they had not received any orientation prior to being placed at their stations; all said they would like to know more about their jobs, the store, the products, and what was expected of them. Most of the people said that because they did not have the necessary information about the store and products, they had little basis for promotion. Promotions from one level to another or transfers from one department to another were indeed few and far between. Most of the employees said they saw working at Claypool as a dead-end job.

Another issue frequently mentioned was the problem of working with other departments. We observed conflicts between the sales and stock personnel and between the sales and credit personnel. The former usually revolved around inventory levels as recorded by the sales department and the actual levels reported by the stock people. Both sales and stock people told us that often items that were not in stock were sold, and also that customers were told that merchandise was out-of-stock when there was an adequate supply. The sales personnel repeatedly told us that the stock people did not "understand what goes on down here." The stock personnel, on the other hand, told us that the sales personnel were creating all the problems by not telling them when items were running low and needed to be reordered or that the sales people did not keep accurate records about what merchandise was on hand. Since records are kept in both departments and since there is little formal communication between the two areas, there is little opportunity to resolve these problems.

The conflicts between the sales department and the credit department revolved around the acceptability of customers' credit. Management's directive to the sales department is not to lose a sale because of poor credit. At the same time that management has been encouraging the sales force to grant credit, it has been telling the credit people to handle the files and the permissions with greater emphasis on profits for the company. Therefore, the salesperson will usually promise the customer credit without first checking with the credit files. However, when a check is made after the merchandise has been purchased on the floor, and the credit department discovers that the customer's credit is poor, the salesperson's acceptance of the credit sales is reversed.

Both of these interdepartmental issues are difficult to resolve because of the lack of formal communication lines between the areas. Most of the managers feel that they cannot make a decision without the expressed consent of either Robert Claypool or Michael Samson. As a result, conflicts at lower levels in the organization are pushed upstairs to be resolved.

A frequently mentioned concern was the lack of adequate restroom facilities in both stores and the condition of the cafeteria and employees' lounge in Atlanta and the lack thereof in Macon.

Still another issue discussed by the sales force was the merchandise return policy. Most felt that the policy was too liberal and that the customers could and did take advantage of the store when they wished. When customers exploited them and the store, this made them angry. They became even angrier when they were undercut by management. This happens when a customer tries to return an item purchased elsewhere, one not even carried by Claypool, which is usually refused by both the exchange counter and the area supervisor, only to be granted by the store manager. Employees said that this sequence of events was not unusual.

There were comments from both the management and the employees about being unable to determine how well one was performing. Employees said they knew only when they did something wrong. Error was brought forcibly to their attention by either the area supervisor, the department manager, the store manager, Michael Samson, or Robert Claypool. However, seldom did any of these people comment on a job that was well done. Managers mentioned that there was a performance appraisal system in operation but that there was little give and take between superior and subordinate. Usually the superior told the subordinate how he had done during the year, what he should do to improve, and then how much his salary would be the following year. Most of the nonmanagement employees said they were never appraised.

The rules which presumably guide people are administered sporadically. Employees commented that only the general rules of business, like being on time and not stealing, were obvious to everyone in the organization. However, they commented that rules were not evenly enforced. People arrived late for work and were not reprimanded. Merchandise was stolen and nothing was done beyond firing the offender if he was caught. Salespeople did not dress according to the wishes of the area supervisors, and little was said. We ourselves observed many salespeople smoking on the sales floor. Employees also said that management "made up rules from day-to-day" to handle special and unique situations. The department managers said that few people bothered to follow the special and emergency rules.

The most oppressive rule or policy to the employees is, "The customer is always right, and it is the function of the employee to meet the customer's wishes." There is a general feeling among the employees that the management cares more about the customers than about their employees. Employees said that the stores would do anything possible to please the customer but were not willing to pay their employees a "decent wage" or give benefits or to "let us know what is going on here." They therefore feel exploited for the sake of the customer.

There are virtually no formal lines of communication at Claypool. Daily information is gathered about sales, inventory levels, and expenses and is regularly analyzed by management. Other than financial data, little information is passed from employees to management. Virtually no information about the operations of the stores is passed on to employees by the management. Even written policies and procedures are not distributed throughout the organization. Claypool relies on supervisors to pass on any necessary information. However, the supervisors, according to the interviews, felt that they do not even have the necessary information to administer their own areas.

As a result, employees rely on the grapevine for "facts" about Claypool. The problem with the grapevine is that most of the information is rumor or gossip, and it is difficult to separate truth from untruth. We ourselves were asked to verify rumors about a "40 percent layoff," an "across-the-board pay increase of $1.00," the "addition of a line of clothing," "the poor health of Robert Claypool" and the "move to unionize the sales force." We could find no basis for any of these rumors, which were persistent in both stores and were told to us by area supervisors and their subordinates.

It may seem at this point that we find only problems at Claypool. Whenever one seeks to help an organization improve itself, inevitably that means concentrating on those issues which it must confront and resolve. However, there is no point talking about problems to be solved if the organization does not have the skills or capacity to solve them. Fortunately Claypool has many assets which it can mobilize to deal with its problems and on which it can build. The fact that it has already successfully resolved four crises in its development reflects its capacity for adaptation.

Among these are flexible financial independence because of the careful and conservative management of resources and customer acceptance. There are some 200,000 active credit customers, and a long history of community esteem and respect. Claypool is located in a booming area of the country which promises to continue its already evident population and economic growth. Furthermore, the kinds of people moving into the area as a result of commercial and industrial development are likely to have even more disposable income than is the case with present residents of Atlanta and Macon.

There is strength in the buyers' merchandising ability. Because of their close personal contacts in the retail industry and their long tenure as buyers, they have developed extensive sources of information as well as great knowledge about retailing furniture and appliances.

The drive, devotion, ability, and determination of both Robert Claypool and Michael Samson are leadership assets. These, combined with the wish to serve and the recognition of organization problems to be solved, are important forces toward positive organizational change.

Not the least of the organization's assets is the wish of so many of its employees to have it become better, to grow in and with it, and to be able to identify more strongly with it.

Summary

Claypool Furniture and Appliances, an organization with a succesful marketing and community service tradition, identified with and respected by a rapidly growing community, has now reached a critical stage in its development. That stage is characterized by changing consumer requirements, shifts in employee attitudes and expectations, loss of opportunities to buy merchandise cheaper than competitors, and the need for expansion to remain competitive while at the same time suffering decreasing profit margins because of increasing costs and more intense competition. Its growth has already strained internal relations and an organizational structure and philosophy of management which was more appropriate to an earlier era. The consequence has been increasing internal pressure and more strenuous efforts to control the organization from the top, which has in turn increased anger, disappointment, disillusionment, apathy, and conflict among employees. As an organization, Claypool must evolve a more adaptive posture toward its problems, one based on collective effort toward a common goal. We offer the following recommendations for your consideration, which we hope will serve as a basis for your continued discussion and collective problem-solving efforts.

Recommendations

We think the first major steps to be taken should be related to establishing common bonds between management and employees and strengthening their collective effort toward coping with environmental changes. Some simple things can be done almost immediately by management, such as establishing a modest cafeteria in Macon and better lounge and restroom facilities in both stores. Rooms should be set aside in both places, with appropriate equipment, for training and conferences. We believe that the representative council should be abolished and that several task forces be created from among personnel in various departments to establish ways of resolving some of the internal conflicts among them.

While this problem-solving process is going on, Claypool should establish job descriptions and standards and objectives for all positions in consultation with incumbents, together with appraisal methods which would enable people and their superiors to assess job performance as well as training and development needs.

The development of job descriptions, standards, objectives, and an appraisal system will constitute a natural basis for the formulation of a salary structure which should be equitable and competitive and open knowledge to everyone in the organization. Ideally a salary structure should include compensation for individual, group, and store performance. This, in turn, means that people will need more information on operations, inventory, volume, expenses, and profitability, to the extent that such information can be given without exposing the organization inappropriately, so that they can act more rationally in keeping with a clear picture of reality.

Once these tasks are completed, it will then become possible both to formally delegate responsibility and authority and to define avenues for promotion, as well as to identify candidates for supervisory and managerial positions.

We believe the company should concentrate heavily on training activities. These should include:

(1) A comprehensive orientation program for all new employees together with conferences with them during their first few weeks on the job.
(2) Sales and product training for all sales personnel.

(3) Supervisory and managerial training.

(4) Special skills training for those too few in number or too specialized for in-house training.

We think training is highly important to the company for it is already evident that people make good use of knowledge to increase sales. It is equally important psychologically to employees, not only for their self-esteem, but also because, given limited education, many look to the company to help them prepare themselves for more responsible work which will enable them to contribute more effectively and to earn more money. Given Claypool's history of concern for employees and community and the employees' need to improve themselves, it is only natural that they expect help from the company in this way and become disillusioned when they do not get it. Furthermore, employees should be able to have the support of and be able to communicate through their supervisors. To do both requires that supervisors and managers be trained.

There is a wide range of practices and problems to be dealt with, ranging from corporate finance to electronic data processing to marketing, in any organization which is moving into a more complex environment. These issues are more properly the concern of those who have specialized responsibilities and of top management. They require much study, discussion, and evaluation. Some will require the help of specialized consultants. We do not, therefore, take them up in this report.

We want to express our appreciation for your interest and help. We hope we have represented your feelings accurately and have emphasized appropriately those issues which are most crucial for both the organization and employees. We hope you yourselves will add other suggestions and recommendations in your discussion of this report. We have enjoyed working with you, and we hope that our contribution will help you develop those effective methods of cooperation which will enable Claypool to grow both larger and stronger, with added luster for its reputation and gratification for its management and employees alike.

APPENDIXES
REFERENCES

Appendix A
INTERVIEWING AND
SAMPLING GUIDES

When a consultant begins to do an organizational case study, it soon becomes apparent that much of the needed data can be obtained from relatively few people. These individuals — in middle and top management, in the union, and in the community — are the sources of information for all of the identifying data, all of the historical data, and all of the examinational data up to "current organizational functioning" in the case study outline.

From this point on, in the outline, the consultant must investigate the organization in depth — and extensively so. He must talk to many people in all parts of the organization. They should be observed as they function on the job, routinely and during emergencies, during their lunch and coffee breaks, and, if possible, when they interact with the community. This part of the study corresponds to the psychological examination of the individual. It is here that the consultant gathers the individual's thoughts about the organization as well as certain perceptions about himself — especially with regard to his relationship to the organization.

In order to expedite the assessment of current organizational functioning, two methods have been utilized — the structured interview and the written questionnaire.

The main advantage of the structured interview lies in the presumption that it is conducted by a skilled behavioral scientist. In such a situation the data are likely to be rich in details, and the validity and appropriateness of the interviewee's verbal and extraverbal responses can be more easily evaluated. Only a personal, private interview, where confidentiality has been assured, can provide such detailed and refined data. Many people will truly "open up," state their opinions, and express their feelings in response to such a situation. However, the structured interview is a form of projective technique. Many people find it difficult to respond to vague questions. The interviewer must support those people to answer in their own way as much as possible.

The written questionnaire is intended to parallel the questions of the structured interview. The main advantage of the written questionnaire is that it can be given to everyone in the organization and yet not consume a great deal of the consultant's time. It provides a means for organization members to express themselves on the issues involved in the study. It has the disadvantage of being a one-way communication and one whose validity cannot always be easily assessed. For example, even though the questionnaire is not signed, many individuals will still remain suspicious of the consultant's motives. This is especially true if it is given early in the study (as it should be) when the employees have not had a chance to get to know, and trust, the consultant. They will be more likely to respond to what they think is the "party line" of the organization, or else they will be noncommittal and not disclose their true feelings about many of the issues. On the other hand, if the written questionnaire is given later on in the study there are still complicating factors. People in the organization may have come to like the consultant and, therefore, they may respond to the questionnaire by wanting to "do a good job" with it — giving him the answers they think he wants to hear. Needless to say, the reverse can also occur if people in the organization come to dislike the consultant. In such a situation, when answering the questions, they might respond more to their personal feelings about the consultant than to their feelings about the organization.

Rationale of the Structured Interview

The general purpose of the structured interview is to learn about the interviewee's thoughts about the organization and certain of his perceptions about himself, especially in relationship to the organization. The following discussion is keyed to the Organizational Study Questionnaire (pp. 530–538).

1. *Tell me about the organization. How did it get to be the way it is?* The answer to this question usually contains the history of the organization, as the person knows it. The amount of history known by the respondent is some indication of his degree of investment in the organization. However, it is also a function of the degree of orientation and indoctrination carried on by training personnel and the degree to which senior members of the organization regard the newer members as playing a part in the history and tradition of the organization.

This question also presents an opportunity to talk about how personal needs are provided for, or not provided for, by the organization; the distance or closeness of the individual to the organization, his reaction to changes within it, and his degree of identification with it. The answer can also indicate what the respondent sees as the forces within the organization, particularly those affecting him, and to what extent he is involved in the realities of the organization which confront him. His discussion of these forces and the means with which he copes with them reveals his perception of his own relationship to the organization.

The prodding question, "Anything else?" may reveal whether the respondent's previous answers are the result of his special preoccupations; and, if so, further facts may be forthcoming. The quantity as well as the quality of this preoccupation may reveal the degree to which an individual feels pressed by what goes on in the organization.

2a. *What do you do here?* This question elicits specific information regarding the individual's task. His view of his task as well as his feelings about it reveal, in essence, his occupational self-image. Does he see himself as being concerned with details exclusively or also with the larger organizational goals? In this, his distance from others and his role conflicts may be revealed.

2b. *What sort of place is this to do your job?* This pertains more to affect and feeling tone, that is, "How do you like it here?" The answer should reveal what it means to this individual to be in the organization; how he fits into the structure; what conflicts, hopes, and aspirations might be engendered through the organization. Will he grow? Will he stagnate? What challenges are present and to what degree does he feel challenged?

2c. *Why?* This should abstract from the answers to 2a the important values (or conflicts) to the individual.

3a. *Tell me about the people here. How are they to work with?* This asks for elaboration on questions 2a and 2b and more specifically deals with what the respondent needs in his relationships with people. Such needs might be fulfilled by supportive functions, power situations, sibling relationships, ego ideals, identification figures, or rewards and punishments. The "why" part of the question allows him to elaborate on the closeness of his relationships, how his dependency needs are gratified, and how he copes with authority relationships.

3b. *What kind of person would be likely to apply for a job here?* The answer implies the respondent's view of the organizational self-image, that is, the collective "who are we." It also reveals why he came here (his self-image), how he fits in society, and "what it (the job or organization) takes." This may illuminate a "typical" personality type in the organization.

3c. *If you were going to hire someone for a job like yours, what kind of person would you hire?* This extracts an aspect of the respondent's ego ideal, "what I should be." It might also suggest what this person fears in terms of who, or what, kind of person will take his job. Sometimes the respondent will go on to elaborate particular stresses or conflicts in his job not explained in response to the preceding questions.

4a. *Tell me what is done here to help a person along once he starts to work in this organization?* This question deals largely with the informal type of help present in the organization. It often reveals the individual's need for support and to what extent his dependency needs are recognized in the organization as well as what his expectations for this are. It may also reveal what mutual coping devices operate between the individual and the organization and what the style of supervision is.

4b. *With respect to helping a person along, how does the organization get people started? What happened to you when you started — and when did you start?* This will elicit specific information about question 4a. This second part of the question personalizes the experience and often also elicits the feelings aroused when the person had to cope with his initial strangeness and helplessness in the organization.

4c. *How much and what kind of training do people get?* This is a more specific inquiry about formal training in the organization. It tends to elicit answers regarding what the individual would like to have and how much he is depending on the company to make him into something, that is, how much he sees the organization as a source of his adult identity.

4d. *How do you find out how your are doing?* The answers to this question often list the feedback mechanisms operating within the organization and suggest the nature and quality of supervisor-supervisee relationships. They deal with such items as the degree and way in which distance or closeness is maintained and how affection and aggression are handled. They also suggest rivalry or openness with peers and where interpersonal gratifications come from. For example, if the chief feedback comes from subordinates or peers, this would suggest that supervisors' feelings of inadequacy are an issue. If an organization is dominated by strong criticism, this suggests that people will have a great deal of fear regarding wishes and impulses that they regard as unacceptable. Conversely, when the rewards are open and people speak freely for themselves, there will be less fright about such impulses emerging, such as being critical of superiors.

4e. *What happens when problems come up?* This elicits dependency relationships and to whom the person turns for support. Also involved in the reply are the individual's relationships to his supervisor, which is called for in specific examples.

4f. *Every organization does certain things to take care of its people — like having health, safety, or retirement programs. Tell me about what they do here.* This question deals with the broad support functions available in the organization, who needs them, and who gets them. It is another version of question 4e. Vague, uncertain, and misinformed answers to the specific details asked for in this question may mean that there has been poor indoctrination about these facts. On the other hand, they may mean that the individual has confidence in the organization that he will be taken care of and is therefore less concerned about such details.

4g. *What do people here do for each other if someone gets sick?* This question deals with the closeness of peers (sibling relationships) to each other, that is, their identification with each other, their feelings about one another, and the degree to which they will mobilize to help one another.

5a. *What are the main rules around here that everyone has to follow?* Answers to this question reveal the key issues regarding control within the organization. They suggest taboos and operational values and indicate how much of these values are introjected and are ego-syntonic to the employees. Rigidity or flexibility within the organization is also indicated.

5b. *How well do they work?* This gives the interviewee opportunity to draw contrasts with his previous answer. It may reveal the degree of denial present in response to 5a.

6a. *What are the busy times around here?* This is to define the external time pressures, their sources, and the realities of such pressures.

6b. *How closely are things scheduled? (What does a typical day look like?)* This deals with how the realities in question 6a are anticipated within the organization. Are they planned for or are they left to occur spontaneously so that the employees must deal with them in the best way they can without help, thus suggesting an attitude of expendability toward the employees. Included in this answer may be a suggestion of how the individual masters his world or is mastered by it.

6c. *Why?* The respondent will list here the realities of these pressures. Are they necessary or are they weapons used within the organization? This question also deals with how the respondent sees the operating forces in his work world.

7. *What ways are there to find out what is going on around here?* Answers to this question will describe communications and their reliability within the organization. Such answers may reveal possible ground for paranoid fantasy (some undefined power up there fouls things up) and helplessness or lack of trust, which lowers self-respect and creates anxiety. The more the employee relies on rumor for information, the more ground there is for distrust and anxiety. Conversely, the more data that are shared with the individual, the more he feels trusted and the more he is capable of expressing his own affection and trust to others. The prodding question, "Any others?" elicits how relevant and how well handled the communications may actually be.

8a. *What do outsiders think of this organization?* This question allows projection, asking in reality, "What do you think others think of the organization?" The answer will thus reveal any disparity between the organization's reputation and what the employees actually think of it, possibly in terms of their feelings regarding fulfillment of their own ego ideals. Specific foci of hostility or energy may also be revealed. The "please specify" part of the question deals more with the political aspects and the organization's relationship to competitors, unions, and regulatory agencies.

8b. *Why?* The second part of the question elicits something about the employee's identification and attitude about the issues to be defended, and it yields as well some idea about how isolated the employees may be from the realities of the business. It allows further opportunity to focus on the important outside figures against whom the company must be defended or, perhaps, who must be manipulated in the interests of the organization.

8c. *How do you know?* This is intended to determine whether the previous answer is based on reality and actual knowledge or on rumor. It also elicits the individual's feelings about the source of his knowledge.

9a. *How does the organization keep up with what's going on elsewhere?* Answers to this question will elicit the degree to which the organization's interests and perceptions are directed outward, thereby suggesting how much the organization wants to know and how much it listens or, conversely, the degree of withdrawal by the organization. Implicit here are such issues as how the organization deals with mastery, curiosity, aggressiveness, progressiveness, innovation, flexibility, security, and change, as well as how it copes with the outside world and how it is coped with.

9b. *What kind of things is it most interested in keeping up with?* This is also outwardly directed and deals with the specific direction, or focus, of question 9a. It might reveal the disparity between the ego ideal and reality.

9c. *How does the organization make use of a person's experience and ideas?* This calls for a more inwardly directed answer, identifying the degree to which the organization makes use of ideas which arise within it. The reply suggests the degree of participation in decision making, stimulation to growth, and respect for the individuals within the organization.

10. *Does the organization make use of the information available?* On one level the response reflects the degree of judgment about what information is available and how well it is used. On another level it will reveal the organization's attitude toward self versus the outside and suggests the quality of defensiveness or amount of drive within the organization.

11a. *What does the organization say it stands for?* This asks for the organizational ego ideal around which people are supposed to cohere. It also indicates how much the employees know about the organization.

11b. *How does it get its message across?* Answers here usually deal with advertising or services and reveal to what extent the ego ideals are supported by fact and behavior, that is, how much disparity there is between the organization's stated ideals and the degree to which it lives up to them. The converse of this may also be suggested, that is, that the employee feels the organization has qualities and ideals that should be, but are not, shown to the outside.

12a. *Make believe this organization is a person . . . Describe that person to me . . .* This elicits an image of the organization. Taken collectively, such images constitute an organizational self-image. This also personifies the relationship of the employee with the organization. His reply is an index of the degree of reciprocation in the psychological contract between the organization and employee, saying what the employee wants from the organization and what he thinks he actually gets. It reveals what the individual experiences from the organization and what the organization may experience from the individual, both in reality and as transference phenomena. The prodding question, "Is he/she always like this?" reveals the consistency and degree of dependability in this relationship.

13a. *How peppy (energetic) is this organization?* This deals with the strength and activity or, conversely, somnolence of the organization. Does the energy vary with realities or with unrealities? The other parts of this question ("b., All the time?" and "c., In what ways is this (pep) useful, or is it just wheel spinning?") reveal the consistency of this behavior and differentiate between diffuse or goal-directed behavior.

14. *How much do the people here really know about this business?* This question has to do with how much people actually invest themselves in the organization, how much responsible communication and participation there is in the

business, and how much the organization is a part of their ego structures. This differentiates between investment in the "company *qua* company" versus in the industry; that is, do they see themselves as "locals" or "cosmopolitans"?

15a. *How strong is this organization?* This question complements number 14 and deals with transference problems. What do the employees think of the business? How much do they depend on it, and how capable do they feel it is? It deals with the degree of compartmentalization or separation between the business and themselves. It also deals with the quality of the organization's strength; that is, is it malevolently attacking or benevolently supportive? The degree to which the employees have identified their future with that of the organization and their conception of the organization's enduring quality will be reflected in the answer to this question.

The second part of this question, "Tell me what you mean," delineates the particular areas in which the employee will look for strength, such as dependency, aggression, ego support.

15b. *How do you know?* This asks the employee to document the sources of his information and thus delineate the solidity of this information. It also elicits how much of his feeling is genuine self-confidence and how much is fantasized trust.

16. *What is he/she (the personified organization) doing?* This deals with how the employee perceives the organization to be coping with reality. What are the problems? What are the goals? What are the assets? To what extent is this coping reality directed; is it aggressive, masterful, passive, and so on?

In response to this question the leader (manager, president, chairman of the board, foreman) is sometimes personified, which suggests that this leader is the primary focus of trust and power to this employee. If the employee himself is personified, it suggests that there is no trust in the leader and that the employee is divorced from, or alienated from, the company. His lack of investment makes him unable to personify the company so he must personify himself. Conversely, if the company itself is personified, it suggests that there is involvement with the total organization rather than any particular person. A lack of any personification suggests an inability to abstract (concreteness) or the absence of a clear image of self or organization.

17a. *Suppose this organization had to stop doing some of the things it now does. Assuming your job would not be affected, what should not be changed?* This question will elicit what the respondent thinks are the most important central functions of the organization and reveal how the employee sees his relationship to those functions.

17b. *Why?* The prodding question deals with the logic to this answer and how much about the realities of the organization the person actually knows.

18a. *Which outside groups does this organization pay attention to?* This question asks where the employee sees the attention of the organization being focused. Who are the reference groups? Where do the felt pressures come from? How much the person knows about this suggests the level of his involvement.

18b. *How? Why?* This tests reality further as well as eliciting the quantity of collective information.

19. *What future do you see for this organization?* This deals with what the employee sees in his own future as well as that of the organization. Where is the organization going, and can the employee go with it? Is the employee's ego ideal clearly established, and does this fit with the organization's ego ideal? How much confidence does the employee have in the organization and in himself? The "Why?" further tests reality.

20. *Suppose you were the head of this organization and had to make long-range plans for it. What do you think would be the most important things about the organization that you would have to keep in mind in making these plans?* This question is an echo of number 17. It deals with the most important problems that the organization faces and how much they are known, thought about, and realistically assessed. It also asks how much the person is involved in the realities of the organization and the interpersonal relationships in it, such as what the employees think about each other's feelings and what the grapevine reveals about each other's complaints.

21a. *Thinking back over the things we've talked about, do you think most people here would look at these things the same way you do?* This asks how much the person feels in tune with, or deviant from, the others in the organization, how much he feels he represents consensus and is a part of the swim of what is happening in the organization. The degree of felt alienation will be revealed.

22. *I've asked you a lot of questions. Do you have any you'd like to ask me?* This question allows the interviewee to ease his anxiety, satisfy his curiosity and obtain approval from the interviewer by asking, in indirect ways, how well he did. It also returns the interviewee to a more equal level with the interviewer and gives recognition to his mature, adult role, to his being engaged with the interviewer in a joint study effort, and recognizes the interviewer's obligation to the interviewee.

Structured Interview Outline

NAME: _____

JOB TITLE: _____

LOCATION OF INTERVIEW: _____

DATE OF INTERVIEW: _____

INTERVIEWER: _____

Opening Statement by Interviewer

As you know, my colleagues and I from (identify consulting organization) are doing a study of (name of organization). Everyone (will be) (has been) asked to fill out a printed questionnaire. In addition some people, like you, are being asked to talk with us individually. You were chosen because of the kind of work you do and by chance. The choice has nothing to do with you personally. Some others will be interviewed personally too. Before we begin, let's review why we are here and what this is all about. Can you tell me your understanding of this study? (Correct misunderstandings.) Do you have any questions about it? (Allow time for questions and explanation.)

All right. Now, I'd like to learn as much as I can about how this organization works. To do that I'd like to ask you a number of questions. By the time we're finished, I'd like to feel I know pretty much how things go around here. Whatever you tell me will be confidential.

1. Tell me about (organization). How did it get to be the way it is? (Anything else?)
2a. What do you do here?
 b. What sort of a place is this to do your job?
 c. Why?
3a. Tell me about the people here. How are they to work with? (Why?)
 b. What kind of a person would be likely to apply for a job here? (Why?)
 c. If you were going to hire someone for a job like yours, what kind of a person would you hire?
4a. Tell me what is done here to help a person along once he starts to work in this (organization). (Anything else?)
 b. With respect to helping a person along, how does (the organization) get people started? What happened to you when you started—and when *did* you start?
 c. How much and what kind of training do people get?
 d. How do you find out how you are doing? (Any other ways?)
 e. What happens when problems come up? (Give me some examples.)
 f. Every organization does certain things to take care of its people — like having health, safety, or retirement programs. Tell me about what they do here.

g. What do the people here do for each other if someone gets sick?

5a. What are the main rules around here that everyone has to follow? (Specify.)

b. How well do they work?

6a. What are the busy times around here?

b. How closely are things scheduled? (What does a typical day look like?)

c. Why? (Spell out.)

7. What ways are there to find out what's going on around here? (Any others?)

8a. What do outsiders think of (this organization)? (Please specify which groups have which attitudes.)

b. Why? (For each.)

c. How do you know?

9a. How does (the organization) keep up with what's going on elsewhere?

b. What kind of things is it most interested in keeping up with? (Note "things" is plural.)

c. How does (the organization) make use of a person's experience and ideas? (Give examples.)

10. Does (the organization) make use of the information available? (Why/Why not?)

11a. What does (the organization) say it stands for?

b. How does it get its message across? (Both what media and how effectively.)

12a. Make believe (this organization) is a person. Think about that person for a minute. Describe that person to me so I can get a good idea of the picture you have in mind.

b. Is he/she always like this? (If not, what other pictures come to mind?)

13a. How peppy (energetic) is (this organization)? (Tell me what you mean.)

b. All the time?

c. In what ways is this (pep) useful, or is it just spinning wheels? (Give examples.)

14. How much do the people here really know about this business?

15a. How strong is (this organization?) (Tell me what you mean.)

b. How do you know? (Explain.)

16. A little while ago I asked you to pretend (this organization) was a person and to describe the person. Think about that person again for a minute . . . think of that person doing something. What is he/she doing?

17a. Suppose (this organization) had to stop doing some of the things it now does. Assuming your job would not be affected, what should not be changed?

b. Why?

18a. Which outside groups does (this organization) pay attention to?

b. How? Why? (For each.) (And others? How? Why?)

19. What future do you see for (this organization)? (Why?)

20. Suppose you were the head of (this organization) and had to make long-range plans for it. What do you think would be the most important things about (the organization) that you should have to keep in mind in making these plans.

21a. Thinking back over the things we've talked about, do you think most people here would look at these things the same way you do?

  b. Why?

22. I've asked you a lot of questions. Do you have any you'd like to ask me? Thank you for your help.

Written Questionnaire

ORGANIZATION AND JOB ATTITUDE INVENTORY

We would like to learn more about how people feel about the company they work for and the job. We do not need to know who you are personally, so do not sign the questionnaire.

Most of the questions ask that you check *one* of the anwers; however, some questions ask that you write the answer in the space provided. The value of this study depends on how honestly and carefully you answer the questions. Remember, *this is not a test,* and there are no right and no wrong answers.

Please answer the questions in order. Do not skip around.
Be sure to answer *all* the questions.
Thank you for your cooperation.

I. Some Things About Yourself
 1. What is your job in the company called _____
 2. In what department, section, or unit of the company do you work _____
 _____
 3. What do you consider to be your usual occupation _____
 4. How long have you worked for the company (check)

  (1) _____ Less than 6 months   (5) _____ 5 years to 10 years
  (2) _____ 6 months to 1 year   (6) _____ 10 years to 20 years
  (3) _____ 1 year to 2 years   (7) _____ Over 20 years
  (4) _____ 2 years to 5 years

 5. How long have you worked in your present department, section, or unit of the company (check)

  (1) _____ Less than 6 months   (5) _____ 5 years to 10 years
  (2) _____ 6 months to 1 year   (6) _____ 10 years to 20 years
  (3) _____ 1 year to 2 years   (7) _____ Over 20 years
  (4) _____ 2 years to 5 years

 6. How far did you go in school (check)

  (1) _____ Less than 8th grade (4) _____ Some college
  (2) _____ 8th through 11th   (5) _____ College graduate
  (3) _____ High school graduate (6) _____ Other (Specify) _____

 7. How old are you (check)

  (1) _____ 18 to 21   (5) _____ 41 to 50
  (2) _____ 22 to 25   (6) _____ 51 to 60
  (3) _____ 26 to 30   (7) _____ Over 60
  (4) _____ 31 to 40

8. Sex (check)

   (1) _____ Male
   (2) _____ Female

II. The Company

9. How old is this company (check)

   (1) _____ Over 100 years old   (5) _____ 5 to 10 years old
   (2) _____ 50 to 100 years old   (6) _____ Less than 5 years old
   (3) _____ 25 to 50 years old   (7) _____ Don't know
   (4) _____ 10 to 25 years old

10. How many people work for this company at this location (check)

    (1) _____ Over 1,000   (5) _____ 50 to 100
    (2) _____ 500 to 1,000   (6) _____ Less than 50
    (3) _____ 250 to 500   (7) _____ Don't know
    (4) _____ 100 to 250

11. In the last five years, how much has this company grown (check)

    (1) _____ A great deal   (3) _____ Not at all
    (2) _____ Somewhat   (4) _____ Don't know

12. How much has the company changed in the last 5 years (other than size) (check)

    (1) _____ A great deal   (3) _____ Not at all
    (2) _____ Somewhat   (4) _____ Don't know

13. How would you rate this company compared to others in the same field (check)

    (1) _____ The very best   (4) _____ Below average
    (2) _____ Above average   (5) _____ The very worst
    (3) _____ Average

14. Compared to other companies in the same field, this company is (check)

    (1) _____ Moving ahead faster   (3) _____ Falling behind
    (2) _____ Holding its own   (4) _____ Don't know

15. How does the community feel about this company (check)

    (1) _____ Very friendly toward it
    (2) _____ Neither friendly nor unfriendly
    (3) _____ Unfriendly toward it
    (4) _____ Don't know

16. Compared to other companies in this community, how would you rate the employment policies and benefits of this company (check)

    (1) _____ Excellent   (3) _____ Average
    (2) _____ Above average   (4) _____ Below average

17. What is this company's most important product or service? _____
_____

18. Who is the most important person in the company and what is his title?
_____

19. What are the three things that this company is working hardest for at this time?

    (1) _____
    (2) _____
    (3) _____

20. What is this company's greatest strength? _____
_____

21. What is this company's greatest weakness? _____
_____

22. What three recommendations would you make to the company that would help it achieve its goals?

    (1) _____
    (2) _____
    (3) _____

III. Your Job

23. What are the main duties of your job? _____
_____
_____
_____

24. What are the three most important things that the company wants in a person doing your job?

    (1) _____
    (2) _____
    (3) _____

25. How many people work in your particular department, division, or unit (check)

    (1) _____ Over 100   (4) _____ 10 to 25
    (2) _____ 50 to 100   (5) _____ 3 to 10
    (3) _____ 25 to 50   (6) _____ Less than 3

26. How many people do you supervise (check)

    (1) _____ Over 100   (4) _____ 10 to 25
    (2) _____ 50 to 100   (5) _____ 1 to 10
    (3) _____ 25 to 50   (6) _____ None

27. How important is your job in the company (check)

    (1) _____ Among the most important
    (2) _____ Very important
    (3) _____ Necessary, but not particularly important
    (4) _____ Unimportant
    (5) _____ Don't know

28. How much supervision do you get (check)

(1) _____ A great deal   (3) _____ Very little
(2) _____ A fair amount   (4) _____ None

29. How would you rate the supervision you get (check)

(1) _____ Excellent   (3) _____ Average
(2) _____ Good   (4) _____ Poor

30. With regard to supervision, would you like to have (check)

(1) _____ More   (2) _____ Same   (3) _____ Less

31. How would you know when you are doing your job well? _____
_____
_____

32. How would you know when you are not doing your job well? _____
_____

33. How would you rate the physical conditions under which you do your job (check)

(1) _____ Excellent   (3) _____ Fair
(2) _____ Good   (4) _____ Poor

34. How would you rate the pay and other benefits you receive, as compared to those doing the same kind of work in other companies in this community (check)

(1) _____ Above average (2) _____ Average (3) _____ Below average

35. How sure do you feel of having a permanent job in this company (check)

(1) _____ Very sure   (4) _____ Rather unsure
(2) _____ Quite sure   (5) _____ Very unsure
(3) _____ Have no idea

36. How much training for your job has the company given you (check)

(1) _____ A great deal   (3) _____ Very little
(2) _____ A fair amount   (4) _____ None

37. With regard to job training, would you like to have (check)

(1) _____ More   (2) _____ Same   (3) _____ Less

38. How much freedom do you have in planning and doing your work (check)

(1) _____ A great deal   (3) _____ Very little
(2) _____ A fair amount   (4) _____ None

39. If problems come up in doing your job, how much help do you get in handling those problems (check)

(1) _____ A great deal   (3) _____ Very little
(2) _____ A fair amount   (4) _____ None

40. Which one of the following would you find most helpful in working out problems connected with your job (check)

(1) _____ Your immediate supervisor
(2) _____ The person above your supervisor
(3) _____ One of your fellow workers
(4) _____ One of the top executives
(5) _____ Somebody outside of the company

41. In doing your job, how much contact do you have with others in your department (check)

(1) _____ A great deal   (3) _____ Very little
(2) _____ A fair amount   (4) _____ None ·

42. In doing your job, how much contact do you have with others in the company outside of your department (check)

(1) _____ A great deal   (3) _____ Very little
(2) _____ A fair amount   (4) _____ None

43. In doing your job, how much contact do you have with people outside of the company (check)

(1) _____ A great deal   (3) _____ Very little
(2) _____ A fair amount   (4) _____ None

44. In connection with your job, would you like to have (check)

(1) _____ More contact with others
(2) _____ The same amount of contact
(3) _____ Less contact with others

45. How well do you like the people in the company that you work with or have contact with (check)

(1) _____ A great deal   (3) _____ Very little
(2) _____ Rather well   (4) _____ Not at all

46. How would you rate the way the people you work with get along (check)

(1) _____ Very close and friendly   (4) _____ Rather unfriendly
(2) _____ Quite friendly   (5) _____ Very unfriendly
(3) _____ Distant but not unfriendly

47. With regard to yourself and your fellow workers would you prefer (check)

(1) _____ Closer relationships   (3) _____ Less close relationships
(2) _____ The way it is now

48. If you had a complaint or "gripe" about something connected with your job, whose attention would you bring it to first (check)

(1) _____ Your supervisor
(2) _____ The person above your supervisor
(3) _____ One of your fellow workers
(4) _____ Union steward or representative

(5) _____ One of the top executives
(6) _____ Someone outside the company
(7) _____ Would keep it to yourself

49. When changes are to be made which affect your job, how much are you consulted (check)

    (1) _____ Always   (3) _____ Seldom
    (2) _____ Usually   (4) _____ Never

50. How would you rate the cooperation you get from others in the company (check)

    (1) _____ Excellent   (3) _____ Fair
    (2) _____ Good   (4) _____ Poor

51. In a typical day, how much tension and friction is there among the people in your department (check)

    (1) _____ A great deal   (3) _____ Very little
    (2) _____ A fair amount   (4) _____ None

52. How much tension and friction is there between your department and other departments of the company (check)

    (1) _____ A great deal   (3) _____ Very little
    (2) _____ A fair amount   (4) _____ None

53. How would you rate the planning, organizing, and scheduling of the work in your department (check)

    (1) _____ Excellent   (3) _____ Average
    (2) _____ Good   (4) _____ Poor

54. How well does your supervisor and those above him understand the technical problems you face in doing your work (check)

    (1) _____ Very well   (3) _____ Not very well
    (2) _____ Rather well   (4) _____ Not at all

55. Considering what the company expects of you in your job and the conditions under which you work, do you think the company (check)

    (1) _____ Expects too much   (3) _____ Expects very little
    (2) _____ Expects about what is right

56. List the three things you like most about your job.

    (1) _____
    (2) _____
    (3) _____

57. List the three things you like least about your job.

    (1) _____
    (2) _____
    (3) _____

58. How much chance do you have for visiting with others in the company during or after working hours (check)

(1) _____ A great deal   (3) _____ Very little
(2) _____ A fair amount   (4) _____ None

59. How many people in the company do you consider to be your personal friends (check)

(1) _____ 10 or more   (4) _____ 1 to 2
(2) _____ 5 to 10   (5) _____ None
(3) _____ 3 to 5

60. If you should change jobs in the company, which job would you like to have? _____

61. How good do you think your chances are for getting a better job in the company (check)

(1) _____ Excellent   (3) _____ Fair
(2) _____ Good   (4) _____ Poor

62. How much do you think the company would help you in preparing for a better job (check)

(1) _____ As much as possible (3) _____ Very little
(2) _____ Quite a bit   (4) _____ Not at all

63. How good is the work done by your department compared to other departments in the company (check)

(1) _____ The very best   (3) _____ Below average
(2) _____ As good as most   (4) _____ The very worst

64. How would you rate the working conditions in your department compared to other departments in the company (check)

(1) _____ The very best   (3) _____ Below average
(2) _____ As good as most   (4) _____ The very worst

65. Who makes the most important decisions in your department (check)

(1) _____ Your supervisor   (3) _____ Top management
(2) _____ The person above   (4) _____ The department as a whole
        your supervisor   (5) _____ Don't know

66. How much turnover have you had in your department during the past two years (check)

(1) _____ A great deal   (3) _____ Very little
(2) _____ A fair amount   (4) _____ None

67. Where do you most often learn what is going on in the company (check)

(1) _____ Official bulletins   (4) _____ People outside the company
(2) _____ Your supervisor   (5) _____ Newspapers
(3) _____ Your fellow workers (6) _____ Rumors, the "grapevine"

68. How free do you feel about talking over job problems with your supervisor (check)

(1) _____ Very free   (3) _____ Not very free
(2) _____ Fairly free   (4) _____ Not at all free

69. How free do you feel about talking over job problems with the person above your supervisor (check)

(1) _____ Very free   (3) _____ Not very free
(2) _____ Fairly free   (4) _____ Not at all free

70. How would you rate the people who run this company as to ability (check)

(1) _____ Excellent   (3) _____ Fair
(2) _____ Good   (4) _____ Poor

71. How much consideration are your ideas or suggestions given by the company (check)

(1) _____ A great deal   (3) _____ Very little
(2) _____ Somewhat   (4) _____ Not at all

72. If, because of unusual problems or emergencies, the company needed you to perform extra duties or work longer hours, would you (check)

(1) _____ Volunteer gladly   (4) _____ Rather not be asked
(2) _____ Wait to be asked   (5) _____ Refuse, if possible
(3) _____ Not mind being asked

73. If there was a conflict or difference of opinion in which you were involved, how much fairness do you think the company would show you (check)

(1) _____ A great deal   (3) _____ Very little
(2) _____ A fair amount   (4) _____ None

74. If you had a serious personal problem that interfered with your work, how much consideration do you think you would get from the company (check)

(1) _____ A great deal   (3) _____ Very little
(2) _____ A fair amount   (4) _____ None

75. How would you rate the strictness of the rules of the company (check)

(1) _____ Very strict   (3) _____ Somewhat easygoing
(2) _____ Average   (4) _____ Very easygoing

76. With regard to strictness of rules, would you like (check)

(1) _____ More strictness   (3) _____ Less strictness
(2) _____ The same

77. How much do you think the company is interested in your welfare (check)

(1) _____ Very much   (3) _____ Not very interested
(2) _____ Quite interested   (4) _____ Not at all interested

78. Would you recommend to a friend that he work for this company (check)

(1) _____ Yes
(2) _____ No

79. Thinking ahead five years, would you want to be working for this company (check)

(1) _____ Yes
(2) _____ No

80. If you could make changes that would make the company a better place for you to work, what three changes would be most important to you?

(1) _____
(2) _____
(3) _____

Date Filled Out _____

Diary Outline

Meeting Location, Date, and Time _____ Reporter _____

Number present ____ Number of questionnaires distributed ____ Dept. _____

1. *Report phase:* attentiveness of audience, evidence of good or poor rapport, mood of reporter (relaxed, tired, tense, comfortable, etc.), comparison with other groups seen.
2. *Discussion phase:* length, questions asked (get as many verbatim as possible), themes emerging from questions or discussion.
3. *Meeting in general:* type of introduction, comparison with other experiences, physical environment (light, heat, noise), degree of time pressure.
4. Other aspects of contact with this group outside the meeting proper but of significance for the study.
5. Rating by reporter:
   (a) Degree of rapport and understanding: high ____ medium ____ low ____
   (b) Degree of acceptance: high ____ medium ____ low ____

Appendix B
ADAPTIVE ACTIVITIES

Adaptation is the aggressive attack on self or the environment to master either or both to serve one's own needs. All living organisms must necessarily attack their environments to survive, for example, a tree spreading its roots, drawing moisture and nutrients from the soil; an animal killing another for food; another digging a home out of the ground or making one of branches; a man cutting wood or mining coal to warm himself. Some organisms must, in effect, attack themselves, compelling themselves to sacrifice present pleasures for future gains, learning skills and competences. Sometimes adaptive mechanisms or activities lose their effectiveness or cost too much in terms of energy or resources for the results they achieve. Sometimes they achieve short-run goals at the cost of long-term survival. Sometimes they are overreactive, destructive to both the actor and the object of his actions. In extreme form adaptive mechanisms result in the literal destruction of the actor.

Adaptation also refers to equilibrium-maintaining activities which an organism undertakes to sustain its integrity against both internal and external threat. For example, fever reflects the equilibrium-maintaining activity of the body against the threat of infection; flight-fight behavior is defensive against external threat. There are many individual and group activities that can be used to maintain psychological equilibrium, ranging from rationalization to creating and attacking external enemies.

Activities devoted to mastering the internal and external worlds may be seen as coping behaviors, or mechanisms. Those directed toward protecting the organism against internal or external threat may be seen as defense mechanisms. All behavior necessarily includes both types of mechanisms in varying degrees (see Harry Levinson, *The Exceptional Executive,* Cambridge, Mass.: Harvard University Press, 1968, ch. 2). The more an organism devotes its energies to defensive behavior, the less it has available for effective and enduring mastery. Similarly, the more an organism devotes itself to its own protection, the more its behavior is stimulated by real or fancied outside forces, and the less it pursues spontaneous mastery efforts. For example, a man who must please others at all costs can hardly be what he wants to be; rather, he is what others want him to be.

Organizations also have coping and defensive behaviors. This appendix lists and categorizes many according to their degree of adaptive effectiveness. These examples are intended to be illustrative, not exhaustive. They may help the consultant weigh more carefully the meaning and cost of the behavior he sees, particularly as he considers organization integrative patterns. The better an organization has integrated its behavior patterns, the more likely it is to adapt and defend successfully.

NORMAL ACTIVITIES

These behaviors permit some discharge of energy, presumably toward solving problems and attaining gratification. They may be divided into those having to do with the product or organization per se, and those having to do with people.

1. *Having to do with product or organization*
   processing materials; rendering services
   periodic reports; quality control
   revision of tasks and processes; changes in space and schedules
   expansion and acquisition
   acquaintance with competitor's products and response thereto
   acquaintance with changes in consumer's wishes and response thereto
   responsiveness to social changes
   research: basic, product, market, economic
   pilot efforts; proving grounds; testing products
   organization planning; projections of future trends
   sales promotion and indoctrination; self-laudatory advertising
   image creating efforts, symbolization, publicity
   public statements by key figures regarding organization's worth

2. *Having to do with people*
   building attractive surroundings; functional physical facilities
   morale building activities; encouraging socialization off the job to foster
      cohesion; company parties and conversational coffee breaks; background
      music
   encouraging shared fantasies of organizational achievement
   providing uniforms and other efforts to foster organization esprit de corps
   personnel selection, training, benefit, and caring functions
   management development
   offering seminars, workshops, training not necessarily connected directly
      with major work goals

participation in professional and trade associations and community activities

seeking support from community and other organizations

exhorting (internal and to community); mild pressure; nagging

expressing overtly internal feelings in advertising ("we like to serve")

complaints of management in public service messages or message seeking public support

protection from arbitrary authority

protection from industrial hazards; care for accidental results

spontaneous and unplanned postponement of tasks (relief)

organizational moratorium periods (minimal activity or productivity to repair, recover, reorganize)

operation of Parkinson's Law (work expands to fill the time for its completion)

occasional absenteeism, breakage, flare-up of hostility in reaction to inadequate problem-solving or due to frustration

FIRST-ORDER ACTIVITIES

These are exaggerations of normal adaptive activities. They are less functional because they tend to cost more in terms of money or energy and to yield proportionately less in results. Usually they increase frustration and anxiety, focus more on short-term than on long-term consequences, and reduce present satisfactions. Therefore they are indicators of stress and the need for intervention. These activities tend to be of two kinds: denials or more intensive efforts at control. Denials shut out information or pretend the threat does not really exist. More intensive control efforts increase the rigidity of the organization. Both are symptoms. Of course, sometimes, increased control efforts are necessary and denials may be temporarily functional. (It does not help the passengers to know that the aircraft pilot is having a difficult time of it in a storm.) The consultant must evaluate whether the activities he observes are normal or first order.

spot audits; PERT systems; times studies

more complex, more frequent reports; more frequent inventory checks

increased security checks, inspections, surveillance of competition, suppliers, operations, processes

reducing intake of information from outside

overtesting; increasing complexity of controls

impulsive revision of tasks and processes

refusal to recognize threat; minimizing threat; unrealistic optimism; pep talks

unrealistic pessimism; chronic griping

decreased philanthropy and community service

extended intervention into community affairs

increased stereotyping (competition, labor, community)

ignoring own history and effects of own behavior

making political commitments unconnected with organizational business

sporadic efforts: abortive cost cutting or sales efforts, often short-lived and inappropriate

overexpansion and acquisition

restricting friendships to company colleagues

needless overemphasis on cleanliness of equipment, plant; cult of poverty with considerable self-praise for making do

increased absenteeism; waste of time and supplies

by-passing of organizational structure

undermining of organizational caring, training, and growth efforts

SECOND-ORDER ACTIVITIES

These are clearly maladaptive and disruptive activities which have a high cost in terms of money, stress for individuals, and organizational survival potential. Usually they suggest a need for different or better leadership.

arbitrary change; sudden cutting of established departments

total rejection of outside information and advice

withdrawal into organizational self; giving up ties to community, professional associations

unduly risky financial manipulations

sacrificing reputation; employee morale; community relations

failure to live up to guarantees, promises

unrealistic fear reactions

repetitive unimplemented discussions and planning

intense chronic concern with a specific internal issue or problem at expense of attention to outside realities

repetitive interpersonal or intergroup conflict

scapegoating some member or part of the organization

self-exploitation in failure to collect accounts receivable

excessive rigidity of routine

repetitive self-sacrifice (cutting off parts of organization, narrowing functions, repetitive contraction)

great effort to conceal problems

loss of key personnel

THIRD-ORDER ACTIVITIES

These maladaptive and disruptive activities are characterized by episodic blatant expressions of hostility. They usually require the organization subseqently to effect a resolution of the difficulty its behavior has created or compensation for its destructiveness.

verbal outbursts in advertising against inappropriate targets

seeking the discharge of public officials or spying on opponents

wanton damage to property of others, reputations of persons, or to community manipulative practices in marketing, motivation, and legal relationships; lying and deception with regard to product

wanton industrial piracy (people, patents)

insincere, inadequate, or superficial compensatory efforts for damage previously done

exaggerated speculation; price-fixing; oligopoly

open violence in labor realtions

extreme behavior (panic, catastrophic demoralization, apathy, resignation, hyperexcitement for no adequate reason)

FOURTH-ORDER ACTIVITIES

These are self-destructive activities resulting in the demise of the organization or the involuntary surrender of control to another organization.

forced merger
bankruptcy
going out of business

REFERENCES

These references are to help the reader who wants more information about specific topics. Not all topics have references; therefore, not all are listed here.

Chapter 1: Overview

Argyris, Chris, *Understanding Organizational Behavior* (Homewood, Ill.: Dorsey, 1960).

Guide for Descriptive Study of Centers for Psychiatric In-Patient Treatment of Children (Washington, D.C.: American Psychiatric Association, 1957).

Seiler, John A., *Systems Analysis in Organizational Behavior* (Homewood, Ill.: Irwin, 1967).

Weiss, Robert S., "Alternative Approaches in the Study of Complex Situations," *Human Organization,* 25:3 (Fall 1966), 198–206.

Chapter 2: Introducing the Study

Obtaining Consent

Schwartzbaum, Allan, and Leopold Gruenfeld, "Factors Influencing Subject-Observer Interaction in an Organizational Study," *Administrative Science Quarterly,* 14:3 (September 1969), 443–450.

544

The Initial Tour

Athos, Anthony G., and Robert E. Coffey, *Behavior in Organizations: A Multi-Dimensional View* (Englewood Cliffs, N.J.: Prentice-Hall, 1968).

Feldman, Sandor S., *Mannerisms of Speech and Gestures in Everyday Life* (New York: International Universities Press, 1959).

Goffman, Erving, *The Presentation of Self in Everyday Life* (New York: Doubleday, 1959).

Hall, Edward T., *The Hidden Dimension* (New York: Doubleday, 1966).

Ruesch, Jurgen, *Therapeutic Communication* (New York, Norton, 1961).

————— and Weldon Kees, *Nonverbal Communication* (Berkeley, Calif.: University of California Press, 1956).

Chapter 3: The Study Procedure

Cook, Stuart W., Morton Deutsch, Marie Jahoda, and Claire Sellitz, *Research Methods in Social Relations* (New York: Holt, Rinehart and Winston, 1959).

Approaches to the Setting and Its Incumbents

Kahn, Robert L., and Charles F. Cannel, *The Dynamics of Interviewing* (New York: Wiley, 1957).

Lopez, Felix, M., *Personnel Interviewing.* (New York: McGraw-Hill, 1965).

Richardson, S. A., B. S. Dohrenwen, and D. Klein, *Interviewing: Its Forms and Functions* (New York: Basic Books, 1965).

Sullivan, H. S., *The Psychiatric Interview* (New York: Norton, 1954).

Work Experience: Rationale

The Person Who Seeks Help

Levinson, Harry, *Emotional Health: in the World of Work* (New York: Harper & Row, 1964), ch. 15.

Chapter 6: Description and Analysis of Current Organization as a Whole

A. Structural Data

1. Formal Organization

Blau, Peter M., and W. Richard Scott, *Formal Organizations* (San Francisco: Chandler Publishing Co., 1962).

Bower, Joseph L., "Descriptive Decision Theory from the 'Administrative' Viewpoint," in Raymond A. Bauer and Kenneth J. Gergen, eds., *The Study of Policy Formation* (New York: Free Press, 1968), pp. 103–148.

Brown, David S., "Shaping the Organization to Fit People," *Management of Personnel Quarterly*, 5:2 (Summer 1966), 12–16.

Gross, Bertram M., *The Managing of Organizations* (New York: Free Press, 1964), pp. 347–387.

Lawrence, Paul R., and Jay W. Lorsch, *Organization and Environment* (Boston: Harvard University, Graduate School of Business Administration, 1967).

Litterer, Joseph A., *Organizations: Structure and Behavior* (New York: Wiley, 1963), pp. 28–136.

Mooney, James D., and Alan C. Reiley, *The Principles of Organization* (New York: Harper & Row, 1939).

Perrow, Charles, "Hospital Techniques, Structure and Goals"; Charles E. Bidwell, "Schools as Formal Organizations"; and Donald R. Cressey, "Prison Organizations," in James G. March, ed., *Handbook of Organizations* (Chicago: Rand McNally, 1965), pp. 910–971; 972–1022; 1023–2070.

Pugh, D. S., D. J. Hickson, C. R. Hennings, K. M. McDonald, C. Turner, and T. Lupton, "A Conceptual Scheme for Organizational Analysis," *Administrative Science Quarterly*, 8 (December 1963), 289–315.

A. Chart

White, K. K., *Understanding the Company Chart* (New York: American Management Association, 1963).

B. Systems concept

Buckley, Walter, *Sociology and Modern Systems Theory* (Englewood Cliffs, N.J.: Prentice-Hall, 1967).

Cleland, David I., and Wallace Munsey, "Who Works with Whom?" *Harvard Business Review*, 45:5 (September–October 1967), 84–90.

Forrester, J. W., *Industrial Dynamics* (Cambridge: M.I.T. Press, 1961).

Katz, Daniel, and Robert Kahn, *The Social Psychology of Organizations* (New York: Wiley, 1966).

C. Formal job description

Beach, Dale S., *Personnel: The Management of People at Work* (New York: Macmillan, 1965), pp. 165–188.

Dale, Ernest, *Organization* (New York: American Management Association, 1967), pp. 306–315.

Hickson, D. J., "A Convergence in Organizational Theory," *Administrative Science Quarterly*, 11:11 (September 1966), 224–237.

Lopez, Felix M., Jr., *Personnel Interviewing* (New York: McGraw-Hill, 1965), pp. 249–251.

2. Plant and Equipment

Factory Management, a monthly journal published by McGraw-Hill.
Maynard, Harold B., *Industrial Engineering Handbook* (New York: McGraw-Hill, 1963).
Reed, Ruddell, Jr., *Plant Lay-Out* (Homewood, Ill.: Irwin, 1967).
Roscoe, Edwin S., *Organization for Production* (Homewood, Ill.: Irwin, 1967).
Staniar, William, *Plant Engineering Handbook* (New York: McGraw-Hill, 1959).

E. Special demands plant and equipment make on people

Turner, Arthur N., and Paul R. Lawrence, *Industrial Jobs and the Worker* (Boston: Harvard University, Graduate School of Business Administration, 1965).
Whyte, William F., *Men at Work* (Homewood, Ill.: Irwin-Dorsey, 1961).
Woodward, Joan, *Industrial Organization: Theory and Practice* (London: Oxford University Press, 1967).

3. Ecology of the Organization

Hawley, Amos, *Human Ecology* (New York: Ronald, 1950).
Lawrence, Paul R., and Jay W. Lorsch, *Organization and Environment* (Boston: Harvard University, Graduate School of Business Administration, 1967).
Levine, Sol, and Paul E. White, "Exchange as a Conceptual Framework for the Study of Interorganizational Relationships," *Administrative Science Quarterly*, 5:4 (March 1961), 583–601.
Thompson, James D., *Organization in Action* (New York: McGraw-Hill, 1967), ch. 3, pp. 25–38.

A. Spatial distribution of individuals

Hundert, Alan T., and Nathaniel Greenfield, "Physical Space and Organizational Behavior: A Study of an Office Landscape," *Proceedings of the 77th Annual Convention of American Psychological Association* (1969), 601–602.
"Making Office Walls Come Tumbling Down," *Business Week* (May 11, 1968), 56–58.

C. Implications of the data on spatial distribution

Sommer, Robert, *Personal Space: The Behavioral Basis of Design* (Englewood Cliffs, N.J.: Prentice-Hall, 1969).

4. Financial Structure

Buhagiar, Marion, "The Xerox Annual Report: A Guided Tour," *Fortune*, LXXC:7 (June 15, 1967), 184–187ff.
Coleman, James S., et al., *Equality of Educational Opportunity* (Washington, D.C.: Government Printing Office, 1966).

Gross, Bertram M., "The State of the Nation: Social Systems Accounting," in Raymond A. Bauer, ed., *Social Indicators* (Cambridge, Mass.: M.I.T. Press, 1966), pp. 154–271.

Hinrichs, Harley H., and M. Taylor Graeme, *Program Budgeting and Benefit Cost Analysis* (Pacific Palisades, Calif.: Goodyear Publishing Co., 1969).

How to Read a Financial Report (New York: Merrill Lynch, Pierce, Fenner & Smith, 1962).

Likert, Rensis, *The Human Organization* (New York: McGraw-Hill, 1967).

5. Personnel

There are many good books on personnel management most of which touch on the topics under this heading. Three are listed here as basic references in addition to specific references for specific topics.

Beach, Dale S., *Personnel: The Management of People at Work* (New York: Macmillan, 1965).

French, Wendell, *The Personnel Management Process: Human Resources Administration* (Boston: Houghton-Mifflin, 1964).

Greenwald, Harold, "Psychoanalytic Profile of a Factory," *Psychoanalysis*, 4:5 (Spring 1957), 27–37.

Miner, John B., "Bridging the Gulf in Organizational Performance," *Harvard Business Review*, 46:4 (July–August 1968), 102–110.

Pigors, Paul, and Charles A. Myers, *Personnel Administration*, 6th ed. (New York: McGraw-Hill, 1969).

B. Where do they come from

Gouldner, A. W., "Cosmopolitans and Locals: Toward an Analysis of Latent Social Roles, I," *Administrative Science Quarterly*, 2:4 (December 1957), 281–306.

C. Educational Levels

Anderson, B. J. Berger, B. P. Cohen, and M. Zelditch, Jr., "Status Classes in Organizations," *Administrative Science Quarterly*, 11:11 (September 1966), 264–283.

F. Absentee rate

Gibson, Oliver R., "Toward a Conceptualization of Absence Behavior of Personnel in Organizations," *Administrative Science Quarterly*, 11:1 (June 1966), 107–133.

Vroom, Victor H., *Work and Motivation* (New York: Wiley, 1964).

G. Turnover rate

Vroom, Victor H., *Work and Motivation* (New York: Wiley, 1964).

H. Accident rate

Hill, J. M. M., and E. L. Trist, "A Consideration of Industrial Accidents as a Means of Withdrawal from the Work Situation," *Human Relations*, 6:4 (Nov. 1953), 357–380.

6. Structure for Handling People

A. Recruitment

Hawk, Roger H., *The Recruitment Function* (New York: American Management Association, 1967).

Mandell, Milton M., *The Selection Process* (New York: American Management Association, 1964).

B. Orientation

Gomersall, Earl M., and M. Scott Myers, "Breakthrough in On-the-Job Training," *Harvard Business Reivew*, 44:4 (July–August 1966), 62–72.

C. Training

Bennett, Willard E., *Manager Selection, Education and Training* (New York: McGraw-Hill, 1959).

Clark, Harold F., and Harold S. Sloan, *Classrooms in the Factories* (Rutherford, N.J.: Fairleigh Dickinson University, Institute of Research, 1958).

Craig, Robert L., and Lester R. Bittel, *Training and Development Handbook* (New York: McGraw-Hill, 1967).

Graham, Robert G., and Milton A. Valentine, "Commitment and the Occupational Cycle," *Personnel Journal*, 48:7 (July 1969), 530–536.

King, David, *Training within the Organization* (London: Tavistock Publications, 1964).

Lynton, Rolf P., and Udai Pareek, *Training for Development* (Homewood, Ill.: Irwin, 1967).

D. Growth on the job

Odiorne, George S., *Personnel Policy: Issues and Practices* (Columbus, Ohio: Charles E. Merrill, 1963), pp. 226–270.

Wirtz, W. Willard, *Report of the Secretary of Labor on Research and Training Activities under the Manpower Development and Training Act* (Washington, D.C.: Government Printing Office, 1963).

E. Promotion

Jennings, Eugene E., *The Mobile Manager* (Lansing, Mich.: Michigan State University Business Studies, 1967).

McCoskey, Dale D., "Ability vs. Seniority in Promotion and Lay-off," *Personnel* 37 (May–June 1960), 51–57.

F. Compensation

Dale, Ernest, "Administration of Compensation," in Ernest Dale, ed., *Readings in Management: Landmarks and Frontiers* (New York: McGraw-Hill, 1965), pp. 291–300.

Jaques, Elliott, *Equitable Payment* (New York: Wiley, 1961).

Patton, Arch, "Top Executive Pay: New Facts and Figures," *Harvard Business Review*, 44:5 (September–October 1966), 94–97.

G. Performance analysis

Barrett, Richard S., *Performance Rating* (Chicago: Science Research Associates, 1966).

Kindall, Alva F., and James Gaza, "Positive Program for Performance Appraisal," *Harvard Business Review*, 41:6 (November–December 1963), 153–167.

Meyer, Herbert H., Emanuel Kay, and John R. P. French, Jr., "Split Roles in Performance Appraisal," *Harvard Business Review*, 43:1 (January–February 1965), 123–129.

Levinson, Harry, "Management by Whose Objectives?" *Harvard Business Review*, 48:4 (July–August 1970), 125–134.

Litterer, J. A., "Pitfalls in Performance Appraisal," *Personnel Journal*, 39:3 (July–August 1960), 85–88.

Whisler, Thomas L. and Shirley F. Harper, eds., *Performance Appraisal* (New York: Holt, Rinehart and Winston, 1962).

Wickert, Frederick R., and Dalton E. McFarland, eds., *Measuring Executive Effectiveness* (New York: Appleton-Century-Crofts, 1967).

H. Kind and intensity of supervision

Day, Robert C., and Robert L. Hamblin, "Some Effects of Close and Punitive Styles of Supervision," and Delbert C. Miller, "Supervisors: Evolution of an Organizational Role," in Gerald D. Bell, ed., *Organizations and Human Behavior* (Englewood Cliffs, N.J.: Prentice-Hall, 1967), pp. 172–184; 282–289.

House, Robert J., and John B. Miner, "Management and Behavioral Theory," *Administrative Science Quarterly*, 14:3 (September 1969), 451–465.

Likert, Rensis, *The Human Organization* (New York: McGraw-Hill, 1967).

Porter, Lyman, and Edward Lawler, *Managerial Attitudes and Performance* (Homewood, Ill.: Irwin-Dorsey, 1968).

Strauss, George and Leonard R. Sayles, *Personnel: The Human Problems of Management* (Englewood Cliffs, N.J.: Prentice-Hall, 1960).

Walker, Charles R., Robert H. Guest, and Arthur N. Turner, *The Foreman on the Assembly Line* (Cambridge, Mass.: Harvard University Press, 1956).

I. Rules and regulations for employees

Anderson, James G., "Bureaucratic Rules: Bearers of Organizational Authority," *Educational Administration Quarterly*, 11:1 (Winter 1966), 7–34.

J. MEDICAL PROGRAM

Felton, Jean Spencer, "Organization and Operation of an Occupational Health Program," *Journal of Occupational Medicine,* 6:1, 2, 3 (January, February, March 1964). (Available as a single reprint.)

Fleming, A. J., C. A. D'Alonzo, and J. A. Zapp, eds., *Modern Occupational Medicine,* 2nd ed. (Philadelphia: Lea & Febiger, 1960).

Hunter, Donald, *The Diseases of Occupations,* 4th ed. (Boston: Little, Brown, 1969).

Johnstone, R. T., and S. E. Miller, *Occupational Disease and Industrial Medicine* (Philadelphia: Saunders, 1960).

Pembertson, Doreen, *Essentials of Occupational Health Nursing.* (London: Arlington Books, 1965.)

Shepard, W. P., *The Physician in Industry* (New York: McGraw-Hill, 1961.)

West, Marion M., *A Handbook for Occupational Health Nurses,* 3rd ed. (London: Edward Arnold Publishers, 1962).

8. Time Span and Rhythm

D. DEGREE REGULATED BY TIME

Goodman, Paul S., "An Empirical Examination of Elliott Jaques' Concept of Time Span," *Human Relations,* 20:2 (May 1967), 155–170.

Jaques, Elliott, *Measurement of Responsibility* (Cambridge, Mass.: Harvard University Press, 1956).

Chapter 7: Interpretative Data

A. Current Organizational Functioning

Nadler, Leonard, "The Organization as a Micro-Culture," *Personnel Journal,* 48:12 (December 1969), 949–956.

1. Organizational Perceptions

A. DEGREE OF ALERTNESS, ACCURACY, AND VIVIDNESS

(1) *To stimuli from within the organization*

(A) FROM PERSONNEL

(ii) Supervisor to subordinate and vice versa

Smith, Peter B., David Moscow, Mel Berger, and Gary Cooper, "Relationships Between Managers and Their Work Associates," *Administrative Science Quarterly,* 14:3 (September 1969), 338–345.

2. Organizational Knowledge

A. ACQUISITION OF KNOWLEDGE

Aguilar, Francis, *Scanning the Business Environment* (New York: Macmillan, 1967).

Blythe, J. William, "Business Forecasting: Where to Get the Facts You Need," *Management Review*, 53:2 (February 1964), 34–41.

B. USE OF KNOWLEDGE

(3) Organizational condition affecting use of intellectual sources

Anshen, Melvin, "The Management of Ideas," *Harvard Business Review*, 47:14 (July–August 1969), 99–107.

3. Organizational Language

C. ADVERTISING THEMES

Greenwald, Harold, "Love and Hate in Rent-a-Car Land," *Playboy*, 14:12 (December 1967), 151–152ff.

E. LANGUAGE OF POLICIES AS DISTINCT FROM THE POLICIES THEMSELVES

Purves, Frederick, "Sacred Cows and Their Management," *Management Review*, 53:8 (August 1964), 43–46.

F. LANGUAGE AS CUSTOMS

Hayakawa, S. E., *Language in Thought and Action* (New York: Harcourt, 1964).

4. Emotional Atmosphere of Organization

Loban, Lawrence N., "Mental Health and Company Progress," *Industrial Medicine and Surgery*, 35:8 (August 1966), 683–687.

Tagiuri, Renâto, and George H. Litwin, *Organizational Climate* (Boston: Harvard University, Graduate School of Business Administration, 1968).

A. PREVAILING MOOD AND RANGE

Sorcher, Melvin and Selig Danzig, "Charting and Changing the Organizational Climate," *Personnel*, 46:2 (March–April 1969), 16–22.

5. Organizational Action

B. QUALITIES OF ACTION

(3) *Planning and time*

"The Corporate Venture Team: New Approach for Choosing New Directions," *Management Review*, 56:3 (March 1967), 34–37.

Chapter 8: Interpretative Data

B. Attitudes and Relationships

"A Conscience in the Boardroom," *Newsweek*, 67:15 (April 11, 1966), 77.

Bower, Marvin, *The Will to Manage* (New York: McGraw-Hill, 1966).

Dale, Ernest, *Organization* (American Management Association, 1967), pp. 49–57.

Eells, Richard, *The Meaning of Modern Business* (New York: Columbia University Press, 1960), pp. 211–403.

Mooney, James D., and Alan C. Reiley, "What Is Meant by Organization and Its Principles?" in Ernest Dale, ed., *Readings in Management: Landmarks and Frontiers* (New York: McGraw-Hill, 1965), pp. 175–177.

1. Contemporary Attitudes Toward, and Relationships with, Others

A. RANGE, DIVERSIFICATION, DEPTH, AND CONSTANCY

(1) *Customers*

Williams, G. J., "The Case for an Integrated Marketing Effort," *Management Review*, 55:4 (April 1966), 38–42.

(3) *Employees*

Greenwald, Harold, "Psychoanalytic Profile of a Factory," *Psychoanalysis*, 4:5 (Spring 1957), 27–37.

(4) *Occupational associations and representatives*

Beal, Edwin F., and Edward D. Wickersham, *The Practice of Collective Bargaining*, 3rd ed. (Homewood, Ill.: Irwin, 1967).

Glaser, William A., and David L. Sills, eds., *The Government of Associations* (Totowa, N.J.: Bedminster Press, 1966).

Selekman, Benjamin M., *Labor Relations and Human Relations* (New York: McGraw-Hill, 1947).

Slichter, Sumner, James J. Healy, and E. Robert Livernash, *The Impact of Collective Bargaining on Management* (Washington, D.C.: Brookings Institution, 1960).

Walton, Richard E., and Robert B. McKersie, *A Behavioral Theory of Labor Negotiations* (New York: McGraw-Hill, 1965).

(5) *Stockholders*

Saxon, O. Glenn, Jr., "Annual Headache: The Stockholders' Meeting," *Harvard Business Review*, 44:1 (January–February 1966), 132–137.

(6) *Legislative bodies*

"Business and Government: A Better Understanding?" *Management Review*, 55:8 (August 1966), 57–61.

Kappel, Frederick R., *Business Purpose and Performance* (New York: Duell, Sloan and Pearce, 1964), pp. 105–108, 126–130.

Smith, Richard Austin, "The Company's Man in Washington," *Fortune*, 73:4 (April 1966), 132–135ff.

(7) *Executive and regulatory bodies (governmental)*

Larson, John A., ed., *The Regulated Businessman: Business and Government. Readings from Fortune* (New York: Holt, Rinehart and Winston, 1966).

Raphael, Jesse S., *Governmental Regulation of Business* (New York: Free Press, 1966).

(8) *Control bodies (internal)*

Price, James L., "The Impact of Governing Boards on Organizational Effectiveness and Morale," *Administrative Science Quarterly,* 8:3 (December 1963), 361–378.

(9) *Suppliers*

Leenders, Michiel R., "Establishing Ground Rules for Suppliers," *Management Review,* 55:11 (November 1966), 72–74.

(10) *Financial community*

Cates, David C. and J. R. Olson, "Do Corporations Analyze Banks Properly?" *Management Review,* 55:10 (October 1966), 60–63.

Wood, Robert J., "New Factors in Financial Public Relations," *Management Review,* 55:4 (April 1966), 19–23.

(11) *Host community*

Vogel, Al, "Urban Crisis: New Focus for Community Relations," *Public Relations Journal,* 23:9 (September 1967), 12–13.

(14) *Consultants*

"How to Conduct a Post-Mortem on a Management Consultant," *Business Management,* 29:3 (December 1965), 47–49. (This article is adapted from a monograph, *How to Get the Best Results from Management Consultants.* Single copies may be obtained without charge from the Association of Consulting Management Engineers, 347 Madison Avenue, New York 10017.)

Seney, Wilson, *Effective Use of Business Consultants* (New York: Financial Executives Institute, 1963).

Tilles, Seymour, "Understanding the Consultant's Role," *Harvard Business Review,* 39:6 (November–December 1961), 87–99.

(15) *Others*

Adler, Lee, "Symbiotic Marketing — Pooling Resources for Mutual Benefit," *Harvard Business Review,* 44:6 (November–December 1966), 59–71.

Linowitz, Sol M., "The Growing Responsibility of Business in Public Affairs," *Management Review,* 55:9 (September 1966), 52–55.

D. Transference phenomena

(2) *Related to the organization*

Marcuse, Donald J., "The 'Army' Incident: The Psychology of Uniforms and Their Abolition on an Adolescent Ward," *Psychiatry,* 30:4 (November 1967), 350–375.

2. Relations to Things and Ideas

B. TIME: HOW IS IT REGARDED

Bird, Caroline, and Thomas D. Yutzy, "The Tyranny of Time: Results Achieved vs. Hours Spent," *Management Review*, 54:8 (August 1965), 34–43.

Fischer Roland, ed., "Interdisciplinary Perspective of Time," *Annals of the New York Academy of Science*, 13:8 (1957), art. 2, 367–915.

(2) *How is the future planned for*

Ewing, David, *The Human Side of Planning: Tool or Tyrant* (New York: Macmillan, 1969); *Long-Range Planning for Management* (New York: Harper & Row, 1964); and *The Practice of Planning* (New York: Harper & Row, 1968).

C. SPACE: HOW IS IT CONCEPTUALIZED

Hall, Edward T., *The Hidden Dimension* (New York: Doubleday, 1966).

D. MEANING OF WORK FOR THE ORGANIZATION

Herzberg, Frederick I., *Work and the Nature of Man* (Cleveland:World Publishing), 1966.

Levenstein, Aaron, *Why People Work* (New York: Crowell-Collier, 1962).

Levinson, Harry, *The Exceptional Executive* (Cambridge, Mass.: Harvard University Press, 1968), ch. 2.

Neff, Walter S., *Work and Human Behavior* (New York: Atherton, 1968).

Shostak, Arthur B., "Business and the Meaning of Work," in Ivan Berg, ed., *The Business of America* (New York: Harcourt, 1968), pp. 338–360.

(2) *As a device for fulfilling psychological contract*

Steiner, Gary A., ed., *The Creative Organization* (Chicago: University of Chicago Press, 1965).

E. AUTHORITY, POWER, AND RESPONSIBILITY

Chamberlain, Neil W., *Enterprise and Environment* (New York: McGraw-Hill 1968).

Cook, Paul W., and George Von Peterfy, *Problems of Corporate Power* (Homewood, Ill.: Irwin, 1968).

Davis, Keith, and Robert L. Blostrum, *Business and Its Environment* (New York: McGraw-Hill, 1966).

3. Attitudes about Self

Athos, Anthony G. and Robert E. Coffey, *Behavior in Organizations: A Multidimensional View* (Englewood Cliffs, N.J.: Prentice-Hall, 1968).

Levinson, Harry, *Executive Stress* (New York: Harper & Row, 1969), ch. 18.

MacLeod, Jennifer S., "The Emphasis is on Corporate Reputation," *Public Relations Journal*, 23:8 (August 1967), 18–20.

4. Intraorganizational Relationships

A. KEY PEOPLE IN THE ORGANIZATION

Dalton, Melville, *Men Who Manage* (New York: Wiley, 1959).
Einstein, Kurt, "The Management Audit," *The Personnel Administrator*, 5:1 (January–February 1970), 16–23.

B. SIGNIFICANT GROUPS WITHIN THE ORGANIZATION

Burns, Tom, and G. M. Stalker, *The Management of Innovation* (London: Tavistock Publications, 1961).
Litwin, George H., and Robert A. Stringer, Jr., *Motivation and Organization Climate* (Boston: Harvard University, Graduate School of Business Administration, 1968).

C. IMPLICATIONS OF A AND B

Zaleznik, Abraham, and David Moment, *The Dynamics of Interpersonal Behavior* (New York: Wiley, 1964).

Chapter 9: Analyses and Conclusions

A. Organizational Integrative Patterns

1. Appraisal of the Effect of the Environment on the Organization

Barker, Roger C., *Ecological Psychology*. (Stanford, Calif.: Stanford University Press, 1968).
Blau, Peter, *Exchange and Power in Social Life* (New York: Wiley, 1964).
Emery, F. E., and E. L. Trist, "The Causal Texture of Organizational Environment," *Human Relations*, 18:1 (1965), 21–32.
Lawrence, Paul R., and J. W. Lorsch, *Organization and Environment* (Boston: Harvard University, Graduate School of Business Administration, 1967).
Levine, S., and P. E. White, "Exchange as a Conceptual Framework for the Study of Inter-Organizational Relationships, *Administrative Science Quarterly*, 5:4 (1961), 583–601.
Rice, A. K., *The Enterprise and Its Environment* (London: Tavistock Publications, 1963).
Selznick, Philip, *TVA and the Grass Roots* (Berkeley, Calif.: University of California Press, 1949).

4. Appraisal of the Organization

A. SPECIAL ASSETS

(2) *Functional (leadership and mental set, or attitude)*

Brown, Michael E., "Identification and Some Conditions of Organizational Involvement," *Administrative Science Quarterly,* 14:3 (September 1969), 346–356.

Drucker, Peter F., *The Effective Executive* (New York: Harper & Row, 1966).

Fiedler, Fred F., *A Theory of Leadership Effectiveness* (New York: McGraw-Hill, 1967).

Guest, Robert H., *Organizational Change: The Effect of Successful Leadership* (Homewood, Ill.: Irwin-Dorsey, 1962).

Levinson, Harry, *The Exceptional Executive* (Cambridge, Mass.: Harvard University Press, 1968).

D. OVERALL EFFECTIVENESS AND FACADE

Mahoney, Thomas A., and William Weitzel, "Managerial Models of Organizational Effectiveness," *Administrative Science Quarterly,* 14:3 (September 1969), 357–365.